GW01368277

PARENTAL RIGHTS AND RESPONSIBILITIES

THE LIBRARY OF ESSAYS ON FAMILY RIGHTS

Forthcoming titles

Marital Rights
Edited with a new introduction by Robert Leckey

Religion and Family Rights
Edited with a new introduction by John Eekelaar

Children's Rights
Edited with a new introduction by Ursula Kilkelly and Laura Lundy

Parental Rights and Responsibilities

EDITED BY
STEPHEN GILMORE

THE LIBRARY OF ESSAYS ON FAMILY RIGHTS

Routledge
Taylor & Francis Group
LONDON AND NEW YORK

First published 2017
by Routledge
2 Park Square, Milton Park, Abingdon, Oxon OX14 4RN

and by Routledge
711 Third Avenue, New York, NY 10017

Routledge is an imprint of the Taylor & Francis Group, an informa business

Editorial material and selection © 2017 Stephen Gilmore; individual owners retain copyright in their own material

All rights reserved. No part of this book may be reprinted or reproduced or utilised in any form or by any electronic, mechanical, or other means, now known or hereafter invented, including photocopying and recording, or in any information storage or retrieval system, without permission in writing from the publishers.

Trademark notice: Product or corporate names may be trademarks or registered trademarks, and are used only for identification and explanation without intent to infringe.

British Library Cataloguing in Publication Data
A catalogue record for this book is available from the British Library

Library of Congress Cataloging in Publication Data
A catalog record for this book has been requested

ISBN: 978-1-4744-6337-1
Series ISBN: 1430

Typeset in Times New Roman MT
by Servis Filmsetting Ltd, Stockport, Cheshire

Publisher's Note
References within each chapter are as they appear in the original complete work

Contents

Acknowledgements ix

Introduction 1

Part I: Who or what is a parent? Underlying rationales

1. Barbara Hall, 'The Origin of Parental Rights' (1999) 13(1) *Public Affairs Quarterly* 73–78   19

2. John Lawrence Hill, 'What Does It Mean to Be a "Parent"? The Claims of Biology as the Basis for Parental Rights' (1991) 66(2) *New York University Law Review* 353–420   29

3. Gillian Douglas, 'The Intention to be a Parent and the Making of Mothers' (1994) 57(4) *The Modern Law Review* 636–641   97

4. Tim Bayne and Avery Kolers, 'Toward a Pluralistic Account of Parenthood' (2003) 17(3) *Bioethics* 221–242   103

5. Jeffrey Blustein, 'Procreation and Parental Responsibility' (1997) 28(2) *Journal of Social Philosophy* 79–86   125

6. James G. Dwyer, 'The Moral Basis of Children's Relational Rights', ch 4.4 in John Eekelaar and Rob George (eds), *Routledge Handbook of Family Law and Policy* (Abingdon: Routledge, 2014), pp. 274–280   133

7. Nigel V. Lowe, 'The Changing Face of Adoption – the Gift/Donation Model versus the Contract/Services Model' (1997) 9(4) *Child and Family Law Quarterly* 371–386   141

Part II: Legal concepts of 'parent' and their linkage

8. Andrew Bainham, 'Parentage, Parenthood and Parental Responsibility: Subtle, Elusive, Yet Important Distinctions', ch 2 in A. Bainham, S. Day Sclater and M. Richards (eds), *What is a Parent? A Socio-Legal Analysis* (Oxford: Hart, 1999), pp. 25–46   159

9. John Eekelaar, 'Rethinking Parental Responsibility' (2001) 31 *Family Law* 426–430   181

Part III: The legal parent – accommodating complexity

10. Craig Lind and Tom Hewitt, 'Law and the Complexities of Parenting: Parental Status and Parental Function' (2009) 31(4) *Journal of Social Welfare and Family Law* 391–406   189

11. Emily Jackson, 'What is a Parent?', ch 4 in A. Diduck and K. O'Donovan (eds), *Feminist Perspectives on Family Law* (London: Routledge-Cavendish, 2006), pp. 59–74   205

12. Andrew Bainham, 'Arguments about Parentage' (2008) 67(2) *Cambridge Law Journal* 322–351   229

13. Leanne Smith, 'Tangling the Web of Legal Parenthood: Legal Responses to the Use of Known Donors in Lesbian Parenting Arrangements' (2013) 33(3) *Legal Studies* 355–381   259

14. Kirsty Horsey, 'Challenging Presumptions: Legal Parenthood and Surrogacy Arrangements' (2010) 22(4) *Child and Family Law Quarterly* 449–474   287

Part IV: The nature and scope of parental rights

15. Phillip Montague, 'The Myth of Parental Rights' (2000) 26(1) *Social Theory and Practice* 47–68   315

16. Colin M. Macleod, 'Conceptions of Parental Autonomy' (1997) 25(1) *Politics and Society* 117–140   337

17. Andrew Bainham, 'Is Anything Now Left of Parental Rights?', ch 2 in R. Probert, S. Gilmore and J. Herring (eds), *Responsible Parents and Parental Responsibility* (Oxford: Hart, 2009), pp. 23–42   361

18. Jonathan Herring, 'The Welfare Principle and the Rights of Parents', ch 5 in A. Bainham, S. Day Sclater and M. Richards (eds), *What is a Parent? A Socio-Legal Analysis* (Oxford: Hart, 1999), pp. 89–105   381

19. Shazia Choudhry and Helen Fenwick, 'Taking the Rights of Parents and Children Seriously: Confronting the Welfare Principle under the Human Rights Act' (2005) 25(3) *Oxford Journal of Legal Studies* 453–492   399

Part V: Shared parental responsibility

20. Nigel V. Lowe, 'The Meaning and Allocation of Parental Responsibility – a Common Lawyer's Perspective' (1997) 11(2) *International Journal of Law, Policy and the Family* 192–215   441

21. Helen Reece, 'The Degradation of Parental Responsibility', ch 5 in R. Probert, S. Gilmore and J. Herring (eds), *Responsible Parents and Parental Responsibility* (Oxford: Hart, 2009), pp. 85–102   465

22. Belinda Fehlberg, Bruce Smyth, Mavis Maclean and Ceridwen Roberts, 'Legislating for Shared Time Parenting after Separation: A Research Review' (2011) 25(3) *International Journal of Law, Policy and the Family* 318–337   483

Part VI: Parental rights and the state

23. Hugh LaFollette, 'Licensing Parents Revisited' (2010) 27(4) *Journal of Applied Philosophy* 327–343   505

24. David Archard, 'Child Abuse: Parental Rights and the Interests of the Child' (1990) 7(2) *Journal of Applied Philosophy* 183–194   523

25. Sonia Harris-Short, 'Making and Breaking Family Life: Adoption, the State, and Human Rights' (2008) 35(1) *Journal of Law and Society* 28–51   535

Index   559

Acknowledgements

The Publishers would like to thank the following for permission to reprint their material:

The University of Pittsburgh for permission to reprint Barbara Hall, 'The Origin of Parental Rights' (1999) 13(1) *Public Affairs Quarterly* 73–78.

New York University Law Review for permission to reprint John Lawrence Hill, 'What does It Mean to Be a "Parent'? The Claims of Biology as the Basis for Parental Rights' (1991) 66(2), *New York University Law Review* 353–420.

John Wiley & Sons for permission to reprint Gillian Douglas, 'The Intention to be a Parent and the Making of Mothers' (1994) 57(4) *The Modern Law Review* 636–641.

John Wiley & Sons for permission to reprint Tim Bayne and Avery Kolers, 'Toward a Pluralistic Account of Parenthood' (2003) 17(3) *Bioethics* 221–242.

John Wiley & Sons for permission to reprint Jeffrey Blustein, 'Procreation and Parental Responsibility' (1997) 28(2) *Journal of Social Philosophy* 79–86.

James G. Dwyer for permission to reprint James G. Dwyer 'The Moral Basis of Children's Relational Rights', ch 4.4 in John Eekelaar and Rob George (eds), *Routledge Handbook of Family Law and Policy* (Abingdon: Routledge, 2014), pp. 274–280.

Jordan Publishing Ltd for permission to reprint Nigel V. Lowe, 'The Changing Face of Adoption – the Gift/Donation Model versus the Contract/Services Model' (1997) 9(4) *Child and Family Law Quarterly* 371–386.

Craig Lind and Tom Hewitt for permission to reprint Craig Lind and Tom Hewitt, 'Law and the Complexities of Parenting: Parental Status and Parental Function' (2009) 31(4) *Journal of Social Welfare and Family Law* 391–406.

Bloomsbury for permission to reprint Emily Jackson, 'What is a Parent?', ch 4 in A. Diduck and K. O'Donovan (eds), *Feminist Perspectives on Family Law* (London: Routledge-Cavendish, 2006), pp. 59–74.

Cambridge University Press for permission to reprint Andrew Bainham, 'Arguments about Parentage' (2008) 67(2) *Cambridge Law Journal* 322–351.

John Wiley & Sons for permission to reprint Leanne Smith, 'Tangling the Web of Legal Parenthood: Legal Responses to the Use of Known Donors in Lesbian Parenting Arrangements' (2013) 33(3) *Legal Studies* 355–381.

Kirsty Horsey for the permission to reprint Kirsty Horsey, 'Challenging Presumptions: Legal Parenthood and Surrogacy Arrangements' (2010) 22(4) *Child and Family Law Quarterly* 449–474.

Philosophy Documentation Center (University of Florda) for their permission to reprint Phillip Montague, 'The Myth of Parental Rights' (2000) 26(1) *Social Theory and Practice* 47–68.

SAGE Publications for permission to reprint Colin M. Macleod, 'Conceptions of Parental Autonomy' (1997) 25(1) *Politics and Society* 117–140.

Hart Publishing for their permission to reprint Andrew Bainham, 'Is Anything Now Left of Parental Rights?', ch 2 in R. Probert, S. Gilmore and J. Herring (eds), *Responsible Parents and Parental Responsibility* (Oxford: Hart, 2009), pp. 23–42.

Hart Publishing for their permission to reprint Jonathan Herring, 'The Welfare Principle and the Rights of Parents', ch 5 in A. Bainham, S. Day Sclater and M. Richards (eds), *What is a Parent?* (Oxford: Hart, 1999), pp. 89–105.

Oxford University Press for permission to reprint Shazia Choudhry and Helen Fenwick, 'Taking the Rights of Parents and Children Seriously: Confronting the Welfare Principle under the Human Rights Act' (2005) 25(3) *Oxford Journal of Legal* Studies 453–492. This study was funded by a grant from the Nuffield Foundation.

Oxford University Press for permission to reprint Nigel V. Lowe, 'The Meaning and Allocation of Parental Responsibility – a Common Lawyer's Perspective' (1997) 11(2) *International Journal of Law, Policy and the Family* 192–215.

Hart Publishing for their permission to reprint Helen Reece, 'The Degradation of Parental Responsibility', ch 5 in R. Probert, S. Gilmore and J. Herring (eds), *Responsible Parents and Parental Responsibility* (Oxford: Hart, 2009), pp. 85–102.

Oxford University Press for permission to reprint Belinda Fehlberg, Bruce Smyth, Mavis Maclean and Ceridwen Roberts, 'Legislating for Shared Time Parenting after Separation: A Research Review' (2011) 25(3) *International Journal of Law, Policy and the Family* 318–337.

Hugh LaFollette for permission to reprint Hugh LaFollette, 2010, 'Licensing Parents Revisited' (2010) 27(4) *Journal of Applied Philosophy* 327–343.

John Wiley & Sons for permission to reprint David Archard, 'Child Abuse: Parental Rights and the Interests of the Child' (1990) 7(2) *Journal of Applied Philosophy* 183–194.

John Wiley & Sons for permission to reprint Sonia Harris-Short, 'Making and Breaking Family Life: Adoption, the State, and Human Rights' (2008) 35(1) *Journal of Law and Society* 28–51.

Disclaimer

The publishers have made every effort to contact authors/copyright holders of works reprinted in *Parental Rights and Responsibilities* (The Library of Essays on Family Rights). This has not been possible in every case, however, and we would welcome correspondence from those individuals/companies whom we have been unable to trace.

Introduction

An editor asked to present a volume of academic writing on 'parental rights' encounters several challenges: a subject matter with a vast body of philosophical and legal literature;[1] a subject matter which is constantly engaging with social change and technological advance; and the difficulty of presenting an account of legal 'rights' in the context of an array of legal jurisdictions. Moreover, these challenges must be addressed within the constraints of the volume size. An editor must therefore take a view on the scope of the subject matter and the nature of the works to be included, and difficult decisions must be taken on what to include and what to leave out.

In this volume an attempt has been made to engage with both philosophical and legal literature, and the choice of works has been informed by an effort to provide examples of perspectives or arguments which may have resonance irrespective of jurisdictional detail, and which offer a starting point for critical engagement and/or comparison.[2] A broad view has been taken of the subject matter of parental rights. In addition to examining philosophically the nature and scope of parental rights and relevant legal terminology for attributing the legal incidents of parenthood, this volume also examines who may be regarded as a parent, the underlying rationales for attributing parenthood, and the complexity of law's engagement with parenthood. This acknowledges that what is meant by being a parent is integral to any discussion of what is meant by *parental* rights.

Part I therefore begins by discussing various rationales that might underpin the attribution of 'parenthood'. These include arguments based upon: a biological connection (principally genetic and/or gestational roles);[3] the intention to become a parent; a person's causal role in producing a child; and the best interests of children.

Barbara Hall, in her piece entitled 'The Origin of Parental Rights', enquires what it is 'about the biological parents (versus the rest of the world) that fuels the intuition that they have initial entitlement to a child'.[4] One explanation, rejected by Hall, is a proprietarian view of the parent/child relationship, relying for example upon John Locke's labour theory that self-ownership of labour entitles one to the fruits of one's labour – in this context the child one has produced.[5] Several arguments can be advanced against such a view, not least that it seems paradoxical in its production of the 'owned' through self-ownership, and that it may conflate 'labour as an activity with labour as product'.[6] Hall offers a further challenge to this labour-based proprietarian view, at least as a universal explanation, in her observation that now, with technological advance, labour is 'neither a necessary nor sufficient factor in the attribution of rights to biological parents'.[7] Rather, 'persons own themselves and, upon pro-creation, this fact entitles these persons to a trusteeship over their children (their derived genetic substance)'.[8] So, the 'fact that the *child represents a genetic part of its parents is what fuels this intuition*'[9] and what 'establishes an initial presumption of parental rights'.[10]

However, John Lawrence Hill in 'What Does It Mean to Be a "Parent"? The Claims of Biology as the Basis for Parental Rights' observes that 'the biological conception does not square with a number of other, equally deep, intuitions. It is not consistent with the modern understanding that parenthood is as much a social, psychological, and intentional status as a biological one.'[11] Unlike Hall, who sees technological advance as a means of underlining biological connection, Hill focuses on the challenge to identification of parental status that social and technological advances pose in the context of surrogacy arrangements, attempting to settle 'conflicting claims to parental status posed by the genetic parents, the gestational host, and the intended parents of the child'. Hill argues that the significance of biological identity and parenthood has manifested itself historically outside of (relatively modern) assisted conception type cases, and that its significance can be interrogated in those contexts. For Hill the 'the right of procreation, as a distinct normative claim, need not be associated with *capacity* to reproduce' but rather 'simply as a normative safeguard to protect the *intention* to create and raise a child'. Hill's article is devoted 'to critiquing the current biology-centred view of the procreative right and defending an intentionalist account of the right of procreation'. In the context of settling the claims mentioned above, Hill rejects any priority for genetic parenthood arising from property rights based on ownership of gametes, and for priority of the gestational mother based on the mother's labour, maternal bonding, the interests of the child, the danger to the mother in relinquishing her child, or risk of her exploitation or commodification in producing children for others. Moreover, he offers three arguments for the moral priority of the intended parents: (1) the importance of the intended parents in the procreative relationship (i.e. but for their initial intention to have the child, the child would not have been created); (2) unfairness in allowing a surrogate to break an agreement; and (3) assuring the identity of the child's parents at the point of conception.[12]

In *Johnson v Calvert*,[13] the Supreme Court of California placed reliance on intention to resolve the conflicting claims between a commissioning couple and a surrogate mother (similar to those examined by Hill).[14] Gillian Douglas's commentary on the case, 'The Intention to be a Parent and the Making of Mothers', considers the wider implications of intention as a determining factor with respect to parenthood, and shows that such an approach may not be without difficulties. As Douglas observes, the corollary is 'to accept that *lack* of intention should be a means of avoiding parenthood'.[15] In addition, if taken as a general approach it would detach procreation from biology and gender requirements.[16] It also raises issues in relation to proof of intention and how it is to be reconciled with protection of the welfare of the child.

Tim Bayne and Avery Kolers in 'Toward a Pluralist Account of Parenthood' also argue against the view that priority should necessarily be given to intentionalism. However, they also attack the view that gestation should be seen as necessary for parenthood (monistic gestationalism). In a similar vein to Hill, they interrogate various reasons put forward in favour of monistic gestationalism, such as ease of identification of the parent, the unique features of pregnancy in respect of labour to produce the child, and emotional bonding. Bayne and Kolers acknowledge that many of these arguments support the view that gestation is a sufficient reason for parenthood, but none stands in defence of gestation as a necessity. In addition, they suggest that monistic gestationalism can be challenged by reference to a meta-principle which they term the parity principle: 'any condition that makes one person a parent should, biology permitting, make anyone a parent'. Thus, they suggest, it 'would seem arbitrary if, say, direct genetic derivation were sufficient for paternity but not maternity'. Directly engaging with Hill's arguments, however, Bayne and Kolers point out that the idea of prime movers in initiating the conception (and ultimate birth) of a child might equally apply to grandparents orchestrating their own daughter's pregnancy, and that a 'but-for' test of causation might equally apply to the role played by the gestational host (mother). The pluralist analysis of Bayne and Kolers leads them to 'an underlying assumption that seems correct, if inchoate: being causally implicated in the creation of a child is the key basis for being its parent ... any such account ought to be broad enough to grant parenthood to genetic, gestational, custodial and intentional parents'.[17]

In 'Procreation and Parental Responsibility' Jeffrey Blustein explores in more detail one aspect of this 'causal view of parental responsibility': 'since biological parents have caused a being to exist, a being who, by its very nature, is dependent and vulnerable to harm, they are mainly responsible for its care'.[18] Blustein points out that proponents of the causal view maintain that 'undertaking obligations is not necessary for parental responsibility and that causation can give rise to it too'.[19] Blustein examines different notions of causation, and how causation as an underlying basis of parenthood plays out in different scenarios: cases of planned parenthood, forced parenthood (through rape), and failed contraception.

James G. Dwyer in 'The Moral Basis of Children's Relational Rights' argues that:

> no adults have a moral right to be in a parent–child relationship with a particular child independently of whether that is in the child's best interests – that is, unless and until the state properly makes a reciprocal choice of that adult on behalf of the child.[20]

The 'state stands in a fiduciary role with respect to each newborn child when it makes the parentage decision, and in that role the state must decide based solely on its best judgment of what is in the newborn child's best interests.'[21] Equally, Dwyer argues, the state sets the terms of parenthood in exchange for bestowing that privilege. For Dwyer, the 'view that legal parents are entitled to set their own terms of engagement with children is morally groundless'.[22]

One area in which the state is directly implicated in deciding in the best interests of children whether carers are accorded parental status is the process of adoption in law. Nigel Lowe's article, 'The Changing Face of Adoption – the Gift/Donation Model Versus the Contract/Services Model', shows how the nature of adoption (in the sense of the reasons for it) can shift over time within a society and may require adaptation.[23] Tracing the development of adoption in England and Wales, Lowe shows how adoption shifted over a period of 70 years from a gift/donation model of providing a baby to a childless couple towards increasing adoption of older children (often through the care system). Lowe suggests that this requires a different, contract/services model in which the adoption agency and adoptive parents work in partnership, recognising that adoption 'is not the end of a process, but merely part of an ongoing and often complex process of family development'.[24]

It can be seen from the array of perspectives presented in Part I that the question of who should be accorded the status of 'parent', and thus potentially the bearer of parental rights and responsibilities, engages many possibilities and underlying rationales or arguments. A particular legal system must decide from among these possibilities to whom the status in law of being a parent is to be attributed,[25] and accordingly who is potentially to be accorded parental rights. Moreover, law's engagement with different notions of 'being a parent' (for example biological, intentional or social/psychological parenthood) may require a layer of legal terminology to designate appropriate status, and to which appropriate legal incidents can be attached. These challenges within a legal system are explored in Part II in Andrew Bainham's chapter, 'Parentage, Parenthood and Parental Responsibility: Subtle, Elusive, Yet Important Distinctions'; and the complex ways in which these different terms can interact within a legal system is illustrated in John Eekelaar's article 'Rethinking Parental Responsibility'.

While the gender neutral terms 'parenthood' and 'parental responsibility' may make sense in some contexts, in others the law may also have to engage with the gendered nature of parenting, with a focus on how 'fatherhood'[26] and 'motherhood'[27] are socially and legally constructed. Moreover, as Susan Boyd has observed, gender can, and should, play 'an important role in mediating both intentionality and bio-genetic ties'.[28]

The overall complexity of law's engagement with parenting is explored in Part III. This presents a challenge to an editor seeking to offer a volume to readers in different jurisdictions, in many of which there is a vast array of detailed and complex legal provisions which may differ even across various states or provinces etc. therein.[29] Therefore, to ensure the coherence and manageability of the account of the law, and the compatibility of the discussions, the legal context within each of the papers chosen in this section is English law.[30] The papers have been chosen, however, as highlighting issues, arguments or themes which are likely to have some resonance across many jurisdictions.

In 'Law and the Complexities of Parenting: Parental Status and Parental Function', Craig Lind and Tom Hewitt – through an examination of the law relating to assisted reproduction parents, same-sex parents and step-parents – reflect on law's use respectively of the status of parent and of the concept of parental responsibility. They note that, despite increased methods of acquiring legal parenthood, the two-parent ideal persists, as do gendered patterns for determination of parental status.[31] Parental responsibility is the concept which is used to extend the notion of parenting beyond this 'parental exclusivity'. Lind and Hewitt argue that parental identity and parental status are important to those who care for children, and that this is not properly acknowledged 'when we reallocate some of the duties of parenting without also broadening the scope of parental status'.[32]

As Emily Jackson comments in her piece 'What is a Parent?', 'the principle of parental exclusivity fails to distinguish between two related but different aspects of parenthood: the status of *being a parent* and the power (or duty) to *act as a parent*'.[33] However, Jackson's point is somewhat different from Lind and Hewitt's: that those who may not currently be recognised in law as a parent or will never have the power to act as a parent (such as an egg donor) are still, in some sense, a parent, which should be recognised (for example by recording on the child's birth certificate). Jackson examines the advantages and disadvantages of parental exclusivity, and argues that '[t]ransparency and descriptive accuracy demand that the law relinquish its principle of parental exclusivity in favour of a model of parenthood that is capable of accommodating its social and technical fragmentation'.[34]

Andrew Bainham in 'Arguments about Parentage' takes a view which chimes with Jackson's point about transparency while also being diametrically opposed to the views of Lind and Hewitt. Bainham argues that there is too strong a tendency to assume that the status required to satisfy the legitimate expectations of those who are looking after children with whom they are not biologically related necessarily needs to be that of parent.[35] Bainham sees the extension of legal parenthood to those who have no biological connection with the child as out of step with the law on establishing paternity, which has increasingly endorsed the need for the biological truth to be disclosed.[36] Bainham comments:

> The fact that someone is doing some of the things which parents do does not make that person the parent. The true claim which same-sex partners and other social parents have is that they should be given the legal powers which are necessary to enable them to look after a child properly and it is the status of possessing parental responsibility which is best designed to achieve this.
>
> [...][37]
>
> The concept of parentage should rather be confined, to reflect as far as possible the unique position of biological parents and, through the child's filiation with them, the wider kinship links to the extended maternal and paternal families.[38]

Tension between the roles of same-sex parents and the child's biological father is explored by Leanne Smith in 'Tangling the Web of Legal Parenthood: Legal Responses to the Use of Known Donors in Lesbian Parenting Arrangements'. Smith examines case law involving disputes between lesbian parents and so-called 'known donors', i.e. men with whom they have made informal insemination arrangements.[39] In that context, she highlights a paradox with respect to the issue of parental exclusivity and same-sex parenting:

> Excluding known donors from legal recognition through a system which recognises only two parents validates and protects lesbian families but also reinforces the dyadic parenting norm based on heterosexual reproduction. Conversely, giving legal recognition to multiple parents undermines the dyadic norm but reasserts heteronormativity by elevating the importance of genetic parentage and fathers.[40]

Smith shows that the case law exhibits judicial uncertainty and inconsistency concerning the extent of legal recognition to which known donors should be entitled. She argues that a legal and regulatory framework facilitating the use of known donors could 'provide a basis for structuring much-needed advice and guidance to inform known donor arrangements at the planning stage, as well as bring stability and clarity'.[41]

Kirsty Horsey, in 'Challenging Presumptions: Legal Parenthood and Surrogacy Arrangements', similarly argues for stability and clarity in the law on legal parenthood surrounding surrogacy arrangements.[42] Horsey argues that in cases of assisted conception and surrogacy the law's foundation for parenthood should be 'intention to parent'. Building upon Hill's arguments and demonstrating the practical implications of such a change in English law, Horsey suggests that the intentions of commissioning parents should be respected by way of enforceable surrogacy agreements. She argues that:

> Grounding the regulation of surrogacy arrangements in contract, relying on the principles of autonomous bargaining, freedom of contract and the built-in ability of contract law to police unconscionable bargains, would offer protection to all parties. In particular, facilitating the making of surrogacy agreements in an environment in which the potential of exploitation is minimised is a constructive use of existing law.[43]

As the first three Parts of this collection illustrate, it is a complex matter for a legal system whether and how it should attach legal incidents to the various claims to be a parent that might plausibly be made. A further difficult issue is how those 'legal incidents' are properly characterised. Is it correct to say that parents have rights over their children in the sense of a right to determine how they are reared?[44] If so, what is their nature and scope? These issues are taken up in Part IV of this collection.

Phillip Montague, in his piece 'The Myth of Parental Rights', denies that parents have 'moral rights to influence the courses of their children's lives in significant ways'.[45] He argues that 'rights are essentially oriented towards their possessors', and thus parental rights 'must serve as protections of parental interests'.[46] This would provide parents with discretion whether or not to promote the welfare of the child. For Montague, however, 'morally speaking, the parent/child relation centers on the interests of children rather than parents' and is therefore better characterised by the idea of parental obligations. Montague observes that, while parents have 'discretion regarding *how* to fulfil their obligations, they do not have discretion regarding *whether* to fulfil them'[47] – so parental obligations 'imply half- rather than whole-liberties'.[48] Ultimately, choices concerning the welfare of children 'fall within the scope of parental obligations rather than rights'.[49]

Insofar as the term 'parental rights' might still be used,[50] Montague's view aligns with what has been termed the 'priority thesis' of parental rights, namely that parental rights derive from and are constrained by prior duty to ensure the child is properly cared for.[51] Montague makes an important point: that one interpretation of the term parental rights risks characterising the 'parental role' as entirely parent-focused, when that role is better characterised as a sphere of parental liberties bounded by parental obligation to the child. Whether it is correct to characterise parental rights as merely child-centred is a matter of debate, and some commentators argue that there is room also for protection of parents' interests in parenting, independent of the welfare of the child concerned (sometimes referred to as the 'independence thesis').[52] Certainly, as a matter of workable law, and of workable day-to-day parent/child relations, it is unrealistic to suggest that parental obligation should be fulfilled by parental liberties controlled by a positive duty to promote the welfare of a child with regard to every parental decision.

In many legal systems, the scope of parental privilege is therefore defined not by reference to positive obligation, but negatively by reference to behaviour which may take a parent's decision or behaviour outside the scope of legitimate parental privilege. The law places limits on parental discretion in various ways, such as: criminal sanctions;

state powers to intervene to protect children; court jurisdiction to take decisions in cases of parental disputes; and legal recognition of a (mature) child's autonomy interest. In day-to-day dealings with children this may translate to 'a parental discretion to employ control over children for purposes not violating children's interests, but equally not advancing their welfare or best interests'.[53] In this way, parents' interests can be accommodated to some extent within the scope of their parental liberties.

In considering the scope of parental autonomy, Colin M. Macleod in 'Conceptions of Parental Autonomy' notes that raising a child is an important element of an adult's life plan, and from this perspective 'parents cannot be seen as mere guardians of their children's interests'.[54] Macleod asks:

> What is the nature and extent of parental prerogatives and responsibilities in raising children in light of the child's interests in leading a good life (both as a child and as a future adult) given independent and potentially conflicting interests parents have in shaping and directing their children's lives?[55]

Subject to the child's basic interests in education and protection from abuse, MacLeod asks: 'To what degree can parents legitimately undertake efforts to ensure that their children become committed to conceptions of the good favoured by their parents?'[56] As Macleod points out, this requires engagement with children's, parents' and societal interests. Macleod interrogates three conceptions of parental autonomy – conservative, democratic and liberal conceptions, finding each in part deficient: the conservative conception rooted in a 'parental right of child-determination' provides 'insufficient recognition of the interests of the democratic community in choosing how a child will be nurtured and educated'; the democratic conception, tempering the conservative 'by the requirement that every child receive a suitable civic education', may preserve democratic pluralism, albeit at the risk of a manufactured pluralism providing too impoverished a commitment to individual autonomy; the liberal conception of parental autonomy 'attempts to speak directly to the child's interests in becoming an autonomous agent',[57] constraining parental autonomy by 'an ideal of neutrality' maximising the child's freedom to choose between ends,[58] yet at its extreme risks alienating parents' distinctive interests and motivations.[59] Macleod therefore suggests a refined liberal conception, replacing the ideal of neutrality with a more permissive conception, extending to parents 'the prerogative of *provisionally privileging* the conception of the good that they favor'.[60] Parents should be:

> permitted to advance a distinctive conception of the good for their children. However, parents must not seek to exempt the ends they wish their children to adopt from rational scrutiny. Nor may parents undertake to foreclose the possibility of deliberation about such matters by tightly insulating children from exposure and access to the social conditions of deliberation.[61]

That is, children must be 'afforded free and full access to the deliberative resources available in the pluralistic public culture'. Children must not be insulated from conceptions of good in the broader community.[62] Of course children must be able to make informed choices, so this conception also places emphasis on 'facilitating the development of children's autonomy'. As noted above, legal recognition of a child's autonomy interest can be a factor limiting the scope of parental discretion. This issue is not pursued in detail in this volume as much of the literature explores this issue from a children's rights, rather than a parents' rights, perspective.[63]

Andrew Bainham, in 'Is Anything Now Left of Parental Rights?', examines the tension in the literature between those who support the priority and independence theses respectively; and, against the background of English law, investigates whether parents' independent interests remain protected. Identifying some erosion of protection of the status of parent, Bainham concludes that there are still 'good reasons for believing that parents have interests in relation to their children which are independent of the child's welfare and which are attributable to their own benefit'.[64] Bainham argues that this should be so, since recognition of parents' independent interests accords with the reality of family life, and is 'appropriate because of the extensive burdens, financial, emotional and practical, which are automatically thrust upon them by law and society'.[65]

One particular area in which the interests of parents can be in tension with those of the child is in court decision-making, particularly where (as not uncommon in many jurisdictions) the guiding decision-making criterion is the welfare of the child. In some jurisdictions the child's welfare is elevated to the paramount consideration (sometimes interpreted to mean the sole consideration), which means that in applying this principle no consideration can be given independently to the interests of parents. Parents' interests are only relevant insofar as they bear upon the child's welfare.[66] In 'The Welfare Principle and the Rights of Parents' Jonathan Herring explores this tension, considering the 'extent to which the courts are and should be entitled to make orders that infringe the rights of parents and others in order to pursue the welfare of the child'.[67] Herring demonstrates the means by which the English courts, despite the welfare principle, have managed to give weight to the interests of parents. Herring appreciates, however, that in some cases parental interests are infringed, but argues that the welfare principle need not be abandoned. Instead, he argues that:

> A full understanding of the welfare principle should include ensuring that the relationship between the parent and child is a fair and just one, with respect to each individual's rights. A child's welfare will be best promoted by being brought up by parents in a family and community based on appropriate mutual co-operation and respect. With this broader understanding of the welfare principle we have no need to seek to undermine or avoid its application and it can take a legitimate and effective pride of place in the law relating to children.[68]

It may be doubted, however, whether this approach adequately meets criticisms of the welfare principle's lack of transparency in its failure to separate out individuals' interests in a dispute before the court.[69] The extent to which, if at all, the welfare principle is compatible with parents' human rights is explored by Shazia Choudhry and Helen Fenwick in 'Taking the Rights of Parents and Children Seriously: Confronting the Welfare Principle under the Human Rights Act' in the European context of the right to respect for family life within Article 8 of the European Convention on Human Rights (ECHR).[70] Choudhry and Fenwick argue that the ECHR requires what they term a 'parallel analysis' in which the requirements of the Article are applied in turn to each parent and the child involved in a dispute, followed by an overarching weighing of the Article 8 rights concerned. In the weighing process, as the European Court of Human Rights has acknowledged, the rights of the child are privileged in the sense that they are seen as of particular importance, and no outcome must prejudice the child's interests. In most cases the outcome will be the same as that applying a child welfare approach; but, importantly, the process is respectful of the independent interests of those involved.

As well as identifying who in law is to be regarded as a parent, and the nature of parental responsibilities, the law has a role in deciding in whom, among parents, parental responsibilities are vested. In cases in which a child's carers separate, the law can also be tasked with deciding on the optimum post-separation parenting arrangements for such children. These issues are examined in Part V of this collection.

In some jurisdictions, the initial allocation of parental responsibility has proved extremely controversial in the distinctions made between mothers and fathers, and between fathers who are married to the child's mother and those who are not.[71] Some of these issues are explored by Nigel Lowe in 'The Meaning and Allocation of Parental Responsibility – a Common Lawyer's Perspective'. Lowe concludes that there seems to be a strong case for vesting parental responsibility in all fathers irrespective of marital status, although this is not an obligation under the ECHR.[72] Another issue explored by Lowe is whether a domestic or international instrument could, and should, define what parental responsibility means. Lowe argues that a meaningful definition could be given.

Such a definition of course would need to include sufficient flexibility to accommodate change over time; and, in the context of allocation of parental responsibilities, Helen Reece in 'The Degradation of Parental Responsibility' shows how the meaning of parental responsibility can develop within a legal system as a result of various shifts of approach. Reece identifies a trend in English law away from parental responsibility as *authority* towards *legitimation*. This trend, she argues, is displayed in the proliferation of non-parents who can acquire parental responsibility; its degradation in some cases from active responsibility towards a mere status; and a shift in the courts' reasons for conferring parental responsibility which are now 'less to do with decision-making and more to do with feelings and emotions'.[73]

A controversial issue in many jurisdictions in recent years in relation to the sharing of responsibility for children has been how the law should address post-separation parenting disputes. Belinda Fehlberg, Bruce Smyth, Mavis Maclean and Ceridwen Roberts – in 'Legislating for Shared Time Parenting after Separation: A Research Review' – summarise research on post-separation shared time parenting, and examine the outcomes of legislating to encourage shared time parenting in Australia. Research shows that shared parenting arrangements can work well when parents cooperate, and communicate and there are low levels of conflict. By contrast, shared care can be a particular risk factor for child well-being where there are issues of child safety, or high ongoing parental conflict, and in the case of children under four years old. Fehlberg et al. suggest that change in Australian law to encourage shared parenting led to an increase in judicially decided shared care arrangements, with a risk that such orders were being made in cases of high risk to children. This is an issue which has resonance across several jurisdictions given a rise in shared parenting and in shared parenting laws.[74]

In the final Part of this collection of works, attention turns to the relationship between parental rights and the state, in the context of child protection. To what extent should state interference with the exercise of parental rights be permitted?

Hugh LaFollette, in 'Licensing Parents Revisited',[75] argues that there are good reasons for licensing the role of parents in the same way as professional activities are licensed (and that parenting does not differ materially in this context from professional activity) – parenting being an activity which is risky, with substantial costs to children, and which requires competence in terms of knowledge, abilities, judgement and appropriate disposition. LaFollette goes on to argue that, if licensing is theoretically appropriate, we should lament not implementing such a system in practice '(a) if we can specify criteria for a competent parent, (b) if we have moderately accurate methods for determining competence, and (c) if there are no special reasons for thinking that the program's costs exceed its benefits'. LaFollette suggests a limited licensing programme, along the lines of an education programme, together with a system of assistance/monitoring in relation to young children in particular. LaFollette's views chime with those of Dwyer (discussed earlier in relation to allocation of parentage) in his characterisation as dangerous the view that 'biological parents have a special moral claim to their children, a claim that outweighs the interests of children in all but rare cases'.

David Archard, in 'Child Abuse: Parental Rights and the Interests of the Child', rejects the suggestion that parents should be 'licensed', but is also critical of the liberal standard for state intervention which provides that the state may only intervene to protect children when alerted to some actual or potential harm to the child. Archard argues that family privacy is of dubious value given the facts of child abuse, and he calls for a much closer monitoring of the family.

Sonia Harris-Short, in 'Making and Breaking Family Life: Adoption, the State, and Human Rights', explores the 'extent to which the state's duties and responsibilities in the context of adoption are framed and reinforced by a rights-based discourse'.[76] Harris-Short notes that through adoption 'the state is uniquely engaged in the process of creating and destroying family life'[77] and that a rights-based discourse ensures that 'the various rights and interests of the parties are carefully articulated and properly and fairly considered at every stage of the decision-making process'.[78] All three members of the 'adoption triad' are potentially vulnerable. As Harris-Short comments:

> Prospective adopters, for example, may face arbitrary and even discriminatory decisions as to their suitability to adopt. Birth parents, often demonized by policy-makers in this area, can be marginalised in the drive towards achieving permanency for the child. Children can find their own rights and interests subsumed within the interests of the adult parties, particularly the adoptive parents.[79]

Harris-Short examines what she sees as the invaluable protections afforded by Article 8 of the ECHR in the context of the making of adoption orders and post-adoption child–birth parent contact, while observing that the obligations of the Convention are not fully met in a domestic context. She notes a tension between a policy drive to seek to achieve permanency for children through adoption and the danger of compromising efforts to reunite a child with his or her birth family as required by Article 8.[80] Harris-Short also observes that the application of a liberal rights-based discourse – with its likely emphasis on the privacy, autonomy and self-sufficiency of the new adoptive family – provides little basis on which to challenge the law's approach to provision of post-adoption support in the context of an increasing move towards a contract/services model of adoption.[81] As Harris-Short comments, '[t]he field of social welfare assistance, including family support, is not a natural home for the human rights paradigm'.[82]

The 25 works in this volume represent a rich 'thicket' of scholarship on the issue of parental rights and responsibilities in a dense forest of literature. It should be clear from the foregoing account that, as editor, I have sought to offer an overview map and a pathway through the forest, via six signposts examining respectively:

(I)   Who or what is a parent? Underlying rationales;
(II) Legal concepts of 'parent' and their linkage;
(III) The legal parent – accommodating complexity;
(IV) The nature and scope of parental rights;
(V)   Shared parental responsibility; and
(VI) Parental rights and the state.

The footnotes and bibliographies in the works themselves, together with the contextualisation and further works highlighted in this Introduction, offer possible diversions from the main route. There are surely many more valuable journeys to be taken; but it is hoped that readers will find this one enjoyable and useful.

Stephen Gilmore, Professor of Family Law, School of Law, King's College London[83]

Notes

1 For an overview of the extensive philosophical literature, see, for example, Elizabeth Brake and Joseph Millum, 'Parenthood and Procreation', in *The Stanford Encyclopedia of Philosophy* (Fall 2014 edn), Edward N. Zalta (ed.), <http://plato.stanford.edu/archives/fall2014/entries/parenthood/>. An accessible entry into the philosophical literature can be found in 'Part III Children, Parents, Family and State' of D. Archard, *Children: Rights and Childhood* (2nd edn, London: Routledge, 2004) and his accompanying bibliographic essay, especially pp. 238ff. A cross-section of perspectives can be found in O. O'Neill and W. Ruddick, *Having Children: Philosophical and Legal Reflections on Parenthood* (New York: Oxford University Press, 1979), and see also G. Scarre (ed.), *Children, Parents and Politics* (Cambridge: Cambridge University Press, 1989). For lawyers' engagements with a variety of perspectives, see C. Barton and G. Douglas, *Law and Parenthood* (London: Butterworths, 1995), especially chapters 1 and 2; J. Herring, R. Probert and S. Gilmore, *Great Debates in Family Law* (2nd edn, Basingstoke: Palgrave Macmillan, 2015), chapter 2; and R. Probert, S. Gilmore and J. Herring (eds), *Responsible Parents and Parental Responsibility* (Oxford: Hart, 2009). For a socio-legal analysis, see A. Bainham, S. Day Sclater and M. Richards (eds), *What is a Parent? A Socio-Legal Analysis* (Oxford: Hart, 1999).

2 It is acknowledged that different starting points could have been taken, but choices must be made.

3 For an account of possible components of the biological connection, see M. Johnson, 'A Biomedical Perspective on Parenthood' in Bainham, Day Sclater and Richards, *What is a*

Parent?, pp. 47–72. For a collection examining experiences, practices and social institutions surrounding childbirth, see F. Ebtehaj, J. Herring, M. H. Johnson and M. Richards (eds), *Birth Rites and Rights* (Oxford: Hart, 2011).

4 Hall, at p. 74. See J. Eekelaar, 'Are Parents Morally Obliged to Care for Their Children?' (1991) 11(3) *Oxford Journal of Legal Studies* 340–353 for the view that the duty to care for children falls upon human society as part of a general duty to promote human flourishing. On this view, the acceptance or otherwise of the intuition argued for by Hall would be a decision for the particular society concerned. For discussion of a legal regime which permits rejection of parental duties through anonymous birth, see N. Lefaucheur, 'The French "Tradition" of Anonymous Birth: The Lines of Argument' (2004) 18 *International Journal of Law, Policy and the Family* 319–342; E. Steiner 'Odièvre v France – Desperately Seeking Mother – Anonymous Births in the European Court of Human Rights' (2003) 15 *Child and Family Law Quarterly* 425–448; and see also K. O'Donovan and J. Marshall, 'After Birth: Decisions about Becoming a Mother' in A. Diduck and K. O'Donovan (eds), *Feminist Perspectives on Family Law* (London: Routledge-Cavendish, 2006), pp. 101–122.

5 For discussion of this perspective, see Archard, *Children: Rights and Childhood*, chapter 10, pp. 141ff. Another view – as expressed by Onora O'Neill in 'Begetting, Bearing and Rearing' in O. O'Neill and W. Ruddick (eds), *Having Children: Philosophical and Legal Reflections on Parenthood* (New York: Oxford University Press, 1979), pp. 25ff. and discussed by Blustein in this volume – is that procreation is a way in which parental obligations can be undertaken, i.e. a voluntarist view of parenthood. On reproductive autonomy, see J. R. Spencer and Antje du Bois-Pedain (eds) *Freedom and Responsibility in Reproductive Choice* (Oxford: Hart, 2006) and S. Day Sclater, F. Ebtehaj, E. Jackson and M. Richards (eds), *Regulating Autonomy: Sex, Reproduction and Family* (Oxford: Hart, 2009).

6 Archard, *Children: Rights and Childhood*, at p. 143.
7 Hall, at p. 75.
8 Ibid., at p. 80.
9 Ibid., at p. 76 (emphasis in original).
10 Ibid., at p. 78 (emphasis removed).
11 Ibid., at p. 419.
12 As Rebecca Probert points out, however, this certainty is not achieved if the surrogate mother is engaging more than one commissioning couple: see R. Probert, 'Families, Assisted Reproduction and the Law' (2004) *Child and Family Law Quarterly* 3(16) 273–288, at p. 285.
13 (1993) 5 Cal 4th 84.
14 The position in England and Wales is different, prioritising the gestational mother as parent, and is subjected to detailed critical examination in Kirsty Horsey's article in this volume.
15 Douglas, at p. 640.
16 See M. Shultz, 'Reproductive Technology and Intent-Based Parenthood: An Opportunity for Gender Neutrality' (1990) 2 *Wisconsin Law Review* 297–398.
17 Bayne and Kolers, at p. 241.
18 Blustein, at p. 79.
19 Blustein, at p. 85. For discussion of the role of causation in parenthood in a legal context, see Probert, 'Families, Assisted Reproduction and the Law'.
20 Dwyer, at p. 276. For a detailed defence of Dwyer's view, see J. G. Dwyer, *The Relationship Rights of Children* (Cambridge: Cambridge University Press, 2006). For a review of this work, see S. Gilmore, 'The Relationship Rights of Children' (2008) 22(2) *International Journal of Law, Policy and the Family* 273–281.
21 Dwyer, at p. 276.
22 Ibid., at p. 279.

23 See also N. V. Lowe, 'English Adoption Law: Past, Present and Future', in S. N. Katz, J. Eekelaar and M. Maclean (eds), *Cross Currents: Family Law and Policy in the US and England* (Oxford: Oxford University Press, 2000). For other accounts of shifts in divorce law and policy, see S. N. Katz and J. Eekelaar, 'Adoption of Children in the United States and England and Wales' in J. Eekelaar and R. George (eds), *Routledge Handbook of Family Law and Policy* (London: Routledge, 2014), pp. 266–273; J. Lewis, 'Adoption: The Nature of Policy Shifts in England and Wales, 1972–2002' (2004) 18(2) *International Journal of Law, Policy and the Family* 235–255.

24 Lowe, at p. 371. The tension between the idea of post-adoption support and a human rights framework for adoption is explored by Sonia Harris-Short in her article in this volume.

25 See, for example, *In re G (Children)* [2006] UKHL 43, in which Baroness Hale of Richmond referred to the distinction between the 'legal parent' and the natural parent, indicating that a person might be the natural parent of a child in various ways: the genetic parent; the gestational parent; and the social or psychological parent (see paras 32–36).

26 See, for example, R. S. Collier and S. Sheldon, *Fathers' Rights Activism and Legal Reform in Comparative Perspective* (Oxford: Hart, 2006); M. Oechsle, U. Mueller and S. Hess (eds), *Fatherhood in Late Modernity: Cultural Images, Social Practices, Structural Frames* (Leverkusen: Barbara Budrich, 2012); R. Collier, 'Fatherhood, Law and Fathers' Rights: Rethinking the Relationship between Gender and Welfare' in J. Herring, S. Choudry and J. Wallbank (eds), *Rights, Gender and Family Law* (London: Routledge-Cavendish, 2010), pp. 119–143; R. Collier, 'Engaging Fathers? Responsibility, Law and the 'Problem of Fatherhood'' in J. Bridgeman, H. Keating and C. Lind (eds), *Responsibility, Law and the Family* (Aldershot: Ashgate, 2008), pp. 169–190.

27 See, for example, S. Boyd, *Child Custody, Law, and Women's Work* (Toronto: Oxford University Press, 2003).

28 S. Boyd, 'Gendering Legal Parenthood: Bio-Genetic Ties, Intentionality and Responsibility' (2007) *Windsor Yearbook of Access to Justice* 25(1) 63–94. Boyd argues that 'thinking about ways to move forward in the field of legal parenthood must be attentive to gender and power differentials and to social relations around parenting. Women and men are differentially situated in relation to parenthood, even now that motherhood and fatherhood are fragmented into various possible components. In order to take such differences into account, analysis, legal frameworks, and dispute resolution must carefully consider the social context and circumstances of each parenting dispute.'

29 For accounts of approaches in some jurisdictions, see, for example, A. Campbell, 'Conceiving Parents Through Law' (2007) 21 *International Journal of Law Policy and the Family* 242–273 (Canadian common law and Quebec civil law); Boyd, 'Gendering Legal Parenthood' (Canadian law); M. Garrison, 'Law Making for Baby Making: An Interpretive Approach to the Determination of Legal Parentage' (2000) 113(4) *Harvard Law Review* 835–923 (US law); K. T. Bartlett, 'Re-Expressing Parenthood' (1988–89) 98 *Yale Law Journal* 293 (US law); I. Karpin and J. Millbank, 'Regulation of Assisted Reproductive Technology and Surrogacy in Australia', chapter 3.2 in Eekelaar and George, *Routledge Handbook of Family Law and Policy*, pp. 201–214 (Australian law).

30 For an overview of English law, see, for example, A. Bainham and S. Gilmore, *Children: The Modern Law* (Bristol: Jordan Publishing, 2013), Part II Children and Families, especially chapters 3 and 4.

31 For a discussion of the normative assumptions underlying the English legislation on parenthood in cases of assisted conception, and questioning the role played by the ideal of the 'sexual family' in the reform process, see J. McCandless and S. Sheldon 'The Human Fertilisation and Embryology Act (2008) and the Tenacity of the Sexual Family' (2010) 73 *Modern Law*

Review 175–207. As Alison Diduck has observed, there is nothing inevitable about predicating parenthood upon the biology of the sexual family: see A. Diduck, '"If only we can find the appropriate terms to use the issue will be solved": Law, Identity and Parenthood' (2007) 19(4) *Child and Family Law Quarterly* 1–23.
32 Lind and Hewitt, at p. 405.
33 See on a similar distinction, J. Masson, 'Parenting by Being; Parenting by Doing – In Search of Principles for Founding Families', in J. R. Spencer and A. Du Bois-Pedain (eds), *Freedom and Responsibility in Reproductive Choice* (Oxford: Hart, 2006).
34 Jackson, at p. 74.
35 See also A. Bainham, 'Status Anxiety? The Rush for Family Recognition' in F. Ebtehaj, B. Lindley and M. Richards (eds), *Kinship Matters* (Oxford: Hart, 2006), p. 58.
36 For a discussion of DNA testing and kinship, see T. Freeman and M. Richards, 'DNA Testing and Kinship: Paternity, Genealogy and the Search for the "Truth" of our Genetic Origins' in Ebtehaj, Lindley and Richards, *Kinship Matters*, pp. 67ff.; for a discussion of the impact in the USA, see M. A. Rothstein, T. H. Murray, G. E. Kaebnick and M. Anderlik Majunder (eds), *Genetic Ties and the Family: The Impact of Paternity Testing on Parents and Children* (Baltimore, MD: Johns Hopkins University Press, 2005). See also H. Draper and J. Ives, 'Paternity Testing: A Poor Test of Fatherhood' (2009) 31(4) *Journal of Social Welfare and Family Law* 407–418.
37 Bainham, at p. 348.
38 Ibid., at p. 349. See also T. Callus, 'First "Designer Babies", Now "a la carte" Parents' (2008) *Family Law* 143 (arguing that extension of assisted conception provisions to same-sex parents creates a deception, concealing the necessary heterosexual element of procreation). A 'head-on challenge to these arguments is that legal parenthood need not be linked to biological parenthood at all': see Herring, Probert and Gilmore, *Great Debates in Family Law*, at p. 30. For the suggestion of a new model which would recognise the social importance of the biological link but reserve legal status for functional parenthood, see T. Callus, 'A New Parenthood Paradigm for Twenty-First Century Family Law in England and Wales?' (2012) 32(3) *Legal Studies* 347–368.
39 For discussion of licensed donor insemination, see C. Jones, 'Parents in Law: Subjective Impacts and Status Implications around the Use of Licensed Donor Insemination', in Diduck and O'Donovan, *Feminist Perspectives on Family Law*, chapter 5.
40 Smith, at p. 378.
41 Ibid., at p. 380.
42 For a useful collection of essays on this topic, see R. Cook, S. Day Sclater and F. Kaganas, *Surrogate Motherhood International Perspectives* (Oxford: Hart, 2003).
43 Horsey, at p. 464.
44 By contrast, the issue of parents' rights against the state is addressed in Part VI of this volume.
45 Montague, at pp. 52–53.
46 Ibid., at p. 55.
47 Ibid., at p. 62.
48 Ibid.
49 Ibid., at p. 64.
50 In England and Wales, for example, section 3 of the Children Act 1989 still refers to 'rights' in its definition of parental responsibility as 'all the rights, duties, powers, responsibilities and authority which by law a parent of a child has in relation to the child and his property'.
51 Archard, *Children: Rights and Childhood*, at p. 149. For a defence of this view, see J. Blustein, *Parents and Children: The Ethics of the Family* (Oxford: Oxford University Press, 1982). For judicial expression of a similar view, see *Gillick v West Norfolk and Wisbech AHA* [1986] AC

112, at 170, per Lord Fraser of Tullybelton: 'parental rights to control a child do not exist for the benefit of the parent. They exist for the benefit of the child and they are justified only in so far as they enable the parent to perform his duties towards the child, and towards other children in the family.'
52 See, for example, A. McCall Smith, 'Is Anything Left of Parental Rights?' in E. Sutherland and A. McCall Smith (eds), *Family Rights: Family Law and Medical Advance* (Edinburgh: Edinburgh University Press, 1990); D. Archard, *Children, Family and the State* (Aldershot: Ashgate, 2003); and Macleod and Bainham in this volume.
53 B. M. Dickens, 'The Modern Function and Limits of Parental Rights' (1981) 97 *Law Quarterly Review* 462, at p. 464.
54 Macleod, at p. 119.
55 Ibid. For a discussion of the child's interests in leading a good life, see Jonathan Herring and Charles Foster, 'Welfare Means Relationality, Virtue and Altruism' (2012) *Legal Studies* 480; and for a recent case exploring this issue in the context of a dispute about children's education and religious upbringing, see *Re G (Education: Religious Upbringing)* [2012] EWCA Civ 123, [2013] 1 FLR 677.
56 Macleod, at p. 120.
57 Ibid., at p. 127.
58 Ibid., at p. 128.
59 Ibid., at p. 129. For a discussion that 'autonomy' should be examined through the lens of our connectedness to others (relational autonomy), see J. Herring, 'Relational Autonomy and Family Law', in Wallbank, Choudhry and Herring, *Rights, Gender and Family Law*, chapter 12.
60 Macleod, at p. 129.
61 Ibid., at p. 130.
62 Ibid.
63 See, for example, R. Lindley, 'Teenagers and Other Children' in G. Scarre (ed.), *Children, Parents and Politics* (New York: Cambridge University Press, 1989); J. Eekelaar 'The Emergence of Children's Rights' (1986) 6 *Oxford Journal of Legal Studies* 161; A. Bainham, 'The Balance of Power in Family Decisions' (1986) 45(2) *Cambridge Law Journal* 262. An influential common law decision is *Gillick v West Norfolk and Wisbech AHA* [1986] AC 112. For a range of perspectives on the impact of the case, see J. Fortin, 'The Gillick Decision – Not Just A High-Water Mark' in S. Gilmore, J. Herring and R. Probert (eds), *Landmark Cases in Family Law* (Oxford: Hart, 2011), chapter 11, and S. Gilmore, 'The Limits of Parental Responsibility' in Probert, Gilmore and Herring, *Responsible Parents and Parental Responsibility*, chapter 4.
64 Bainham, at p. 30. An example provided by Bainham is the interest which both parent and child may have in maintaining contact with each other.
65 Ibid., at p. 33.
66 For criticism of the welfare or paramountcy principle, see R. H. Mnookin, 'Child-Custody Adjudication: Judicial Functions in the Face of Indeterminacy' (1975) 39(3) *Law and Contemporary Problems* 226–293; H. Reece, 'The Paramountcy Principle: Consensus or Construct? (1996) 49 *Current Legal Problems* 267–304; S. Parker, 'The Best Interests of the Child – Principles and Problems' in P. Alston (ed.), *The Best Interests of the Child: Reconciling Culture and Human Rights* (Oxford: Clarendon, 1994); and J. Herring, 'Farewell Welfare?' (2005) 27(2) *Journal of Social Welfare and Family Law* 159–171.
67 Herring, at p. 89.
68 Ibid., at p. 104.
69 For an alternative approach should the principle be abandoned, which would take account of adults' interests while privileging the welfare of the child, see J. Eekelaar, 'Beyond the Welfare Principle' (2002) 14(3) *Child and Family Law Quarterly* 237–249.

70 See also J. Herring, 'The Human Rights Act and the Welfare Principle in Family Law: Conflicting or Complementary?' (1999) 11(3) *Child and Family Law Quarterly* 223–235.
71 See articles on allocation of parental responsibility.
72 The debate has been particularly strong in England and Wales. For the historical perspective, see A. Bainham, 'The Illegitimacy Saga' in R. Probert and C. Barton (eds), *Fifty Years in Family Law Essays for Stephen Cretney* (Cambridge: Intersentia, 2012) and S. Cretney, *Family Law in the Twentieth Century: A History* (Oxford: Oxford University Press, 2003), chapter 15; A. Bainham, 'When is a Parent Not a Parent? Reflections on the Unmarried Father and His Child in English Law' (1989) 3 *International Journal of Law, Policy and the Family* 208–239; R. Deech, 'The Unmarried Father and Human Rights' (1992) 4 *Journal of Child Law* 3; G. Branchflower, 'Parental Responsibility and Human Rights' (1999) 29 *Family Law* 34–37; R. Pickford, 'Unmarried Fathers and the Law' in Bainham, Day Sclater andRichards, *What is a Parent?*, chapter 8; S. Sheldon, 'Unmarried Fathers and Parental Responsibility: A Case for Reform?' (2001) 9 *Feminist Legal Studies* 93; S. Gilmore, 'Parental Responsibility and the Unmarried Father – A New Dimension to the Debate' (2003) *Child and Family Law Quarterly* 15(1) 21–93. For a comparative perspective, see J. M. Scherpe, 'Establishing and Ending Parental Responsibility: A Comparative View' in Probert, Gilmore and Herring, *Responsible Parents and Parental Responsibility*, chapter 3.
73 Reece, at p. 98.
74 H. Rhoades 'The Rise and Rise of Shared Parenting Laws: A Critical Reflection' (2002) 19 *Canadian Journal of Family Law* 75; H. Rhoades and S. B. Boyd, 'Reforming Custody Laws: A Comparative Study' (2004) 18(2) *International Journal of Law, Policy and the Family* 119.
75 See also LaFollette's earlier article on this topic, H. LaFollette, 'Licensing Parents' (1980) 9 *Philosophy and Public Affairs* 182. For other works on this topic, see C. P. Mangel, 'Licensing Parents: How Feasible?' (1988) 22 *Family Law Quarterly* 17; J. C. Westman, *Licensing Parents: Can We Prevent Child Abuse and Neglect?* (Cambridge, MA: Perseus Books, 1994); M. Freeman, 'The Right to Responsible Parents' in Bridgeman, Keating and Lind, *Responsibility, Law and the Family*, pp. 21–40.
76 Harris-Short, at p. 28.
77 Ibid.
78 Ibid., at p. 29.
79 Ibid., at p. 30.
80 Amendments effected by the Children and Families Act 2014 have further sought to speed up the process of taking children through the care system and providing permanency through adoption. For a critical account, see A. Bainham and S. Gilmore, 'The English Children and Families Act 2014' (2015) *Victoria University of Wellington Law Review* 46(3) 627–648.
81 See the discussion by Lowe in this volume.
82 Harris-Short, at p. 48.
83 I am very grateful to the series editor, Professor Alison Diduck, Professor of Law at University College London, for inviting me to compile this volume; for her patience and encouragement in its preparation; and for her very helpful comments on an earlier draft of this Introduction, which have significantly improved it.

Part I:

Who or what is a parent? Underlying rationales

1

THE ORIGIN OF PARENTAL RIGHTS

Barbara Hall

The remarkable growth of reproductive technology is steadily unhinging a Pandora's Box of questions and difficulties regarding the essential nature of human procreation. Moral and legal dilemmas regarding the liabilities and entitlements associated with procreation seem inevitable. How are we to characterize the relationship between the procreator and the reproduced?

In a less technologically advanced time the above question could only have been understood as an inquiry into the nature of the parent/child relationship. Today the makeup of the parties is more ambiguous. Perhaps the relationship contemplated by the question would be the one between the sperm donor and fetus, the surrogate mother and newborn, the divorcing couple and the frozen embryos.

In this paper I examine the relationship of parent and child. I do so because, ultimately, how we judge the rights and responsibilities associated with these newly emerging sets of procreational relationships will be a reflection of our beliefs about the privileges and obligations of the prototype parent/child relationship.

Every culture has certain assumptions about what parents can and cannot do with and to their progeny. In our own culture these ideals are given constitutional protection. For instance, parents have the right to the physical possession of the child, including the day-to-day care and companionship of the child; the right to discipline the child, including the right to inculcate in the child the parents' moral and ethical standards; and the right to prevent adoption without parents' consent.[1]

These are just some of the benefits to which most of us believe that parents as such are entitled. They are not absolute; and there are undoubtedly others. But, are these beliefs morally justified in addition to being legally sanctioned? What is the moral basis of the tie that binds the procreator to the begotten? Is the right relevantly like a property right? How tenuous is it? How immutable?

The issue of what specific moral rights parents have vis-a-vis their progeny is itself a matter of controversy. However, it is not necessary for our purposes to broach this topic. The fact is that we do think, all things considered, that biological parents should have the original charge of children. By "original charge" I mean the initial legal and moral *claims to* and *responsibilities for* their progeny. What is it about the biological parents (versus the rest of the world) that fuels the intuition that they have initial entitlement to a child?

One feature distinguishing the parents from everyone else is that they (and no one else) have acted distinctly in begetting the child. Perhaps it is these unique actions that yield them special rights. Let us explore what these actions might be and how they could generate rights.

John Locke in his Theory of [Just] Acquisition[2] offers an explanation of how it is that an individual may come to rightfully acquire or possess a thing—to have rights over and above the claims of anyone else to that thing. According to Locke, an individual's actions vis-a-vis Thing X generate his rights to that thing. Specifically, when one acts to mix one's labor with X (X being unowned) one justly obtains X.[3] Moreover, Locke says, "[J]ustice gives every man a title to the product of his honest industry."[4] Can this "labor theory" provide an adequate explanation of the basis for parents' rights to children?

Lawrence Becker succinctly outlines the basics of the "mixing" argument. The initial premise upon which Locke rests his conclusions is that everyone has a right in his own person that no other person can claim.[5] Given this, the labor he produces with his body also belongs to him. Locke mentions only labor in this context, but presumably whatever a body generates is "from that body" (i.e., of that person). Thus, a smile, an idea, or a chemical secretion can be described as things being "of" or from a person's body and, therefore, things belonging to that person.[6]

Locke's theory of property rights is based on the presumption that a person, by mixing his labor (what he owns) with an unowned thing, comes to own that thing to which the labor has been attached. This "leap" Locke makes is not without its critics.[7]

Putting aside the problems associated with the idea of "mixing" labor with a thing, let us assume that we are indirectly and retroactively afforded protection for our labors when we are allowed property rights to the thing on which we have labored.[8] Can we argue that the reason that parents have "first dibs" on the children they produce is that they have labored to bring these children into existence?

Perhaps it should be stated here that Locke himself did not use his theory of property rights to justify parental rights. Parental rights were not akin to property rights. Parents were charged with the care of their

THE ORIGIN OF PARENTAL RIGHTS

children only because of the latter's imperfectly developed faculties of reason.[9] Commentators have argued that Locke's attempt to distinguish between property rights and parental rights is unsuccessful and contradictory.[10]

A critical assessment of Locke's theories of parental and property rights may indeed lead one to the conclusion that his theory arbitrarily distinguishes between children and vases.[11] But the question is simply whether the relationship between parents and children, however it is conceived, rests on the notion of a begetter's privilege which is tied to a Lockean notion of property rights requiring labor as a necessary condition.

In the next few pages I will argue that labor is neither a necessary nor a sufficient factor in the attribution of rights to biological parents. Hence, *Locke's labor theory cannot justify our notion that initial parental rights belong to the biological progenitors.*

Consider the following. Suppose a woman, Gertrude, agrees to serve as a surrogate mother. That is, she agrees to gestate and give birth to a child for the couple with whom she contracts. Should Gertrude have any parental entitlement to the child? If the contribution of labor is the determining factor in the allowance of parental entitlements, then Gertrude should have parental rights. Certainly, the amount of labor she expended in gestating and giving birth to the child exceeds that expended by the couple for whom the baby is delivered. What if the child is genetically unrelated to Gertrude?

There are essentially two ways in which a woman may provide surrogacy services for a couple wishing to have a child.[12] One, she may agree to have her own ovum artificially inseminated by the male, then surrender the child upon its birth to him. His wife, who (typically) is infertile, then legally adopts the child. This has been the customary scenario for surrogacy arrangements. In the United States, courts have held that the surrogate mother and the biological father are the natural parents of such children.[13]

These rulings have undoubtedly given pause to infertile couples who might wish to choose the surrogacy option. They hold that no surrogate mother can contractually be compelled to abrogate her maternal rights, nor can she receive money for her services as a surrogate mother. (It would be tantamount to selling her child. She may, however, donate her services.[14]) These rulings have protected women who decided, upon giving birth to a child, that they did not wish to give up their rights to that child.

The courts' holdings do not seem out of accord with our moral intuitions. Why? Is it because the labor of the surrogate perhaps warrants her having some maternal rights? Now, consider a second, more problematic scenario.

The surrogate, in essence, agrees to make a loan of her womb. She is implanted with the ovum of the prospective mother (donor female) which is fertilized with the prospective father's sperm either in vitro or in vivo.[15]

Here, *the surrogate is not genetically related to the child she carries.* The courts, however, still maintain that the surrogate is the natural mother of the child in these cases.[16] Again, the surrogate might seem to deserve rights to the child given that she has labored more than the intended mother in the gestation and birth of the child. But when we consider the biological father's labor in producing the child we can see that he has labored no more (and probably less) than the intended mother in donating her genetic material.[17]

If we are ascribing parental rights by the amount or type of labor expended in the reproduction process, then, perhaps, the child's parents ought to be the surrogate mother and the donor female. After all, the latter went through the uncomfortable labor of having her ovum extracted while it is doubtful that the prospective father experienced such discomfort in contributing his sperm. Certainly, it is not obvious that the biological father deserves more rights than the donor female. Yet she is not considered to be the natural mother, while he is deemed the natural father.

If it seems unfair that the sperm donor has presumed legal rights to the child but the ovum donor does not, it is because intuitively we believe that labor is not truly the determining factor in the ascription of parental rights. *It is not the actions or labors of the natural parents that warrant their entitlement to their children, but something more fundamental.* If Gertrude gives birth to a child that is the genetic progeny of Roger and Sally, and that has no genetic affiliation to herself, the child seems to be Roger's and Sally's, even though, legally, Gertrude is considered the biological mother and Sally must adopt the child.

The fact that the *child represents a genetic part of its parents is what fuels this intuition.* Parents are entitled to *their* children for the same reasons that they are entitled to anything that is a part of themselves. *Thus, it is ultimately a belief in the notion of self-ownership or self-integrity that fuels our presumption in favor of a natural parent's entitlement to her child.* If the concept of self-ownership is valid, then certainly whatever is constitutive of a person's body and self belongs to that person.[18]

Earlier I stated that the notion of self-ownership buttressed Locke's labor theory of acquisition: if a person owns himself, then he owns his labor. When he expends his labor, he is mixing something that he owns with some other thing and that is why he comes to acquire that other thing. Here, my claim is not about ownership of our labor, but about ownership of our genetic material. As I stated previously, labor turns out to be neither a necessary nor a sufficient condition for establishing parental rights. But, perhaps, the reader is not yet convinced that this point is correct. So, consider the following two scenarios:

THE ORIGIN OF PARENTAL RIGHTS

Scenario 1

Zerba, an evil but ingenious scientist, invents a device that can extract people's body parts unbeknownst to them. Zerba does not steal vital organs such as hearts and brains, but he does have a rather lucrative business selling misappropriated kidneys and lungs. He is soon discovered by the Filched Organ Police. He has a stockpile of unsold kidneys and lungs. Who, legally and morally, should be entitled to claim these organs? Justice seems to require that the unwilling donors be entitled to reclaim the organs or at least to receive compensation for them should they so desire. Why? Because the concept of self-ownership (or self-possession) gives them a superior claim to the organs from their bodies.

Scenario 2

The organ-heisting business becomes too risky for Zerba. He decides that there is less risk and more money in selling babies. He discovers that if he implants a human embryo into a cow's womb, the cow can gestate and give birth to a human child. Rather than using his organ-extracting device to purloin embryos from pregnant women, he prefers, instead, to extract ova and sperm from unsuspecting men and women and combine them through in vitro fertilization. He does this to allow his customers to "design" the children they wish to purchase. He then implants the embryo into a cow's womb for gestation.

Zerba's operation is eventually discovered by the Genetic Crimes Police who close down his business. What, now, should become of the unsold, soon-to-be-born fetuses?[19] Who, legally and morally, should be entitled to claim these babies? Does justice in this case dictate a different or more complex answer than it did in the case of the pilfered organs? If so, why? I suggest that it is still the individuals from whom the genetic materials were stolen who are entitled to lay claim to the neonates. This is true, even though none of these individuals labored to produce the children.

If it is true that someone is entitled to the infants, what would justify not allowing the genetic parents the presumption of entitlement to them? These "parents" have suffered a loss of a part of their persons. If they are not allowed at least some form of recompense for their loss, then we are not acknowledging that they have sustained a loss. Anyone suggesting that the genetic material losers represent a different type of case than do the organ losers seems to have the burden of proving why the cases are dissimilar.

Someone could suggest that the cases are different because in one situation you have a person who loses a kidney and can claim back that kidney, while in the other case you have a person who has lost an egg or some sperm and is claiming back a child. In the latter case, the recompense far exceeds the actual loss.

My response, however, is that there is no way that the lost genetic material can be recovered. It has obviously undergone substantial changes! If we acknowledge that these persons are due compensation because they have lost something that once belonged to them (however great or minor we might consider the loss) then we are admitting that these persons have at least some claim to/on the children artificially produced from their genes. And this claim exists independent of their labor since they did not labor.

Why should the loss/theft of their ovum and sperm entitle these individuals to a presumption of parental rights instead of, say, a presumption of a $50 remuneration? Not everyone is capable of being a good parent, so why should they be entitled even to the supposition of rights to the possession of a child just because s/he has their genes?

My basic contention here is not that the biological parents *are* entitled to parental rights to their children because of the genetic connection. Rather, *my argument is that it is the biological connection that establishes an initial presumption of parental rights to the children.* The parents can forfeit the claim by not fulfilling or assuming their parental duties of care for the child.[20] When the questions, "Whose child is it?" and "Who is entitled to the child?" have different answers, it is because of some biological parent's forfeiture. Thus, we may recognize that little Billie is Jed and Ida's son, but that because the courts put him in foster care they are not entitled any parental rights.

But, why the presumption of parental rights and not the presumption of $50? To answer this, let us return to the example of the people who lost their bodily organs. Suppose one of the people from whom a kidney was extracted is an alcoholic. The kidney is still in relatively good condition. Would anyone suggest that because of his alcoholism he would not be a good caretaker of the kidney and, therefore, should not be entitled either to the kidney or to full remuneration for it, thereby failing to acknowledge his prior claim to it? People do not take the best care of their bodies; yet, we would still give credence to their demands for the return of their organs. Why is it different with the loss of genetic matter that has become a child?

"The consequences of mistreating a child are potentially more dire than are the consequences of mistreating a kidney," comes the response. "This is why we can return a kidney to an alcoholic, but cannot give a child to people who are either unwitting procreators or unproven parents." But this is exactly what we do! The parents of children born from wombs in the "normal" way are presumed to have entitlement to their children when they are born, even given prior evidence of poor parenting skills. Child abusers are not automatically required to relinquish their newborns. How and why should the method of birth affect the premise of parental rights?

To restate: what I am asserting is that it is the concept of self-ownership (integrity/possession) and the ensuing biological connections between parents and their offspring, not the concept of labor, that gives parents the initial presumption of rights or entitlements to the children. When we say that B is A and C's child, we are saying that B is (composed) of A and C and that A and C, therefore, are presumed to have certain privileges regarding B that no one else can initially claim.[21]

The answers to the questions "Whose child is it?" and "Who is entitled to it?" are not always the same, but the answer to the first question is presumed to be the answer to the second. This presumption can be overcome (given some malfeasance or abnegation by the biological parents), but it is not a presumption that can be initially averted.[22]

I am not maintaining that self-ownership is a valid notion. Perhaps the materialist is right after all. My claim is that our acceptance of the concept of self-ownership (or some materialist equivalent) buttresses our notion that parents have original claim to the children born from their genetic substances.

One might reasonably assume the Lockeanesque position that self-ownership generates ownership of labor which in turn generates entitlement to the fruit of one's labor which could be one's children. Indeed, this was the view I initially examined; but the evolution of technology shows the need for more fine-tuned distinctions. Until recently, it was not possible in case of childbirth to separate the labor of parents from the process of reproduction. Now, however, it is clearly possible that a child may be produced from a male and female without either person having to labor in the process. Yet the child derived from the male and female would, by the principle of self-ownership, belong to that couple. Thus, the scenario I suggest is *self-ownership —> ownership of genetic material —> rights to child* as opposed to the Lockean notion of *self-ownership —> ownership of labor —> rights to child*.

Earlier I discussed some of the problems with the concept of self-ownership. There is another more perplexing problem arising from the concept. The notion that all persons own themselves seems glaringly incompatible with the notion that parents own their children. The latter statement precludes the former. I cannot own myself because my parents own me. And they cannot own themselves because their parents own them . . . and so on. How do we come to own ourselves, given our parents' prior claim?

One could hold the view that as the child grows it becomes less physically derivative of the parents and more self-constituted.[23] By the child's age of majority the genetic substance actually derived from the parents constitutes a truly minimal part of the adult progeny. Unfortunately, this argument quantifies genetic material as if it were something that could be measured in amounts diminished through the years. Parental rights as I have argued, though, do not accrue because of the amount of genetic contribution to the offspring. They are, instead, rights arising due to the *fact* of parental genetic contribution to the child.

We might reasonably say that persons own themselves and, upon procreation, this fact entitles these persons to a trusteeship over their children (their derived genetic substance), a la Locke.

It seems reasonable to assume that it is at the child's age of majority that the parental "hold" might conflict with the child's self-ownership and autonomy, and because we believe that the latter is of greater importance than the former, parental governance should dissipate. But if this were truly the case, we would not be able to find fault with grown children who abandon their needy parents or who feel no sort of filial duty or responsibility. Arguably, we do recognize some sort of parental claim on children even after adulthood. That claim may amount to no more than a right to a certain degree of respect or deference, or maybe more. So, rather than suggest that the parents do not have any sort of rights regarding their adult children, I suggest that the parental entitlements diminish significantly upon the child's majority, but they do not dissipate.[24] The parent, thus, is allowed to declare to the child, "You were once a part of me. The initial claim I have to/on you as a product of my genes does not disappear, but fades significantly once you have become an adult."

Summary

I have suggested that the notion of property, or, more properly, of self-ownership serves as the rudimentary justification for parental rights. It might, initially, seem to be the parents' act of creating the child that generates their rights over the child, but more fundamentally it is that the child is a product of the parents' own selves that generate the parental rights. These might be called rights of ownership, or more appropriately, rights of governance or trusteeship.[25]

Georgia State University

NOTES

1. *Black's Law Dictionary* (St. Paul: West Publishing Co., 1990).

2. *Two Treatises of Government.*

3. "As much land as a man tills, plants, improves, cultivates and can use the product of, so much is his property. He by his labor, does, as it were, inclose it from the Common." John Locke, *Two Treatises of Government*, Second Treatise, sects. 27, 32.

4. First Treatise, sect. 42, line 10.

5. Lawrence Becker, *Property Rights: Philosophical Foundations* (London: Routledge & Kegan Paul, 1977) p. 33. This first premise, that human beings have property rights in their own persons (their "own persons" being their bodies and I assume anything constitutive of their bodies), is not unproblematic given Locke's views about God as the creator. I shall return to this point later.

6. Copyright and patent laws in affording protection to a person's unique ideas, etc. seem to exemplify this notion.

7. Jeremy Waldron argues, "[S]ome sort of category mistake is involved in speaking of literally mixing one's labor with an object. Actions (labor) cannot be mixed with objects." See A. John Simmons, *The Lockean Theory of Rights* (Princeton: Princeton University Press, 1992), p. 267, fn. 110. Citing Jeremy Waldron, "Two Worries About Mixing One's Labor," *Philosophical Quarterly*, January, 1983. The contention seems to be that labor can no more be mixed or joined with a piece of wood (or any object) than can, say, a frown be mixed or joined with water. Also see John Nozick, who argues: "[W]hy isn't mixing what I own with what I don't own a way of losing what I own rather than a way of gaining what I don't? If I own a can of tomato juice and spill it in the sea so that its molecules . . . mingle evenly throughout the sea, do I thereby come to own the sea, or have I foolishly dissipated my tomato juice?" Robert Nozick, *Anarchy, State, and Utopia* (New York: Basic Books, 1974), p. 175.

8. See A. John Simmons, *The Lockean Theory of Rights* (Princeton: Princeton University Press, 1992), p. 267.

9. Second Treatise, section 58.

10. Becker, p. 37.

11. Becker: "It seems unlikely that anything will be found in the nature of the labor involved in conception, gestation, birth, and nurturing which will distinguish it sufficiently from the labor involved in cultivating a garden to justify using the latter in a Lockean argument but forbidding the use of the former." (p. 38)

12. Aubrey Milunsky and George J. Annas, eds., *Genetics and the Law III* (New York: Plenum Press, 1985), pp. 186–87.

13. Ibid. The reasons for this have to do with social considerations rather than any theory about labor expended. The courts have voided surrogate contracts for money because it amounted to the mother's selling her offspring. See Wesley H. Winborne,

ed., *Handling Pregnancy and Birth Cases/Family Law Series* (Colorado Springs: Shepard's/McGraw-Hill, 1995 supplement), pp. 70–72.

14. *Genetics and the Law,* pp. 186–87.

15. In vitro: outside of a living organism (i.e., in a test tube); in vivo: within a living organism (i.e., within a womb).

16. *Genetics and the Law,* p. 186.

17. The process of extracting the female's ovum can be very uncomfortable and time-consuming for her. *Genetics and the Law,* p. 213.

18. The concept of self-ownership, of course, poses its own problems. It seems to presuppose a Cartesian dualism: the subject and the object; the owner and the owned; the person and her body. If the materialist is right, however, then I am identical to my body and the notion of owning myself is unintelligible. Perhaps this debate can be sidestepped by acknowledging that even if materialism is true, so that strictly speaking one cannot be said to own one's self, the whole person is, nonetheless, constituted of a variety of parts. Thus, I am my kidneys, my brain, my toes, etc. And, if a part of me is removed, I am no longer wholly me. I might then argue that by a theory of self-possession or self-integrity we all have a *prima facie* right to be "whole" and, thereby reclaim (this piece of) *me*. Whereas, if I am a Cartesian, I reclaim it because it is *mine*.

19. The babies who have already been sold pose problems that need not be dealt with here.

20. Or by the commission of a crime, etc.

21. This would explain the legal conventions establishing the priority of kinship in matters of probate and other affairs.

22. Thus, in a case where a child is born from rape, everyone might agree that the child is John's (the rapist) and yet no one hold that John is entitled to rights to that child.

23. Thanks to Jim Humber for this point.

24. Also by this point in the child's life the issue of parental entitlements must be based on more than just sheer genetics. The amount of labor expended in rearing the child must surely, with the passage of time, solidify the parent's "hold on" the child. So, in effect, it is genetics that first gives parental entitlement to the child, but it is the parents' *labor* vis-a-vis the child that *maintains* the entitlement through the years.

25. I would like to thank everyone whose valuable time and thoughtful insights helped me complete this paper. Including, but not limited to, Joel Feinberg, Tom Christiano, Robert Almeder, and Jim Humber.

2

WHAT DOES IT MEAN TO BE A "PARENT"? THE CLAIMS OF BIOLOGY AS THE BASIS FOR PARENTAL RIGHTS

JOHN LAWRENCE HILL

Modern technology has wreaked havoc on conventional and legal notions of parenthood. For example, the traditional legal presumption granting parental rights to a child's biological mother seems at least questionable when the biological mother differs from the intended mother. As a result, courts employing traditional constitutional and family law doctrines have not adequately sorted out the claims of biological, gestational, and intended parents. In this Article, Professor Hill argues that the claims of those who first intend to have a child should prevail over those who assert parental rights on the basis of a biological or gestational relation. Such a view, he argues, is consistent with existing case law on the constitutional rights to procreation and privacy and supported by moral theory and modern scientific evidence.

INTRODUCTION

In 1799, the first reported use of artificial insemination took place.[1] With this event, the once-insoluble link between coitus and procreation was severed. However, while sporadic experimentation with artificial insemination continued through the first third of the twentieth century,[2] it was not until the 1930s and 1940s that artificial insemination by donor (AID) began to be recognized and employed on a widescale basis as a response to the problem of male infertility.[3] Within the past two de-

---

[1] U.S. Cong. Office of Technology Assessment, Infertility: Medical and Social Choices 36 (1988) [hereinafter OTA, Infertility]. Artificial insemination is a process by which sperm from a donor is injected, usually via syringe, into the vaginal opening. Artificial insemination consists of two varieties: artificial insemination by donor (AID) and by husband (AIH). AID is used where a woman's husband is sterile or where a woman wishes to avoid sexual intercourse. Id. at 126-28. AIH is used where normal coital methods of procreation are, for a variety of reasons, ineffective. Id.

[2] In the 1860s, for example, Dr. J. Marion Sims experimented with AID but later renounced the work as immoral. Note, Legal Recognition of Surrogate Gestation, 7 Women's Rts. L. Rep. 107, 119 n.88 (1982).

[3] It is estimated that anywhere from 6000 to 10,000 births a year result from AID. See Curie-Cohen, Luttrell & Shapiro, Current Practice in Artificial Insemination by Donor in the United States, 300 New Eng. J. Med. 585, 588 (1979). One estimate places the number at 20,000 a year. See Note, supra note 2, at 119. Approximately 250,000 Americans now living were born through the use of AID or AIH. Keane, Legal Problems of Surrogate Motherhood, 1980 S. Ill. U.L. Rev. 147, 148. See generally J. Fletcher, Morals and Medicine 101-16 (1954)

cades, the process of procreation has been fragmented further by the development of a number of techniques, most notably in-vitro fertilization, which separate the conceptive and gestational phases of reproduction.[4] Thus, the genetic and gestational mothers of a child are no longer necessarily the same individual.[5] In this manner, science has distilled the various phases of procreation—coitus, conception, and gestation—into their component parts, wreaking havoc on our prevailing conceptions of parenthood.

This is not to suggest that parenthood always has been recognized as being coextensive with the biological relationship. While legal adoption is a statutory creation not existing at common law,[6] in practice it undoubtedly has taken place from time immemorial.[7] Thus, a strong social tradition recognizes the purely social and psychological dimensions of parenting, even where these occur in the absence of biological ties. Yet even with adoption, adoptive parents may acquire parental status with respect to a particular child only after termination of the parental rights of the child's biological parents, particularly those of the natural mother.[8] With the new reproductive technologies and arrangements,[9]

(discussing and defending artificial insemination).

[4] In-vitro fertilization (IVF) involves the removal of mature oocytes (female germ cells) through a surgical procedure known as laparoscopy or a nonsurgical procedure such as ultrasound-guided oocyte retrieval. Once removed, the ova are combined with sperm in the laboratory. After fertilization, a number of preembryos, generally at the two to 16 cell stage, are transferred to the uterus of the woman who will bear the child. OTA, Infertility, supra note 1, at 123.

[5] The woman to whose uterus the fertilized preembryo is transferred need not be the original egg donor. The first child born in the U.S. of gestational surrogacy—a surrogate arrangement where the surrogate gestates but does not conceive the child—took place in 1985. Id. at 36.

[6] See Smith v. Org. of Foster Families, 431 U.S. 816, 845-46 (1977).

[7] See I. Sloan, The Law of Adoption and Surrogate Parenting 5-10 (1988).

[8] The "presumption of biology" serves as an irrebuttable legal presumption that the birth mother of the child is its legal mother and that adoption can take place only consequent to a termination of the parental rights of the birth mother. See Andrews, Surrogate Motherhood: Should the Adoption Model Apply?, 7 Children's Legal Rts. J. 13, 14-16 (1986) (discussing adoption laws as applied to surrogacy); notes 74-89 and accompanying text infra (discussing presumption of biology).

[9] I distinguish the reproductive "technologies" from "arrangements" to highlight that, while many of these procedures such as AID and IVF involve some use of technology, surrogate parenting involves a social and legal, rather than a technological, innovation. While surrogacy typically uses AID to impregnate the surrogate with the sperm of the intended father or a third-party donor, the characteristic feature of surrogacy is the social arrangement whereby a woman agrees to conceive (in most, but not all cases), to carry, and to relinquish the child upon birth. See Brophy, A Surrogate Mother Contract to Bear a Child, 20 J. Fam. L. 263, 268-91 (1981-82) (explaining surrogate arrangement); see also Hill, The Case for Enforcement of the Surrogate Contract, 8 Pol. & Life Sci. 147, 150-57 (1990) (discussing policy issues surrounding surrogacy); Suh, Surrogate Motherhood: An Argument for Denial of Specific Performance, 22 Colum. J.L. & Soc. Probs. 357, 362-71 (1989) (arguing that bonding process experienced during pregnancy gives woman inalienable right as parent).

however, a more fundamental question arises: where various parties have made distinct contributions to the procreative process, who should be recognized as the parents of the child?

We now live in an era where a child may have as many as five different "parents." These include a sperm donor, an egg donor, a surrogate or gestational host, and two nonbiologically related individuals who intend to raise the child. Indeed, the process of procreation itself has become so fragmented by the variety and combinations of collaborative-reproductive methods that there are a total of sixteen different reproductive combinations, in addition to traditional conception and childbirth. This total is the product of varying the source of the male gametes (whether by husband or third-party sperm donor), the source of the female gametes (whether by wife or third-party egg donor), the location of fertilization (whether in the wife, the laboratory, or the surrogate host), and the site of gestation (either in the wife or the surrogate).[10]

The importance of parental status, and the accompanying controversy where the identity of the parent is not determined, can be observed in a number of currently debated issues concerning collaborative repro-

[10] ALTERNATIVE REPRODUCTIVE METHODS

	Source of gametes Male	Source of gametes Female	Site of fertilization	Site of pregnancy	Notes
1	H	W	W	W	Customary, AIH
2	S	W	W	W	AID
3	H	W	L	W	IVF
4	S	W	L	W	IVF with donated sperm
5	H	S	L	W	IVF with donated egg
6	S	S	L	W	IVF with both gametes donated (or donated embryo)
7	H	S	S	W	AIH with donor woman plus uterine lavage (semi-donated embryo)
8	S	S	S	W	AID with donor woman plus uterine lavage (donated embryo)
9	H	W	W	S	⎫
10	S	W	W	S	⎬
11	H	W	L	S	⎬
12	S	W	L	S	⎬ Surrogate
13	H	S	L	S	⎬ Motherhood
14	S	S	L	S	⎬
15	H	S	S	S	⎬
16*	S	S	S	S	⎭

H = Husband; W = Wife; S = Third-party substitute, or surrogate;
L = Laboratory

* Planned procreation for placement; traditional adoption is not part of the schematic.
Chart developed by William B. Weil, Jr. and LeRoy Walters.

Walters, Editor's Introduction, 10 J. Med. & Phil. 209, 210 (1985) (although in theory 24 permutations are possible, only 16 actually would occur because of various overlaps).

duction. For example, one may question whether surrogate-parenting arrangements constitute a highly contrived form of baby-selling.[11] The answer depends upon which parties to the procreative process are deemed to be the "parents" of the child at birth. If the intended parents[12] are recognized as the parents of the child, then it is difficult to see how they could be guilty of buying their own baby. Similarly, if the surrogate is deemed not to be the mother of the child, she cannot, as a logical matter, be culpable for baby-selling.[13]

Determination of parental status also may have great significance in deciding who possesses the right of procreation. Arguably, only a "parent" can exercise the right of procreation[14] with respect to any particular child. Indeed, it is exactly this proposition that this Article defends.[15] It follows that the application of the constitutional right of procreation depends upon an antecedent definitional conclusion regarding the meaning of parenthood. This determination will have fundamental significance where the genetic progenitors, the gestational host, and the intended parents (where the intended parents are not also the genetic parents) all claim parental status based on their respective roles in the procreative process.[16]

Finally, competing conceptions of the rights of the biological parents, and most particularly the gestational host, animate the stormy debate concerning the enforceability of the surrogate contract. Where the

---

[11] "Baby-selling" laws make it a criminal offense to exchange money or other material consideration for the promise of a parent of the child to relinquish custody and parental rights in the child. See Katz, Surrogate Motherhood and the Baby-Selling Laws, 20 Colum. J. L. & Soc. Probs. 1, 8-9 (1986).

[12] I use the term "intended parents" here to describe the person or couple who initially intended to raise the child. Three conditions must be met for persons to be considered intended parents: (1) the intended parents must plan to have a child before the conception of the child; (2) they must take morally permissible measures, not limited to biological procreation, to bring a child into the world; and (3) they must meet certain minimally adequate conditions to be able to raise and care for the child. This last requirement embodies the condition that parents obtain the "constructive consent of the child." See text accompanying notes 171-72 infra.

[13] This outcome would be a departure from the Baby M court, which stated that the egg donor/gestational host was "the natural mother inappropriately called the 'surrogate mother.'" In re Baby M., 109 N.J. 396, 411, 537 A.2d 1227, 1234 (1988). Having decided the issue of motherhood, the court went on to state that the surrogacy contract was "the sale of a child, or, at the very least, the sale of a mother's right to her child." Id. at 437-38, 537 A.2d at 1248.

[14] See Skinner v. Oklahoma, 316 U.S. 535, 541 (1942) (currently viewed as establishing right of procreation by holding involuntary sterilization statute unconstitutional); note 67 and accompanying text infra (discussing decisions of Baby M court regarding parenthood and right of procreation); see also text accompanying notes 129-30 infra (biological connection offers unique opportunity for parental relationship).

[15] See notes 61-62 and accompanying text infra.

[16] See Allen, Privacy, Surrogacy and the Baby M Case, 76 Geo. L.J. 1759, 1774-81 (1988) (discussing four models for privacy-right attribution).

connotations associated with motherhood invariably are linked with the role of the birth mother, the prospect of compelling her to relinquish the child takes on the proportions of a crime against nature. However, where parental status is deemed to attach to the persons who have sought, by whatever means they could marshal, to cause a child to be born so that they could raise it and care for it—in short, where parental status is viewed as distinct from biological consanguinity—enforcement of the surrogate contract will be viewed as a necessary prerequisite to achieving justice.

This Article attempts to arrive at a conception of parenthood which settles conflicting claims to parental status posed by the genetic parents, the gestational host, and the intended parents of the child. Part I begins by posing the paradigmatic procreative scenario in which such conflicting claims to parental status will arise. This Part then evaluates a number of definitional considerations relating to the use of the term "parent," arguing that appeals to traditional definitions are of little use in answering what is essentially a normative question: who should be considered the parent in collaborative-reproduction arrangements? It also argues that, while we lack a concept of parenthood sufficiently definite to resolve modern controversies about *who* is the parent, we nevertheless have a working legal definition of parental rights that can help reveal what is at stake in the controversy. Thus, this Part examines the rights which attach to persons legally recognized as parents, as demonstrated by the parental-rights doctrine.

Whereas Part I concludes by focusing on what rights parents have, Part II turns to the central question of who, legally, may be a parent. Seemingly uncontroversial claims to parental rights can be made by the procreators of a child. Indeed, the Constitution has long recognized that parental status inures to procreators.[17] A problem arises, however, in attempting to define who counts as a procreator. Under existing legal doctrine, although a biological connection between adult and child is not always a sufficient condition to establish procreator status, it is virtually a necessary condition, at least in the ascription of maternal rights. Yet as the remainder of Part II demonstrates, to link biology and procreation so closely is to confuse the right of procreation with the right of privacy. In fact these rights are distinct, and recognition of this distinction suggests that intended parents[18] have a respectable claim to being procreators. Part II concludes that the legal right to procreation can be read to support parental-rights claims of intended parents over the claims of biologi-

---

[17] See, e.g., *Skinner*, 316 U.S. at 541 (procreation is basic, fundamental civil right); *Baby M*, 109 N.J. at 449-52, 537 A.2d at 1254-55 (considering only procreators when discussing parental rights).

[18] See note 12 supra.

cal parents, where the two types of claims conflict.

Part III looks beyond the law to determine if empirical evidence and moral arguments favor the right of biological progenitors to be accorded primary legal recognition as the parents of a child. More specifically, Part III assesses the claims that a person possesses a parental right in a child by virtue of the following: the genetic relationship which exists between them, the efforts inherent in the gestational relationship, the "bond" which develops between the birth mother and the child as a result of the gestational relationship, and a variety of predicted psychological harms to mother and child resulting from their separation. This Part also evaluates the general claim that it is in the child's best interests to be placed with its natural parents. In addition, Part III investigates a number of extrinsic social and moral arguments focusing not on the rights of particular parties per se, but on a variety of consequences which may follow the adoption of a definition of parent which would favor one group over another. This Part argues that many of the claims posed in defense of the priority of the genetic progenitors or gestational host carry little moral weight and that the case for the primacy of the rights of biological parents is considerably weaker than it might first appear.

Finally, Part IV sketches three arguments favoring the claims of the intended parents—even where they lack any biological ties with the child born of the procreative relationship. This Part argues that, under an "intentional" view of parenting, the claims of the intended parents outweigh those of the gestational host. Thus, the parental rights of the intended parents should be legally recognized from the time of conception.

I

What Does It Mean to Be A "Parent"?

A. The Problem

Imagine the following scenario. A married couple wishes to have a child. Unfortunately, both spouses are infertile. As the result of testicular cancer, the husband physically is incapable of producing sperm. Similarly, due to a condition known as endometriosis, the wife is incapable of producing ova. The condition also has affected her capacity to bring to term a previously conceived embryo.[19] In essence, the couple lacks the biological ability to produce a child genetically or gestationally.

Nevertheless, after repeated unsuccessful attempts at adoption, the couple decides to "have a child of its own." They proceed by contacting

---

[19] See OTA, Infertility, supra note 1, at 65-66 (discussing endometriosis and its effects on women's capacity both to produce ova and to bring fetus to term); id. at 72-73 (discussing effects of cancer on male and female fertility).

a facility which collects and stores donor sperm for artificial insemination. The couple carefully reviews the records indicating a number of general characteristics of the prospective donor including height, weight, age, race, eye color, hair color, occupation, talents, and hobbies. They choose the sperm of an individual whose general physical appearance and professional biography most closely approximate that of the husband. Next, the couple contacts one of the recently established ova banks. They choose ova contributed by a woman with physical and intellectual attributes strikingly similar to that of the wife.[20]

The couple then selects a suitable woman who has expressed an interest in assisting an infertile couple to bring a child into the world. The surrogate is to be paid $10,000 and, to increase the probability of pregnancy, agrees to have three preembryos surgically implanted, after which she will carry and bear the child, relinquishing the child to the couple upon birth. Through the process of in vitro fertilization, the sperm and ova of the two anonymous donors are united. Three days after conception, the preembryos are transferred to the surrogate who carries one of them to term and bears a healthy baby girl. Shortly after birth, the surrogate turns the child over to the commissioning couple. The new "parents" have "brought a child into the world."

But who are the "parents" in the preceding scenario? Should the answer depend upon whether the surrogate willingly relinquishes her claim to the child? Indeed, who is more like a parent here? Are the husband and wife, who carefully and intentionally orchestrated the procreational act, bringing together all the necessary components with the intention of creating a unique individual whom they intend to raise as their own, the parents? Or is the gestational host, who bore the physical burden of pregnancy and the pain of labor, more properly the "mother" of the child? Or should the genetic parents—the anonymous donors—if they knew of the existence of the child, take legal priority as its parents? Thus we are led to inquire: what relevance do the various intentional, genetic, and gestational components of procreation have for the concept of parenthood? The answer depends upon our definition of "parent."

B. *The Limits of Definition*

The use of definitions in any empirical area poses a curious dilemma.[21] We seek to define a particular concept so that, among other

---

[20] While the couple would have preferred an in-depth psychological and intellectual sketch of each of the two donors, this is not yet available. Consequently, they construct a general psychological picture of each donor based upon the other information present in the biographies.

[21] I classify definitions into the "analytic" and the "empirical." Analytic definitions are those which are true as a matter of logic. The definition is "contained" within the concept.

reasons, we can accurately distinguish uncertain or borderline examples of that concept from counterexamples or instances falling outside of the scope of that concept. In the process of arriving at a definition, we must make antecedent determinations of the scope of the concept. In other words, if we could be certain when a particular object, X, falls within the operational scope of a concept, F, the need to define F would be eliminated, or at least greatly mitigated. Thus, in arriving at a definition of any concept, we must come to some preliminary conclusions about which particular examples fall within the definitional scope of that concept. In short, we seek definition in order to distinguish instances of a concept from noninstances. But we must make these distinctions prior to the definition, in effect deciding in advance whether certain instances fall within the scope of the concept.

In attempting to define the term "parent," for example, we must make certain assessments about uncertain cases. Is a person who raises a child, but who is not biologically related to the child, truly a "parent"? Is an egg donor who does not carry the child to term the "mother" of the child? In deciding these uncertain cases, we implicitly appeal to some preanalytic concept of parenthood, as if presupposing the definition.[22] Yet the entire reason for seeking a definition in the first place is to permit us to know whether an egg donor, for example, is a "mother." Thus, the entire process is circular.

It might appear that we should surmount this obstacle simply by stipulating a definition of parenthood. Thus, we could provide, almost by fiat, that the term "parent" is to be understood as designating a biological parent of the child, or a party who actually raises the child, or some other party. This would provide order where it formerly was ab-

---

But see D. O'Connor & B. Carr, Introduction to the Theory of Knowledge 145-63 (1982) (questioning existence of separate category of analytic truths). So, for example, according to the analytic definition, a triangle is a three-sided closed-plane polygon. To know what a triangle is, is to know whether or not any particular object is in fact a triangle.

Empirical definitions, by contrast, have uncertain boundaries. The concept "chair," for example, appears to have no necessary and sufficient conditions for application. It is uncertain how many legs a chair must have. Similarly, by analyzing the concept of a chair, we cannot determine at what precise width a chair becomes a sofa. Parenthood is an empirical concept. By analyzing the term we cannot arrive at a set of necessary and sufficient limiting criteria for its application.

[22] Concerns such as these led Plato and his followers to posit a realm of the Forms; a nonspatial, nontemporal domain in which the perfect Forms of every particular object exist. See Plato, Paramenides, in The Dialogues of Plato (B. Jowett trans. 4th ed. 1953). Each concept is, in some sense, a mental representation of this transcendental Form. See id. By remembering these Forms we gain a kind of a priori knowledge. Aristotle modified this thesis to exclude the notion of a transcendental realm in which the Forms exist but retained the notion of universals as a representation of the essence of each concept. See Aristotle, The Metaphysics, in The Works of Aristotle (W. Ross ed. 1949); Woozley, Universals, in 8 The Encyclopedia of Philosophy 194 (P. Edwards ed. 1967).

sent since whichever definition of parenthood is chosen, all parties will have prospective notice of the governing definition and will be aware of their corresponding status in light of the definition.

There is, however, a significant problem with this approach. If the definition which we stipulate does not comport with the way in which the term actually is used, the definition may provide theoretical order, but only at the price of alienating the term from its traditional use. For parenthood to continue to be recognized as perhaps the most fundamental social relationship in our culture, carrying with it the basis for a number of basic human rights with which it has historically been associated,[23] a continuity of core meaning must be maintained. To stipulate a meaning for "parenthood" which is fundamentally distinct from the traditional way in which the term is used is to open the door to a changed, and perhaps diminished, social significance for parenthood as an institution. Moreover, the stipulative definition is, in a significant sense, arbitrary. It thus can be challenged as merely asserting by fiat that which it is supposed to answer.

Rather than providing a stipulative definition, we could seek what Professor Copi calls a "lexical" definition.[24] This is a definition of a term reflecting the way people use it in common parlance. The common use of the term, however, may be ambiguous, lacking clear boundaries, and may be equivocal, having conflicting meanings. Moreover, common usage may manifest certain "gaps" in meaning. In the case of the term "parent," for example, the very fact that common usage is unclear in a number of novel situations has motivated this entire definitional search. Consequently, we need something more than an appeal to the lexical use of the term "parent."

Perhaps what is required is what Copi dubs a "precising" definition.[25] A precising definition is, in effect, a hybrid of the stipulative and lexical definitions. It is used in an effort to remain as faithful as possible to the common usage of the term while simultaneously stipulating its scope.[26] In ambiguous cases, the precising definition sets forth a meaning

---

[23] See notes 44-51 and accompanying text infra (discussing constitutional rights accorded by virtue of parental status).

[24] Professor Copi distinguishes five types of definitions: stipulative, lexical, precising, theoretical, and persuasive. Each has a different function and can result in disparate meanings for the same term. The primary logical distinction between a stipulative definition and a lexical definition is that a truth value can be assigned to the latter, but not to the former. In other words, it either is or is not true that a certain term is used in common parlance in a particular way. Conversely, the stipulative meaning need not conform to common usage at all. See I. Copi, Introduction to Logic 140-47 (7th ed. 1986).

[25] See id. at 144-45.

[26] Thus, there is only a partial truth value with precising definitions. To the extent that the definition departs from clearly established common usage, it is similar to the stipulative definition. See id. at 144.

which is consistent with lexical use, while also providing some stipulation clearly limiting the definitional parameters of the term.[27]

The problem with utilizing the precising definition to define terms such as "parent," "mother," and "father," however, is that these terms are not merely ambiguous terms; they are equivocal as well.[28] The term "parent," for example, is used to denote both biological progenitors who do not raise the child ("natural parent") and persons who are not biologically related but who do care for the child ("adoptive parent"). Indeed, it is precisely in disputes between diverse parties such as these that legal conflicts arise. Therefore, a definition that will distinguish these conflicting claims to parental status is required. The precising definition falters because it does not serve to delineate the better of the inconsistent uses of a term that is used in everyday language.

In our attempt to arrive at a cogent definition for the term "parent," we confront a basic dilemma. On the one hand, if we attempt to remain faithful to the everyday use of the term, we are prevented from arriving at a set of necessary and sufficient conditions for its use because the term commonly is used to describe both the noncustodial biological progenitor and the nonbiologically related custodian of the child. On the other hand, if we depart from these everyday uses of the term, we run the risk of abandoning an important part of its meaning. To the extent that the rights of "parents" and the tradition of parenthood are contingent upon this meaning, abandoning the lexical meaning abjures the very basis for these rights and traditions. Ultimately, the problem with finding a purely formal definition of "parent" is that the formal definition ignores the social, moral, and legal contingencies which have shaped our shared social intuitions about parenthood. Thus, the delineation of an appropriate definition must account for the contingent factors which have shaped this social meaning. In essence, the search for a unifying conception of parenthood cannot be simply an exercise in semantics; instead, it must be a genuinely normative quest that accounts for a great deal of empirical evidence and moral assessment.

---

[27] For example, the term "person" might be defined as a human being after the point of viability. The term reflects common usage but also sets a definite line which delimits the scope of the definition, thereby recognizing that the previable fetus is not a "person" under the definition.

[28] Ambiguity may be distinguished from equivocation as follows. Ambiguity, on the one hand, refers to vague definitional boundaries. At what width does a chair become a sofa? At what stage of development does a fetus become a person? When does facial hair become a beard? These various issues, ranging from the mundane to the profound, are all examples of conceptual ambiguity. Equivocation, on the other hand, is where one term is used in two different and perhaps conflicting ways. Thus, the term "guilty" is used to denote both individuals who have committed a crime, whether or not they are convicted—this is "factual guilt"—and those who are convicted of a crime, even if they did not in fact commit the crime—"legal guilt." See I. Copi, supra note 24, at 113 (discussing ambiguity and equivocation).

C. The Parental-Rights Doctrine

Creating a legal definition of "parent" is problematic because it is virtually impossible to delineate a list of necessary and sufficient conditions with which to define "parent." Given that the problem of parenthood cannot be resolved by definitional fiat, perhaps we would do better to look for a provisional definition that focuses on what we expect parents to do, that is, by examining the legal rights which parents possess and the extent to which these rights are limited by other doctrines. Immediately, however, one faces a new complexity—the fundamental dichotomy underlying our present system of family law between the rights of the parent in the child and the interests of the child. This dichotomy has been played out in modern legal practice as a conflict between the parental-rights doctrine and the best-interests-of-the-child test.[29]

The parental-rights doctrine holds that the fit parent has a right to the custody, care, and companionship of his or her child even if the interests of the child would be better served by being placed with a third party.[30] The best-interests test, by contrast, does not focus on the claims of the competing potential custodians but instead attempts to define the interests of the child in being placed with one or another party.[31] The conflict between these two custody approaches is most poignant when the best interests of the child clearly require the child's removal from the parent or, even more dramatically, the irrevocable termination of parental rights.

Traditionally, the parental-rights doctrine took nearly absolute priority. In early English history, parental rights were remarkably similar to property rights; indeed, as late as the tenth century, parents held life

---

[29] See Russell, Within the Best Interests of the Child: The Factor of Parental Status in Custody Disputes Arising from Surrogacy Contracts, 27 J. Fam. L. 587, 620-27 (1988-1989) (discussing tension between these two doctrines); see also McGough & Shindell, Coming of Age: The Best Interest of the Child Standard in Parent-Third Party Custody Disputes, 27 Emory L.J. 209, 212-14, 230-44 (1978) (examining changing balance between these two doctrines in parent/third-party custody disputes).

[30] In deciding custody between parents, courts consider the child's best interests, but they generally do not when deciding custody between a fit parent and a third party. Professor Russell states:

> Courts have long held that primary custody should be granted to the parent who would best serve the interests of the child, and that when the parent's and child's interests conflict, the child's interests must prevail. Courts and scholars also agree, however, that these principles should not operate to remove a child from a fit parent merely to enhance the child's life chances.

Russell, supra note 29, at 600.

[31] See Mnookin, Child-Custody Adjudication: Judicial Functions in the Face of Indeterminacy, 39 Law & Contemp. Probs. 226, 257-61 (1975) (discussing difficulty of determining child's best interests); see also Ruddick, Parents and Life Prospects, in Having Children: Philosophical and Legal Reflections on Parenthood 124-37 (O. O'Neill & W. Ruddick eds. 1979) (providing philosophical account of nature of parenthood and child's interests).

and death sway over their children, at least while the children were young.[32] Recently, however, the priority of the parental-rights doctrine has been placed in question.[33] In particular, considerations of parental unfitness[34] and the child's best interests have acted as limits on parental rights.[35] Indeed, many states have statutes which provide for awards of custody to nonparents if it is in the best interests of the child.[36]

Still, even the more limited, modern parental-rights approach reflects our basic intuition that the parents of the child should not be deprived of their right to nurture their child.[37] For example, all states apply a presumption that placement of the child with its natural parent is in the best interests of the child.[38] While custody awards to nonparents occasionally are made over the claims of fit parents,[39] the fit parent re-

---

[32] See McGough & Shindell, supra note 29, at 210.

[33] See Mnookin, supra note 31, at 246-49 (arguing that, in some contexts, best-interests test appears to have taken precedence over parental rights); Page, Parental Rights, 1 J. Applied Phil. 187, 188 (1984) (arguing that notion of parental right denigrated by holding that parents possess rights in their children only as long as they do not conflict with other social interests).

[34] See McGough & Shindell, supra note 29, at 226-28 (explaining parental-unfitness doctrine).

[35] See Page, supra note 33, at 188.

[36] See Mnookin, supra note 31, at 237.

[37] See id. Mnookin poses the following hypothetical.

Suppose there are two couples, the Smiths and the Joneses. The Smiths wish to adopt a child. The Joneses have a four-day-old baby daughter whom they wish to keep

. . . .

Suppose both Smith parents were well educated, wealthy, and healthy; loved children; and appeared to be highly successful parents with two older children. Suppose the Joneses were older; had no experience at child rearing; had severe financial problems; and Mr. Jones was in bad health. There are certainly plausible and perhaps even persuasive reasons to believe the child's "life chances" would be greater if placed with the Smiths. And yet, a decision to remove the daughter from the Joneses for placement with the Smiths would be considered by most in our society to be monstrously unjust.

Id.

[38] See Russell, supra note 29, at 622; see also notes 245-46 and accompanying text infra (discussing this presumption).

[39] See, e.g., Painter v. Bannister, 258 Iowa 1390, 1400, 140 N.W.2d 152, 158 (custody of minor granted to maternal grandparents over father's objection so as not to disrupt child's development), cert. denied, 385 U.S. 949 (1966). Cases where a grant of custody is made to a nonparent usually involve situations where the child has been living with the nonparent and has established a psychological relationship. See Note, Psychological Parents vs. Biological Parents: The Courts' Response to New Directions in Child Custody Dispute Resolution, 17 J. Fam. L. 545, 550 (1979). This is plainly distinguishable from a case where a child is removed from the custody of a fit parent to be placed with a nonparent. Such a decision would likely be unconstitutional. See notes 44-51 and accompanying text infra (discussing constitutional status of parents); cf. In re May, 14 Wash. App. 765, 769, 545 P.2d 25, 27 (1976) (refusing to place child under state guardianship, stating that mother had right to attempt parenting before removal proceedings could be instituted). But see In re East, 32 Ohio Misc. 65, 69, 288 N.E.2d 343, 346-47 (1972) (newborn infant removed from custody of its mother on theory of dependency, without showing of parental neglect).

tains a number of rights independent of custody.[40] A nonparent may be awarded full parental status despite the competing claim of a natural parent where the natural parent of an illegitimate child has failed to establish rights in the child.[41] This placement often occurs where the natural father has failed to establish a relationship with the child, either because of indifference or as a result of not knowing about the existence of the child,[42] and where his parental rights already have been extinguished prior to the award of parental rights to a third party.[43]

The parental-rights doctrine, a creature of common law and more recently statutory law, is reinforced by its constitutional analogue. The Supreme Court has stated that parental rights are " '[r]ights far more precious . . . than property rights.' "[44] More specifically, " 'freedom of personal choice in matters of . . . family life is one of the liberties protected by the Due Process Clause of the Fourteenth Amendment.' "[45] The zone of family privacy and parental authority has been afforded both substantive and procedural protection under the due process clause.[46] This cluster of constitutional protections includes the right of the family to live together,[47] the right of parents to raise their children as they deem fit,[48] and the right of parents to educate their children without state interference.[49] The procedural protections recognized pursuant to the due process clause require that parental rights may not be terminated without notice and a hearing,[50] and without at least clear and convincing evidence of parental unfitness.[51]

---

[40] See Note, The Legal Relationship of a Nonbiological Father to His Child: A Matter of Equity, 66 U. Det. L. Rev. 97, 98 (1988) (examining limits on grants of paternal status to nonbiologically related fathers).

[41] See Quilloin v. Walcott, 434 U.S. 246, 256 (1978), in which a woman's new husband was allowed to adopt her child where the child's biological father had forfeited his parental rights by not marrying the mother or seeking to establish a relationship with the child. Essentially, the Court relied upon the best-interests test to permit the adoption where there was, in effect, no father in existence. See id. at 251.

[42] See, e.g., M.H.B. v. H.T.B., 100 N.J. 567, 579, 498 A.2d 775, 781 (1985) (per curiam) (biological father of child, unaware of child's existence, lacked parental rights).

[43] See notes 90-155 and accompanying text infra (discussing parental rights of unwed father).

[44] Stanley v. Illinois, 405 U.S. 645, 651 (1972) (quoting May v. Anderson, 345 U.S. 528, 533 (1953)).

[45] Smith v. Org. of Foster Families, 431 U.S. 816, 842 (1977) (quoting Cleveland Bd. of Educ. v. LaFleur, 414 U.S. 632, 639-40 (1974)).

[46] See id.

[47] See Moore v. City of E. Cleveland, 431 U.S. 494, 505-06 (1977).

[48] See Wisconsin v. Yoder, 406 U.S. 205, 214 (1972).

[49] See Pierce v. Soc'y of Sisters, 268 U.S. 510, 534-35 (1925); Meyer v. Nebraska, 262 U.S. 390, 400 (1923).

[50] See Stanley v. Illinois, 405 U.S. 645, 655-57 (1972).

[51] See Santosky v. Kramer, 455 U.S. 745, 758-68 (1982) (preponderance-of-evidence standard insufficient to deny parental rights).

Parents, in short, retain a significant bundle of rights with respect to their children. These legal rights, while not defining "parent," help identify what is at stake in this debate over parenthood. Nevertheless, before resolving this controversy more vexing questions need to be examined. Who is eligible to be a parent? Does the law currently recognize any necessary or sufficient conditions for ascribing parental status?

II

THE EXISTING LAW OF PARENTHOOD

A consideration of the indicia of parental status should commence with an analysis of the legal issues surrounding procreation. This requires an examination of two fundamental issues. First, what is the right of procreation and to which activities does the right extend? More specifically, does the right of procreation encompass collaborative-reproduction technologies? Second, to whom does the right of procreation apply? These issues are considered in the two sections which follow.

A. The Right of Procreation

In *Skinner v. Oklahoma*,[52] the Supreme Court held unconstitutional an Oklahoma statute providing for the involuntary sterilization of certain classes of offenders whose crimes were characterized by "moral turpitude."[53] While the case was decided on equal protection grounds,[54] it since has been incorporated unofficially into substantive due process analysis as part of the privacy right elaborated years later in *Griswold v. Connecticut*[55] and its progeny.[56] However, despite these subsequent de-

---

[52] 316 U.S. 535 (1942).
[53] Id. at 537.
[54] See id. at 541.
[55] 381 U.S. 479, 485-86 (1965) (law forbidding use of contraceptives intrudes upon right to marital privacy).
[56] See, e.g., Roe v. Wade, 410 U.S. 113 (1973); Eisenstadt v. Baird, 405 U.S. 438 (1972). The Supreme Court has not ruled on the right of procreation since *Skinner*. Thus, the Court has never stated that the procreative right is an aspect of the privacy right. Nonetheless, the right to procreation does have all the indicia of a privacy right. First, analogous pre-*Griswold* privacy rights have been subsumed into modern substantive due process analysis. Thus, early cases such as Meyer v. Nebraska, 262 U.S. 390 (1923), which invalidated a law prohibitting instruction in any language other than English, and Pierce v. Soc'y of Sisters, 268 U.S. 510 (1925), which held unconstitutional a law forbidding education outside of public schools, have been recognized as part of the right to privacy. See, e.g., *Roe*, 410 U.S. at 159 (relying upon *Griswold*, *Meyer*, *Pierce*, and *Skinner* in privacy-right analysis).

Second, the right of procreation, at least superficially, involves similar issues as those encountered in other privacy-right cases. The rights to use contraception, to have an abortion, and to live with one's family—are all aspects of the privacy right as it has developed over the past quarter-century. See Allen, supra note 16, at 1786-91 (analyzing right of procreation as traditional privacy right); Note, A Taxonomy of Privacy: Repose, Sanctuary, and Intimate Decision, 64 Calif. L. Rev. 1447, 1466-78 (1976) (privacy right of intimate decisions includes

velopments in the area of privacy rights, *Skinner* remains the only Supreme Court decision explicitly addressing the right of procreation.

Skinner is ambiguous for a number of reasons. First, the right of procreation elaborated in *Skinner* appears as a negative right to make procreational decisions without government interference. This is quite distinct from a positive right requiring government assistance to enforce reproductive-services contracts between commissioning couples and surrogates.[57] Second, it is not clear whether the right of procreation extends beyond the scope of traditional two-party sexual reproduction. Specifically, although some state courts have taken a position on these matters,[58] the Supreme Court has not determined whether the right extends to the use of artificial insemination by donor, in vitro fertilization, or surrogate-parenting arrangements.[59]

Two further ambiguities in *Skinner's* procreative-rights analysis more directly related to the present discussion likewise remain unresolved. First, the substantive content of the right is unclear: does it protect only the biological act of reproduction, or also the corresponding right to parent the child? Second, even if the right applies in the context of collaborative reproduction, and particularly in surrogate-parenting arrangements, to whom does it apply? Does the right attach only to the biological progenitors—the sperm donor, whether or not he is also the intended father, and the surrogate in genetic surrogacy—or does it also extend to the couple possessing the prebirth intention to raise the child? The answer to each of these questions generally will depend on whether procreation is cast purely in biological terms or, alternatively, whether it encompasses an intentional dimension.

The first of these two issues concerns the extension of the right of procreation beyond biological reproduction to include the right to raise the child born through the procreative act. At least one scholar has argued that the right of procreation is not simply a right to beget and bear

---

rights of procreation, cohabitation, child-rearing, bodily integrity, in-home possession, and private sexual activities between consenting adults). But see Robertson, Procreative Liberty and the Control of Conception, Pregnancy, and Childbirth, 69 Va. L. Rev. 405, 414-20 (1983) (distinguishing freedom to procreate from freedom to control every related activity).

[57] See In re Baby M, 109 N.J. 396, 447-49, 537 A.2d 1227, 1253-54 (1988) (rejecting claim of intended parent that his right of procreation required government enforcement of surrogate contract).

[58] See, e.g., Doe v. Kelley, 106 Mich. App. 169, 173-74, 307 N.W.2d 438, 441 (1981) (right of procreation does not extend to surrogate arrangements); *Baby M*, 109 N.J. at 448, 537 A.2d at 1253 ("[t]he right to procreate very simply is the right to have natural children, whether through sexual intercourse or artificial insemination").

[59] If the right of procreation is deemed to extend to collaborative reproduction, yet is treated as a negative right, the effect would be to limit greatly any government involvement in procreational choices—either to enforce or to criminalize collaborative-reproductive agreements.

a child but includes the right to be a parent.[60] This conclusion comports with the commonsense intuition that the procreative right is virtually empty unless it ensures progenitors the right to acquire parental rights in the child. While the contrary interpretation, which construes that right as nothing more than the right to pass along one's genes without a corresponding right to have custody of or to make decisions affecting the child, seems untenable, a range of intermediate positions entitling procreators to parental rights in certain situations has received support in various courts.[61]

The recent case of *In re Baby M*[62] will help formulate an intermediate approach to the right of procreation. The *Baby M* case is one of the few decisions in which a court faced directly the task of elaborating the substantive content of the right of procreation. In *Baby M*, the Sterns commissioned Mary Beth Whitehead to act as a surrogate for them.[63] Ms. Whitehead was artificially inseminated with the sperm of Mr. Stern and gave birth to a baby girl.[64] Ms. Whitehead then changed her mind and attempted to retain custody of the child.[65] Construing the scope of the right of procreation, the New Jersey Supreme Court stated:

> The right to procreate very simply is the right to have natural children, whether through sexual intercourse or artificial insemination. It is no more than that. Mr. Stern has not been deprived of that right. Through artificial insemination of Mrs. Whitehead, Baby M is his child. The custody, care, companionship, and nurturing that follow birth are not parts of the right to procreation . . . .[66]

Thus, according to the court, the right to procreation protects only the right to reproduce physically and possibly some limited aspects of parental rights. The court's ruling makes clear that the right of procreation does not include the right to raise and nurture the child. If it did, then conflicting claims to the custody of a child, as in divorce or contested surrogate arrangements, could not be resolved.[67] The right, nonetheless, does render its possessor a legally recognized "parent."[68]

---

[60] See O'Neill, Begetting, Bearing, and Rearing, in Having Children: Philosophical and Legal Reflections on Parenthood 25-26 (O. O'Neill & W. Ruddick eds. 1979) (intent to procreate creates right, as well as duty, to raise child).

[61] See *Baby M*, 109 N.J. at 466, 537 A.2d at 1263 (demonstrating intermediate position by granting visitation rights to Mrs. Whitehead, egg donor/gestational host).

[62] 109 N.J. 396, 537 A.2d 1227 (1988).

[63] Id. at 411, 537 A.2d at 1235.

[64] Id. at 412, 414, 537 A.2d at 1235-36.

[65] Id. at 415-16, 537 A.2d at 1237.

[66] Id. at 448, 537 A.2d at 1253.

[67] This is clear because while Mrs. Whitehead ultimately did not receive custody of the child, she was accorded visitation privileges as a parental right. See id. at 466, 537 A.2d at 1263.

[68] The decision to award custody of Baby M to the intended parents, the Sterns, was based

More specifically, the right of procreation elaborated in *Baby M* is analogous to that possessed by noncustodial parents: it includes the minimum rights to take part in certain fundamental child-rearing decisions, to visit the child,[69] to bring an action modifying the custody award,[70] and the duty to provide child support.[71] In short, exercising the right of procreation is sufficient to make one a "parent" in the legal sense. Of course, where no conflicting claims exist by parties who have exercised the right, the right to raise the child will inure to both parents. Thus, the pivotal question now becomes: does the right of procreation extend to biological progenitors or intended parents, and for what reason?[72] The analysis prompted by this question can be distilled into two questions under current legal doctrine. First, is genetic consanguinity a sufficient condition for recognizing the biological progenitor as a parent? Second, is it a necessary condition of parenthood?

B. To Whom Does the Right of Procreation Attach?

The right of procreation attaches to those parties identified by the courts as the mother and father of the child at birth.[73] This section examines common-law doctrines, recent statutory law, and constitutional law to determine which participants courts currently designate as parents. This section considers to what extent current concepts of mother-

---

on the additional determination of the child's best interests, not an absolute right to custody on the part of the Sterns. Thus, Mr. Stern's genetic contribution to the arrangement rendered him a "parent" under the court's analysis. The ultimate decision regarding custody, however, was determined under the best-interests test. See id. at 448-54, 537 A.2d at 1254-57.

[69] See J. Areen, Family Law 462-506 (2d ed. 1985) (discussing visitation rights).

[70] See id. at 536-51 (discussing modification of custody awards).

[71] See id. at 591-675 (discussing child support).

[72] See Allen, supra note 16, at 1760-68, 1771-81, 1786-92 (analyzing parental rights in light of privacy rights and procreative rights of intended parents and surrogate); Jackson, *Baby M* and the Question of Parenthood, 76 Geo. L.J. 1811, 1813-16 (1988) (examining definition of parent and role of intent in determining parental status); Robertson, supra note 56, at 427-36 (discussing right of procreation in context of collaborative reproduction). One commentator has put forth one of the most cogent analyses of the right of procreation and the stages of conception, pregnancy, and childbirth, proposing a scheme for reconciling the rights and interests of diverse parties in reproductive arrangements. She argues for an intentional analysis of the right of procreation limited by the privacy-right concerns of the surrogate. As such, her article is one of the few to draw a conceptual distinction between the right of privacy and the right of procreation. See Note, Redefining Mother: A Legal Matrix for New Reproductive Technologies, 96 Yale L.J. 187, 192-202 (1986).

[73] For example, in the *Baby M* case, the right of procreation attached to Mr. Stern and Mrs. Whitehead, the two parties that would be considered the mother and father of Baby M under traditional legal rules. Because Ms. Stern would not be considered the mother of the child under traditional law, the right of procreation did not extend to her. See In re Baby M, 109 N.J. 396, 447-48, 537 A.2d 1227, 1253 (1988) (concluding that egg donor/gestational host was "natural mother . . . entitled to retain her rights as a mother," then discussing Mr. Stern's right of procreation without any indication that Mrs. Stern also could possess this right).

hood and fatherhood are biological constructs and questions whether biology should act as either a necessary or sufficient condition to parenthood.

1. Who is Mother: The Presumption of Biology and the Role of Gestation

The "presumption of biology" manifests the once monolithic and still pervasive legal principle that the mother of the child is the woman who bears the child.[74] This principle reflects the ancient dictum *mater est quam gestation demonstrat* (by gestation the mother is demonstrated).[75] This phrase, by its use of the word "demonstrated," has always reflected an ambiguity in the meaning of the presumption. It is arguable that, while gestation may demonstrate maternal status, it is not the sine qua non of motherhood. Rather, it is possible that the common law viewed genetic consanguinity as the basis for maternal rights.[76] Under this latter interpretation, gestation simply would be irrefutable evidence of the more fundamental genetic relationship.

The debate and, indeed, the distinction itself were in the past only a matter of academic interest, but today, with the increased use of reproductive technologies, it is a matter of palpable significance. For example, in the context of gestational surrogacy,[77] different women play the genetic and gestational roles. The egg donor, who is not capable of bringing the fetus to term, provides a number of fertilized ova to the surrogate with the intention that, upon the birth of the child, the egg donor will assume parental obligations for the child. However, if the surrogate changes her mind and wishes to retain custody of the child, how should the law respond?

Application of the presumption of biology as it traditionally has been understood would give legal priority as mother to the surrogate. But it is not clear that this application comports with either the deeper meaning of the presumption of biology or modern sensibilities regarding this conflict. Indeed, the term "biology" itself is susceptible to equivocal use, implicating both the genetic and the gestational aspects of procreation.

Commentators who have considered this problem have come to op-

---

[74] See Note, supra note 72, at 190-92 (discussing ineffectiveness of presumption of biology in resolving surrogate-mother issues).

[75] See OTA, Infertility, supra note 1, at 282.

[76] See Johnson v. Calvert, No. X 633190 (Cal. App. Dep't Super. Ct. Oct. 22, 1990) (holding that egg donor/intended mother had parental rights over surrogate and discussing common-law background) (on file at New York University Law Review).

[77] This is a surrogate arrangement accompanied by the use of in vitro fertilization, where the surrogate gestator is not the same woman as the egg donor. See id. at 3.

posite conclusions. A number of scholars argue that the egg donor should take precedence because the hereditary and biological characteristics of the child are derived from her.[78] Others, however, argue that the surrogate's greater physical and emotional involvement in carrying the fetus, along with the advantage of simplicity in identifying the gestational host, gives the surrogate a greater right to be designated the legal mother of the child.[79] The relative merits of these alternatives are evaluated in Part III of this Article.[80] The analysis in the remainder of this subsection focuses on the legal rights that flow from the gestational role.

The courts have confronted explicitly the conflict between the egg donor/intended mother and gestational host only twice.[81] In each case, a decision was rendered favoring the egg donor/intended mother. In the first case, *Smith v. Jones*,[82] the proceeding was a "set-up" to allow the egg donor to adopt the child, and, in accordance with the surrogate agreement, the surrogate did not contest the ruling.[83]

In the second and more recent case, *Johnson v. Calvert*,[84] the parties actively disputed the same issue. In *Calvert*, the surrogate, Anna Johnson, had agreed to act as gestational host for the Calverts, the intended parents and sperm and egg donors.[85] However, near the end of her pregnancy, Ms. Johnson changed her mind and decided that she wanted to retain custody of the child.[86] In a loosely reasoned oral opinion, the court awarded full parental rights to the Calverts, analogizing the role of Ms. Johnson to that of a foster parent.[87] Thus, the *Calvert* court implicitly recognized that in a dispute between the egg donor/intended mother and the gestational host, the former has the superior legal claim. Aside from these two cases, the presumption of biology provides for an irrebut-

---

[78] See, e.g., Brahams, The Hasty British Ban on Surrogacy, 17 Hastings Center Rep. 16, 18-19 (1987); Samuels, Warnock Committee: Human Fertilisation and Embryology, 51 Medico-Legal J. 174, 176 (1983).

[79] See, e.g., Annas, Redefining Parenthood and Protecting the Embryos: Why We Need New Laws, 14 Hasting Center Rep. 50, 50-51 (1984) (presumption favoring surrogate mother provides certainty of identification at time of birth); Note, Rumpelstiltskin Revisited: The Inalienable Rights of Surrogate Mothers, 99 Harv. L. Rev. 1936, 1950-51 (1986) (social and emotional bonds formed in childbirth process favor surrogate mother's rights).

[80] See notes 190-307 and accompanying text infra.

[81] While the two cases represent the only existing law on this issue, numerous legislative proposals have been made to remedy the uncertain state of the law in this respect. See OTA, Infertility, supra note 1, at 284 (discussing some legislative proposals).

[82] No. 85-532014 DZ (Mich. Cir. Ct. Mar. 14, 1986) (on file at New York University Law Review).

[83] Id. at 2.

[84] No. X 633190 (Cal. App. Dep't Super. Ct. Oct. 22, 1990) (on file at New York University Law Review).

[85] Id. at 3.

[86] Id. at 11.

[87] See id. at 5-6.

table presumption of motherhood in favor of the birth mother in all states except Arkansas and perhaps Nevada. In these states, the irrebuttable presumption appears to have been abrogated in the case of surrogate arrangements.[88] Additionally, the status of the birth mother is protected in a variety of other ways including the prohibition in every state against enforcing prebirth agreements to consent to adoption.[89]

While both *Smith* and *Calvert* were decided in favor of the egg donors/intended mothers, in other contexts the birth mother appears to retain various rights. Thus, the legal significance of the gestational role is uncertain. As for the genetic role, its relevance is best developed in the context of a discussion of paternal rights.

2. *Who is Father: The Presumption of Legitimacy and the Significance of the Genetic Relationship*

We now turn to a consideration of two related issues. First, what are the legal requisites for ascription of parental rights? Second, what rights does a natural parent possess by virtue of the genetic relationship between parent and child? It is significant that these two questions are elaborated separately, because, as it turns out, there is only a loose legal relationship between legally recognized fatherhood and genetic consanguinity. The second question is posed and distinguished from the first so that some general conclusions can be drawn regarding the legal significance of the genetic relationship for the egg donor, as well as the sperm donor.

In general, fatherhood is a status which is predominantly a function of the family relationship. More specifically, it is a status accorded to men who entertain certain kinds of relationships with the mother and the child. Ultimately, there is only a contingent relationship between this relational status and the genetic connection between putative father and child.[90]

At common law, the "presumption of legitimacy" provided that any child born to a woman while she was married would be considered the

---

[88] The Arkansas statute provides in relevant part:
(b) A child born by means of artificial insemination . . . shall be presumed to be the child of the woman giving birth . . . except in the case of a surrogate mother, in which event the child shall be that of: 1) The biological father and the woman intended to be the mother if the biological father is married; or 2) The biological father only if unmarried; or 3) The woman intended to be the mother in cases of a surrogate mother when an anonymous donor's sperm was used for artificial insemination.

Ark. Stat. Ann. § 9-10-201 (1991); see also Nevada Rev. Stat. Ann. § 127.287(5) (Michie & Supp. 1989) (lawful surrogacy contract exception to bar against using money to secure adoption).

[89] See OTA, Infertility, supra note 1, at 281, table 14-2 (containing chart of applicable adoption laws).

[90] See notes 96-105 and accompanying text infra.

child of her husband.[91] Indeed, the husband did not have to be physically present at the time of conception. In the words of one court: "If a husband, not physically incapable, was within the four seas of England during the period of gestation, the court would not listen to evidence casting doubt on his paternity."[92]

Correlatively, at common law, a third party possessed no right to bring an action to establish his paternity; rather, this right is a relatively recent creation of statutory law.[93] The common-law presumption would bar a man who wanted to acknowledge responsibility for a child born to a married woman even if one or both of the spouses testified that the child was that of the third party.[94] Despite its harsh ring to the modern ear, this irrebuttable presumption of legitimacy, enshrined as Lord Mansfield's Rule,[95] was well-motivated. The rule not only protected the integrity of the family but also served to ensure the legitimation of the child in a period when illegitimacy carried with it a terrible social stigma and resulted in severe legal consequences.[96]

Under modern statutory law, paternity still is largely presumed. Indeed, in a number of states the presumption of legitimacy remains irrebuttable.[97] Thus, despite the invention of scientific methods conclusively establishing nonpaternity[98] and positively establishing paternity to within a small fraction of certainty,[99] third parties still are precluded from bringing actions to establish paternity. In the majority of

---

[91] See M. Field, Surrogate Motherhood 118-21 (1988).

[92] In re Findlay, 253 N.Y. 1, 7, 170 N.E. 471, 472 (1930).

[93] See A v. X, 641 P.2d 1222, 1222 (Wyo.) (under Wyo. Stat. § 14-2-104 (1977), child, her mother, or man presumed to be her father may bring paternity action to determine whether there is father-child relationship), cert. denied, 459 U.S. 1021 (1982).

[94] See, e.g., State ex rel. H. v. P., 90 A.D.2d 434, 437, 457 N.Y.S.2d 488, 490-91 (1982) (upholding husband's paternal rights where separated wife claimed to have withdrawn from artificial insemination program and instead conceived baby with unnamed third party).

[95] See Goodright v. Moss, 2 Cowp. 591, 98 Eng. Rep. 1257 (1777).

[96] See Sass, The Defense of Multiple Access (*Exceptio Plurium Concubentium*) in Paternity Suits: A Comparative Analysis, 51 Tul. L. Rev. 468, 498-99 (1977) (discussing historical legal status of illegitimate child). During the early period of the common law, illegitimate children had no rights against their male progenitors: the "bastard" could neither inherit nor claim support and was even deprived of legitimation by the subsequent marriage of its natural parents. See id. at 499. Thus, these children were called *filii nullius* ("children of no one"). Id. at 498. In the sixteenth century, however, the Poor Laws partially ameliorated this situation. See Poor Law Act, 18 Eliz. lc. 3 (1576). Under the Poor Laws, illegitimate children were accorded the right to seek support, although they still were not permitted to inherit. See Sass, supra, at 499.

[97] See M. Field, supra note 91, at 118 n.12 (by Oklahoma statute, wife denied opportunity to establish husband's nonpaternity); id. at 119 n.19 (California and Oregon law apply conclusive presumption that cohabiting husband is father of child).

[98] See The Chi. Daily L. Bull., July 21, 1989, at A5.

[99] See id. (predicting that paternity trials eventually will become unnecessary).

those states in which the presumption of legitimacy is rebuttable,[100] the presumption can be challenged only by the mother of the child or her husband.[101] Thus, third parties attempting to establish paternity require the cooperation of one of the spouses. Only in a minority of states can a third party challenge the presumption on his own.[102]

Under the Uniform Parentage Act (UPA or Act),[103] a third party may bring an action to establish paternity only when there is no presumed father under another section of the Act.[104] Thus, the husband of the mother of the child retains legal rights simply by virtue of his relationship with the mother.[105] The legal nexus between a nonbiologically related father and child also is recognized by permitting consensual artificial insemination by donor.[106] This rule protects the paternal status of

---

[100] See, e.g., Cal. Evid. Code § 621(b)(West Supp. 1991).
[101] See, e.g., Cal. Evid. Code § 621(c)-(d) (West Supp. 1991).
[102] See M. Field, supra note 91, at 118-21 (discussing issues involved in third-party challenges).
[103] Unif. Parentage Act §§ 1-29, 9A U.L.A. 579-622 (1973).
[104] Id. § 6(c), 9A U.L.A. at 594. Section 4 of the Act provides, in part:
  (a) A man is presumed to be the natural father of a child if:
   (1) he and the child's natural mother are or have been married to each other and the child is born during the marriage, or within 300 days after the marriage is terminated . . . ;
   (2) before the child's birth, he and the child's natural mother have attempted to marry each other by a marriage solemnized in apparent compliance with law, although the attempted marriage is or could be declared invalid . . . ;
   (3) after the child's birth, he and the child's natural mother have married, or attempted to marry, each other by a marriage solemnized in apparent compliance with law, although the attempted marriage is or could be declared invalid, and
      (i) he has acknowledged his paternity of the child in writing filed with the [appropriate court or Vital Statistics Bureau].
      (ii) with his consent, he is named as the child's father on the child's birth certificate, or
      (iii) he is obligated to support the child under a written voluntary promise or by court order;
   (4) while the child is under the age of majority, he receives the child into his home and openly holds out the child as his natural child; or
   (5) he acknowledges his paternity of the child in a writing filed with the [appropriate court or Vital Statistics Bureau], which shall promptly inform the mother of the filing of the acknowledgment, and she does not dispute the acknowledgment within a reasonable time after being informed thereof, in a writing filed with the [appropriate court or Vital Statistics Bureau]. If another man is presumed under this section to be the child's father, acknowledgment may be effected only with the written consent of the presumed father or after the presumption has been rebutted.
Id. § 4, 9A U.L.A. at 590-91. Section 4(b) provides that the presumptions are rebuttable by clear-and-convincing evidence. Id. § 4, 9 U.L.A. at 303-04.
[105] See, e.g., County of San Diego v. Brown, 80 Cal. App. 3d 297, 303, 145 Cal. Rptr. 483, 486 (1978) (conclusive presumption that defendant was child's father barred defendant from adducing evidence that he did not father child).
[106] Consensual AID requires that the husband's consent to artificial insemination be in writing. See OTA, Infertility, supra note 1, at 244. In addition, under the UPA, the procedure

the surrogate's husband while simultaneously providing that the sperm donor is not to be considered the father of the child.[107] It is worth underscoring that this presumption applies only in marital relationships and does not extend to either heterosexual or homosexual cohabitation.[108]

While recognition of the presumption of legitimacy, in its various manifestations, has been conducive to the development of artificial insemination, it poses a significant obstacle to surrogate arrangements. While the wife of an infertile husband, with the assistance of the sperm donor, may plan to conceive and raise the child born of the AID arrangement, the situation is different where an infertile wife and her fertile husband seek the assistance of a married surrogate. In the latter instance, the presumption of legitimacy prevents the sperm donor/intended father from a claim to paternity of the child. Thus, in at least eighteen states, the husband of the surrogate will be considered the child's father.[109]

Understanding the legal framework for determining paternal rights also requires an examination of the constitutional dimension. Within the last two decades, the Supreme Court increasingly has involved itself in the process of explicating the constitutional rights of the unmarried male in establishing paternity. Two general rules have emerged from this case law. First, where the mother of the child is unmarried, the biological connection does afford the biological father a "foot in the door," permit-

---

must be performed under the supervision of a licensed physician. See Unif. Parentage Act § 5(a), 9 U.L.A. 301.

A number of cases have arisen where women artificially inseminated themselves at home. See, e.g., Jhordan C. v. Mary K., 179 Cal. App. 3d 386, 394, 224 Cal. Rptr. 530, 535 (1986) (provisions of UPA held inapplicable where woman used friend's sperm to inseminate herself, thereby allowing friend to petition to establish paternity). Before the Uniform Parentage Act and relatively early in the period in which AID became popular, the status of AID was uncertain. In one case, an Illinois superior court found that consensual AID failed to legitimize the child and rendered the wife guilty of adultery. Doornbos v. Doornbos, 23 U.S.L.W. 2308 (1954), appeal dismissed, 12 Ill. App. 2d 473, 139 N.E.2d 844 (1956). The first case to recognize that the presumption of legitimacy extended to consensual AID was Strnad v. Strnad, 190 Misc. 786, 787, 78 N.Y.S.2d 390, 392 (1948).

For specific discussions of AID issues, see Andrews, The Stork Market: The Law of the New Reproductive Technologies, 70 A.B.A. J. 50, 53 (1984); Hollinger, From Coitus to Commerce: Legal and Social Consequences of Noncoital Reproduction, 18 U. Mich. J.L. Ref. 865 (1985); Robertson, supra note 56; Wadlington, Artificial Conception: The Challenge for Family Law, 69 Va. L. Rev. 564 (1983); Note, Reproductive Technology and the Procreative Rights of the Unmarried, 98 Harv. L. Rev. 669 (1985); Special Project, Legal Rights and Issues Surrounding Conception, Pregnancy and Birth, 39 Vand. L. Rev. 597 (1986).

[107] See Unif. Parentage Act § 5, 9A U.L.A. 592-93.

[108] See *Jhordan C.*, 179 Cal. App. 3d at 395, 224 Cal. Rptr. at 535 (presumption of legitimacy does not accord parental status to man with whom biological mother lived).

[109] See Andrews, supra note 106, at 53 (discussing history of presumption of legitimacy in AID cases); In re Baby Girl, 9 Fam. L. Rep. (BNA) 2348 (Ky. Cir. Ct. Jefferson City Apr. 5, 1983) (presumption of legitimacy operates to deny paternity even when both surrogate and sperm donor/intended father wished to have parental rights accorded to intended father and his wife).

ting him to establish a relationship with the child and justifying certain procedural safeguards of that relationship.[110] Failure to establish this relationship, however, will result in the eventual extinction of these rights.[111] Second, the biological progenitor of a child does not enjoy a constitutional right to establish paternity or to seek any form of legal recognition of the relationship if the mother of the child is married to another man, even where he has actively sought to establish a relationship with the child.[112]

Stanley v. Illionis,[113] the first of four Supreme Court cases to address the right of an unmarried father to establish or maintain a legally recognized relationship with his child, involved a challenge to the constitutionality of an Illinois statute that conclusively presumed every unwed father unfit to care for his children.[114] Appellant Stanley had lived with his children and their mother for eighteen years without benefit of marriage.[115] Upon the mother's death, the State declared the children its wards and assumed responsibility for their care and custody without affording Stanley a hearing or establishing his unfitness.[116] The effect of the state rule was to deny Stanley status as the legally recognized parent of the children.[117] The Supreme Court rejected this statutory scheme because it violated both procedural due process and equal protection guarantees.[118] Implicit in the Court's decision was the view that Stanley was indeed a "parent" for constitutional purposes, notwithstanding the State's more restrictive legislative definition.[119] According to the Court, therefore, under the Constitution, a state may not make marriage a sine qua non for ascription of paternal rights.

This first elaboration of the paternal rights of unmarried men conceivably could have been interpreted as a constitutional protection of the genetic relationship itself. By this theory, a man achieves constitutional

---

[110] This is apparent as a synthesis of the following cases: Lehr v. Robertson, 463 U.S. 248 (1983); Caban v. Mohammed, 441 U.S. 130 (1979); Quilloin v. Walcott, 434 U.S. 246 (1978); Stanley v. Illinois, 405 U.S. 645 (1972). See notes 111-43 and accompanying text infra.

[111] See *Lehr*, 463 U.S. at 248 (1983); *Quilloin*, 434 U.S. at 246 (1978); notes 119-28, 135-41 and accompanying text infra.

[112] See Michael H. v. Gerald D., 491 U.S. 110, 129-32 (1989); notes 144-149 and accompanying text infra.

[113] 405 U.S. 645 (1972).

[114] See id. at 648.

[115] Id. at 646.

[116] Id.

[117] The statutory definition of "parent" at issue in *Stanley* included "the father and mother of a legitimate child, or the survivor of them, or the natural mother of an illegitimate child." The definition did not include unwed fathers. Id. at 650.

[118] See id. at 657-58.

[119] The Court held that the "state's interest in caring for Stanley's children is de minimis if Stanley is shown to be a fit father." Id. Thus, part of what it means to be a "parent" for constitutional purposes is a presumption of fitness.

protection as parent of his child by virtue of the genetic relationship alone.[120] As we shall see, however, this interpretation later was rejected as unduly broad.

The next step in the almost dialectical development of this uncertain area came six years later in *Quilloin v. Walcott*.[121] *Quilloin* involved a Georgia statute permitting the adoption of a child born out of wedlock over the objection of the male progenitor if he had not taken steps to legitimize the child.[122] Here, the mother had married when the child was three years of age and sought to have her husband adopt the child eight years later.[123] The biological progenitor sought to block the adoption of the child upon the filing of the adoption petition,[124] which occurred eleven years after the birth of the child. Even then, the petitioner-biological progenitor did not seek custody but only objected to the adoption of the child by its mother's husband with whom the child had lived for most of its life.[125]

A unanimous Supreme Court upheld the state court's finding that the adoption petition was granted properly over the petitoner's objection, rejecting petitioner's due process and equal protection claims.[126] Significantly, the Court distinguished *Stanley* by invoking the best-interests-of-the-child standard under which it determined that the adoption was appropriate, because it gave legal recognition to an already established family unit.[127]

As previously noted, however, the best-interests test cannot be the basis for terminating parental rights in the absence of a showing of unfitness.[128] Indeed, the *Quilloin* Court noted this, stating that due process would be offended if the state were to attempt to force the breakup of a natural family in the name of the child's best interests.[129] Therefore, the only plausible interpretation of *Quilloin* consistent with the parental-rights doctrine is that, for constitutional purposes, the petitioner was not a "parent" of the child. By failing to assume any significant responsibility in the eleven years since the child's birth, the petitioner had lost, or had never fully actualized, his status as the parent of the child. While the

---

[120] See Lehr v. Robertson, 463 U.S. 248, 271 (1983) (White, J., dissenting) (father's interest entitled to constitutional protection because biological relationship exists, not because of that relationship's quality).
[121] 434 U.S. 246 (1978).
[122] See id. at 248-49.
[123] Id. at 247.
[124] Id. at 250.
[125] Id. at 247.
[126] See id. at 254-56.
[127] See id. at 255.
[128] See note 30 and accompanying text supra.
[129] See *Quilloin*, 434 U.S. at 255.

Quilloin Court did not adopt this view explicitly, subsequent developments render this the most meaningful interpretation of the Court's reasoning.[130]

Caban v. Mohammed,[131] decided one year later, involved the conflicting claims of two unmarried parents both of whom had maintained joint custody of their children until the mother left to marry another man.[132] In *Caban*, the Court upheld the father's constitutional challenge, on equal protection grounds, to a New York statute permitting an unwed mother, but not an unwed father, to prevent adoption by withholding consent.[133] While the New York statute was similar to the Georgia statute under attack in *Quilloin*,[134] the Court struck down the New York statute as an overbroad gender-based classification.[135] Operative in the Court's decision was its finding that the petitioner's relationship with his children was sufficiently "substantial" to warrant protection.[136]

In *Lehr v. Robertson*,[137] the last of its four cases addressing a biological father's claims of parental rights to a child born out of wedlock, the Court elaborated upon the scope of the constitutional recognition of an unmarried man's parental rights. In *Lehr*, the Court explicitly rejected petitioner's claim that the due process and equal protection clauses of the fourteenth amendment, as interpreted by *Stanley* and *Caban*, gave an unwed father an absolute right to notice and an opportunity to be heard before the child could be adopted by the subsequent husband of the child's mother.[138] Again, the Court's decision turned on the relationship of the genetic father to the child. Rejecting petitioner's due process claim, the majority stated that he had "never supported and rarely seen" the child in the two years between the child's birth and the petition for

---

[130] See Lehr v. Robertson, 463 U.S. 248, 261-62 (1983) (suggesting that parental rights can be extinguished by failure to exercise them); cf. Caban v. Mohammed, 441 U.S. 380, 389 n.7, 393 n.14 (1979) (noting appellant's failure in *Quilloin* to act as father toward his child as important factor).

[131] 441 U.S. 380 (1979).

[132] Id. at 394.

[133] See id. at 382, 394. Under the New York statute, to block an adoption, an unwed father was required to prove that the adoption would not be in the child's best interests. See id. at 386-87. In *Quilloin*, by contrast, the Georgia statute allowed an unwed father to legitimate a child and gain parental rights, including the right to block an adoption. See *Quilloin*, 434 U.S. at 249.

[134] See *Quilloin*, 434 U.S. at 248.

[135] See *Caban*, 441 U.S. at 388 n.7 (noting that Georgia statute in *Quilloin* was similar to New York statute in *Caban*).

[136] See id. at 393-94 & n.14; see also Note, *Caban v. Mohammed*: Extending the Rights of Unwed Fathers, 46 Brooklyn L. Rev. 95, 109-10, 115-16 (1979) (concluding that *Caban*'s recognition of qualitative aspects of parental relationship will provide guidance for legislation).

[137] 463 U.S. 248 (1983).

[138] See id. at 250.

adoption by the mother's subsequent husband.[139] The *Lehr* Court also addressed the relevance of the biological relationship directly:

> The significance of the biological connection is that it offers the natural father an opportunity that no other male possesses to develop a relationship with his offspring. If he grasps that opportunity and accepts some measure of responsibility for the child's future, he may enjoy the blessings of the parent-child relationship and make uniquely valuable contributions to the child's development. If he fails to do so, the Federal Constitution will not automatically compel a State to listen to his opinion of where the child's best interests lie.[140]

Thus, according to the *Lehr* majority, the biological tie provides a foundation upon which the progenitor may build, if he wishes, a parent-child relationship and become a legal "father."[141]

The *Lehr* dissent, which took issue with the majority's characterization of the significance of the biological relationship, noted that a "'mere biological relationship' is not as unimportant in determining the nature of liberty interests as the majority suggests."[142] Indeed, the dissent appeared to argue that the biological relationship warrants protection of the father's rights regarding the child.[143] The disparity in the respective views of the majority and dissent may be reduced to two varying conceptions of the basis of parental rights—one requiring a psychological component characterized by a measure of emotional and financial commitment to the child, the other strictly biological.

Taken together, *Stanley, Quilloin, Caban,* and *Lehr* require something more than a biological link between progenitor and child to award

---

[139] Id. at 249. The Court noted:
> As we have already explained, the existence or nonexistence of a substantial relationship between parent and child is a relevant criterion in evaluating ... the rights of the parent. ... Because appellant, like the father in *Quilloin*, has never established a substantial relationship with his daughter, the New York statutes at issue in this case did not operate to deny appellant equal protection.

Id. at 266-67 (citations omitted). The dissent raised the same inquiry, but read the facts differently, alluding to a pattern of deliberate concealment of the child by the mother, accompanied by persistent attempts on the part of appellant to locate mother and child and to establish a relationship with the child. See id. at 269 (White, J., dissenting).

[140] Id. at 262.

[141] Of course, the progenitor, by himself, may not absolve himself of the *duties* of parenthood, such as the payment of child support. See J. Areen, supra note 69, at 665-76 (examining enforcement of child-support orders). Where, however, another is willing to assume these duties, the Court has appeared to embrace the possibility that the biological progenitor may irrevocably lose the *right* to parental status.

[142] *Lehr*, 463 U.S. at 271 (White, J., dissenting) (citations omitted).

[143] Justice White's dissent stated: "Whether Lehr's interest is entitled to constitutional protection does not entail a searching inquiry into the quality of the relationship but a simple determination of the *fact* that the relationship exists." Id. at 272 (White, J., dissenting) (emphasis in original). But see text accompanying note 137 supra (discussing further *Lehr* dissent).

even noncustodial parental rights to an unwed man. Moreover, it is unlikely that the *Lehr* dissent stands for the bald pronouncement that genetic consanguinity alone is sufficient for ascribing parental rights. After all, *Quilloin*, decided just five years earlier, was a unanimous opinion.[144] Further, it is unlikely that even the *Lehr* dissenters would hold unconstitutional a provision similar to article five of the Uniform Parentage Act, providing that a sperm donor is not to be treated as the legal father of a child conceived through artificial insemination.[145] Thus, it is clear that neither statutory law nor the Federal Constitution protects a man's parental status based solely upon the genetic connection.

The rights of a biological father are even more restricted where the mother of the child is married to another man. In *Michael H. v. Gerald D.*,[146] the Supreme Court held that California's presumption of legitimacy did not violate the due process rights of the biological progenitor of a child by preventing him from establishing his status as the child's father.[147] Although the putative father had established through blood tests a probability greater than 98 percent that he was the natural father of the child,[148] the Court invoked the common-law tradition of placing the integrity of the family unit and the status of the child above the claims of the natural father.[149] The Court reached its holding despite the progenitor's commitment to the child and his active assertion of paternity,[150] in contrast to the appellants in *Quilloin* and *Lehr*.

Michael H. represents a potent endorsement of the common-law limitation of the natural father's paternal rights. More importantly, it clearly reiterates the theme that parental rights are not solely a function of one's status as a genetic progenitor. With this case, the Supreme Court rejected a strictly biological conception of parenthood in favor of broader considerations.

The significance of the decision must not be overstated. Neither *Michael H.* nor its predecessor decisions render the genetic relationship of the father to the child irrelevant. It is very unlikely, for example, that

---

[144] See Quilloin v. Walcott, 434 U.S. 246, 247 (1978).

[145] See Unif. Parentage Act § 5, 9A U.L.A. 593. Thus, the unwed father's relationship with the mother of the child establishes rights that the sperm donor clearly lacks. Indeed, it might not even be necessary that a "father" have had sexual relations with the child's mother. See, e.g., Jhordan C. v. Mary K., 179 Cal. App. 3d 386, 224 Cal. Rptr. 530 (1986) (friend of mother permitted to establish paternal relationship with child born after mother inseminated herself with his sperm, partly because parties' conduct reserved his status as family member).

[146] 491 U.S. 110 (1989).

[147] See id. at 118-20.

[148] Id. at 114.

[149] See id. at 124. The Court concluded by wryly stating that the biological father's claim "is not the stuff of which fundamental rights qualifying as liberty interests are made." Id. at 127.

[150] See id. at 114-15.

the Court would object to state laws that dilute the presumption of legitimacy—and therefore strengthen the claims of the genetic father—by permitting either spouse to rebut it[151] or to state laws that permit a challenge by the putative natural father.[152] Finally, even where the presumption remains conclusive, in actuality most legal fathers are biological fathers. Thus, even if it is true by contingent coincidence that most fathers are genetically related to their children, the fact has achieved recognition and legitimacy in the law.

In sum, fatherhood is a function of the confluence of three factors: the man's biological relationship with the child,[153] his legal or social relationship with the child's mother,[154] and the extent of his social and psychological commitment to the child.[155] While in reality the first factor rarely is isolated from the latter two, the purpose of this exercise has been

---

[151] See text accompanying notes 97-102 supra. However, even where permitted, the ability of the spouse to rebut the presumption of legitimacy has been limited in certain situations. For example, where a man has held himself out as the father of a child born during marriage, only to have his wife inform him, upon divorce, that the child is not his, the wife will be estopped from testifying that the child was not that of her former husband. See, e.g., Atkinson v. Atkinson, 160 Mich. App. 601, 609-12, 408 N.W.2d 516, 519-20 (1987) (relying upon doctrine of "equitable parent" to achieve result); M.H.B. v. H.T.B., 100 N.J. 567, 568, 498 A.2d 775, 775 (1985) (husband equitably estopped from denying paternity after child had come to rely on relationship); New York ex rel. H. v. P., 90 A.D.2d 434, 440-41, 457 N.Y.S.2d 488, 492-93 (1982) (equitable estoppel precluded wife from requiring blood test to establish her husband's nonpaternity); cf. Berrisford v. Berrisford, 322 N.W.2d 742, 745 (Minn. 1982) (equitable estoppel not applied against husband where child was too young to rely upon relationship).

[152] See M. Field, supra note 91, at 120 n.23 (Illinois and Wisconsin statutes construed to let putative father try to establish rights).

[153] Controversy has arisen regarding the due process rights of foster and adoptive parents. While the Supreme Court has not ruled on the constitutional status of adoptive parents, it did address the question as to whether foster parents have the same due process rights as natural parents. In Smith v. Org. of Foster Parents, 431 U.S. 816 (1977), the Court strongly suggested in dicta that foster parents lack due process rights equivalent to those possessed by natural parents. The Court stated, "[n]o one would seriously dispute that a deeply loving and interdependent relationship between an adult and a child in his or her care may exist even in the absence of blood relationship." Id. at 844. Nevertheless, "the usual understanding of 'family' implies biological relationships, and most decisions treating the relation between parent and child have stressed this element." Id. at 843. In the end, the Court appeared to create a distinction based on natural law, arguing that the relationship between foster parent and child is a creation of the state, whereas the biological relationship between parent and child is grounded in a "liberty interest in family privacy [which] has its source, and its contours . . . not in state law, but in intrinsic human rights, as they have been understood in 'this Nation's history and tradition.' " Id. at 845 (quoting Moore v. City of E. Cleveland, 431 U.S. 494, 503 (1977)).

[154] While marriage traditionally has been the most important type of relationship, ascription of paternal rights also may depend upon the type of nonmarital relationship. See, e.g., Jhordan C. v. Mary K., 179 Cal. App. 3d 386, 397-98, 224 Cal. Rptr. 530, 537-38 (1986) (despite statute precluding sperm donors from asserting paternity, friend of mother permitted to establish paternal relationship with child born after mother inseminated herself with his sperm, partly because relationship was between social acquaintances).

[155] See notes 109-10 and accompanying text supra.

to attempt to draw some general conclusions about the way in which the law currently treats this variable in isolation.

3. *In Re Baby M:*[156] *The Biological Interpretation of the Right to Procreate.*

The arguments above demonstrate that a biological link is not, as a matter of the constitutional right to procreation, sufficient to create parental rights. Not all biological parents are procreators. However, the *Baby M* court clearly suggested that a biological link is a *necessary* condition for procreators. Thus, it held that the right of procreation applied only to Mrs. Whitehead, the surrogate, and Mr. Stern, the sperm donor/ intended father, by virtue of their respective biological contributions to Baby M, and not to Mrs. Stern, the intended mother.[157] This biological interpretation of the right to procreate inextricably links the *right* to reproduce with the *biological capacity* to do so.

This approach raises numerous questions. First, one may inquire whether a gestational host, who is not genetically related to the child, is also a procreator. The recent ruling in *Johnson v. Calvert* strongly suggests that this is not the case.[158] Note that if gestation alone is deemed sufficient to give the host a stake in the child,[159] then three conflicting claims founded upon the right of procreation are possible: the claims of the sperm donor, the egg donor, and the gestational host. Second, interpreting the right of procreation to apply solely to those having made a biological contribution to the child, as opposed to those who may have had some instrumental, though nonbiological, role in creating the child, arguably is both overinclusive and underinclusive in scope. It is overinclusive by allowing those with a relatively insignificant role in the procreative process to acquire a right in the child.[160] For example, a sperm

---

[156] 109 N.J. 396, 537 A.2d 1227 (1988).

[157] See id. at 441-44, 537 A.2d at 1248-50 (contract was held ineffective for granting parental rights to Mrs. Stern, who had no biological connection to child).

[158] See notes 84-89 and accompanying text supra (discussing *Calvert* case). Gestational surrogacy is still relatively infrequent; the first reported instance in the United States took place in 1985. See OTA, Infertility, supra note 1, at 36. The process typically involves the use of in vitro fertilization and embryo transfer to the womb of a woman other than the egg donor. See id. at 255.

[159] See Annas, supra note 79, at 50-51 (arguing that gestation alone should trump claims of other parties to procreative relationship).

[160] The relative insignificance of the biological contribution as a basis for ascribing the right of procreation can be seen by comparing the facts of the *Baby M* case with those of our opening scenario where the intended parents biologically were unrelated to the child. From the intended father's standpoint in each of the two scenarios, the only distinction is that, in the *Baby M* case, the intended father contributed his own sperm while the sperm of an anonymous third party was used in the opening scenario. But surely this factor alone should not be the basis for according full parental rights to the intended father and custodial privileges to the intended mother in the former case, while denying them in the latter.

donor contributing his issue to third parties wishing to have a child would satisfy a necessary condition to acquire parental rights in the child even though he never may have intended to parent the child.[161] Simultaneously, the biological interpretation of the right is underinclusive by precluding those who lack the biological capacity to reproduce from exercising the right in a constitutionally protected manner. This interpretation precludes even the intended parents in the procreative relationship from asserting their right to procreate and their corresponding interest in the child simply because they lack the biological ability to reproduce.[162]

As the law currently exists, the legitimate exercise of the right of procreation includes the right to parent a child.[163] If the rationale in *Baby M* is followed, however, only those who possess the biological capacity to reproduce are deemed to possess the right to procreation.[164] Thus, only those with the capacity to reproduce have a constitutional guarantee to do so. Ironically then, the right protects those who are least likely to need its protection.

C. Questioning the Reliance on Biology: Privacy versus Procreation

The right of procreation typically is construed as one aspect or dimension of the right of privacy.[165] And yet, the rights of privacy and procreation are distinct both in their nature and in the types of activities each protects. As Professor Robertson has maintained:

> [C]hoices about who may conceive, bear, or rear a child are distinct from choices about the conduct that occurs in the process of conceiving, bearing and rearing. In other words, the freedom *to* procreate is distinct from freedom *in* procreation. Freedom to control every activ-

---

[161] See notes 100-09 supra (discussing laws limiting right of sperm donors to claim paternity).

[162] Significantly, this is not a situation where a party possesses a right in theory but lacks the capacity to exercise it, as with certain economic or social rights. The distinction is important. If the infertile party possessed a constitutional right to procreate, the state could not prohibit collaborative-reproductive arrangements absent a compelling state interest. Thus, infertile persons with the resources to pay others for their biological contributions to the procreative act, but forbidden to do so by statute, differ from indigent persons who cannot afford an education, for in the latter case, the barrier is economic, while in the former, the barrier is legal. It illustrates the difference between economic and legal barriers to note that, in Roe v. Wade, 410 U.S. 113 (1973), the Court held that women had a constitutional right to abortion in certain circumstances, but in Harris v. McRae, 448 U.S. 297 (1980), the Court held that there was no constitutional mandate for the state to provide abortion services when women could not afford them.

It may turn out that the positive/negative right distinction is philosophically unsound. If so, the distinction between possessing a right without the opportunity to exercise it and not possessing a right at all will fall.

[163] See text accompanying notes 60-61 supra.

[164] See text accompanying notes 156-57 supra.

[165] See notes 56-57 and accompanying text supra.

ity related to procreation—to determine how conception will occur, to manage the pregnancy, to decide how, when, where, and with whom parturition occurs, or how the neonatal period will be managed—may be of great significance to individuals and may also deserve protection. Although these activities may be lumped under the broad rubric of procreative freedom, analytically they involve choices distinct from the decision to procreate, which is the decision to conceive, gestate, or rear another person.[166]

In short, the right of privacy, which encompasses the right to use contraceptives,[167] the right to an abortion,[168] and a variety of other activities associated with a right *not* to procreate,[169] is distinct conceptually from the right to procreate. More specifically, the right of privacy is nonrelational while the right to procreate is relational in character.[170] Thus, while the exercise of the right of privacy is not dependent upon the consent or cooperation of others—for example, a woman need not seek the consent of another, even her husband, to obtain an abortion during the first trimester of her pregnancy[171]—the right of procreation does depend upon the acts of others in at least one respect and, arguably, in a second as well. First, because it takes two to procreate, the exercise of the right is dependent upon the cooperation of another.[172] Second, the procreative right arguably is contingent upon the constructive consent of the resulting child. A parent must meet certain minimal conditions in order to acquire the right to be a parent.[173] While actual consent by an unborn child is an obvious impossibility, the notion of constructive consent is an accurate metaphorical reflection of the general intuition that parents must meet a minimum condition of fitness. While failure to meet this condition cannot undo the physical act of procreation, the rights of the parent in the child may be terminated as a result of the parent's failure to meet this minimal condition of fitness.[174]

---

[166] Robertson, supra note 56, at 410.
[167] See Griswold v. Connecticut, 381 U.S. 479 (1965).
[168] See Roe v. Wade, 410 U.S. 113 (1973).
[169] See note 56 supra (discussing right of procreation as part of privacy right).
[170] Relational rights can be exercised only with the assistance of, at a minimum, the consent of others. Nonrelational rights, by contrast, are individual rights the legitimate exercise of which is not contingent upon the consent or participation of others. See Floyd & Pomerantz, Is There a Natural Right to Have Children?, in Morality and Moral Controversies 135-136 (J. Arthur ed. 1981).
[171] See Planned Parenthood v. Danforth, 428 U.S. 52, 69 (1976).
[172] Thus, the act of rape can never be a legitimate exercise of the procreative right. See text accompanying notes 186-88 infra (discussing relevance of rape).
[173] See notes 34-36 and accompanying text supra (discussing parental unfitness).
[174] The right to family integrity is a fundamental right protected by the fourteenth amendment. See Roe v. Conn, 417 F. Supp. 769, 779 (D. Ala. 1976). Thus, statutes permitting the removal of a child from the home or the termination of parental rights on grounds of neglect or parental unfitness are subject to the compelling state-interest test. Id. But where the state

The rights of privacy and procreation also differ conceptually in the nature of their respective relations to other rights. The right of privacy is derivative of a generalized notion of personal autonomy or bodily integrity,[175] whereas the right of procreation is fundamental, and does not flow from some other, more fundamental right.[176] The right to procreate is the right to bring a child into the world in an effort to have a family.[177] As such, it is more than a right of personal expression.[178]

The distinction being drawn here has important ramifications for determining who should be treated as the parent of a child. Even if the right of privacy is intimately associated with the biological concomitants of procreation, pregnancy, and childbirth, the right of procreation, as a distinct normative claim, need not be associated with the biological *capacity* to reproduce. The right of procreation instead can be viewed simply as a normative safeguard to protect the *intention* to create and raise a

---

can show parental unfitness by clear-and-convincing evidence, the termination of parental rights is constitutionally permissible. See Santosky v. Kramer, 455 U.S. 745, 747-48 (1982).

[175] See Comment, A Taxonomy of Privacy: Repose, Sanctuary, and Intimate Association, 64 Calif. L. Rev. 1447, 1471-73 (1976) (discussing which matters related to bodily integrity receive constitutional protection); id. at 1482 (discussing various interpretations of right of privacy). It is not clear which of these two varying notions, personal autonomy or bodily integrity, more clearly approximates the right of privacy. In Roe v. Wade, 410 U.S. 113 (1973), the Court stated that the right to an abortion is not predicated upon a right to do with one's body as one wishes:

> The privacy right involved, therefore, cannot be said to be absolute. In fact, it is not clear to us that the claim asserted by some *amici* that one has an unlimited right to do with one's body as one pleases bears a close relationship to the right of privacy previously articulated in the Court's decisions. The Court has refused to recognize an unlimited right of this kind in the past.

Id. at 154. The right of privacy also does not approximate a right of personal autonomy similar to John Stuart Mill's harm principle. Mill's principle states:

> [T]he sole end for which mankind are warranted, individually or collectively in interfering with the liberty of action of any of their number, is self-protection. That the only purpose for which power can be rightfully exercised over any member of a civilized community, against his will, is to prevent harm to others. . . . In the part which merely concerns himself, his independence is, of right, absolute. Over himself, over his own body and mind, the individual is sovereign.

J.S. Mill, On Liberty 16 (Promoetheus Books ed. 1986) (n.p. 1859). The right of personal autonomy, encompassing psychological and life-style choices, is broader than a right of bodily integrity, strictly speaking.

[176] See O'Neill, supra note 60, at 26 (discussing distinction between basic and derived rights).

[177] In this respect, the view of the right of procreation put forth here diverges from Robertson. Under my view, the intention to parent the child is necessary for the legitimate exercise of the right of procreation. This intention is not necessary in Robertson's view. See Robertson, supra note 56, at 460-61. It appears that even the desire to pass one's genes along to a succeeding generation is sufficient for the right to be exercised under Robertson's interpretation. See id. at 408-10.

[178] Compare C. Fried, Right and Wrong 151-52 (1978) (parental rights are an extension of personal rights) with Page, supra note 33, at 192 (rejecting this view).

child.[179] Biological capacity, on this view, is neither necessary nor sufficient for ascribing the right to procreate. Thus, while surrogate hosts, such as Mary Beth Whitehead in *Baby M*, are protected by constitutional privacy rights in a wide range of decisions regarding whether and how to continue the pregnancy,[180] it is not correct to ascribe the right to procreate automatically to the gestational host or to the sperm or egg donors as the *Baby M* court did in its recent decision.[181]

Adopting this intentional interpretation of the right of procreation would have fundamental significance for the issue of parental rights. Since the legitimate exercise of the right of procreation would accord parental status to the possessor of the right, those to whom the right of procreation does not apply would not have a cognizable claim to parent the child. Thus, where a conflict develops, as in the *Baby M* case, between claims based upon intentionality and those predicated upon biology, the intentional parents[182] would take legal priority as the parents of the child. In *Baby M*, if Mr. Stern possessed a right to procreate and an interest in the child at all, it should have been based not upon the slender thread of genetic consanguinity, but upon his actions initiating the procreative relationship.[183] By this alternative analysis, Mrs. Stern, the intended mother, would have possessed the same right and interest.

The remainder of this Article is devoted to critiquing the current biology-centered view of the procreative right and defending an "intentionalist" account of the right of procreation outlined above. Before proceeding to these arguments, however, it will be helpful to consider two preliminary objections to an intentionalist justification for parental rights. First, one might be concerned that, if the intentional exercise of the right of procreation is the basis for parental rights, those who have not taken part in the creation of the child would be precluded from being

---

[179] See notes 309-18 and accompanying text infra (discussing arguments predicated upon intentional aspect of parenting).

[180] For example, the surrogate retains the right to an abortion. See Note, supra note 72, at 203 n.61 (discussing implications of this division of rights).

[181] See In re Baby M, 109 N.J. 396, 448-49, 537 A.2d 1227, 1254 (1988). Thus, since a surrogate cannot constitutionally waive her right to an abortion, for example, this could not be the basis for a valid contractual provision. Whether the surrogate could be contractually liable for obtaining an abortion, however, is uncertain. See Simons, Rescinding a Waiver of a Constitutional Right, 68 Geo. L.J. 919, 919-24, 945 (1980) (examining propriety of allowing rescission of waiver of constitutional right). As a practical matter, it is likely that the intended parents would be entitled, at a minimum, to a return of any compensation paid to the surrogate. See Hill, In Defense of Surrogate Parenting Arrangements: An Ethical and Legal Analysis 284-94 (discussing legal issues surrounding surrogate's breach of contract) (dissertation available from UMI, 1990). Whether there also would be a cause of action for the intentional infliction of emotional distress, among other theories, for example, is unclear.

[182] For the definition of intentional (or intended) parents, see note 12 supra.

[183] See notes 309-18 and accompanying text infra (defending intentional view of parental rights).

considered parents. For instance, would this approach exclude adoptive parents from the claim to parental rights? Clearly not. Exercising the right of procreation is *sufficient* as the basis for parental rights, but it is not *necessary*. There are other ways of becoming a parent in addition to procreating. Through death, adoption, or involuntary termination of parental rights, as in the case of a determination of unfitness, third parties may acquire parental rights after the fact. However, it is the procreators—the party or parties responsible for bringing the child into the world with the intention of raising it, the prime movers in the procreative relationship—who are the "parents" of the child at birth.

A second concern is that this reconstruction of the right of procreation will deny the biological progenitors of an unplanned, but ultimately wanted, child the opportunity to be considered the legal parents of that child. Once again, however, the objection is unwarranted. Intentionality acts as a trump for the intended parents when conflicting claims are made by parties who have contributed biologically to the creation of the child. Intentionality, however, is not the only way to acquire parental status.[184] Where no party has intended to create a child, as in the case of the unplanned child, there are no intentional parents. Thus, the claims of the biological parents would take precedence.

To sum up the argument to this point, any coherent theory regarding the right of procreation must resolve first, what parental rights the right of procreation entails; second, whether biological consanguinity is either necessary or sufficient to claim the right of procreation; and third, which conditions limit the parental rights stemming from procreation. As to the first, it was suggested above that the right to procreation plausibly entails the parental rights to make decisions affecting the child and, other things being equal, custody rights.[185] Further, once the right of procreation has been exercised, the person or persons exercising this right should be deemed the parents of the child at birth.

With regard to the second issue, biological consanguinity clearly should not be *sufficient* for application of the right of procreation.[186] The

---

[184] To protect the sanctity of the family, high standards should be established for proof of an intentional relationship. Thus, in the case of surrogate gestation, not only should the parties evince their understanding contractually, but also the contract should be reviewed by a court. This would require both the surrogate and the intentional parents to manifest publicly their intentions regarding the procreational relationship. Aside from the evidentiary benefits of judicial review, such a hearing would have the added psychological advantage of requiring the surrogate to come to terms with, and to declare publicly, her stated intention to relinquish the child. This hearing, which would take place prior to the process of artificial insemination, could be instrumental in weeding out prospective surrogates who are uncertain of their ultimate ability to carry out the agreement.

[185] See text accompanying notes 60-72 supra.

[186] See text accompanying notes 179-83 supra (critiquing *Baby M*'s reliance on biology for ascribing parental rights).

case of pregnancy by rape makes this clear. Though the assailant may be the genetic progenitor of the child, he cannot be deemed to have exercised his right to procreate in the course of the act of rape. Similarly, the Supreme Court's ruling in *Michael H.*[187] suggests that biological consanguinity does not itself guarantee its possessor the right to procreate.[188] Thus, biological consanguinity is not sufficient for application of the right of procreation. But neither should biological consanguinity nor capacity be considered *necessary* for one to possess and exercise the right of procreation. The right of procreation should extend to anyone intending to have a child and capable of producing a child, either biologically or by putting together the necessary biological components with the assistance of others. As to the third issue mentioned above, while others subsequently may acquire parental rights in the child, as in the case of adoptive parents, this acquisition can happen only after the parental rights of the procreative agents have been terminated either voluntarily or in order to protect the child.

III

THE CLAIMS OF BIOLOGY RECONSIDERED

We have a technology that takes Susan's egg and puts it in Mary's body. And so we ask, *who* is the mother? Who is the surrogate? Is Mary substituting for Susan's body, growing Susan's baby for Susan? Or is Susan's egg substituting for Mary's, growing into Mary's baby in Mary's body? Our answer depends on where we stand when we ask the question.[189]

The "presumption of biology" and cases like *Baby M* must be read as endorsing a view of parental rights that gives primacy to those who are related biologically or gestationally to the child. This Part considers and rejects a number of arguments which could be made for the priority of the genetic donors or the gestational host over the claims of the intentional parents.

A. *The Genetic Donor's Claims for Priority*

A number of commentators addressing the conflicting legal claims to parental status between an egg donor and a gestational host have come

---

[187] Michael H. v. Gerald D., 491 U.S. 110, 129-32 (1989) (rejecting constitutional challenge to state laws extending presumption of legitimacy to child of marriage, holding third party with 98% chance of being child's father has no parental rights).

[188] See id. at 121-23 (rejecting claim that natural father outside marriage has substantive liberty interest in obtaining parental recognition); notes 144-50 and accompanying text supra.

[189] B. Katz-Rothman, Recreating Motherhood: Ideology and Technology in a Patriarchal Society 44 (1989) (emphasis in original).

down squarely on the side of the egg donor.[190] While these commentators have adverted to a number of interrelated and overlapping considerations in their defense of the genetic bond, none has undertaken a systematic explication of these arguments. The following discussion sets forth what appear to be the two most compelling claims that can be made in defense of the genetic donor's priority. The first is predicated upon the unique biological relationship shared by parent and child.[191] The second is a property-oriented argument based upon the person's right to any products of his or her body.[192]

1. The Genetic-Identity Argument

It is beyond dispute that an important aspect of parenthood is the experience of creating another in one's "own likeness." Part of what makes parenthood meaningful is the parent's ability to see the child grow and develop *and see oneself in the process of this growth*. Through this process, the parent views himself or herself as a creative agent in nature. This genetic identity accords the parent a kind of limited, genetic immortality, which one commentator has called "the sense of living on *through* and *in* one's sons and daughters and their sons and daughters."[193]

The significance of the genetic connection between parent and child undoubtedly is part of what makes infertility a painful experience.[194] While adoption may satisfy one's desire to provide nurturance for a child, adoption cannot satisfy the yearning to create the child and to watch as a version of oneself unfolds and develops. It is, without doubt, this desire which impels some to use reproductive technologies and arrangements, including surrogate parenting, to create a child rather than to adopt.[195] The fundamental nature of this generative role may have inspired one commentator to argue that, while gestational surrogacy poses no insurmountable moral problems, genetic surrogacy—where the surrogate conceives the child with the intention of giving it up to another—is morally condemnable.[196]

The blood bond between parent and child has achieved both histori-

---

[190] See, e.g., Brahams, supra note 78, at 18-19; Samuels, supra note 78, at 176.
[191] See notes 193-205 and accompanying text infra.
[192] See notes 206-17 and accompanying text infra.
[193] R. Lifton, The Life of the Self 32 (1983) (emphasis in original).
[194] The harmful symptoms of infertility include depression, avoidance of social occasions celebrating the birth or growth of children, the side effects of drugs used to combat the condition causing infertility, and marital tension. OTA, Infertility, supra note 1, at 37. Divorce is not an uncommon result of infertility where the fertile party wishes to remarry and start a family. Id.
[195] See A. Overvold, Surrogate Parenting 81 (1988) (stating that genetic input is important motive in genetic parenting).
[196] See Krimmel, The Case Against Surrogate Parenting, 13 Hastings Center Rep. 35, 35, 38 (1983).

cal and mythological significance in every culture.[197] This connection is a manifestation of both the act of creating the child and the ongoing similarity between parent and child.[198] The significance of this latter feature is experienced both by parent and child, most noticeably when the natural parent and child meet for the first time.[199] The importance of biological similarity is augmented by scientific developments over the past fifty years which strongly suggest that even variables such as psychological dispositions and personal proclivities in such intimate matters as spousal preference and occupational choice may be determined, at least in part, genetically.[200] In sum, it is only natural that our sublime and complex feelings regarding this issue reflect precisely the sentiment that law should preserve as a family unit that which nature has rendered genetically similar.

While the foregoing manifests our general intuitions for the roles of genetic parents as they have developed historically in our culture, the historic basis for these rights is distinct from the type of situation under consideration in this Article. Here we are considering the genetic link unto itself, distinct from the cultural connotations attending the genetic relationship. Our hypothetical situation poses a sperm or ova donor who has no other involvement in the procreative relationship against a number of parties with competing claims. The genetic relationship itself should not be the basis for evaluating the parental claims of genetic donors above these other claims.

First, the sperm donor, who merely hands over a vial of sperm, typically is denied parental rights.[201] The contribution of the egg donor, of course, requires a greater level of physical involvement and risk.[202] While this factor may give that donor a claim intuitively stronger than

---

[197] See N. Chodorow, The Reproduction of Mothering: Psychoanalysis of Gender (1978) (discussing masculine and feminine parental roles in different societies).

[198] See J. Bluestein, Parents and Children: The Ethics of the Family 142 (1982) (stating that conception and birth are direct cause of emotional attachment to biological child).

[199] For example, one adoptee, upon locating her biological mother, expressed delight simply at hearing a voice identical to hers emanating from the other end of the telephone line for the first time. A. Sorosky, A. Baran & R. Pannor, The Adoption Triangle 159 (1984).

[200] See E. Wilson, On Human Nature 15-51 (1978) (discussing claim that personal and, ultimately, social practices are predicated upon genetic foundation). I do not take a stand here on the ever-present nature-nurture debate. The point is simply that, just as physical traits are heritable, it is likely that the physical processes which underlie psychological functioning also are heritable. This is not rendered any less plausible by social conditions in the child-rearing environment which may reinforce certain psychological dispositions. Thus, a child with a psychological propensity toward learning may be reinforced in her pursuits by a mother with a similar disposition. See R. Lewontin, S. Rose & L. Kamin, Not in Our Genes 83-130 (1984) (discussing influence of genes versus environment on intelligence).

[201] See note 104 supra.

[202] Ova are removed through a surgical process known as laparoscopy. See OTA, Infertility, supra note 1, at 105-06.

that of the sperm donor, that intuition rests on an argument regarding the greater psychological and physical involvement of the egg donor, rather than the genetic connection per se. The active role of parent as the *creator* of the child is lacking in the contribution of the genetic donors here. The sperm or egg donor plays the passive role of providing the seed from which the child will develop. This contribution, in itself, cannot be the basis for a claim to parental rights.

Second, it should not be relevant that the donor and child share similar physical or even psychological characteristics. As one commentator has pointed out, there is no difference genetically between the relationship of the donor and child and the relationship between full siblings.[203] In either case, there is a fifty percent probability, with regard to any particular gene, that the pair will share that gene.[204] By itself, sharing fifty percent of a child's genetic make-up should give the biological progenitor no greater right to parent than it does a sibling. Indeed, if genetic similarity alone were sufficient for ascribing parental rights, an identical twin would possess a greater claim than the parent.[205] The absurdity of this result demonstrates that genetic similarity alone should not serve as a basis for recognizing parental rights.

2. *The Property-Rights Argument*

The property-rights argument can be put into simple syllogistic form. The major premise states that persons possess property rights in the products, processes, and organs of their bodies and in any commodities developed from these sources.[206] The minor premise provides that a child is a product of a person's genetic issue. Therefore, the syllogism concludes that the genetic progenitor should have property rights or quasi-property rights in the child.

There are, however, a number of preliminary difficulties with this argument. First, because a child is the genetic expression of two persons, a genetic progenitor would have only a half-interest in the child. Second, most sperm and eggs are sold to commercial sperm banks.[207] Consequently, even under traditional principles of property law, the sperm and ova would belong to the purchaser who would have the right to dispose of them as he or she sees fit, within existing legal constraints, free and

---

[203] See B. Katz-Rothman, supra note 189, at 37.
[204] Id.
[205] Identical twins carry all the same genes. Id.
[206] This proposition must be qualified. Persons do not have an absolute right to dispose of their bodies as they deem fit. For instance, there are significant limitations on the sale of organs. See R. Scott, The Body as Property 179-97 (1981); Andrews, My Body, My Property, 16 Hastings Center Rep. 28, 28 (1986).
[207] See Jansen, Sperm and Ova as Property, 11 J. Med. Ethics 123, 124 (1985) (examining ethical implications of unauthorized use of donated sperm, ova, and embryos).

clear of any claims on the part of the gamete donor.[208] Third, even if the sperm or ova had not been sold but had been appropriated accidentally as part of the reproductive process of another, the doctrine of accession might bar the claims of the genetic progenitors. Where a raw material has been remade so as to completely change its nature or greatly increase its value, accession requires that title in the object vests with the person who has performed the labor—in this case either the intending parents or, more literally, the gestational host.[209] Thus, even if the property-rights metaphor were appropriate in this situation, the sperm and ova donors would have no claim to the child.

Overlooking these objections, however, a more fundamental difficulty with the property-rights argument remains. While people may possess property rights in their genetic issue, they certainly do not possess property rights in the results of their genetic contributions. Put more simply, children are not property. While it is true that at common law parental rights were in many ways strikingly similar to property rights,[210] this similarity no longer exists.[211] Thus, while a sperm or egg donor may have something approximating a property right in his or her gametes, their status with respect to an embryo is less certain.[212] The continuum running between the jurisprudential categories of property and personhood is unclear. For example, the progenitors of a frozen embryo awaiting implantation in the uterus may be treated as property owners in some contexts and as prospective parents in others.[213] But

---

[208] See R. Brown, The Law of Personal Property § 9.2 (3d ed. 1955) (discussing passage of title in sale-of-goods context).

[209] Before a court will apply the doctrine of accession, it must find that the raw material was used accidentally or in good faith. See 1 Am. Jur. 2d Accession and Confusion § 2 (1962). Also, the object must be substantially changed or increased in value. See Wetherbee v. Green, 22 Mich. 311 (1871) (rejecting plaintiff's replevin action for hoops made from wood cut from his land).

[210] See McGough & Shindell, supra note 29, at 209-17 (discussing development of state intervention in parent-child relationships). "As late as the tenth century in England, a parent ... could sell a child under seven into slavery." Id. at 209. Even as recently as the nineteenth century, a parent had a legal right over the child's property, services, and earnings. See id. at 210.

[211] Parental rights now may be terminated, for example, when a parent is deemed unfit. See notes 33-36 and accompanying text supra.

[212] The Warnock Report in Britain recommended that legislation be passed providing that embryos should not be treated like property. See Jansen, supra note 207, at 125.

[213] For example, while the progenitors of a frozen embryo together share the right to dispose of the embryo as they deem fit, this right may be lost to both parties in the event of divorce or passage of time. See Davis v. Davis, No. 180 (Tenn. App. Sept. 13, 1990) (LEXIS, States library, Tenn. file) (divorcing couple litigated disposition of frozen embryos which had not been implanted prior to divorce), leave to appeal granted sub nom. Stowe v. Davis, No. 180 (Tenn. App. Dec. 3, 1990) (LEXIS, States Library, Tenn. file); see also Andrews, The Legal Status of the Embryo, 32 Loy. L. Rev. 357, 402-03 (1989) (analysis of legal issues surrounding frozen embryos).

certainly, upon birth, the property metaphor is no longer apposite.

Perhaps the property-rights argument could be amended to meet this objection by acknowledging that the parents do not retain property rights in the child but rather that their property rights in their gametes "mature" into parental rights with the growth of the fetus. However, the moral intuition underlying the doctrine of accession[214] undermines the modified version of the property-rights argument. The link between gamete and newborn child is too attenuated to support a claim to parent the child by virtue of the genetic contribution alone. Where the genetic donor solely relinquishes his or her issue for the purpose of another carrying the child to term, with the understanding that the genetic donor will raise the child, the genetic donor has a compelling argument. In the absence of this intention, however, the claim is much weaker; and where there exists a clear intention that another will raise the child, the claims of the genetic progenitors are negligible.

This is not to say that the gamete donor has no interest in the use to which the sperm or ovum is put. For example, it has been suggested, perhaps crassly, that the right of the gamete producer is similar to the right of the manufacturer of a computer chip, or the distributor of some copyrighted material.[215] While a party may sell the right to use, view, or listen to the material, the right to duplicate or alter it is not included.[216] Analogously, the genetic progenitor would possess an interest in restricting the uses of his or her genetic material. The progenitor, for example, might have an interest in preventing the purchaser from using his or her gametes to create a race of genetically-engineered automatons or to develop some interspecies hybrid.[217]

That the producers of sperm and ova have a interest in preventing certain uses of their issue, however, does not establish that they should be accorded parental rights. Where the gamete producer has transferred to another the right to use his or her issue for legally permissible forms of collaborative reproduction, he or she has relinquished any rights or interest in the issue as long as it is used as provided for by agreement. The genetic source may retain an interest in seeing that the bodily product is not used improperly, just as the publisher may prevent copyright infringement, but this interest gives the genetic source no right to parent the child, just as a publisher has no right to reclaim a book purchased for a legitimate purpose by another.

Thus, the argument for the priority of the genetic progenitor as parent of the child is not, in itself, compelling. To the extent that the genetic

---

[214] See text accompanying note 209 supra.
[215] See Jansen, supra note 207, at 124.
[216] See id.
[217] See id.

progenitor does have a colorable claim to parent the child, it must be by virtue of some other form of contribution to the procreational arrangement.

B. *The Gestational Host's Claims for Priority*

> God gave her the child, and gave her, too, an instinctive knowledge of its nature and requirements . . . which no other mortal being can possess. And, moreover, is there not a quality of awful sacredness in the relation between this mother and this child.[218]

The claims for the moral and legal priority of the gestational host are much more compelling than are those of the genetic progenitors. At least five distinct genres of argument can be brought to bear in favor of the primary parental status of the gestational host. These include claims predicated on the prenatal and postnatal bonding between the birth mother and child; the best interests of the child; the harmful psychological effects to the birth mother resulting from compelled relinquishment of the child; the physical involvement of the birth mother in bringing the child into the world; and the extrinsic social and moral considerations which portend harmful consequences predicted to result from permitting the legal separation of birth mother and child. Each of these claims will be considered in turn.

1. *The Maternal-Bonding Argument*

The claim that a deep attachment or bond develops in the course of the prenatal and postnatal relationship between mother and child is, perhaps, the most popular and most controversial argument favoring the priority of the gestational host.[219] The controversy is due, in part, to the

---

[218] N. Hawthorne, The Scarlet Letter 113 (H. Levin ed. 1960) (n.p. 1850).

[219] The bonding claim lies at the very heart of the attack on the proposed enforcement of surrogate contracts. See Suh, supra note 9, at 362 (bonding is among strongest human ties, profoundly affecting birth mother).

The claim is also the subject of numerous articles. See Belsky & Rovine, Nonmaternal Care in the First Year of Life and the Security of Infant-Parent Attachment, 59 Child Dev. 157 (1988) (child's behavioral responses to others influenced by level of care rendered by primary caretaker); Chess & Thomas, Infant Bonding: Mystique and Reality, 52 Am. J. Orthopsychiatry 213 (1982) (critiquing evidence supporting uniqueness of mother-infant attachment and idea that there is critical period for bonding); Egeland & Farber, Infant-Mother Attachment: Factors Related to Its Development and Changes Over Time, 55 Child Dev. 753 (1984) (studying effect of socioeconomic factors on infant-mother bond); Fein, Men's Entrance to Parenthood, 25 Fam. Coordinator 341 (1976) (discussing parental duties as factor in reducing anxiety in paternal role); Fletcher & Evans, Maternal Bonding in Early Fetal Ultrasound Examinations, 308 New Eng. J. Med. 392 (1983) (discussing how sensory contact with fetus facilitates bonding); Goldberg, Parent-Infant Bonding: Another Look, 54 Child Dev. 1355 (1983) (critical look at whether bonding hypothesis has been proven); Herbert, Sluckin & Sluckin, Mother-To-Infant Bonding, 23 J. Child Psychology & Psychiatry 205 (1982) (arguing that evidence fails to support critical-bonding-period hypothesis, especially in light of socioeco-

fundamental implications that the bonding hypothesis has for our view of human nature and for our conception of the nature of the parent-child relationship.[220]

Accordingly, the bonding hypothesis is susceptible to a variety of interpretations and has taken on a corresponding number of diverse theoretical manifestations. First, an ancient claim, now recast in the parlance of sociobiology, asserts that there is a maternal instinct which biologically predisposes a woman to want to bear and nurture a child.[221] A second view suggests that pregnancy and childbirth precipitate a battery of powerful psychoanalytic forces that facilitate the maternal bond.[222] Third, several competing psychosocial theories view the maternal-child relationship as the result of a matrix of social influences.[223] And, of

---

nomic factors and successful adoptions); Isabella, Belsky & von Eye, Origins of Infant Mother Attachment: An Examination of Interactional Synchrony During the Infant's First Year, 25 Dev. Psychology 12 (1989) (arguing that mother-infant interaction is self-reinforcing: behavior of one influences and reinforces responses of other); Kennell & Klaus, Mother-Infant Bonding: Weighing the Evidence, 4 Dev. Rev. 275 (1984) (arguing for critical-bonding-period hypothesis); Lamb, Early Mother-Neonate Contact and the Mother-Child Relationship, 24 Child Psychology and Psychiatry 487 (1983) (arguing that critical-bonding-period hypothesis is not supported by evidence); Lamb & Hwang, Maternal Attachment and Mother-Neonate Bonding: A Critical Review, 2 Advances in Dev. Psychology 1 (1982) (same); Leifer, Psychological Changes Accompanying Pregnancy and Motherhood, 95 Genetic Psychology Monographs 55 (1977) (discussing change in maternal self-image during first pregnancy and early postpartum period); Lewis & Feiring, Infant-Mother and Mother-Infant Interaction Behavior and Subsequent Attachment, 60 Child Dev. 831 (1989) (examining synchronic aspect of mother-infant interaction); Myers, Mother-Infant Bonding: The Status of the Critical Period Hypothesis, 4 Dev. Rev. 240 (1984) (arguing that, on balance, early sensitivity period for maternal bonding has not been proven) [hereinafter Myers, Status]; Myers, Mother-Infant Bonding: Rejoinder to Kennell and Klaus, 4 Dev. Rev. 283 (1984) (same) [hereinafter Myers, Rejoinder]; Shtarkshall, Motherhood as a Dominant Feature in the Self-Image of Female Adolescents of Low Socioeconomic Status, 22 Adolescence 565 (1987) (arguing that plans for becoming parent and feelings about maternity are affected by socioeconomic status); van Ijzerdoorn & van Vliet-Visser, The Relationship Between Quality of Attachment in Infancy and IQ in Kindergarten, 149 J. Genetic Psychology 23 (1988) (positive correlation found between quality of infant-to-mother attachment and child's IQ).

[220] Where the bonding hypothesis is viewed as a claim that parental feelings are the product of biologically preprogrammed factors, the implication is that social factors are less important than usually thought. Therefore, parenting, and the feelings of nurturance that accompany it, cannot be learned. See Shtarkshall, supra note 219, at 568-69 (discussing social and economic factors affecting feelings of adolescent girls concerning their self-image as potential mothers).

[221] Kennell and Klaus come close to this position but are not unqualified biological reductionists because they admit that the bonding process may be affected by psychosocial factors. See Kennell & Klaus, supra note 219, at 276-77 (reviewing evidence of biologically produced sensitivity period and arguing for critical-bonding-period hypothesis); see also E. Wilson, supra note 200, at 15-53 (theoretical account of sociobiology and claim that biological mechanisms underlie social behavior).

[222] See, e.g., S. Freud, Some Psychological Consequences of the Anatomical Distinction Between the Sexes, in 5 Collected Papers 195 (J. Strachey ed. 1959) (discussing penis envy, its renunciation, and female desire to nurture child).

[223] Many commentators, particularly feminists, have attacked the biological conception in favor of a psychosocial or social learning view of motherhood. See, e.g., N. Chodorow, supra

course, there are variations and combinations of these diverse themes which further frustrate any attempt to arrive at a univocal conception of the bonding phenomenon.[224] Thus, the meaning of the term "bond" varies from one theoretical orientation to another. This lack of uniformity has important implications for the claim that bonding is an inevitable concomitant of pregnancy and childbirth.[225]

In addition to these theoretical difficulties, confusion exists as to whether bonding occurs before birth, after birth, or throughout both pregnancy and the neonatal period.[226] The answer to this question appears to depend upon the researcher's theoretical orientation—biological determinists place much greater emphasis on prenatal factors than do those from a social-learning perspective. The question is confused further by conflating the mother-to-infant bond and the infant-to-mother bond.[227]

---

note 197, at 40 (study of psychodynamic considerations advances sociological understanding of women's assumption of maternal role); G. Corea, The Mother Machine 283-99 (1985) (examining significance of social factors in development of gender identity and assumption of maternal role).

[224] For example, bonding has been viewed as a fundamentally biological phenomenon which may be affected by social factors. See Kennell & Klaus, supra note 219, at 276-77 (bonding affected by cultural and socioeconomic background as well as hospital-care practices); R. Lewontin, S. Rose & L. Kamin, supra note 200, at 289 (human development is result of complex array of factors).

[225] Biological theories generally suggest that the bond is immutable and inevitable provided there is contact during the critical period. Similarly, psychoanalytic theories appear to render behavior a function of unconscious motivational processes over which the woman has no conscious control. See, e.g., S. Freud, supra note 222, at 191-92. Social-learning theories, by contrast, suggest that behavior can be changed by altering psychological and social conditions which bring about certain behavior. See, e.g., N. Chodorow, supra note 197, at 205-06. For example, the maternal-infant bond may be simply the product of social influences which condition a woman to behave in certain ways toward her baby. If so, where social expectations toward the gestational host do not compare with those directed toward the biological mother who has intended to keep her child, the surrogate may not bond with the child. In short, the social-learning theories interpret human behavior as flexible and more amenable to social influences. See Myers, Rejoinder, supra note 219. Thus, according to social-learning theory, the implications of the bonding hypothesis are less dramatic, at least where the social influences which affect the birth mother's relationship with the child can be altered. Id.

[226] From the standpoint of mother-infant bonding, there are proponents of both the prenatal bond and the postnatal bond. Compare Fletcher & Evans, supra note 219, at 392 (discussing development of prenatal mother-infant attachment) with Kennel & Klaus, supra note 219, at 277-78 (discussing presence of postnatal mother-infant sensitivity period).

[227] Four distinct types of bonds may be distinguished logically: a prenatal infant-to-mother bond, a prenatal mother-to-infant bond, a postnatal infant-to-mother bond, and a postnatal mother-to-infant bond. It is difficult to see how the first of these could be tested. For a discussion of the prenatal mother-to-infant bond, see Fletcher & Evans, supra note 219, at 392-93 (bonding facilitated by ultrasound and sensory contact). For a consideration of the postnatal infant-to-mother bond, see Belsky & Rovine, supra note 219, at 164-65 (child's behavior influenced by level of care); Egeland & Farber, supra note 219, at 769 (socioeconomic factors affect child's attachment to parent). The postnatal mother-to-infant bond is the focus of the present discussion.

Our knowledge of the emotional impact of pregnancy strongly suggests that there are as many feelings and experiences accompanying pregnancy as there are pregnant women. For some women, pregnancy is a time of significant emotional upheaval, psychological disequilibrium, and profound uncertainty in self-identity as their role changes from wife to mother and, possibly, from working woman to child caretaker.[228] Others experience pregnancy, birth, and childcare with an unparalleled sense of personal wholeness.[229] For still other women, the early phase of parenthood is a time of crisis exceeding even that of pregnancy.[230]

Still, despite these variations, the *prenatal* version of the bonding hypothesis is supported by a great deal of evidence, both scientific and anecdotal. Thus, women often report feelings of loyalty toward the fetus early in pregnancy, sometimes as early as the end of the first trimester.[231] Quickening, the point at which a woman begins to feel the movements of the fetus, is important to the development of maternal feelings of attachment to the fetus.[232] Reactions to quickening appear to be an example of the general correlation between the woman's increasing sensory awareness of the fetus and her feelings of loyalty and attachment to it.[233] While both parents interact greatly with the fetus—touching, rubbing, and talking to it, often in response to fetal movements—women have a greater sense of the fetus as a separate individual, often attributing emotional responses to fetal movements.[234] Finally, there is empirical support for the claim that women mourn after the loss of a baby, even a nonviable fetus.[235]

---

[228] See Leifer, supra note 219, at 57-60 (1977) (analyzing empirical evidence on pregnant women's psychological mutations). These changes are particularly significant with the birth of a woman's first child. See A. Oakley, Women Confined 179-80 (1980).

[229] See Leifer, supra note 219, at 89-90; see also K. Rabuzzi, Motherself 48-59, 109-20 (1988) (discussing changes in roles and self-perception brought about by pregnancy and childcare).

[230] See Leifer, supra note 219, at 89.

[231] See Fletcher & Evans, supra note 219, at 392.

[232] See Leifer, supra note 219, at 76. Quickening takes place some time around the end of the first or the begining of the second trimester, from 12 to 16 weeks of gestation. See Hellegers, Fetal Development, in Contemporary Issues in Bioethics 125, 127 (T. Beauchamp & L. Walters eds. 1989).

[233] Thus, it is suggested that ultrasonography, by which ultrasonsic pictures of the fetal form are taken, may facilitate feelings of attachment for the fetus on the part of both parents. See Fletcher & Evans, supra note 219, at 392-93.

[234] See Stainton, The Fetus: A Growing Member of the Family, 34 Fam. Rel. 321, 322-24 (1985) (studying prospective parents' impressions of appearance, communication, gender, temperament, and sleep-wake cycle of their fetus).

[235] See Kennell, Slayter & Klaus, The Mourning Response of Parents to the Death of a Newborn Baby, 283 New Eng. J. Med. 344 (1970) (reporting feelings of attachment before tactile contact between fetus and mother).

There appears to be a high correlation between attachment to the baby and anxiety directed toward the fetus. See Leifer, supra note 219, at 91. Further, high self-concern is corre-

Yet the implications for parental-rights arguments are unclear. First, much hinges on the nature-nurture variations of the bonding hypothesis. Notwithstanding this evidence, there is widespread disagreement concerning the bonding hypothesis—or even whether bonding exists as a discrete phenomenon.[236] As a preliminary matter, there are profound conceptual difficulties in the concept of bonding.[237] It is not clear whether the bonding hypothesis, as conceived by its proponents, must necessarily entail some kind of biological link which transcends social factors and influences. For example, if bonding is simply the result of complex social factors which condition or motivate a woman to feel and behave in certain ways toward the child, then these factors can be mitigated by changing the social contingencies which shape the expectations of the gestational host. Indeed, numerous studies strongly suggest that socioeconomic circumstances affect a woman's emotional predisposition to the child.[238] Even the most ardent proponents of the biological interpretation of the bonding hypothesis have qualified their earlier positions to admit that socioeconomic factors affect the mother-infant relationship.[239] Other research refutes the claim that the prenatal bond is a universal concomitant of pregnancy. In one study, researchers asked ninety-seven new mothers when they first felt love for their babies. Only 41% first felt love during pregnancy.[240] This response suggests that prenatal attachment is not an immutable biological imperative that supports a universal legal commitment to the priority of the gestational host.

Nonetheless, even if the prenatal-bonding hypothesis cannot support a general presumption in favor of the gestational parent, in many cases the gestational host does develop strong feelings toward the fetus before birth, and there is some indication that depriving her of the child will result in serious psychological consequences.[241] These cases warrant serious moral consideration. Legal rights are not created in a vacuum.

---

lated with a low level of attachment to the fetus. See id. Also, there appears to be a correlation between maternal feelings early in pregnancy and the disposition toward the fetus much later in pregnancy. See id. at 91-92. Thus, a woman's attitude toward pregnancy early on may affect her subsequent level of attachment.

[236] See note 219 supra.

[237] See Herbert, Sluckin & Sluckin, supra note 219, at 206 (analyzing difficulties in bonding hypothesis).

[238] See, e.g., Egeland & Farber, supra note 219, at 769; Herbert, Sluckin & Sluckin, supra note 219, at 218-19; Myers, Status, supra note 219, at 256, 268; see also Shtarkshall, supra note 219, at 568 (women of low socioeconomic backgrounds tend to have greater desire to become mothers).

[239] See Kennell & Klaus, supra note 219, at 276.

[240] Id. at 281. Twenty-four percent first felt love for their children at birth, 27% felt love during the first week after birth, and the remaining 8% first felt love at some point after the first week. Id.

[241] See notes 270-87 and accompanying text infra (discussing psychological effects of relinquishment).

Rights must account for tangible human feelings and relationships, particularly in an area such as this, where these feelings and relationships are most vulnerable. The weight that these considerations deserve, however, will depend upon the extent to which these feelings may be vitiated or prevented by changing the social expectations of the surrogate. Correspondingly less weight should be given to these considerations where the surrogate's attachment to the child can be precluded by her knowledge that she will not be recognized as the mother of the child.

As for the notion of a postnatal-bonding process or critical period in which the new mother is particularly susceptible to deep feelings of attachment as she interacts with the child, recent research has cast serious doubt on this hypothesis. Minimally, it is clear that there is no magical point at which the bonding process occurs.[242] Moreover, numerous researchers have stated bluntly that there is no evidence to support the critical-period hypothesis.[243]

Arguments predicated upon the bonding hypothesis simply raise more questions than answers regarding the moral status of the gestational host. In addition to the theoretical problems mentioned thus far, it remains to be proven that the bonding process is *qualitatively* distinct from feelings of attachment for the child developed by others in the procreative process. The birth mother obviously is involved most directly with the physical development of the fetus and is the only one physically to experience tactile contact with the fetus. Nevertheless, there is little evidence for the claim that there is a qualitative difference between the feelings of the birth mother and those of another party to the procreative relationship. If there is no qualitative difference, then the claims of the gestational host predicated upon the prenatal-bonding hypothesis may be reduced to the contention that the birth mother has a superior claim to parent the child by virtue of her greater involvement with, and feelings of attachment for, the child at birth. While this may be an important argument in her favor, it does not carry the absolute moral weight conveyed by the onerous connotations of the term "bonding."

As for the argument predicated upon the postnatal-bonding hypothesis, two responses serve to answer the claims for the superiority of the

---

[242] See Chess & Thomas, supra note 219, at 215.
[243] Professor Lamb noted:
>[I]t is clear that claims regarding the effects of early contact on mother-infant bonding are not well-supported by the empirical evidence. Most charitably, one could say that advocates of mother-infant bonding have yet to prove their case. More critically, one could say that early contact has no enduring effects on maternal attachment, but may sometimes have modest short-term effects on *some* mothers in *some* circumstances.

Lamb, supra note 219, at 294 (emphasis in original). For other research, see, e.g., Herbert, Sluckin & Sluckin, supra note 219, at 209-12 (evidence fails to support critical-period hypothesis); Myers, Rejoinder, supra note 219, at 283-84 (sensitivity-period hypothesis not proven).

gestational host. First, the very notion of postnatal bonding as a discrete phenomenon empirically is suspect.[244] Parents typically love and nurture their children whether they are natural or adoptive parents. There appears to be nothing intrinsic to the biological parent-child relationship which does not similarly occur in an adoptive relationship. Moreover, difficulties in operationalizing the concept of bonding, together with the lack of evidence for the postnatal-sensitivity period, render the hypothesis an entity of dubious scientific status.

Second, even if the postnatal-bonding hypothesis is correct and new mothers experience a period of sensitivity shortly after birth which readies them for the task of mothering, this sensitivity would give the gestational host the morally superior claim to be a parent of the child if the process of bonding is experienced only by natural parents. If the process of bonding is experienced by all new parents, natural and adoptive, then the intended parents would possess the same propensity to bond with the child as does the birth mother. However, if the bonding process takes place only between the birth mother and the child, because bonding is brought about not by contact with the child but as a physical consequence of pregnancy itself, what would be the negative consequences of placing the child with someone other than the birth mother? There is little moral significance in the claim that relinquishment of the child precludes a bond that *would have* developed had the birth mother retained custody. The only real claim that can be marshalled on behalf of the birth mother is that breaking or precluding the postnatal bond *ab initio* will result in some psychological harm to her. In essence, this reduces to a claim that compelled relinquishment of the child may have severe consequences for the psychological health of the birth mother. Whether or not this is true—and we shall turn to this question shortly— this issue is conceptually distinct from claims predicated upon the bonding process per se.

2. The Best-Interests-of-the-Child Argument

As noted previously, every state has recognized a presumption that it is in the best interests of the child to be placed with its natural parents.[245] While the legal impetus for this presumption may be the parental-rights doctrine,[246] some empirical evidence has linked several psychological problems among adopted children and adolescents to difficulties in the reproductive and early postnatal history of the child.[247] In

---

[244] See notes 242-43 and accompanying text supra.
[245] See notes 38-43 and accompanying text supra.
[246] See notes 29-51 and accompanying text supra (discussing parental-rights doctrine).
[247] See Isabella, Belskey & von Eye, supra note 219, at 12.

general, it is argued that separating the child from the birth mother may affect the child adversely in two ways. First, the child may incur irrevocable psychological harm because the parent and child fail to develop an emotional "bond."[248] These problems have been linked to the inability of both the mother to develop an attachment to the child and the child to develop a bond with its parents. Second, the child may experience psychological harm due to uncertainty regarding its biological heritage.

Throughout the 1960s and 1970s, researchers began to observe an apparent increase in the number of cases of child abuse suffered by prematurely born children.[249] A developing body of evidence suggested that a bond must develop between parent and child during a critical period early in infancy—according to some, within twelve hours of birth.[250] In considering what possible connection might exist between premature births and subsequent parental behavior toward the child, researchers hypothesized that vital medical treatment given to premature babies, requiring the separation of mother and infant, prevented the mother from bonding with the child. They concluded that the failure to bond resulted in a higher incidence of child abuse later in life. Thus, if a mother were precluded from interacting with her child soon after birth, there would be less likelihood that the mother-infant bond would develop.

A great deal of evidence also suggests that a symbiotic relationship between newborns and mothers develops throughout infancy.[251] In particular, it appears that the level of maternal responsiveness to the behavioral and verbal signals of the child may affect the child's sense of attachment[252] and the child's subsequent level of sociability.[253] Thus, the bonding hypothesis posits that early maternal contact with a child is necessary to foster the mother's feelings for the child and, consequently, that development of the mother-to-infant bond is vital for the child's well-being. The crux of this first claim for the rights of the gestational host, then, is that the intended mother, not having experienced the mother-to-infant bond, may lack the nurturing qualities of the birth mother.

Insofar as this best-interests-of-the-child argument relies on the

---

[248] See notes 219-44 and accompanying text supra (discussing bonding).

[249] See T. Verney & J. Kelly, The Secret Life of the Unborn Child 149-50 (1981).

[250] See id.; Kennell & Klaus, supra note 219, at 276-77 (authors, research pioneers who propounded bonding hypothesis, reevaluate evidence for sensitivity period, concluding that early mother-infant contact facilitates bonding but is not irreplaceable). But see Lamb, supra note 219, at 488-92 (arguing that sensitivity-period hypothesis is not well-founded).

[251] See Isabella, Belsky & von Eye, supra note 219, at 18 (study of one, three, and nine-month-old infants concluding that secure attachment is fostered where mothers respond consistently and appropriately to infants' signals); Lewis & Feiring, supra note 219, at 832, 836 (studying relationship between three-month-old infants and mothers and infants' later attachment behavior and sociability).

[252] See Isabella, Belsky & von Eye, supra note 219, at 18.

[253] See Lewis & Fiering, supra note 219, at 836.

mother-to-infant bonding hypothesis, it is susceptible to the empirical and philosophical criticisms raised above.[254] Moreover, studies of attachment between adoptive mothers and children report no difference in the quality of attachment between adoptive and natural parent-child relationships.[255] After reviewing the literature on the bonding issue, one group of researchers noted that early contact between mother and child has no provable long-term psychological consequences for the mother's feelings toward the child and, at best, only marginal short-term advantages.[256] In light of these studies, the postnatal mother-to-infant bond cannot be an adequate basis upon which to ground an argument for the best interests of the child.

Alternatively, one might examine bonding from the standpoint of the child, i.e., the infant-to-mother bond. There is little doubt that the development of secure emotional ties between parent and child has fundamental and long-lasting significance. It is well-established that infants failing to form a bond with any adult are likely to lack the ability to form deep and enduring relationships later in life.[257] One study found a strong correlation between insecurely attached infants and those who experience a higher level of nonmaternal care in the first year of life.[258] Another study maintains that *all* infants who are placed for adoption after nine months of age have difficulties with a variety of "socioemotional" matters, including establishing certain kinds of relationships with others.[259] Still other studies indicate that the quality of attachment in infancy may affect the IQ of the child[260] and the development of the child's sense of self-identity, thereby affecting the child's ability to cope with various environments including schools.[261]

---

[254] See text accompanying notes 221-44 supra.

[255] See, e.g., Singer, Brodzinsky & Ramsay, Mother-Infant Attachment in Adoptive Families, 56 Child Dev. 1543, 1544, 1550 (1985) (claiming that while early mother-neonatal bonding is not necessary, adoption should take place in infancy to facilitate attachment).

[256] See Lamb & Hwang, supra note 219, at 21, 29.

[257] See S. Fruiberg, Early Childhood Birthright: In Defense of Mothering 51-62 (1977); Singer, Brodzinsky & Ramsay, supra note 255, at 1544.

[258] See Belsky & Rovine, supra note 219, at 164-65.

[259] See Yarrow & Goodwin, The Immediate Impact of Separation: Reactions of Infants to a Change in Mother Figures, in The Competent Infant: Research and Commentary 1032, 1036-39 (L. Stone, H. Smith & L. Murphy eds. 1973) (study of infants placed in adoption finds that, prior to three months, few infants react to changes in environment; between three and six months, number affected and severity of effect increased; and after nine months all infants demonstrated some adverse effect). But see Singer, Brodzinsky & Ramsay, supra note 255, at 1549-50 (study of adopted infants finding no correlation between timing of adoption and mother-infant attachment). The latter study did not question the general empirical claim that the child must develop a strong relationship with an adult figure in order to mature properly. See id.

[260] See van Ijzendoorn & van Vliet-Visser, supra note 219, at 27.

[261] See Singer, Brodzinsky & Ramsay, supra note 255, at 1544. This study considered a

These studies clearly indicate the importance to the child of developing a secure relationship with at least one parent figure early in childhood. There is absolutely no evidence, however, that the child must form this relationship with a *biological* parent. What is important is the psychology, not the biology, of the relationship.[262] Thus, if a party, other than the gestational host, can render the same care and devotion as do most natural mothers, considerations of the child's best interests give the gestational host no inherently superior claim to the child. Moreover, it appears that younger children require less time to form ties with a new caretaker.[263] Some have suggested that a very young infant may take as little as an hour to form a new bond with another person.[264] Thus, even where a surrogate mother has formed a preliminary relationship with the child soon after birth, this factor alone fails to trump the claims of other participants in the procreative relationship.

The second genre of arguments favoring the gestational host and focusing upon the best interests of the child is founded not upon the prediction that the child will fail to form a bond with the nonbiologically related parent, but upon the argument that the child will suffer psychological harm as a result of the circumstances of birth. Thus, it is argued that the child will feel a sense of psychological "rootlessness" at not knowing her biological identity,[265] or that a child will be disadvantaged by the "unnatural" procreative process that brought her into the world.[266]

There are a number of responses to the charge that a child will suffer long-term psychological harm as a result of its uncertain biological identity. Insofar as this claim appears to address the uncertainty regarding the child's *genetic* heritage, this concern is unwarranted where the intended parents are the genetic parents of the child, as in gestational sur-

---

number of possible reasons why adopted children experience a much higher percentage of psychological problems. These include: (1) a more problematic prenatal and reproductive history, (2) complications associated with the social stigma surrounding adoption, (3) the nature of the transition from foster care to the adoptive home, (4) the effects of adoption placement beyond infancy, (5) difficulties associated with the adoption-revelation process, and (6) the confusion surrounding the adoptee's search for identity. See id. at 1543-44.

[262] See J. Goldstein, A. Freud & A. Solnitz, Beyond the Best Interests of the Child 105-11 (1973) (arguing that child's interests in psychological relationships with its caretaker parents should be protected in custody determination).

[263] See Note, supra note 39, at 546-47 (discussing time factor in child's ability to break old bonds and form new relationships).

[264] See T. Vernay & J. Kelly, supra note 249, at 148.

[265] See Robertson, Surrogate Mothers: Not So Novel After All, 13 Hastings Center Rep. 28, 30 (1983) (concluding that child may experience rootlessness if unable to contact surrogate, but that similar situation is tolerated with adoptions).

[266] Krimmel, for example, argues that because the surrogate conceives without wanting a child, the child suffers knowing that it was "conceived in order to be given away." See Krimmel, supra note 196, at 35.

rogacy. The claim also does not give the surrogate an advantage where neither she nor the intended parents are the genetic progenitors of the child, as where the sperm and eggs of anonymous donors are used. Moreover, even where the surrogate is the genetic progenitor, the child can receive information regarding her biological legacy precisely because surrogacy, unlike adoption, permits the intended parents to develop a complete medical record of the child's history and development.[267]

Finally, and perhaps most fundamentally, while the child may experience a natural curiosity regarding her parentage and biological legacy, there are problems with the prediction that this might affect the child's basic sense of self-identity throughout life. One commentator, for example, has argued that "[c]larity about [one's] origins is crucial for self-identity, itself important for self-respect."[268] This claim is predicated upon a troublesome view of personal identity, which implies that every adopted child is hopelessly insecure and devoid of self-respect. It appears to confuse the psychological notion of self-identity with the relatively more superficial knowledge of one's biological legacy. As such, this view is not only dubious empirically but also an atavistic throwback to the priority of blood ties over all else as a determinant of one's sense of self.

As for the claim that the child may experience psychological self-doubt or alienation as a result of knowing that it was born through collaborative reproduction, it is not clear that this gives the gestational host any advantage over other participants in the procreative relationship. Indeed, since the surrogate initially has agreed to bear and relinquish the child, the child may feel less comfortable with her than with the intended parents. At any rate, this same charge was made against artificial insemination forty years ago.[269] It is no more compelling now than it was then. In conclusion, notwithstanding the prevailing popular belief and the legal fiction that it is in the child's best interests to be raised by its natural mother, the best-interests argument provides little support for according parental rights in the gestational host above the claims of all others. We must, therefore, turn to another consideration raised by our initial dis-

---

[267] See A. Overvold, supra note 195, at 92 (noting willingness of some couples to allow their children to meet surrogate who bore them). Alternatively, a file could be established containing the biological and medical history of the surrogate. This file could be constructed in a manner that would not identify the surrogate, if this is what the parties to the arrangement prefer. Cf. B. Lifton, Twice Born: Memoirs of an Adopted Daughter (1975) (providing personal account of adopted child's difficulties in finding natural parents).

[268] Kass, *Making Babies* Revisited, 54 Pub. Interest 32, 47 (1979).

[269] See J. Fletcher, supra note 3, at 126-27 (reviewing common arguments against artificial insemination and collaborative-reproductive techniques, including claim that child will experience psychic dislocation from its unusual origins). Fletcher rejects this claim by arguing that this issue is actually more problematic in adoption, where the child's original parents may not have wanted it, than in collaborative reproduction, where both parents consent to love and care for the child and desire to bring it into the world. See id.

cussion of the bonding argument: whether the harm caused to the gestational mother by relinquishment of the child warrants granting her parental rights.

3. The Relinquishment Argument

One of the most poignant arguments favoring the right of the gestational host to be considered the mother of the child concerns the effects upon her of relinquishing the child. The effects of relinquishment on the birth mother in the case of adoption are well-documented.[270] Indeed, there is evidence that new mothers experience a kind of separation anxiety when they are separated from their children even for relatively short periods of time.[271] When the separation is permanent, the experience may take on extreme, even pathological proportions, including a deep sense of loss which pervades daily activities.[272] Depression, anxiety, and a host of other emotional consequences may result.[273] In one study, surrendering mothers reported recurring dreams of loss, fantasies involving rescue and reunion, heightened ecstasy in contemplation of the relationship with future children, and a greater than normal level of protectiveness toward their other children.[274] These experiences were reported even by women who were not permitted to see their babies upon birth.[275]

Additional evidence indicates that the surrender of a child may remain a source of conflict and interpersonal difficulties for many years.[276] In one study, 96% of all surrendering mothers reported that they had considered searching for the child while 65% actually had initiated a search.[277] Moreover, secondary infertility was higher among couples in which the woman previously had relinquished a child.[278] Other reported

---

[270] See Deykin, Campbell & Patti, The Post-Adoption Experience of Surrendering Parents, 54 Am. J. Orthopsychiatry 271, 276-78 (1984) (women who surrender child for adoption perceive negative influence on marriage, fertility, and parenting); Millen & Roll, Solomon's Mothers: A Special Case of Pathological Bereavement, 55 Am. J. Orthopsychiatry 411, 418 (1985) (experience of mother relinquishing child is similar to pathological mourning, including feelings of intense loss, panic, anger, and incompleteness); Rynearson, Relinquishment and Its Maternal Complications, 139 Am. J. Psychiatry 338, 340 (1982) (relinquishment of child appears to be disjunctive event for women; subsequent maternal attachment is sought intensely).

[271] See Hock, McBride & Gnezda, Maternal Separation Anxiety: Mother-Infant Separation from the Maternal Perspective, 60 Child Dev. 793, 794 (1989) (confirming separation anxiety and finding that many factors, including mother's basic personality, genetically determined biases, and cultural background are relevant).

[272] See Millen & Roll, supra note 270, at 411-12 (discussing effects of relinquishment in extreme cases).

[273] See id. at 413-17; Rynearson, supra note 270, at 338-39.

[274] See Rynearson, supra note 270, at 339-40.

[275] See id. at 339.

[276] See Deykin, Campbell & Patti, supra note 270, at 272.

[277] See id. at 274.

[278] Secondary infertility is infertility among couples who already have had children. See

effects include marital disharmony (though the divorce rate among these couples was markedly lower) and both positive and negative child-bearing consequences.[279] Finally, there is an increasing body of anecdotal evidence concerning relinquishment as a result of the experiences of Mary Beth Whitehead and other surrogates.[280]

In contrast to voluntary adoption, studies also suggest that the negative effects of relinquishment actually may be exacerbated by a compelled surrender of the child. One study found that parents were more likely to search for the child when external factors, such as family pressure, were instrumental in their decision to relinquish the child.[281] By analogy, one might infer that the consequences of relinquishment may be even more difficult for surrogates required to surrender the child pursuant to a contractual promise than for those who relinquish the child in the absence of external legal coercion. Yet it may be at least as plausible to suggest that surrendering mothers in the adoption situation are more susceptible to the trauma of relinquishment than gestational hosts in the collaborative-reproductive arrangement precisely because the adoptive mother is under no legal compulsion to surrender a child even where she informally has agreed to do so before birth.[282] Indeed, it is likely that many surrendering mothers vacillate as to their decision for some time up to, and in some cases even after, the birth of the child.[283] This wavering may aggravate feelings of loss once the decision is made to surrender the child. In short, expectations may influence feelings. If the postrelinquishment experience of birth mothers is at all related to their previous feelings regarding the child, then it is possible that women who do not expect to raise the child may be relatively less affected by relinquishment. This possibility is suggested by one poll of surrogate mothers in which only one in five reported that relinquishment was the most difficult aspect of the arrangement.[284]

OTA, Infertility, supra note 1, at 50. It is distinguished from primary infertility, where the couple has had no children. See id. The rate of secondary infertility among the study participants was 16% as compared with 6% of the general population. See id. at 276.

[279] See id.

[280] Mary Beth Whitehead was the surrogate in the *Baby M* case. See In re Baby M, 109 N.J. 396, 537 A.2d 1227 (1988). For a narrative of her experiences immediately precipitated by her surrender of Baby M, see M. Whitehead & L. Schwartz-Nobel, A Mother's Story: The Truth About the Baby M Case 17-37 (1989). For the experiences of another surrogate, see A. Overvold, supra note 195, at 33.

[281] See Deykin, Campbell & Patti, supra note 270, at 274.

[282] Prebirth consent to adoption on the part of the birth mother is unenforceable in all fifty states. See Andrews, supra note 8, at 15-16.

[283] If there were not such vacillation before birth and for some period afterward, there would be little need for laws rendering void prebirth consent to adoption as well as laws permitting the birth mother to revoke her consent for a period of time after relinquishment. See id. at 19 (discussing these statutes).

[284] See A. Overvold, supra note 195, at 130.

The relinquishment argument is a vital component of the case for the priority of the gestational host. Nevertheless, more empirical evidence is necessary to evaluate the weight that should be accorded this claim and, in particular, the nature of postrelinquishment emotional effects upon the birth mother. We must determine whether these effects are intrinsic concomitants of the biological changes that occur during and after pregnancy, or whether they may be ameliorated by social influences and the birth mother's expectations regarding her role in the procreative arrangement.

Even if further research suggests that the harm of relinquishment is tangible, however, it is not clear that this effect should give the surrogate legal priority as the mother of the child. First, whatever harm redounds to the surrogate in the event of relinquishment must be weighed against a similar harm to the intended parents in the event that the surrogate does not turn over the child. Particularly where the intended parents are childless and infertile, the emotional significance of the loss of the child they expected to raise is undoubtedly great.[285] Second, and perhaps most important, the surrogate's claims for legal priority resulting from the harms of relinquishment must be evaluated in the context of her earlier contractual agreement to relinquish the child. Parties to contracts often regret having entered into enforceable agreements. In some cases, they may be disadvantaged greatly by the agreement; but as long as the agreement is entered into voluntarily,[286] the argument that the surrogate now regrets having made this choice lacks the moral force it otherwise might have.[287]

4. The Physical-Involvement Argument

It has been suggested by a number of writers that the physical process of bearing the child in itself, independent of considerations of bonding and the effects of relinquishment, carries significant moral weight in determining who should be considered the parent.[288] As one writer has stated:

> And from the woman's point of view? We can use this man's sperm or that one's to have our children. With this or that man as father, our bellies will swell, life will stir, milk will flow. . . . For a man, what makes the child *his* is his seed. For women, what makes the child ours

---

[285] See Kennell, Slayter & Klaus, supra note 235.

[286] See notes 294-303 and accompanying text infra (discussing exploitation and claim that surrogate's decision to enter into agreement is not voluntary).

[287] See notes 284-85 and accompanying text supra (weighing relinquishment argument against claims of intended parents).

[288] See, e.g., P. Chesler, Sacred Bond: The Legacy of Baby M 53-54 (1988) (comparing contribution of birth mother vis-á-vis that of sperm donor).

is the nurturance, the work of our bodies. Wherever the sperm came from, it is in our bodies that our babies grow, and our physical presence and nurturance that make our babies ours.[289]

Inextricably intertwined with the notion of the birth mother's physical contribution are claims predicated upon the bonding hypothesis, the effects on the mother of relinquishment, and other related issues which have been considered in previous sections. This subsection attempts to abstract from this nest of issues an argument based simply upon the physical involvement of the gestational host.

The reality and extent of the physical involvement of the gestational host in the procreative process is obviously paramount. The birth mother risks sickness and inconvenience during pregnancy. She faces the certain prospect of painful labor. She even risks the small but qualitatively infinite possibility of death. Throughout all of this discomfort and uncertainty, it is her body which remains the cradle for the growing fetus. By comparison, the physical involvement of the sperm donor is de minimis. While the egg donor physically risks more[290] than the sperm donor, her level of physical involvement pales in comparison with that of the gestational host. Consequently, the argument postulates that this greater involvement should be the basis for recognizing the gestational host as the mother of the child.

Notwithstanding the obvious fact that the gestational host is the most important physical link in the procreative process, this argument encounters difficulties similar to those of the arguments for the priority of the genetic progenitors.[291] The nature of this claim is that the gestational host has a kind of property right in the child. But, if so, then where she has entered a contract to act as gestational host for another, she has transferred this right.[292] Even assuming she could have property rights in the child, the surrogate has no more of a claim to the "property" by virtue of this argument than a builder has in a house constructed for another.[293]

---

[289] B. Katz-Rothman, supra note 189, at 44 (emphasis in original).

[290] The egg is taken by laparoscopy, a surgical procedure by which ova are removed from the ovaries of the woman. See OTA, Infertility, supra note 1, at 106.

[291] See notes 206-17 and accompanying text supra (reviewing arguments favoring genetic progenitors on a "property rights" approach).

[292] See notes 206-17 and accompanying text supra (discussing property-rights argument and transfer-of-rights argument in context of genetic progenitor). Where no contract exists, however, the surrogate's greater level of physical involvement should be entitled to great weight as evidence of the woman's intention to raise the child. See notes 308-20 and accompanying text infra (analyzing relevance of intention in procreative process).

[293] At a presentation which I gave recently at IIT-Chicago Kent Law School, various participants took issue with this metaphor. "Children are not houses," it was stated, "nor are pregnant women housebuilders." I fully appreciate the relevance of this comment. Indeed, I am arguing that children are not the subject of property rights, though one's procreational

If the argument of the gestational host's greater physical involvement is not a property claim, to what does it amount? One suspects that it is actually an argument predicated upon bonding, relinquishment, or the best interests of the child, or perhaps a combination of these other arguments. Excluding from the present argument claims based on the mother-infant bond, the effects of relinquishment, considerations of the child's best interests, and any theory predicated upon a kind of property analysis, virtually eliminates the argument of the greater physical involvement of the gestational host. Indeed, the argument appears to be a mere restatement of these other considerations.

5. The Exploitation and Commodification Arguments

Scholarly and legislative proposals defending the moral right of a woman to sell her gestational services have been the object of lively, if not vituperative, responses on the part of numerous writers, both in the legal literature[294] and the academic press.[295] The range and scope of these objections are too numerous and too deep to develop and to address systematically in this discussion.[296]

Despite their sheer number and variation, however, these diverse arguments have two main recurring themes. The first, the "exploitation argument," posits that women who enter into surrogate agreements, as a general matter, somehow are unfree with respect to this decision. This moral assessment typically is predicated upon a matrix of social and economic factors which are held to predispose the prospective surrogate to her decision. In the words of one commentator:

> When money animates the transfer of a human substance, the issue of exploitation arises. The danger is that the transferor is exploiting the

---

services are. My sole point here is that, *even if* the property metaphor were applicable to the transfer of a child, the gestational host would have no claim where the intended couple had compensated her.

[294] See O'Brien, Commercial Conceptions: A Breeding Ground for Surrogacy, 65 N.C.L. Rev. 127 (1986); Olsen, The Family and the Market: A Study of Ideology and Legal Reform, 96 Harv. L. Rev. 1497 (1983); Radin, Market-Inalienability, 100 Harv. L. Rev. 1849 (1987); Wikler, Society's Response to the New Reproductive Technologies: The Feminist Perspectives, 59 S. Cal. L. Rev. 1043 (1986); Note, supra note 79; Note, Surrogate Mother Agreements: Contemporary Legal Aspects of a Biblical Notion, 16 U. Rich. L. Rev. 467 (1982); Note, supra note 2; Recent Developments, An Incomplete Picture: The Debate About Surrogate Motherhood, 8 Harv. Women's L.J. 231 (1985).

[295] See Annas, Baby M: Babies (and Justice) for Sale, 17 Hastings Center Rep. 13 (1987); Annas, Contracts to Bear a Child: Compassion or Commercialism?, 11 Hastings Center Rep. 23 (1981); Ince, Inside the Surrogate Industry, in Test-Tube Women (R. Arditti ed. 1984); Krimmel, supra note 196; Merrick, Selling Reproductive Rights: Policy Issues in Surrogate Motherhood, 8 Pol. & Life Sci. 161 (1990); Rothman, The Meanings of Choice in Reproductive Technology, in Test-Tube Women (R. Arditti ed. 1984); Woliver, Reproductive Technologies and Surrogacy: Policy Concerns for Women, 8 Pol. & Life Sci. 185 (1990).

[296] For a legal and philosophical defense of surrogacy, see Hill, supra note 181.

desperate need of the transferee and that the transferee is exploiting the financial need of the transferor.... For some of the same reasons that organ donation is prohibited, commercial surrogacy should be prohibited.[297]

Unlike the exploitation argument, which focuses upon whether the surrogate's decision was the product of causally determinative influences, the second general theme, the "commodification argument," focuses upon the object of the transfer. The commodification argument holds that certain intrinsic capacities or properties of the individual should not be alienable or commodified on the open market, and that a woman's reproductive ability is one such capacity. Professor Radin, a proponent of this view, has stated:

> Market-inalienability [of surrogacy] might be grounded in a judgment that commodification of women's reproductive capacity is harmful for the identity aspect of their personhood and in a judgment that the closeness of paid surrogacy to baby-selling harms our self-conception too deeply. There is certainly the danger that women's attributes, such as height, eye color, race, intelligence, and athletic ability, will be monetized. Surrogates with "better" qualities will command higher prices by virtue of those qualities.[298]

The frequent allusions to organ donation,[299] prostitution,[300] and baby-selling,[301] are tempting and powerful analogues. These allusions run throughout the exploitation and commodification arguments. While this Article has undertaken an examination of the philosophical justification for these claims elsewhere,[302] it is worth noting the basic difficulties with each of these two arguments.

The difficulties come in two forms, internal and external. The external difficulty, which will be discussed at the end of this subsection, is that these arguments are too powerful—they do not argue in favor of the gestational host. Rather, they militate against the very legitimacy of surrogacy as a legally permissible institution. The internal difficulties, by contrast, stem from flaws in the internal structure of these arguments. For example, proponents of the exploitation argument never elaborate a theory of exploitation. This failure sometimes manifests itself in the con-

---

[297] O'Brien, supra note 294, at 142-43.

[298] Radin, supra note 294, at 1932.

[299] Barbara Katz-Rothman claims that "surrogacy is exactly the same as organ donation." See Levine, Whose Baby Is It?, Village Voice, Nov. 26, 1986, at 17.

[300] One writer has equated the freedom to sell one's reproductive services with "the freedom to prostitute oneself." See G. Corea, supra note 223, at 227.

[301] See Radin, supra note 294, at 1932.

[302] See Hill, supra note 181, at 109-34 (examining coercion and exploitation as applied to surrogate arrangements); id. at 134-46 (examining commodification argument).

flation of the concepts of exploitation and coercion.[303] More fundamentally, however, situations involving exploitation are not adequately distinguished from those which do not. For example, how is the situation of a woman from a lower-middle income family who enters a surrogate arrangement distinguished from the situation of this same woman who instead takes a job cleaning bathrooms in a bus station—assuming that this latter alternative is not itself exploitative? Let us assume that the compensation is at a similar rate and that the woman has similar alternative prospects. What distinguishes these two scenarios? If the answer depends upon morally distinguishing the two activities—that cleaning bathroom floors is a morally permissible use of one's body while becoming a surrogate is not—then the respondent is confronted with a fundamental difficulty. The opponent of surrogacy is arguing that surrogacy is wrong because it is exploitative. She cannot then claim, when asked what makes surrogacy exploitative, that the two situations are distinguishable because surrogacy is wrong. This would constitute a blatantly circular argument. If surrogate arrangements are wrong because they are exploitative, then they cannot be exploitative because they are wrong.

However, if what distinguishes these two situations is that surrogacy involves the use of some intimate personal capacity which should not be the subject of barter, while bathroom cleaning does not, then the exploitation argument collapses into the commodification argument. Once the opponent of surrogacy makes this move, she relinquishes the claim that the decision to become a surrogate is, in some sense, *unfree*. Rather, it is wrong because it alienates a fundamental aspect of one's personhood. This reasoning, however, replaces the claim of exploitation with that of commodification.

The commodification argument similarly encounters a number of fundamental philosophical difficulties. The notion of commodification is functionally dependent upon drawing a distinction between a realm of personal capacities and properties which may be the subject of market alienation and those which may not. In one of the most careful and systematic elaborations of the commodification argument, Professor Radin states:

> A better view of personhood should understand many kinds of particu-

---

[303] Coercion could be said to occur whenever one's options are reduced by forces external to oneself. See A. Wertheimer, Coercion 40 (1987). Exploitation does not reduce options. Indeed, the exploitative situation typically occurs where an individual is given an additional choice which she cannot easily refuse. See id. at 39 (discussing exploitation of another's existing dilemma); Feinberg, Noncoercive Exploitation, in Paternalism 201 (R. Sartonius ed. 1983) (distinguishing coercion and exploitation by whether subject's options or interests are affected).

lars—one's politics, work, religion, family, love, sexuality, friendships, altruism, experiences, wisdom, moral commitments, character, and personal attributes—as integral to the self. To understand any of these as monetizable or completely detachable from the person ... is to do violence to our deepest understanding of what it is to be human.[304]

Notwithstanding her painstaking historical and philosophical analysis devoted to distinguishing "integral" or "intrinsic" from "extrinsic" personal attributes, Radin's view suffers from three fundamental flaws. First, no principle is presented by which essentially internal, noncommodifiable attributes may be distinguished from external, commodifiable attributes. There is little reason to believe that the attributes which Radin cites—political action, work, love, sexuality, family, experience, and wisdom—are anything more than an ad hoc assortment of incongruous elements invested with varying degrees of importance in our culture. Moreover, without a principle distinguishing the internal and external, it is impossible to make future determinations as to which elements are basic to our sense of self.

Second, Radin admits that drawing the line between the internal and the external, the inalienable and the alienable, is ultimately a moral judgment.[305] If one's reproductive capacity is an attribute which should not be subject to commodification, reproductive capacity will be deemed an essentially internal attribute. But this logic reverses the role of premise and conclusion. It attempts to determine whether a certain attribute is sufficiently internal to our personal identity so that we can render a moral conclusion about whether the attribute should be commodifiable. But Radin's analysis appears to *begin* with this moral assessment regarding the permissibility of commodifying an attribute.[306] In essence, there would be no need to employ the commodification argument if we knew in advance that a particular capacity or attribute should not be commodified. Yet Radin's argument appears to require exactly this prior determination.

Finally, as a practical matter, we cannot sort neatly between inherently intrinsic and extrinsic attributes on the basis of the attribute itself. For example, while Radin suggests that personal attributes should not be commodifiable,[307] they are routinely the subject of commodification. Indeed, it is difficult to imagine anything other than personal attributes which are commodified any time anyone is hired to do a job. The model uses her face and physique, the construction worker uses her physical

---

[304] Radin, supra note 294, at 1905-06.
[305] See id. at 1908.
[306] See id. at 1859.
[307] See id. at 1905-06.

strength, and the professional utilizes her intelligence, character, and motivation—all attributes which go to the very heart of their personhoods. It is striking that those attributes which typically are denigrated as the more superficial or less intrinsic to the individual, such as physical beauty, eye color, and height, are the same attributes which so trouble the proponent of the commodification argument. Indeed, it would be more logical, on this view, to place attributes such as character, personality, and intelligence, which generally are thought to be central to our innermost being, beyond the reach of the market and to permit the commodification of physical attributes such as eye color and sexual attractiveness. On such a view, prostitution would be permitted while teaching philosophy would be placed outside the realm of the market.

In general, the exploitation and commodification arguments raise profound ethical questions which require careful attention and analysis. Unfortunately, this attention has been lacking, even in scholarly appeals to these arguments.

The arguments surveyed in this subsection take us somewhat far afield from the central focus of this piece. We have examined them briefly, however, because of their purported relevance to the parental status of the gestational host. Nevertheless, these arguments encounter a more fundamental difficulty for purposes of the present Article. Even if the exploitation and commodification arguments have some merit, they ultimately are not arguments favoring the parental priority of the gestational host. While they suggest that collaborative-reproductive arrangements should be regulated, even banned, they do not establish that the gestational host is the real "parent." In short, an argument against the social or ethical permissibility of surrogate arrangements is not necessarily an argument in favor of the moral priority of the surrogate as the mother of the child. If such arrangements are valid, the claim of the gestational host as the true mother of the child will have to depend upon other considerations.

IV

The Claims of Intentionality

The previous section considered the claims for the moral priority of the biological progenitors of the child, both the genetic sources and the gestational host. It is time now to consider briefly the possible claims favoring the priority of the intended parents. In this section, I pose the situation of the couple from the opening scenario.[308] This is the case of the intended parents who have no biological connection with the child,

---

[308] See text accompanying notes 19-20 supra.

but who have orchestrated the procreative relationship from the outset. They have brought together sperm and egg through in-vitro fertilization, and they have contracted for the services of a surrogate to bear the child they intend to raise. What reasons favor recognizing the intended parents as the procreators and, therefore, as the legal parents of the child?

Three arguments can be made for the moral priority of the intended parents. The first focuses upon the prima-facie importance of the intended parents in the procreative relationship. The second concerns the unfairness of permitting the surrogate to break the promise to relinquish the child. Finally, the third addresses important policy considerations in assuring the identity of the parents of the child from the time of conception. These arguments should trump the relatively weaker claims of either the gestational host[309] or the biological progenitors.[310]

A. The "But For"-Causation Argument

Notwithstanding the competing claims of the various biological progenitors of the child, there is one essential fact favoring the moral and legal priority of the intended parents. The intended parents are, so to speak, the "first cause" of the procreative relationship; they are the ones who have engineered the birth of the child. Their desire and intention set into motion the entire process that begins with securing gamete donors and proceeds through the arrangement to have a woman bear the child.

The importance accorded to the intended parents' role as the first cause in the procreative relationship thus depends on adopting a nonbiologically based view of parenthood. What is essential to parenthood is not the biological tie between parent and child but the preconception *intention* to have a child, accompanied by undertaking whatever action is necessary to bring a child into the world. On this view, biological procreation is one way, albeit the most common one, to proceed in having a child. What is fundamental in rendering a biological progenitor a parent is not the biological tie itself, however, but the preconception intention and the preconception and postconception acts which the biological relation evinces.

It might be argued that this is a peculiar approach to the determination of parental status since it places a mental element, intention, over the tangible, biological tie. But just as mental state is relevant in other

---

[309] See notes 219-44 and accompanying text supra (maternal-bonding argument); notes 245-69 and accompanying text supra (best-interests-of-the-child argument); notes 270-87 and accompanying text supra (relinquishment argument); notes 288-93 and accompanying text supra (physical-involvement argument); notes 294-307 and accompanying text supra (exploitation/commodification argument).

[310] See notes 193-205 and accompanying text supra (genetic-identity argument); notes 206-17 and accompanying text supra (property-rights argument).

areas of the law, including contracts, torts, and criminal law, perhaps it is time that the determination of parental status similarly depend upon the preconception intent of the parties.[311]

Slightly recast, the first argument maintains that, while all of the players in the procreative arrangement are necessary in bringing a child into the world, *the child would not have been born but for the efforts of the intended parents.* The efforts of the biological progenitors are instrumental to the act of procreation, but the status of "parent" should go to the persons who constitute the "but for" cause of the child's birth.

It might be argued in response that the child would not have been born but for the assistance of the gamete donors and the gestational host. Thus, the position of the intended parents is not superior in this respect. Still, the position of the intended parents is distinct from that of the biological progenitors in two ways. First, the intended parents are the first cause, or the prime movers, of the procreative relationship. The others are participants only after the intention and actions of the intended parents to have a child. Second, while *some* gestational host and genetic progenitors are necessary to achieve the intention of the intended parents to have a child, no *particular* biological progenitors are necessary. Where one prospective biological contributor is not available, the couple can always seek the services of others. Thus, no one but the intended parents stands in the relationship with the child of being the *but for* cause of the child's existence. This unique causal relationship with the child should afford the intended parents primary status as the parents of the child.

B. *The Contract Argument*

The second argument in defense of the priority of the intended parents focuses upon the preconception commitment of others, most notably, the gestational host, to refrain from claiming parental rights. The argument here is familiar: the gestational host and the genetic progenitors should be held to their original promises not to seek any form of parental rights in the child. There are two aspects to this argument, one deontological or rights-based and the other consequentialist. The deontological strain holds that people generally should be held to their promises simply because promise-keeping is a good in itself. The predicament of the intended parents is poignant precisely because the surrogate's promise is the very basis for her involvement in the procreative relationship in the first place. Absent a commitment on her part, the intended parents could seek the assistance of another. But where the

---

[311] See Note, supra note 72, at 195 (family law traditionally has not relied upon mental elements).

gestational host, or the genetic progenitor, for that matter, has gained access to the procreative relationship initiated by another, she should not be permitted the double injustice of reneging and, more importantly, retaining custody of the child.

The consequentialist strain of this argument emphasizes the reliance of the intended parents upon the promise of the other parties in the procreative relationship. The intended parents rely, both financially and emotionally, to their detriment on the promises of the biological progenitors and gestational host. They rely financially by purchasing the material essentials of child-rearing, including baby furniture, clothes, toys, and other accessories. They may even move or expand their home to accommodate the new arrival. If the promise of the other parties were not enforceable, the intended parents could not make these preparations without the possibility of losing their investment.

More importantly, the intended parents rely emotionally on the promises of the others to refrain from claiming parental rights in the child. They rely by preparing themselves psychologically for parenthood and all that it entails. They also rely emotionally to the extent that they have interacted with the surrogate and anticipated the birth of the child.[312]

It has been argued that the gestational host, in particular, should not be held to her promise because of the unpredictable nature of the development of feelings for the child while she is pregnant.[313] Elsewhere, I have proposed guidelines to mitigate this possibility.[314] At any rate, whether the claims of the gestational host should be honored above the claims of the intended parents depends upon a weighing of the broader issues raised by the bonding hypothesis and the compelled-relinquishment argument.[315]

---

[312] Even here, the intended parents' reliance cannot be absolute. The surrogate retains her constitutional rights to obtain an abortion. See text accompanying notes 165-81 supra (discussing surrogate's right of privacy). Nevertheless, particularly during the last trimester, after the point of viability, the surrogate's commitment to having the child will be clear. Reliance on the part of the intended parents after this point would be justified.

[313] See Suh, supra note 9, at 363.

[314] I have proposed a rule that only women who previously have had children should be permitted to become surrogates. See Hill, supra note 181, at 361. This rule would enable the prospective gestational host to predict more adequately her feelings during pregnancy. Also, the process of psychological screening of applicants should be made more rigid to weed out those who would be expected to have a particularly difficult time with relinquishment. See id. at 362. Finally, surrogate contracts should receive judicial screening and approval. See id. at 366. This judicial oversight would require the surrogate to affirm publicly her promise and intention to relinquish the child. This requirement might reduce further the number of surrogates who are uncertain about relinquishing the child.

[315] See notes 219-44 and accompanying text supra (discussing bonding hypothesis); notes 270-87 and accompanying text supra (discussing compelled-relinquishment argument); conclusion infra (discussing relative weights given to these claims).

C. The Avoidance-of-Uncertainty Argument

Where the identity of the parents is not determined at the time of conception, all parties are affected adversely. If the gestational host or the genetic progenitors of the child legally are permitted to claim parental rights in the child, contrary to their earlier promises, then the identity of the child's parents will remain unanswered as litigation may drag on for years after the birth of the child. The ultimate solution may render all concerned parties—the intended parents, the biological progenitors, and the child—victims of the uncertainty.

If there is any truth to the notion that the feelings of the gestational host toward the child are influenced by her expectation of raising the child, then the surrogate may develop proprietary feelings toward the child because she retains the possibility of challenging the claims of the intended parents. However, if this prospect is not open to her, the gestational host will be less likely to entertain such sentiments toward the child. Of course, this claim is dependent upon the empirical observation that the development of maternal feelings is influenced by social factors such as the expectation of raising the child.

From the standpoint of the intended parents, I have argued already that it is important that they be able to rely on their expected status as parents in making preparations, both financial and emotional, for the arrival of the child.[316] Where the prospect remains open that their claims may be subordinated to those of one of the biological progenitors, the logistic and emotional preparation by expectant parents may be inhibited, rendering the transition to parenthood more difficult.[317]

Finally, the uncertainty regarding the identity of the parents takes its most compelling form from the standpoint of the child. In cases where litigation over parental rights takes years, the child may grow up with uncertainty regarding the identity of her parents. This uncertainty only is aggravated by the likely solution to the conflict—a decision dividing the child's time among joint custodians or, as in *Baby M*, a disposition which grants custody to one couple and visitation privileges to another.[318] Permitting challenges to the parental status of the intended parents virtually ensures that the child will grow up in the functional equivalent of a broken home.[319] For all of these reasons, the identity of

---

[316] See text accompanying notes 312-15 supra.

[317] Studies indicate that paternal anxiety is inversely related to the extent of participation on the part of a new father. See Fein, supra note 219, at 341. In other words, once the role of the father is established, he is more likely to feel a part of the child-rearing process with a concomitant reduction of psychological anxiety. This phenomenon might be analogous to that which the expectant intended parents undergo.

[318] See In re Baby M, 109 N.J. 396, 466, 537 A.2d 1227, 1263 (1988).

[319] Of course, a rule providing that the intended parents will take the child unless the surro-

the parents should be determinate *ab initio* from the time of conception.[320]

CONCLUSION

With the expanding popularity of the various collaborative-reproductive techniques and arrangements, including surrogate parenting, it is increasingly imperative to settle the question of parental status in collaborative-reproduction arrangements. Having considered the arguments in defense of the claims of the genetic progenitors, the gestational host, and the intended parents, it is clear why the intended parents should be considered the "parents" of the child born of the reproductive arrangement in the opening scenario.

This Article has argued that the genetic relationship, in itself, should be accorded very little moral weight in the determination of parental status. Claims based on the biological similarity of genetic progenitor and child and those predicated on a kind of quasi-property right in the child simply do not withstand sustained scrutiny. Thus, though the genetic tie historically has been accorded great significance, the genetic link per se places the genetic progenitor in the least-compelling position of all parties in the procreative relationship.

What can be said of the claims of the gestational host? The genre of arguments which predicates the surrogate's priority as parent upon the best interests of the child are not convincing. Similarly, the claims based upon her greater physical involvement in the procreative process, as well as those based upon a number of social and ethical concerns, are of little moral force. At best, the social and ethical arguments suggest only that certain forms of collaborative reproduction, particularly surrogate arrangements, should be regulated or prohibited altogether. They do not speak to the moral priority of the gestational host.

This leaves the arguments founded upon the bonding hypothesis and the harms predicted to result from compelled relinquishment of the child. As we have seen, empirical support for the postnatal mother-to-

---

gate changes her mind, in which case she will be awarded full parental rights, would eliminate this uncertainty from the standpoint of the child. The difficulty with this rule, however, is that with traditional surrogacy, where the intended father is also the sperm donor, parental rights would be split between him and the surrogate. The child would continue to live a life divided between two families. This outcome would be the case unless the proposed rule not only gave the surrogate full rights as mother, but also cut off all rights possessed by the sperm donor/ intended father.

[320] The gestation host should be permitted to renounce the contract at any time before conception has occurred. Furthermore, because the designation of parental status in the intended parents does *not* entail that the gestational host forfeits her constitutional privacy rights, she will retain the right to have an abortion. See notes 165-81 and accompanying text supra (discussing distinction between right of privacy and right of procreation).

infant bond is equivocal at best. Indeed, a preponderance of the more recent evidence contradicts the hypothesis. Nonetheless, it would be preposterous to argue categorically that the gestational host harbors no feelings for the child at birth. The gestational host interacts intimately and directly with the fetus with increasing frequency from the time of quickening. Thus, in some cases, the surrogate possesses strong attachment to the child by the time of birth. But even if these feelings amount to a prenatal mother-to-infant bond, they fail to trump the claims of others. The bonding hypothesis is significant only to the extent that it suggests that it will be more difficult for the gestational host to relinquish the child than for the intended parents to give up their dream of parenting the child. Thus, it appears that the bulk of the claims for the priority of the gestational host boils down to the deleterious consequences of relinquishment, exacerbated as this may be by the lingering effects of the prenatal bond.

It is not likely that the relinquishment argument itself will be sufficient to accord the gestational host legal recognition as the child's mother. Ultimately, the weight of the relinquishment argument will depend in part upon further empirical assessment of the harms of relinquishment. Minimally, however, the argument for the priority of the gestational host has been overstated. Unexamined assertions predicated upon the best interests of the child, the bonding hypothesis, and the greater physical involvement of the gestational host in bearing the child, among others, have been the result of both a mischaracterization of the empirical evidence and a superficial assessment of the moral weight of this evidence.

This Article concludes that the balance of equities favors the claims of the intended parents over those of the gestational host. The moral significance of the intended parents' role as prime movers in the procreative relationship, the preconception promise of the biological progenitors not to claim rights in the child, and the relative importance of having the identity of the parents determined from conception onward outweigh the potential harm to the gestational host in compelled relinquishment. This conclusion, of course, will not be well-regarded in all quarters. An important reason for this skepticism is that a fundamentally biological conception of parenthood is ingrained deeply in the ethos of our culture. It continues to influence our most profound intuitions concerning the nature of parenthood and parental rights.

Nevertheless, the biological conception does not square with a number of other, equally deep, intuitions. It is not consistent with the modern understanding that parenthood is as much a social, psychological, and intentional status as it is a biological one. It also is inconsistent with the sentiment that persons are not invariably and irrevocably predisposed to a role in life—even that of parenthood—by virtue of the inexorable workings of biology. Finally, and most fundamentally, the biological conception of parenthood cannot be reconciled with the belief that other moral considerations sometimes may override claims predicated upon the biological relationship. In essence, the claims of biology cannot be deemed to trump invariably the moral claims of those who entertain no biological connection with the child.

3

The Intention to be a Parent and the Making of Mothers

Gillian Douglas

Deciding who is to be recognised as the parent of a child is an important matter because it provides the starting point for determining who has the right to bring up that child and who will be liable for his or her support. The development of assisted reproduction techniques whereby the genetic, gestational and social aspects of motherhood can be separated has complicated this decision, and has required new legal provisions to settle the ascription of parental status. In the United Kingdom, s 27 of the Human Fertilisation and Embryology Act 1990 provides that the 'woman who is carrying or has carried a child as a result of the placing in her of an embryo or of sperm and eggs, and no other woman, is to be treated as the mother of the child.' This preference for the gestational over the genetic mother upgrades the common law assumption that proof of maternity could be supplied by the fact of giving birth to a rule of law.

It has been argued that the common law might merely have

> viewed genetic consanguinity as the basis for maternal rights. Under this ... interpretation, gestation simply would be irrefutable evidence of the more fundamental genetic relationship.[1]

This assumption was never tested in the English courts[2] but, in *Johnson v Calvert*,[3] the Supreme Court of California has ruled that in a case involving gestational surrogacy,[4] whereby an embryo created from the gametes of a couple who intend to raise the child is transferred to another woman who carries and gives birth to the child, the legal mother of that child is the genetic mother. California law is therefore the opposite of that in the United Kingdom. This note examines the reasoning of the California court and considers what the conflicting answers to the question of who is a mother reveal about the similarities and differences in attitudes to parenthood in the two jurisdictions.[5]

---

1 Hill, 'What Does it Mean to be a "Parent"? The Claims of Biology as the Basis for Parental Rights' (1991) 66 NYU L Rev 353, 370.
2 A case, known as the Cumbria case and reported as *Re W (Minors) (Surrogacy)* [1991] 1 FLR 385, did in fact arise which would have required the matter to be determined, but it was settled. See the letter from the parties' solicitor to *The Times*, 28 February 1990.
3 (1993) 5 Cal 4th 84, Cal LEXIS 2474.
4 In this note, surrogacy means an arrangement whereby a woman — the 'surrogate mother' — carries a child for the 'commissioning couple,' 'commissioning mother' or 'commissioning father' — the persons who commission the surrogate. In 'gestational,' 'host' or 'full' surrogacy, the surrogate does not provide the egg; in 'partial' surrogacy, she provides the egg and is therefore the genetic as well as gestational mother.
5 Other jurisdictions have tended to take a cautious, if not hostile, approach to surrogacy arrangements and hence have tended to prefer the gestational mother as the legal mother — eg the National Bioethics Consultative Committee of Australia would strictly regulate surrogacy and legal parenthood would not be transferred until the surrogate had been given one month after the child's birth to make up her mind; the New York State Task Force on the Life and the Law would refuse to recognise surrogacy contracts and give the surrogate the *prima facie* right to custody of the child (see the discussion by Franklin, 'Surrogacy on Three Continents' (1991) 65 Bull Med Eth 13). In France, the Cour de Cassation revoked an adoption order made in favour of a commissioning couple, holding that a surrogacy agreement (paid or not) is illegal as constituting an unauthorised disposal of the human body: see *Procureur Général v Madame X*, 31 May 1991, Cass Ass Plenière, J417, discussed by Steiner, 'Surrogacy Agreements in French Law' (1992) 41 ICLQ 866.

The Law in California — *Johnson* v *Calvert*

The *Johnson* case was a straightforward example of 'womb-leasing' or 'gestational surrogacy.' The commissioning mother, Crispina Calvert, had undergone a hysterectomy and therefore could not carry a child, but still produced eggs. The surrogate, Anna Johnson, offered to carry a child for her and her husband Mark, and it was agreed that they would pay the surrogate $10,000 in return. One of the commissioning mother's eggs was fertilised *in vitro* with her husband's sperm and transferred to the surrogate who successfully carried it to term, giving birth to a boy. During her pregnancy, she and the commissioning couple fell out and each applied to the courts for a declaration of parentage of the child. It was accepted that blood tests showed the commissioning parents to be the genetic parents of the child. The California Supreme Court held that under the California Civil Code, incorporating the Uniform Parentage Act, both the surrogate and the commissioning mother had presented evidence which could support a finding that either was the child's 'natural mother,' the former by means of giving birth and the latter by means of blood testing. Since the Court declined to accept the argument of the American Civil Liberties Union, acting as *amicus curiae*, that the child had *two* legal mothers, it had to choose between two equal claims.[6]

The Court's reason for preferring the claim of the genetic mother was not a preference for the blood tie, as might perhaps have been thought, and which had formed the basis of the decisions in the lower courts.[7] Rather, it was that the commissioning parents had had the *intention* to procreate a child whom they could bring up. Panelli J, giving the judgment of the majority, argued that the commissioning parents:

> affirmatively intended the birth of the child, and took the steps necessary to effect in vitro fertilization. But for their acted-on intention, the child would not exist . . . The parties' aim was to bring Mark's and Crispina's child into the world, not for [them] to donate a zygote to Anna . . . Although the gestative function Anna performed was necessary to bring about the child's birth, it is safe to say that Anna would not have been given the opportunity to gestate or deliver the child had she, prior to implantation of the zygote, manifested her own intent to be the child's mother . . . she who intended to procreate the child — that is, she who intended to bring about the birth of a child that she intended to raise as her own — is the natural mother under California law.[8]

This reasoning caters both for surrogacy, where the surrogate does not *intend* to raise the child, and egg donation, where the egg donor does not intend to do so either, whereas the position under s 27 of the Human Fertilisation and Embryology Act fails to cater for surrogacy, since it makes the surrogate the legal mother even though she has no wish to be. This outcome was a deliberate measure designed to discourage people from entering into surrogacy arrangements.

The California Court regarded the *intellectual* conception of the child as being the fundamental cause of his creation. 'But for' the commissioning parents setting out to find a surrogate to carry their embryo, this child would never have come into existence. However, as Kennard J, who dissented, pointed out, the gestational mother's role in the child's creation was just as indispensable to the child's birth as

---

6 English law similarly does not recognise that a child can have more than two parents at a time, although *parental responsibility* may be shared by several persons — Children Act 1989, s 2(5).

7 *Anna J* v *Mark C* (1991) 286 *Cal Rptr* 369. Preference for the genetic link pervades the approach to adoption law in the United States: for a striking illustration, see the 'Baby Jessica' controversy reported in the media, eg *The Independent*, 5 August 1993.

8 (1993) Cal LEXIS 2474, 16–17.

that of the genetic mother. Relying upon causation does not provide a satisfactory means of distinguishing the competing claims, and one must examine more closely the Court's reliance upon intention itself as the determinant.

Intention is not usually recognised as being of significance in determining issues in Family Law. However, the trend in the law relating to parental status in both this country and others throughout this century has been to grant greater recognition to the *social* rather than the biological aspects of parenthood. Unlike biological parenthood which can occur without being planned and intended, social parenthood is an act of will (albeit that it may be done for a variety of reasons, ranging from the altruistic desire to provide a home for a needy child, to a grudging acceptance of a *felt* obligation to, say, a relative's child left orphaned by a car crash). The law provides a variety of means of accommodating the intention to assume social parenthood. For example, the law of adoption enables people not genetically related to a child to become her legal parents in order that they may act as her social parents. Adoption cannot take place without the prospective parents *applying* for an adoption order, ie manifesting their intention and desire[9] to acquire parental status. An unmarried father who seeks to play a full role in his child's life must manifest that intention by either making an agreement with the child's mother, or by persuading a court that he has a contribution to make to the child justifying a parental responsibility order under s 4 of the Children Act 1989. Indeed, calls for such fathers to be granted automatic parental responsibility are based in part at least upon the view that weight should be given to their *desire* to act as social parents.[10] The Human Fertilisation and Embryology Act 1990 enables those who wish to become social parents, but are unable to provide their own genetic material to do so, to acquire parental status if they procreate through assisted reproduction using donated gametes.[11]

The Implications of Intention as the Determining Factor in Parentage

The California Court's reliance on intention may therefore be seen to be as much a recognition of its already established importance in forging a legal relationship between parent and child as an instance of breaking new ground. Nonetheless, it has potentially interesting consequences for our attitudes to parenthood and family formation in general. For instance, it has been argued that using intention in this way is a means of avoiding gender-based stereotypes and biologically-determined differences when determining issues of parenthood. While men and women cannot physically play the same role in the procreation of children, both can have the intention to become a parent. Giving weight to intention, rather than to biological roles, therefore provides a means to treat claims to parenthood equally, regardless of gender difference.[12] On the other hand, it could be argued that focusing upon intention is very much a *male* approach to parenthood because it fits far more closely to men's experience of procreation than to that of most women. Just as the commissioning mother was unable to carry and give birth to her own child, so too

---

9 The two in this context are interchangeable.
10 See, for example, the Scottish Law Commission, *Report on Family Law* (1992) No 135, para 2.37 — 'the existing rule . . . seems to ignore the fact that an unmarried father may be just as motivated to care for and protect his child as a married father, or indeed as the mother of the child.'
11 ss 27–29 of the Act.
12 Shultz, 'Reproductive Technology and Intent-Based Parenthood: An Opportunity for Gender Neutrality' (1990) Wisconsin L Rev 297.

was her husband; for men, *all* women who carry children are surrogates. Relying upon their intention to produce and raise a child is a very convenient way for men to assert their parentage over children.[13]

Although the Court used intention as the means of distinguishing what it viewed otherwise as equal claims to parenthood through genetic and gestational links, logically, if the intention to create a child is the 'controlling factor in its creation and the originators of that concept merit full credit as conceivers,'[14] then those who set out to use assisted reproduction (or simply to use others) to give them a child with whom they have no genetic *or* gestational tie, deserve equal recognition. Intention would also serve as a tiebreak in the no doubt extremely rare but perfectly imaginable case of an identical twin carrying a child for her sister, where (assuming that the gestational mother is capable of producing eggs herself) genetic testing would *not* be able to distinguish between the two possible mothers.[15]

If the intention to have and rear a child were to be the main criterion for legal parenthood, anyone who had this intention could seek out gamete donors and a surrogate and claim the 'product' of these people's labours when the child was born. This would render irrelevant the assumption that to be the parents of a particular child presupposes a relationship (sexual or not) of not more than two persons of different sex. There would be no reason why more than two people could not be recognised as 'parents,' nor why they should be of different sex.

But there may be practical difficulties in the emphasis on intent. First, how does it relate to the welfare and interests of the child who is produced? The California majority relied upon the argument that 'the interests of children, particularly at the outset of their lives, are unlikely to run contrary to those of adults who choose to bring them into being.'[16] This view underpins our own law on parentage and is the basis of the Children Act 1989 which grants parental responsibility to 'parents' on the assumption that they are generally better placed to exercise it than anyone else. Yet our preference for the 'natural' or genetic basis of parenthood and a suspicion of assisted reproduction, especially surrogacy (at least when used by those not deemed 'deserving'), lead us to pay lip-service to the welfare of a child born as a result of assisted reproduction by requiring account to be taken of that welfare in the decision whether to offer treatment.[17] Where surrogacy is to be employed, then we go further by requiring a court to rule on the desirability of allowing a transfer of legal parenthood *after* the child is born.[18] This was Kennard J's solution to the dilemma in *Johnson* v *Calvert*. Although he would have preferred to see a regulatory regime to vet surrogacy arrangements before they took place,[19] in

---

13 However, it could also be argued that this is exactly what marriage already does, by identifying those children for whom the man is prepared to accept responsibility: see further below.
14 At p 19, quoting 'Note, Redefining Mother: A Legal Matrix for New Reproductive Technologies' (1986) 96 Yale LJ 187, 196.
15 For discussion of the particular complexities of intra-familial gamete donation, see Goodwin, 'Determination of Legal Parentage in Egg Donation, Embryo Transplantation and Gestational Surrogacy Arrangements' (1992) 26 *Family Law Quarterly* 275, pp 289–291.
16 At p 19, quoting Shultz (above), at p 397.
17 s 13(5) of the Human Fertilisation and Embryology Act 1990, discussed by Douglas, 'Assisted Reproduction and the Welfare of the Child,' 46 *Current Legal Problems 1993 Part 2: Collected Papers* 53–74.
18 s 30 of the 1990 Act provides a cumbersome process whereby a court may grant an order in favour of commissioning parents — so long as at least one of them has a genetic link with the child — that the child be treated in law as their child. It was drawn up after media attention was given to the Cumbria case (which was also a case of gestational surrogacy) referred to above.
19 As proposed by the National Conference of Commissioners on Uniform State Laws (in their Uniform Status of Children of Assisted Conception Act) (1992) 98 West's U Laws Ann (supp) pp 122–137, discussed by Goodwin (n 15 above).

639

the absence of such a scheme, he would have referred the case back to the first instance court to determine parentage on the basis of the best interests of the child. But this seems the worst of all worlds. It leaves the parentage of the child uncertain, and dependent upon the view of a single judge as to where the child's best interests will lie. The 'best interests' test is open to criticism as being unpredictable and subjective and, at least in the context of American surrogacy cases, appears apt to favour the middle-class, 'traditional' commissioning parents over the surrogate and her family.[20]

Secondly, how would proof of intention be established? The easiest way is by written agreement between the parties and there is certainly nothing new about this. A marriage licence provides evidence of the intention to form a legally recognised relationship which extends not just to the married couple themselves but to their offspring as well.[21] A parental responsibility agreement between unmarried parents is evidence of their willingness to share parental responsibility for their children. But a surrogacy agreement which provides that the surrogate is to relinquish all parental rights over the child is of a different order and more open to dispute. It is evidence of the surrogate's willingness to waive, rather than to share, her parental rights. In English law, parental rights (or responsibility) may not be surrendered except by court order.[22] Basing parenthood on intention implies a preparedness to recognise the free alienability of parental responsibility and hence the acceptability of surrogacy agreements. It comes closer to characterising children more openly as a form of property which can be transferred to others.

Thirdly, the corollary of recognising intention as the determining factor of parenthood is to accept that *lack* of intention should be a means of avoiding parenthood. Hitherto, the law in the United Kingdom has generally refused to permit someone to avoid liability (if not responsibility) for a child on the ground that he or she had not *intended* the child's conception or birth. It is no answer to the Child Support Agency for an absent parent to say that he thought the child's mother was on the pill, or even that his condom split during intercourse.[23] But, on the other hand, it is possible for a sperm or egg donor to waive their parental status and responsibility in respect of any resulting child under the terms of the Human Fertilisation and Embryology Act 1990. Parents may also give their child up for adoption. So our law does recognise the intention *not* to be a social parent in certain circumstances.

Why, then, not take the more straightforward route of the California court and accept that the intention to act as parent should be the key indicator for parental status? The short answer is because of the disapproval of surrogacy as a form of assisted reproduction. English law views the gestational mother as the legal mother because this will produce the right result in terms of parentage for all cases except

---

20 For discussion of the problems of the welfare principle, see Cretney and Masson, *Principles of Family Law* (London: Sweet & Maxwell, 5th ed, 1990) pp 525–526; Mnookin, 'Child Custody Adjudication: Judicial Functions in the Face of Indeterminacy' (1975) 39 *Law and Contemporary Problems* 226. For discussion of welfare with specific reference to *Johnson v Calvert* in the lower courts, see Dolgin, 'Just a Gene: Judicial Assumptions about Parenthood' (1993) 40 UCLA L Rev 637.
21 It also *presumptively* commits the man to a legal relationship with any children produced by the wife, whether genetically his or not — *pater est quem nuptiae demonstrant*.
22 s 2(9) of the Children Act 1989.
23 The question of whether a man could avoid being required to provide financial support for a child born after he had been assured that he did not need to use contraception was answered in the negative in Scotland in *Bell v McCurdie* (1981) SC 64.

for surrogacy. Reliance on intent would also destroy the prohibitions on private adoption placements which underpin our adoption law. But underlying these restrictions is a deeper assumption. We still require, or at least prefer, some sort of biological link to a child, be it genetic *or* gestational, because we view children as in some way the physical recreations of their parents. We still refuse to face up to the reality of our acceptance of the importance of social parenthood — to an idea of parenthood as departing from the traditional, pseudo-biological model of two people of the opposite sex creating and rearing their offspring. In *Johnson* v *Calvert*, probably unintentionally, the Supreme Court of California appears to have moved a little closer to such recognition.

4

TOWARD A PLURALIST ACCOUNT OF PARENTHOOD

TIM BAYNE AND AVERY KOLERS

ABSTRACT

What is it that makes someone a parent? Many writers – call them 'monists' – claim that parenthood is grounded solely in one essential feature that is both necessary and sufficient for someone's being a parent. We reject not only monism but also 'necessity' views, in which some specific feature is necessary but not also sufficient for parenthood. Our argument supports what we call 'pluralism', the view that any one of several kinds of relationship is sufficient for parenthood. We begin by challenging monistic versions of gestationalism, the view that gestation uniquely grounds parenthood. Monistic and necessity gestationalism are implausible. First, we raise the 'paternity problem' – necessity gestationalists lack an adequate account of how men become fathers. Second, the positive arguments that necessity gestationalists give are not compelling. However, although gestation may not be a necessary condition for parenthood, there is good reason to think that it is sufficient. After further rebutting an 'intentionalist' account of parenthood, in which having and acting on intentions to procreate and rear is necessary for parenthood, we end by sketching a pluralist picture of the nature of parenthood, rooted in causation, on which gestation, direct genetic derivation, extended custody, and even, sometimes, intentions, may be individually sufficient for parenthood.

1.1 INTRODUCTION

What makes someone a parent? Three distinct views have emerged in answer to this question: *geneticists* claim that parenthood arises from direct genetic derivation; *gestationalists* claim that parenthood arises from gestation and childbirth; and *intentionalists* claim that parenthood arises from intentions to create, nurture, and rear.

Each of these positions can be endorsed in a number of forms. The strongest of each are *monistic* accounts of parenthood, which hold that parenthood has a single ground. For example, monistic gestationalism is the view that gestation is the sole ground of parenthood: gestating is both necessary and sufficient for parenthood. All other views are *pluralist*, but pluralism may be more or less inclusive. Some versions of pluralism are *necessity* views, in which one or more of genetic, gestational, or intentional relations are necessary (but not also sufficient) for parenthood. More inclusive are *sufficiency* versions of pluralism, in which one or more types of relations are sufficient (but not necessary) for parenthood.

We have argued elsewhere[1] that genetic relations are not necessary for parenthood, and so neither monistic nor necessity geneticism can be correct. Insofar as genetic relations ground parenthood, they can do so only within an inclusively pluralistic view of parenthood. In this paper, we extend the case for inclusive pluralism: neither gestation nor intentions are plausibly regarded as necessary, and *a fortiori*, as necessary and sufficient, for parenthood. Having rejected these accounts, we then draw out what is plausible in each – namely, that each is sufficient but not necessary for parenthood. We suggest that the sufficiency of gestation and intentions derive from the causal role of gestation and intentions in the creation and survival of dependent children. As we argue in the concluding section, there is reason to think that parenthood is ultimately grounded in causal relations.

I.2 PARENTHOOD: NATURAL AND LEGAL

By 'parenthood' we mean what is often called 'natural' or 'original' parenthood, as opposed to social or custodial parenthood. Persons can become parents without standing in gestational or genetic relations to infants – as when they adopt them – but it is often assumed that, at least in the first instance, parenthood is grounded in a natural relation of some kind.

The relationship between natural parenthood and legal parenthood is both complicated and fluid. Roughly speaking, natural parenthood puts one in position to be considered for parental

---

[1] A. Kolers & T. Bayne. 'Are You My Mommy?' On the Genetic Basis of Parenthood. *Journal of Applied Philosophy* 2001; 18: 273–85. In the earlier paper, we referred to 'monistic geneticism' and 'monistic gestationalism' as 'strong geneticism' and 'strong gestationalism' respectively.

rights, and it may make one liable for parental responsibilities. Custody is not always given to a child's natural parents, nor are a child's natural parents necessarily required to provide for her *as* her parents; the point is simply that being a natural parent gives one an initial claim to parental rights and makes one initially liable for parental responsibilities. Both claims and liabilities are defeasible (rebuttable), but the point is that natural parenthood suffices to generate a presumption of legal parenthood in the first instance. Natural parenthood is not simply legal parenthood, but it does carry legal implications.

We use the term 'parenthood' rather than divide parenthood into constituent rights (or claims) and responsibilities. We do this in part because we are trying to fix on a basic moral notion rather than a legal relation. We also speak of parenthood because we assume that insofar as parenthood brings both rights and responsibilities it brings them *together* – that is, one does not get all the rights but none of the responsibilities, or vice versa. This is not to say that parenthood *does* bring either rights or responsibilities, or that it does not bring one without the other. Nor is it to say that one cannot *lose* rights and responsibilities separately; an abusive parent, for instance, may lose custody but be compelled to pay child-support. Our assumption is only that *if* parenthood brings both rights and responsibilities, then it brings them together.

1.3 WHY NATURAL PARENTHOOD MATTERS

Despite the fact that various accounts of parenthood have fundamental implications for the nature of fatherhood, the debate about the basis of natural parenthood has emerged only since genetic and gestational motherhood became separable through reproductive technologies such as 'surrogate' or 'contract' motherhood, gamete donation, the freezing of embryos, and attempts to develop an artificial uterus (which would permit ectogenesis, disembodied gestation). Monistic gestationalism implies that infants gestated in an artificial womb would be orphans – which might provide an argument against ectogenesis. For their part, monistic geneticists – even those who oppose surrogacy contracts – regard gestation as such as mere babysitting, and therefore find (mere) gestational surrogacy morally unproblematic.[2] Many

---

[2] See: H. Krimmel. 1998. The Case against Surrogate Parenting. In *Classic Works in Medical Ethics*. G. Pence, ed. Boston. McGraw-Hill: 127–137. See also: J.L. Nelson. Parental Obligations and the Ethics of Surrogacy: A Causal Perspective. *Public Affairs Quarterly* 1991; 5: 49–61.

gestationalists, on the other hand, oppose surrogacy on the basis of gestationalism.[3] While no view on the nature of parenthood by itself *entails* any position on these other issues, accounts of parenthood clearly shape the character of these debates. A plausible account of natural parenthood could help move these debates in fruitful directions.

II.1 THE PARITY PRINCIPLE AND THE PATERNITY PROBLEM

In the face of reproductive technologies, medical and legal institutions have had to address new kinds of parental disputes. Although there is no consensus on the nature of parenthood, there is widespread support for monistic gestationalism *about motherhood*. Legislation in the United Kingdom, South Africa, Bulgaria and Spain holds that the gestational mother should be considered the sole mother.[4] According to the Council of Europe, 'maternity should be determined by the fact of giving birth, rather than genetics (origin of the ova).'[5] Similarly, the Warnock Report – perhaps the most influential public document on reproductive technology – also endorses some form of gestationalism: 'legislation should provide that when a child is born to a woman following donation of another's egg the woman giving birth should, for all purposes, be regarded in law as the mother of the child, and that the egg donor should have no rights or obligations in respect of the child.'[6] Where they have addressed the issue,

---

[3] See: R. Tong. The Overdue Death of a Feminist Chameleon: Taking a Stand on Surrogacy Arrangements. *Journal of Social Philosophy* 1990; 21: 40–56; M. Moody-Adams. On Surrogacy: Morality, Markets and Motherhood. *Public Affairs Quarterly* 1991; 5: 175–191. See also several of the papers discussed below.

[4] On the UK, see: United Kingdom Department of Health and Social Security. 1986. *Legislation on Human Infertility Services and Embryo Research: A Consultation Paper.* London. H.M. Stationery Office. On South Africa and Bulgaria, see: R.A. Charo. 1990. Legislative Approaches to Surrogate Motherhood. In *Surrogate Motherhood: Politics and Privacy.* L. Gostin, ed. Bloomington. Indiana University Press: 106. And on Spain, see: K.H. Rothenberg. 1994. Gestational Surrogacy and the Health Care Provider. In *The Beginning of Human Life.* F.K. Beller & R.F. Weir, eds. Dordrecht. Kluwer: 101–113.

[5] Rothenberg, *op. cit.* note 4.

[6] M. Warnock. 1985. *A Question of Life: The Warnock Report on Human Fertilisation and Embryology.* New York. Basil Blackwell: 37. The Report is ambiguous between sufficiency and monistic gestationalism, for it does not say whether egg donors *alienate* their parental claims, or whether they have no such claims to alienate.

medical associations have also generally endorsed monistic gestationalism (for motherhood).[7]

The legal approach to motherhood is not clearly compatible with the legal approach to fatherhood.[8] Most jurisdictions strongly presume that the husband of the 'natural' mother is the child's father, where the natural mother is usually understood to be the gestational mother.[9] This 'mother's husband' presumption may suggest that the law regards paternity as an indirect relation, acquired via a man's relationship with a (gestational) mother rather than his relation to the child. However, the mother's-husband presumption is not always decisive, and courts (at least in America) are becoming increasingly willing to proclaim the rights of genetic fathers. For instance, the Colorado Supreme Court has claimed that the 'natural father, no less than the mother, must have the right to establish the significant relationship of paternity to the child he has allegedly sired.'[10] In addition, several courts have overturned adoptions to which the genetic father had not consented (because he did not know he was a father), thus explicitly assuming that mere genetic parenthood does ground a man's claim to parental custody.[11] In short, the legal perspective on parenthood is both equivocal and fluid.

Whatever view theorists or laws take on parenthood, they ought to accept a meta-principle regulating such determinations, which we call the *parity principle*: any condition that makes one person a parent should, biology permitting, make anyone a parent. It would seem arbitrary if, say, direct genetic derivation were

---

[7] Both the Working Party on Human Infertility Services of the British Medical Association, and the Committee on Ethics of the American College of Obstetrics and Gynecology, deem genetic parentage less weighty than gestational parentage. See: Rothenberg, *op. cit.* note 4.

[8] For an extensive review of American legal precedents on fatherhood, see: J.L. Hill. What Does it Mean to Be a 'Parent'? The Claims of Biology as the Basis for Parental Rights. *New York University Law Review* 1991; 66: 353–420, at 372–83.

[9] B. Cohen. Surrogate Mothers: Whose Baby IS it? *American Journal of Law and Medicine* 1984; 10: 243–285.

[10] Cohen, *op. cit.* note 9, p. 270.

[11] For discussion and criticism of three infamous contested-adoption cases where courts found in favour of genetic fathers, see: A.S. Rosenman. Babies Jessica, Richard, and Emily: The Need for Legislative Reform of Adoption Laws. *Chicago Kent Law Review* 1995; 70: 1851–95. In the first gestational surrogacy case, the court granted the genetic parents the right to have their names put on the birth certificate and be recognised as the legal parents. See: L.B. Andrews. 1989. Alternative Modes of Reproduction. In *Reproductive Laws for the 1990s*. S. Cohen & N. Taub, eds. Clifton, NJ. Humana Press: 361–404.

sufficient for paternity but not maternity. Institutions that recognise the parenthood of genetic fathers should also recognise the parenthood of genetic mothers, and vice versa.

Some people might reject the parity principle based on the following two claims: (1) the gestational mother has a better claim to be the mother than the genetic mother does; and (2) a person cannot have multiple (natural) mothers. Whatever is the case with (1), (2) is implausible. Monistic gestationalists, for their part, may remain silent on claim (2), or even join us in rejecting it, if shared gestation becomes possible. Monistic gestationalists (trivially) endorse the parity principle by asserting a stronger claim: (1*) the gestational mother has the *only* claim to be the mother. Thus because it (trivially) supports the parity principle, monistic gestationalism has initially plausible implications. However, this way of respecting the parity principle faces the *paternity problem*: if the gestational relation is necessary for parenthood, how do men become fathers?[12] The best account of parenthood should both respect the parity principle and solve the paternity problem.

Monistic gestationalists might offer two solutions to the paternity problem. One solution would make 'non-gestational parenthood' derivative on gestation. In this view, 'fatherhood' can be acquired only indirectly, in virtue of the man's relationship with the child's only genuine parent, its gestational mother. In essence, this move aligns paternity with social parenthood: a 'genetic father' has neither a prima facie claim to parental rights, nor liability for parental responsibilities. This position is quite counter-intuitive, and so defending it requires a powerful argument in favour of necessity gestationalism; in the rest of this section, we examine three potential arguments. Because this position makes natural parenthood rest on some inherent aspect of gestation, we call it the 'inherent' approach.

A second approach to the paternity problem would make a subtle but important emendation to gestationalism. Instead of grounding parenthood in a property unique to gestation, one might ground parenthood in a feature that accompanies or 'tracks' gestation, but which men can also possess. Indeed, monis-

---

[12] The paternity problem is a special case of a general challenge to the *exclusivity* of monistic gestationalism. Other species of this problem would ask whether (mere) genetic mothers are to be regarded as mere gamete-suppliers rather than parents; or whether adoptive parents can ever be the real parents of their adoptive children. In our view, however, the problem is sharpest for the case of paternity, so in what follows we focus on that version.

tic gestationalists might even hold that men can *easily* possess this feature – for instance, when they participate as equals in child-rearing – but that this feature does not supervene on genetic derivation (and so denies the paternity of sperm donors and men who contract with surrogate mothers, where parenthood is most disputed). In this approach, then, gestation generates parenthood only because it tracks those properties that really ground parenthood. This 'tracking' strategy must specify: i) which property or properties gestation tracks, and ii) why those properties generate parenthood. Section III below examines three plausible candidates for such a property.

II.2 THE INHERENT APPROACH TO PARENTHOOD

Monistic gestationalists often endorse the indirect conception of paternity we mentioned above. According to Barbara Katz Rothman, 'If men want to have children, they will have to either develop the technology that enables them to become pregnant (and so be 'legal' mothers of children they gestate themselves) or have children through their relationships with women.'[13] In effect, in Rothman's view fatherhood (given current technology) is merely an ascriptive relation grounded in social, economic, or legal considerations, rather than a natural relation grounded in biology.[14] The problem is that Rothman defend this view of paternity by appeal to the legal context mentioned earlier, in which a husband is presumed to be the father of any child born to his wife.[15] Similarly, defending the indirect account, Ruth Macklin notes that in cases of artificial insemination by donor (AID) the law recognises the husband of the sperm recipient as the father.[16] However, these considerations are not clearly to the point, since they address legal conventions rather than natural relations; moreover, as we noted, the legal context is ambiguous. As for Macklin's point about AID, it is at least arguable that gamete donors *transfer* their parental

---

[13] B.K. Rothman. 1989. *Recreating Motherhood: Ideology and Technology in a Patriarchal Society*. New York. W.W. Norton: 257.

[14] It is debatable whether a sharp natural/ascriptive distinction can be sustained. Rothman seems to assume that it can be, and we follow her here. Note, however, that our account of parenthood in section V does not depend on this distinction.

[15] See Rothman, *op. cit.* note 13, pp. 230, 254.

[16] R. Macklin. 1996. Artificial Means of Reproduction and Our Understanding of the Family. In *Biomedical Ethics* (4th edition). T.A. Mappes & D. DeGrazia, eds. New York. McGraw Hill: 514.

rights and responsibilities, rather than they never had these rights and responsibilities at all (as Macklin assumes).[17]

It is, of course, still open to defenders of the inherent approach to offer positive arguments for limiting parenthood to gestational mothers. What, then, can be said in favour of the view that gestation is uniquely necessary for parenthood?

II.3 THE IDENTIFIABILITY ARGUMENT

One familiar basis for gestationalism is that gestational mothers, unlike genetic 'parents', are guaranteed to be identifiable at birth. This 'identifiability' argument is one of two that the Council of Europe offers in defence of monistic gestationalism.[18] It also finds support from George Annas and other commentators.[19]

We have two worries about the identifiability argument. First, we have qualms about appealing to consequentialist considerations in theorising about natural parenthood. While such considerations ought to play a key role in custody decisions, it is less clear that they should be given a central role in grounding natural parenthood. However, even if we grant the consequentialist orientation of the argument, it still does not go through. One wouldn't want to endorse *monistic* gestationalism if one wanted to ensure that children enter the world with a network of people who have an interest in, and responsibilities for, their welfare. Monistic gestationalism ensures that children have (at most) one parent, while recognising that the moral force of genetic relations will usually bring in two 'parents' and a whole network of 'kin.'[20] A pluralist account of parenthood, according to which gestational and genetic relatedness are individually sufficient for parenthood, better ensures that children have adequate protection from birth. To be sure, this inclusiveness could generate custody disputes, which in this context would seem like an embarrassment of riches for a child who (one previously worried) might lack *any* guardian.

---

[17] T. Bayne. Gamete Donation and Parental Responsibility. *Journal of Applied Philosophy* 2003; 20: 77–87.

[18] See: Rothenberg, *op. cit.* note 4, p. 103.

[19] G. Annas. Redefining Parenthood and Protecting Embryos: Why We Need New Laws. *The Hastings Center Report* 1984; 51 (October): 106. See also: Charo, *op. cit.* note 4, p. 105. The consequentialist nature of the identifiability argument is explicit in: S. Feldman. Multiple Biological Mothers: The Case for Gestation. *Journal of Social Philosophy* 1992; 23: 98–104.

[20] See: U. Narayan. 1999. Family Ties: Rethinking Parental Claims in the Light of Surrogacy and Custody. In *Having and Raising Children*. U. Narayan & J. Bartkowiak, eds. University Park, PA. Pennsylvania State University Press: 76.

However, provided gestation remains sufficient for parenthood travesties such as the *Baby M* case would not occur.[21]

Of course, the identifiability of genetic parents might raise issues of privacy. But privacy concerns need not be significantly challenged if genetic testing and other methods of identification were limited to cases where the gestational mother requests it, or (what is more likely) can identify the genetic parent(s). It should also be noted that cases where the genetic parents are hard to locate are likely to be cases in which, for whatever reason, no one wants or feels able to assume responsibility for the child. Assuming that parenthood brings rights and responsibilities together if at all,[22] monistic gestationalism implies that the *only* person with parenthood-based responsibilities for an unwanted child would be its gestational mother. It seems to us that this would be a troubling result.

II.4 THE INCORPORATION ARGUMENT

One of the unique features of pregnancy is the physical relation between the foetus and the gestational mother. Three aspects of this physical relation are relevant here. First, the foetus is *physically contained* within its gestational mother. Second, the foetus is *physiologically integrated* with the gestational mother – she provides its nutrients and eliminates its waste. Because of this, the foetus is, at least in the early stages of development, directly dependent on its gestational mother for life. Third, the foetus is *materially derived* from the mother's body. Given these three considerations, it is plausible to view the embryo-foetus as, quite literally, 'part of the woman's body, regardless of the source of the egg and the sperm.'[23] And from there the move to the special moral relationship between gestational mother and child is quick; the liberal doctrine of sovereignty over one's person, for instance, supports the idea that one bears a special relation to things that are, or used to be, part of one's body.

According to the incorporation argument, the gestational mother is the parent of her child because it was once part of her. So there are two premises to the incorporation argument: (1) at least in the early stages of its development, a foetus is quite literally part of its gestational mother's body; (2) being, or having been, someone's body part is necessary for being that person's child.

---

[21] G. Annas. Baby M: Babies (and Justice) for Sale. *Hastings Center Report* 1987; 17 (June): 13–15.
[22] See section I.1 above.
[23] Rothman, *op. cit.* note 13, p. 238; cf. 258.

Although the notion of a body part is not unproblematic, there seems to be something to (1).[24] The foetus does have its own blood supply, but it lacks an independent supply of oxygen, and this is as important as blood. One might object that since a foetus is an organism in its own right, it cannot be part of its mother. Granting – if only for the sake of argument – that a foetus is an organism in its own right, it does not follow from this that it could not also be part of its mother. Something can be both an organism in its own right and, at the same time, part of another organism. Our cells, for instance, are organisms that are parts of other organisms, and perhaps the foetus bears this relationship to its mother. Although problematic then (1) is not implausible. Premise (2), however, is unattractive. While incorporation may be *sufficient* for parenthood, it is unclear why it should be necessary.

Monistic gestationalists might argue that the important phenomenon is not bodily incorporation *per se*, but the fact that foetuses are materially derived from their gestational mother in a way that they are not derived from genetic or custodial 'parents.' This point is clearly true, but it lacks probative force: a foetus is *materially* derived from its gestational mother but it is *genetically* derived from its genetic 'parents.' And of course, the environment provided by the social 'parent(s)' and the larger society has deep and powerful effects on the growing child's physical and emotional development. There is little *prima facie* reason to regard any one of these relations as primary, though surely each takes its turn in the experiential limelight. It seems arbitrary to regard any one kind of contribution to creation and development as necessary for parenthood, when clearly each is necessary for a child's flourishing and growth. Arguments from derivation support sufficiency gestationalism, but they also support sufficiency geneticism, and even some form of social parenthood.

Identifiability and incorporation, then, each supports sufficiency gestationalism – and indeed can be extended to support pluralism – but neither stands up as a defence of the claim that gestation is *necessary* for parenthood.

III. THE TRACKING APPROACH

Earlier we distinguished two general strategies for answering the paternity problem. We have seen that the inherent strategy

---

[24] See: E. Olson. 1997. *The Human Animal.* Cambridge. Cambridge University Press: 142–153, for discussion of some of the difficulties involved in giving an account of what makes something part of one's body.

does not support monistic gestationalism, because the positive defences of monistic gestationalism are inadequate. We now turn to the second strategy, according to which gestational mothers are parents because they possess some feature that not only tracks gestation but may also track other relations some of which may be carried out by would-be genetic and social parents. Three plausible features might be appealed to here: 'sweat equity', an affective relation of some kind, and social expectations. We take these in order.

III.1 SWEAT EQUITY

A number of authors argue that gestation grounds parenthood on account of the labour that the gestational mother performs. In Narayan's words, a gestational mother undergoes 'considerable discomfort, effort, and risk in the course of pregnancy and childbirth.'[25] Moody-Adams defends monistic gestationalism on the grounds that gestation is a *sui generis* form of labour, unique because of its duration and constancy, its effects on the life of the labourer, and its product. In contrast, genetic 'parents' do not perform any comparable labour, for although genetic parents help to *cause* the child, the *labour* they invest in the child is minimal.

The sweat equity argument may suggest an unattractive children-as-property conception of parenthood, but the argument can in fact be made without appeal to property in oneself or one's creations. Someone who donates much of their time and effort to community work deserves recognition for their work, but they do not thereby acquire property rights through their efforts.

However, there is a problem with the sweat equity argument and it is this: while mapping onto our intuitions about the fruits of one's labour, it ignores the fact that the direction of fit can also go in the other direction. Consider the situation of a genetic father who refuses to contribute to the well-being of his genetic child. We would be inclined to regard such a person as failing to fulfil his parental responsibilities. This, of course, assumes that such a person has an obligation to invest his labour in a certain child *because* this child is his, i.e., because he is its genetic father.

---

[25] She goes on to say that 'gestation is an intimate process during which a woman could quite understandably develop a deep attachment to the child she carries and gives birth to.' Narayan, *op. cit.* note 20, p. 81. This second claim is a version of what we call the affective argument, which we discuss below.

Monistic gestationalism cannot explain why being a genetic parent can make the investment of sweat equity morally incumbent.

It may be, then, that the sweat equity argument throws into question the assumed symmetry between the origins of parental rights and the origins of parental responsibilities. A monistic gestationalist might argue that through successful gestation, gestational mothers gain defeasible rights over, but not defeasible obligations to, their children. We find this proposal implausible. For one thing, this argument distinguishes gestation from any other kind of action, in that the agent would bear no responsibility for its consequences even when the action is voluntary. To be sure, some defenders of the sweat equity argument, such as Moody-Adams, emphasise the putative *sui generis* character of gestational labour, but to ground such an odd moral conclusion in the sheer uniqueness of gestation could only add to the mystery. Moreover, from a teleological perspective, this rights-only position endangers the child, whose only genuine parent is now taken to have no obligations with respect to it.

III.2 BONDING AND AFFECTIVE RELATIONS

The sweat equity argument emphasises the physical relation between the gestational mother and her foetus. By contrast, the affective argument emphasises their psychological relationship. In this view, gestation grounds parenthood because it tracks an emotional relationship between mother and child, a relationship that does not follow upon genetic relationships as such.

Bonding and attachment play a role in custody disputes and the assignment of social parenthood, and it doesn't seem unreasonable to suppose that they should also play a role in generating natural parenthood. According to Rothman:

> Any pregnant woman is the mother of the child she bears. Her gestational relationship establishes her motherhood . . . [Children] enter the world in a relationship, a physical and social and emotional relationship with the woman in whose body they have been nurtured.[26]

Do children really enter the world in a social and emotional relationship with their gestational mother? One can consider the mother-child relation from two perspectives: that of the infant (attachment) and that of the mother (bonding). Let us begin with attachment. The monistic gestationalist might attempt to derive

---
[26] Rothman, *op. cit.* note 13, p. 475.

some support from attachment theory.[27] Attachment theorists hold that early mother-infant attachment is essential for the development of the infant. Although 'official' versions of the view tend to date the beginnings of attachment to birth, attachment theorists sometimes suggest that attachment might begin during pregnancy.[28]

Attachment theory, however, has come in for significant criticism in recent years.[29]

> [R]esearch on early emotional bonding suggests that parents can become highly involved with their infants during the first few hours if they are permitted to touch, hold, cuddle, and play with their babies . . . However, it appears that this early contact is neither crucial nor sufficient for the development of strong parent-to-infant or infant-to-parent attachments. Stable attachments between infants and caregivers are not formed in a manner of minutes, hours or days: they build rather slowly from interactions that take place over many weeks and months.[30]

Although it is certainly possible that future research may show that significant attachment can occur only if it begins *in utero*, or in the hours immediately following birth, there is currently little support for either claim.

While there is little evidence that infants become attached to their gestational mothers either in the womb or in the birth process, it may be that gestation and childbirth are crucial in the bonding process, that is, in the *mother's* felt relationship with her child. While it is certainly true that many gestational mothers bond with their foetus or new-born, many mothers are indifferent to their new-borns, and it is often a week or so before this indifference gives way to deep feelings of concern.[31] More

---

[27] See: J. Bowlby. 1969. *Attachment and Loss*. London. Hogarth Press. M.D. Ainsworth, M.C. Blehar, E. Waters & S. Wall. 1978. *Patterns of Attachment*. Hillsdale, N.J. Lawrence Erlbaum. M.H. Klaus & J.H. Klennell. 1983. *Bonding*. St. Louis, MO. Mosby. See also: Hill, *op. cit.* note 8, pp. 394–400, and works cited there.

[28] See: Bowlby, *op. cit.* note 27, p. 181; Ainsworth, *op. cit.* note 27, p. 23; and Klaus & Kinnell, *op. cit.* note 27, p. 9.

[29] See: D.E. Eyer. 1992. *Mother-Infant Bonding: A Scientific Fiction*. New Haven, CT. Yale University Press. See: M. Daly & M. Wilson. 1988. *Homicide*. New York. A. de Gruyter: 69–73. S. Goldberg. Parent-Infant Bonding: Another Look. *Child Development* 1983; 54: 1355–1382.

[30] D. Shaffer. 1989. *Developmental Psychology: Childhood and Adolescence* (2nd edition). Pacific Grove, CA. Brooks/Cole: 399.

[31] See Daly & Wilson, *op. cit.* note 29, pp. 71–72.

generally, we do not think that emotional intimacy is necessary for parenthood. Consider the example of an emotionally cold and distant parent. We might describe such a person's emotional state as being inappropriate or impoverished in some way: one ought to love and care for one's children simply because they are one's children. However, if this response is appropriate then emotional attachment cannot be necessary for parenthood.

In addition, we should also note that emotional commitment is not sufficient for parenthood. Many individuals can bond with an infant (and perhaps even a foetus), albeit in different ways. Relatives, family friends, and hospital staff can all bond with an infant, but they do not for this reason become parents of the infant in question. Bonding and attachment are not helpful for the monistic gestationalist, because they are not properties that parenthood plausibly tracks.

III.3 SOCIAL NORMS AND EXPECTATIONS

A final argument for gestationalism appeals to the social norms that govern pregnancy and childbirth. Perhaps gestational mothers are mothers because they are regarded as such. Elizabeth Anderson puts this point nicely: 'Pregnancy is not simply a biological process but also a social process. Many social expectations and considerations surround women's gestational labor, marking it off as an occasion for the parents to prepare themselves to welcome a new life into their family.'[32] Social institutions, formal rules, and informal norms, can have powerful effects on people's conception of their roles and themselves. It might be that this attitude – combined with its origin in social norms and pressures – grounds parenthood. A pregnant woman is likely to change her diet in the interests of the foetus, and may change her job in its interests as well. Whether or not she *does* act in the interests of her foetus, she will be expected to do so by many people, and in some jurisdictions she can be prosecuted for failing to do so in certain ways. Not only does society in general regard gestational mothers as mothers, but they see themselves in this light. The self-conception of many pregnant women is in large part as mothers – or, at least, as mothers-to-be.

Although the social argument seems to provide some support for sufficiency gestationalism, it does not show that gestation is

---

[32] E.S. Anderson. Is Women's Labor a Commodity? *Philosophy and Public Affairs* 1990; 19: 81 (cf. 87).

necessary for parenthood. Clearly social norms of parenthood do surround gestational mothers, but they also surround genetic fathers and adoptive 'parents.' Men are expected to have a certain attitude toward their genetic children, whether or not they live with the gestational mother or have ever met the child. Paternal abandonment is generally the subject of censure, even if the father helps ensure that the mother and child are economically secure. And in the same way that gestational mothers internalise the general conception of them, so too do genetic fathers. The social norms surrounding pregnant women in particular and parenthood in general do not regard gestation as the sole ground of parenthood.

A second point to note about the social argument is that, as Laura Purdy has noted, there may be a rather high cost in grounding gestationalism in our social norms concerning gestation and childbirth. The social norms around childbirth and rearing are among the more regressive, with respect to gender, in our society.[33] This remains true even if, as Anderson argues, those norms serve the valuable function of encouraging mothers to love and identify with their children. Laying a great deal of moral weight on them may therefore be counterproductive in other respects. In particular, women who intend to terminate their pregnancy or give up their child for adoption might want to resist seeing themselves as – and being seen as – mothers-to-be.

We have surveyed an array of arguments for monistic gestationalism and found each one lacking. At most, these arguments support *sufficiency* gestationalism, which is friendly to the pluralism about parenthood that we endorse. We have not, it should be noted, argued that sperm (or egg) donation and gestation are equally arduous, nor have we argued that gestational mothers have no better claim to be awarded custody of a child than its genetic 'parents.' We have argued only that each relation gives its possessors a defeasible claim to parental rights and responsibilities. In this respect, 'parenthood' is a success term – its applicability is a function of its bearer having a certain status, not how hard she must work to attain that status. Similarly, 'pregnancy' is a success term. Some people try for a long time with no results (hence the fertility industry), while others 'succeed' without even trying (hence the shotgun wedding). We do not disrespect those whose pregnancies require exhaustive biological and

---

[33] L.M. Purdy. Surrogate Mothering: Exploitation or Empowerment? *Bioethics* 1989; 3: 18–34.

technological effort when we regard accidental pregnancies as no less pregnancies than theirs; similarly, we do not disrespect or devalue gestational mothers when we regard genetic 'parenthood' as no less a form of parenthood than gestational parenthood.

IV. INTENTIONALISM

Although less prominent in the philosophical literature, intentional approaches to parenthood have been popular among legal theorists.[34] In its broadest form, an intentional account of parenthood takes the intentions to rear and nurture as relevant (i.e. necessary, sufficient, or both) to the ascription of parenthood. As one proponent writes, 'it is the procreators – the party or parties responsible for bringing the child into the world with the intention of raising it . . . – who are the "parents" of the child at birth'.[35]

Intentionalism strikes many as intuitively odd, so it may be appropriate to say a few words in its favour. First, intentionalism offers the appealing prospect of integrating natural and social parenthood. Social parenthood is plausibly regarded as resting on parents successfully carrying out the intention to parent. Second, intentionalism promises to make sense of how parental rights and responsibilities are acquired. This can look somewhat mysterious from the standpoint of geneticism and gestationalism.

---

[34] Hill, *op. cit.* note 8. Other intentionalist approaches to parenthood include: A. Stumpf. Redefining Mother: A Legal Matrix for New Reproductive Technologies. *The Yale Law Journal* 1986; 96: 187–208; M.M. Shultz. Reproductive Technology and Intent-Based Parenthood: An Opportunity for Gender Neutrality. *Wisconsin Law Review* 1990: 297–398; P. Parker. Surrogate Motherhood: The Interaction of Litigation, Legislation and Psychiatry. *International Journal of Law and Psychiatry* 1982; 5: 341–54; and L.M. Silver & S.R. Silver. Confused Heritage and the Absurdity of Genetic Ownership. *Harvard Journal of Law & Technology* 1998; 11: 593–618. Nelson, *op. cit.* note 2, discusses and rejects a theory that he calls 'intensionalism' (with an 's'). He characterises this view as a theory of how parental obligations are incurred, rather than a theory of what makes someone a parent (though he does not distinguish between these two issues). This distinction matters here because intensionalism for Nelson amounts to an instance of the general view that all obligations are (hypothetically) voluntary, which Nelson rejects. But intentionalism (with a 't') does not share this premise. To wit, Nelson and (as we shall see below) Hill both defend causal accounts of the origins of parental obligations, though Nelson thinks that this 'causalism' entails monistic geneticism.

[35] Hill, *op. cit.* note 8, p. 387.

TOWARD A PLURALIST ACCOUNT OF PARENTHOOD 237

How could a purely biological relationship such as genetic derivation or gestation generate rights and responsibilities? By contrast, it is much more comprehensible how rights and responsibilities could arise out of the effective achievement of manifest intentions.[36]

In arguing for intentionalism, Hill considers a five-person surrogacy arrangement involving two persons who intend to rear a child ('intended parents'), two gamete donors, and a woman who will gestate the foetus (three 'biological progenitors'). Hill offers two reasons for thinking that (only) the intended parents are the real parents. First, they are the 'first cause, or the prime movers, of the procreative relationship.' Second, 'while some gestational host and genetic progenitors are necessary to achieve the intention of the intended parents to have a child, no particular biological progenitors are necessary.'[37] But for the intended parents, there would be no child at all.

Neither of these claims is convincing.[38] The 'prime mover' argument is not to the point, for persons who were eager to be grandparents might act as 'prime movers' in orchestrating their daughter's or daughter-in-law's pregnancy. It would not follow that the grandparents thereby became parents. Nor is Hill's second point persuasive. Hill's 'but-for' causal argument is invalid because it equivocates on the identity of the particular child in question. Hill is correct that no particular biological progenitors are 'necessary to achieve the intention of the intended parents to have *a* child', but it does not follow that the particular biological progenitors do not stand in the 'but-for' causal relationship with the child that they do in fact have.[39] To the contrary, at least on the most plausible current theory of identity, each person's genetic material – the particular gametes that fused at conception – is essential to that person, and thus each person's genetic parents stand in a 'but-for' causal relationship to her or him.[40] It may be true that but for the orchestration of the intended parents, no child would have been born, and *a fortiori* that *the*

---

[36] O. O'Neill. 1979. Begetting, Bearing, and Rearing. In *Having Children*. O. O'Neill & W. Ruddick, eds. Oxford. Oxford University Press: 25–38.

[37] Hill, *op. cit.* note 8, p. 415. Emphasis in original.

[38] For a penetrating critique of Hill see: M. Roberts. Good Intentions and a Great Divide: Having Babies by Intending Them. *Law and Philosophy* 1993; 12: 287–317.

[39] Hill, *op. cit.* note 8, p. 415. Emphases added.

[40] S. Kripke. 1972. *Naming and Necessity*. Cambridge, MA. Harvard University Press: 113–14.

child would not have been born, but it does not follow that the intended parents are the only 'but-for' causes of the child.[41]

Intentionalism also suffers from other problems. First, and most simply, many people become pregnant unintentionally and this does not make them any less the parent of the ensuing child than if they had planned the pregnancy. Thus, preconception intentions to procreate are not necessary for parenthood. The same can be said for pre*birth* intentions to procreate, or for that matter, procreative intentions whenever they arise. If, as we have argued, genetic fathers are fathers, they are such whether or not they know they have conceived a child. (It does not follow that the father is a *good* father, or that the acts whereby he participated in procreation were exercises of a putative right to procreate.) However, if genetic 'fathers' are fathers, they are such whether or not they intend to be. It seems to follow that no particular intentions are necessary for parenthood.

V. CAUSALISM

The argument against necessity intentionalism leaves open the possibility that a weaker form of intentionalism – sufficiency intentionalism – might take its place alongside sufficiency geneticism and gestationalism as one of several bases for ascribing parenthood. Indeed, it could be that (sufficiency) intentionalism is, at root, plausible for the same reasons that (sufficiency) geneticism and gestationalism are plausible, viz., procreative intentions can be causally linked in the right sort of way to the creation of children. Our goal here is not to defend a causal account of parenthood in any detail. Rather, we want to suggest that whatever shape a causal account of parenthood takes, it must be pluralistic, because several kinds of activities make significant causal contributions to procreation.

The gestational mother plays the most obvious causal role: inside her, the embryo-foetus is actually created and, at significant expense, she provides the oxygen, nutrients, and shelter required to bring the foetus to term. There is also little mystery in the causal role of genetic parents, whose chromosomes are essential to the particular being that comes to exist. Though at this point

---

[41] Hill offers two other arguments for intentionalism. These are the 'contract argument' and the 'avoidance-of-uncertainty' argument. These two arguments, while not wholly implausible as far as they go, are much more plausibly read as defending particular frameworks for legal rights, rather than as an account of parenthood. Thus, we leave these arguments aside here.

we have no account of the 'right way' of being causally implicated, it seems that including the gestational and genetic parents is a litmus test of any account of the right sort of causal linkage.

Less obvious is the causal role of custodial 'parents.' Causal accounts of parenthood may be more or less inclusive, and we suggest that they ought to be at least inclusive enough to admit certain custodial 'parents' fully into the realm of parenthood. Custodial parents – however many there are, and whether or not they are also 'biologically' related to the child – are causally important in the developing child's personality, opportunities, physical and mental health, and every other aspect of the child's life. Neoteny – long-term dependence upon others after birth – is as 'natural' an aspect of the human species as viviparous reproduction. For this reason, the widely held conviction that adoptive parents – at least when they adopt very early in the child's life, and at least after the passage of sufficient time – are parents on a par with 'birth' parents, seems correct. While we emphasise that simply determining the basis of natural parenthood does not entail any particular policies concerning parenthood, and so adoptive parents may be *legal* parents even if they are not *natural* parents, it seems that the causal role of adoptive parents in the creation of live, healthy children (and eventually adults), merits inclusion within a theory of natural parenthood.

Still less clear is the causal role of intended 'parents.' Although intentionalists fail to show that intended parents play a uniquely important causal role in the generation of a surrogate child, it is clear that intended parents are crucial to the creation of children in cases of 'assisted reproduction' (though even this term risks begging the question of who is doing the reproducing). For this reason, the plight of intended parents – who go to great pains orchestrating a process that results in the creation of a child, and who prepare for the coming child just as expecting gestational parents do – is surely a sympathetic one. However, it is by no means clear that the role of intended parents is in these respects any more 'parental' than the role of expectant grandparents. As we noted earlier, sometimes grandparents, too, can be the 'prime movers' in the creation of grandchildren. It should be remembered, too, that, provided the causal theory is sufficiently inclusive to cover custodial parents, intended 'parents' can expect to become genuine parents not long after they take custody of the child.[42]

---

[42] The *Glover Report* reaches a similar conclusion on surrogacy. See: Jonathan Glover. 1989. *Fertility and the Family: The Glover Report on Reproductive Technologies to the European Commission*. London. Fourth Estate: 77–80; 151.

Then again, custodial parents become parents (as opposed to mere legal guardians) solely on account of actions taken *after* gaining custody through, say, adoption. In contrast, intended parents take procreative actions before gaining custody, indeed, before conception. And as Hill notes, intended parents may even be causally necessary in the creation of the child. We are therefore inclined toward a brand of pluralism that is sufficiently inclusive to admit intended parents as parents.

This conclusion represents an attempt to resolve a conceptual problem, not a custody dispute. However, our resolution – mildly favouring intended parenthood as sufficient for parenthood – may seem threatening, in the context of contested cases where legislatures and courts have often favoured genetic and intended parents over gestational mothers. We should say, then, something about the implications of our pluralist position for these sorts of contested cases. Our position does not, recall, entail any position on custodial disputes. Nor does it entail any conclusion about the morality of surrogacy or any other technique of reproduction. One may be an inclusive pluralist – and so, in principle, consider intended parents genuine parents – but nonetheless reject reproductive technologies altogether. (Inclusive) pluralism implies only that genetic, gestational, custodial, and sometimes even intended parents, are all parents, and for that reason should be regarded as having *prima facie* responsibilities and rights as parents.

We do think that in the most controversial cases, the relevant interests of the gestational mother should generally be accorded priority over those of the genetic and intended parents. Our reasons for taking this position have to do with the power relations between genetic, gestational, and intended parents, rather than with any view about degrees or kinds of parenthood. In the contested cases that provide the backdrop to this debate, gestational mothers will typically have less voice, exit potential, and power than genetic/intended parents.[43] Thus, if legal priority is to be accorded to any party it should be the gestational mother.

---

[43] Intended mothers of their husbands' genetic children in surrogacy cases may also find themselves lacking voice, exit potential, and power. Indeed our pluralist view may be cold comfort in such cases: imagine the intended mother protests that her husband regards his genes as more important than hers, and his reply is that she can become a genuine parent by taking primary responsibility for child-rearing! For good reason, then, Rosemarie Tong has suggested that the practice of surrogacy inhibits solidarity among women who have more in common with each other than they do with their husband, genetic father, or intended father. See: R. Tong, *op. cit.* note 3, p. 48.

This priority might be regarded as an equalising force, intended to counterbalance the risk that the gestational mother's interests will not get their due consideration.

A more straightforward implication of pluralism is that a child can conceivably have a number of natural parents – two (or, technology permitting, more or fewer) genetic parents and one (or, technology permitting, more or fewer) gestational mother(s). However, this does not seem objectionable. After all, children can have an indefinite number of custodial parents, whose relationships to their children fall on a continuum from relatively informal to the most formalised, namely adoption. Toward the most-formalised end of this continuum, there may be few moral or legal differences between natural and social parenthood; and given high degrees of 'parental investment' and bonding, it is hard to see that social parenthood is any less 'real' a relation than natural parenthood. Thus, even those who defend 'natural' accounts of parenthood must admit that to some degree, parenthood is what we make it.

VI. CONCLUSION

We have argued against two widely held views of parenthood, monistic gestationalism and necessity intentionalism. However, in gestationalism and intentionalism, as well as geneticism, we found an underlying assumption that seems correct, if inchoate: being causally implicated in the creation of a child is the key basis for being its parent. Although we have neither defended nor developed a causal account of parenthood in any depth, we have suggested that any such account ought to be broad enough to grant parenthood to genetic, gestational, custodial, and intentional parents.

Acknowledgements

We are grateful to two referees from this journal, members of the Center for Applied Philosophy and Professional Ethics (Canberra), and Steve Gardiner and Maria Taylor for their helpful comments. We are also grateful to the University of Pittsburgh Philosophy Department for summer research support. Finally, we would like to thank Giuliana Fuscaldo for calling our attention to the intentionalist literature.

5

Procreation and Parental Responsibility

Jeffrey Blustein

1. "Adam," says John Locke, "was created a perfect Man, his Body and Mind in full possession of their Strength and Reason, and so was capable from the first Instant of his being to provide for his own Support and Preservation, and govern his Actions according to the Dictates of the Law of Reason."[1] Actual human beings, however, depend on the care of adults over a relatively long period in order to develop capacities for rational choice and even to survive, and the obligation to care for children arises from this dependence. Some obligations are owed *by* all *to* all children. For example, the members of society collectively have a duty to protect children from abuse and neglect. But the care of a particular child, it is widely believed, should normally be the primary responsibility of those who give it birth.

It is of course no justification of this arrangement to say merely that this is how children are customarily cared for in our society or that it is only "natural" that biological parents should be the ones who have this responsibility. Without additional normative premises, appeals to custom or nature never establish moral conclusions. A more promising suggestion begins with the assumption that the only significant factor in settling the question of responsibility is what arrangement is likely to best satisfy the interests of children.[2] If being cared for by one's biological parents is in the best interests of children—and so it is alleged to be—then biological parents should be the primary caretakers. Another suggestion, and the one I want to explore in this paper, is that since biological parents have caused a being to exist, a being who, by its very nature, is dependent and vulnerable to harm, they are mainly responsible for its care. Causing a helpless and vulnerable being to exist is sufficient, on this view, for moral responsibility. I call this the "causal view of parental responsibility."

Procreation, however, may be thought to have moral significance for a different sort of reason, not because it causes a needy being to exist but because it is one way in which parental obligations may be undertaken. This is how Onora O'Neill explains the role of procreation:

> Biology is not irrelevant to parental obligations, for a standard way of acquiring obligations is to undertake them, and a standard way of undertaking parental obligations is to decide to procreate.[3]

Another way of acquiring parental obligations is adoption, more formal and regulated than procreation, to be sure, and the exception rather than the rule. But on the present view, when procreation gives rise to parental responsibility, it is for the same reason that adoption does: in procreating, one chooses to become a caretaker. I call this the "voluntarist view of parental responsibility."

The distinction between the causal and the voluntarist views can be further sharpened by considering the implications of different background institutions for the rearing of children. In a society in which the whole upbringing of children is assigned to specially trained agents of the society, the decision to procreate is not standardly a decision to undertake the rearing of a child. The decision to procreate would not have its usual meaning, that is, the meaning it has in a society like ours where biological parents are and are known to be the normal childrearers. By contrast, on the causal view, even if procreation takes place within such a society, there is an obligation to care for the child one has created. This would not necessarily be an all-things-considered obligation, however, since in this society vulnerable children are standardly cared for by persons who are not their biological parents.

In an earlier work, I presented an institutional theory of parental obligation in which questions about who has parental duties are addressed in two stages.[4] In the first stage, we ask about the justifiability of social arrangements that assign responsibility for the care and upbringing of children in specific ways. The justification of social practices of childrearing, I argued, is a higher-order account that takes into consideration, and seeks an appropriate balance between, three distinct yet closely interwoven sets of interests: the (legitimate) interests of parents, of children, and of society at large. In the second stage, we provide an explanation for how particular individuals acquire parental duties under a justifiable set of childrearing practices. But even if the social arrangement whereby natural parents are responsible for the care of their offspring turns out on this analysis to be seriously flawed, this does not carry the implication that particular natural parents have no duties of parenthood. Parental duties might still be incurred either because persons have undertaken to rear a child or, alternatively, because they have caused a needy being to exist.

In this paper, I will not be concerned with the evaluation of the social and institutional arrangements that connect specific children to specific others. I will instead be principally interested in working through some different ways of interpreting the causal view of parental responsibility to see if it can illuminate a dimension of parental responsibility that has been overlooked by the voluntarist view. I do this by examining three vignettes which describe various conditions under which reproduction takes place and asking what the causal and the voluntarist views would say about the responsibility of the procreators in each case.

2. I begin with a case of planned childbirth.

Procreation and Parental Responsibility 81

> Joel and Diane have been married five years and have frequently discussed starting a family. They agreed early on, however, to postpone having children until they are well-established in their careers and have saved enough money to comfortably afford the expenses of childrearing. They have used contraceptives faithfully, but they have no moral or other objections to abortion, and in fact Diane had one some years back when she became pregnant due to contraceptive failure. Joel and Diane are now both successful professionals and decide that the time is right to start working on the family they have so long desired. Diane becomes pregnant. She goes regularly for prenatal care and follows all her obstetrician's orders. She and Joel arrange parental leaves with their employers, attend Lamaze classes together, and prepare a special room in their home for the nursery. Diane gives birth, and with a mixture of joy and apprehension, she and Joel begin their lives together as parents.

Both causal and voluntarist views, as I understand them, agree that Joel and Diane are duty-bound to nurture and care for their child; that their duty is special in the sense that it is a duty of a different kind—having a distinct basis—from whatever general duty strangers may have to the child; and further that being duty-bound in this way does not preclude their being justified in transferring all or some of the nurture and care of their child to others. But the two explanations diverge in that on the voluntarist approach, unlike the causal, causing the child to exist is not itself a ground of parental duty. Joel and Diane are duty-bound as parents only because they have voluntarily chosen to have a child and in so doing have assumed responsibility for it (assuming again that reproduction takes place in a society where natural parents are and are known to be normally responsible for their offspring).

Though the case of Joel and Diane is clearly one of voluntary choice because of the careful planning that went into their decision to have a child, it would be a mistake to suppose that, on a reasonable construal of the voluntarist position, biological parents have parental duties only when their decision to procreate is of such a deliberate nature. Individuals can, in a somewhat looser sense, freely choose to do things that they do not aim to do. For example, if I let my insurance policy lapse, out of sheer laziness, when I could easily have paid the premium on time, we would quite naturally say that I have chosen to let the policy expire. Similarly, a woman might be said to choose to have a child, even if, unlike Joel and Diane, she did not seek this as her goal. A plausible voluntarist view, I believe, would count a range of situations as satisfying the voluntary choice condition.

3. Let us now consider a hypothetical case that is the polar opposite of the story of Joel and Diane, what I call a case of forced childbirth:

> Marcia becomes pregnant as a result of rape and is imprisoned by her rapist for nine months until she gives birth. Immediately after birth, the rapist abandons both mother and child, leaving them to fend for them-

82   Jeffrey Blustein

Would Marcia violate some duty to her child if she too abandoned it? Since voluntarists about parental responsibility are not committed to the view that *all* duties to others are a result of our voluntary acts, it is open to them to appeal at this point to some general duty of beneficence. Every person, as an expression of our common humanity, has a duty to help any other person who is in need or jeopardy, at least when he or she can so without excessive risk or loss to self. Assuming there is something Marcia could do to protect the helpless child that meets this threshold condition, she has a (natural) duty to do it.

Thus, a voluntarist would have Marcia think about her situation in the following way: "I didn't choose to become pregnant or to have this child. Both were the result of force. Of course, now that there is this helpless infant before me, I can't just walk away. Like anyone, I have a duty to protect needy persons from harm. But I have no duty to care for it that derives from its being my offspring. My duty to it, as one might put it, is only accidentally *parental*." Indeed, it might be added that it would be unfair to saddle Marcia with such a duty. Biological parents have parental duties, when they do, because they have decided to procreate and so have assumed responsibility for its care and upbringing. But Marcia has in no way elected to become a parent.

Would Marcia have parental duties on the causal view of parental responsibility? She certainly has played a causal role in the production of a vulnerable human being. But we would hesitate to designate her *the* cause of this needy being. (Similarly, when an otherwise dying patient is not resuscitated in the event of cardiac arrest, *the* cause of death is said to be the underlying disease, not the failure to resuscitate.) We reserve this designation for that condition which, among the various factors empirically determined to have causally contributed to an event, is its "proximate" or "material" cause, and judgments about proximate cause are not prior to and independent of judgments about rights, duties, and obligations.[5] An inquiry into the proximate cause of an event, in other words, is one that takes into account normative standards (legal or moral, as the case may be). Some of these standards relate to the use of force and fraud: we do not consider a person to be a proximate cause of event E if—as in Marcia's case—her bringing about E is the result of deception, coercion, or violence on the part of others.

The plausibility of the causal view of parental responsibility depends on the conception of cause it employs. A counterfactual or "but for" test of causality is a notoriously broad and liberal test for identifying cases of causal dependence. It identifies any background or circumstantial factor without which an event would not have occurred as a cause of that event, and if parental responsibilities were incurred by anyone who was a cause of the child's existing in this sense, there would be a tremendous proliferation in the number of persons who could be considered the child's "parents." Alternatively, we can formulate the causal view more narrowly in terms of the notion of proximate cause: anyone who is a proximate cause of a child's existing, and so being vulnerable to harm, is responsible for keeping this child safe from harm.

In addition to "but for" causation and proximate causation, there is a third way of defining cause that is stricter than the former and not normatively loaded like the latter: a cause of event E is an indispensable part of a sufficient condition of E. Alison McIntyre explains:

> A complete sufficient condition of some event E would include all of the relevant antecedent events, background circumstances, and laws of nature that must be described in a set of sentences that would logically entail a sentence asserting that E occurred. Any component of this condition that is indispensable, in the sense that without the sentence describing it, the sentences describing the other elements would not entail that E occurred, is a necessary part of a sufficient condition of E.[6]

Using this notion of cause, the causal view would assign parental responsibility to anyone who causes a child to exist by being a necessary part of a sufficient condition of that child's existing. (Note that this is not the same as being a necessary condition of the child's existing.)

On this interpretation of the causal view, Marcia would seem to be morally responsible as a parent for the well-being of the child to which she gave birth. Marcia is both the genetic and the gestational mother of the child. Without her procreative contribution, no set of otherwise sufficient conditions for the existence of this child would in fact have been sufficient to produce it. (If we find this result counterintuitive, I suspect it is because of the fact that Marcia in no way consented to or had control over her becoming a parent.) The same can be said about the rapist's genetic contribution, and more: his rape and imprisonment of Marcia were indispensable as well.

4. Finally, consider a case of failed contraception:

> Anthony and Joan make love. They agree that they do not want to have a child and they both use contraceptives, she a spermicidal gel, he a condom. Soon after, the two separate. Despite having taken reasonable care to avoid conception, Joan becomes pregnant, and since she cannot bring herself to have an abortion or to give the child up for adoption, decides to have and raise the child, at no small cost to herself. She has no family to help her take care of the child and struggles to make ends meet, so she reluctantly contacts Anthony. "You're the father," she tells him, "and a father ought to contribute something toward the upbringing of his child."

In this scenario, intercourse was voluntary and Anthony was not deceived by Joan. When she said she did not want to have a child and that she was being careful to use a contraceptive, she was telling the truth. The failure of contraception and her unexpected pregnancy simply led her to reevaluate her situation. Yet Anthony did not choose to procreate either and so has not fulfilled the condition that, on the voluntarist view, generates parental responsibility. Does he have any parental obligations?

An analogy might help. Suppose you accidentally hit a pedestrian with your car, even though you are driving alert, sober, within the speed limit, and in a well-maintained automobile. You have not chosen to injure the pedestrian (in any reasonable sense of the term) and are not blameworthy for doing so. It was, from your point of view, simply a case of bad luck. Yet you seem to be in a very different position, morally speaking, from the driver who was equally careful and did not have an accident. In a well-known passage, Bernard Williams draws attention to this difference:

> The lorry driver who, through no fault of his, runs over a child, will feel differently from any spectator, even a spectator next to him in the cab, except perhaps to the extent that the spectator takes on the thought that he himself might have prevented it, an agent's thought....We feel sorry for the driver, but that sentiment co-exists with, indeed presupposes, that there is something special about his relation to this happening, something which cannot merely be eliminated by the consideration that it was not his fault.[7]

What is special is that he caused harm. Moreover, this fact, Williams claims, is relevant to moral responsibility. Ascription of responsibility is not only appropriate to the extent that the person in question is to blame. Causing something bad to happen is also relevant, even when this is unintentional and not the result of some failure to exercise due care.

However, the circumstances in which the driver causes harm to a pedestrian are very different from those in which one unwittingly causes harm to another by engaging in a safe activity that, through some freakish sequence of events, leads to harm. Whether one has obligations in the latter case may be uncertain, but not in the former. Driving is an inherently risky activity, however careful the driver may be, and an automobile accident is a forseeable risk of it. When an individual unintentionally causes harm by forseeably risky actions, he or she is morally obligated to compensate the victim (an insurance company may discharge this obligation on the driver's behalf). Similarly, construction companies that engage in blasting with high explosives must be prepared to compensate any innocent parties who may incidentally be harmed, even if the blasters exercise all due care. The price one must pay for permissibly engaging in risky or dangerous activities is what in the law is called strict liability for causing harm.

To return to the case of Anthony and Joan, the analogy with strict liability is imperfect, but it may nevertheless be sufficiently strong to suggest that Anthony is a parent in more than just a biological sense. Unlike the driver example, Anthony does not make someone worse off just by participating in the creation of a child, and he does not have a duty to compensate the child merely for having participated in its creation. However, the child will be harmed if it is not protected, and by participating in the creation of such a being, it may be argued, Anthony incurs at least a prima facie obligation to *prevent* harm from coming to it. To be sure, there is a difference between pointing out that pregnancy is a reasonably forseeable risk of intercourse with many contraceptive methods and claiming that the birth of a child is a reasonably forseeable risk of intercourse with these methods. But supposing that Joan's going through with the pregnancy (should it occur) is a realistic possibility of which Anthony should have been aware, then the principle of strict liability can plausibly explain why Anthony is obligated to care for the child that is born.

In saying this, I am obviously questioning the adequacy of the voluntarist view of parental responsibility. On the strict liability model, Anthony is not specially obligated to care for his offspring because he *chose*, either explicitly or by indirection, to become a father. Having some control over the reproductive process may be a necessary condition of incurring obligations to the child that is born, as my discussion of the case of forced childbirth suggested. But choosing to procreate is not the only way of being in control of one's reproductive life. Anthony too had some control over becoming a parent, some choice whether to engage in risky activity, and some power to diminish the risk by being more careful than he might otherwise have been.

5. Clearly a causal account of the ground of parental responsibility cannot be the whole story about how parental obligations are acquired, if adoption is also acknowledged as a way in which individuals can become parents. Another moral principle is needed to explain how adoptive parents become responsible for those they adopt. For the voluntarist, those who cause a child to exist are responsible for it insofar as, and only insofar as, they have chosen to procreate and so assumed responsibility for it, and the principle linking procreation and responsibility also explains how persons who are not procreators can acquire parental obligations. Admittedly, the voluntarist will say, when adoptive parents undertake obligations, they frequently have a clearer idea of what their child will require of them, and are less likely to misjudge their desires and capacities, than biological parents. This is not surprising, since those who want to adopt a child can only do so after they undergo a protracted and rigorous investigative process to determine their suitability as parents. But as I noted in section 2, voluntarists are not committed to a narrow view of choice according to which only especially well-thought-out decisions, arrived at after careful consideration of their consequences, count as genuine choices.

This does not satisfy proponents of the causal view, however. They do not deny that one way of acquiring parental obligations is by undertaking them and that this principle can account for the existence of parental obligations in a significant number of cases. They only maintain, against the voluntarists, that undertaking obligations is not necessary for parental responsibility and that causation can give rise to it as well. In addition, it is no part of the causal view as I present it that biological parenthood is somehow preferable to (because more "natural" than?) adoptive parenthood or that adoptive parents are only parents by default. Arguably, as Hugh LaFollette has suggested, it would be better for children if we took adoption as the model for all parenting and required all parents, not just adoptive ones, to be licensed.[8] But these are extremely controversial claims, and they go well beyond the scope of this paper.

I believe enough has been said to suggest that voluntarism about parental responsibility is too restrictive. Playing a causal role in the creation of a child can give rise to parental obligations. But playing a causal role is only part of the explanation, and it is only when this is joined with other conditions that causation becomes morally relevant. These include the decision to procreate (the only one allowed by the voluntarist view), as well as others discussed in sections 3 and 4.

An earlier draft of this paper was presented at the conference, Building Families: Ethical and Policy Issues in Adoption, *sponsored by the Center for Biomedical Ethics, University of Minnesota, November 13-14, 1994. I am grateful to members of the audience for their comments, and particularly to James Lindemann Nelson, who was my co-panelist at the conference and with whom I have had several lengthy and stimulating discussions about the issues addressed in this paper.*

Notes

[1] *Two Treatises on Civil Government*, Peter Laslett, ed. (Cambridge: Cambridge University Press, 1960, with amendments, 1963), section 56.

[2] This is the view of Patricia White in *Beyond Dominion: An Essay in the Political Philosophy of Education* (London: Routledge and Kegan Paul, 1983), chap. 5.

[3] "Begetting, Bearing, and Rearing," in *Having Children: Philosophical and Legal Reflections on Parenthood*, Onora O'Neill and William Ruddick, eds. (New York: Oxford University Press, 1979), p. 26.

[4] *Parents and Children: The Ethics of the Family* (New York: Oxford University Press, 1981), part 2, chap. 2.

[5] For a brief discussion of "proximate" or "substantial" cause, see *Deciding to Forego Life-Sustaining Treatment*, President's Commission for the Study of Ethical Problems in Medicine and Biomedical and Behavioral Research (Washington, DC: U.S. Government Printing Office, 1983), pp. 68-73; and Alison McIntyre, "Guilty Bystanders? On the Legitimacy of Duty to Rescue Statutes," *Philosophy and Public Affairs* 23 (1994): pp. 161-62.

[6] Ibid., pp. 162-63.

[7] "Moral Luck," in *Moral Luck* (Cambridge: Cambridge University Press, 1982), p. 28.

[8] See "Licensing Parents," *Philosophy and Public Affairs* 9 (1980): 182-97.

6

The moral basis of children's relational rights

James G. Dwyer

Introduction

'Children's rights' connotes to many a plea for special assistance, a claim to sympathy and charity for a vulnerable population. They are positive rights, dependent on adults' choosing to be generous, and thus inherently weaker than the negative liberties that respect for autonomous individuals entails. In addition, when thinking about children's rights many imagine only particular aspects of upbringing that arise after children are embedded in a family, such as schooling, medical care and discipline. Children's coming to be in one particular family rather than another in the first place is not a concern of political theorists, and is generally not thought to be something to which they have rights; the family setting is taken for granted, parenting by biological parents assumed as a natural, supra-legal condition.

In fact, however, most of what children need for their healthy development is best viewed as a matter of moral entitlement quite like what autonomous adults demand for themselves, resting on notions of negative liberty, contract, and equality. Only modest conceptual modification is necessary to account for children's lack of autonomy – namely, allowing for their rights more routinely to be exercised by a proxy (rather than only occasionally, as with autonomous adults). Moreover, the scope of children's moral rights extends to all aspects of their family life, including formation and termination of family relationships, just as does the scope of adults' rights. From the first moment of a child's life, we should ask not (just) what can we who happen to care about the child do to improve his or her life, but what rights does that child have that prohibit us, individually or collectively, from doing things detrimental to his or her well-being and life prospects, including a poor choice of caregivers.

This chapter schematises the moral rights of children relevant to their basic welfare and protection from harm. It first addresses formation of children's family relationships, then regulation of particular aspects of their upbringing.

Children's rights to enter or avoid family relationships

A newborn child is a separate human being with needs and interests distinct from those of birth parents. In fact, the child's interests can be in conflict with those of birth parents; the

The moral basis of children's relational rights

latter typically wish to serve as the child's legal parents and custodians, but they might not be the best choice for that role among available potential caregivers. And it is a choice. Birth parents make a choice: whether they will make themselves available for a family relationship with the child; and the state makes a choice: whether it will confer legal parent status on the birth parents or on someone else. With state-conferred status, legal parents can call on state officials to help them retain possession of the child and exclude others who might wish to take possession of or simply interact with the child. In short, the state creates parent–child relationships, and not only in the adoption context but also when biological parents serve as legal parents and custodians.

The state thus takes action in the case of every child, which largely determines the child's life course and well-being, given the decisive role parents play in any person's life. That particular state actors, such as legislators or judges, might make a particular choice regarding legal parenthood – for example, to confer it automatically on biological parents – based on their own notions of natural law or moral rights does not mean they are not choosing. State actors play a crucial causal role in formation of children's family life even if they believe they could not morally make a different choice. As a practical matter, they could make a different choice, and whatever reasons they have for the choice they make should be subject to examination.

Choosing family members for someone is an extraordinary thing for the state to do. We adults have a right against the state presuming to do that for us. There is no question of the state's forcing us to be in social relationships with any other human beings. With respect to parent–child relationships, although western states today extract money from some unwilling biological parents (in the form of child support, see Chapters 2.6, 2.7 and 3.3 of this book), in an effort to privatise the cost of raising children, they do not force those adults to assume a parenting role. And with respect to legal relationships between adults, the state does not force people into marriages they have not chosen themselves. For the state to do so would clearly violate negative moral rights, rights embodied in modern constitutions and human rights Conventions. This would be so even if the state's aim was just to gratify an individual's wish to be in a relationship with another individual.

Children also have this negative moral right against forced intimate association, because they too have tremendous interests at stake in connection with their social relationships, especially family life. Children are also persons under the constitutions and Conventions which embody that moral right. This would be clear to all in the context of adoption; if the state were to place children in parent–child relationships with adults other than birth parents in an arbitrary fashion or in disregard of children's welfare (e.g. giving them to infertile mentally ill adults as a therapeutic measure), everyone would perceive the violation of children's rights.

There is nothing different about the state's choice of a child's first caregivers; children have a right against the state's presuming to force them into *any* relationship. It is simply the case that children's predicament necessitates the state's nevertheless doing so, such that if done properly the state's infringement of that right is not a violation of it. We might say that placing children into a parent–child relationship with good caregivers is a justified infringement. Or we might impute to children a limited waiver of their right, the crucial limitation being that the state act with the sole aim of benefiting the children and do so competently. The state could not reasonably justify its infringement of this right by saying it is aiming to gratify desires of other individuals or to further collective aims, any more than it could do so to justify infringing the same right of adults. And we could not reasonably impute to children a waiver of their right for the purpose of enabling the state to gratify other persons or to serve state ends.

James G. Dwyer

Regardless of how conceptualised, then, the state's infringing a newborn child's negative right against forced association is justified only if and to the extent that the state aims to serve the child's interests. Thus, parentage laws morally must aim to choose the best available parents for any given child. As a practical matter, we cannot expect the state to do this perfectly, but we can expect it not to knowingly make very bad choices when good choices are available. Yet the state in modern western societies routinely does this; it knows some birth parents have seriously problematic histories of child maltreatment and/or severe dysfunctions such as drug addiction that will prevent them from caring adequately for a child, but it confers legal parent status on them anyway, with permanently damaging consequences for the children. It does this despite the great over-supply of good applicants for adoption. The state might reasonably assume it is best for most newborn children to be raised by biological parents, but it is patently false to suppose this true for all children, and it is inexcusable not to exclude birth parents as to whom it is manifestly untrue. Existing parentage laws are morally condemnable and in need of reform.

In sum, we should not overlook the huge role parentage laws play in children's lives, and we should recognise that children have a negative moral right against the state's applying to them parentage laws that force some into family relationships with adults unfit to care for them. Keeping children out of the custody of dysfunctional birth parents is not gratuitous on the part of the state, neither in the context of adoption nor in creating a child's first family, and insisting that the state do so is not a matter of asserting positive rights. In essence, the state stands in a fiduciary role with respect to each newborn child when it makes the parentage decision, and in that role the state must decide based solely on its best judgment of what is in a newborn's child's best interests. A corollary of this view of children's situation is that no adults have a moral right to be in a parent–child relationship with a particular child independently of whether that is in the child's best interests – that is, unless and until the state properly makes a reciprocal choice of that adult on behalf of the child. The right we adults have against forced association does not evaporate when some other person who wishes to initiate an intimate relationship with us has made some extraordinary effort to benefit us; we remain entitled to refuse that partnership on no other grounds than we think it not in our best interests going forward. No plausible moral principle supports a different view of children's right against forced association.[1] (See further Chapters 3.3–5 of this book).

Regulating children's upbringing

To survive and thrive, children need to avoid harmful conduct toward them and to receive several basic goods. Do children have any negative rights to underwrite a demand for these things?

Popular and scholarly discussion of child maltreatment commonly ascribes to children a negative moral right against gratuitous violence, with a corresponding duty on the part of legal parents to refrain from such violence. Many people, however, view the state's status vis-à-vis child maltreatment as that of an innocent bystander. On this view, it violates no negative

---

[1] For fuller treatment of biological parents' moral position in connection with legal parentage, including refutations of arguments based on hypothetical contract or duty of gratitude, see J.G. Dwyer, *The Relationship Rights of Children*, Cambridge: Cambridge University Press, 2006, ch. 7. For description of their constitutional position, see J.G. Dwyer, 'A Constitutional Birthright: The State, Parentage, and Newborn Persons', *UCLA Law Rev.* 56, 2009, 755–835, 812–20.

The moral basis of children's relational rights

right of children to leave them unprotected from parental abuse or neglect, and a demand for state protection amounts to an assertion of positive right against the state, a claim for assistance rather than forbearance, something the Anglo-American legal system is generally loath to ascribe to individuals.

But this is a quite inaccurate perception of the state's situation. As shown earlier, the state plays a crucial role in creating parent–child relationships in the first place. The state also plays a crucial role in children's daily lives after legal and social parent–child relationships are in place, because it establishes the legal rules that govern those relationships, including rules that confer on legal parents extraordinary power over various aspects of children's lives. Negative rights of the child constrain the state's choices as to the content of that power, just as negative rights of incompetent adults constrain the state's conferral of power over their lives on guardians. The default legal regime in western society is that everyone, including children, possesses a negative right against encroachment on their lives and bodies by other private parties. We all also possess a negative right against others interfering with our efforts to obtain the basic necessities of life in a legal manner, such as employment or soliciting help from others. For certain adults to be legally free to take a child, into their home, restrain the child, remove the child's clothing, physically discipline the child and otherwise engage in normal parenting behaviour, to the exclusion of other adults who might wish to help a child, they require special legal dispensation. The state must attach various legal privileges and powers to the legal parent role. Someone without legal parent status and such legal dispensation who took a child home and confined the child, removed the child's clothing and spanked the child, would be subject to prosecution for serious crimes. As with conferral of legal parent status, the state must be able to justify its bestowal of particular privileges and powers on parents, which is concomitant with a withdrawal of certain rights and immunities from the child, by reference to children's needs. No other legitimate basis exists for giving private parties licence to infringe children's negative rights to bodily integrity, privacy and liberty. Children have a negative right against the state's legally authorising any other private party to inflict gratuitous violence or sexual acts on them or the state's giving exclusionary powers to adult custodians who are not prepared to fulfill all a child's developmental needs.

The analogy to adult intimate relationships again helps reinforce this position. As a general matter, adults possess negative rights against physical incursions and forced isolation, and they presumptively carry these with them into marriage. For marrying to limit or eliminate those negative rights would require the state to enact special legal rules authorising one spouse to do things to the other that would violate a negative right absent the marital relationship. The state in Anglo-American legal culture in fact once did this; it authorised husbands to physically chastise, force sex on and confine their wives. If the law gave such authorisation today, the legal community and advocates for women would characterise it as a gross violation of women's negative rights *by the state*. This would be so even though women are legally and practically free not to enter into a legal marriage at all if they wish to remain immune to such withdrawal of rights. It is even more clearly an infringement of children's negative rights for the state, after forcing a child to be in a family relationship with particular adults, additionally to give those adults a legal licence to hit the child and to prevent the child from interactions with other people which would benefit the child.

A somewhat different question, though, is whether the state owes any obligation to children or wives to *enforce* any legal prohibitions on violence against them in ongoing family relationships. Are vulnerable persons' negative rights fully respected if the state simply refrains from forcing them into relationships with people known at the time to pose a danger of abuse or neglect and refrains from legally *authorising* other private parties to harm them? Do vulnerable people have a right to the state's assistance in avoiding private *illegal* harmful behaviour?

One answer rests on the equal protection right all persons possess against the state's arbitrarily treating some group less favorably than other persons. If the state enacts and generally enforces a prohibition against private violence but adopts a policy and practice of enforcing it less or not at all when the victim is the perpetrator's child, there is unequal treatment the state must justify. It certainly could not do so on the grounds that protection from violence is unimportant for or less needed by children. The state should bear the burden of showing that children would somehow be made even worse off if the state enforced child abuse laws more vigorously, and empirical support for such a showing does not exist.

Another way to answer these questions is to emphasise that children, at least young ones, are incapable of exiting from a parent–child relationship. In contrast, spouses are generally are able to leave a marriage if their partner engages in harmful behaviour. Children's inability to exit means the state's placing them in a particular family and then declining to remove them from that family despite learning of abuse plays a crucial causal role in their suffering. Conceptually, the state effectively every day renews its decision to place each child in the care of particular adults; it is always either deciding to continue a given child's custody with the same people or deciding to switch custody to other persons. If state actors become aware that existing custodians are abusing a child, to an extent that the child would be better off if permanently removed from those custodians and placed in a different home, children's *negative* rights require the state to do that rather than continuing to confer custodial rights on known abusers.

Lastly, there is question as to the state's obligation to ensure children receive goods conducive to their healthy development, such as shelter, clothing, food, supervision, schooling of a certain quality and medical care. (See further Chapters 6.1–6.2 of this book.) This is the realm of neglect law. Most political theorising relating to child rearing has focused narrowly on education and whether the state *may* ensure children receive a secular education promoting autonomy and broad knowledge by imposing compulsory schooling laws and substantive regulation of private school instruction. Theorists fail to recognise that the analysis is the same whether the issue is school curriculum or food. As to either, parents might have reasons, religious or secular, for denying children what the state thinks children ought to receive. As to either, proponents of parents' rights or religious freedom might contend that the state may not force parents either to provide or to allow the state to provide what the parents do not wish children to have. In addition to this question of *permissibility* of state action, though, there is also the question whether the state *must* ensure these things for children – that is, whether children have a right to these goods and to state action that ensures they receive them.

The permissibility question is relatively easy. Just as an adult is entitled to demand certain things as a condition for entering into and then remaining in a marriage, every child has a moral right, which the state would effectuate, to condition acceptance of a family relationship with particular adults (whether birth parents or adoptive parents) on their agreement to abide by certain reasonable conditions. So long as it is consistent with the welfare of children generally (e.g. will not deter too many would-be parents), the state must be free to say to all persons wishing to become legal parents, 'These are the terms, enshrined in law, to which you must agree in exchange for our bestowing on you legal parent status. If you find these terms unacceptable, you are free not to serve as parents to any child; other people can raise this child, on the terms the law has set'. The view that legal parents are entitled to set their own terms of engagement with children is morally groundless.[2]

The harder question is whether the state could choose *not* to require of parents that they provide certain goods to children. Would it thereby violate any right of children? Again, the analysis should be the same for food and education; both are necessary to positive development, yet some parents might be indifferent or believe their children should receive something radically different from what the state values. Could the state confer legal parent status and custody as to a child on particular adults and then remain indifferent as to whether those adults gave the child any food? Or do children have a right to the state's imposing a feeding duty on custodians? If parents' religion tells them children should subsist only on lettuce, is the state permitted to indulge their faith?

The best answer to these questions might rest on a contract rationale and on the concept of fiduciary duty. As explained above, when the state chooses persons to serve as legal parents and custodians, it effectively acts as a proxy or agent for the child, authorised to make this decision for children solely because they cannot make it themselves, and required to exercise that authority solely to further the child's well-being. The state acts in a fiduciary capacity, bound to choose the best parents from among adults willing to serve; there is no justification for it substituting or adding any other aim in carrying out this function. And it should seek to establish the best possible terms for children in effectively striking a bargain with potential parents. So we should ask what is the best deal, in terms of expectations for provision of goods, that the state, as agent for children, can demand of prospective parents. That could vary depending on social and economic circumstances, but in modern western societies, the expectation could certainly include a parental commitment to provide adequate housing, clothing, nutrition, supervision, and protection; to secure the preventive and remedial medical treatment professionals recommend; and to not get in the way of children receiving a liberal education. For the state not to demand these things of parents would violate the right of children correlative to the state's fiduciary duty owed to them, just as a lawyer would breach a fiduciary duty to a client by negotiating a contract in which the client provides goods and services to the other party but gets nothing in return. Enforcing neglect laws against deficient parents amounts in a sense to contract enforcement, holding parents to the terms they implicitly agreed to when they asked to be made legal parents to a child, and the state would also fail in its fiduciary duty to children by failing to monitor and police contract compliance.

Does that leave room for accommodating parental values or ideological beliefs that diverge from the state's secular values and mainstream beliefs? Yes, but less room than current law in most Anglo-American jurisdictions gives. Some differences in values or beliefs are not of great significance to children's well-being, and it would be unwise for the state to refuse to concede parental freedom as to those. For example, medical professionals might not think occasional fasting periods some religions dictate are optimal for children, but any detriment might be so insignificant that a wise agent for children would indulge that practice, to avoid driving away too many potential parents or making the parental role unnecessarily unpleasant. In addition, the value for children of being raised by biological parents might outweigh the value to children of being raised by people who have no such minor differences of value or

---

2 For more thorough critique of the concept of parental child-rearing rights, see J. G. Dwyer, 'Parents' Religion and Children's Welfare: Debunking the Doctrine of Parents' Rights', *California Law Review* 82, 1994, 1371–447.

belief, so some biological parents will be the best available legal parents for their offspring despite their departure from what the state deems ideal. Further, children learn much from exposure to different values and beliefs and from experiencing particularistic culture within the family. These reasons for accommodation are not sufficiently strong, however, to warrant accommodations that would cause substantial detriment to children. They are insufficient to justify, for example, empowering parents to deny children immunisations, medical care for treatable injuries and illnesses, or a liberal education. What we know about child development suggests newborn children would be better off on the whole if the state, as their agent, chose biologically unrelated adults to serve in the parental role rather than birth parents who would deny them these important goods.

Conclusion

Children's moral (and constitutional) rights are stronger in content than is generally supposed. The main obstacle to achieving for them the better parentage decision making and protection from abuse and neglect to which they are entitled is their inability to advocate on their own behalf coupled with lack of substantial adult constituency advocating forcefully on their behalf. The lack of support among adults for reformation of parentage and maltreatment laws, in turn, reflects a general adult-centric mentality and failure to perceive the negative-rights nature of children's entitlements. The flip-side of misconstruing children's moral position as that of beggars pleading for help is a mistaken view that conferring legal parent status and custody on biological parents, and empowering legal parents to do harmful things to children, is a necessary deference to the negative rights of those adults. In fact, it is the adult members of parent–child relationship who effectively ask the state to give them an extraordinary and gratuitous benefit – namely, possession and control of another human being.

7

The changing face of adoption – the gift/donation model versus the contract/services model[†]

INTRODUCTION

This article first examines how much adoption has altered during the 70 or so years of its existence under English law. In particular, it will examine how the nature of the work has changed, how the organisation of adoption work has developed, how practice has altered, and, finally, how the law itself has been modified. These enquiries, however, are really a means to an end, which is to explore whether in the light of the changed nature of adoption, the current law and practice are adequate. It will be my contention that the 'mind set' which is, rightly or wrongly, associated with the adoption of babies, still permeates thinking not only behind the law and, possibly to a lesser extent, practice, but also the attitudes of the adopters themselves. Under this 'mind set', which in this article is labelled the 'gift/donation model', adoption is seen very much as the last and irrevocable act in a process in which the birth parent – normally, of course, the mother – has 'given away' her baby via the adoption agency to the adopters, who are then left to their own devices and resources to bring up the child as their own. Associated with this model is the 'exclusive' view of adoption, ie that the child is both *de jure* and *de facto* transplanted *exclusively* to the adoptive family, with no further contact or relationship with the birth family. This model, however, sits uneasily with the adoption of older children, and it will be my contention that in these instances, at least, a different model is needed in which it is recognised that adoption is not the end of the process, but merely part of an ongoing and often complex process of family development.

I should explain also by way of introduction that the underlying thesis has been prompted by research, funded by the Department of Health, that my colleague Professor Mervyn Murch and I have been conducting into 'support services for families of older children adopted out of care'.[1] In the course of this research, which was about support *during* the adoption process, ie from the time that adoption was proposed until one year after the order in relation to children aged five or over, we received detailed questionnaire returns from 115 out of 160 adoption agencies (85 statutories and 30 voluntaries), followed up by an intensive study comprising 45 interviews with agency workers, and from 226 families with whom a child aged five or over had been placed between 1 January 1992 and 31 December 1994, followed up by 48 interviews.

[†] This article is the text of a lecture given at a seminar organised by *Child and Family Law Quarterly* and held at All Souls College, Oxford on 1 July 1997.

[‡] The author is indebted to his colleague, Professor Mervyn Murch, for his many helpful comments on earlier drafts of this article.

[1] This project was conducted at Cardiff Law School from January 1993 until July 1997. The research team, apart from the directors, comprised Margaret Borkowski, Verna Beckford, Caroline Thomas, and Anna Weaver. A full report of the project will be published in due course. A preliminary report was presented to the project's advisory committee on 24 July 1997. The final part of the project resulting from interviews of 40 children (aged eight or over) who have recently been adopted is due to be completed in the spring of 1998.

THE CHANGING FACE OF ADOPTION

The changing nature of the work

The changing face of adoption is, in part, well-illustrated by the statistics.[2]

Two messages are clear: first, adoption is in decline, at the moment deep decline; secondly, baby adoptions have virtually disappeared. Whereas from its creation by the Adoption of Children Act 1926 until the late 1960s the numbers rose steadily from 2943 in 1927, 7775 in 1940, 12,739 in 1950 (there had been a marked, post-war surge in 1944–48), 15,099 in 1960, to a peak of 24,831 in 1968 (the 1960s saw an explosion of adoptions), since then it has declined – from 22,373 in 1970, under 10,000 in 1980 (7908, excluding magistrates), 7452 in 1992, to 4936 in 1996 which, incidentally, is comparable to the figures of the mid 1930s.

So far as baby adoptions are concerned, ie children under the age of 12 months, whereas in 1970 some 8833 babies were adopted, amounting to 39 per cent of the total number, in 1977 there were only 3000, amounting to 23 per cent of the then total of 13,000 adoptions, and in 1991 there were said to be 900, amounting to 12 per cent of the then total of at least 7059 adopters.[3] At any rate, according to the marriage and divorce statistics in 1992 there were just 660 baby adoptions, amounting to approximately nine per cent, while in 1995 that figure again dropped to 332, amounting to six per cent of the total.

The obvious corollary of the decline in baby adoption is the rising *proportion* of older child adoptions. In 1970, for example, 20 per cent of the children adopted were aged between five and nine with a further 10 per cent aged 10 or over. By 1995 these proportions had risen to 37 per cent and 31 per cent respectively. These figures, however, mask another important change: in 1970, for instance, whereas most adoptions by non-relatives were of babies or toddlers, most of the adoptions of older children – in fact 90 per cent of the five to nine age group and 84 per cent of those aged 10 or over – were by step-parents. Today the profile is different. About half of all adoptions are step-parent adoptions (in 1996, 55 per cent of adoption orders were made in favour of step-parents) and half by strangers. However, in a recent study by the Social Services Inspectorate,[4] half the children referred to the adoption service of the agencies inspected were aged six or over. In our own study, out of a national sample of 1525 children placed for adoption by adoption agencies, both statutory and voluntary, in 1993–94, 42 per cent were aged five or over. In other words, as far as adoptions by non-relatives are concerned, baby adoptions have now become relatively unusual, while the adoption of older children, those aged five or above, has become quite normal.

The changing organisation of adoption work

When adoption was first introduced into England and Wales by the Adoption of Children Act 1926 it was remarkably unregulated. The 1926 Act essentially provided, as Stephen Cretney has put it, 'a process whereby, under minimal safeguards supervised by the court, a civil contract was registered and recognised'.[5] There were no provisions regulating who could

---

[2] One has to be say that the official statistics have become less informative and even vary from one source, for example annual judicial statistics, to another, for example the marriage and divorce statistics. The following statistics are based on those found in the Houghton Committee Report, *Report of the Departmental Committee on the Adoption of Children* (HMSO, 1972) Cmnd 5107, at appendix B; the relevant *Judicial Statistics Annual Reports*, and the *Marriage and Divorce Statistics* (Office for National Statistics, 1995), Series SM2, No 22.

[3] Query the accuracy of this figure – it was quoted in Department of Health, Welsh Office, Home Office, Lord Chancellor's Department, *Adoption: The Future* (HMSO, 1993), Cm 2288.

[4] *For Children's Sake: An SSI Inspection of Local Authority Adoptions Services* (Department of Health, 1996). In its second report, *For Children's Sake II* (Department of Health, 1997), 62.9 per cent of the children placed for adoption were aged six or over, and only three per cent were under the age of 12 months.

[5] 'From Status to Contract?', in Rose (ed), *Consensus Ad Idem* (Barry Rose, 1996), at p 252.

arrange adoptions. However, following the recommendations of the Horsburgh Committee[6] section 1 of the Adoption of Children (Regulation) Act 1939 made it an offence for a body of persons other than a registered adoption society or a local authority to make any arrangements for the adoption of children. By section 2 a system of local registration of adoption societies was introduced. Under section 4 the Secretary of State was empowered to make regulations, *inter alia*, to: (a) ensure that parents wishing to place their children for adoption were given written explanation of their legal position; (b) prescribe the inquiries to be made and reports to be obtained to ensure the suitability of the child and adopter; and (c) to secure that no child would be delivered to an adopter until he had been interviewed by a case committee.

Although the 1939 Act made express provision for local authorities to arrange adoptions, the major work continued to be done by the voluntary societies, although the law was later clarified, by section 7(2) of the Adoption of Children Act 1949, to make it clear that the local authorities had power 'under any enactment relating to children to make and participate in arrangements for the adoption of children'. The Hurst Committee, which reported in 1954,[7] recommended that local authorities should be empowered to arrange for the adoption of any child without that child having to be in care. The Committee made that recommendation not because it wished to see local authorities usurp the function of voluntary adoption societies but because it had been 'impressed by the fact that it is clearly impossible for the small number of societies [then numbering 60–70] to cover the needs of the whole country'.

The Hurst Committee was particularly concerned with the placement stage which it saw as the crucial stage since, 'Once the child is placed, much harm and unhappiness may result if a change has to be made'. It was the Committee's view that adoptions arranged by persons of special experience and training stood a much better chance of success. However, whilst it recommended that social workers employed by societies be fully trained, it stopped short of recommending the prohibition of private or third party placements. That particular bullet was bitten by the Houghton Committee[8] and, following its recommendation, private placements of children for adoption by non-relatives became an offence with effect from 1982, when section 28 of the Children Act 1975 was brought into force.

It was at the moment that one might say the process of the 'professionalisation of adoption work' was completed. The Houghton Committee wanted to see the establishment of a *nationwide* comprehensive adoption service. As it noted, at the time of its Report in 1972, only 96 of the 172 local authorities in England and Wales acted as adoption agencies. What the Committee wished to see was a comprehensive service available to 'all those needing it in any part of the country'. The Committee accordingly recommended that *all* local authorities should have a statutory duty to provide an adoption service as part of their general child care and family case work provision. Further, having acknowledged that voluntary adoption societies had been pioneers of adoption and that they had a valuable continuing role to play, *inter alia*, to provide a choice of service, the Houghton Committee recommended that local authorities should have a statutory duty 'to ensure, in co-operation with voluntary societies, that a comprehensive adoption service is available throughout their area'.[9] Registration of voluntary societies was recommended to be national rather than local.[10]

These recommendations were accepted and, so far as the adoption service was concerned, were implemented in 1988 under what became section 1 of the Adoption Act 1976. Although

---

[6] *Report of the Departmental Committee on Adoption Societies and Agencies* (HMSO, 1937), Cmd 5499.
[7] *Report of the Departmental Committee on the Adoption of Children* (HMSO, 1954), Cmd 9248, at para 24. See also Goodacre *Adoption Policy and Practice* (Allen and Unwin, 1966), who advocated that all adoptions by strangers be handled by local authorities.
[8] Op cit, n 2, at paras 84–90, and recommendation 13.
[9] Ibid, at para 42, and recommendation 3.
[10] Ibid, at paras 51–55, and recommendation 5. Registration was recommended to be renewable every three years.

voluntary societies continued to deal with the majority of agency adoptions through to the 1970s – in 1966, for example, of adoptions arranged by agencies, 73 per cent were arranged by voluntaries, as against 29 per cent by local authorities – by 1971 the gap was already closing, with voluntaries dealing with 60 per cent of cases. Now, with the demise of baby adoptions, the majority of agency work is done by the statutory agencies, although exact figures are not available. In our study, for example, out of a national sample of 1557 children placed for adoption in 1993–94 84 per cent were placed by statutory agencies, compared with 16 per cent by voluntary agencies.

In fact, our study showed wide variations in the workload of agencies, both statutory and voluntary alike. For example, three agencies, two statutory and one voluntary, had not approved a single family in the last year of their records while at the other end of the scale one statutory agency approved 67 families. As far as children were concerned the numbers ranged from none to 91 'approvals'[11] in one year. This variation in load has led us to speculate what is a viable number for agency practice – our preliminary thinking is about 15–20 placements per year.

Another important development in the organisation of adoption work is the move towards consortia, network or association of agencies, which is an increasing feature of the adoption world but which falls outside the scope of this article.

As far as individuals seeking to adopt a non-relative are concerned, adoption is fully regulated. They must first be approved by an agency, which entails a thorough screening process conducted by what are now known as adoption panels[12] both as to the applicants' commitment to and motive for seeking to adopt, as well as of their lifestyle, stability of their relationships and, of course, their ability to provide a loving and permanent home for any child. Having been approved, applicants must then wait, often for several months, until the agency has found what it considers to be a suitable match. There are then various and sometimes elaborate and imaginative introduction processes before placement and then, if the placement is successful, after a minimum period of 13 weeks, an application can be made to the court for an adoption order. Each of these stages is fraught with difficulty and anxiety, and often requires considerable support. Our research certainly echoes what was recognised by all three Committees, the Horsburgh, Hurst and Houghton, just what a crucial stage the matching and introduction process is. To back this up we obtained an interesting analysis by agencies replying to our questionnaire of the disruptions occurring in the last year of the agencies' records, as to the stage when those disruptions occurred, as follows.

	Statutory agencies	Voluntary agencies
During placements (pre-order)	94 per cent	80 per cent
One year after order	three per cent	seven per cent
More than one year after order	three per cent	13 per cent

Overall sample size: 188 cases

---

[11] In the case of statutory agencies 'approved' means approved for adoption by an adoption panel in their agency. In the case of voluntary agencies 'approved' refers to children who were placed for adoption or who were found adoptive placements.
[12] For the constitution of which see the Adoption Agencies Regulations 1983 (SI 1983/1964), reg 5 as substituted by SI 1997/649.

Changing practice

As already mentioned, a key change in adoption practice was that of placing older children out of care for adoption. That, in turn, sprang from the child care policy which, in the 1970s, began in the UK to be termed permanency planning.[13] It was undoubtedly stimulated by the seminal work of Goldstein, Freud and Solnit, *Beyond the Best Interests of the Child*[14] in which they challenged the then prevailing traditional mode of thought that biological and legal parenthood should take precedence over psychological parenthood. Their thesis was intended to reinforce the security of the adoptive, psychological parent/child relationship. Many of their – at the time revolutionary – notions subsequently came to be accepted by social work and legal practitioners working in the child care and adoption fields, and although such ideas were later questioned and qualified, a powerful residue has permeated professional thinking ever since. Certainly, they strengthened the view that children from neglectful, disrupted and severely disordered families might often do much better if placed permanently with loving, secure and more stable families.

This change of attitude was accompanied by a much more determined effort to secure adoption placements for so-called hard to place children – to the extent of having extensive publicity campaigns, one of the best known being the 'Be my Parent' scheme organised by British Agencies for Adoption and Fostering. To agencies' initial surprise, they were able to find people willing to take on children with all sorts of disadvantages and such willingness would now no longer be commented upon – even being taken for granted – although this, in turn, can create its own difficulties.

Adoption of older children meant, of course, that the legal fiction of a family transplant was more difficult to sustain, and it is no accident that adoption with some form of continuing contact began in the 1970s while, at the same time, there were stronger efforts and entreaties that children should be told of their adoption (although in this respect it might be noted that the Hurst Committee specifically recommended[15] that all adopters should be required to give a formal undertaking to tell the child about his/her adoption) and the eventual enactment of the 'right' of the adult adopted child to obtain his original birth certificate.[16]

Today, the practice of so-called 'open adoption' is very much a fact of adoption life.[17] Of the respondents to our family questionnaire we found that about half had met the birth mother, and 21 per cent the father. There were also a substantial number who had had some form of contact with other birth relatives, and nearly as many had ongoing contact after the adoption order. Indeed, considerable post-adoption work is involved with various forms of contact, whether it is direct or indirect – and, if the latter, through letter-box and telephone schemes.[18] Reflecting this *de facto* growth in post-adoption contact and evident change of policy is the change of recruiting practice. As one social worker told to us:

> 'The whole issue of contact, letter-boxes, post-adoption work and that sort of thing has just come into our practice. It is also a standard feature of our assessment. There is a line in our agreement with prospective adopters which says Mr and Mrs Smith would be very happy for you to exchange information [ref to letter-box contact scheme]. That's just par for the course now. In fact if Mr and Mrs Smith weren't happy with that then we would wonder whether we should be approving them as adopters.'

---

[13] See, particularly Parker, *Planning for Deprived Children* (National Children's Homes, 1971).
[14] Free Press, 1973.
[15] Op cit, n 7, at para 150.
[16] Discussed further below.
[17] That is not, however, meant to imply that continued contact is *always* in the child's interests.
[18] A detailed discussion of contact will be included in our full report.

This last point was echoed by another comment, 'Our agency has a policy of only recruiting prospective adopters who understand what openness means and are prepared to actively work with it'. This is not to say that we did not find consumer resistance to this; indeed, one adoptive couple questioned the whole rationale for contact and whether it is really helpful to a child's development, especially as the child has to hold in mind and understand so many relationships. When the couple sought to explain this to adoption agency staff they were told in no uncertain terms that their views were 'old fashioned' and unacceptable in the light of the agency's policy on open adoption and supporting contact. They had, therefore, in their own words 'to soft peddle' and keep their mouths shut. But, in fact, the couple accept letter-box contact with their adoptive daughter's half-brother and a great aunt in her eighties.

Changing legal position

INTRODUCTION

Under Adoption Act 1976, sections 12(1), (3) and 39 an adoption order effects a complete and irrevocable transfer of legal parentage. In other words it is of the very essence of adoption that the prior legal relationship between the adults (usually the birth parents) or institution (ie local authorities) and the child is permanently extinguished and replaced by a new legal relationship between the adopters and the child. It is this permanence and totality of the transferred relationship that distinguishes adoption from fostering, residence orders under the Children Act 1989 and even guardianship. It is to be observed, however, that in the past the legal effects of adoption have not always been the same, while the central notions of permanence and legal severance, particularly the latter, have to some extent been softened or come under recent attack.

Although I would maintain that from the beginning adoption meant the irrevocable transfer of legal parentage, there are those,[19] who maintain that because Adoption of Children Act 1926, section 5(2) expressly refrained from altering an adopted child's succession rights, in its early years adoption could best be described as creating a special kind of guardianship. Be that as it may, such arguments ended when sections 9 and 10 of the Adoption Act 1949 (a Private Members Bill) provided that adopted persons should be treated for the purposes of the devolution or disposal of real or personal property as if they were children of adopters.[20]

Notwithstanding these foregoing statements, adoption has never been absolutely irrevocable, nor has it ever provided for complete severance in the sense of totally ignoring the *de facto* origins of the child. This article will not explore those cases where an adoption has been set aside; suffice to say that there have been some truly extraordinary cases where it has,[21] but there are limits to this power[22] in that it cannot be exercised many years after the order.

I want to explore in a little more detail what I have called the *inroads to severance*. First, there are some long-established incidences, ie that the adopted child remains within the same prohibited degrees of his natural family, that the order does not affect the law relating to incest, and that a child of British citizenship does not lose it if adopted by a foreign natural.[23]

---

[19] See, for example the Hurst Committee, op cit, n 7, at para 196.

[20] Although as Stephen Cretney has pointed out *total* integration of the child into the adoptive family for succession purposes was only finally achieved by the Children Act 1975: *Consensus Ad Idem*, op cit, n 5, at p 266.

[21] Not the least of which is the so-called 'Bosnian child case', *Re K (Adoption and Wardship)* [1997] 2 FLR 221. Note also that former parents are not necessarily prevented from seeking a residence or contact order under s 8 – although, like any other stranger, they will require court leave.

[22] As illustrated by *Re B (Adoption: Jurisdiction to Set Aside)* [1995] Fam 239.

[23] See Adoption Act 1976, s 47(1) and (2), and the Sexual Offences Act 1956. For the effect on pensions and insurance see ss 48 and 49 of the 1976 Act. For the background to some of these points see Stephen Cretney, *Consensus Ad Idem*, op cit, n 5, at pp 266–268.

However, aside from these rather specialised issues, and more importantly, from the point of view of this article, are four areas, namely, post-adoption contact, tracing parents, adoption allowances, and post-adoption support, which do need to be explored further.

INROADS INTO SEVERANCE

Post-adoption contact

The first reported case in which it was held that continued contact was not fundamentally inconsistent with adoption was *Re J (A Minor) (Adoption Order: Conditions)*.[24] In that case Rees J said, 'the general rule which forbids contact between an adopted child and his natural parent may be disregarded in an exceptional case where a court is satisfied that by so doing the welfare of the child may be best promoted'.[25] The access order was made to avoid lengthy litigation which would otherwise have damaged the child.

This decision was authoritatively confirmed by the House of Lords in *Re C (A Minor) (Adoption Orders: Condition)*[26] in which Lord Ackner said:

> 'The cases rightly stress that in normal circumstances it is desirable that there should be a complete break, but that each case has to be considered on its own particular facts. No doubt it will not, except in the most exceptional case, impose terms or conditions as to access to members of the child's natural family to which the adopting parents do not agree.'[27]

Before the Children Act 1989 any regime of contact had to be made under the power conferred by section 12(6) to attach conditions to an adoption order. Although this power still exists, the obvious and simpler method now is to couple an adoption order with a section 8 contact order.[28] Notwithstanding this power, the courts are generally reluctant to use it, particularly if it means imposing an order on unwilling adopters. Where they are agreed that contact should continue, it has been said in *Re T (Adoption: Contact)*[29] that there is no need for an order. Although this approach seems eminently reasonable given the well known difficulty of enforcing contact orders, it is not at all clear that this is the sole reason behind the reluctance. Note, for example, the comment of Butler-Sloss LJ in *Re T (Adoption: Contact)* in which she said, ' ... the finality of adoption and the importance of letting the new family find its own feet ought not to be threatened in any way by an order [for contact] in this case'.[30] This comment is not exactly consistent with the *de facto* practice of open adoption.

In important contrast is *Re T (Adopted Children: Contact)*[31] in which Balcombe LJ held that adopters cannot agree to indirect contact and then simply resile from it without explanation. Where they do, the court might well be disposed to grant the former parents leave to apply for a section 8 contact order. In this case leave was given, the court being satisfied that the proposed application would not disrupt the children's lives, although all that was in issue was the adopters' promise to provide the birth parents with annual reports.

---

[24] [1973] Fam 106.
[25] Ibid, at p 115.
[26] [1989] 1 AC 1.
[27] Ibid, at p 17.
[28] In fact this is the only way contact can be provided for on a freeing order since the power under s 12(6) to attach conditions applies only to full adoption orders.
[29] [1995] 2 FLR 251.
[30] Ibid, at p 257.
[31] [1995] 2 FLR 792.

Tracing parents

An important inroad into severance is the provision under section 51 of the Adoption Act 1976 by which adult adopted children can obtain a copy of their original birth certificate from which they may be able to trace their parents.[32] This had been first recommended by the Hurst Committee – it was the Houghton Committee recommendation – based on John Triseliotis' work on the Scottish provisions, which permitted it – that finally prompted reform. This provision came into force in 1975 and was controversially retrospective.

By 1990 it was estimated[33] that some 33,000 adopted children had taken advantage of this provision, while according to Stafford 3500 people received birth records counselling in 1991.[34]

Although access to birth records enables some adopted persons to trace and make contact with their birth parents, until the creation of the Adoption Contact Register in 1991[35] it was difficult to discover whether that contact would be welcome. The purpose of the Register is 'to put adopted people and their birth parents or other relatives in touch with each other where this is what they both want. The Register provides a safe and confidential way for birth parents and other relatives to assure an adopted person that contact would be welcome and give a contact address'.[36]

The Register comprises two parts:[37] Part I, upon which is maintained the name and address of any adopted person who is over 18 and has a copy of his birth certificate and who wishes to contact a relative; and Part II, upon which is entered, subject to certain prescribed conditions,[38] the current address and identifying details of a relative[39] who wishes to contact an adopted person. The proposed Adoption Bill contains in clause 65(2) the provision that the Contact Register be extended to allow birth parents and relatives to register their wish *not* to be contacted.

It may be noted that there is no facility for exchanging limited information, such as medical information, nor is an agency required to retain records, let alone disclose to the adopted person or others information it has about adoption. However, as Cretney and Masson observe,[40] some agencies are prepared to disclose the information they have about the adoption, although this depends upon 'its nature, the perceived ability of the adopted person to cope with it and their intentions'. Under clause 48 of the proposed Adoption Bill agencies would be required to provide specified, non-identifiable information to the adoptive parents when the adoption order is made.

---

[32] Although not as an absolute right: see *R v Registrar General ex parte Smith* [1991] 1 FLR 255 – danger to birth mother.

[33] Inter-Departmental Review of Adoption Law, Discussion Paper No 1, *The Nature and Effect of Adoption* (Department of Health, 1990), at note 140.

[34] Stafford, 'Section 51 counselling' (1993) 1 *Adoption & Fostering* 4, at p 5.

[35] Under Adoption Act 1976, s 51A (added by Children Act 1989, Sch 10, para 21) the Registrar General is required to maintain such a Register. In fact the Register is operated on behalf of the Registrar General by the Office of Population Censuses and Surveys.

[36] Department of Health, *The Children Act 1989: Guidance and Regulations* (HMSO, 1991), vol 9: *Adoption Issues*, at para 3.2.

[37] Adoption Act 1976, s 51A(2).

[38] Upon payment of a prescribed fee, that the applicant is aged 18 or over, that the Registrar General has either a record of the applicant's birth or sufficient information to obtain a certified copy of the record of the birth, and that the applicant is a relative: Adoption Act 1976, s 51A(3)–(6).

[39] Ie 'any person (other than an adoptive relative) who is related to the adopted person by blood (including half-blood) or marriage': Adoption Act 1976, s 51A(13)(a).

[40] *Principles of Family Law* (Sweet & Maxwell, 6th edn, 1997), at p 885, in turn relying on Haines and Timms, *Adoption, Identity and Social Policy* (Gower, 1985).

Adoption allowances

Consistent with the notion that adoption severs all previous legal relationships, including that with the local authority where the child was previously in care,[41] there was for a long time no provision for the payment of adoption allowances by an agency. The suggestion that some provision might be made was first floated in the working paper produced by the Houghton Committee[42] on the basis that more adoptive homes might be found for children in need. This suggestion was not well received,[43] the principal objection being that it would amount to discriminating against natural parents.[44] In any event it was argued that the subsidising of adoption went against the notion that the child should be put in precisely the same position as a child born to the adopters. Notwithstanding this opposition, the Houghton Committee recommended that 'the law should be amended to permit pilot schemes of payment of allowances to adopters under the general oversight of the Secretary of State'.[45]

The issue proved equally controversial in Parliament and, indeed, in Standing Committee it was only the chairman's casting vote that saved the provision.[46] Nevertheless, a provision permitting an adoption agency to submit a scheme for the payment of an adoption allowance for approval by the Secretary of State was enacted under section 32 of the Children Act 1975, which was brought into force on 15 February 1982. Later this provision was replaced by section 56(4)–(7) of the Adoption Act 1976.

At the time of implementation the expectation was that there would be relatively few schemes, but it rapidly became apparent that most agencies would seek to have a scheme[47] and in fact by the 1990s virtually all statutory agencies and many voluntary agencies had successfully applied for a scheme.[48] Reflecting this overall position, the law was changed by the Children Act 1989[49] so as to empower all agencies to pay an adoption allowance provided such payments conform to the requirements set out by the Adoption Allowance Regulations 1991.[50] In other words, instead of a series of individual schemes there is now uniform provision covering all payments of adoption allowances. Under the present law, all agencies have a discretion both whether to pay an allowance at all[51] and, if so, how much.[52] However, reflecting the original intention of the scheme, which was to target payments for a minority of children whose chances of being adopted needed special encouragement, the current guidance

---

[41] See Adoption Act 1976, s 12(3)(aa), added by Children Act 1989, Sch 10, para 3(3).
[42] Houghton, *Working Paper on Adoption of Children* (HMSO, 1970), at paras 119–122.
[43] In fact, as the Committee acknowledged in its final report (op cit, n 2, at para 94), most witnesses were opposed to the suggestion.
[44] As the British Association of Social Workers later put it: 'It would be an intolerable situation if financial resources were made available to subsidise adoption when an allocation of similar resources to the natural parents may have prevented the break up of the family in the first place': *Analysis of the Children Bill* (British Association of Social Workers, 1975), at p 22 – cited by Bevan and Parry, *The Children Act 1975* (Butterworths, 1979), at para 121.
[45] Op cit, n 2, at recommendation 17.
[46] Standing Committee A (Ninth Sitting), cols 447–480.
[47] Within two years 58 applications had been made of which 24 had been approved, see Lambert, 'Adoption allowances in England: an interim report' (1984) 8(3) *Adoption & Fostering* 12.
[48] For details of the early practice, see Lambert and Seglow, *Adoption Allowances in England and Wales: The Early Years* (HMSO, 1988).
[49] Substituting s 57A for s 56(4)–(7) of the Adoption Act 1976.
[50] SI 1991/2030.
[51] However, as *The Children Act 1989: Guidance and Regulations*, op cit, n 36, vol 9: *Adoption Issues*, at para 2.3 points out, voluntary agencies who do not hold themselves out as normally paying allowances, unlike statutory agencies, are not even under an obligation to decide whether or not to pay an allowance, although they are not prevented from doing so in any particular exceptional case.
[52] In no event, however, can the allowance exceed the fostering allowance that would have been payable: reg 3(4)(b) of the Adoption Allowance Regulations 1991.

states: 'Adoption allowances continue to be the exception rather than the norm'. However, like the schemes they replace, the 1991 Regulations are intended to give agencies 'sufficient flexibility to respond to individual needs and circumstances within this overall objective'.[53]

Virtually nothing was said about adoption allowances in the *Review of Adoption Law Consultative Document*[54] other than that it was a 'valuable service' which should continue.[55] However, in clause 13 of the proposed Adoption Bill, the power to pay adoption allowances would be extended to enable allowances to continue to be paid to someone with parental responsibility for the child should the adopters die.[56]

Post-adoption support

Mention has already been made of the Houghton Committee's vision of a nationwide *comprehensive* adoption service. What the Committee had in mind was that such a service:

> 'should comprise a social work service to natural parents, whether married or unmarried, seeking placement for a child ... , skills and facilities for the assessment of the parents' emotional resources, and their personal and social situation; short-term placement facilities for children pending adoption placement; assessment facilities; adoption placement services; aftercare for natural parents who need it; counselling for adoptive families. In addition, it should have access to a range of specialised services, such as medical services (including genetic, psychological assessment services, arrangements for the examination of children and adoptive applications, and medical adviser) and legal advisory services.'[57]

Wide though the Houghton Committee envisaged a comprehensive adoption service to be, it made no mention of *post*-adoption support at all. However, although based on the Houghton Committee's recommendations, the wording of section 1 of the 1976 Act is wide enough to impose a duty on local authorities to provide post-adoption support.

Under section 1(1) of the Adoption Act 1976:

> 'It is the duty of *every* local authority to establish and maintain within their area a service designed to meet the needs in relation to adoption of —
>
> (a) children *who have been* or may be adopted,
>
> (b) parents and guardians of such children, and
>
> (c) persons *who have adopted* or may adopt a child and for that purpose to provide the requisite facilities, or secure that they are provided by approved adoption societies.'[58]

---

[53] *The Children Act 1989: Guidance and Regulations*, op cit, n 36, vol 9: *Adoption Issues*, at para 2.2.
[54] *Review of Adoption Law, Report to Ministers of an Interdepartmental Working Group: A Consultative Document* (Department of Health and Welsh Office, 1992).
[55] Ibid, at para 27.11.
[56] *Adoption Bill: A Consultative Document* (Department of Health and Welsh Office, 1996). This proposal is apparently based on the lesson learned from the operation of the 1991 Regulations. An example might be where, following the death of the adopters, an older sibling decides to take care of the adopted child and applies for a residence order: see the notes to clause 13 of the proposed Bill.
[57] Ibid, at para 38.
[58] Emphasis added.

It is now[59] accepted that by referring to children who '*have been adopted*' as well as those who may be adopted and to persons '*who have adopted*' as well as to '*persons who may*' adopt, section 1(1) imposes an obligation to provide a *post*-adoption service. These somewhat general provisions are supplemented to a certain extent by the Adoption Agencies Regulations 1983[60] and further guidance as to what an adoption service should comprise is to be found in the Local Authority Circular LAC (87) 8. However, notwithstanding the Regulations and guidance, the fact remains that under the current law there is precious little detailed requirements or guidance as to what a *general* adoption service should comprise. There is, as the Inter-Departmental Review of Adoption Law[61] pointed out, a lack of clarity about what post-adoption services adoption agencies are supposed to provide. This, in turn, has led to a variety of interpretations as to what is required and thus to a consequential patchy provision of services which are 'more often likely to be available from voluntary sources'.

The *Review of Adoption Law* Consultative Document made a number of detailed proposals in relation to the provision of an adoption service.[62] In particular, it recommended that the legislative framework should underline an adopted child's right to know that he or she is adopted and that the agency or guardian should provide a package of information about the child's background to be given to the adoptive parents to make available to the child. The consultative document also recommended that agencies should be under a duty to give birth parents the opportunity to have their own social worker so as to be able to participate in decisions about their child's future. A system should be set up whereby medical information may be passed to the child's doctor, and to inform the adopter that this has been done. The document also recommended that legislation should make it clear that any user of a local authority adoption service should have access to the complaints procedure, and that approved societies should be under a duty to operate a similar complaints procedure. Finally, the document recommended that inspection and approval of voluntary societies should revert to local authorities.

As far as post-adoption services are concerned the Consultative Document recommended that there should be a general counselling service for birth parents, adopters and adopted children.

Notwithstanding the aforementioned recommendations, the Government White Paper, *Adoption: The Future*[63] in fact said little about adoption services, except the following:

> 'Adoptive parents have a right to as much information about their adopted child as is possible. Agencies will therefore be given a duty to prepare for the adopters a package of information including health and family history. The information will also be retained in court records to which the adopted child will have access as of right having reached the age of 18. *Agencies will be encouraged to offer post-adoption support to new families.* This is particularly appreciated by adoptive parents of children with special needs.'[64]

---

[59] One of the first to mention this was Bevan and Parry, *Children Act 1975*, op cit, n 44, at p 15. Post-adoption support is specifically mentioned but only for adult adopted people in the list of services that must be provided in Local Authority Circular LAC (87) 8, *Adoption Act 1976: Implementation*, and Welsh Office Circular 35(8), *Adoption Act 1976: Implementation*.

[60] SI 1983/1964.

[61] Inter-Departmental Review of Adoption Law, Discussion Paper No 3, *The Adoption Process* (Department of Health, 1991), at para 88.

[62] Op cit, n 54. See, generally recommendations 24–33, discussed in Part VII.

[63] Op cit, n 3.

[64] Ibid, at para 4.25. Emphasis added.

Whilst the idea of requiring agencies to provide adopters with a package of information was welcomed, alarm was expressed at the phrase that agencies will be '*encouraged*' to provide post-adoption support, which seems to imply that, unlike the current law, there will be no obligation to do so. In the event, these fears seem unfounded since clause 2(1) of the proposed Adoption Bill provides, in similar terms to section 1(1) of the current law, that:

'Each local authority must continue to maintain within their area a service designed to meet the needs, in relation to adoption, of—

(a) persons who have been or may be adopted,[65]

(b) parents or guardians of such persons, and

(c) persons who have adopted or may adopt a child ... '

Again, the obligation to provide post-adoption support hangs in the phrases '*persons who have been adopted*' and '*persons who have adopted*'. It would surely be better if the obligation to provide post-adoption support were expressly provided for in the statute. It may be noted that to allay any doubts as to whether there is an obligation to provide an adoption service in relation to intercountry adoption, clause 2(5) expressly so provides. A similar provision should surely be added to cover post-adoption support.

ARE THE CURRENT LAW AND PRACTICE ADEQUATE?

The need for a new model

At the beginning of this article reference was made to the 'mind set', which seems to stem from the practice of baby adoptions, that essentially adoption is a gift and is the final and irrevocable act in which the mother has given away her child. The mentality is perfectly captured by Ellison:[66]

'Once an adoption order is made ... the infant passes irrevocably into the family of the adopter. After that neither the adopter nor the natural mother can revoke what has been done; that is the final step. The work of the adoption agency ends in every case with the granting of the order, although adopters sometimes wish to maintain a friendly contact with an agency, particularly when they intend to follow up a first adoption with a second or a sequence. Many people prefer to bring up a family together, rather than an only child who would lack the companionship of brothers and sisters. But once this process has been completed, most adoptive parents prefer to take the advice contained in Mrs Leah Manning's wise remark in the House of Commons – "the most important thing in regard to adoption is that the book should be closed and the curtain come down absolutely".'[67]

It is the thesis of this article that this 'mind set' is certainly inadequate for the adoption of older children and, even possibly, for all types of adoption, yet, notwithstanding the virtual ending of baby adoption, this type of thinking still permeates the law, and legal and social work practice.

As far as legal thinking is concerned, this 'gift mentality' is evident in the contact cases already cited but a further example is *Re S (A Minor) (Blood Transfusion: Adoption Order*

---

[65] The reference to 'persons' rather than to 'children' as in s 1(1)(a) of the Adoption Act 1976 arguably extends the obligation to provide a general support service into adulthood, although whether this is intended, is unclear.
[66] *The Deprived Child and Adoption* (Pan, 1963).
[67] Ibid, at p 76.

Condition)[68] which establishes that conditions should rarely be imposed under section 12(6) of the Adoption Act 1976. Staughton LJ, in that case, commented, 'The best thing for the child in the ordinary way is that he or she should become as near as possible the lawful child of the adopting parents'.[69] The 'gift' mentality is also evident: (a) in the State's thinking both in its ambivalence towards post-adoption support in general, and its reluctance to treat adoption allowances as being appropriate only in unusual circumstances; (b) in social work practice, in that it is essentially geared towards preparing the child and adopters for entry into the family – but not necessarily into the community nor in some ways for after life in the family; and (c) in some adopters who – perhaps naturally enough – consider the adopted child theirs, to the exclusion of all others.

The 'gift/donation' model sits uneasily with the adoption of older children (which current adoption agency practice is increasingly all about) and it seems clear that a new model is needed. At the very least with regard to older children (if not for all children) it needs to be accepted that adoption is not the end of the process but only a stage (albeit an important stage) in an ongoing and often complex process of family development. It is further suggested that adoption of older children out of care is best understood as some kind of informal 'contract' between the birth family, the child and the adoptive family – a 'contract' which brings with it a pattern of reciprocal obligations between the 'parties' and between the adoption agency which performs a brokering role, as well as providing continuing support, while the court holds the ring in this process and puts an important symbolic and official seal to the arrangements.

Under this 'contract/services' model the State should expect to provide substantial support both before, during and after the adoption; the adopters should expect to be informed fully of all the circumstances of the child and to be warned properly of the risks of 'failure' both for the child and for themselves. They should also expect that adoption will not necessarily mean the end of contact with members of the birth family and, although this proposition is made much more tentatively, they may also have to expect that the price of ongoing support is that they may not be in complete control of the child's upbringing. It remains now to examine some of the implications of this new model in more detail.

Some implications of the contract/services model

LEGAL POLICY

Consistent with the general thesis that adoption should not be regarded as the end of the process, the State cannot consider that its obligations towards such children as being *ipso facto* discharged by the making of the order. In other words, its duty to support these needy children and those who take on the task of looking after them, must *prima facie* continue even after the adoption order has been made. Accordingly, it is submitted that it is simply not good enough for the legislation only to impose an *implicit* obligation upon local authorities to provide post-adoption support as part of the general adoption service. The legislation should be changed so as to make provision of post-adoption support an *express* obligation. Furthermore, it will be necessary to accompany this change by providing in subordinate legislation guidance as to precisely what is expected of a post-adoption service.

With regard to adoption allowances it is submitted that it is wrong that: (a) they are regarded as the exception rather than the norm; (b) they are generally lower than fostering allowances; and (c) they should be dependent upon individual agency policy. There is surely a compelling case for society to continue to bear the costs of looking after these especially vulnerable and frequently highly damaged children, particularly those who have previously been removed

---

[68] [1994] 2 FLR 416.
[69] [1994] 2 FLR 416, at p 421.

from their birth family into local authority care on the basis of 'significant harm'[70] and for whom, therefore, the State took on the responsibility to look after them into adulthood. At the very least these children should be entitled to the same level of support as if they were still fostered – the adoption process should surely not financially prejudice such children, nor their adopters. Ideally, a national standardised system of eligibility and level of support should be introduced.

JUDICIAL APPROACH
There remains a judicial assumption that adoption marks the end of the process which is evident in the approach to post-adoption contact, the application of section 12(6) of the Adoption Act 1976 to impose conditions on adoption orders, and with regard to continued contact with the birth family when the long-term plan is for the local authority to place a child for adoption. Although it is submitted that such an assumption needs reassessing that does not necessarily mean that the judicial reluctance to *impose* contact orders on unwilling adopters, for instance, is wrong because there is evident sense in being realistic about ensuing problems of enforcement. Nevertheless, even in this regard care needs to be taken lest pragmatism effectively overrides the child's welfare. There will be cases where it is in the child's interests that he both be adopted and have continued contact with his birth family, and sometimes resort may have to be had to the imposition of a contact order.

Difficulty of enforcement is also a legitimate concern with regard to the imposition of conditions under section 12(6), but it is noticeable that in this area a dominant concern has been neither to derogate from nor enhance the parental responsibility conferred on the adopters by an adoption order. This has led the courts, it is submitted, to make some questionable decisions, such as the refusal to impose a condition to require adopters to provide an annual report[71] or a six-monthly photograph to the birth parents.[72] One might similarly question the Court of Appeal decision in *Re D (A Minor) (Adoption Order: Validity)*[73] that there was no power to grant an injunction under section 12(6) to restrain contact with the child by the natural grandparents since that would give the adopters more extensive rights than those to which the natural parents of the child are entitled.[74] Of course, in all these cases it is far better if the adopters are willing to accept contact or other conditions and where this is the case it equally seems right that no order is needed,[75] especially in the light of the welcome ruling in *Re T (Adopted Children: Contact)*[76] that parties agreeing to such conditions cannot subsequently resile from them without explanation. Nevertheless, there will remain cases where conditions will need to be imposed.

AGENCY PRACTICE
As part of the 'contract/services' model it is vital that adopters are informed fully about the child's circumstances, and about the risks that they are undoubtedly undertaking both to themselves and to other members of the family. They should also be able to expect to be told of all the support that is available from or through the agency. Although, and this needs to be

---

[70] Ie under the criteria set out in s 31 of the Children Act 1989, which is now the only route into care under English law.
[71] *Re C (A Minor) (Adoption Order: Condition)* [1986] 1 FLR 315.
[72] *Re D (A Minor) (Adoption Order: Condition)* [1992] 1 FCR 461.
[73] [1991] 2 FLR 66. Although as Bromley and Lowe, *Family Law* (Butterworths, 8th edn, 1992), at p 450 point out, this ruling might be academic anyway since the court undoubtedly has a power to make a prohibited steps order under s 8 of the Children Act 1989.
[74] Ibid, at pp 76 and 150 respectively per Balcombe LJ.
[75] As held by Butler-Sloss LJ in *Re T (Adoption: Contact)* [1995] 2 FLR 251, discussed at p 377 above.
[76] [1995] 2 FLR 792, discussed at p 377 above.

stressed, we encountered during our research many examples of good and dedicated practice, it must be recorded that we also came across examples of bad practice. In particular, we were alarmed at what can only be described as the deliberate concealment of information from the prospective adopters. In its worst form we came across cases in our study where information about the child's development, for example of the child's violence or propensity for sexual abuse, had either been withheld or concealed from the prospective adopters. Apart from the question of whether this withholding of information is actionable,[77] it is clearly unacceptable practice. Also unacceptable is the apparent reluctance, at least in some agencies, to give information about what practical (including financial) support is available. Indeed, it was our impression that this reluctance was at least in part motivated by a desire to reduce the level of demand upon the service.

In line with the 'contract/services' model it is suggested that there should be some type of adoption agreement under which the placing agency should, *inter alia*: (a) give the adopters an 'information pack' clearly explaining precisely what support is available, including information about adoption allowances and other financial support, and how and from where it can be claimed; (b) guarantee that the information about the child is complete and up to date – and that it will continue to be updated – and is clearly explained to the adopters; (c) respect the adoptive applicants' own wishes (in relation to the type of child they wish to adopt) and only to depart from them by agreement; and (d) continue to offer support both after the adoption or, after the child has left, if the placement has 'disrupted'.[78]

THE ADOPTERS

As has been mentioned, many adopters still hold to the idea that upon adoption the child becomes 'theirs' and that there should be no further contact with the birth family. This 'exclusive' view of adoption, however, is not easily sustainable in respect of older children, and most agencies make this clear both at the recruitment and placing stage. What cannot be denied, however, is that as a matter of law an adoption order vests parental responsibility exclusively in the adopters – in other words, they are legally in control of the child. Even so, it has to be asked whether the price to be paid for continuing support after the order should be the surrender of some of that control. It has been suggested, for example, that the courts should perhaps be less reticent about imposing conditions, and it might be argued that provision of ongoing support carries with it a reciprocal obligation to use that support to benefit the child, for example continuing with therapeutic treatment.

CONCLUSION

As this article has sought to demonstrate, modern adoption practice in the England and Wales is more about adopting older children than about adopting babies or toddlers, yet the 'mind set' associated with the latter still permeates legal and social work thinking. The time has surely come for this thinking to take on board the reality of adopting older children. To do this it has been suggested that the 'contract/services' model of adoption would more appropriately take account of modern practices. This model, however, poses awkward questions: for the State it means having to come to terms with the fact that adoption is not a cheap option for bringing up

---

[77] Compare *W v Essex County Council* [1997] 2 FLR 535 in which Hooper J held that a social worker had a duty of care to provide foster-parents with 'reasonable' information about the child and that a local authority could be vicariously liable for a breach of that duty. Accordingly, four children, who were sexually abused by a teenager fostered by the family, were given leave to sue the council.

[78] Some moves, it must be acknowledged, have already been made along these lines with the introduction in July 1997, under reg 13A of the Adoption Agencies Regulations 1983, of the obligation on agencies to provide after the making of an adoption order, such information about the child as they consider appropriate. However, the proposals in this article go a lot further than those just introduced.

children currently languishing in care; for adoption agencies it may mean having to make agreements with the adopters, *inter alia*, undertaking to give full and up-to-date information both about the child's circumstances and about the risks to the adopters and their family about taking such a child on, and having to come to terms with the fact that breach of that agreement might be actionable; for the adopters it may mean having to accept that they are not in complete control of their adopted child's upbringing; for the law it begs the question of whether we should retain the concept of adoption for older children and, if so, how adoption can then sensibly be distinguished from long-term fostering.

What should the object of adoption be? Certainly, its overall aim should be to continue to provide a legal mechanism by which a new and independent functional family, without the need for public support, can be created. At the same time, however, we should expect that for many of these very damaged children such a transition will not be straightforward and that, therefore, the State should expect, and the law and practice should ensure, that adoptive placements continue to receive full support even after the order.

Part II:

Legal concepts of 'parent' and their linkage

8

Parentage, Parenthood and Parental Responsibility: Subtle, Elusive Yet Important Distinctions

ANDREW BAINHAM

1. INTRODUCTION

What is a parent? Judge De Meyer, giving judgment in the European Court of Human Rights in 1997, was quite confident that he knew the answer to this question.[1] The issue was whether the United Kingdom had violated rights to family life and had discriminated against a female-to-male transsexual (X) in refusing to register him as the father of a child (Z) born to his female partner (Y) following insemination by donor sperm. In holding that the UK authorities had not breached the Convention he said that the "principles and rules are quite simple . . . It is self-evident that a person who is manifestly not the father of a child has no right to be recognised as her father". So, the implication is, we all know a father when we see one—it is the man who has the genetic link with the child—the man whose sperm brings about the child's conception. The difficulty with this view is all too apparent and several other judges in the European Court drew attention to it.[2] If X had been born a biological *male* there would have been no question that he could have been registered as the father under the status provisions of the Human Fertilisation and Embryology Act 1990. This treats as the *legal* father of a child the man who undergoes licensed treatment together with a woman who conceives with the use of donated gametes.[3] The result seems to be that to qualify as a "father" (and hence a "parent") it is not necessary to be the genetic *father* but it is necessary to start life as a biological *male*. This view of the legal position of transsexuals is open to question but is beyond the scope of the present discussion.[4]

My concern in this chapter is whether it is just possible that Judge De Meyer was right after all—that being a parent is a genetic notion and that the mistake

---

[1] *X, Y and Z v The United Kingdom* (1997) 24 EHRR 143.
[2] See particularly the dissenting judgment of Judge Foighel.
[3] 1990 Act s. 28(3).
[4] For further discussion of the implications of this decision for transsexuals see Bainham (1997).

26 *Andrew Bainham*

we have made as a society is to treat or regard as *parents* many social carers of children who lack this genetic connection.

Before examining the issues it is necessary to say something about the terminology used in this chapter. Judges and legal commentators frequently use the terms *genetic parent* and *biological parent* interchangeably as if they were synonymous. There are frequent references also to the *natural parent* and the *blood tie*. All these expressions have been used to distinguish those who have a genetic connection with a child from those who do not but may be caring for that child. The latter are usually described as *social parents*. The primary thrust of this chapter is to explore the legal significance of this distinction and, in this sense, any of these expressions would do equally well. However, it must be acknowledged that there are scientifically important distinctions to be drawn between the existence of a *genetic link* and what may be thought to be the wider components of *biological parentage*. These components are analysed in depth by Martin Johnson (in Chapter 3 below). The distinction between what is *biological* and what is *genetic* may be particularly important in the context of assisted reproduction.

Distinctions may also need to be drawn between *mothers* (who will usually, but not always, satisfy all the components of *biological parentage*) and *fathers* (who will frequently, but not always, have only a *genetic* connection with a child). Since the key arguments in this chapter surround the presence or absence of a genetic link, the expression *genetic parent* is generally preferred to that of *biological* or *natural parent*. But the reader should bear in mind that many *genetic parents* will clearly be *biological parents* in the wider sense identified by Johnson. Further, in the case of mothers, the various techniques of assisted reproduction can result in the four components of biological parentage being shared by more than one woman (most obviously the genetic and gestational components). In these instances careful thought needs to be given to the legal significance which is attached to each of these distinctive contributions.

I shall explore these issues by looking at the subtleties inherent in the concepts of *parentage, parenthood* and *parental responsibility*. One of my aims is to draw attention to the incongruity between the social and legal uses of these terms. In particular I suggest that in social usage a meaningful distinction can be drawn between the ideas of *parentage* and *parenthood* which is not currently reflected in the law. Legislation does not use the term *parenthood* as such and rarely uses *parentage*,[5] preferring instead to concentrate on the concept of *being a parent*.[6] I speculate on whether there could be value in establishing separate legal concepts of *parentage* and *parenthood* as a means of recognising the distinctive

---

[5] Under Family Law Act 1986, s. 56 a person may apply to the court for, *inter alia*, "a declaration . . . that a person named in the application is or was his parent". Such declarations are referred to in the legislation, in the heading to the section, as "Declarations of Parentage".

[6] This is true, for example, of the Children Act 1989, the Adoption Act 1976 and the Child Support Act 1991, although under this last mentioned legislation it is possible to refer *disputes about parentage* (s. 26) to court for a *declaration of parentage* (s. 27). I am very grateful to Stuart Bridge for this insight.

interests which children have in establishing and sustaining links with genetic parents where the social parenting role is performed by someone else.

My chapter attempts to cut across the familiar debate about "genetic" versus "social" parenthood by focusing more closely on the above distinctions. It will be my contention that, with growing recognition of the child's fundamental right to knowledge of genetic origins,[7] it will be necessary to have a clear concept that gives expression to this link. Alongside this, I accept that there ought to be equally clear recognition of the significance and importance of what has been termed *social parenthood* to children and that this status must also be given proper weight in law. Increasingly the question will not be whether to *prefer* the genetic or social parent but how to accommodate *both* on the assumption that they both have distinctive contributions to make to the life of the child. In essence I shall argue that, as far as possible, the notion of *being a parent* should turn on a presumed or actual genetic connection with the child, leaving *parental responsibility* as the device for giving to *social parents* most but, crucially, not all of the status which attaches automatically to genetic parents—at least where the child is born to a married couple.[8] Thus, although it would remain perfectly usual to describe those performing the social role of parents as *social parents* they would usually not be *legal parents*. Put another way, the concept of *social parenthood* would embrace the legal powers and duties associated with *parental responsibility* and its exercise but not the wider legal status of *being a parent*.

A difficulty arises in relation to those instances in which the law has already gone beyond conferring *parental responsibility* on social parents and has indeed allowed them to become *legal parents*. This is true in both adoption and certain instances of assisted reproduction where the link between genetic and legal parenthood has been broken. It is here that I will suggest there might be some utility in separating out the concepts of *parenthood* and *parentage* in law. In short it might, in cases like adoption and assisted reproduction, be important to find two independent concepts which can, respectively, give effect to the legal status of, say, the adopters as parents and the child's interest, perhaps right, to a certain level of knowledge about and contact with the genetic parent. The former we might call *legal parenthood* and the latter *legal parentage*.

2. IS IT ALL JUST SEMANTICS?

An obvious question to pose at the outset is whether it really matters at all that someone is *called* a "parent" or not. Suppose, for example, that following

---

[7] See particularly United Nations Convention on the Rights of the Child, Article 7.

[8] Where a child is born to a married couple both will be *parents* and both will have *parental responsibility* Children Act 1989, s. 2(1)). Where the mother and father are unmarried they will both be *parents* but only the mother will, initially at least, have *parental responsibility* Children Act 1989, s. 2(2)).

28 *Andrew Bainham*

divorce a mother sets up home with a man whom she may or may not marry. In due course the children come to regard this man as their father and they call him "Dad". He is regarded as the father of the children by friends and others in the community. The law cannot, and would not want to, attempt to prevent the step-father or cohabitant from being known *informally* as the parent of the children. But *formally* the position is quite different even though this may not be fully appreciated by those concerned (see Pickford, Chapter 8 below). "Dad" remains in law as merely the *social* father, in no stronger position than any other *de facto* carer of children. The *legal* father is the genetic, now divorced, father. A recent decision of the High Court brings out this distinction between *informal* and *formal* parenthood rather well.[9] A mother had, independently, changed the surname of the children without the knowledge or consent of the natural father. It was ordered that, although the mother had behaved unlawfully, the children could continue to be known informally by the new surname but the mother was prohibited from taking any steps to "cause, encourage or permit any person or body to use the new surname without the prior consent of the father or the court". In effect the continuing legal parental status of the natural father was preserved through his name when it came to official dealings with educational, medical authorities and other outsiders.

So *being a parent* is not just a matter of language but something which confers a legal status. It therefore becomes important to consider closely the precise legal significance of establishing maternity or paternity, the circumstances in which the law should confer the full status of parent and what this ought to entail and, likewise, the circumstances under which parental responsibility should be obtained and how this might differ from being a legal parent. But, before doing so, it may be helpful to compare the way in which we generally use the expressions *parentage, parenthood* and *parental responsibility* with their technical legal uses.

3. SOCIAL AND LEGAL USAGES

(a) Being a parent: parentage and parenthood

We sometimes speak of the *parentage* of children. It is quite common to find legal commentators using the expression *parentage* interchangeably with *parenthood*. This is perfectly understandable since, as noted above, the law does not distinguish between the two and legislation instead usually refers to *parents* or, occasionally, to *mothers* and *fathers*. Yet *socially*, I suggest, we tend to use them somewhat differently. If we say "X's parentage is unknown" what we are talking about is *genetic* parentage. We are not usually raising questions about who has the right to look after the child. The dictionary definition of *parentage*

[9] *Re PC (Change of Surname)* [1997] 2 FLR 730.

which refers to "descent from parents, lineage" seems to confirm this view. Arguably, therefore, *parentage* is an exclusively genetic idea and it may be that we have here a concept capable of giving effect to the child's alleged right or interest in genetic origins.

The notion of *parenthood* in everyday usage is more problematic and ambiguous. While many people referring to *parenthood* would immediately associate it with the status held by the child's genetic father and mother, others might well associate it with those who are acting out the *social role* of parents by looking after a child. Often the expression *parenthood* is accompanied by a prefix. We talk of *step*-parenthood, *foster*-parenthood or *adoptive* parenthood. An umbrella term often used by commentators, though not, I suggest, in wider society, is *social parenthood*. One distinction then between *parentage* and *parenthood*, at least as a matter of everyday language, may be that the former, but not the latter, is an *exclusively* genetic idea. But this is not, in my view, the only point of distinction. *Parentage*, I suggest, has a "one-off" character. It is about genetic truth, or at least a *presumed* genetic link—as in marriage. Once parentage has been established following the birth of the child we tend not to continue using the term—unless perhaps someone in the family dies and it becomes important to resurrect the question of genetic links for the purposes of succession to property[10] or, more commonly, someone is denying financial liability for child support under the Child Support Act. *Parenthood* is arguably different. It conveys an on-going status in relation to the child and, in particular, is associated with the responsibility for raising a child.

So far as the law is concerned, *being a parent* is a legal status which has traditionally been associated with a presumed or actual genetic link.[11] But adoption (introduced in England in 1926) has long represented an exception to the principle that *genetic* and *legal* parenthood should coincide. In this context it is clear to everyone that the legal, adoptive parent is not the genetic parent. Since 1990 the instances of non-genetic parenthood have increased in the context of assisted reproduction. Under the Human Fertilisation and Embryology Act 1990 there are several instances in which a person who is patently not the *genetic* parent will be treated as the *legal* parent.[12] (See Bridge, Chapter 4 below). It should also be said that artificial insemination by donor (AID) has been around for half a century and that many children born into marriages will have been presumed (wrongly) to be the genetic children of the respective husbands. These cases are however distinguishable from those under the 1990 legislation since legal parenthood still arose in the pre-1990 cases from a *presumed genetic connection*,

---

[10] For a particularly striking illustration see *Re Overbury (deceased)* [1955] Ch 122.

[11] Within the context of marriage there is a legal presumption that a child born to a married woman is the child of her husband. The presumption is encapsulated in the Latin maxim *Pater est quem nuptiae demonstrant*.

[12] Thus under s. 28(2) the husband of a woman who did not object to her receiving various forms of infertility treatment will be treated in law as the father. The same is true of an unmarried man under s. 28(3) where there has been a course of treatment services provided for the mother and that man together.

30 *Andrew Bainham*

albeit an inaccurate one. What made the 1990 legislation so special was the willingness of Parliament to acknowledge openly the *legal parenthood* of those who lacked *genetic parentage*.

The position is complicated further in that the legal parent may, in the case of a genetic father not married to the mother, lack parenthood in the full sense, in that the law withholds from him parental responsibility. Thus it is necessary, at least from a legal perspective, to distinguish between being a parent and having parental responsibility—a subtlety which is probably not appreciated by many in society including those most directly affected (see Pickford, Chapter 8 below).

(b) Parental responsibility

If we consider how the expression *parental responsibility* might be used in society we can again observe a distinction between its social and its legal usage. Let us take the example of a young unmarried mother whose parents (the baby's grandparents) look after the baby while the mother gets on with her life—perhaps, shall we say, by going off to college. If we were to ask people generally who has "parental responsibility" for the baby in these circumstances, we could reasonably expect that some would see the grandparents as exercising it. They would be, as it were, *in loco parentis* to the child. Yet they do not have *legal* parental responsibility. Parental responsibility, in the technical legal sense, remains vested in the mother and the grandparents have only those powers and duties which other *de facto* carers possess.[13] Parental responsibility in law is not therefore just about the fact of looking after a child. But equally it is not just about being a parent either. The unmarried father is undoubtedly a parent with the status of legal parenthood but he lacks the powers and duties which go with having parental responsibility[14] (see Pickford, Chapter 8 below). Conversely many social parents succeed in obtaining parental responsibility in the legal sense but do not thereby acquire the full status of being parents and the very expression "parent" is in this context a legal misnomer.

To summarise, therefore, we can say that the social usage and perceptions of *parentage, parenthood and parental responsibility* may not always coincide with the legal significance of these concepts and that the first two (though perhaps socially distinguishable) are legally conflated in the notion of *being a parent*. If therefore we want to ask the question "what is a parent?" we need to ask further questions about whether we are seeking to establish genetic parentage, invest someone with the status of legal parent or merely give to that person the

---

[13] Under Children Act 1989, s. 3(5) a person who does not have parental responsibility but has care of a child may "do what is reasonable in all the circumstances of the case for the purpose of safeguarding or promoting the child's welfare".

[14] He can however acquire parental responsibility by agreement with the mother Children Act 1989, s. 4(1)(b) or by obtaining from the court a parental responsibility order Children Act 1989, s. 4(1)(a)).

legal powers and duties which are associated with raising a child and are encapsulated in the legal concept of "parental responsibility". These are not just questions of terminology since there are real distinctions of substance between merely having genetic parentage established, being a legal parent and possessing parental responsibility.

4. WHAT IS THE LEGAL SIGNIFICANCE OF PARENTAGE, PARENTHOOD AND PARENTAL RESPONSIBILITY?

What makes the legal situation so complex is that genetic parentage, legal parenthood and parental responsibility may be split between different individuals or institutions in relation to a particular child. This is, of course, frequently not the case. Perhaps the best example is again the situation of the unmarried mother (or two married parents). Where an unmarried woman gives birth (assuming she conceived by sexual intercourse) she will be the genetic parent, the legal parent and she will possess parental responsibility. However, the genetic father, if established, will also be the legal parent but will not have parental responsibility. To take a second example, if the mother and her unmarried partner had "produced" a child together with the use of licensed donor sperm, the partner would *not* be the genetic parent (this would be the sperm donor); the partner would be the legal parent but would still not have parental responsibility. Suppose that the mother then separated from the partner and married another man with whom she successfully obtains a joint residence order. Now the former partner is still the *legal* parent but her husband, who is neither the legal nor genetic parent, shares parental responsibility with the mother by virtue of the residence order. In this last example genetic parentage, legal parenthood and parental responsibility are split between three different men. It would not be difficult to dream up more complicated situations than this (Eekelaar, 1994).

What these examples suggest is that careful thought needs to be given to the legal consequences which flow from the establishment of genetic parentage, the attribution of legal parenthood and the granting of orders which give parental responsibility. Perhaps, more importantly, there needs to be a re-evaluation of the circumstances in which it is appropriate to allocate to individuals the status which goes with these distinctive concepts.[15] Thus, for example, when it is argued that being a parent is nowadays more about the *intention* to perform the role of a parent, rather than the fact of procreation (Barton and Douglas, 1995), we need to be clear about whether we are concerned merely with the acquisition of parental responsibility or with the wider status of legal parenthood.

---

[15] There has, in particular been much debate about the legal status of step-parents which raises questions about whether they should be allowed to acquire the full legal status of parent (through adoption), parental responsibility (automatically, by agreement with the genetic parent or by court order) or whether they should merely have the legal status of other *de facto* carers.

32 *Andrew Bainham*

(a) **The legal significance of establishing genetic parentage**

The establishment of *genetic parentage* will generally result in the attribution of *legal parenthood* with the consequences which attach to this status but, as discussed above, it will not always do so since there are instances in the context of assisted reproduction and adoption, in which the genetic parent either will not become, or will cease to be, the legal parent. Furthermore, whether or not the establishment of genetic parentage will create the *full* legal status of parenthood (inclusive of parental responsibility) will depend, in the case of the father, on the presence or absence of *marriage* to the mother.[16] Where the father, being married to the mother, acquires this full legal status of parenthood, it is not necessary to distinguish between the effects of legal parenthood and those of parental responsibility—he gets *both* since they are subsumed or conflated in the general notion of *being a parent*. Where however, he is *not* married to the mother, it is necessary to make this distinction. Hence we need to be able to separate the legal consequences of *being a parent* from those which derive from having *parental responsibility*. It is of course the case that many now argue that the unmarried father should automatically have a full parental status but this has thus far been resisted in England. (See Pickford, Chapter 8 below and on the different position taken by the Scottish Law Commission, see Scottish Law Commission (1992) and Bainham (1993)). The debate about this and other matters, such as liability for child support, largely hinges on the question of what consequences, if any, should flow from the *mere fact* of establishing genetic parentage; it might arguably be helpful to have an independent concept of *legal parentage* (as distinct from legal parenthood) as a mechanism for defining these consequences.

(b) **The attribution of legal parenthood**

As noted above, genetic parentage will usually trigger the legal status of parent. But we have now broken the necessary connection between the two. Legal parenthood may be attributed to social or intentional parents, as where a commissioning couple obtain a "parental order" under the Human Fertilisation and Embryology Act 1990.[17] Except in the case of the unmarried father, those who are legal parents will also have parental responsibility, but the distinction between the two concepts has an importance which goes well beyond this. This is because the legal effects which are peculiar to *parenthood* will not pass to *social parents* who get *parental responsibility*. Let me reinforce this point. Leaving aside the exceptional situation of the unmarried father, legal parent-

[16] Being married at the time of the child's birth here carries an extended meaning in accordance with Children Act 1989, s. 2(3) and Family Law Reform Act 1987, s. 1. The expression includes some children of void marriages, legitimated and adopted children and children who are treated as legitimate.

[17] 1990 Act, s. 30.

hood *includes within it* parental responsibility—but the reverse is not true. Parental responsibility *does not include* the wider legal effects of parenthood. This leads me to one of the most important issues for the future. In allocating parental responsibility to more and more social parents, is it necessary or desirable to go the extra mile and confer on them legal parenthood? It will be my strong contention that this is neither necessary nor desirable and that legal parenthood, with some exceptions, ought to be confined to genetic parents. This is because those legal effects, which are peculiar to parenthood, are fundamental to the genetic link and provide a basis for continuing to recognise this while parental responsibility, at the same time, can give a measure of legal security to social parents.

What are these fundamental effects of legal parenthood which do not pass with parental responsibility? The first is arguably the most important and is also the most frequently neglected. This is that legal parenthood, but not parental responsibility, makes the child a member of a family, generating for that child a legal relationship with wider kin going well beyond the parental relationship. This is expressed most concretely in the law of succession where entitlements on intestacy depend on being able to establish these kinship links. Beyond this, the social or psychological value of belonging to a particular family is a nebulous subject for lawyers and is more the terrain of the anthropologist or psychologist. What the lawyer *can* point out is that the loss of the legal status of parent will entail the loss, at least in law, of these wider relationships. Let us suppose, for example, that a mother divorces H1 and remarries H2. Both men have siblings. The mother and H2 apply to adopt the mother's children who are the genetic children of H1. If the adoption is granted, the children will lose their legal relationship with the uncles and aunts derived from H1. They will acquire new uncles and aunts from H2. If, on the other hand, a joint residence order is made rather than an adoption order, the children will retain the legal link with H1's siblings and any relationship with H2's siblings will be social rather than legal. It may be that this does not matter but it is surely a factor which should be considered before we allow too readily those who have performed a social role to become legal parents.

Other effects which arise specifically from legal parenthood are financial liability for child support,[18] the right to object or consent to adoption[19] (though this also depends on possessing parental responsibility), and the right to object to a change of the child's surname and to removal of the child from the jurisdiction,[20] the right to appoint a guardian[21] (although guardians themselves also have this right and the parent must possess parental responsibility), a presumption of

---

[18] Social Security Administration Act 1992, s. 78(b) and Child Support Act 1991, s. 1(2).
[19] Adoption Act 1976, s. 16.
[20] These rights, recognised at common law, are not lost where a residence order is made in favour of the other parent or someone else. See Children Act 1989, s. 13(1).
[21] Children Act 1989, s. 5(3).

contact where a child is in care[22] and an automatic right to go to court.[23] One might have thought that there would be an equivalent presumption of contact in the private context but decisions of the courts have cast doubt on this.[24]

Are these distinctive legal effects just anomalies, historical accidents of the piecemeal development of the law? Surely they should all now be subsumed under the central organising concept of parental responsibility? (Lowe, 1997). It is my contention that, on the contrary, they continue to serve a vital purpose in that they give expression to the continuing importance of the genetic link. What they all have in common is that they relate to fundamentals which go beyond the everyday decisions involved in upbringing. Allowing the child to be adopted severs the parental link completely (at least traditionally in English law); allowing the child to be taken permanently out of the country or changing the child's name threatens its existence, in the case of the latter perhaps only symbolically. If we are to move in the direction of giving effect to a child's right to knowledge of genetic origins we are going to need some legal means of preserving the genetic connection and it is the concept of legal parenthood which currently achieves this. As noted earlier there are limited exceptions to this principle in which some other distinctive mechanism is perhaps required, since legal and genetic parenthood have become divorced from one another.

(c) The effect of conferring parental responsibility

Parental responsibility is now a technical legal concept. It conveys a status which is held automatically by both parents where they are married and by the mother alone where the child is born out of wedlock. Yet many people who are not genetically related to children, but are looking after them, can acquire parental responsibility through court orders or, in the event of the death of a natural parent, through being privately appointed guardian by that parent (Douglas and Lowe, 1992). The most usual order will be the residence order, the effect of which is automatically to give parental responsibility to the person in whose favour it is made—but only for so long as the order lasts.[25] Orders will usually terminate when the child attains sixteen years of age.[26] Here we can see immediately one very clear distinction between being a legal parent and holding parental responsibility. The legal parent will remain a parent for life. Although many of the legal effects of parenthood will terminate when the child attains majority at eighteen, the legal family relationship of parent and child will

---

[22] Children Act 1989, s. 34(1)(a).
[23] Thus a parent may apply, without leave, for any "Section 8 order" under the Children Act 1989 (s. 10(4)) and this includes the unmarried father despite his lack of parental responsibility (see *M v C and Calderdale Metropolitan Borough Council* [1994] Fam. 1).
[24] See the House of Lords decision in *S v M (Access Order)* [1997] 1 FLR 980.
[25] Children Act 1989s. 12(2).
[26] Children Act 1989, s. 91.

endure for good.[27] Thus, in quite a number of countries (and formerly under the English Poor Law), adult children have legal obligations in certain circumstances to provide for the financial support of elderly parents. In contrast parental responsibility is really a sort of trusteeship over the child which is more limited and, since the Children Act 1989, will usually cease even before the child reaches majority. Under the draft Adoption Bill 1996 it would be possible for orders over children to be extended to the age of eighteen thus ensuring a continuation of parental responsibility (Department of Health and Welsh Office, 1996). But this has not been brought before Parliament.

So what exactly is *parental responsibility*? A great deal has been written on the subject and while the Scots have attempted in their 1995 legislation to define its content,[28] the English approach has been to leave things rather vague, at least on the statute book, and to presuppose some knowledge of the effects of being a parent which the courts have formulated over a long period of time at common law. But, for what it is worth, the Children Act defines *parental responsibility* as

"all the rights, duties, powers, responsibilities and authority which by law a parent of a child has in relation to the child and his property".[29]

The definition does not tell us what these are, which is why some question its usefulness, but it is, in a broad sense, fairly clear what it is talking about. At the risk of over-simplification, the person possessing parental responsibility will have a right to look after the child (unless this has been removed by a Court order)[30] and the right and duty to take all major decisions relating to the child's upbringing including such matters as where the child is to live, which school the child should attend or what medical treatment the child should, or should not, receive.[31]

Thus, where a social parent succeeds in obtaining parental responsibility he or she will have the legal right to look after the child and to take all the everyday and important decisions about upbringing which a parent could take. But the social parent will not *become* the legal parent in the fullest sense and one obvious question for policy-makers is why the social parent might feel the need to press for full legal parenthood. Why isn't having parental responsibility

---

[27] It was largely for this reason that an adoption order was made in *Re D (A minor) (Adoption Order: Validity)* [1991] 2 FLR 66. The child here was only six days short of majority when the adoption application was made but suffered from severe mental handicap. It should also be noted that some jurisdictions still allow the adoption of adults.

[28] Children (Scotland) Act 1995, ss. 1 and 2 set out, respectively, the *responsibilities* and *rights* of parents. English law subsumes the rights of parents, insofar as they exist, in the general notion of *parental responsibility*.

[29] 1989 Act, s. 3(1).

[30] The effect of a residence order or care order could be to prevent a person with parental responsibility from having the right to look after the child.

[31] These rights or powers are not absolute (*Gillick v West Norfolk and Wisbech Area Health Authority* [1986] 1 AC 112) but they do confer a good deal of discretion with which the courts may be reluctant to interfere (see, for example, *Re T (Wardship: Medical Treatment)* [1997] 1 FLR 502).

enough in itself? Why is it, for example, that so many step-parents, following the liberalisation of divorce in 1969, sought to adopt their step-children rather than merely to acquire the equivalent of what is now parental responsibility through a joint custody (or, latterly, a residence) order with their spouses? (Houghton, 1972). At least part of the explanation must surely lie in the fact that orders that confer what is now parental responsibility are *revocable* whereas adoption (which creates full legal parenthood) is *permanent* other than in very restricted circumstances.[32] This is particularly striking in the case of the unmarried father who, having acquired parental responsibility, may subsequently have it revoked by the court. So adoption offered greater *security* to *de facto* carers like step-parents, foster-parents and others, and the wish to have this security is readily understandable. But there is more to the push for parenthood than this. It seems entirely likely that many of those raising children have a psychological need to be regarded as, or called, *parents* and here we are perhaps back to the semantic debate alluded to earlier in this chapter. For many people, perhaps especially step-parents in a reconstituted family, it is not enough to be given the powers and duties of parents—they want to *be* parents.

The policy of the law has been to restrict the circumstances, again with step-parents particularly in mind, in which the *de facto* carer should be able to go beyond acquiring parental responsibility and actually attain full legal parenthood. I believe this policy to have been well-founded in view of what is increasingly recognised as the importance of the genetic link to the child. I turn to this in the next section. But before doing so, it should not go unnoticed that there has been some erosion of this policy and that the Children Act amended earlier provisions that were designed explicitly to discourage step-parent adoption and adoption by natural relatives (Bainham, 1990). Another point which ought to be raised here is that the concern of social parents for legal security in the process of raising a child is real and justifiable. It certainly suggests that further consideration should be given to the introduction of an *irrevocable* order, such as an irrevocable residence order or a form of *inter vivos* guardianship, which would stop short of making the social parent the legal parent but would also erase any real fear that the child could be removed from the social parent during the child's minority.

5. IS THERE A RIGHT TO KNOWLEDGE OF GENETIC ORIGINS?

Exactly what is the value of the genetic link to children or indeed to adults in later life is not something upon which lawyers are fit to pronounce. This is surely a matter for others such as geneticists and psychologists. But it does seem to be accepted that there are perhaps two major reasons why knowledge of

---

[32] For an unsuccessful attempt to revoke an adoption order see *Re B (Adoption: Jurisdiction to Set Aside)* [1995] 2 FLR 1. For a rare successful revocation see *Re K (Adoption and Wardship)* [1997] 2 FLR 221.

genetic background is thought to be important (O'Donovan, 1998). The first relates to information about an individual's medical history in the context of the wider family, and the second stresses the psychological need of individuals to have knowledge of their background in acquiring a sense of identity. Any uncertainty over the value of the genetic link has not stopped the international community from passing an extremely widely ratified Convention which appears to acknowledge the child's fundamental right to establish connections with his or her genetic parents. Article 7(1) of the United Nations Convention on the Rights of the Child provides that:

> "The child shall be registered immediately after birth and shall have the right from birth to a name, the right to acquire a nationality and, as far as possible, the right to know and be cared for by his or her parents".

Article 8(1) reinforces the previous article by providing obligations relating to the preservation of the child's identity, family relations etc. It provides that:

> "States Parties undertake to respect the right of the child to preserve his or her identity, including nationality, name and family relations as recognised by law without unlawful interference".

It might be argued that the expression "parents" in Article 7 is wide enough to include not only genetic parents but also those performing the social role of parents. What is not in dispute is that the purpose behind Article 7 was an attempt to combat the problem of children's statelessness. Article 7, as Jane Fortin puts it, "makes it clear that states parties must provide a method whereby the child is 'labelled' or named immediately she is born and thereby linked accurately and quickly to the people who brought her into the world, her birth parents" (Fortin, 1998). It is equally clear that Article 8 was inspired by the international community's need to respond to "the abuses committed by the military regime in Argentina during which babies had been abducted from their mothers at birth, before their births could be registered and illegally given to childless couples, associated with the armed forces and police" (Fortin, 1998; see also Le Blanc, 1995; Van Bueren, 1995).

Notwithstanding this background, the Convention contains no definition of "parents" and its meaning is therefore legitimately a matter of interpretation upon which opinions may differ. It is argued here, for a number of reasons, that the expression should be interpreted in the conventional sense of genetic parents. First, the history of Articles 7 and 8 reveals that the concern of the international community was with the rights of children from the moment of birth and in relation to their birth parents. It was precisely the threat of removal of the child from the birth parents by others which was the *raison d'être* of Article 8. Secondly, we must remember that the Convention is a *legal* document. In 1989, when it was adopted, there was, for example, no legislation anywhere in the world regulating assisted reproduction which has been the engine for the re-evaluation of traditional definitions of parenthood. Leaving aside adoption,

38 *Andrew Bainham*

legislation worldwide has traditionally defined parenthood as genetic parenthood. The legal tie has closely followed the genetic connection. Thirdly, as noted below, the jurisprudence generated under another international Convention, the European Convention on Human Rights, again supports the notion of "family life" from birth and has confirmed that this includes the potential relationship of a child with his or her genetic father even where unmarried. Finally, as discussed below, the conventional interpretation was adopted by the Court of Appeal in the one reported decision which directly invokes Article 7. For all these reasons it is submitted that "parents" in the Convention was intended to mean genetic parents and that the onus is very firmly on those who would argue for an unconventional interpretation.

Although the United Nations Convention is not directly incorporated into English law, it does require the government to adopt a social policy that is consistent with its international obligations, and Article 7 has already had a significant, perhaps decisive, influence on the outcome of one paternity dispute which reached the Court of Appeal.[33] In that case the mother, who had both a lover and a husband who had had a vasectomy, was told robustly by Lord Justice Ward that "honesty was the best policy", that she ought not to be telling lies and that the child had the right to know the truth of his paternity and "the sooner the better". Lord Justice Ward was at pains to distinguish between the two separate rights in Article 7. For him, the fact that the genetic father was not in a position to care for the child did not detract from the child's *independent* right to know of his genetic origins. A succession of decisions by the European Court of Human Rights have also made it plain that under the European Convention there are *positive* obligations on states to foster the "family life" of children from birth and that this "family life" is not confined to relationships within marriage.[34] These decisions are also founded in part on the importance of the genetic link which generates mutual fundamental rights for both children and parents in or out of marriage.

What the lawyer can therefore say with some confidence is that there are legal obligations which mean that it will not be lawful for states to devalue or ignore the link between the child and his or her genetic parents, though the extent of these obligations, especially positive obligations to take action, remains unclear.

How far English law currently complies with these international obligations is open to doubt. Adopted adults have a legal right of access to their original birth certificates but they do not, as the law stands, have a right to be told that they are adopted nor access to their original birth certificates *during childhood*. Children born with the use of donated gametes do not have the right to be told, while children, that they were conceived in this way but there are limited rights to "non-identifying information" to establish that there is no risk of marrying someone to whom a person is closely genetically related (Maclean and Maclean,

[33] *Re H (Paternity: Blood Test)* [1996] 2 FLR 65.
[34] See, for example, *Johnston v Ireland* (1986) 9 EHRR 203 and *Keegan v Ireland* (1994) 18 EHRR 342.

Parentage, Parenthood and Parental Responsibility 39

1996). There is no general obligation to establish genetic paternity in all cases of childbirth and there is some ambivalence in the attitude of the courts to the direction of blood testing or DNA tests in the event of paternity disputes.[35] It should perhaps be said that, with the ready availability of DNA testing and the possibilities for surreptitious removal of small quantities of genetic material such as hair roots, the role of the courts may in future be somewhat pre-empted by resort to such DIY measures.

The extent to which the law does or should accommodate biological parenthood alongside social parenthood is therefore going to be the subject of ongoing debate and in the next two sections I attempt to outline two possible approaches.

6. A RADICAL APPROACH—SHOULD PARENTHOOD BE EXCLUSIVELY GENETIC?

A radical and extreme response to the emerging right of the child to knowledge of genetic origins (and perhaps the logical conclusion from the existence of such a right) would be to regard as *parents* only those who can establish the genetic relationship. We should perhaps note, in passing, that Article 7 is not simply about knowledge—it talks of the right of the child "to know *and be cared for* by his or her parents" but only "as far as possible". This would seem to imply that the Convention is concerned not merely with establishing the initial link (what I have called the *parentage* issue above), but also with the on-going status of being a parent (what I have identified with *parenthood*).

I should say immediately that I am not advocating the following approach and it is my view that there is no possibility whatever of its adoption in England. The clock simply could not be turned back in this way. But there is value in speculating on what changes would flow from a reconceptualisation of our view of legal parenthood. I emphasise that I am only talking about the *legal* status of parenthood since, as discussed above, the law has no real control over the *social* usages of the term.

What, then, would have to change if we woke up tomorrow morning with the startling news that *only* those with an established genetic link with a child would, in law, be regarded as *parents*? The first and most obvious point is that it would make no difference whatever to the situation which applies already to the majority of children. Most children born into marriages are *in fact* the genetic children of both parents. Birth registration and indeed birth within marriage are not, of course, conclusive proof of a genetic connection with the men concerned, but these events do give rise to a *presumption* that this is the case. If we wanted to be absolutely sure we would have to test everyone, including the child, in every case of childbirth but, as far as I am aware, no-one has seriously

---

[35] Contrast particularly *Re F (A minor) (Blood Tests: Parental Rights)* [1993] Fam 314 with *Re H* (n. 34 above).

40 *Andrew Bainham*

proposed this. Certainly the radical approach would suggest that if anyone decided to *contest* paternity and put these presumptions in doubt, scientific tests should always be directed by the courts. This would certainly involve a change from current practice and I return to this issue in the next section. However, one point which ought not to be lost is that, in my view, legal paternity under these rules does not arise *because* of marriage or *because* of birth registration. It arises from the *presumed genetic link* which is triggered by these events. To that extent these rules are consistent with the radical thesis that parenthood is genetic.

The first real problem the radical approach would have to face is adoption. The effect of adoption under English law is what has been called a "legal transplant". The birth parents are replaced by the adoptive parents who step into their shoes. So *legal parenthood,* and not merely parental responsibility, is transferred. This form of adoption, as we know it in England, would have to go. But we should not make the mistake of believing that there is something inevitable or sacrosanct about the "transplant" model. Many civil law countries (essentially those whose legal systems derive from Roman law) have long recognised a distinction between *full adoption*, which broadly corresponds with the English version, and *simple adoption*, which does not extinguish the child's links with the wider birth family. In recent years a number of Latin American countries have reformed their adoption laws and the future of the dual system of adoption seems somewhat uncertain (Grosman, 1998; Alzate Monroy, 1998). The point is that it would not be impossible to conceive of a new kind of adoption order which gave long-term legal security to the adoptive parents but which also continued to preserve the legal link with the birth family in some way.

What about assisted reproduction? If legal parenthood were to be exclusively genetic, the anonymity of gamete donors would have to go—radical indeed, and calculated to reduce the number of volunteers, but scarcely revolutionary. Sweden has done it and Switzerland has enacted legislation which gives to the sixteen-year-old child, born of medically assisted procreation, the right to know a sperm donor's identity (Guillod, 1997). Surely surrogacy would represent a massive problem. On a closer examination perhaps the problem would not be as great as it seems at first sight. Under current legislation a commissioning couple can obtain a "parental order", the effect of which is similar to adoption in that it makes that couple the legal parents of the child and extinguishes the parental status of the surrogate mother.[36] The requirements for making such an order are themselves an interesting reflection of official ambivalence about what parenthood is, since at least one commissioning parent must have a genetic link with the child, they must be married and they must already be acting as the child's social parents. We may well speculate, in the light of this, whether it is the fact of procreation, family life within marriage or the intention to act as social parents which generates the greatest claim to legal parenthood. If legal parenthood were to be exclusively genetic, a "non-genetic" member of the

[36] Human Fertilisation and Embryology Act 1990, s. 30(1) provides that the effect of the order is that the child is "to be treated in law as the child of the parties to a marriage".

commissioning couple could no longer be the legal parent but this would not prevent him or her from being given parental responsibility. In the context of heterosexual unmarried cohabitation, we already have one intriguing decision which has allowed the male partner to adopt while giving the female partner only parental responsibility under a residence order.[37] Where a surrogacy arrangement breaks down, the law already arguably attaches greatest importance to the biological position since the surrogate mother, who carries the child and gives birth, will be the legal mother.[38] Cases of full surrogacy do, of course, raise questions as to whether the genetic link is to be regarded as more important than the biological contribution involved in carrying a pregnancy and giving birth.

The determination of fatherhood in cases of assisted reproduction would undoubtedly present a major problem. The attribution of legal fatherhood to the husband or partner[39] who receives licensed treatment services "together with" his wife or partner would have to be abolished. But, again, this would not necessarily involve denying that man any legal status. He too could be given parental responsibility rather than being made a parent and this would give him the legal powers and duties he would need to raise the child.

What this review perhaps reveals is that, although there would be substantial doubts about the desirability of reserving legal parenthood as an exclusively genetic concept and, although this is clearly not going to happen, it would not be impossible to achieve. It might be somewhat easier to achieve than would be commonly supposed with an intelligent use of the alternative legal notion of parental responsibility.

7. A MODERATE APPROACH—HOW CAN WE ACCOMMODATE GENETIC AND SOCIAL PARENTHOOD?

If we reject the radical approach, as now we surely must, how else might due weight be given to the genetic link alongside the very proper recognition of social parenthood? Again we perhaps need to focus on those instances in which the law separates genetic from legal parenthood by giving the legal status of parenthood to the social parent. The broad question which needs to be asked is whether the law adequately upholds the child's right to knowledge of genetic origins and preservation of that link.

What about adoption? The law and practice of adoption has already been moving slowly but surely towards a more "open" system although, as Bridget Lindley has pointed out, there are different manifestations of "openness" and the meaning of "open adoption" is not wholly clear (Lindley, 1997). Nor is the

---

[37] *Re AB (Adoption: Joint Residence)* [1996] 1 FLR 27.
[38] Human Fertilisation and Embryology Act 1990, s. 27(1). In some of these instances of course the gestational mother will not be the genetic mother.
[39] Human Fertilisation and Embryology Act 1990, ss. 28(2), (3).

42 *Andrew Bainham*

precise shape of adoption reform.[40] But we do seem to have arrived at the point where we are prepared, in some circumstances, to countenance on-going contact of a limited kind with the birth family following adoption.[41] It has also been proposed that a child should have a legal right to be told that he or she has been adopted—but the question of precisely when the child should be given information, and how much, remains contentious. It is even more contentious in the case of the children of assisted reproduction, but we need to continue to ask hard questions about why adopted children are allowed access to much more information about their genetic beginnings than are these children (Freeman, 1997; Maclean and Maclean, 1996).

More, much more, needs to be done about the process of establishing genetic paternity but already there are signs that the courts are beginning to shift the balance more towards genetic truth and are less obsessed with preserving family stability. As Lord Justice Ward has put it, when deciding to direct blood tests in the "vasectomy" case, "the issue of biological parentage should be divorced from psychological parentage . . . Mr B's parental responsibility should not dent Mr H's social responsibility".[42] Thus Lord Justice Ward was of the opinion that we should not *necessarily* assume that to establish the genetic parentage of an outsider will "upset the apple cart" as far as the social family situation is concerned. The child may have interests, perhaps rights, in an *inclusive* approach which acknowledges the different but complementary roles of genetic and social parenthood. With the growing societal acceptance of social parenting, and the very great range of family arrangements in which children move in and out of different kinds of households (Maclean and Eekelaar, 1997), there may be much less stigma attached to paternity outside marriage than there used to be.

I would go further than this. We need to look more closely at the responsibility of *the state* in establishing the genetic connection. If the child does have fundamental rights, this is a matter which perhaps ought not to be left to the various adults concerned. In Scandinavia and, until recently, Germany, the state has taken on a much more active role in attempting to establish genetic paternity in *all* cases of child birth—although the *pater est* presumption is still applicable to births in wedlock (Eriksson and Saldeen, 1993). The German case is an interesting one since the state, perhaps surprisingly, has traditionally had a much more assertive function in the former West Germany than in the former German Democratic Republic (Frank, 1997, 1998). It now seems, following reunification, that the state's role will recede at least in part because the kind of investigations carried out by social welfare agencies in the West would be found unacceptable by East Germans. In France and many other civil law jurisdictions there is much greater opportunity for a man to acknowledge his paternity

---

[40] The 1996 Draft Adoption Bill has never been presented to Parliament and, at the time of writing, there is no indication that the Labour Government intends to make adoption reform a priority.

[41] See, for example, *Re C (A minor) (Adoption Order: Conditions)* [1988] 2 FLR 259 and *Re T (Adopted Children: Contact)* [1995] 2 FLR 792.

[42] See n. 34 above at 82.

independently and without the initial need for co-operation by the mother or a court order (Senaeve, 1993; Meulders-Klein, 1990). Compare these approaches with the stance taken in England. I think it is fair to say that the only circumstances in which the state, in the guise of the Child Support Agency, bothers to get interested in the establishment of paternity is where the mother is dependent on social security. Otherwise she is under no obligation to register the name of the father and a man believing himself to be the father has no right to acknowledge his paternity without either the mother's consent or a court order.[43] There is not so much as a whiff of any independent right of the child in all this.[44]

A final consideration might be that we should continue to scrutinise carefully the circumstances under which social parents are actually allowed to become legal parents. Top of the list here is the position of step-parents. It is a matter of regret that the strong recommendations of the Houghton Committee (Houghton, 1972) which led to provisions in the Children Act 1975 designed to discourage step-parent (and relative) adoption,[45] were first subverted by the courts[46] and then eroded by Parliament, without much discussion, in the Children Act 1989 (Bainham 1990). The vast majority of step-parents become step-parents following the divorce of their spouses. In most of these cases the divorced parent will still be on the scene and perhaps involved with the children to a greater or lesser extent. We should be vigorously defending the parental status of the divorced parent in these cases and not pretending that a step-parent is a parent. To do otherwise would be directly contrary to the philosophy of continuing parental status following divorce.[47] Neither am I personally convinced that we should even go so far as to confer parental responsibility on the step-parent—at least not routinely. I think Brenda Hale got it exactly right when she said that the step-relation is not the same as the "normal" family constituted within marriage and "perhaps we should not pretend that it is" (Hoggett, 1987, p.126). The step-relationship may, however, arise in rather different circumstances. Perhaps the mother is widowed or the relationship with the natural father broke down before the child was born. In cases like this there is a much stronger case for giving parental responsibility to the step-father or, even perhaps, parenthood through adoption. These last examples do perhaps suggest that a general distinction should be drawn between cases in which the genetic parent is known and "on the scene" from those in which he or she is either unknown or has disappeared. The case for creating a new parent for the child

---

[43] Births and Deaths Registration Act 1953, s. 10, as amended.

[44] The child does not, for example, have a right to require the state to disclose information about his father's whereabouts which it has obtained as a result of its investigations for the purposes of enforcing his liability to support the child financially. See *Re C (A minor) (Child Support Agency: Disclosure)* [1995] 1 FLR 201.

[45] Children Act 1975, s. 37(1), (2) and Adoption Act 1976, ss. 14(3), 15(4).

[46] *Re D (Minors) (Adoption by Step-parent)* [1980] 2 FLR 102, *Re S (A minor) (Adoption or Custodianship)* and *Re A (A minor) (Adoption. Parental Consent)* [1987] 1 WLR 153.

[47] The theory of the Children Act is very clear and is that parents remain parents despite divorce. Thus, both parental status and parental responsibility are unaffected by termination of the marriage.

44 *Andrew Bainham*

to replace one which has been effectively lost is, I suggest, much stronger than where the child already has both parents intact. But this itself involves a deep philosophical question about why it is that children are apparently not entitled to more than *two* parents and sometimes have less than two.[48]

8. CONCLUSION

The great irony of the present time is that just at the moment when it has become possible to establish genetic parentage virtually conclusively it seems to matter less to do so since we are now much more accepting of social parenthood in its many manifestations. This has given rise to a good deal of debate about whether we should attach more importance to the one rather than the other. In the context of paternity disputes it has been presented as an issue of truth versus stability. Elsewhere there is much talk of genetic versus social parenthood.

A primary aim of this chapter has been to suggest that as we move into the twenty-first century we are not really going to be confronted with this polarised "either/or" dilemma. Because of the acceptance internationally of the child's fundamental rights regarding his/her genetic origins, to say nothing of domestic concerns about medical knowledge and psychological well-being, it is going to be necessary to take an *inclusive* approach. The Children Act 1989 is in fact full of inclusive ideas of partnership and the notion that children can relate to a range of adults.[49] Yet we remain stoutly resistant to the idea that a child could have more than two parents. On the other hand it is a feature of the new concept of parental responsibility that it can be shared out among a potentially unlimited range of adults. The real question in this sharing process will be who gets legal parenthood and who gets only parental responsibility, if anything. It could have been exceptionally neat and tidy to say that those with a proven genetic connection are the parents and everyone else gets parental responsibility and no more. But this is not the course we have followed in England and it is too late to change course now. Given that legal and genetic parenthood will not coincide in a number of instances, it may just be that thought needs to be given to resurrecting or creating a legal concept which could be exclusively genetic and could thereby serve the independent rights or interests of children to knowledge of origins in these cases. I tentatively put forward the idea that *parentage* might in law be distinguished from *parenthood* and be given a technical importance which would, I believe, bring it closer to its ordinary social usage.

---

[48] Under the provisions of the Human Fertilisation and Embryology Act 1990, s. 28, where no man is deemed to be the legal father the child can be "fatherless" viz. without a legal father.

[49] A principle which applies particularly to the relationship between the state and parents and which is also reflected in the provision that "a person who has parental responsibility for a child at any time shall not cease to have that responsibility solely because some other person subsequently acquires parental responsibility for the child".

REFERENCES

Bainham, A., "The privatisation of the public interest in children" (1990) 53 *Modern Law Review* 206.
Bainham, A., "Reforming Scottish children law—sense from north of the border" (1993) 5 *J. of Child Law* 3.
Bainham, A., "Sex, gender and fatherhood: does biology really matter?" (1997) 56 *Cambridge Law Journal* 512.
Barton, C. and Douglas, G., *Law and Parenthood* (London, Butterworths, 1995).
Department of Health and Welsh Office, *Adoption—A Service for Children: Adoption Bill—A Consultative Document* (London, March 1996).
Douglas, G. and Lowe, N. V., "Becoming a parent in English law" (1992) 108 *LQR* 414.
Eekelaar, J., "Parenthood, social engineering and rights" in D. Morgan and G. Douglas (eds.), *Constituting Families: A Study in Governance* (Stuttgart, Franz Steiner Verlag, 1994).
Eriksson, A. and Saldeen, A., "Parenthood and science—establishing and contesting parentage" in J. Eekelaar and P. Sarcevic (eds.), *Parenthood in Modern Society* (The Hague, Martinus Nijhoff, 1993).
Fortin, J., *Children's Rights and the Developing Law* (London, Edinburgh and Dublin, Butterworths, 1998).
Frank, R., "Germany: the need for reform in parentage law" in A. Bainham (ed.), *The International Survey of Family Law 1995* (The Hague, Martinus Nijhoff, 1997).
Frank, R., "Germany: a fundamental reform of parentage law is pending" in A. Bainham (ed.), *The International Survey of Family Law 1996* (The Hague, Martinus Nijhoff, 1998).
Freeman, M. D. A., *The Moral Status of Children* (The Hague, Martinus Nijhoff, 1997).
Grosman, C. P., "The recent reform of Argentine adoption law" in A. Bainham (ed.), *The International Survey of Family Law 1996* (The Hague, Martinus Nijhoff, 1998).
Guillod, O., "Switzerland: Choosing its own way or following others?" in A. Bainham (ed.), *The International Survey of Family Law 1995* (The Hague, Martinus Nijhoff, 1997).
Hoggett, B. M., *Parents and Children: The Law of Parental Responsibility*, 3rd edn. (London, Sweet and Maxwell, 1987).
Houghton Report, *Report of the Departmental Committee on the Adoption of Children* (Cmnd. 5107, 1972).
Le Blanc, L. J., *The Convention on the Rights of the Child* (Lincoln and London, University of Nebraska Press, 1995).
Lindley, B., "Open adoption—is the door ajar?" (1997) 9 *Child & Family Law Quarterly* 1997.
Lowe, N. V., "The meaning and allocation of parental responsibility—a common lawyer's perspective" (1997) 11 *International Journal of Law, Policy & the Family* 192.
Maclean, M. and Eekelaar, J., *The Parental Obligation* (Oxford, Hart Publishing, 1997).
Maclean, S. and Maclean, M., "Keeping secrets in assisted reproduction—the tension between donor anonymity and the need of the child for information" (1996) 8 *Child & Family Law Quarterly* 243.
Meulders-Klein, M. T., "The position of the father in European legislation" (1990) 4 *International Journal of Law & the Family* 131.

46 *Andrew Bainham*

Alzate Monroy, P., "Adoption law in Colombia" in A. Bainham, (ed.), *The International Survey of Family Law 1996* (The Hague, Martinus Nijhoff, 1998).

O'Donovan, K., "Who is the father? Access to information on genetic Identity" in G. Douglas and L. Sebba (eds.), *Children's Rights and Traditional Values* (Aldershot, Ashgate, Dartmouth, 1998).

Scottish Law Commission, *Report No. 135* (1992).

Senaeve, P., "Reform of affiliation law in France and the Benelux countries" in J. Eekelaar and P. Sarcevic (eds.), *Parenthood in Modern Society* (The Hague, Martinus Nijhoff, 1993).

van Bueren, G., *The International Law on the Rights of the Child* (The Hague, Boston and London, Martinus Nijhoff, 1995).

9

RETHINKING PARENTAL RESPONSIBILITY

JOHN EEKELAAR Pembroke College, Oxford

Clause 91 of the Adoption and Children Bill 2001 contains provisions implementing the reform first officially floated by the Lord Chancellor's Department in 1998, whereby an unmarried father would acquire parental responsibility for a child by entering his name on the child's birth register jointly with the mother (*Consultation Paper: Court Procedures for the Determination of Paternity; The Law on Parental Responsibility for Unmarried Fathers* (Lord Chancellor's Department, 1998), at para 59). Although the present position has been held to be 'human rights compliant' (*B v UK* [2000] 1 FLR 1), some change seemed inevitable when it began to be realised that there are thousands of unmarried fathers, living together with their children and their mothers, acting in exactly the same way as married fathers do, but who do not have parental responsibility for those children because they do not appreciate the need to take legal steps to acquire it. The consultation paper (at paras 52 and 53) gave a figure of 135,282 men entering this position in 1996. If we appreciate that these numbers build up year on year, and then consider the whole child population under the age of 16, we must reach a figure of over a million such fathers, even discounting for lower rates of unmarried cohabitation prior to 1996 and the fathers who subsequently leave the home. It is obviously unsatisfactory that the status of these fathers *vis-à-vis* their children should be different from that of married fathers, and this in itself justifies reform. However, matters might not be completely straightforward and some further reflection is called for.

THE RIDDLE OF PARENTAL RESPONSIBILITY

One powerful impetus for the reform was the research of Ros Pickford. She discovered that unmarried fathers who were acting as fathers on a daily basis were surprised and angry, understandably, to discover that they did not have parental responsibility. One father had experienced difficulties in giving consent to necessary medical treatment on behalf of his children (see Pickford 'Unmarried Fathers and the Law' in Bainham, Day Sclater and Richards (eds) *What is a Parent?* (Hart Publishing, 1999)). The assumption made not only by the hospitals, in that case, but also by Pickford, is that 'only a person with "parental responsibility" has the right to make decisions about a child's upbringing'. But is this common assumption correct? It is not entailed by statute. The fact that s 3(1) of the Children Act 1989 states that parental responsibility means 'all the rights, duties, powers, responsibilities and authority which by law a parent of a child has in relation to the child and his property' does not prevent some such rights etc being held by persons who do not have parental responsibility. One has to look to statute and common law to find out what these rights are. In other words, having parental responsibility is not a necessary condition for possessing some important attributes of parenthood. Nor, it turns out, despite the word 'all' in s 3(1), is it a sufficient condition for holding some such attributes.

(A) Parental responsibility neither a necessary nor a sufficient condition

It is well known that the duty to support a child under the Child Support Acts 1991 and 1995 is imposed on 'any person who is in law the mother or father of the child' (Child Support Act 1991, s 54); having parental responsibility is neither necessary, nor (if the person with it is not in law the mother or father) sufficient. The same is true with respect to succession rights (Law Commission, Law Com No 172, *Review of Child Law: Guardianship and Custody* (HMSO, 1988), para 2.7 and Children Act 1989, s 3(4)(b)).

(B) Parental responsibility a sufficient but not necessary condition

Sometimes, having parental responsibility confers certain rights etc, but those rights could be held quite apart from it. In such cases, either having parental responsibility is sufficient, or being a legal parent is sufficient; neither is necessary. For example, either a legal parent (with or without parental responsibility), or someone who is not a legal parent, but who has parental responsibility, may apply, without leave, for certain orders with respect to the child (Children Act 1989, ss 10(4)and 12(2)). Similarly, parents (with or without parental responsibility) and non-parents with parental responsibility have the right to be kept in reasonable contact with children who are in local authority care (Children Act 1989, ss 34(1)(a) and 12(2)) and to be consulted by a local authority when it reviews the position of a child it is looking after (Children Act 1989, ss 26(2)(d) and 12(2)). The same is true with respect to education: either a parent or someone with parental responsibility is under a duty to ensure the child receives efficient full-time education (Education Act 1996, ss 7 and 576).

(C) Parental responsibility a necessary but not a sufficient condition

Rarely will it be necessary to have both parental responsibility and legal parenthood to exercise a right, etc. The most important example is the right to consent, or to refuse consent, to adoption. A person with parental responsibility who is not the legal parent does not have this right (Children Act 1989, s 12(3)), but being the legal parent without parental responsibility is not enough either (Adoption Act 1976, ss 16 and 72. This is maintained in the Adoption and Children Bill 2001, clause 44(3)(c)). Another example is the right to appoint a guardian (Children Act 1989, ss 5(3) and 12(3)).

(D) Parental responsibility both a necessary and sufficient condition

Sometimes, holding parental responsibility alone will not only be necessary to exercise a right, but will also be enough. This is the case with respect to the right to object to the issue of a passport to a child (see Lowe and Douglas (eds) *Bromley's Family Law* (Butterworths, 9th edn, 1998), at p 361) and to consent to the marriage of a child under the age of 18 (Marriage Act 1949, s 3(1A)(a) and (b)). Other examples are the right to apply for a discharge of a care order (Children Act 1989, s 39(1)(a)) and the right to object to a local authority providing accommodation on a voluntary basis to a child and the right to remove the child from such accommodation (Children Act 1989, s 20(7) and (8)). Like the case of adoption, these are rather unusual circumstances. A more common one is where, usually after the separation of the parents, a residence order is made. Then a child cannot be known by a new surname or removed from the country without the written consent of every person who has parental responsibility, or with the leave of the court (Children Act 1989, s 13(1)).

It will be evident, therefore, that the rights etc associated with parental responsibility and with legal parenthood are not simply stated. In order to know what rights an unmarried father without parental responsibility has concerning a child he is bringing up, it is necessary to establish into which of the above four categories this situation falls. There seem to be good reasons to place it under (B); that is, where having *either* parental responsibility *or* legal parenthood is sufficient. For if it is the case that an unmarried father, as legal parent, has a duty to cause his child to receive efficient full-time education, it would be absurd to withhold from him the right to take the decisions necessary to carry out that duty. 'Ought' necessarily implies 'can'. Indeed, Education Act 1996, s 9 requires children, as far as possible, to be educated in accordance with their parents' wishes. This includes parents without parental responsibility as well as non-parents with parental responsibility (Education Act 1996, s 576: definition of 'parent'). The same must be true regarding medical treatment. It surely cannot be denied that, if the father has a duty to see his child is educated, he is also under a duty to tend to his health. He must, therefore, be able to make decisions necessary to promote the child's health. We can go further. In *Re O (A Minor) (Custody: Adoption)* [1992] 1 FLR 77 the Court of Appeal upheld an unmarried father's claim to bring up his child in preference to that of prospective adopters. The court decided he had the better right to bring up the child. It must follow that he possessed the necessary powers to carry that right out, whether or not he applied for parental responsibility. Whatever may have been the experience of some unmarried fathers in Pickford's research, the law must bear some reasonable relationship to social life. The fact that around one million fathers are daily making decisions concerning their children's upbringing cannot surely go unrecognised by the law. The conclusion is irresistible that they do, indeed, have the legal rights necessary to bring up their children.

If this is the case, one may reasonably ask what point there is in having the separate concept of parental responsibility, in addition to legal parenthood. One clear purpose is to enable parental authority to be conferred on non-parents, such as grandparents, same-sex partners, or step-parents. (The Adoption and Children Bill contains a provision allowing parental responsibility to be conferred on a step-parent by agreement: clause 92.) But what of the case of legal parents? What is the effect of distinguishing between those unmarried fathers who have parental responsibility and those who do not? We have seen, in categories C and D above, some consequences which do flow from that distinction. These are relatively rare circumstances, but important none the less. When unmarried fathers are granted parental responsibility, their position will, therefore, improve. However, it is fair to suppose that fathers who apply for parental responsibility are unlikely to have the circumstances of categories C and D very much in mind. So what is it that they think they are acquiring, which they do not already have, when they seek parental responsibility?

The courts have been rather vague about the answer to that question. They have talked mystically about the acquisition of a 'status' (without specifying its incidents) or of conferring a 'stamp of approval'. It may all boil down to symbolism, but it is unsatisfactory to use scarce legal resources to engage in gestures. It must be remembered that cases where fathers make applications for parental responsibility are invariably those where they are living apart from their children. Sometimes they have been in prison. The truth, therefore, is probably that they believe they are acquiring rights to be directly involved in their children's upbringing, despite living apart from them: that is, a right to be consulted. That would, indeed, be something more than the right to take decisions necessary for bringing up a child, which I have just argued they would have anyway if they were actually bringing the child up. So does parental responsibility give them that right?

The answer, laid down clearly by statute, and enunciated by the Law Commission when it formulated the concept of parental responsibility, is 'no'. Section 2(7) of the Children Act 1989 states that 'where more than one person has parental responsibility for a child, each of them may act alone and without the other (or others) in meeting that responsibility'. The only exception is where statute otherwise provides (see also *Review of Child Law*, at para 2.10). The trouble is, the judges do not like this answer. They believe that a parent with parental responsibility has the right to be consulted on important matters regarding the child's upbringing. Hence in *Re PC (Change of Surname)* [1997] 2 FLR 730 Holman J effectively ignored s 2(7) in deciding that a parent with parental responsibility should have the right to be consulted over a change of surname, even though no residence order had been made, as the statute required as a condition for conferring such a right (see Eekelaar 'Do Parents have a Duty to Consult?' (1998) 114 *Law Quarterly Review* 337). Other cases have supported this position. In *Re T (Change of Surname)* [1998] 2 FLR 20 Thorpe LJ, without referring to s 2(7), held that a mother who had changed the child's surname without consultation had acted 'unlawfully'. In *Re H (Parental Responsibility)* [1998] 1 FLR 855 Butler-Sloss LJ said that if a father had parental responsibility, 'he would have the right to be consulted on schooling, serious medical problems and other important occurrences in the child's life'. In *Re J (Specific Issue Orders: Child's Religious Upbringing and Circumcision)* [2000] 1 FLR 571 the Court of Appeal upheld Wall J in saying that 'circumcision must join the exceptional categories where disagreement between holders of parental responsibility must be submitted to the court for determination'. Yet disagreement on any issue may need judicial resolution. It seems that the court was assuming that consultation on this issue must occur, and the court would have to make the decision if the parties could not agree.

IMPLICATIONS FOR THE REFORM

However desirable the result which the courts are seeking to achieve might seem to be, it flies in the face of the clear words of s 2(7) of the Children Act 1989. But while I wish to maintain that the outcome is indeed wrong in law, I also wish to argue that it is undesirable. The mistake is to attempt to cast into legal form an aspiration of good conduct. No one could possibly argue that it would not be a 'good thing' for separated parents to co-operate together as far as possible, and as amicably as possible, over their children's upbringing. So also we could not but applaud a parent who lives apart from his child and who visits the child regularly and lovingly. But we do not impose a legal duty to visit. Even if we believed that imposing such a duty would 'send the right message', the risk would be that by clothing the features of co-operative behaviour in the form of legal duty, people would be encouraged to resort to lawyers over perceived infractions. In any case, how could it be enforced? So we wisely leave this to moral persuasion and the dynamics of the relationship. Precisely the same considerations apply to consultation between separated parents. Provided the relationship is good, and especially where contact takes place, either consultation will occur or the non-residential parent will know what is going on. Cases where problems arise tend to be those where the contact has ceased or is rare.

Suppose there was a generalised legal duty to consult, such as that articulated by Butler-Sloss LJ above. What amounts to consultation? Is provision of information enough (and would reasonable notice need to be given before action was taken), or must there be agreement over outcome? There will always be uncertainty over what matters are sufficiently 'serious' to attract the duty. Will it apply if the non-resident parent has virtually lost touch, or shown no interest in previous communications? What must the parent under the duty do to comply with the duty? What if consultation exacerbates conflict? Clearly there must be flexibility in interpretation, but could we really allow the parents with the children to decide whether they were under the duty? And what would such parents think when they realise that the non-residential parents are under no corresponding duty to take an interest in the children? These are all hard enough questions. They would be made harder by giving the parties an added opportunity for dispute, and incentives to consult solicitors if they believe there has been failure to comply. In any event, it is difficult to see what enforcement mechanism could be used that is not already available to a non-residential parent who is dissatisfied with how the children are being brought up.

These comments should not be read as a generalised objection to the use of law or to concepts of rights within family disputes. I have frequently pressed the case for protecting legal rights in this context. But proper appreciation of the importance of the law must be accompanied by similar recognition of its limits. On the matter of consultation, as in the case of compelling the non-residential parent to take an interest in the children, the law reaches those limits. These are not the kinds of disputes solicitors feel they have the expertise to handle (see Eekelaar and Maclean *Family Lawyers* (Hart Publishing, 2000), at pp 102 and 112–3). This is not to say that a court could not impose a requirement for consultation appropriate to the circumstances when disposing of a specific dispute within the context of a specific issue order. But a generalised duty is another matter. It threatens to subject parents caring for children to an unnecessary risk of legal harassment and the added anxieties and pressures that would cause in already conflicted situations.

When the Lord Chancellor's Department made the suggestion which the Bill implements, it was concerned that it might have the effect of deterring fathers from having their names recorded on the birth register (see the consultation paper, at p 18). As Wikeley has pointed out, this provision could make it easier to identify fathers who are liable to pay child support, even though having parental responsibility is not a condition of such liability ('Child Support, Paternity and Parentage' [2001] Fam Law 125). But mothers, whose consent is necessary before the father's name is recorded, could be more vulnerable, especially if they are not living with the father at the time. These relationships tend to be fragile (see Maclean and Eekelaar *The Parental Obligation* (Hart Publishing, 1997)). If the registration gives the father a generalised legal right to be consulted, the mother could be opening herself up to potential trouble in the future. She would be well advised not to agree to have his name recorded, although this would need to be balanced against any difficulty non-registration of his name might cause in establishing his paternity, should she subsequently seek child support (see Ashley 'Parental Responsibility – A New Deal or Costly Exercise?' [1999] Fam Law 175).

Since I am of the view that having parental responsibility does not alter the legal position of the unmarried father very much, this might be taken as a case against the proposed reform. In fact, my preferred solution is that once advocated by the Scottish Law Commission: that unmarried fathers should have parental responsibility automatically. That would remove the few remaining distinctions (categories C and D) between married and unmarried fathers. It would make less depend on the fact of registration, which should be merely a recording exercise (with possible evidential consequences), and not a mode of conferring legal rights. However, this solution is only feasible if the judges repudiate suggestions that there exists a generalised duty to consult, even over 'serious' matters. And that applies equally to the reform set out in the Bill. It is not much to ask. After all, it is what the statute unambiguously says.

The Grandparents' Federation is a charity doing effective and much needed work with children and their grandparents.

Working for Children

Registered Charity Number 802850

On the evening of Monday 2 July we are holding our first annual dinner in the historic Middle Temple Hall, London. The guests of honour are the Rt. Hon. Dame Elizabeth Butler-Sloss and her husband. There will be a champagne reception followed by dinner.

Tickets are being sold at £65 each. We are also seeking to recruit sponsors and benefactors, prices from as little as £1000 which includes tickets and a mention in the evenings literature.

Further details on purchasing tickets or being one of our sponsors/benefactors are available from:
Grandparents' Federation, Moot House, The Stow, Harlow, Essex CM20 3AG. Tel: 01279 428040.
Email: grandfed@talk21.com

Part III:

The legal parent – accommodating complexity

10

Law and the complexities of parenting: parental status and parental function

Craig Lind and Tom Hewitt

In this paper we explore three types of parental relationships which have grown in importance over the course of the last quarter of a century. Our object is to explore the extent to which assisted reproduction parents, same-sex parents and step-parents, assist us in our reconsiderations of the legal status of parents and of the responsibilities that they fulfil in law. We argue that thinking about these parental types will encourage us to embrace a formal fragmentation of parental status. This in turn will help us to restore clarity to the concept of parental responsibility and address the need to create legal hierarchies of parental status for children. It will also cause us to reconsider the extent and uniformity of the legal consequences of parental status.

Introduction

In this paper we wish to explore the legal and social significance of attributing parental status to people who might fulfil an active parental role in the lives of children but who have no status to do so. That role may, in some cases, be quite central to the child's upbringing while in others it might be only peripheral to it. At the heart of this paper lies a concern about the distinction that the law draws between parents, on the one hand, and the people who have parental responsibility for children, on the other. We will try to defend this distinction as one which valuably contributes to the well being of children. But we will also ask whether or not the law has gone far enough in allowing parental responsibility to be shared by many, but limiting parenthood to at most two people. We will argue that the time has come to allow for the fragmentation of parental status so that we are able to keep abreast of social developments and to continue to serve the interests of children.

We will begin by making some observations about the state of the law on parenthood in England and Wales. At this point we will use a confused language of parenthood, parentage, and parental responsibility; we will not attempt to define each of these terms or to use them as distinctly separate concepts (see Bainham 1999 for a closer analysis of the distinctions between these terms). For the most part our comments will cover both mothers and fathers. However, it will become apparent that there is a gendered dimension to the problems that must be resolved. The concerns we raise impact differently on women and men creating special challenges for lawyers and policy makers.

Some observations about *parental status* and *parental responsibility*

Many of the observations we will make in this section are empirically verifiable, although they are (as Collier and Sheldon 2008 have argued convincingly) rarely uniformly or uncontrovertibly true.

Identifying legal parents in law is a relatively simple matter. Mothers are women who give birth and fathers are those who are the male genetic progenitors of children (*Ampthill Peerage Case* [1977] AC 547). Very occasionally these status relationships are reallocated either because of the formal involvement of scientific technologies which assist reproduction (Human Fertilisation and Embryology Act 2008 (HFEA 2008), Part 2) or because children have been adopted (Adoption and Children Act 2002 (ACA 2002), s. 67).

The status of legal parent remains important – inheritance rights and support obligations, for example, turn largely on family status (s. 1, Inheritance (Provision for Family and Dependants) Act 1975 and s. 1, Child Support Act 1991). But parental status has declined in importance in the last few decades. Parental responsibility, a statutory concept introduced in the Children Act 1989 (CA 1989) (s. 2), has made it possible for the rights and duties that were automatically attached to that status to be redistributed to others; parental responsibility, as a legal concept, is therefore quite malleable.

Since the advent of the 1989 Act, our law has been (relatively) clear about the conditions under which more than two people – all of whom are involved in the work of raising children and fostering their well-being – might share legal responsibility for them. However, it is submitted that this particular 'fragmentation' of parenthood (moving much of the legal significance of parental status to the concept 'parental responsibility') has caused us to neglect the importance that people themselves attach to parental status. The social significance of 'parent' has not waned since the introduction of the notion of parental responsibility. And, although the law is finally beginning to rediscover the importance of parental status, it is doing so in an *ad hoc* way without any thorough consideration of what it would like that status to accomplish. A proper analysis of the social significance of parental status and of its legal consequences is, therefore, necessary.

New parents and their effect on legal and social parental norms

Before trying to grasp the importance of thinking differently about parental status and parental responsibility we will consider assisted reproduction parents, same-sex parents and step-parents as paradigm illustrations of the difficulties that arise when we fail to reassess radically our traditions of parental status.

a. *Assisted reproduction parents*

i. *Identifying the parents*

Reproductive technologies clearly have the ability to complicate the status and function of parents by disrupting the genetic, gestational and social links between adults and children (Collier and Sheldon 2008, Ch.3). However, although the enactment of the Human Fertilisation and Embryology Act 1990 (HFEA 1990) demonstrated the law's desire to engage in a radical rethink of the allocation of parental status, the Act also saw the law resolve to settle that allocation in a profoundly conservative way. Initially parental status was extended to adults who were not parents, but only if they resembled traditional nuclear family members. Despite the expansion of the concept of parental responsibility in the CA 1989 the HFEA 1990 retained parental status as binary and heterosexual (see ss. 27–30 HFEA 1990). Even where profound gender uncertainty might have allowed the law to expand its concept of parental status for transsexual parents it was not prepared to betray its traditional, narrowly conceived, heterosexual roots (in *X, Y and Z* v. *UK* (1997) 24 EHRR 121 the European Court of Human Rights refused to require English law to recognise the paternity of a transsexual man).

But the traditional gender constraints on parenthood – that a child have a mother and a father – were to change with the passing of the Gender Recognition Act 2004. Moreover, the revisions to infertility regulation in the HFEA 2008 opened the way to the legal recognition of same-sex parents (ss. 42-44, 54 HFEA 2008). However, even now, we will argue, the allocation of parental status in the case of assisted reproduction remains unduly narrow.

The 2008 HFEA sets out the rules for determining parental status where clinical reproductive services succeed in helping people to have children. Maternal status is allocated simply to those who give birth (s. 33) and paternal status is allocated to a (just one) man who is in a closely defined relationship with the mother (ss. 35–37). Any legal parental relationship between the child and the gamete donor (whether egg or sperm) is explicitly excluded (ss. 41, 47).

Interestingly, in all cases of assisted conception involving a man the father's position is secured through the mother. Her husband is the father but only if he was a willing participant in her treatment (s. 35), and any other man can only be a father if she supports his wish to be a parent (ss. 36, 37). Indeed, the central importance of the mother in determining fatherhood extends to the creation of second mothers. Where a child has no father a second female parent – even if she was the genetic progenitor – can only achieve parental status by satisfying conditions that rely on the consent of the legal mother. Her own biological role in procreation is immaterial (s. 47).

Although the façade of a two-parent family remains fairly securely in tact, the Act does fragment parental status. Despite extricating gamete donors from their parenthood, the identity of those donors remains important in the 2008 parental scheme. Donors may be traced by children when they become adults (Human Fertilisation and Embryology Authority (Disclosure of Donor Information) Regulations 2004, SI 2004/1511). There is, therefore, an acknowledgement – as there is in Adoption Law (s. 79 ACA 2002, Smith and Logan 2002) – that the genetic parent has some status in the minds of children and that that status must be respected. However, that status is not, in law at least, parental. It does not entail access to parental responsibility and is, at best, a tag of identity.

There is one circumstance in which this scheme for determining parenthood may be averted. In the case of a successful surrogacy arrangement, in which a child has been commissioned and the surrogate has, in fact, handed the child to the commissioning parents after giving birth, the commissioning parents may obtain a 'parental order' (s. 54 HFEA 2008) which will make them the child's legal parents. This is the one instance in which an egg donor (the genetic mother) might acquire a legal maternal status. However, her capacity to do so relies, as ever, on the consent of the legal mother (s. 54).

ii. Parental responsibility

By the late twentieth century, children were often being raised in households which did not include both of their parents (Eekelaar and Maclean 1997). The creation of parental responsibility in the CA 1989 (s. 3), therefore, was a significant step heralding a remarkable change in the importance of parents to children. The CA 1989 invented the concept precisely to disaggregate parental status from the important role that adults – usually parents – fulfilled in the lives of children. It allowed those who were raising or wished to raise children to enhance their power to exercise responsibility for them (Bridgeman *et al.* 2008, Probert *et al.* 2009). Parental responsibility is, therefore, often a much more significant attribute of adults caring for children than is parental status. According to the Act it is the traditional 'rights, duties, powers, responsibilities and authority' of parents (s. 3 CA1989). Allocating those powers to people other than parents was the impetus to the legal fragmentation of parenthood (Smart and Neale 1999, Collier and Sheldon 2008). It allowed non-parents to make (or participate in making) fundamentally important decisions about children's upbringing and to involve themselves in children's lives.

In relation to children born as a result of clinically assisted conception parental responsibility follows parental status (Lind 2008). Those who become mothers and fathers by virtue of the provisions of the 2008 Act gain responsibility by virtue of their being parents (under ss 2, 4, CA 1989). Because the genetic parents have no legal relationship with the children they have no parental responsibility for them. At best they may – like any other stranger –apply for leave to apply for a section 8 order (CA 1989) which would give them some of the trappings of parental responsibility.

Although the allocation of parental status and responsibility in circumstances of assisted conception is fairly straight forward (the rules are clear and detailed), problems sometimes arise in assisted conception circumstances that cast doubt on the efficacy of the rules. Two cases decided under the 1990 HFEA are illustrative. In both the court found the particular men were not the fathers of children born as a result of assisted conception; they did not satisfy the statutory conditions for paternity. However, in both the court also found that they deserved (at least some) attributes of parental responsibility.

In *Leeds Teaching Hospitals NHS Trust* v. *Mr and Mrs A* [2003] 1 FLR 1091, two married couples had approached a clinic for assistance in conceiving. Both couples wished to have children using the respective husbands' sperm. However, because of a clinical error the sperm of one husband was used in the insemination of the other wife. Twins were born and the question of fatherhood arose. By the time the case came to court it was clear that the mother's husband and not the sperm 'donor' would raise the children as their father. The court even anticipated that he would successfully adopt the children. But it allocated fatherhood – under the statutory rules – to the sperm 'donor'.

Re D (a child) [2005] UKHL 33 was strikingly different. The mother and her partner, who had approached the clinic for assistance in conceiving, had separated by the time embryos were successfully implanted. By that time the mother did not wish her now ex-partner to participate in raising the child. As he was not, either in law or in fact, the child's father (under the rules) the mother saw no need for his involvement. And yet the court granted him a contact order. It found that he had a valuable contribution to make to the child's upbringing, particularly in relation to helping her understand the circumstances of her birth.

In both these cases aspects of parental responsibility were awarded to men who were not parents. And in *Leeds* the man who was the father was never going to play any parental role in the children's live at all.

The separate allocation of parental status and parental role in these cases should not be surprising. That is, after all, what the 1989 creation of parental responsibility had made possible. However, the misplaced status in *Leeds* and the limitation of parental status in *Re D* raises questions as to why it is necessary to insist on such tightly drawn, narrowly conceived rules for parental status. Why is it possible for parental responsibility to be so generously drawn while parental status remains so constrained (and so distant from the social reality of children's lives)?

iii. The meanings of parental status

Collier and Sheldon (2008) have demonstrated the complex fragmentation of fatherhood. They have traced that fragmentation to the increasing social acceptance of a variety of diverse family structures and to the alteration in the social meanings and social importance that is associated with family membership. Yet, despite this fragmentation in the norms of family life there remains something stubbornly old-fashioned about the way in which the law regards the parental status of those adults who conceive using assisted reproduction clinics. Instead of simply transferring parental responsibility to those who would be parents by assisted conception the law has determined to adjust both status and responsibility. These could not just be unrelated people who, for good reasons, acquired parental responsibility. They had to be parents with those responsibilities.

However, the rising significance of genetics as a mechanism for creating personal identity (Collier and Sheldon 2008, p. 225) has seen the law resurrect the spectre of genetic parents. In a close analysis of *Re G (children) (residence: same-sex partner)* [2006] UKHL 43 Diduck (2007) has demonstrated that courts are not above reinvigorating genetics as a marker of children's welfare. Even where the law has removed or reduced the significance of genetics as a marker of status (as it does in the cases of assisted reproduction and adoption) it does this. This has resulted in the need to craft a language to describe people who are parents, but whose status as parent has been removed. What do we call the genetic father of a child who is simply a sperm donor? Or the genetic mother who is a philanthropic egg donor? (*Re B (Role of Biological Father)* [2007] EWHC 1952, especially at para. 23). In adoption we refer to birth parents while in assisted conception we have begun to refer to genetic parents. And, if Diduck is right, we may begin to see some weak forms of responsibility being allocated to genetic parents who no longer have legal parental status in the lives of 'their' children. Hedley J. ends his judgment in *Re B* with these words: 'The concept of family is both psychological and biological and, in my judgment, a court would be unwise not to have regard to both aspects' (para. 33).

b. Same-sex parents

Where same-sex couples have children without formal clinical intervention they are like other parents: their parental status and role is determined under the ordinary rules for their allocation (*B* v. *B (Custody, Care and Control)* [1991] 1 FLR 402; *Re G (children) (residence: same-sex partner)* [2006] UKHL 43; *Re B (Role of Biological Father)* [2007] EWHC 1952). Where same-sex couples use assisted reproduction services to have children (because they need the reproductive gametes of another person to procreate) their parental status is like all other assisted reproduction parents, determined by the HFEA 2008. However, whenever same-sex couples have children there are additional factors justifying separate consideration of their parenthood. Perhaps most significant of these is the pronounced gendering of parenthood that is always present in the same-sex parental setting. For that reason the discussion in this section will focus on the way in which the ascription of parental status to same-sex parents revolves around and reinforces gender difference.

i. Lesbian couples: having children and becoming parents

Where two women plan to have children they need donor sperm. If they have children informally – if they arrange privately for the (non-clinical) insemination of one of them – one of them will be the child's mother and the 'donor' will be the child's legal father. The second lesbian parent will have no parental status and she will only acquire a legal parental role if she approaches a court. The mother will have parental responsibility for the child while the father will acquire it, or at least some of its attributes, quite easily (see *Re H (Local Authority: Parental Rights)* [1991] 1 FLR 214, and *Re S (Parental Responsibility)* [1995] 2 FLR 648 CA; *Re D (Contact and Parental Responsibility: Lesbian Mothers and Known Father)* [2006] EWHC 2 (Fam); Gilmore 2003; however, see *Re B (Role of Biological Father)* [2007] EWHC 1952 for a case in which the father was granted contact, but not a parental responsibility order because the court was concerned that he might use his parental responsibility to undermine the child's well-being).

If the assistance of a clinic is sought in order to conceive two options present themselves, one more complicated than the other. The simpler option would be to have one of the couple inseminated using donor sperm. The more complicated alternative would be to harvest eggs from one of the couple, create embryos using donor sperm and have them implanted into the other prospective parent. In the first instance the child would be the genetic child of only one of the couple. In the second, however, the child would have a biological relationship with both women. In both instances there is, of course, a genetic relationship with a man. But his legal status as father will be terminated if he provides formal consent to the use of his sperm by others so that they can become parents (s. 41 HFEA 2008). Although the second option is a more complicated and invasive way to have children, it is readily apparent why a couple might choose it, given society's growing attachment towards reifying our biological antecedents (*Re D* and *Re B* (above), and the (factually similar) Australian case of *Re Patrick* (2002) 28 *Fam Law Reports* 579 and US case of *Thomas S.* v. *Robin Y.* 599 NYS 2d 377 (Fam Ct 1993) are all illustrative of the importance that people attach to genetic heritage when arguing about parenting; see too Diduck 2007, Wallbank 2002, Takala and Gylling 2000, Wilkinson 2010).

For the purposes of allocating parental status to the couple, the law does not distinguish between these two options. It allocates motherhood to the woman giving birth (s. 33 HFEA 2008). In order for her partner to be a 'second female parent' she would have to be in a civil partnership with the mother and have consented to her treatment (s. 42 HFEA 2008) exactly as a married man would have had to do. Or she would have to satisfy the 'female parenthood' conditions (ss 43, 44 HFEA 2008). These conditions mirror the 'agreed fatherhood' conditions of section 37 (HFEA 2008). Whether or not the 'non mother' is, in fact, the genetic progenitor of the child is irrelevant to the legal determination of parenthood (ss 33, 47 HFEA 2008).

In the words of Diduck (2007):

> Like fatherhood under the Human Fertilisation and Embryology Act 1990, lesbian parenthood is acquired on a basis that mimics rather than overcomes traditional norms and biology. It applies a type of presumption of paternity to partnered lesbian women and instantiates rather than challenges hetero normativity and 'nature'. It both biologises and heterosexes 'parent' by ascribing that status on the basis of a person forming an exclusive sexual link with the biological parent ... [W]e are left with a situation in which legal parenthood remains limited in number and subtly gendered. (notes removed) (p. 465)

Instead of taking advantage of the combination of science and biology that makes it possible for two women to be physically related to a child, and to ascribe parental status and responsibility on that basis, the law deliberately adopts a binary gendered framework for parental status. The nomenclature of 'parent' (s. 42 HFEA 2008), 'second female parent' (s. 43 HFEA 2008) and 'female parenthood' (ss 43, 44 HFEA 2008) rather than of (additional) 'mother' and 'motherhood' is adopted (as if to replace the nomenclature of fatherhood where the second parent is a man). And the conditions that must be satisfied to become a 'second parent' reiterate the conditions that were designed, and are particularly appropriate, for infertile men who wish to become fathers. This framework for parenthood is unnecessary and (arguably) inappropriate for lesbian parents who have both contributed biologically to a child's creation and who will both fulfil a mothering role in raising their child. The legal rules have no basis in the life of the family and, therefore, appear to hanker after a binary female/male ideal of parenthood. Perhaps most peculiarly, the law does this in the process of recognising a child's additional mother.

ii. Gay male couples: commissioning children and becoming parents

The variety of ways in which two men might become parents is considerably more (practically) limited than it is for two women. If they do not wish to adopt a child (ss 50, 144(4), ACA 2002) a gay male couple would have to approach a surrogate mother to bear one for them. The advantage of the latter option – in this era of raised genetic significance – is that the child would be genetically related to one of the couple (see Alghrani 2008, forthcoming, on the legal complications that arise if the future does hold out the prospect of male pregnancy). Although surrogacy arrangements are unenforceable (s. 1, Surrogacy Arrangements Act 1985) the parental status of those who commissioned the surrogacy can be adjusted if the resulting child is handed over to the commissioning couple (s. 54, HFEA 2008). However, where the child is not handed over (and parental status is not adjusted to reflect the surrogacy arrangement) the law uses its ordinary rules to determine parental status (either under the common law or, where clinical assistance is used, under the HFEA 2008). The child's mother will be the woman giving birth and one of the couple (if he provided sperm) will be the child's father (Otlowski 1999, Wallbank 2002).

Although the gendering of parenthood for male couples is less pronounced than it is for female couples, a gendered assumption of parental preference or parental importance does appear to exist. Most significantly, although two men can become parents, their ability to do so always depends upon (legal) mothers. If a child is born as a result of a surrogacy arrangement the mother is pre-emptively the person either to raise the child, or to control her destiny. This is true even in disputes between the (surrogate) mother and a genetic father who has commissioned the surrogacy (with his partner) (Otlowski 1999, Wallbank 2002).

c. Step-parents

i. Parental status and the complexities of step-parenting

Of the parents we have chosen to discuss, step-parents have the longest social heritage. Yet, their modern manifestation seems to pose the greatest difficulty for lawyers and policy-makers trying to regulate parental relationships for the benefit of children. The difficulties derive from a combination of three factors. One is the contemporary prevalence of step-parenting (Smith 2008, Smart and Neale 1999, Gibson 1996; Wardle 1993; Agell 1993). The second is the competition between (legal or genetic) parents for on-going relationships with their children after they – the parents – separate (Bainham *et al.* 2003, Flowerdew and Neale 2003, Smart and Neale 1999, Smart and Sevenhuijsen 1989). And, third, the quality of step-parental relationships themselves vary widely: there are those in which step-parents take a full and active sharing role in raising their step-children; and there are those in which they fulfil a much more limited role which may involve no more than seeing their step-children during rare contact visits (Smith 2008, Sosson 1993, Wardle 1993, p. 387).

These factors are further complicated by the politics that surrounds post-separation parenting. The unfortunate social perception seems to be that, if the status of step-parents were enhanced, the status of absent parents would be undermined (Agell 1993, p. 412). Given the prevalent social perception of an already precarious post-separation relationship between children and their absent parents (Collier and Sheldon 2006, Bainham *et al.* 2003, Smart and Neale 1999, Smart and Sevenhuijsen 1989) that development would be politically difficult to achieve.

These difficulties have hampered attempts to enhance the legal status of step-parents. The closest the law comes to doing so is to create an environment in which step-parents can adopt their step-children without disrupting the children's relationships with one of their legal parents (ss 51(2), 67(2) and (3) ACA 2002).

ii. Step-parents and parental responsibility

Because the variety of step-relationships that children encounter is complicated by the varying degrees to which step-parents involve themselves in raising the children of their partners (Smith 2008) the legal extension of responsibility to step-parents has been developed gingerly (Wardle 1993, Sosson 1993, Agell 1993). While most legal parents acquire parental responsibility automatically (s. 2 CA 1989) and the rest acquire it relatively easily (s. 4 CA 1989, *Re H (Local Authority: Parental Rights)* [1991] 1 FLR 214, *Re S (Parental Responsibility)* [1995] 2 FLR 648 CA) step-parents must take more onerous steps to acquire it. They must either reach a formal agreement with the parents or approach a court for a parental responsibility order (s. 4A CA 1989). It is worth noting that the rules on the acquisition of parental responsibility by step-parents (introduced into the CA 1989 by ACA 2002) only apply to formal step-parents (that is, to people married to a parent); they do not apply to those who are in an unmarried cohabiting relationship with parents (s. 4A CA 1989).

When unmarried fathers were only able to acquire parental responsibility in the two ways in which step-parents may now acquire it, researchers showed that they did not, in significant numbers, make use of those rules (Barlow and Duncan 2000, p. 139; Barlow *et al.* 2005). Reaching formal agreement or approaching courts to extend powers which are, without their formal extension, being exercised anyway, seemed to be futile to most unmarried men. It is submitted, therefore, that step-parents who are, in fact, parenting are also unlikely to concern themselves with the formalities of the law. Until, that is, a dispute arises. And it is likely to be at this time only that they realise the precariousness of their position.

There are two respects in which the step-parental acquisition of parental responsibility (or aspects of it) has broadened beyond the statutory facility created in section 4A of the Children Act 1989. The first relates to the acquisition of parental responsibility itself. Before the new section was enacted (in s. 112 ACA 2002) the courts had begun, almost routinely, to make shared residence orders as a way of giving step-parents (and their unmarried counterparts) parental responsibility (see, for example, *Re A (A Child: Joint Residence/Parental Responsibility)* [2008] EWCA Civ 867, especially at para. 36, *Re G (shared residence order: parental responsibility)* [2005] EWCA Civ 462; see too Reece 2009 who, although critical of this development, acknowledges that it has taken place). The second relates to the financial obligations of supporting step-children. Where a step-parent treats a child as 'a child of the family' it has become possible for a legal financial support obligation to arise. This obligation may even be extended to a time when the step-parent is no longer a step-parent. A court asked to make financial provision on divorce may require a step-parent to continue to provide financial support to the child of his former spouse (ss 25(4), 41 MCA 1973).

It is clear that step-parents do acquire aspects of parental responsibility, if not by court order then by social and, very occasionally, legal accretion. And often they establish exceptional, lasting, parental relationships with their step-children. Yet acquiring formal parental responsibility is not easy, and, short of adoption, acquiring parental status is impossible. These defects in the legal framework for step parenting are in need of repair.

iii. The significance of gender in the step-parental relationship

There is, once again, a significant gender dimension to the way in which step-parenting responsibilities are borne (Smart and Neale 1999, Smart and Sevenhuijsen 1989). Step-fathers are much more likely to be intimately involved in rearing their step-children than are step-mothers who are more likely to be only peripherally involved in raising their step children (Smith 2008, Flowerdew and Neale 2003). This means that, despite retaining their parental responsibility, absent fathers will rarely exercise the full range of powers, or meet the full range of obligations, that are encapsulated in parental responsibility. Many of those powers and obligations will, instead, be exercised or met by step-fathers. But they will most often be doing so without (formal) parental responsibility and without any parental status in relation to their step-children.

This statistical observation must make us reflect on the mechanisms by which men – both parents and step-parents – come to have parental responsibility for children. Fathers acquire it easily (s. 4 CA 1989, Gilmore 2003). Step-fathers, on the other hand, have a slightly more onerous task acquiring it (s. 4A CA 1989). And yet, in the circumstances of step-parenting, step-fathers are often more likely than fathers to need and to deserve parental responsibility. The final gendered observation, therefore, relates to an irony in the politics of fatherhood. Until now father's rights activists have represented the views of genetic fathers. They have yet to take up the cause of social fathers. This has meant that the political struggles for parental responsibility have an unavoidably gendered dimension. They pit men against women. Perhaps the advent of a struggle for step-parental responsibility will allow us to consider the allocation of power to parents in a way that is less contentiously framed by issues of gender.

Observations on the nature of parental status

In this paper we have tried to outline the ways in which both parental status and parental function have important implications for the potential, real and legal relationships that parents have with their children. In the final section of this paper we wish to consider, thematically, some of the ideas that have been raised so far.

a. Gendering and the fragmentation of parenthood

In Western societies parenting remains gendered (Smart and Sevenhuijsen 1989). There is, therefore, no doubt that parental responsibility follows gendered patterns (Collier and Sheldon 2008). The discussion so far has highlighted the extent to which the allocation of parental status is itself deeply gendered. The conditions that establish motherhood and those that establish fatherhood in law are different. Even in the case of same-sex parents the law has fostered a gendered division for the allocation of parental status (Diduck 2007, discussed above). Additional mothers must satisfy father-like conditions to be parents, and additional fathers require the consent of mothers to have their position as parent confirmed. Where parental status for same-sex couples is beyond the scope of the HFEA 2008 donor parents are often able, because of their gender, to assert a right to participate in a child's life (Arnup and Boyd 1995).

These gendered patterns for the determination of parental status extended to different-sex couples as well. In the context of surrogacy arrangements mothers appear to have greater power to link their parental status to parental responsibility than do fathers (Otlowski 1999). And, in the context of step-parenting relationships legal (gestational), mothers are much more likely to perform a mothering role than are step-mothers, and legal fathers are often usurped as engaged fathers by step-fathers (even though they have no legal parental status to do so).

In discussing the gendered nature of parenthood our aim has been to highlight the importance of expanding the concept of parental status to embrace the variety of kinship relationships to which social parenting has given rise.

b. Status and responsibility

In different ways Reece (2009), Gilmore (2003) and Eekelaar (2001) have each demonstrated the profound revisions that have been made to the nature and scope of parental responsibility since its creation in the CA 1989. Eekelaar has argued that parental responsibility and parental status are of limited use as independent, segregated concepts. Instead their significance derives from their position at the centre of a complex matrix of powers over, and duties towards, children. Gilmore has pointed out that, in some circumstances, parental responsibility has become a badge of status (and not, as s. 3 CA 1989 dictates, a concept allocating real power and tangible obligations to adults who care for children). Because of these journeys away from its original objectives Reece has gone so far as to wonder whether or not parental responsibility is becoming meaningless.

In this paper we have tried to reflect on similar problems but refracted, not through the concept of parental responsibility, but through the older notion of parental status. It seems to us that much of the work that judges, in particular, are trying to get parental responsibility to do is better subsumed under the rubric of parental status. In our view the complications (and possibly growing meaninglessness) of parental responsibility derive from the failure of law to re-assess the parameters of parental status. If, as in the case of assisted reproduction parents and same-sex parents, we were prepared to countenance the allocation of parental status to other adults, and if we were prepared to do so without disrupting the parental status of those who are already parents, we could begin to restore meaning to parental responsibility. That concept could, again, be about the roles that adults play in the lives of children. Parental status, on the other hand, could be the concept that names those who have some significance for children, but who are not (necessarily) actively engaged in rearing them. We do not envisage that a complete separation between these concepts is possible. Parents will, still, most often be responsible for raising children. However, cleaner conceptual tools would help us – and our judges – understand what it is that they are allocating when called upon to do so.

c. More than two parents?

As we have indicated above, the law still subscribes to a two parent ideal for parental status. Our discussion of assisted reproduction parents, same-sex parenting, and step-parenting, however, lead us to believe that the two parent ideal is often some distance from the social reality of parents and children. While the advent of parental responsibility has enabled the fragmentation of parental role to be replicated in law, the absence of a similar fragmentation of parental status has undermined the law's ability to be clear on what it does when it tries to allocate power and status to adults in relation to children. Law needs to reconsider the need for a binary parental status. If status itself could be allocated to more than two people, each inhabiting different attributes of that status, we believe the law would provide society with clearer conceptual tools for the allocation of parental significance to the adults that are involved in raising children.

In this respect same-sex parenthood and gestational surrogacy are instructive. But their lessons might easily be translated into the spheres of infertile parents, step-parents and even adoptive parents. There is some evidence to suggest that a three parent triad was often contemplated in the 1970s and 1980s when lesbian couples used informal insemination to have children (often using gay sperm donors: *Thomas S. v Robin Y.* 599 NYS 2d 377 (Fam Ct 1993); Arnup and Boyd 1995, p. 84). Despite the advent of clinically assisted conception for lesbian couples (which would remove the father from parenthood) there continue to be instances of informal insemination in which parental contests occur between lesbian parents and donor 'fathers' (*Re D (Contact and Parental Responsibility: Lesbian Mothers and Known Father)* [2006] EWHC 2 (Fam); *Re B (Role of Biological Father)* [2007] EWHC 1952). Similar struggles between mothers and commissioning couples in failed surrogacy arrangements occasionally reach the courts (Wallbank 2002, Otlowski 1999, Kandel 1994).

Although the HFEA 2008 has resolved to redistribute parental status from the two parents to, at most, two new parents, Wallbank (2002) and Kandel (1994) have argued convincingly for a broader view of parental status. Judges clearly have great difficulty in constraining fathers who attempt to challenge the authority of non-parents who are raising 'their' children. In both *Re D* and *Re B* the courts expressed great sympathy towards the women who wished to protect their (nuclear) family status from an invasive father. And yet, in both cases, the courts acknowledged the importance to the child of having that father. In *Re Evelyn* (unreported) (Otlowski 1999) the Australian courts were similarly sympathetic to the surrogate mother and the commissioning parents when the mother changed her mind about handing her child to the child's father and his wife. These sympathies – born out of the absence of legal tools to deal with the complexities of these parental situations – are also often present in step-parenting cases: in *Re A (A Child: Joint Residence/Parental Responsibility)* [2008] EWCA Civ 867 the court clearly had sympathy for the step-father's desire for an ongoing status relationship with the child of the woman from whom he was separated. It made a contact order in his favour for that reason. But it had no power to make a status order and the mother's response to that inability was clearly to regard him as less important to their child.

Such cases cry out for the fragmentation of parental status. If courts had the power to enhance the legal standing of adults whose significance to their children is not simply material but ethical, they might finally have a better legal vehicle for the sympathy they express; if parental status could be allocated to more than two people, the need to use parental responsibility to give 'status' might finally reach an end.

There is an added dimension to parental status that bolsters the argument for its fragmentation. Status relationships are long lasting in a way that parental responsibility is not. They linger longer than a child's childhood. The law's concession that children should be able to trace their genetic heritage when they are adults is, therefore, clearly a concession that is about parental status (and not role). If status were allocated without any role content, and if it could be addressed to more than two adults, the 'birth parents' in adoption and 'genetic parents' in assisted reproduction would never need to lose their status link with children. Furthermore, the need to enhance the long term relationships of (some) step parents would also be met. The profound importance that step-parents often have in the lives of their children would have the kind of long term ramifications that they deserve and that parental status offers.

Given the close attachment – whether real or imagined – between children and the various people who are in many different ways involved as their parents it may be time to breach our attachment to the two parent paradigm. Perhaps some children really do have – and deserve to have – more than two people with a real and enduring stake in their lives rather than a tenuous short-lived responsibility for them. Perhaps the complete transfer of (status) parenthood from one or two people to another set of (no more than two) people is no longer the necessity it was when adoption was brought into the realms of law in the early twentieth century. Perhaps it is time to think of both responsibility and parental status in broader, more flexible terms.

d. The consequences of status and its hierarchical restructuring?

There are two potential problems with extending an inherent parental status beyond the confines of (two) narrowly defined adults. One is that status raises a social assumption of parental responsibility. And the other is that status has long-term legal consequences, sometimes extending beyond the parents and children in question. If parental status is to be fragmented each of these problems will have to be addressed.

i. Social assumptions of parental authority

Once people consider themselves to be the parents of a child, they think they ought to have some say in the child's upbringing. The fact of a genetic or legal relationship, alone, seems to create a claim to compete for parental authority (no matter how well ordered our rules removing parental authority from them are). The fear of adoptive parents seems always to have been based on the absence of legitimacy that their parental claim has when compared with the parental claim of the 'birth parents' (Smith and Logan 2002). Adoption gives adoptive parents a sense of security in their relationship with the child. Openness in adoption undermines that sense of security. Similarly, the fear of same-sex couples seems frequently to be that the absent genetic parent might, by virtue of the genetic relationship with the child, demand greater involvement in rearing the child than the resident non-parent (*Re D (Contact and Parental Responsibility: Lesbian Mothers and Known Father)* [2006] EWHC 2 (Fam); *Re B (Role of Biological Father)* [2007] EWHC 1952); *Re Patrick* (2002) 28 *Fam Law Reports* 579, *Thomas S.* v. *Robin Y.* 599 NYS 2d 377 (Fam Ct 1993), Dempsey 2004, Wallbank 2002, Arnup and Boyd 1995). Although these fears might be exacerbated by the prejudice that same-sex couples feel they suffer in society (*Re D* (above), paras 61, 62, Dempsey 2004) it is noteworthy that similar genetic assumptions arise in cases involving heterosexual relationships. In *Re A (A Child: Joint Residence/Parental Responsibility)* [2008] EWCA Civ 867, the mother had deliberately sought genetic testing of her child to undermine her ex-partner's claim to a continuing parental relationship with her. And in *Re T (Paternity: Ordering Blood Tests)* [2001] 2 FLR 1190 a man sought (and was granted) genetic testing in order to bolster his claim to a parental relationship with a child (Northover and Dennison 2002).

If it is true that the social perception is that genetic parental status enhances a claim to parental authority the law will have to address this issue if it is to extend parental status to more than two people. Somehow, legal parental status will need to have a similar social impact. Indeed, in some instances legal parental status will have to have a more profound social impact than genetic status now appears to have. If the law comes to use a refined concept of parental responsibility to order parental authority, the confirmation or allocation of legal parental status to other adults cannot be allowed to undermine that hierarchy of parental authority.

ii. The legal consequences of parental status

At present parental status has wide ranging legal consequences; parents do not, for example, require leave to apply for orders in relation to children (as non-parents do: s. 10 CA 1989). And these legal consequences often extend to other status relationships which arise out of the parental relationship. The rules on intestacy, for example, extend beyond parents and children to other family members traced through legal kinship ties. Because parental status has legal significance any decision to expand the number of people to whom it is extended must accept that those consequences will apply to all of those to whom it is extended. Alternatively, a system must be established which will allow for the creation of a hierarchy of status (in the way that a hierarchy of responsibility can be arranged under s. 8 CA 1989).

iii. Creating immaterial legal consequences for parental status

The advent of genetic tracing in assisted reproduction and openness in adoption has demonstrated that the significance of genetic parental status sometimes exists only to provide a child with a badge of identity. Genetic information is required because children want to know their origins. It is not attached to an expectation that the 'relationship' will have a material consequence. It is submitted, that any hierarchy of parental status must be able to accommodate legal parents like these (those whose identity has no material affect on children at all). The developing rules that allow children to trace their birth parents in adoption (s. 79 ACA 2002) and their genetic progenitors in assisted reproduction (Human Fertilisation and Embryology Authority (Disclosure of Donor Information) Regulations 2004, SI 2004/1511) have already begun to do this. It is clear that genetic parental status is gaining a dimension of legal significance that has no material consequence. Instead it is rooted simply in a renewed interest in genetic origins (Diduck 2007, Collier and Sheldon 2008).

e. The usual absence of law in parenting: law's role

The final observation we wish to make relates to the role of law in parenting. Parents and the other adults who participate in raising children usually conduct themselves beyond the gaze of the law. Law tends to become involved in the parenting of children only when things go wrong. Because families are diverse and their problems complicated the particular event that requires legal intervention can be infinitely diverse. And the responses of individuals to those problems are equally diverse. Each of the cases we have discussed in this essay demonstrates aspects of this assertion.

The cases also show how the resolutions that the law provides to the problems that families present continue to have a life beyond the day on which the legal problem reaches its culmination (much of the judgment in *Re D (Contact and Parental Responsibility: Lesbian Mothers and Known Father)* [2006] EWHC 2 (Fam) is given over to discussing the changing circumstances of the family following their responses to the court's earlier ruling). In other words, the solutions that law provides may become the kernel of new family problems and result in new negotiations to resolve those family problems. They themselves may, later, have to be resolved in legal forums (as the 'final' decisions in *Re G* and *Re D* attest).

At least as significantly, legal resolutions have ramifications in society. People see legal decisions as indicators of the way in which similar family disputes are (or ought to be) resolved. The media report judicial pronouncements in family cases and their reports have a life beyond the actual dispute. Media reporting on father's rights movements, for example, impacts upon the way in which people understand the law to allocate parental responsibility to parents (Collier and Sheldon 2006). The way our society thinks about family problems is framed by these rumblings about those problems.

We are ending with these observations simply to reflect on the limited power of the law to assert control over the family problems that it wishes to resolve (see King and Piper 1995, especially Ch. 2). Parenthood is a diverse social activity. Social actors and their discourses about parents are as likely to shift the boundaries of parental activity as are legal rules and legal rulings. It is for this reason that lawyers and policy makers should acknowledge the limitations of their power. Law's ambitions must be tailored accordingly. It cannot hope to resolve all problems. Instead the law should set out to provide a framework for resolution which allows problems to be 'self solving'. In this respect the work of Teubner (1989) may be useful. For Teubner law must limit its substantive involvement in decision making because it has a limited understanding of and a limited power to address substantive issues. Instead it should set out to design a framework for dispute resolution which will allocate some of the power of resolution to actors better able to exercise substantive influence than the law is able to do. Law simply provides forums for dispute resolution, and procedural guidance for their satisfactory resolution. The hope is that the need for more intrusive official interventions will thereby be circumvented.

f. Fathers (and mothers)

In each of the thematic discussions above, the distinction between fatherhood and motherhood looms large. When we talk of the fragmentation of parenthood as something gendered we raise, particularly, the spectre of complicated notions of fatherhood (Collier and Sheldon 2008). Motherhood remains a much more stable and consistent concept. When we discuss the link between parental status and parental responsibility, again, the impact of their disaggregation is different for women than it is for men. Women are much more likely to be parents who are actively enjoying parental responsibility than are fathers. Paternal status is more often segregated from paternal parental responsibilities. Step-fathers are the complicating 'fathers'; for these men their parental role is often active, but they lack parental status. Even here, however, we find that there is a breach between their parental status and their parental responsibilities.

Even our discussions about children having more than two parents impacts differently on fathers than it does on mothers. Because mothers usually perform as mothers, third parents are more likely to be fathers who share their parental position with two more involved parents (step-fathers and gamete donor fathers are the most obvious examples). We have also argued that parental status hierarchies are necessary because the competition for paternal status will have an impact on perceptions of parental power. Once again, the necessity of a hierarchy applies much more obviously to fathers (because of their role) than it does to mothers. Finally, the discussion on the limitations of law in its regulation of family relationships revolves principally around a social world which sees fatherhood as problematic.

Thus, although our discussions about fragmenting parenthood have been gender neutral, it is clear that the need to re-examine the parameters of parental status is driven by a need, principally, to re-evaluate the law's attitude to fathers.

Conclusion

In this paper we have tried to set out reasons for expanding parental status in ways that parallel the late twntieth century transformation of parental responsibility. If we embrace the fragmentation of parenthood and if we wish to celebrate the myriad ways in which people relate to and care for children, it is, we believe, necessary to think much more creatively about the ways in which parental status can be brought into the matrix of fragmented parental relationships. This is particularly important for fathers – in all their varieties. Given the rising interest in our genetic origins and our ancestry (probably for no better reason than that we are inquisitive beings and that science is able to enlighten us) the biological fact of parenthood – and fatherhood in particular – will, it is submitted, continue to have growing social currency. But it does not detract from the breach that now often exists between genetic links and parental performance. And that breach, we have argued, demands more than just a legal role reallocation. People who spend decades performing a parental role deserve parental status far more that those who do not, but who are parents by virtue of their genetic status or some, limited, legal reallocation of that status. They deserve that status because its longer term legal consequences ought to be applied to them. What assisted reproduction, same-sex parenting, and step-parenting (and adoption and fostering and other kinds of parental caring) teach us is that parental identity and parental status are both important to us. We do not, it is submitted, properly acknowledge that importance in law when we reallocate some of the duties of parenting without also broadening the scope of parental status.

References

Agell, A., 1993. Step-parenthood and biological parenthood: competition or cooperation. *In*: T. Eekelaar and P. Sarcevic, eds. *Parenthood in Modern society: legal and social issues for the twenty first century*. Dordrecht, Germany: Martinus Nijhoff Publishers.

Alghrani, A., 2008. Regulating the reproductive revolution: ectogenesis – a regulatory minefield. *Law and bioethics: current legal issues*, 11, 303–329.

Alghrani, A., forthcoming. Assisted reproductive technologies and family formation: how womb transplant technology will transform the concept of the 'family' in far greater ways than the state could have envisaged. *In*: C. Lind, H. Keating and J.Bridgeman, eds. *Taking responsibility: law and the changing family*. London: Ashgate.

Arnup, K. and Boyd, S., 1995. Familial disputes? Sperm donors, lesbian mothers, and legal parenthood. *In*: D. Herman and C. Stychin, eds. *Legal inversions: lesbians, gay men, and the politics of law*. Philadelphia, PA: Temple University Press.

Bainham, A., 1999. Parentage, parenthood and parental responsibility: subtle, elusive yet important distinctions. *In*: A. Bainham, S. Day Sclater and M. Richards, eds. *What is a parent?* Oxford: Hart Publishing.

Bainham, A., Lindley, B., Richards, M. and Trinder, L., eds, 2003. *Children and their families: contact, rights and welfare*. Oxford: Hart Publishing.

Barlow, A. and Duncan, S., 2000. New Labour's communitarianism, supporting families and the 'rationality mistake': Part II. *Journal of social welfare and family law*, 22 (2), 129–143.

Barlow, A., Duncan, S., James, G. and Park, A., 2005. *Cohabitation, marriage and the law: social change and legal reform in the 21st century*. Oxford: Hart Publishing.

Bridgeman, J., Keating, H. and Lind, C., eds, 2008. *Responsibility, law and the family*. Aldershot: Ashgate Publishing.

Collier, R. and Sheldon, S., eds, 2006. *Fathers' rights activism and law reform in comparative perspective*. Oxford: Hart Publishing.

Collier, R. and Sheldon, S., 2008. *Fragmenting fatherhood: a socio-legal study*. Oxford: Hart Publishing.

Dempsey, D., 2004. Donor, father or parent? Conceiving paternity in the Australian family court. *International journal of law, policy and the family*, 18, 76.

Diduck, A., 2007. 'If only we can find the appropriate terms to use the issue will be solved': law, identity and parenthood. *Child and family law quarterly*, 19, 458.

Eekelaar, J., 2001. Rethinking Parental Responsibility. *Family law*, 31, 426.

Eekelaar, J. and Maclean, M., 1997. *The Parental obligation: a study of parenthood across households*. Oxford: Hart Publishing.

Flowerdew, J. and Neale, B., 2003. Trying to stay apace: children with multiple challenges in their post-divorce family lives. *Childhood*, 10 (2), 147–161.

Gibson, C., 1996. Contemporary divorce and changing family patterns. *In*: M. Freeman, ed. *Divorce: where next?* Aldershot: Dartmouth Publishing.

Gilmore, S., 2003. Parental responsibility and the unmarried father – a new dimension to the debate. *Child and family law quarterly*, 15, 21.

Kandel, R.F., 1994. Which came first: the mother or the egg? A kinship solution to gestational surrogacy. *Rutgers law review*, 47, 165.

King, M. and Piper, C., 1995. *How the law thinks about children*. Aldershot: Arena.

Lind, C., 2008. Responsible fathers: paternity, the blood tie and family responsibility. *In*: J. Bridgeman, H. Keating and C. Lind, eds. *Responsibility, law and the family*. Aldershot: Ashgate Publishing, 191–210.

Northover, A. and Dennison, G., 2002. Genetic testing and the impact on the family. *Family Law*, 32, 752.

Otlowski, M., 1999. *Re Evelyn* – reflections on Australia's first litigated surrogacy case. *Medical law review*, 7, 38–57.

Probert, R., Gilmore, S. and Herring, J., 2009. *Responsible parents and parental responsibility*. Oxford: Hart Publishing.

Reece, H., 2009. The degradation of parental responsibility. *In*: R. Probert, S. Gilmore and J. Herring, eds. *Responsible parents and parental responsibility*. Oxford: Hart Publishing.

Smart, C. and Neale, B., 1999. *Family fragments*. Cambridge: Polity Press.

Smart, C. and Sevenhuijsen, S., 1989. *Child custody and the politics of gender*. London: Routledge.

Smith, C. and Logan, J., 2002. Adoptive parenthood as a 'legal fiction' – its consequences for direct post-adoption contact. *Child and family law quarterly*, 14 (3), 281.

Smith, M., 2008. Resident mothers in stepfamilies. *In*: J. Pryor, ed. *The international handbook of stepfamilies: policy and practice in legal, research and clinical environments*. Hoboken, NJ: Wiley.

Sosson, J., 1993. The legal status of step-families in continental European countries. *In*: J. Eekelaar and P. Sarcevic, eds. *Parenthood in modern society: legal and social issues for the twenty first century*. Dordrecht, Germany: Martinus Nijhoff Publishers.

Takala, T. and Gylling, H., 2000. Who should know about our genetic makeup and why? *Journal of medical ethics*, 26, 171–174.

Teubner, G., 1989. How the law thinks: towards a constructivist epistemology of law. *Law and society review*, 23 (5), 727–758.

Wallbank, J., 2002. Too many mothers? Surrogacy, kinship and the welfare of the child. *Medical law review*, 10, 271.

Wardle, L., 1993. The evolving rights and duties of step-parents: making new rules for new families. *In*: J. Eekelaar and P. Sarcevic, eds. *Parenthood in modern social issues for the twenty first century*. Dordrecht, Germany: Martinus Nijhoff Publishers.

Wilkinson, R., 2010. When is my genetic information your business? biological, emotional, and financial claims to knowledge. *Cambridge quarterly of healthcare ethics*, 19, 1–8 (forthcoming).

11

What is a Parent?

Emily Jackson

As a result of changes - both social and technological - in the ways in which we reproduce, a growing number of children have more than two 'parents'. Legally, however, it is only possible for a child to have one mother and one father. In this article I investigate the law's inability to accommodate the reality of multiple parent/child relationships. I argue that the law's reliance upon a superficially factual inquiry into the identity of a child's parents obscures the policy choices that might be revealed if we were to abandon the now-outdated principle of parental exclusivity.

1.   Introduction

Because parents possess a bundle of important rights and duties, clear and unambiguous legal definitions of mother and fatherhood are self-evidently desirable. And yet the law has tended to assume that the existence of a parent/child bond will simply be obvious. While this may be true in the paradigm case of a child conceived through sexual intercourse and brought up by both her genetic progenitors, for an increasing number of children there may be genuine uncertainty about the identity of their parents. Reproductive technologies, as is commonly observed, have the potential to fragment our definitions of mother and fatherhood. Science, according to John Lawrence Hill, has 'distilled the various phases of procreation - coitus, conception and gestation - into their component parts, wreaking havoc on our prevailing conceptions of parenthood' (Hill, 1991). Where there are a number of possible mothers and/or fathers, how should we choose between them in order to identify a child's *legal* parents?

At the outset, it is of course important to acknowledge that most children know who their parents are without any need to resort to a complex legal definition. This is because all of the various criteria that we associate with mother and fatherhood are crystallized in the same two people. Such parents fall within what we might refer to as the 'core of certainty' and represent what I intend to call the paradigm case. Outside of this core of certainty lies a 'penumbra of uncertainty' in which the normal incidents of parenthood are more widely distributed. Here we may have more than one woman who has a plausible reason to believe that she is a particular child's mother. For example, following egg or embryo donation, or IVF surrogacy, a woman gives birth to a child to whom she is not genetically related. Two women might then claim to be the *biological* mother of the same child. In such cases the identity of the child's legal mother is not obvious. Rather, outside of the paradigm case, we must *decide* which of the various candidates has the better claim to be considered the child's legal mother.

Yet framing the question in this way uncritically accepts what I believe to be the law's principal stumbling block, namely its assumption that a child can only have two legal parents: one mother and one father. Conventionally, legal parenthood has been an indivisible and exclusive status: you either are a child's mother or father, or you are not (Bartlett, 1984, 879). Provided that one woman is recognised as a child's legal mother, no other woman can have her 'motherhood' of the same child acknowledged simultaneously. This is, I shall argue, unnecessarily confusing for children, who may find it harder to understand that one of their 'mothers' is a legal stranger than they would living with the reality that two women stand in a maternal relationship towards them.

In this chapter, I propose to examine what we mean by the word 'parent', both in the paradigm case, and within the penumbra of uncertainty. A number of different criteria ground our definition of parenthood, and while in the paradigm case these are all present within the same two people, within the penumbra of uncertainty, they may be split between different individuals. Because the law has been stymied by the principle of parental exclusivity, its response to the splitting of the normal incidents of parenthood has been to try to identify a hierarchy of criteria which will result in one putative parent's claim trumping the others. In so doing, it has become spectacularly confused and confusing, not least because different hierarchies operate in different circumstances. So, for instance, the intention to become a parent will sometimes trump genetic relatedness, while at other times, the genetic link is decisive. I will suggest that the quest to identify one mother and one father within the penumbra of uncertainty has been a profoundly misguided enterprise. If instead we were to acknowledge the reality that some children have more than one mother and/or father, I think that we might be able to reach a solution that would have both practical and symbolic advantages for children and their parents.

In addition to the existing technological and social reordering of family life, new pressures on the legal meaning of parenthood can be foreseen. It seems that within a few years, it will be possible to create gametes artificially, the most likely source being stem cell lines which have been extracted from human embryos. This will mean that same-sex couples will be able to have children who are genetically related to both of them. It is already possible to create what are known as parthonotes, that is eggs which appear to begin the process of cell division without having been fertilised. Parthogenesis - from the Greek for Virgin birth - may not be that far away. If human reproductive cloning becomes a reality, there will inevitably be considerable confusion over the resulting child's parentage. Is the DNA source the child's sole parent? Is the woman's whose denucleated egg was used also a biological parent, and what about the woman who gestates the pregnancy? Alternatively, if a clone is perceived to be a delayed twin of the DNA source, are her parents in fact the same people as the DNA source's parents?

My first task in this chapter is to think about why we might need to identify a child's parents, and to offer some criticism of the way in which the law has tended to approach this question. I intend to argue that the law has become hopelessly muddled and incoherent, and that it is time to rethink what we might mean when we use the word 'parent'.

2. The Legal Significance of Being a Parent

Why does the identity of a child's legal parents matter? It would be impossible to list every situation in which we might want to know who a child's legal parents are, but a few examples may be useful. First, succession on intestacy is governed in part by the parental bond, and the connections with other relatives that flow from this primary relationship. Second, the right to claim damages for the tortiously caused death of a parent or child is clearly dependent upon knowing what counts as a parent/child relationship. Third, the duty to pay child support is owed by a child's legal parents.[1] Fourth, a person is a British citizen if at the time of her birth, her father or mother is a British citizen or settled in the United Kingdom,[2] which again makes parental identity a matter of considerable importance. Fifth, parents have certain rights to make applications to the Courts for orders relating to their child. They can, for example, apply without the leave of the court for residence and contact orders.

In sum, since parents have certain rights and responsibilities *as* parents, it is obviously important to know who they are from the moment of the child's birth, and preferably before. Given that - for a variety of reasons - uncertainty exists, the law must devise some mechanism(s) through which legal parenthood can be fairly and clearly allocated. Before offering some criticism of the English law's approach to this question, I first describe how the law currently identifies a child's legal parents.

---

[1] Child Support Act 1991, s.1
[2] British Nationality Act 1981 s. 1(1)

3   The Paradigm Case: What are the defining features of parenthood?

There are a number of ways in which we might identify a child's parents. For mothers these are currently: (1) giving birth; (2) contributing the egg; and (3) intending to raise the child. For fathers, they are: (1) contributing the sperm; (2) intending to raise the child; (3) being married to the child's mother; and (4) being registered on the child's birth certificate.[3] Almost all mothers satisfy all three criteria, and many - though by no means all - fathers will fulfil all four. Where each of the three defining features of motherhood vest in one woman, and all four defining features of fatherhood vest in one man, we have an example of the paradigm case in which the parenthood of a child is entirely straightforward. Of course, that child might subsequently be adopted, which would result in the separation of, *inter alia,* the intention to raise the child and genetic relatedness. Given the availability of legal adoption, even within the paradigm case, legal parenthood is necessarily potentially impermanent.

Nevertheless, where a man and a woman conceive a child sexually, within marriage, whom they intend to raise, we can unproblematically accept that they are that child's parents. Some parents who differ only marginally from this paradigm case will also very obviously be a child's parents. An unmarried father, for example, who is registered on the birth certificate; genetically related to his child and intends to raise her is unquestionably that child's father. He may not be subject to the common law presumption of legitimacy within marriage, but he undoubtedly still falls within the core of certainty that we might attribute to the word 'father'.

But what if we move slightly further away from the paradigm case. What it, for example, a child is conceived using donated sperm? Here we might have a man who intends to raise the child; is married to the child's mother; and registered on the birth certificate, and *another* man whose sperm was used to fertilise the mother's egg. Who is the 'father' of this child? Following a surrogacy arrangement, we will have a woman who intends to raise the child and who may have contributed the egg, and *another* woman who gestated the pregnancy and gave birth. Which woman is this child's mother? Because the principle of parental exclusivity insists that one mother and one father must be singled out, the conventional approach to answering these questions has been to try to work out which of the features that we normally associate with parenthood should be decisive. While this might be relatively straightforward if a universally applicable hierarchy could be devised through which one factor - such as the genetic link - always took priority, as we see in the next sections the law has instead used different tests in different circumstances, resulting in an extraordinarily incoherent approach to the identification of parents.

4 The current law

(a) Paternity

At common law, the husband of a married woman is presumed to be the genetic father of any child that she bears (*pater est quem nuptiae demonstrant*), and is therefore automatically treated as the child's legal father from birth. This presumption was, however, always rebuttable by proof that the mother's husband could not be the child's genetic father. Before blood tests were available, the sort of evidence that might displace the presumption would be that the husband was sterile or impotent, or that he had been *extra quator maria* (beyond the four seas of England) at the time of conception. While the presumption of paternity within marriage usually simply confirms the genetic father's identity, at times it results in a legal fiction. A child's mother and 'father' may both know that another man is her biological father, but the presumption enables them to conceal her extra-marital conception. This common law rule works, therefore, not to promote truth about a child's genetic origins, but rather to safeguard the traditional family unit.

Since the 1940s, blood tests have been able to assist in identifying the child's genetic father. Until fairly recently, blood tests could only rule out a man's paternity. A man who shared the child's blood group might be her father, but so might any other man with the same blood group. Only if a man's blood group revealed that he could not have fathered this child was decisive evidence available that he could not be her father. Over the last 20 years, DNA fingerprinting has enabled paternity to be proved with a degree of accuracy which now comes very close to complete certainty. Under section 20(1) of the Family Law Reform Act 1969, as amended, the Court may 'give a direction for the use of scientific tests to ascertain whether such tests show that a party to the proceedings is or is not the father or mother of that person'. Inferences are drawn from a putative parent's refusal to be tested.[4] The purpose of a section 20 direction is therefore now to *establish* paternity, rather than to exclude it as a possibility.[5]

Yet despite the availability of proof of genetic fatherhood, the presumption of paternity within marriage has not been entirely displaced. Rather there have been a few times when the courts

---

[3] Births and Deaths Registration Act 1953 s. 34(2)
[4] Family Law Reform Act 1969, s. 23(1). *In re A (A Minor) (Paternity: Refusal of Blood Test)* [1994] 2 FLR 463
[5] *Re H (A Minor)(Blood Tests: Parental Rights)* [1996] 3 WLR 505; *Re J (A Minor)(Wardship)* [1988] 1 FLR 65.

have persisted in using the man's *relationship* with the child's mother and/or his *intention* to raise the child as the primary indicators of legal paternity. In *Re F (A Minor) (Blood Tests: Parental Rights)*,[6] for example, E's mother had been having sexual intercourse with both her husband and the applicant at the time of E's conception. Her relationship with the applicant had ended before the birth, and there had been no contact. The presumption of legitimacy within marriage meant that the law recognised the mother's husband, who was bringing up E as his own child, as her father. According to the Court of Appeal, the chances of the putative father being granted parental responsibility or contact with the child were slim. They therefore refused to grant a direction for blood tests to determine paternity, on the grounds that this would 'disturb ..the stability of the family unit within which E has lived since her birth', with no countervailing benefits to E.

Hence a man's relationship with the child's mother, coupled with his intention to raise the child, can sometimes trump genetics as the test for paternity. Legal fatherhood consists in both a genetic and a social relationship, and when the two are severed, biology is not necessarily decisive. A similar approach has been evident in other jurisdictions. In the US case *Department of Health and Rehabilitative Services v. Privette*, for example, the Court stated that

> It is conceivable that a man who has established a loving, caring relationship of some years' duration with his legal child later will prove not to be the biological father. Where this is so, it seldom will be in the children's best interests to wrench them away from their legal fathers and judicially declare that they now must regard strangers as their fathers. The law does not require such cruelty toward children.[7]

Genetics as the test for paternity is also routinely trumped by intention following donor insemination. When treatment is provided in licensed clinics, the sperm donor will have signed a consent form agreeing to waive his right to be recognised as the father of any children conceived using his gametes. Donation is then conditional upon the donor's clearly expressed intention *not* to become a father. If the woman being treated in a licensed clinic with donated sperm is married, the presumption is that her husband has agreed to be treated as the father of any child that may be born as a result of the treatment.[8] He can only avoid being recognised as the child's legal father if he can establish that he did *not* consent to the treatment received by his wife. If the woman is unmarried, her heterosexual partner will be the legal father of any child that may be born provided that the couple were treated 'together'. On a literal interpretation, this latter

---

[6] [1993] Fam 314
[7] 617 So. 2d 305 (Fla. 1993) 308
[8] Human Fertilisation and Embryology Act 1990 s.28(2)

provision is misleading because the male partner will not have received any treatment himself. Instead,

> what has to be demonstrated is that, in the provision of treatment services with donor sperm, the doctor was responding to a request for that form of treatment made by the woman and the man as a couple, notwithstanding the absence in the man of any physical role in such treatment.[9]

Despite the statute's rather ambiguous wording, the purpose of this rule is clear: if the clinic are aware of the unmarried man's *intention* to become the father of any child born following treatment, the law will recognise him as the child's legal father. Because it is routine to demand that both husbands and unmarried male partners sign consent forms agreeing to be treated as the father of any child who might be born following treatment, there is usually decisive proof of intent. As a result, disputes about paternity following fertility treatment are uncommon, although as demonstrated by *Re R (a child)*[10] and *Leeds Teaching Hospital NHS Trust v A*,[11] not unprecedented.

In *Re R (a child)*, a woman sought treatment with donated sperm after she and her partner, with whom she had previously sought treatment together, had split up. She did not tell the clinic that the relationship was over, and as a result the clinic relied upon the earlier consent forms which had been signed by her and her ex-partner. The Court of Appeal held that whether a couple were being 'treated together' under section 28(3) should be judged at the time of embryo transfer or insemination, and not when the couple were first accepted for treatment. Hence in this case the ex-partner was not being treated together with the child's mother at the relevant time, so he could not be recognized as the child's legal father. A different sort of dispute arose in *Leeds Teaching Hospital NHS Trust v A*, where Mr B's sperm was used to fertilise Mrs A's eggs by mistake. Mr A had consented to the use of his own sperm to fertilise his wife's eggs, and not to the treatment which his wife actually received, and he was therefore unable to acquire paternity under section 28(2). So while intention can trump genetic fatherhood under the 1990 Act, this will be possible only if the facts fit squarely within the terms of section 28.

Intention is also only able to trump genetic fatherhood if the sperm has been provided in accordance with the consent requirements laid out in both the Human Fertilisation and Embryology Act 1990[12] and the HFEA's Code of Practice (HFEA, 2004: part 6). If these conditions are not met – for example if a woman inseminates herself at home with sperm obtained through a private arrangement or purchased over the internet - genetic paternity takes priority

---
[9] *U v W (Attorney General Intervening)* [1998] Fam. 29, per Wilson J at 40
[10] [2003] EWCA Civ 182, [2003] Fam 129
[11] [2003] EWHC 259, [2003] 1 FLR 1091

over intention. Should this woman be married, her husband will be treated as the child's father, although this common law presumption might be trumped by genetic tests which identify the sperm donor. If she registers a different man - her unmarried partner, for example - as the child's father, there is again a presumption of his paternity which could be rebutted by genetic evidence. Once identified, the sperm donor will be under a duty to maintain his child throughout her minority.

Following a surrogacy arrangement, the child's legal father will initially be the surrogate mother's husband, who is neither the intended nor the genetic father, but acquires his paternity through the common law presumption of legitimacy within marriage. This might subsequently be rebutted by genetic tests that reveal him to be unrelated to the child. And fatherhood can be formally transferred either through adoption or the special procedure introduced by section 30 of the Human Fertilisation and Embryology Act 1990. Nevertheless, from the moment of the child's birth, a man who did not instigate the child's conception, is not genetically related to her, and who usually has no desire or intention to play any part in her life, will have the right to take decisions about her upbringing, and will be obliged to maintain her. Conversely, the genetic and intended father will initially bear no responsibility for 'his' child. Because neither adoption nor the section 30 procedure is straightforward, not all surrogacy arrangements culminate in the formal transfer of legal parenthood. For obvious reasons, it is impossible to tell how many unofficial transfers of children take place each year. Worryingly, however, the Brazier Report concluded that 'a substantial proportion of commissioning couples are failing to apply to the courts to become the legal parents of the child.' (Brazier *et al*, 1998: para 5.7). In such situations the surrogate mother's husband (if she has one) remains the legal father, and the man who is bringing up the child is treated as a legal stranger to 'his' child.

A compelling illustration of the illogicality of the UK's rules on paternity following surrogacy is provided by applying them to the infamous American case, *In re Marriage of Buzzanca*.[13] In his divorce petition, John Buzzanca asserted that his marriage to Luanne Buzzanca had been childless. Luanne Buzzanca responded by claiming that a surrogate mother (SM) was expecting the couple's first child. Jaycee Buzzanca, who was born six days later, had been conceived using sperm and eggs from anonymous donors (let us call the sperm donor SD and the egg donor ED). The surrogate and her husband (SM and SH) did not seek to become Jaycee's parents. The question for the court was a complex one. Out of the three plausible candidates for fatherhood

---

[12] Schedule 3
[13] 72 Cal. Rptr. 2d 280 (Ct. App. 1998), review denied, No. S069696, 1998 Cal. LEXIS 3830 (June 10, 1998)

(John Buzzanca, SD, SH) and the three possible mothers (Luanne Buzzanca, ED and SM), who are Jaycee's legal parents?

At first instance, the trial judge reached the rather surprising conclusion that, despite this surfeit of possible mothers and fathers, none could be considered Jaycee's legal parents and Jaycee must be judged to be a legal orphan. This was reversed on appeal when the Court held that because Mr and Mrs Buzzanca had jointly initiated Jaycee's conception, they were her legal parents and they were both therefore under a duty to contribute to her support. As a matter of justice, this seems right. John Buzzanca had deliberately instigated Jaycee's unconventional conception, and it would seem iniquitous for the law to allow him to shrug off any legal responsibility for the resulting child. John Buzzanca is Jaycee's father because without the Buzzanca's decision to become parents through this bizarre arrangement, Jaycee would never have been born. Identifying the surrogate mother's husband as Jaycee's father (as English law would have done) would absolve John Buzzanca of his responsibility for the life he deliberately created, and instead pass legal responsibility for Jaycee's wellbeing for the next 18 years to a man who is not genetically related to her, and who never intended or wanted to become her father.

So we can see that, outside of the paradigm case, the test for legal fatherhood varies according to the circumstances. A *genetic* link will usually - though not always – determine fatherhood in cases of disputed paternity, where the mother was having sexual intercourse with two men at the time of conception. If a child is conceived using donated sperm, *intention* will trump the genetic link provided that insemination took place in a licensed clinic. But if the sperm donation was accomplished informally, *genetic* relatedness will be decisive. Following a surrogate birth, it is the man's *relationship* with the child's mother that normally determines the identity of the child's father. Given this hotchpotch of competing presumptions and hierarchies, the identity of a child's legal father is patently not a self-evident question of fact.

(b)   Maternity

In English law, while motherhood may subsequently be transferred by adoption or the section 30 procedure, *ab initio* a child's legal mother will always be the woman who gave birth to her. Although now also given statutory effect,[14] this common law rule derives from the maxim *mater est quam gestation demonstrat* (by gestation, the mother is demonstrated). Or in the words of

---

[14] Human Fertilisation and Embryology Act 1990 s. 27

Lord Simon in the *Ampthill Peerage* case, maternity is 'proved demonstrably by parturition'.[15] Yet we immediately have a source of confusion here. Is it gestation itself that is decisive, or does gestation merely *demonstrate* or offer proof that the woman who gives birth is the *genetic* mother of the child? So while usually assumed to mean that legal motherhood always vests in the gestational mother, an alternative interpretation of this common law rule could therefore be that the test for motherhood is in fact genetic relatedness, rather than gestation. Until the development of *in vitro* fertilisation techniques, gestation simply constituted irrefutable evidence of the decisive genetic link.

The adoption of a universal gestational test for maternity is usually, of course, unproblematic. Its principal defect is its application to undisputed surrogacy arrangements, when the rule will vest maternal status in a woman who never intended to be the child's mother. Because most surrogate mothers do want to hand over the baby after birth, the practical consequence of the universal gestation-based test are that the child is born into a legal limbo which will continue until parental status and responsibility is formally transferred via judicial proceedings. And as noted earlier, since no formal transfer will ever take place in a 'substantial proportion' of cases, this legal limbo may continue throughout her life. This sort of uncertainty, even if relatively short-lived, is self-evidently not in the best interests of the child. In the absence of a dispute, it would therefore seem sensible for intention to be decisive. In the handful of cases where there is a disagreement over the child's parentage, some mechanism to resolve the dispute must be found. This could consist in a default test (gestation or intention, for example), or in some sort of 'best interests' assessment.

In England, depending upon the context, a variety of tests can be employed in order to identify a child's legal father. In sharp contrast, the definition of mother is rigidly inflexible and inattentive to the different contexts in which children are conceived. Of course women's gestational capacity is clearly a material difference between the sexes, and therefore adopting differential tests for mother and fatherhood is not presumptively discriminatory. But if we think about some of the reasons for gestational priority, a powerful argument against differential treatment of men and women emerges. Both men and women can, via gamete donation, voluntarily surrender their parental status prior to a child's conception. Whereas the gestational mother's decision to relinquish her parental status will be ineffective until at least six weeks after her child's birth. The only plausible explanation for the difference is that women are assumed to be incapable of making this decision before and during pregnancy, and within the first six weeks of the child's life. There is, in short, a danger that women might change their minds, and that their subsequent

---

[15] [1977] AC 547, at 577

regret would be intolerable. But there are a great many other life-changing decisions that we allow people to make despite the possibility that they may have second thoughts and experience considerable distress as a result. Marriage and sterilisation are obvious examples. Of course, there might be circumstances in which consent to sterilisation would be ineffective. Asking for consent from a woman in the throes of labour would be improper because she would not have the opportunity to reflect upon the consequences of permanent sterility. But in relation to agreements to relinquish motherhood, we assume that women are incapable of making this decision *for several months,* thus reinforcing 'the sexist stereotype that women are ruled by unpredictable emotion' (Shultz, 1990, 352). For men and non-pregnant women, parenthood can be acquired and transferred by clear expressions of intent on the part of the social and genetic parents. For gestating women, 'biology is still destiny' (Shultz, 1990, 394).

While a number of other countries, such as France and Germany, also adopt a uniform gestational test for motherhood, some courts in the United States have attempted to vary the definition of motherhood according to the circumstances of the child's conception. So, for example, intention was decisive in the *Buzzanca* case, when the surrogate, the egg donor and the intended mother were three different women, only one of whom (the intended mother) was interested in raising the child. In an earlier case, *Johnson v Calvert*,[16] the California Supreme Court was faced with two possible mothers, each seeking a declaration of maternity. Following an IVF surrogacy arrangement, Anna Johnson had given birth to a child who had been conceived *in vitro* using Mr and Mrs Calvert's gametes. In the UK, Anna Johnson's gestational role would have been decisive. In California, on the other hand, Justice Panelli concluded that both women had 'presented acceptable proof of maternity'[17], and he then used intention as the factor which tipped the balance in favour of Crispina Calvert:

> The [Uniform Parentage] Act recognizes both genetic consanguinity and giving birth as means of establishing a mother and child relationship, when the two means do not coincide in one woman, she who intended to bring to procreate the child - that is, she who intended to bring about the birth of a child that she intended to raise as her own - is the natural mother under California law.[18]

Not only did intention offer a convenient mechanism with which to distinguish between two equally credible claims, but the Court also suggested that an intention-based test might promote the child's best interests because 'a rule recognizing the intended parents as the child's legal, natural parents should best promote certainty and stability for the child'.[19] In addition, the court

---

[16] *Johnson v Calvert* 851 P 2d 776, 782 (Cal. 1993)
[17] ibid at 782
[18] ibid at 782
[19] ibid at 783

also reasoned that 'by voluntarily contracting away any rights to the child, the gestator has, in effect, conceded that the best interest of the child is not with her'.[20]

For many of its critics, the principal explanation for the decision in *Johnson v Calvert* is not a preference for planned parenting, but rather the existence of a racial difference between Anna Johnson, who was black, and the Calverts and 'their' child, who were not.[21] Whatever the underlying justification for the decision in *Johnson*, it is important to note that other US courts have doubted both the universal applicability and the wisdom of an intention-based test. In *In the Marriage of Moschetta*,[22] for example, the Court noted that intention could only be employed as a 'tie breaker' when gestation and genetics did not coincide. When the surrogate mother is also the genetic mother, there is no 'tie' and intention is therefore irrelevant.

Other US courts have expressed a preference for genetics as the decisive test for maternity. In *Belsito v Clark*,[23] the court criticised the *Johnson* decision for its uncertainty in circumstances when more than one woman adduces proof of her intention to raise the child. Instead, the Court preferred the certainty offered by a genetic test and found that in Ohio 'the natural parents of the child shall be identified by a determination as to which individuals have provided the genetic imprint for that child', unless they have expressly waived or relinquished their parental rights. A different reason for preferring a genetic definition of legal motherhood was offered in *Soos v Superior Court of Maricopa*.[24] The Appellate Court found that an Arizona statute which specified that the gestational surrogate is the legal mother of the child violated the genetic mother's equal protection rights because there was no compelling reason to justify the dissimilar treatment of similarly situated men and women (the child's genetic father and mother).

This brief summary of a handful of US cases is simply intended to show that legal motherhood has been attributed using gestation (UK), genetics (*Belsito/Soos*), intention (*Johnson/Buzzanca*) or some combination or all three (*Moschetta*). Motherhood, it seems, has become profoundly uncertain. Whether or not a woman can be considered the legal mother of a child depends upon whether the child is born in London or San Francisco. While family law has always varied between different countries, cross-national variation in the *identity* of a child's parents seems both new and puzzling.

---

[20] ibid at 782
[21] J. Raymond, *Women as Wombs: Reproductive Technologies and the Battle over Women's Freedom* (1993) 69; M. Field, 'Surrogate Motherhood' in *Parenthood in Modern Society: legal and social issues for the twenty-first century*, (eds) J. Eekelaar and P. Šarčević 228; A. Cherry, 'Nurturing in the Service of White Culture: Racial Subordination, Gestational Surrogacy, and the Ideology of Motherhood', (2001) 10 *Texas Jounal of Women and the Law* 83-128
[22] (1994) 25 Cal. App. 4th 1218; 30 Cal. Rptr. 2d 893 17,32, 34,
[23] 644 N.E.2d 760 (Ohio Com. Pl. 1994)
[24] 897 P.2d 1356 (Ariz. App. Div. 1 1994)

Nor is it obvious that any of these various solutions is preferable to the any of the others. To value intention or genetics over gestation is to disregard the contribution made by the woman who carried the fetus to term and underwent childbirth. To privilege gestation is to ignore a commissioning mother's instrumental role in bringing about the child's birth, and perhaps also her genetic parentage. The reason that none of the various possible solutions seems entirely satisfactory is because, in truth, the child born following a surrogacy arrangement has (at least) two mothers.

5   The advantages and disadvantages of parental exclusivity:

By restricting the number of parents a child may have to one mother and one father, the law is unable to adequately accommodate increasingly complex reproductive arrangements. Children born following surrogacy arrangements, or children who have been adopted have *two* mothers. When donated gametes are used, the genetic parent and the social parent are different people, but both are in some important sense *parents*. Pretending that these additional 'parents' are actually strangers to the child may help to preserve the fiction of the biological nuclear family, but by misrepresenting the reality of a child's origins, the law undoubtedly causes children unnecessary confusion. For example, the 'total transplant' model of adoption relies upon the legal fiction that the child's genetic mother and father are no longer her parents. While this may have had some perceived advantages when most adopted children were illegitimate babies, now that the vast majority of adoptions are of older children - either from local authority care or in adoptions by step parents - this legal fiction is bewildering for children who know and have had a relationship with their original parents.

Why has the law continued to rely upon an exclusive model of parenthood despite the technical and social fragmentation of the normal incidents of maternity and paternity? The obvious answer is itself revealing. If a child has only one mother and one father, we can be certain about who possesses the various rights and obligations that attach to the status of being a parent. Were we to recognise multiple parents, we would have to decide which 'parents' should be obliged to maintain the child; which should be her primary caretakers, and so on. Parental exclusivity thus appears to have the merit of certainty. Yet this superficially appealing explanation in fact presupposes what it seeks to prove.

Consider, for example, our assumption that - barring the child's serious ill-treatment - her parents have the right to be her primary caretakers throughout her childhood. As Lord Templeman famously explained in *Re KD (A Minor) (Ward: Termination of Access)*

> the best person to bring up a child is the natural parent. It matters not whether the parent is wise or foolish, rich or poor, educated or illiterate, provided the child's moral and physical health are not endangered.[25]

If we are genuinely uncertain about who a child's parents might be, then their 'right' to be recognised as the child's primary caretakers is essentially meaningless. It will point only to a number of candidates who cannot logically *all* have the *prima facie* right to care for the same child. Where there is more than one woman with a credible claim to be considered the child's mother, there is no escaping the need to *decide* which woman should acquire the right to be considered the child's principal caretaker. To say that this right vests with the child's mother simply begs the question. With baffling circularity then, in trying to decide between a number of possible mothers and/or fathers, the law in fact assumes that every child will have two (and no more than two) clearly identifiable parents.

The identification of parents is conventionally believed to be a question of fact rather than judgment, and so the test we employ in order to identify a child's mother and father is supposed simply to locate the truth about the child's origins. The problem of course is that there may be no obvious 'truth' to be discovered. Following egg donation, it is not necessarily self-evident whether the genetic mother or the woman who gives birth is properly described as the child's mother. If parenthood is not a fact waiting to be discovered, we are going to have to make some decisions about the relative importance of various different aspects of mother and fatherhood. But introducing this element of *choice* into the identification of parents is profoundly counter-intuitive, and as a result, it is probably unsurprising that the law has been reluctant to abandon the idea of a clear, factual test for parenthood. Judge De Meyer advocated just such a simple but ultimately circular definition of fatherhood in the judgment of the European Court of Human Rights in *X, Y and Z v United Kingdom* when he said that 'it is self-evident that a person who is manifestly not the father of a child has no right to be recognised as the father'[26] as if, as Andrew Bainham has pointed out, 'we all know a father when we see one' (Bainham, 1999: 25). Illogically, then, when identifying a child's parents, we 'implicitly appeal to some simple preanalytic concept of parenthood' (Hill, 1991: 360), when the reason why we need this definition in the first place is that genuine uncertainty exists. And of course, we can only be

---

[25] [1988] AC 806 at 812
[26] (1997) 24 EHRR 143

uncertain about who should be considered a child's parents if our concept of parenthood is much more fluid than we may have supposed.

So despite its apparent clarity, the principle of parental exclusivity does not enable us to avoid deciding in whom the various rights and obligations of parenthood should vest. Rather it obscures this decision-making process by presupposing that every child's parents can be identified with the same certainty as exists within the paradigm case. The decision about who should have the *prima facie* right and duty to look after a particular child is no less a decision just because we present it as a question of fact (i.e. who *is* the child's mother?) rather than judgment (i.e. who do we think *deserves* to have their parental claim given priority?). Admittedly, the law does not engage in a case by case determination of parenthood in order to allocate it to the persons who are best able to meet a particular child's needs. But making intention - rather than the genetic link - the factor which determines the paternity of children born following sperm donation is nonetheless a *decision* rather than a straightforward question of fact. Preferring to give surrogate mothers and their husbands first refusal on the rights and obligations of parenthood is a *choice* which is obscured by the law's insistence that gestation - as opposed to genetic relatedness or the intention to raise the child - is the defining feature of motherhood.

In addition to its obfuscatory function, the 'all or nothing' quality of parental status creates a further problem. Where the normal incidents of parenthood are distributed more widely than in the paradigm case, but the law has identified just one mother and one father, what is the status of the non-parents who nevertheless possess one or more of the normal incidents of parenthood? Because the law admits no middle-ground here, such people are *prima facie* legal strangers to the child. So - to take IVF surrogacy as an example - the gestational mother is *the* legal mother, and the genetic and intended 'mother' is in fact not a mother at all. Yet on a common sense understanding of motherhood, of course the woman whose fertilised egg develops into a child is in some important sense her mother. She may not ever be the child's social mother, and may have none of the rights and duties that we normally associate with parenthood, but it makes very little sense to say that she is as unrelated to that child as a total stranger.

It might be argued that the problem here is essentially linguistic. Perhaps legal language simply has insufficient elasticity to accommodate the cultural and technological disintegration of the biological nuclear family. The principle of parental exclusivity means that the law has no concept of 'partial' or 'incomplete' mother or fatherhood: you either are or are not a child's legal parent. Not only does this inaccurately describe many children's parentage, but it is also out of step with prevalent non-legal understandings of parenthood. It is certainly not now uncommon for children conceived sexually to have more than one adult man who might be identified as their father, and/or more than one mother-figure. Millions of children have a stepfather, *and* a biological father. Although the numbers are smaller, children who have been adopted are almost always told that they also have a birth mother whose identity they can discover when they reach adulthood. For children the presence of multiple parents is undoubtedly less confusing than the law's denial of their existence. A child who knows that she was conceived using donated sperm understands - for example - that she has two different sorts of father, one genetic and one social.

In essence, the principle of parental exclusivity fails to distinguish between two related but different aspects of parenthood: the status of *being a parent* and the power (or duty) to *act as a parent*. Of course, in the paradigm case, these two features of parenthood are inevitably blurred because the power to act *as* a parent derives precisely from *being* a parent. But where the normal incidents of parenthood are distributed between a number of different individuals, while not all of them will have the power to act *as* a parent, each one *is*, in some sense at least, a parent.

In fact, although the principle of parental exclusivity is indeed deeply entrenched, the law already distinguishes between the status of being a parent and the power to act as a parent, through possession of parental responsiblity. To be a parent is to have a connection with your offspring that will endure throughout both your lifetimes. Parental responsibility, on the other hand, is a more transitory and flexible concept. It will last only during the child's minority, and it can be acquired by a variety of non-parents. Anyone who is granted a residence order automatically also gains parental responsibility for the duration of the order,[27] so step-parents or grandparents can be granted parental responsibility despite not being the child's legal parents. Parental responsibility can also vest with a local authority after a child has been taken into care. Mothers (and in some circumstances fathers) will continue to have parental responsibility despite its acquisition by other parties. Thus, the number of people who can have parental responsibility for a child is not limited in the same way as the number of people who can be identified as her legal parents.

Being a parent is therefore not synonymous with *possessing* parental responsibility. Indeed not all parents actually have parental responsibility for their children. Only mothers and married fathers acquire parental responsibility automatically from birth. Unmarried fathers will only have parental responsibility for their child if they are registered on the child's birth certificate, or have made a parental responsibility agreement with the mother, or obtained an order from the court.[28] In contrast, unmarried fathers are always *financially* responsible for their children regardless of their lack of formal parental responsibility. Duties, such as the obligation to maintain one's offspring, are owed by parents *as parents*, rather than by those with parental responsibility.

---

[27] Children Act 1989 s. 12
[28] Children Act 1989 s. 4, as amended.

Parental responsibility is, in essence, the right and duty to look after a child during her childhood. It includes, for example, the right to give consent to a child's medical treatment and to take decisions about her education. In contrast to parenthood, parental responsibility - with its capacity to be shared, transferred and acquired - is flexible enough to accommodate the social reality of the child's domestic circumstances where these do not conform to the traditional nuclear family. A social 'parent' does not have to become a legal parent in order to offer a child the security and support that she needs. But while the concept of parental responsibility may have more elasticity than the attribution of parenthood, Jonathan Herring has suggested that it too may be insufficiently 'fine-tuned' to accommodate the various diverse tasks it now fulfils (Herring, 2004). In the absence of serious misconduct by the father, parental responsibility court orders are routinely granted to unmarried fathers as a stamp of approval for the commitment entailed in making the application in the first place, even if the father's practical involvement in caring for the child has been and will continue to be minimal. But once parental responsibility is acquired, it gives this potentially absent and distant parent the right to be consulted about certain major decisions, such as changing the child's surname, or leaving the country.[29] Instead, Herring suggests that a two-tier model for parental responsibility might be developed so that the symbolic recognition of parental commitment could exist separately from the right to play a significant role in the child's upbringing. My argument here is that it is not just parental responsibility that is insufficiently flexible. Our definitions of mother and fatherhood are also too rigid to accommodate the diversity of modern family life. By severing parenthood from parental responsibility, the law has acknowledged that the biological model of family life in which each child lives with her genetic mother and father no longer fits the complex and multiple parent-like relationships that a child may form during her life. My proposal in this chapter is that we should take this existing legal recognition of parental variety a stage further.

The law has tended to assume that the bundle of legal rights and duties that *normally* flow from being a parent do so *necessarily*. So that recognising someone's parental status would automatically vest them with a range of powers and obligations which might - in the case of a sperm donor, for instance - be inappropriate. But the rule that everyone who is recognised as a parent is under an obligation to maintain their child until she reaches adulthood is a legal creation rather than a natural consequence of human reproduction. It would be perfectly possible to fix only certain parents with duties of support, or rights to be involved in the child's upbringing.

We already have an example of legislation which facilitates the purely symbolic acknowledgment of a parental bond. Under the Human Fertilisation and Embryology (Deceased Fathers) Act 2003

---

[29] Children Act 1989 s.13

it is possible for a man to be registered as the father of a child conceived after his death. The recognition of these deceased fathers' paternity is only for the purpose of registration on the child's birth certificate. None of the other normal incidents of paternity, such as inheritance rights, apply, thus avoiding the problem of testamentary uncertainty that might arise if a child could be conceived many years after her 'father's' death. For my purposes, the importance of this Act is its introduction of a new sort of parental status which is limited to the *acknowledgment* of paternity. Obviously none of the rights and duties that normally flow from being a parent can apply to these deceased fathers, instead the Act simply allows the reality that these children *did* have fathers to be formally recognised. Lifting the numerical restriction upon the number of parents a child might have would enable this sort of symbolic recognition of parenthood to be extended to other 'parents'.

The law has also already taken one small step away from the biological model of legal parenthood through the rules governing the paternity of children born following the artificial insemination in licensed clinics of women without husbands or consenting opposite-sex partners. Despite having a biological father, these children are legally *fatherless*: their mother is their only legal parent. Could we further extend this recognition that the 'natural' two-parent family is not always an appropriate way to describe the parentage of a child? Might the law additionally recognise that, in certain circumstances, a child has *more* than one mother or father?

6   Non-Exclusive Parenthood?

In sum, acknowledging that the normal features that we associate with being a parent might be distributed among a number of individuals poses two important questions for the law. First, how should we choose which of the various possible 'parents' should also acquire the right and duty to care for and support the child. And second, having singled out the principal parent/s, exactly what is the status of the other individuals who possess one or more parental characteristics? Neither question is at all easy to answer, but my point has been that we should admit that these are matters of choice and judgment, rather than hiding behind a superficially factual inquiry into the identity of a child's parents.

So, for example, making the intention to become a parent the decisive factor in allocating the rights and duties of parenthood following an IVF surrogacy arrangement would be synonymous with making surrogacy contracts specifically enforceable. Whereas if gestation determines the identity of the principal mother, then we are deciding that surrogate mothers should always have the right to change their mind. My purpose here is not to express an opinion on either option, but rather to point out that our current preference for gestation reflects our *decision* to give surrogate mothers the right to renege on their agreements. It may be more convenient to say that the gestational mother is the only mother, and that the woman who contributed the egg and instigated the conception is therefore a stranger to the child, but the price to be paid for this simplicity is a fundamental misrepresentation of the reality of this child's parentage.

The recognition of multiple parents certainly more accurately describes the parenthood of children born following gamete donation. A sperm donor is, in an important sense, the child's genetic father, but this does not necessarily mean that he should have parental responsibility, or owe any other obligations to 'his' child. Instead, by signing the requisite consent form, he has voluntarily agreed to give up *any* parental rights and obligations, and the couple or individual who received treatment have (also by signing the requisite consent form) voluntarily agreed to assume full responsibility for the child from birth. It is therefore only the intended parents who possess the rights and duties we associate with parenthood. Acknowledging the paternity of the sperm donor is especially important given the removal of donor anonymity from April 2005.[30] When donors become identifiable, it would seem sensible to admit that they are the genetic parents of their offspring. In the future children may trace and meet their gamete donors making acknowledgment of their parenthood, albeit only in a genetic sense, more important. But if the law were capable of recognising multiple parents, this need not displace the parental rights and obligations of the intended or social parents.

Following surrogacy, acknowledging the existence of multiple parents might also be advantageous. When a child is born as the result of a surrogacy agreement, the couple or individual who recruited the surrogate mother are the intended, and often also the genetic parents, and either of these tests could be sufficient to allow them to be recognised as the child's parents from birth. Of course, the surrogate mother will always be the child's gestational mother, and will sometimes additionally be genetically related to her. She undoubtedly also has a compelling claim to have her maternity formally acknowledged. In most surrogacy arrangements, where the surrogate is happy to hand over the child at birth, a non-exclusive model of parenthood would permit the commissioning mother and father to be recognised as the child's parents with parental responsibility from birth. The surrogate mother would continue to be the child's birth mother, but she would have voluntarily waived all of the rights and duties we would normally associate with parenthood. Parental duties would instead vest only in the couple or individual with whom the child will be living.

But if the surrogate mother changes her mind about handing over the child, my model would lead us to ask which of the child's parents should possess the rights and obligations of parenthood. The answer to this question depends upon whether one believes that surrogacy contracts should be specifically enforceable or not. If the arguments in favour of specific enforcement are preferred, we could say that the commissioning couple should *always* be recognised as the child's parents with parental responsibility. It might, for example, be argued that the surrogate mother agreed to waive her acquisition of parental responsibility and the other incidents of parental status, in the same way as a sperm or egg donor, and that her agreement should likewise be binding upon both her. The commissioning couple's agreement to assume responsibility for the child's upbringing might also be enforceable, so that a man like John Buzzanca would not be permitted to shrug off his obligations towards a child whose conception he instigated. But if specific enforcement is believed to be intrusive, oppressive or otherwise undesirable, parental responsibility could vest initially in the woman from whose body the child emerges. She would then continue to have the right to renege on her agreement to relinquish her parental responsibility.

If a surrogate mother changes her mind about handing over the child to the commissioning parents, we cannot avoid the need to *choose* where the child should live. No test for the identification of parents is capable of effacing the human tragedy of this sort of dispute. There is no easy or obviously right solution, rather when surrogacy agreements break down, the party who is deprived of 'their' child will inevitably suffer profound distress. Whether we decide that the 'losing' party should be the surrogate mother or the commissioning couple, their disappointment will be intense. I would, however, maintain that they should be entitled to recognition, albeit largely symbolic, of their parental status. If the child is to be brought up by the surrogate mother and her husband, it might nevertheless be important for that child to know something of the circumstances of her conception, especially since at least one of her intended parents will normally also be genetically related to her. On reaching adulthood, their identity might be revealed. If the commissioning couple's claim is preferred, again the gestational mother's identity might be disclosed when the child reaches the age of majority. It is worth restating, however, that very few surrogate mothers change their minds. So while I admit that my proposed shift towards the recognition of multiple parents is incapable of providing a solution to disputed surrogacy arrangements, it would solve the much more common practical problem that arises following surrogate births, namely the need for the child's parentage to be formally transferred via judicial proceedings. Because, as we saw earlier, this cumbersome legal process creates an

---

[30] Human Fertilisation and Embryology Authority (Disclosure of Donor Information) Regulations 2004

incentive for informal transfers, unknown numbers of children are currently living with 'parents' who are in fact legal strangers to 'their' child.

It is important to remember that the recognition of multiple parents would not only apply when the normal features of parenthood are split by collaborative reproduction. A non-exclusive model of parenthood might also add clarity to cases of disputed paternity, because it would allow us to admit that the child may have *two* fathers, one genetic and one social. Once doubt has been case upon the genetic paternity of her 'father', I am unpersuaded that it is not in the child's best interests to have their genetic parentage revealed by blood tests. The advantage of non-exclusive parenthood would be that acknowledging the genetic paternity of the mother's ex-lover need not displace the paternity of the social father. On the contrary, as a result of his ongoing relationship with 'his' child, the social father should be formally recognised as the only legal father who *also* has parental responsibility. In *Re H (Blood Tests: Parental Rights)*[31], Ward LJ struggled to achieve precisely this sort of result. He argued that 'the issue of biological parentage should be divorced from psychological parentage'. A direction for blood tests was issued because knowing the truth about his genetic paternity would not necessarily 'undermine his attachment to his father figure and he will cope with knowing that *he has two fathers*'[32] (my emphasis). But because under English law, the discovery that the mother's ex-lover is her son's genetic father completely displaces the social father's 'paternity', the only way in which he could retain parental responsibility would be to apply for a residence order for 'his' child. A better solution, and one that Ward LJ himself appears to endorse, would be to admit evidence that the ex-lover is the genetic father, but to simultaneously affirm the social father's status as the only *father* who also possess the rights and obligations of parenthood.

Of course, recognising multiple parents will leave us with some extremely difficult questions. We would, for example, have to devise some mechanism for choosing which of the various individuals who possess the normal incidents of parenthood should be principally responsible for the child's upbringing. My point is that we are already making these difficult decisions, but we are hiding them within the supposedly neutral, objective and purely factual inquiry into the identity of a child's parents.

## 7	Conclusion:	A right to know the identity of all of your parents?

---

[31] [1996] 3 WLR 505, at 523
[32] ibid

A child's 'right to know and be cared for by his or her parents' is enshrined in Article 7(1) of the United Nations Convention on the Rights of the Child. While the Convention was ratified by the UK in 1991, it has not been directly incorporated into English law. Nevertheless, the concept of a right to know the identity of one's parents has received judicial approval,[33] and may additionally be protected by the right to respect for private and family life, now guaranteed by Article 8 of the Human Rights Act 1998. In the words of Wall J,

> [k]nowledge of their paternity is increasingly seen not only as a matter of prime importance to children, but as being both their *right* and in their interests.[34] (my emphasis)

Obviously, giving effect to this right is only possible if we have a clear understanding of what defines a parent. Neither the UN Convention on the Rights of the Child, nor the Human Rights Act offers any definition, which could either mean that their drafters assumed that a child's parentage would be a self-evident question of fact, or alternatively, it could indicate that states have a 'margin of appreciation' in the rules governing the identification of parents. Importantly, the right to know the identity of one's parents does not necessarily imply any numerical limit upon the number of parents that might exist. Moreover, no practical rights or obligations automatically flow from the right simply to know the identity of one's parents.

Of course, one consequence of a non-exclusive model of parenthood would be that a child's birth certificate might have to record more than one mother and/or father. However counter-intuitive this might initially seem, my point is simply that some children *do* have more than one mother or father, and that by failing to acknowledge this, and to address its practical consequences, the law is unable to adapt to the complexity of family life in the twenty-first century. While the idea of parenthood as a divisible status would, in some respects, be a radical departure for the law; given that parenthood now *is* a divisible status, rethinking the legal conception of parenthood is a necessary, albeit difficult, task. Transparency and descriptive accuracy demand that the law relinquishes its principle of parental exclusivity in favour of a model of parenthood that is capable of accommodating its social and technical fragmentation. If people no longer reproduce and raise children within the conventional biological nuclear family, the law should stop pretending that the answer to the question 'what is a parent' is a fact waiting to be discovered. Rather, however challenging, the law should address the messy reality of multiple parent/child bonds and relationships.

---

[33] See, for example, *S v McC (orse S) and M (D S intervener); W v W* [1972] AC 24; *In re G (A Minor) (Parental Responsibility)* [1994] 2 FCR 1037; *In re H (A Minor) (Blood Tests: Parental Rights)* [1996] 3 WLR 506
[34] *In re O (A Minor) (Blood Tests: Constraint)* [2000] Fam. 139, at 144

Bibliography

Bainham, A (1999) 'Parentage, Parenthood and Parental Responsibility: Subtle, Elusive Yet Important Distinctions' in *What is a Parent: A Socio-Legal Analysis*, A. Bainham, S.Day Sclater and M. Richards (eds) 25

Bartlett, KT (1984) 'Rethinking Parenthood as an Exclusive Status: The Need for Legal Alternatives when the Premise of the Nuclear Family has Failed' 70 *Virginia Law Review* 879

Brazier, M; Campbell, A and Golombok S (1998) *Surrogacy: Review for Health Ministers of Current Arrangements for Payments and Regulation*, London: HMSO Cm 4068

Herring, J (2004) *Family Law* 2nd edition Harlow: Pearson

Hill, JL (1991) 'What does it mean to be a 'Parent'? The Claims of Biology as the Basis for Parental Rights' 66 *New York University Law Review* 353

Shultz, MM (1990) 'Reproductive Technology and Intent-Based Parenthood: An Opportunity for Gender Neutrality' *Wisconsin Law Review* 297

12

ARGUMENTS ABOUT PARENTAGE

Andrew Bainham

I will not draw a distinction between biological and non-biological – we are not buying Persil or Daz (Stephen Quinn)[1]

Separating a person from his parents must only happen as a last resort, and separation before birth is thoroughly unjustifiable...It is not the place of government or the place of legislation to declare that gamete donors are not parents. Parenthood is a fact of biology (Tom Ellis)[2]

STEPHEN Quinn and Tom Ellis could hardly have more differing views on what it is to be a parent. Mr.Quinn was quoted following the then recent revelation by DNA testing that the former Home Secretary, David Blunkett, was not the biological father of Mr.Quinn's wife's second son. For Mr. Quinn, it apparently mattered not whether the biological father of the child was Mr. Blunkett, the Indian media tycoon or the political columnist also mooted by the press as possible candidates[3], some other man or himself. What mattered was that he intended to stay with his wife and perform the role of father to her children. It was this which made him the father and, in relation to the child in question, the *legal* father too, since the *pater est* presumption attributes parentage to the mother's husband unless and until it is rebutted. Biological truth might continue to elude us, but what John Eekelaar has called "legal truth" could and should be allowed to prevail.[4] Mr. Ellis is a donor-conceived person who gave evidence to the recent Joint Committee on the Human Tissue and Embryos (Draft) Bill. For Mr. Ellis, anyone performing the social role of parent, but lacking the biological connection, cannot be legitimately regarded as a parent. As he puts it in his evidence, specifically in relation to gamete donation:

> A man or woman whose gametes are not used to create a child should not be referred to as simply a "parent". If that man or woman raises the child it should be made clear that the man or

---

[1] 'Blunkett "did not father child"' *BBC News/Politics*, Saturday 5 March 2005. http://news.bbc.co.uk/1/low/uk_politics/4320827.stm.
[2] *Joint Committee on the Human Tissue and Embryos (Draft) Bill 2007, Volume II: Evidence*, HL Paper 169-II, HC Paper 630-II, Ev 16, paragraphs 2 and 24.
[3] See, for example, "Kimberly Fury over Blunkett Smear", *The Mail on Sunday*, March 6 2005.
[4] John Eekelaar, *Family Law and Personal Life* (Oxford 2006), ch. 3.

woman is an "adoptive parent" or a "step-parent". Likewise, sperm or egg "donors" are never just donors. They are genetic parents. It is wrong that this legislation attempts to sever this relationship between parent and child.[5]

The rival claims of biological and social parents have been neatly summed up by Judith Masson as "parenting by being" and "parenting by doing".[6] The latter functional approach to family relationships, which supports the notion of social parenthood, has gathered considerable ground in recent years. If it looks like a family it must be a family, if people behave in a "marriage-like" way they should be treated as if married (or if they are of the same sex, as civil partners) and, so the argument goes, if someone behaves as a parent he or she *is* a parent. Important recent developments both in England and elsewhere provoke a reappraisal of this argument in the context of parentage and invite consideration of how far it is appropriate or desirable to transport this functional approach into the relationship of parent and child. These developments, which relate to paternity, assisted reproduction, same-sex parenting and adoption, raise the question of what recognition ought to be given to biological and social parenting arrangements. This article focuses principally on developments in relation to paternity, assisted reproduction and same-sex parenting. For reasons of space it does not consider in depth the choice between adoption and its alternatives, though the recent jurisprudence of the English courts on this matter is noted in the concluding section.

What legal status or priority then is it appropriate to give to biological and social parents?[7] Common to all these developments is the question whether the commitment to human rights has made, or should make, any difference and whether there is any case for modifying the traditional welfare principle which governs disputes concerning the upbringing of children.[8] A further question, somewhat less debated, is what values ought to govern the determination of parentage. It will be suggested here that the guiding principles should be a commitment to truth,[9] individual autonomy and priority for the

---

[5] Above, note 2, at paragraphs 25 and 26.
[6] Judith Masson, "Parenting by Being; Parenting by Doing – In Search of Principles for Founding Families", in J.R. Spencer and Antje Du Bois-Pedain, *Freedom and Responsibility in Reproductive Choice* (Oxford 2006), ch. 8.
[7] The question of status generally in English family law is pursued further by the author in Andrew Bainham, "Status Anxiety? The Rush for Family Recognition", in Fatemeh Ebtehaj, Bridget Lindley and Martin Richards (eds.), *Kinship Matters* (Oxford 2006), ch. 3.
[8] See, particularly John Eekelaar, "Beyond the Welfare Principle" (2002) 14 C.F.L.Q. 237.
[9] The importance of truth and transparency in the context of parentage has been recognised judicially on a number of occasions, notably by Hale L.J. (as she then was) in *Re R (Surname: Using Both Parents')* [2001] 2 F.L.R. 1358, 1362. In a dispute over surnames she offered the view that it was not the name which was the crucial issue rather "that it is important for a child that there should be transparency about his parentage and for it to be acknowledged that a child always has two parents; and if it turns out (as it often does) that children have both social and birth parents, it is important that that fact too is acknowledged".

rights and interests of those primarily affected. These are the children or adults who result from reproduction, whether through sexual intercourse or assisted reproduction and those who are adopted. This last principle might be thought contentious since there are undoubtedly those, among them many childless people, who would question why priority should be accorded to children over adults. If a justification is needed, it might reside primarily in the power imbalance which exists between children and the adults with whom they are in a relationship.[10] Nowhere is this disparity in power more clearly demonstrated than in the fact of birth and its implications over which, self-evidently, the child concerned has no choice or control. But for the purposes of this paper it is sufficient to note that both international conventions and the domestic laws of virtually all developed countries acknowledge that the interests of children are, at the very least, a primary consideration in matters directly affecting them.[11]

I. PATERNITY

Advances in technology have made it increasingly difficult for the law to justify an approach to establishing paternity which is characterised by fiction and presumption. Conventional blood tests and other evidence might have *disproved* paternity but they could never definitively establish it. The availability of DNA testing, which can now establish the biological truth with near certainty, has caused a number of jurisdictions to review their legal frameworks for establishing and disputing paternity.[12] The strength of the *pater est* presumption has in particular been weakened by a greater willingness on the part of states to remove, or loosen, the restrictions which historically prevented challenges to it. These restrictions were of course influenced by considerations of preserving the stability of the child's family situation which biological revelations might be thought to have threatened.[13]

---

[10] It is this power imbalance which is often relied upon, for example, to justify giving priority to the child's interests where medical intervention is sanctioned against the express wishes of a parent. For fuller discussion in the medical context see Michael Freeman, "Whose Life is it Anyway?" (2001) 9 Medical Law Review 259 and Caroline Bridge,"Religion, Culture and Conviction – the Medical Treatment of Young Children" (1999) 11 C.F.L.Q. 1.

[11] The United Nations Convention on the Rights of the Child, Article 3(1) provides: "In all actions concerning children, whether undertaken by public or private social welfare institutions, courts of law, administrative authorities or legislative bodies, the best interests of the child shall be a primary consideration."

[12] On the significance of DNA testing in the context of paternity and kinship see Tabitha Freeman and Martin Richards, "DNA Testing and Kinship: Paternity, Geneology and the Search for the 'Truth' of Genetic Origins", in Ebtehaj, Lindley and Richards, above note 7, chapter 4.

[13] For a relatively modern case exhibiting judicial concern about stability which proved to be the decisive factor see *Re F (A Minor) (Blood Tests: Parental Rights)* [1993] Fam. 314.

In Norway, legislation in 1997 allowed for the first time a man claiming to be the father of a child to bring a paternity suit within the first three years of the child's life.[14] In 2002, amendments to this legislation removed this time restriction. The Norwegian Act on Children and Parents now allows, without time restriction, an action by either parent, the child or a third party claiming to be the father notwithstanding that the child has an existing legal father. Lødrup has described the basic philosophy of the legislation, "that it is in the best interests of the child that the man who is the biological father should also be considered the legal father, even if it means that an existing father's parenthood is challenged".[15] Early statistics on the result of actions brought under the new law yield the fascinating conclusion that just two-thirds of existing legal fatherhoods corresponded with the biological position while in the remaining third it was proved conclusively that the legal father was not the biological one.[16] We could not of course begin to draw the general conclusion from this that as many as one third of those registered as legal fathers are not the biological fathers, since the very fact of a challenge to paternity indicates doubt about the original determination. These doubts were principally felt by the legal fathers themselves in Norway who brought the action in 109 of the 129 Norwegian cases. But the Norwegian experience does substantiate what is commonly appreciated – that legal fatherhood frequently does not correspond with biology.

France is not a country noted for its unwavering commitment to the right to knowledge of biological origins. It remains the case, for example, that a French mother may give birth anonymously[17] and the European Court of Human Rights has found, albeit by majority, that *L'accouchement sous X* does not violate the child's rights under the ECHR.[18] It is also the case that French law prohibits the establishment of an incestuous affiliation despite the fact that this may be the biological truth. Even so, when the French radically reformed their filiation laws in 2005 to reflect the principles of *egalité, vérité et stabilité*, there is no doubt that the principle of *verité* took precedence and is given the greatest emphasis in the new code.[19] French law has long accepted "sociological parenthood" through the concept of

---

[14] For a discussion of the legislation see Peter Lødrup, "Norway: Challenges to an Established Paternity – Radical Changes in Norwegian Law" [2003] International Survey of Family Law 353.

[15] *Ibid.*

[16] Peter Lødrup, "Changing Paternity" [2006] International Survey of Family Law 321.

[17] For a penetrating analysis of the history and arguments surrounding anonymous birth in France see Nadine Lefacheur, "The French 'Tradition' of Anonymous Birth: The Lines of Argument" 18 I.J.L.P.F. 319.

[18] *Odièvre* v. *France* [2003] 1 F.C.R. 621.

[19] See Hugues Fulchiron, "Égalité, Vérité, Stabilité: The New French Filiation Law after the Ordonnance of 4 July 2005" [2006] International Survey of Family Law 203.

possession d' état.[20] But under the new filiation law a challenge may be brought by the child, either legal parent or a person claiming to be the parent even where there is *possession d'état* provided that the latter has not lasted for more than five years from the birth or subsequent recognition of the child. Regarding recognition, French law may also be said positively to encourage the establishment of paternity by permitting the *unilateral* recognition of a child by a man claiming to be the father. This act of recognition may be effected in the process of birth registration, in a document received by the civil registration officer or in any document authenticated by a notary.

Although civil law jurisdictions generally provide for recognition or acknowledgement of children[21] French law, unlike the law in some other jurisdictions, allows paternal recognition *without* the agreement of the mother and indeed perhaps without her knowledge. The position contrasts sharply with that in England where there is no provision for unilateral registration or other formal acceptance of a child by a man without the co-operation of the mother. We should not however conclude from this that the underlying purpose of recognition in civil law jurisdictions is to establish biological fatherhood or truth. The aim seems rather to facilitate finding *a* father for the child rather than *the* father. As Fulchiron has explained:

> There is a sort of French tradition of recognition of convenience, generally followed by marriage and legitimation to give a father to the child of the woman with whom one is living. "Take the woman, take the child", as the saying goes.[22]

The ECHR now appears to require that those countries which continue to place severe restrictions on challenges to existing paternity, especially on challenging the *pater est* presumption within marriage, should relax those restrictions at least to the extent that an individual must be given *at least one opportunity* to dispute the matter. In a stream of cases the European Court has found violations of the Convention where the imposition of strict time limits does not strike a fair balance between the legitimate interests of the state in protecting legal certainty of family relationships and the interests of legal fathers in having their paternity reviewed in the light of biological evidence.[23]

---

[20] "*Possession d'etat* refers to the fact that the child enjoys the status of a child, in relation to a particular man or woman, whether or not this situation corresponds to the legal reality." *Ibid.*, at p.209.

[21] For a comparison of the approach to establishing paternity in continental civil law jurisdictions and in common law jurisdictions see the seminal article by Marie-Thérèse Meulders-Klein, "The Legal Position of the Father in European Legislation" (1991) 4 I.J.L.F. 131.

[22] Above note 19, at p. 207.

[23] See particularly, *Shofman* v. *Russia* [2006] 1 F.L.R. 680, *Mizzi* v. *Malta* [2006] 1 F.L.R. 1048, *Paulik* v. *Slovakia* [2007] 1 F.L.R. 1090 and *Tavli* v. *Turkey* [2007] 1 F.L.R. 1136. For commentary on these cases see Andrew Bainham, "'Truth will Out': Paternity in Europe" [2007] C.L.J. 278.

It must be a matter of doubt whether the French five-year limit would survive challenge under the Convention. Moreover, where it can be shown that an incorrectly assigned paternity arose from deliberate deception on the part of the mother, an action for damages based on the tort of deceit may now lie in England.[24] Elsewhere too "paternity fraud" is also now recognised as giving rise to a cause of action.[25]

The individual's interest in biological truth may then be the *negative* one of disproving paternity as these cases reveal, but may just as likely be the *positive* one of seeking to establish a relationship with a biological child or parent.[26] The United Nations Convention on the Rights of the Child, in Article 7 asserts the child's right from birth, "as far as possible...to know and be cared for by his or her parents." The European Court has held that, where "family life" is established between a man and a child, the state is under a positive obligation to act in a manner calculated to enable an established family tie to develop. This may mean providing directly accessible procedures to establish paternity. The Court has, however, controversially taken the consistent line that "family life" is not established with the child merely on account of being the genetic father.[27] But it has accepted in *Mikulić* v. *Croatia*[28] that the concept of *private life*, also enshrined in Article 8, is apposite to include the child's right to knowledge of biological origins and that this can apply to a case where the child is conceived as a result of a casual sexual relationship. Whether the Court would reach the same conclusion if the applicant were the genetic father rather than the child is open to doubt. Would it hold that a genetic father also has a private life interest in his connection with the child capable of protection under the Convention?

English law has enthusiastically embraced the principle of biological truth, qualified only in the context of paternity issues by

---

[24] *P* v. *B (Paternity: Damages for Deceit)* [2001] 1 F.L.R. 1041; *A* v. *B (Damages for Paternity)* [2007] 2 F.L.R. 1051. In the latter case the male cohabitant who had been deceived by the mother into believing he had fathered her second child was awarded £7,500 in general damages for "the substantial and continuing degree of distress and deep sense of loss suffered".

[25] In a spectacular case of paternity fraud from Argentina, a husband was awarded damages where for twenty years the wife had led him to believe that he was the father of the three children born during the marriage, when in fact they were the biological children of her lover. See Cecilia Grosman and Marisa Herrera, "The Right to One's Identity in Recent Judicial Decisions on Filiation and Adoption" [2005] International Survey of Family Law 23, at pp 24–27. However, the High Court of Australia has rejected an action based on the tort of deceit for paternity fraud in the context of a married couple in *Magill* v. *Magill* (2006) 231 A.L.R. 277. For commentary see Nick Wikeley and Lisa Young, "Secrets and Lies: No Deceit Down Under for Paternity Fraud" [2008] C.F.L.Q. 81.

[26] See *Rozanski* v. *Poland* [2006] 2 F.L.R. 1163 in the European Court of Human Rights. For a notable English case see *Re T (Paternity: Ordering Blood Tests)* [2001] 2 F.L.R. 1190.

[27] In *G* v. *The Netherlands* (1990) 16 E.H.R.R. 38 a sperm donor to a lesbian couple was found by the European Commission not to have established "family life" with the resulting child. The existence of further ties between the father and child are required and there is a gathering jurisprudence from the European Court on what amounts to sufficient ties. See particularly *Lebbink* v. *The Netherlands* [2004] 2 F.L.R. 463.

[28] [2002] 1 F.C.R. 720.

considerations of the child's welfare. The latter will now normally be seen as requiring the truth to be established. A long line of cases, with few exceptions, have supported directions for testing and in the leading decision in *Re H and A (Paternity: Blood Tests)*[29] the Court of Appeal made clear its view that paternity was now to be established by science and not by legal presumption. There would be few cases in which the child's best interests would be served by the suppression of truth. Curiously, two of the exceptional cases in which it has been held that it was not immediately in the bests interests of the child to be told the truth, were cases in which the identity of the father was not in doubt and was known to all relevant parties except the child.[30] These cases, and the recent decision of Hedley J. in *Re D (Paternity)*[31], raise an important temporal question. If the child does have a right to be told or an interest in the biological truth, exactly when does this right or interest come into being? It is a question which arises not merely in the context of paternity but also in relation to assisted reproduction and we must return to it in that context. Suffice it to say that Hedley J. took the view in *Re D* that to direct that tests immediately be carried out would not serve the best interests of the child, but that in the longer term (and probably sooner rather than later) it would be in the best interests of the child to know the truth about disputed paternity. He therefore directed samples to be taken from the man claiming to be the father and stored and ordered samples to be taken from the child, stayed that order without limit of time but gave liberty to restore.

The government has also recently taken a keen interest in procedures for establishing paternity though it is clear that this interest is derived as much, if not more, from the financial interest of the state than from any enthusiastic commitment to human rights. In June 2007 the Department for Work and Pensions published a Green Paper on joint birth registration[32] in the wake of new legislation which will (yet again) radically reform the child support scheme.[33] But, on this occasion, the reform is to emphasise the importance of private

---

[29] [2002] 1 F.L.R.1145.
[30] In *Re K (Specific Issue Order)* [1999] 2 F.L.R. 280 the man concerned was a well-known disc jockey based in King's Lynn. The mother had consistently informed the child (aged 12 at the time of the proceedings) that his father was dead. The mother's hatred of the father was such that it was not thought to be in the child's best interests to inform him of the truth. In *Re J (Paternity: Welfare of Child)* [2007] 1 F.L.R. 1064, the decisive factor against ordering revelation of the child's true paternity was thought to be the risk this would pose to the mother's mental condition. The Court of Appeal has recently made it clear however in *Re F (Paternity: Jurisdiction)* [2008] 1 F.L.R. 225 that the family courts do have jurisdiction to decide whether or not a child should be told the truth of his paternity and that, in a case where the mother is unreasonably failing to comply with a court order to do so, the court may put in place alternative professional arrangements for imparting the truth to the child.
[31] [2007] 2 F.L.R. 26.
[32] *Joint Birth Registration: Promoting Parental Responsibility*, Department for Work and Pensions, Cm. 7160 (June 2007).
[33] Child Maintenance and Other Payments Bill 2007.

ordering and agreement between parents concerning child support as well as private responsibility.[34] In the same vein, the Government wishes to encourage more joint registration of births outside marriage. At the present time, where a child is born to an unmarried mother, it is she alone who has the legal duty to register the birth.[35] Registration of a man as the father (which now carries with it the consequence that he obtains parental responsibility[36]) can only take place with the co-operation of *both* that man and the mother. If either is unwilling to accept that man's paternity, there will be a sole registration by the mother with the name of the father left off the birth certificate. Sole registrations currently account for about 7 % of total birth registrations each year, involving approximately 45,000 children. The government points to research evidence which establishes a link between sole registration and social exclusion. The mothers concerned are likely to be younger, poorer and with lower levels of educational attainment. The government now proposes to establish a norm of *joint* registration. The aim is to emphasise the equal parental status of mother and father, the positive role of fathers in children's development and especially to promote early engagement in their lives and encouragement of an ongoing relationship between fathers and children:

> Father-child relationships, be they positive, negative, or lacking, have profound and wide ranging impacts on children that last a lifetime, particularly for children from the most disadvantaged backgrounds.[37]

If the government legislates on the basis of these proposals *both* parents, outside marriage, will be under a legal duty to register the birth of the child subject to statutory exemptions designed to protect vulnerable women. These exemptions are however wide-ranging and include situations where the mother does not know, or is not clear about, who is the father of the child; does not know where the father is; alleges that the father is, or could become, violent or abusive; alleges that the child was conceived as a result of rape, non-consensual sex or incest; or where she alleges that the man claiming paternity is not the father of the child. An exemption will also arise where a man alleges that he is not the father of the child.[38] In these exceptional cases, where either party wishes to pursue joint registration the matter would have to be determined by the courts. Otherwise only sole

---

[34] Following the recommendations of the Henshaw Report. See D. Henshaw, *Recovering Child Support: Routes to Responsibility*, Cm. 6894 (2006).
[35] Births and Deaths Registration Act 1953, s.10(1).
[36] Children Act 1989, s.4(1)(a), as introduced by the Adoption and Children Act 2002.
[37] Above note 32, at paragraph 15.
[38] *Ibid.*, paragraphs 56–61.

registration by the mother would be permitted. In Australia, where a similar approach to birth registration has been adopted, there was a significant decrease in sole registrations of approximately 20 % between 1994 and 2004.[39]

There are several features of this proposal which are worthy of note in the context of the arguments presented in this paper.

First, the proposal for a norm of joint registration acknowledges that the state has an interest in the establishment of biological parentage in as many cases as possible. Secondly, it is considered to be in the child's best interests to have knowledge of parentage from as early a point as possible and to have the opportunity of developing a relationship with *both* parents. Thirdly, although the Green Paper does not support the right of any man to effect a sole registration where it is either opposed by the mother or without her knowledge, the norm of joint registration and the imposition of a legal duty on both parents to register, does water down to some extent the mother's control over the birth registration process and with it her control of the acquisition of parental responsibility by the father. In the light of the exemptions, this loss of control by the mother may be viewed by some as more symbolic than real, but it is notwithstanding an important assertion of the equality of parentage. Finally, there is scant reference (if any) in the Green Paper to human rights which could have been the most important driving force behind the proposal. There is no apparent appreciation in the paper that there might be a right on the part of the child to have biological parentage established and no attempt accordingly to evaluate how the many exemptions which would lead to sole registration might be squared with any independent rights which the child or father might have. It is not clear, for example, whether the mother's word that she does not know who the child's father is or his whereabouts would be taken at face value. It does seem clear however that the Government does not favour a full investigation of the circumstances both because of its concern about the vulnerability of parents, especially mothers, and the practical challenges which a more proactive "tracing" of fathers would pose for the Registrar Service.[40] Neither is it clear in this context, any more than it is in the French context, exactly why the child's right to knowledge of parentage (if such right exists), would be lost in the context of rape or incest. Of course it is true that there would be the opportunity of recourse to the courts where the exemptions are applied, but there must at least be some question about whether this range of exemptions is consistent with the state's positive obligations under the ECHR.

[39] *Ibid.*, paragraph 7.
[40] *Ibid.*, paragraph 67.

What conclusions if any can we draw from these developments in paternity laws?

First, it is clear that biological parentage is important to a significant number of people. In the case of men anxious to dispute an established legal paternity, the application is often motivated by financial and property considerations. Liability for child support will usually depend on biological fatherhood, whether presumed or proved. If disproved, liability will usually cease along with the status of parent. Likewise inheritance rights depend on legal family membership, specifically here the relationship of parent and child. Conversely, those seeking to establish a biological relationship may be driven by curiosity, the desire to forge a relationship or possibly again by financial or property considerations. But what is quite clear is that, for these people, the claim that being a parent is about doing the job of a parent is explicitly rejected. Secondly, recent changes in England and elsewhere reflect a heavy emphasis on the importance of biological truth. Ascertaining the truth, if not seen as a right of the child, is certainly viewed as being in the child's best interests most of the time. Indeed, the only generally-accepted qualification to the principle of biological truth in this context appears to be based on a welfare determination that it would not be in the child's best interests to reveal the truth at the relevant time. But even then, the courts have accepted that the truth will eventually need to be disclosed and the only issue is when is the right time. Moreover, there is concern for the beginnings of life and the child's rights and interests at that crucially important stage. Just as the Government has expressed its view that the parentage of both parents should be fostered from the start, so there is evidence that the judiciary too, at least in this paternity context, believe that there is a lot to be said for revealing the truth of parentage sooner rather than later.[41] Thirdly, there is evidence too of a

---

[41] In *Re J*, above note 30 at p 1066, Sumner J., although refusing to order the mother to reveal the name of the father, was clearly concerned about the problems this might be storing up for the future. As he put it, "the longer J remains in ignorance, the greater the chance that he will learn the truth from some other source. That could be potentially very damaging for him. Secondly, by 16 [when the mother was proposing to tell him] he will have been through puberty. Given the turmoil that this can cause, the impact of then learning that his mother has kept from him the truth about his paternity could well cause him even greater upset than had he learned earlier...for J to know sooner rather than later may well be to his advantage." The strongest judicial statement of the importance to children of not delaying revelations about paternity is probably that of Ward LJ in *Re H (Paternity: Blood Test)* [1996] 2 F.L.R. 65 in which he said that it was in the child's best interests to know the truth unless the child's welfare justified a "cover up", that the mother ought not to be "living a lie" but that she ought to be teaching her children "at her knee" that "honesty is the best policy". He also took the view that the sooner the child was told the truth the better. A similar judicial attitude was exhibited recently by the Court of Appeal in relation to a father's change of gender in *Re C (Contact: Moratorium: Change of Gender)* [2007] 1 F.L.R. 1642. Here Thorpe L.J. (at p.1646) offered the following view: "If the children discover from casual talk or chance discovery, they will not only have to come to terms with a shocking discovery, but also the fact that they have been deceived by their own mother." And he went on that the "question of imparting truth to children simply cannot thus be deferred".

commitment to individual autonomy in that, for the various adults concerned, the view seems to be taken that they also have a right to at least a reasonable opportunity to establish the truth. Finally, there is very clear evidence that, in the matter of establishing paternity, the wishes of the mother are no longer (if they ever were) sovereign. The view that it is the mother's absolute, or even qualified, right to withhold information about the paternity of the child is now increasingly questioned and bears comparison with what is often seen as the mother's traditional right to give up her child for adoption and her entitlement to confidentiality in doing so. We will return to this matter briefly in the concluding section.

II. Assisted Reproduction and Same-Sex Parentage

The issue of the relative importance which should be attached to biological and social parenting relationships has surfaced again in relation to same-sex relationships. Is a lesbian "co-parent" to be treated as equal to the child's biological parent? Should same-sex partners be permitted to adopt? Does the child have a right to a connection, and if so what kind of connection, with the donor father in the case of lesbian parenthood, or with the mother in the more unusual context of two men using surrogacy to produce a child? What rights, if any, do these surrogate mothers and fathers themselves have in relation to the child? These and other questions are exercising both Parliament and the courts.

The Human Fertilisation and Embryology Bill 2007 (hereafter "the Bill"), currently before Parliament, would increase the circumstances in which legal parentage could be conferred on those who are not the biological parents of the child.[42] Specifically it would in essence extend to women in civil partnerships and lesbian couples the provisions currently in the 1990 legislation which give legal parentage to the husband of a married woman or the male partner of a woman who receives fertility treatment in the context of a joint enterprise to produce a child.[43] There have been difficulties over the wording of the 1990 legislation[44] and the new provisions, whether applying to a man

---

[42] The Bill was introduced into the House of Lords on November 8, 2007 following pre-legislative scrutiny, then as the Human Tissue and Embryos (Draft) Bill, by a Joint Committee of both Houses of Parliament. At the time of writing, the Bill is awaiting its second reading in the House of Commons.

[43] The current provisions are to be found in s.28(2) and (3), Human Fertilisation and Embryology Act 1990. The new parenthood provisions are in clauses 33–48 of the Bill.

[44] Particular difficulty has been cause by the wording in s.28(3) requiring that treatment should have been provided to an unmarried woman "in the course of treatment services provided for her and a man together". This has exercised the courts on a number of occasions. See, for example, *Re Q (Parental Order)* [1996] 1 F.L.R. 569; *Re B (Parentage)* [1996] 2 F.L.R. 15; *U v. W (Attorney-General Intervening)* [1997] 2 F.L.R. 282; *Leeds Teaching Hospital NHS Trust v. A* [2003] 1 F.L.R. 1091 and the House of Lords decision in *Re R (IVF: Paternity of Child)* [2005] 2 F.L.R. 843.

and woman or a lesbian couple, hinge on consent being given to the parentage of the partner by both parties and which has not been withdrawn at the time when an embryo or gametes are placed in the woman concerned or she is artificially inseminated.[45]

In the case of those who are married or civil partners, parentage is automatic unless the husband or female civil partner, as the case may be, is shown not to have consented to the mother's treatment.[46] In the case of unmarried partners, whether heterosexual or female same-sex partners, the previous test in the 1990 Act of being "treated together" is replaced by a requirement of express consent by both parties to the partner being treated in law as the parent.[47] These provisions do not of course apply directly to male same-sex couples since, by definition, in that context a surrogate mother must be involved and the legal position remains there that the gestational mother will always be regarded as one of the child's legal parents whether or not she is also the genetic mother.[48] In fact the Bill makes it explicit that a woman is not to be treated as a legal parent by reason of egg donation.[49] Nonetheless, the Bill would also reform s.30 of the 1990 legislation and extend the procedure for obtaining parental orders, presently available only to married couples, to civil partners and to unmarried couples (whether opposite-sex or same-sex) provided that the gametes of at least one member of the couple were used in the assisted birth.[50] This s.30 procedure, which has been referred to as "fast-track adoption", is similar in its effect to adoption in that legal parentage is conferred on the applicants.[51] What this means in simple language is that a male civil partner or unmarried male partner could acquire legal parentage where his partner's sperm was used in a surrogacy arrangement, but only after a welfare determination by the courts.[52]

These provisions have been inserted in part because the government wishes to "recognise the wider range of people who seek and receive assisted reproduction treatment in the early 21st century".[53]

---

[45] The new "fatherhood conditions" are to be found in clauses 36 and 37. The "female parenthood conditions" are in clauses 43 and 44.

[46] This maintains the current position under s.28(2) of the 1990 Act and extends it to female civil partners.

[47] Express consent to parentage is here replacing the unsatisfactory concept of receiving treatment services together. See above note 44.

[48] The rule is currently contained in Human Fertilisation and Embryology Act 1990, s.27(1).

[49] Clause 47. Where a woman has not carried a child she will only be treated as the legal parent if she is the mother's partner and the female parenthood conditions apply or if she has adopted the child. Egg donation alone will not lead to legal parentage.

[50] Clause 54.

[51] Human Fertilisation and Embryology Act 1990, s.30(1) provides that the effect of a parental order is "for a child to be treated in law as the child of [the applicants]."

[52] As in the case of adoption by two men, this is to create a new category of legally "motherless" children and is quite revolutionary in English law in this respect – although, as noted above, it has been possible for children to be legally motherless in France for some time.

[53] White Paper, *Review of the Human Fertilisation and Embryology Act*, Department of Health, Cm. 6989 (December 2006), at paragraph 2.67.

They have also been influenced by changes to the law which have enabled unmarried and same-sex couples to adopt,[54] unmarried fathers to acquire parental responsibility through joint birth registration[55] and the "policy to create parity between civil partners and married couples".[56]

These reforms, if enacted, would increase the circumstances under which biological parentage is divorced from legal parentage and in which the social or intentional parent is treated in law as the parent. As such they raise fundamental questions about their consistency with the principle of biological truth so widely accepted now in other contexts, especially as noted above in the determination of paternity. The Bill acknowledges the importance of access to information about biological origins which the law has for some time accepted in the case of donor-conceived persons, albeit subject to major qualifications. As under the present law, the HFEA will be required to keep a register of information about people born as a result of treatment services.[57] In relation to donations made after March 31st 2005, it is already the law that certain identifying, as well as non-identifying, information about the donor must be given to donor-conceived persons if requested.[58] At present, information may be requested at the age of 18 but the government has accepted in part the recommendations of the Joint Committee on the Human Tissue and Embryos (Draft) Bill (hereafter "The Joint Committee") that the age of access to information should be lowered from 18 to 16.[59] The government, however, takes the position that only *non-identifying* information should be provided at 16 since those donors who have already donated and provided identifying information would have done so on the basis of disclosure at 18. It is also concerned that future donors might be deterred by the possibility of 16 rather than 18 year olds having access to identifying information.[60] The Bill also now provides for the establishment of a voluntary contact register[61] which in essence corresponds with the adoption contact register for adopted persons and birth relatives.[62]

---

[54] Adoption and Children Act 2002, s.50(1) and s.144(4).
[55] Children Act 1989, s.4(1)(a), as introduced by Adoption and Children Act 2002.
[56] Above note 53, at paragraph 2.69.
[57] The current law, which *inter alia* requires the HFEA to maintain a register of information, is contained in the Human Fertilisation and Embryology Act 1990, s.31. The new provisions governing this register are set out in Clause 24 of the Bill and Clause 25 imposes certain restrictions on disclosure of information. The details are beyond the scope of this article.
[58] See the Human Fertilisation and Embryology Authority (Disclosure of Donor Information Regulations) 2004, SI 2004/1511.
[59] *Joint Committee on the Human Tissue and Embryos (Draft) Bill, Volume I; Report*, HL Paper 169-I, HC Paper 630-I (2007), paragraphs 261–262.
[60] *Government Response to the Report from the Joint Committee on the Human Tissue and Embryos (Draft) Bill*, Cm. 7209 (October 2007), paragraph 68.
[61] Clause 24 would insert a new s.31ZF into the 1990 Act.
[62] The provisions are now contained in the Adoption and Children Act 2002, s.80.

There are therefore some advances here in the direction of upholding the principle of knowledge of biological truth, but there is also a fundamental qualification to this. The Bill does not provide donor-conceived persons with any legal right *to be told* that they are donor-conceived any more than the adoption legislation gives to adopted persons the right to be told that they are adopted,[63] nor does it place the legal parents under any duty to disclose the circumstances of conception to the child. Adoption is in practice far less problematic in that it is accepted good practice to inform adopted children that they are adopted as soon as it is thought to be in their best interests to do so. The overwhelming majority are told. In contrast, the great majority of donor-conceived persons are not told of their status and the legal parents are held out in most cases as the biological parents. In the case of donor-conceived persons therefore, as the author put it in evidence to the Joint Committee:

> The most immediate and obvious reason why these rights and obligations should exist is that the right to information at the age of eighteen [or at sixteen] is largely illusory in the case of donor-conceived children unless they know that they are donor-conceived.[64]

The Committee was clearly concerned about what it felt could be seen as complicity by the state in deception. The facts of conception and birth are known in the case of assisted reproduction but a deliberate choice is being made to keep the donor-conceived child in the dark, certainly during childhood, raising again the temporal question about exactly when the child should be told the truth and the implications of delay. As it was put by the Committee: "unlike where children are born through natural conception, assisted conception by its nature involves the authorities and we are deeply concerned about the idea that the authorities may be colluding in a deception".[65] The Committee, however, rejected the idea of imposing a duty on the legal parents to reveal the facts to the child believing, as the government does, that this is rather a matter of good practice. But it is worthy of note that the Joint Committee did take the view that it was in the best interests of the child to know that he or she was donor-conceived:

> We believe that it is in the best interests of the child to know of their donor conception. Parents should be encouraged to be open

---

[63] Contrary to the recommendations of the *Review of Adoption Law*, Report to Ministers of the Interdepartmental Working Group, Department of Health and Welsh Office (1992).
[64] *Joint Committee on the Human Tissue and Embryos (Draft) Bill, Volume II: Evidence*, HL Paper 169-II, HC Paper 630-II, Ev.14, paragraph 7.
[65] *Report*, paragraph 276.

and honest, and counselling and intermediary services should be available to them.[66]

The Joint Committee recognised the force of the argument, put forward by a number of witnesses, that the fact of donor conception should be registered on a person's birth certificate. In the view of the Committee:

> This would create the incentive for the parents to tell the child of the fact of his or her donor conception and would go some way to address the value of knowledge of genetic history for medical purposes.[67]

The government has in the event rejected this proposal and it is not incorporated in the Bill. Its current position is "that it is preferable that parents are educated about the benefits of telling children that they were donor-conceived rather than forcing the issue through the annotation of birth certificates." However, recognising the Committee's concern, the government has undertaken to keep the matter under review.[68]

The likelihood therefore is that, apart from the situation in which legal parents can be persuaded to reveal the facts of conception to the child, the child and indeed the donor-conceived adult will in many cases remain in ignorance of the true position. Ironically, as the author pointed out in evidence to the Joint Committee, this is capable of discriminating in favour of the children of same-sex parents and against those of heterosexual parents:

> This is because it will become clear, at a relatively early age to the children of same-sex parents, but not to those of opposite-sex parents, that those parents cannot both be the biological parents. The right to acquire information at eighteen [or at sixteen] in the case of children of same-sex parents is therefore a real right in the sense that they will be on notice that a third person must have been involved in their conception. This is not the case in relation to children of opposite-sex parents, except perhaps in an unusual case such as where there is a racial difference between the child and the legal parents (as occurred by accident in the Leeds case where the hospital concerned confused donated sperm). Given that the children of same-sex legal parents will be aware that the biological and legal positions diverge and can effectively exercise their rights in due course to obtain information about the donor, the question needs to be asked whether the much larger group of children of opposite-sex legal parents should not be given the legal right to be told of their conception so that they too may meaningfully exercise their rights to information when the time comes.[69]

---

[66] *Ibid.*, paragraph 272.
[67] *Ibid.*, paragraph 276.
[68] *Government Response*, above note 60 at paragraphs 69–70.
[69] *Volume II, Evidence*, Ev.14, paragraph 11.

The techniques of assisted reproduction are strongly supportive of the notion of individual autonomy in that they facilitate one of the most important life choices which adults can make – the decision to have a child. What needs to be questioned is how supportive they are of the child's own personal autonomy and in particular his or her right to knowledge of biological origins. It can surely be argued that since "these couples will be acquiring the ultimate status in relation to children, that of legal parentage...in return they should be placed under a legal obligation to disclose to the child the true biological position."[70] But this begs the question whether they should in any event be acquiring the status of legal parent. This is especially problematic in the case of same-sex couples since it involves a departure from the historically entrenched position that a child has one legal mother and (at least where identity is established) one legal father.

Does the argument for more or less automatic legal parentage for the lesbian partner stand up to scrutiny? Superficially it might appear discriminatory to withhold this status given the civil partnership legislation and the capacity of same-sex partners now to adopt.[71] As we have seen, these were policy factors which influenced the government in its view. It is submitted, however, that the attempted analogies with civil partnership and adoption are not true analogies.

Civil partnership is about regulating the relationship between two adults, as is marriage, and is not about the relationship between adults and children. Indeed, those countries which pioneered registered partnerships were careful not to include provisions which affected the parent-child relationship.[72] Marriage as a status is quite distinct from parentage and civil partnership, which apes marriage, should also be distinct from it. What about adoption? Prima facie, there would seem to be a powerful argument that if a same-sex partner can adopt a child on the basis of his or her intentional or social parenthood, then he or she should also be able to acquire parentage through the alternative means of assisted reproduction. Yet, again, the analogy is false. First, the claim of the potential adopter is based not merely on intention but also on an existing social relationship with the child as well as a relationship with the biological parent which is judged to be "an

---

[70] Ibid., paragraph 12.
[71] On the rise of same-sex partnerships in terms of legal recognition see Stephen Cretney's 2005 Clarendon Lectures published as *Same Sex Relationships: From 'Odious Crime' to 'Gay Marriage'* (Oxford 2006).
[72] Denmark, which was first to introduce the registered partnership for same-sex couples on October 1, 1989, explicitly provided that registered partners were not to be treated as a married couple either with respect to adoption or for the purposes of obtaining joint legal custody of a child. The concern was that it was thought to be in the interests of children to have a male father and a female mother. See Morten Broberg, "The Registered Partnership for Same-Sex Couples in Denmark" [1996] 8 C.F.L.Q. 149.

enduring family relationship".[73] Adoption involves a probationary period being spent with the child, serious social welfare scrutiny of the suitability of the potential adopter and a court order which will not be made unless the welfare of the child is judged to require it.[74] These safeguards do not exist in the context of parentage acquired through assisted reproduction although it is fair to say that judicial scrutiny is required where a parental order is made following a surrogacy arrangement. It is also the case that the European Court of Human Rights has held in *Fretté* v. *France*[75] that Article 8 of the ECHR does not cover the desire to found a family but presupposes the existence of a family. That being the case there is no Convention right to adopt and France did not violate the rights of a single homosexual applicant by refusing his adoption application. Yet, there is another reason why acquiring parentage through assisted reproduction ought not to be seen as analogous, far less equated, with that of adoption. This is because adoption is by definition concerned with an *existing* child whereas assisted reproduction is concerned with a *potential* child. As Mary Warnock put it twenty years ago:

> It is plausible to talk about the good of the child when the child exists and there are alternative futures before it, between which someone must choose. To choose whether or not a baby should be born in the first place is a different kind of choice altogether. The whole undertaking is *in fact* for the sake of the infertile would-be parents. It is *they* who want the baby.[76]

Adoption then, like all social parenting, comes about not as the option of first choice but because (in an entirely non-pejorative sense) the natural family has failed. Assisted reproduction involving donation, in contrast, is a deliberate choice to create for the child, from birth, a family in which at least one biological parent will never be recognised as the parent of the child.

If these analogies are not true analogies, we are still left with the policy question whether there are, or are not, good reasons for conferring legal parentage automatically on a female partner or for "fast-tracking" it by court order in the case of a male partner. Here we need to consider whether the position of the biological parent gives to that parent a superior claim in relation to the child and, if so, whether

---

[73] "Couple" for these purposes is defined by the Adoption and Children Act 2002, s.144 (4) as:
"(a) a married couple, or,
(aa) two people who are civil partners of each other, or
(b) two people (whether of different sexes or the same sex) living as partners in an enduring family relationship."
[74] The Adoption and Children Act 2002, s.1(2) provides that "the paramount consideration of the court or adoption agency must be the child's welfare throughout his life".
[75] [2003] 2 F.L.R. 9.
[76] Mary Warnock, "The Good of the Child" (1987) 1 Bioethics 141, at p.144.

it is appropriate to confer parentage, or some lesser form of legal status, on his or her partner.

In *Re G (Children)*[77] the House of Lords was faced with a dispute between a lesbian mother and her partner and found itself drawn into the debate about exactly what it is which makes one a parent. The dispute concerned a "time-sharing" order under which the biological mother had originally been awarded 70 % of the time with the two children (who were conceived by donation in joint enterprises involving the mother and her partner) and the lesbian partner 30 %. This was then changed on appeal to Bracewell J. Her order reversing the percentages and giving primary care to the partner was upheld by the Court of Appeal which rejected the argument that there must be cogent reasons for preferring the claims of a person who is not a parent over those of a natural parent. The House of Lords allowed the mother's appeal and restored her primary care in accordance with the original percentages. It was acknowledged, at all stages of the litigation, that the partner had a strong emotional and social relationship with the children and this was reflected in the shared residence order which also gave her parental responsibility for the children to be shared with the mother.[78]

Lord Scott of Foscote offered the view that "mothers are special".[79] Lord Nicholls of Birkenhead emphasised that "a child should not be removed from the primary care of his or her biological parents without compelling reason".[80] But the case is most noteworthy for the detailed analysis of Baroness Hale of Richmond of the different components of parenthood.[81] She identified three such components in relation to a biological mother, namely the *genetic, gestational* and *social and psychological* contributions. The biological mother (except in the case of egg donation) combines all three. The biological father certainly has the genetic component and in many, if not most cases, will also perform the social and psychological role. He does not of course conceive and bear the child, but it is a moot point whether his role at the gestational stage should be completely ignored.[82] It is of course fair to say that many fathers who leave the scene when the mother becomes pregnant, perform no role beyond the genetic and the same can be said for the licensed sperm donor. So far as the lesbian

---

[77] [2006] 2 F.L.R. 629.
[78] Under the Children Act 1989, s.12(2), where a residence order is awarded to someone who is not already the child's parent or guardian, one of its effects is to give to that person parental responsibility.
[79] Above note 77, at p 631.
[80] *Ibid.*
[81] *Ibid.*, at p 641.
[82] The author has argued elsewhere that the father's contribution in pregnancy ought not to be ignored completely in discussing the components of parenthood. See Andrew Bainham, "Who or What is a Parent?" [2007] C.L.J. 30, 31.

partner is concerned, she is only the social or psychological parent, subject to the same point which applies to many fathers that she would also be very likely to have supported the mother at the gestational stage, *viz.* during pregnancy. None of this, in the view of the Judicial Committee, meant that there was a legal presumption favouring the biological parent because that would detract from the application of the welfare principle which applies equally to disputes between parents and non-parents. But that same welfare principle was held to be broad enough to accommodate the "special contribution" of the natural parent which should be an important and significant factor in the court's determination.

The speech of Baroness Hale is also noteworthy for the significance it appears to attach to the beginnings of life. Two out of three components of natural parenthood are concerned with the conception of the child, pregnancy and the child's peri-natal care. It is those contributions which make the natural parent special and it is those contributions which, first and foremost, should receive a significant level of support from the state and the legal system. As we have seen, the government appears to acknowledge this in its proposals for joint birth registration.

We therefore have it on high authority that we should pause before equating the position of the biological parent with that of the lesbian partner. This is, of course, exactly what the Human Fertilisation and Embryology Bill is seeking to do in the case of assisted reproduction but without any prior judicial scrutiny. The question we need to ask, given that there is general agreement that the partner of a parent should be given recognition and support in her psychological role, is what is the *appropriate* legal response. This is not a question confined to lesbian partners, but clearly one which also applies to heterosexuals in the context of assisted reproduction and to step-parents and the partners of parents outside the context of assisted reproduction. In order to answer this question we need to focus on the contribution which is being made.

The partner of a parent is in effect participating, to a greater or lesser degree, in the upbringing of the child. In some cases, like *Re G*, the level of participation in parenting will be high. In other cases involving some step-parents and partners of parents it may be quite low if that person is with the children not from any desire to be with them but because he or she is in the relationship with the parent. One is reminded here of the French tradition, "Take the Woman, Take the Child". It is very far from clear that the right legal response to these extremely varied social arrangements should be to facilitate the acquisition of parentage and indeed English law has for some time been highly sceptical about the value of step-parent adoption especially following divorce.[83] Where the level of involvement in parenting by the parent's partner is high, there is a strong case for facilitating the acquisition of parental responsibility since this is the legal device for conveying the powers and responsibilities associated with upbringing.[84] The mother's partner in *Re G*, as noted above, had parental responsibility through the residence order. Parents may now share parental responsibility with step-parents by agreement and without court order[85] and consideration might be given to whether this facility should be available in relation to others in more informal relationships with parents.[86] But to go further and make the partner of a parent the legal parent is a different matter altogether.

Parentage is not principally about the powers and duties of upbringing though, of course, most parents will also have parental responsibility. The distinctive features of parentage relate to the establishment of filiation and the wider kinship links deriving from the parent-child relationship. These kinship links clearly have significance for the notion of family membership but also for the purposes of inheritance and liability for child support. It is these last two features of parentage which lie behind most of the applications made by men seeking to disprove their paternity. The argument, therefore, is that while it may be appropriate to give to the lesbian partner and other social parents parental responsibility (depending on the extent to which the individual actually performs parenting functions), it is *inappropriate* to make that person the legal parent because this is to distort and misrepresent kinship.[87] The lesbian partner's mother and father, for example, would become the child's grandparents and her brothers and sisters the child's uncles and aunts. Meanwhile, the biological father drops out of the legal picture as do everyone in what would have been the paternal family.

---

[83] The Houghton Committee in the *Report of the Departmental Committee on the Adoption of Children*, Cmnd. 5107 (1972) wanted to discourage step-parents from adopting because of the effect of adoption on the divorced parent, and the courts were directed, initially in the Children Act 1975, to have regard to alternatives.

[84] "Parental responsibility" in the Children Act 1989, s.3(1) is an umbrella concept which includes within it:
"all the rights, duties, powers, responsibilities and authority which by law a parent of a child has in relation to the child and his property."

[85] Children Act 1989, s.4A, as inserted by the Adoption and Children Act 2002.

[86] Consideration might also be given to reforming the current concept of "child of the family" (defined in the Children Act 1989, s.105(1)) which can generate certain rights and responsibilities in relation to social parents but only where the relationship is formalised through marriage or civil partnership. There is a case for saying that the relationship between a child and a step-parent or the civil partner of a parent is not greatly different (if different at all) from that between a child and the heterosexual or same-sex partner of a parent. The Law Commission does not however favour such a reform in the context of its recent report on the financial consequences of breakdown of cohabitation. See Law. Com. Report No. 307, *Cohabitation: The Financial Consequences of Relationship Breakdown* (2007), Cm. 7182, especially at para. 4.108.

[87] This is essentially the view also taken, specifically in relation to the status provisions of the Human Fertilisation and Embryology Bill, by Thérèse Callus in "First 'Designer Babies', now À La Carte Parents" [2008] Family Law 143.

This brings us to the whole question of the donor's or biological father's position in the context of female same-sex parenting. The Joint Committee received a great deal of conflicting, even impassioned, evidence on the question of the child's need for a father.[88] The current legislation governing clinics provides as follows:

> A woman shall not be provided with treatment services unless account has been taken of the welfare of any child who may be born as a result of treatment (including the need of that child for a father), and of any other child who may be affected by the birth.[89]

The HFEA Code of Practice which provides guidance to clinics advises in the following terms:

> Where the child will have no legal father, the treatment centre should assess the prospective mother's ability to meet the child's/children's needs and the ability of other persons within the family or social circle willing to share responsibility for those needs.[90]

The Human Fertilisation and Embryology Bill 2007 retains the requirement that clinics must have regard to the welfare of any potential child (though as at present the child's welfare will not be paramount) and other children who might be affected by the treatment services, but removes from the licence condition the reference to the child's need for a father.[91] The Joint Committee was influenced by research evidence concerning the importance to children of fathers[92] but, in the end, was more impressed by the research which appears to demonstrate that it is the presence of a *second parent* of whatever gender in the child's life, rather than a father as such, which has the greatest impact on outcomes for children.[93] Accordingly the Committee proposed that the question whether the statutory reference to the need for a father should be retained or removed in the reformed legislation should be put to a free vote of both Houses of Parliament. It was the balance of view of the Committee that it would be detrimental to remove the reference entirely and that the provision should be retained in an amended form which makes it clear that it is capable of being interpreted as the "need for a second parent". The Committee was at pains to emphasise that it was not its intention to discriminate against single women seeking treatment and it took note of the fact that under the present law, the existing provision had not operated as a barrier to the treatment of single women.[94] The

---

[88] This evidence is discussed at paragraphs 224–243 of the *Report*.
[89] Human Fertilisation and Embryology Act 1990, s.13(5).
[90] *HFEA Code of Practice*, 7th Edition, G.3.3.3.
[91] Clause 14(2)(b).
[92] See *Report*, paragraphs 229–231.
[93] *Ibid.*, paragraphs 233–234.
[94] *Ibid.*, paragraphs 225–226.

government, however, in its response to the Joint Committee's Report has opted in the Bill, albeit in the face of immediate protest[95], to remove the reference entirely. The government's view is that amending the reference to refer instead to a second parent "would not add significantly to the Government's proposal to retain a mandatory licence condition requiring that the welfare of the child be taken into account before providing treatment".[96]

The government's position is consistent with the general view of regulated sperm donation that this should not, and does not, result in legal parentage for the donor and this essential legal position will be maintained under the Bill.[97] It is however rather more difficult to square with its rhetoric regarding the importance to children of fathers, most recently articulated in its Green Paper on Joint Birth Registration.[98] The willingness to accept father absence, which clearly is the implication of female same-sex parentage, also jars somewhat with the developments here and elsewhere facilitating the establishment of biological paternity.

While the absence of a father is something which can apparently be ignored in the case of an anonymous sperm donor, it will be apparent that this cannot as readily be the case where there is a *known* donor under a private, unregulated arrangement which may involve sexual intercourse with the mother or so-called "home insemination". In this case it is clear that the "donor" will be the legal father, whatever may have been intended, and he may *inter alia* be liable for child support. This may be inconvenient enough to the parties concerned;[99] but even more inconvenient is the situation where a lesbian couple are confronted with a man who wishes to play a larger role in the upbringing of the child than they had ever intended.

This was the scenario facing Black J. in *Re D (contact and parental responsibility: lesbian mothers and known father)*[100] where a lesbian couple advertised for a man interested in fathering a child. The child

---

[95] An alliance of senior politicians and churchmen are set to oppose the removal of the reference from the legislation. See "Battle for a Child's Right to a Father", *The Mail on Sunday*, November 18, 2007.

[96] *Government Response*, supra note 60 at paragraph 57. Clause 14(2)b would now amend the reference to refer merely to the child's need for "supportive parenting".

[97] Where legal parentage is conferred on the mother's husband or partner, the 1990 Act, s.28(4) provides that "no other person is to be treated as the father of the child". See clauses 38 and 41 of the Bill which maintain this position and expressly provide that a sperm donor is not to be treated as the legal father. Where the mother's female partner acquires parentage the Bill provides in clause 53 that references to a child's father in legislation, other documents and relevant cases should be read as references to the child's parent by virtue of the Bill's provisions relating to female parenthood.

[98] Above, note 32.

[99] See, for example, the recent, widely reported case of Mr. Andrew Bathie who provided sperm to a lesbian couple on the express understanding that that would be the end of his parental duties. It did not, however, stop the Child Support Agency from successfully pursuing him. See "Lesbian Sperm Donor Must Pay Child Support", *Daily Mail*, December 4 2007.

[100] [2006] 1 F.C.R. 556.

was conceived following intercourse between the father and the mother. The mother's partner had already obtained parental responsibility under a shared residence order with the mother before the father also applied for this. There had been an agreement between the three that the father would play some part in the child's life, but it soon became apparent that his perception of what this involved was not that of the mother and her partner. He had seen himself as in an analogous position to a divorced father with an appropriate amount of contact and participation in decisions affecting his daughter, whereas the women had not anticipated that level of contact or involvement. The disagreement between them was exacerbated by references to the father by the women as a "sperm donor" and by the father's apparently hierarchical view that, as a parent, his position in relation to the child was superior to that of the mother's partner. There was evidence that the women were troubled by their fear that, as an unusual family, they would not be accepted as a proper family or as two parents by society and they clearly considered applying to adopt the child to overcome this anxiety. There was what was seen as inappropriate and insensitive intervention by the father in medical and educational matters affecting the child. In these circumstances, Black J. granted parental responsibility to the father, largely as a question of status[101] in view of his undeniable interest in and commitment to the child, but only on his undertaking not to visit or contact his daughter's school or any health professional involved in her care without the prior written consent of the mother or her partner.

There is a notable discussion by Black J., drawing on the expert evidence of Dr. Claire Sturge (a consultant child and adolescent psychiatrist), of the expectations of the various parties in their roles and of the significance of language or terminology to them. Dr. Sturge referred particularly to the "deficiencies of our language" in dealing with societal developments which embraced this kind of parenting arrangement. These include "whether two women can be 'parents', whether children's psychological thinking can accommodate three 'parents', and what the biological father should be called if not a 'parent'".[102] These difficulties over appropriate terminology are also evident in Parliament's reluctance, both in the Adoption and Children

---

[101] The possession of parental responsibility puts the father, for example, in a stronger legal position to resist the adoption of the child which would require his consent, in relation to invoking the Hague Convention governing child abduction and in relation to the local authority if the mother proposes to agree to the child being looked after by it. It also fulfils what is thought to be a symbolic function in conveying as positive an image of the father to the child as is possible. The leading decision in which these features are highlighted is the Court of Appeal decision in *Re S (Parental Responsibility)* [1995] 2 F.L.R. 648.

[102] Above note 100, at p 571.

Act 2002[103] and in the Human Fertilisation and Embryology Bill,[104] to acknowledge in the case of same-sex adoption and same-sex parentage respectively, that the child may have two legal "fathers" or two legal "mothers", opting in each case for "parent". This might be seen in a positive light as a commitment to gender-neutrality and the equality of parental status as between men and women. Others will view it as cowardice and an attempt to dodge the sensitive issues involved in explicitly providing, for the first time, that a child need not have one legal mother and one legal father.

So far as the "three parent" question is concerned, English law has thus far set its face against the notion of more than two parents for a child though, as is illustrated by *Re D* itself, there is nothing to prevent more than two people holding parental responsibility, or indeed more than three. In North America we are seeing the first signs of acceptance of the notion that the law might recognise three parents as such. The Superior Court of Pennsylvania in *Jennifer L. Shultz-Jacob v. Jodilynn Jacob and Carl Frampton*[105], following an earlier decision in Ontario, has held that for the purposes of child support a child may have *three* legal parents. The difficulty with this approach, apart from the obvious one that it contradicts the traditional view that a child has one father and one mother, is that it also has the potential for proliferating legal parents. If three, why not four, five or six? It is an approach which is not supported in this paper, the principal arguments here being that the law should be confining the notion of legal parentage as far as possible to biological parents and not expanding it further.

Re D is a case which is very much concerned with questions of language and status and is a good example of the desire which people have for a superior status in relation to children and their concern about where they are in the hierarchy of those who have a relationship with them.[106] The paradigm case of this desire, demonstrated many times, is that of those who wish to adopt and who make it plain that no arrangement short of adoption will enable them to feel that they are

---

[103] See particularly section 68(3) which provides:
"A reference (however expressed) to the adoptive mother and father of a child adopted by-
(a) a couple of the same sex, or
(b) a partner of the child's parent, where the couple are of the same sex, is to be read as a reference to the child's adoptive parents."
This is in contrast to the position of heterosexual adopters where section 68(1)(a) openly acknowledges that:
"an adopter may be referred to as an adoptive parent or (as the case may be) *as an adoptive father or mother*" (emphasis added).

[104] This is most spectacularly demonstrated by the Bill's references to "the *fatherhood* conditions" (Clauses 36 and 37) in the case of heterosexual partnerships but "the female *parenthood* conditions" in the case of lesbian partnerships (clauses 43 and 44) (author's emphasis).

[105] 207 PA Super. 118.

[106] For the author's views on this phenomenon see "Status Anxiety? The Rush for Family Recognition", above note 7.

a "true" family and "real" parents.[107] We must touch on the question of how the arguments presented in this paper relate to the institution of adoption in the concluding section.

III. Conclusions

How far do these developments relating to paternity, assisted reproduction and same-sex parenting reflect commitment to the values of truth, individual autonomy and priority for the rights or interests of children?

Laws now governing paternity in England and elsewhere demonstrate an already strong and increasing commitment to truth and recognition that knowledge of the truth will usually be in the best interests of children. This commitment is qualified only by an appreciation that in a minority of cases it may be better not to reveal the truth immediately. Although the issue of direction of tests is not governed directly by the welfare principle, it is accepted that tests should not be directed where that is thought to be *against* the child's best interests.[108] Yet, even in those cases, the judiciary have a tendency to note that putting off discovery of the truth for too long may not promote the child's welfare. There is a general view that disputed paternity is better resolved sooner rather than later.[109] There is recognition here too of the individual autonomy of adults who wish to resolve the issue often years after legal fatherhood has been determined. Human rights, as we have seen, now require that those wishing to dispute paternity be given at least one opportunity to do so. The government has also accepted the importance of establishing the truth of paternity at the first available opportunity, when the child's birth is registered, and the importance of both parents to the child from the very beginning of life is emphasised.

In the context of assisted reproduction, the commitment to truth is far less strong. In particular there is no general acceptance that a child has a right to know, or an interest in knowing, the truth about the circumstances of his or her birth at least *while a child*. As we have seen, the Human Fertilisation and Embryology Bill would reduce the age of access to certain information about donors from eighteen to sixteen, but only in relation to non-identifying information. One view of the failure to reveal the truth to the child at an earlier stage is, to put it no higher, that the state is participating in a misrepresentation. The legal parents are assumed to be the biological parents and no-one, it seems,

---

[107] The most striking example of this attitude being *Re M (Adoption or Residence Order)* [1998] 1 F.L.R. 570 where two Oxford academics who were fostering a child made it clear that they would not continue to do so unless they were permitted to adopt her.
[108] *S* v. *McC* [1972] A.C. 24.
[109] Above note 41.

is under any obligation to tell the child the real situation. This is instead to be governed by "good practice". This approach certainly gives full weight to the autonomy of the adults who desire a child by these means, but it can be criticised for failing to give priority to the interests of the child. The child's interests in this situation are again first and foremost rooted in the concept of individual autonomy. The infant or young child cannot of course be said to possess actual autonomy, but respect for human rights surely requires that it is the child's *capacity or potential* for autonomy which needs to be protected.[110]

What specifically is the child's autonomy interest here? We know that in adulthood a certain proportion of adopted persons seek out their biological origins and some also go further and attempt make contact with their birth relatives.[111] We can conclude from this and also from the paternity cases discussed above, that for some people at least biological relationships are important though by adulthood this is probably better described as an interest in biological history. The benefits of having knowledge about biological origins are most commonly asserted to be psychological and medical.[112] But whether or not there are psychological or medical benefits is not the crucial question. The key point is that individuals wish to exercise personal autonomy and to take their own decision about whether or not biological links are important to them. They are not required to give any reason for this. It is not for the state, or their parents or anyone else to dictate whether biological parentage is, or is not, important to them. It is fundamentally an individual choice which ought to be respected. The issue is how the child's choice can be meaningfully protected *during childhood*. It can be argued that the state should be under a positive obligation to establish and conserve biological heritage in as many cases as possible and that this is not something which should be left to chance. The child's opportunities for establishing and fostering a relationship with the biological family are also surely reduced where knowledge of that family is postponed to adulthood. Here we should remind ourselves of the state's positive

---

[110] It is this potential for maturing into a rationally autonomous adulthood which has been argued to lie at the heart of state paternalism concerning children. See Michael Freeman, *The Rights and Wrongs of Children* (London 1983), especially at pp.54–60.

[111] See generally David Howe and Julia Feast, *Adoption, Search and Reunion* (London 2000). On the use made of access to original birth certificates by adopted persons see Rupert Rushbrooke, "The Proportion of Adoptees who have Received their Birth Records in England and Wales (2001) 104 Population Trends 26. On the use made of the Adoption Contact Register by adopted persons and relatives see John Haskey and Roger Errington, "Adoptees and Relatives who Wish to Contact One Another: the Adoption Contact Register" (2001) 104 Population Trends 18.

[112] See, for example, Katherine O'Donovan, "A right to know one's parentage?" (1988) 2 I.J.L.F. 27 and Sarah Maclean and Mavis Maclean, "Keeping Secrets in Assisted Reproduction – The Tension between Donor Anonymity and the Need of the Child for Information" (1996) 8 C.F.L.Q. 243.

obligations under the ECHR, underlined in *Görgülü* v. *Germany*,[113] to attempt reunification of parent and child where family life has been established and the potential for breach of the Convention where the state is inactive. The case for a legal obligation to inform the donor-conceived child of the fact of donation as soon as is reasonably possible is therefore a strong one, though there can be legitimate arguments about exactly when, by what means and by whom.

The key legal question in the context of same-sex parenting is the same question which can be posed in relation to all social parents. What kind of legal status is required to satisfy the legitimate expectations of those who are looking after children with whom they are not biologically related? Here it can be argued that there is too strong a tendency to assume that this status necessarily needs to be that of parent. The fact that someone is doing some of the things which parents do does not make that person the parent. The true claim which same-sex partners and other social parents have is that they should be given the legal powers which are necessary to enable them to look after a child properly and it is the status of possessing parental responsibility which is best designed to achieve this. Where appropriate, parental responsibility can be bolstered by making the social parent the special guardian of the child to provide greater security in long-term caring arrangements. The lesbian partner in *Re G* was given parental responsibility and the right to care for the children 30 % of the time. Some may think that this was quite enough and that the House of Lords was right to reject her demand not merely for equality with the mother, but for *more* than equality.[114] The reasons given by Baroness Hale about why the social or psychological parent is not in an equivalent position to the biological mother (or for that matter the father) are entirely convincing. And it is manifestly not the case that the ECHR requires parentage to be conferred on the female or male same-sex partner. Their positions are quite distinct from those of biological parents. It is therefore not discriminatory for the state, and well within its margin of appreciation, to treat them differently in terms of their legal status whether in the context of assisted

---

[113] [2004] 1 F.L.R. 894. The case concerned an unmarried father who, despite being originally unaware of the pregnancy and birth, subsequently found out and proposed that he adopt the child himself as alternative to adoption by unrelated adopters. The ECtHR found a violation of his article 8 rights where he was refused custody and access and emphasised that it was in the child's interests for his family ties to be maintained so as not to cut the child off from his roots.

[114] Though evidently not Elizabeth Woodcraft who described the dicta attaching importance to the biological mother as "tragic". She felt "driven to the conclusion that the House of Lords has allowed the unusual context of this case to send it scurrying back to the mid-twentieth century and distract it from properly dealing with the 'undefined family connections' that the lower courts are wrestling with every day." Elizabeth Woodcraft, "Re G: A Missed Opportunity" (2007) Family Law 53.

reproduction or generally. The concept of parentage should rather be confined, to reflect as far as possible the unique position of biological parents and, through the child's filiation with them, the wider kinship links to the extended maternal and paternal families.

Where does this leave adoption? The logical conclusion of this approach would be to abolish the institution of adoption. While it is not suggested that this is a realistic or desirable option, we should note that adoption as we know it is a relatively recent phenomenon in the English legal system and that not every jurisdiction has supported the "transplant model" of adoption which terminates the legal relationship between the child and the birth family. Simple adoption, which does not have this effect, has historically been recognised in some civil law jurisdictions[115] and Islamic law rejects adoption preferring instead the institution of *kafalah*.[116] Commentators too are increasingly calling into question the suitability of adoption in the context of modern family structures.[117] Much of the case for adoption seems to rest on meeting the insecurities of long-term carers, but it is questionable whether the only or best means of addressing these understandable insecurities is through what has been called a 'constructed affiliation'.[118]

Perhaps there is a place for adoption, especially in the context of a genuine orphan lacking any existing family, but this does not mean that we should view adoption as synonymous with permanence. Neither does it mean that we ought to be promoting it, as the

---

[115] Simple adoption does not involve complete dissolution of the legal ties with the birth family and is more akin, in this respect, to long-term fostering in English law.

[116] In Islam, *kafalah* means sponsoring or guardianship of a child while preserving the child's awareness of his birth family. There is a priority for the extended family. It is considered to be the child's right to know his parents and accordingly what is prohibited is any suggestion that the child is the carers' own child. They are not permitted to change the child's name; something which is clearly allowed and considered important in the context of legal adoption. The institution of *kafalah* is acknowledged in Article 20.3 of the United Nations Convention on the Rights of the Child. This article also requires that 'when considering solutions, due regard shall be paid to the desirability of continuity in a child's upbringing and to the child's ethnic, religious, cultural and linguistic background'. For an accessible judicial discussion of the institution of *kafalah* see the judgment of Munby J. in *Re S; Newcastle City Council* v. *Z* [2007] 1 FLR 861, especially at p.872 *et seq*, and the sources cited there. In that case he held (perhaps controversially) that a devout Muslim mother, whose faith in Islam was not in doubt, was nonetheless unreasonably withholding her consent to adoption since a parent's religious belief, however profound, could not be determinative of the outcome in children cases.

[117] Jane Lewis has, for example, commented: "In the increasingly messy world of family formation and change, children may have a number of mother figures and father figures. Furthermore the messiness is no longer hidden and gives rise to less and less stigma. In this context, the notion of giving the child a new legal status in a new family looks increasingly anachronisitic." Jane Lewis, "Adoption: The Nature of Policy Shifts in England and Wales, 1972–2002" (2004) 18 I.J.L.P.F. 235, at 252.

[118] C. Van Nijnatten and W. de Graaf, "The Legal Management of (Social) Parenthood: Adoption and Dutch Family Policy" (2002) 24 J.S.W.F.L. 263.

government has been doing[119], nor "fast-tracking" it as the Court of Appeal has seemed to favour in a recently reported decision. In *Re C (A Child) (Adoption: Duty of Local Authority)*[120] the Court of Appeal held that there is no mandatory duty on local authorities (when acting as adoption agencies) to inform the mother's wider family, the father (if identified) or the wider paternal family of the child's birth, where the placement is with the mother's consent and initiated by her.[121] The statutory duty to explore the resources of the wider family which applies where the child is "looked after" by the local authority[122], was held not to apply to what the Court characterised as the essentially *private* adoption placement in which the mother is requesting total confidentiality. Thorpe L.J. referred to cases like this, with evident approval, as "fast-track adoption". The decision, contrary to the theory that modern adoption is child-centred, is glaringly mother-centred. The decisive criterion governing involvement of the father or the wider birth family on either side is effectively the mother's own decision.[123] It is clear, in contrast, that where the father *does* find out about the birth and wishes to have an involvement there may be significant human rights arguments in relation to himself and the wider family. It is also clear that where the child is looked after by the authority there may be a preference for care in the extended family.[124]

Human rights obligations, far from requiring the facilitation of adoption, militate against it and towards some less drastic alternative which can preserve the child's existing kinship links and contacts.

---

[119] The then Prime Minister, Tony Blair, took a personal interest in the promotion of adoption believing that it represented the best solution for children in long-term care where it has been adjudged that they should not return to their birth family. See *Performance and Innovation Unit, Prime Minister's Review: Adoption: Issued for Consultation* (Cabinet Office, July 2000). This policy was reflected in particular by the setting of targets designed to increase the numbers of children looked after by local authorities being adopted and by new statutory duties to establish 'adoption support services' in the Adoption and Children Act 2002. Others have pointed out that the empirical evidence does not support the view that adoption necessarily produces better outcomes for children than other long-term arrangements. See, for example, John Eekelaar, "Contact and the Adoption Reform" in A. Bainham, B. Lindley and M. Richards (eds.), *Children and their Families: Contact, Rights and Welfare* (Oxford 2003), ch. 13 and, for an Australian perspective on the same question see Patrick Parkinson, "Child Protection, Permanency Planning and Children's Rights to Family Life" (2003) 17 I.J.L.P.F. 147.

[120] [2007] 3 F.C.R. 659. For commentary see Brian Sloan, "Adoption, Welfare and the Procreative One-Night Stand" [2008] CLJ 33.

[121] Placement for adoption under the Adoption and Children Act 2002 may now take place either by consent (s.19) or without the parent's consent under a placement order (s.21).

[122] Children Act 1989, s.22(4) and s.23.

[123] The Court cites with approval the recent decision of Munby J. in *Re L* [2007] EWHC 1771 to the effect that the court ought not to seek to compel, as opposed to persuade, a mother to reveal the name of the father which, for whatever reason, she has decided to withhold.

[124] Compare, for example, the decision of Sumner J. in *Birmingham City Council v. S, R and A* [2007] 1 F.L.R. 1223. Here the child was removed from her mother's care and was in foster care following emergency police protection and local authority intervention. The father was known and had some contact with the child. It was held, *inter alia*, that the child had a right to be brought up within her own family unless there was good reason why not and the paternal family also had a right to put themselves forward as potential carers in order that the child might remain in the family.

Perhaps the Court of Appeal is right that the welfare principle is neutral as between adoption and its alternatives, but respect for human rights requires no such neutrality but rather a preference for keeping alive the legal link with the birth family wherever feasible. The reported decisions concerning the choice between special guardianship and adoption[125] only reveal how ill-adapted and unfit for purpose the welfare principle is in the modern era of human rights.[126]

Mr.Quinn and Mr.Ellis are, in the final analysis, both correct to assert the importance of social and biological parents respectively. Both should receive appropriate support. The mistake is to assume that they must be treated identically.

---

[125] The leading authorities are a "triptych" of Court of Appeal decisions handed down the same day and intended to be read together. See *Re S (Adoption Order or Special Guardianship Order)* [2007] 1 F.L.R. 819; *Re AJ (Adoption Order or Special Guardianship Order)* [2007] 1 F.L.R. 507; and *Re M-J (Adoption Order or Special Guardianship Order)* [2007] 1 F.L.R. 691.

[126] For the author's view on this see Andrew Bainham, "Permanence for Children: Special Guardianship or Adoption?" [2007] C.L.J. 520.

13

Tangling the web of legal parenthood: legal responses to the use of known donors in lesbian parenting arrangements

Leanne Smith

This paper explores cases involving disputes between lesbian parents and known donors with whom informal insemination arrangements were made. It observes that the current legal framework for recognising parents following assisted reproduction is incapable of dealing adequately with known donors, notwithstanding a host of recent developments in the law relating to lesbian parenting. As a result, the case-law exhibits judicial uncertainty and inconsistency about the extent of the recognition to which known donors should be entitled. In spite of the difficulties posed by using known donors, the paper argues that there is a strong case for finding an appropriate way of accommodating them within the legal framework for recognising parents. It explores some of the possible legal responses and highlights their potential advantages and disadvantages from theoretical and practical perspectives.

INTRODUCTION

In recent years the law relating to lesbian parenting has undergone a series of developments which culminated in the Human Fertilisation and Embryology Act 2008 (hereafter 'the 2008 Act') making provision for lesbian couples to qualify as joint legal parents in certain circumstances. This move means that the law now recognises lesbian parents on terms equal to heterosexual parents when their children are conceived through artificial insemination.[1] However, this paper examines a number of recently reported cases which involve disputes between lesbian couples and known sperm donors. The cases highlight a new problem concerning recognition of parental roles in lesbian parenting arrangements that the 2008 Act does not address. Moreover, the factually complex web of relationships that is revealed in the cases has been further complicated by the judicial decisions in them.

1. Some technical points of difference do remain. See C Jones 'The (im)possible parents in law' in C Lind, J Bridgeman and H Keating (eds) *Taking Responsibility: Law and the Changing Family* (Farnham: Ashgate, 2011) pp 201–220 and S Sheldon and J McCandless 'The Human Fertilisation and Embryology Act (2008) and the tenacity of the sexual family form' (2010) 73 Modern Law Review 175. Details of the relevant provisions will be outlined later.

The paper therefore argues that recognition on equal terms should not be seen as the end of the road in terms of the development of the law on lesbian parenting. It begins by explaining why this is so in theoretical terms before moving on to examine how the cases demonstrate continuing shortcomings in law's capacity to respond to the full complexity of lesbian parenting arrangements. The final part of the paper considers ways in which those shortcomings could be addressed to facilitate a more constructive response to the problems posed by known donors.

Central to the discussion are two contentions which make a strong case for formulating a more constructive response. First, the difficulties presented by the cases are as attributable to the lack of an appropriate framework to facilitate and regulate the use of known donors as they are to the intrinsic complexities of the resulting parenting arrangements. Second, validating lesbian parenting means going beyond providing recognition on equal terms with heterosexual parents and making space for their differences to 'reflexively transform' the legal framework for recognising parents. The paper concludes with a suggestion that a tentative step towards formal recognition of multiple parents would address these concerns and might also be of significance for the practice and regulation of heterosexual parenting.

1. THE DEVELOPMENT OF THE LAW ON LESBIAN PARENTING: FROM INTOLERANCE TO RECOGNITION – AND BEYOND

Historically, the stance of the courts did not bode well for lesbian parents. A belief that children may be 'permanently scarred'[2] as a result of being brought up by non-heterosexual parents informed the earliest judicial decisions. These concerned the fitness of mothers to care for their children after developing lesbian relationships. Judicial hostility continued to be evident in the rhetoric of *C v C*.[3] There, it was held that a mother's lesbian relationship does not necessarily render her unfit to care for her child but the judge still stressed that he regarded it as 'axiomatic that the ideal environment for the upbringing of a child is the home of loving, caring and sensible parents, her father and her mother'.[4] As Reece has noted, the case effectively established 'a presumption in favour of heterosexual parenting'.[5]

C v C was heard in 1991 but no further cases involving lesbian parents were reported for fifteen years afterwards. Moreover, in that case (and all the cases preceding it), the court was only presented with a single biological mother; lesbian co-parents remained a legal anomaly during that time.[6] Planned lesbian parenting presented a new legal dilemma – namely whether and how to recognise the co-parent

---

2. Wilberforce LJ in *Re D (an infant)* [1977] AC 602 (CA) at 629. This position was supported in *S v S* (1980) 1 FLR 143.
3. *C v C (a minor) (custody: appeal)* [1991] FLR 223 (CA).
4. Per Glidewell LJ, ibid.
5. H Reece 'Subverting the stigmatisation argument' (2006) 23 J Law and Society 484 at 486.
6. This is in spite of the fact that in the interim years a rise in the number of lesbian planned births can be traced in figures showing that the number of donor insemination treatment cycles provided for lesbian couples in the UK increased fourfold between 2000 and 2005, amounting to 14.4% of the total cycles provided at the end of that period: Human Fertilisation and Embryology Authority *Figures for Treatment of Single Women and Lesbian Couples 2000–2005*, available at http://www.hfea.gov.uk/docs/Figures_for_treatment_of_single_women_and_lesbian_couples_2000-2005.pdf.

who was neither biologically nor legally related to the child.[7] This matter came before the court of Appeal in *Re G (residence: same sex partner)*.[8] The case was brought by W, the co-parent of two children conceived by anonymous donor insemination during W's relationship with their biological mother, when the mother restricted her contact with the children following the breakdown of the relationship. No means existed by which she could legally be recognised as a parent so she sought a shared residence order which would have the indirect effect of giving her parental responsibility.[9] The Court of Appeal granted the order, comparing the co-parent's situation to that of an unmarried father seeking parental responsibility in the same circumstances.[10] It was hoped that the order would send 'a clear and strong message to the mother that she could not achieve the elimination of W, or even the reduction of W from the other parent into some undefined family connection'.[11]

Re G was important because it was the first case to project the dilemma of lesbian co-parents clearly into the legal arena. It illustrated judicial support for a direct means of legally acknowledging the parental role of lesbian co-parents, thereby diverting attention away from the question of whether lesbian biological mothers were suitable parents and clearing the way for focus on the possibilities for recognition. The 2008 Act was introduced soon afterwards. Under its provisions, women in W's position may now be treated as the second legal parent of their partner's child and the problem of how to recognise lesbian co-parents that *Re G* highlighted has been responded to.[12]

Thus far, the pattern of development in the law relating to lesbian parenting has moved from intolerance of the idea, through the reluctant tolerance demonstrated in *C v C*, to support and recognition in the outcome of *Re G* and the terms of the 2008 Act. This pattern corresponds closely to the 'standard sequence' in the legal recognition of same-sex relationships in different jurisdictions that has been observed by Waaldijk.[13]

---

7. In America, a body of academic writing on this difficulty was already in existence, underpinned by an emerging body of case-law on the issue, by the early 1990s. See, eg, N Polikoff 'This child does have two mothers: redefining parenthood to meet the needs of children in lesbian mother and other non-traditional families' (1990) 78 Georgetown Law J 459; K Arnup 'Living in the margins: lesbian families and the law' in K Arnup (ed) *Lesbian Parenting: Living With Pride and Prejudice* (Charlottetown: Gynergy Books, 1995).
8. *Re G (Residence: same sex partner)* [2005] EWCA Civ 462.
9. Section 12(2) Children Act 1989 states that parental responsibility is conferred on anyone with a residence order. Parental responsibility is defined in s 3(1) as 'all the rights, duties, powers, responsibilities and authority which by law a parent of a child has in relation to the child and his property'. This does not amount to legal parental status, however.
10. It was stated that that the outcome would have been evident if W had been an unmarried father seeking parental responsibility under the same circumstances (although an unmarried father would have been able to apply directly for parental responsibility under s 4 Children Act 1989).
11. Per Thorpe LJ at [27].
12. Though note that some ambiguity might remain when disputes arise between separated lesbian parents. An early indication that this was the case came when the parties from *Re G* returned to court in a residence dispute which progressed to the House of Lords (*Re G (Children) (Residence: Same-sex Partner)* [2006] UKHL 43; [2006] 1 WLR 2305). The case has been extensively commented upon elsewhere and is only tangentially relevant to the focus of this article, so it will not be considered in depth here. Discussion can be found in L Smith 'Re G (Children) (Residence: Same-sex Partner) [2006] UKHL 43' (2007) 29 J Social Welfare and Family Law 307.
13. K Waaldijk 'Standard sequences in the legal recognition of homosexuality: Europe's past, present and future' (1994) 4 Australasian Gay and Lesbian Law J 50 at 72.

His sequence describes a chain of development in the law which, in broad terms, reflects the shift from intolerance, to tolerance, to recognition.[14] He further illustrates how his overarching sequence can be sub-divided into different 'fields' of development, including same-sex parenthood. The standard sequence of development in this 'field' follows the same trajectory from intolerance, to tolerance, to recognition. Moreover, the recognition of same-sex parenthood features as the final stage of Waaldijk's sequence, a trend which has led Weeks et al to conclude that 'parenting has become the touchstone issue for attitudes towards non-heterosexual relationships, the yardstick by which social acceptance may be judged'.[15] Does this mean that with the 2008 Act English law reached the end of the road in terms of the recognition of same-sex relationships and parenting, that the sequence of developments is now complete? It is submitted that it would be a mistake to assume that this is the case.

One obvious question, beyond the scope of this paper, is whether parenting by two men has been adequately dealt with because differences remain in the legal approach to same-sex parenting by men and by women.[16] Beyond that, the legal approach to recognising lesbian parenting is now broadly equivalent to the approach to opposite-sex parenting. The important point about Waaldijk's sequence, however, is that it places developments in the recognition of same-sex relationships on a continuum; each development is to be understood as a step in an evolutionary process.[17] If recognition has been an evolutionary process, why should the evolution of attitudes and regulation stop here? Why should we assume that equality is the endgame of the evolutionary process? Once it is accepted that law's response to different types of family and parent evolves over time, it is logical to expect further changes to ensue in response to further innovations in parenting practices.

In light of this, it is suggested that there is the potential for a further stage of *reflexive transformation* to be added to Waaldijk's evolutionary chronology of the recognition of same-sex relationship practices. This new stage would see the principles and practices of conventional family relationships being questioned with reference to different relationship principles and practices adopted by gay men and lesbians.[18] To illustrate, a useful analogy can be drawn with critiques of the Civil

14. This is a distilled interpretation of the sequence, which, in Waaldijk's terms, moves from *criminalisation, to decriminalisation, to equalising the age of consent, anti-discrimination legislation and legal recognition of partnership.*
15. J Weeks, B Heaphy and C Donovan *Same Sex Intimacies: Families of Choice and Other Life Experiments* (London: Routledge, 2001) p 158.
16. Parenting between two men remains problematic legally, not least because it requires adoption or the use of a surrogate. The 2008 Act does, however, remove the previous restriction on applying for parental orders following a the birth of a child to a surrogate to commissioning couples who were married. Unmarried couples, both opposite and same-sex, may now apply to be treated as the parents of a child born to a surrogate.
17. In line with this it makes sense that *Re G* and the 2008 Act did not occur in a vacuum. They were precipitated by the legalisation of same-sex adoption in the Adoption and Children Act 2002, the introduction of the first anti-discriminatory legislation applicable to gays and lesbians (Employment Equality (sexual orientation) Regulations 2003), the repeal of the infamous section 28 of the Local Government Act 1988, and the Civil Partnership Act 2004. These steps contributed to a legal and social climate more sensitive to same-sex relationships, thus preparing the ground for better receptiveness to the idea of lesbian parenting.
18. I do not intend to suggest here that all same-sex couples construct their intimate and family relationships according to principles and practices which differ from conventional heterosexual relationships. However, plenty of research demonstrates that many same-sex

Partnership Act 2004. Many commentators have observed that the assimilating effect of introducing an institution which recognises same-sex relationships on a virtually identical basis to married relationships failed to capitalise on the 'transformative potential' of same-sex relationships.[19] Freed from the traditions of monogamy, dependency and gendered behaviour which form a blueprint for heterosexual marriage, many same-sex couples carve out their own relationship norms which shun these relationship characteristics.[20] Consequently, some have expressed hope that civil partnerships will gradually displace the hegemonic norms of marriage as they 'introduce a reflective element into expectations of behavior in relationships' and 'reveal different ways of being married'.[21] Others have challenged the likelihood of this aspiration, arguing instead for the necessary introduction of an entirely different type of relationship recognition, with different criteria and consequences, not just a different title. Less than a decade after the introduction of civil partnership, neither goal has come to fruition.[22] Nevertheless, the advent of civil partnership has opened the door to debate and fed high-profile legal challenges to the basis and nature of adult relationship recognition in law. The cases include *Burden and Burden v UK*, in which the legitimacy of the conjugal basis of relationship recognition was unsuccessfully questioned.[23] There have also been calls for civil partnership to be made available to opposite-sex couples, some of whom find the new title more palatable than marriage with all its hegemonic, patriarchal and religious connotations.[24]

Just as civil partnership prompted discussion of whether marriage itself, as the gold-standard of relationship recognition, is an institution in need of reform, shifts in the law on lesbian parenting could do the same for the general recognition of parenthood. The known donor cases discussed below add a new strand to the debate on how parents, lesbian and otherwise, are recognised. The 'problems' raised and unsolved by the cases only qualify as such because the parenting arrangements they relate to have been organised along lines and ideals which differ from traditional heterosexual parenting practices and do not fit into the frameworks established for recognising them. They highlight outstanding questions concerning the basis and scope of the legal recognition afforded to different parents, the intrinsic significance of genetic parentage and how to balance the roles of parents in conflict. The cases therefore present an

---

couples do make a conscious decision to shun conventional heterosexual relationship norms. See, eg, K Weston *Families We Choose: Lesbians, Gays, Kinship* (New York: Columbia University Press, 2nd edn, 1998).
19. C Lind 'Sexuality and same-sex relationships in law' in B Brooks-Gordon et al (eds) *Sexuality Repositioned* (Oxford: Hart, 2004) p 109 and A Diduck 'A family by any other name . . . or Starbucks comes to England' (2001) 28 J Law and Society 290.
20. See Weston, above n 18, and Weeks et al, above n 15.
21. Lind, above n 19, p 126.
22. This is perhaps unsurprising given that a great deal of the debate has been focused on whether there can be full equality without opening up same-sex marriage.
23. *Burden and Burden v United Kingdom* (App No 13378/05, ECHR) 2008. For discussion see L Glennon 'Obligations between adult partners: moving from form to function?' (2008) 22 Int J Law, Policy and the Family 22.
24. In November 2009, Tom Freeman and Katharine Doyle applied to register a civil partnership and the inevitable refusal of permission on the grounds that they were not of the same sex was highly publicised. The couple, who are in part protesting against the continued exclusion of same-sex couples from marriage, later coordinated a more widespread challenge under the banner of the 'Equal Love Campaign'.

opportunity to question the parenting norms and models which currently underpin the legal regulation of parenthood.

In a normative sense it is necessary to do this for the benefit of lesbian parents. The decision of some lesbian parents to include a known donor in their parenting arrangements shuns the exclusivity of the dyadic parenting model that is based on heterosexual reproduction.[25] Insofar as the current legal framework for recognising parents struggles to accommodate this choice, it fails to value the difference in lesbian parenting practices.[26] In order to move beyond this situation, it is necessary to embrace the capacity of lesbian parents to 'remake the normative family'[27] by *reflexively transforming* the existing template for parenting practices and regulation.[28] In a broader sense, responding to the known donor cases has the potential to bring new insights and open up new possibilities for practising and regulating parenthood which are relevant beyond the particular circumstances of lesbian parenting arrangements.

2. TANGLING THE WEB OF LEGAL PARENTHOOD: THE KNOWN DONOR CASES

(a) The Cases

This section examines six known donor cases that have been reported since 2006. It was clear that the lesbian couple were intended to be the primary carers in all the cases, though there was variation in the degrees of involvement planned for the fathers.[29] In each case conflicts arose when the father sought more involvement in the child's upbringing than that with which the lesbian couple was comfortable. Each of the couples involved had planned conception of their child(ren) together, but before the 2008 Act came into force, meaning that none of the lesbian co-parents were legal

---

25. See S Sheldon 'Reproductive technologies and the legal determination of fatherhood' (2005) 13 Feminist Legal Studies 349; R Probert 'Families, assisted reproduction and the law' [2004] Child and Family Law Q 273, for discussion of how this model is emulated in the 2008 Act and its predecessor, the Human Fertilisation and Embryology Act 1990.
26. Difference feminists were the first to critique the assimilationist consequences of recognition of different relationships, experiences and behaviours on equal terms. For a discussion of their ideas see chapters 6 and 7 of N Lacey *Unspeakable Subjects: Feminist Essays in Legal and Social Theory* (Hart: Oxford, 1998).
27. A Diduck *Law's Families* (London: Butterworths, 2003) p 210.
28. In other words, the goal should not be simple recognition on equal terms, but a chance to contribute to the construction and meaning of the terms. This is part of what the feminist project of 'normative reconstruction' (see Lacey, above n 26, ch 8) exhorts us to do. It is a practical, reformist manifestation of the 'utopian' project of reimagining identities and the terms of social and regulatory practices that theorists such as Drucilla Cornell have engaged in: D Cornell *Beyond Accommodation: Ethical Feminism, Deconstruction and the Law* (Lanham, MD: Rowman & Littlefield, 1999) and *The Imaginary Domain: Abortion, Pornography and Sexual Harrassment* (London: Routledge, 1995).
29. There is scope for reasonable debate over whether the term 'father' is preferable to 'known donor' in these cases. The term 'father' features in the judgments of all the cases discussed in this article, though it is sometimes qualified in a phrase such as 'donor father' or 'biological father'. For consistency and straightforwardness, the term 'father' will therefore be used in the discussion of the cases here. It is not the intention of this article to enter into lengthy debate over the significance of the terminology, though this is not to say that such a debate would not be worthwhile.

parents. A further complicating feature of the cases is that, because informal insemination arrangements were made, the fathers did qualify as legal parents.

RE D (CONTACT AND PARENTAL RESPONSIBILITY: LESBIAN MOTHERS AND KNOWN FATHER)[30]

This was the first reported English case to deal with a lesbian couple using a known donor.[31] Relationships were difficult from the outset and the father, B, applied for contact and parental responsibility a year after the birth. His application for parental responsibility was unsuccessful but he was granted limited monthly contact. The judge also made a joint residence order in favour of the mother and co-parent to confer parental responsibility on the latter. *Re D* arose when the child was five and the parental responsibility application was renewed. The lesbian couple were concerned that granting parental responsibility to B would symbolically undermine the status of their nuclear family and diminish the co-parent's role in the eyes of outsiders. Although the concern was considered valid by the judge and an expert witness, parental responsibility was granted. However, Black J was mindful of the need to protect the child's primary family and home with the lesbian couple, particularly as incidents had occurred in which B had caused problems with arrangements for her schooling and healthcare. In a solution that Black J described as 'creative', the order was hedged about with a series of conditions designed to 'strip it of practical effect'.[32] She considered that this outcome would recognise the father as a parent, but 'a parent of a very different sort'[33] while retaining the stability and integrity of the child's primary home with the mother and co-parent.

RE B (ROLE OF BIOLOGICAL FATHER)[34]

Again, relationships soured early on and the father applied for contact and parental responsibility when the child was 18 months old, by which time supervised contact had occurred twice.[35] In contrast to *Re D*, Hedley J declined to make a parental responsibility order, which he described as 'wholly inconsistent'[36] with the reality that the nuclear family comprised the child and the lesbian couple. He also rejected the father's wish for sufficient contact to enable him to play a significant role in the child's life. However, asserting that it would promote the child's best interests to have

---

30. [2006] EWHC 2 (Fam); [2006] 1 FCR 556.
31. The earlier cited Scots case of *X v Y (Parental Rights: Insemination)* 2002 SLT (Sh Ct) 161, dealt with this issue, however. In addition, at least one unreported case of this nature was previously heard by the Family Division of the High Court: *Re M (sperm donor father)* Family Division, 15 November 2001 (unreported). See G Douglas [2003] Family Law 94 for a summary casenote.
32. [2006] 1 FCR 556 at 582. Specifically, B was prohibited from seeking any involvement with the child's education or medical care without the prior written permission of the lesbian couple.
33. Ibid, at 583.
34. [2007] EWHC 1952 (Fam); [2008] 1 FLR 1015.
35. It is not possible to tell from the judgment whether there was a clear and unequivocal intention to bring the child up knowing who his father was in this case but some contact was certainly envisaged as a minimum.
36. [2008] 1 FLR 1015 at 1022.

knowledge of his father, he made an order for limited contact, to take place several times a year. It was felt that this would enable the child comfortably to 'satisfy his curiosity about his origins'[37] if and when he wished to do so.

R V E AND F (FEMALE PARENTS: KNOWN FATHER)[38]

The father in this case was named on the birth certificate but did not have parental responsibility.[39] The mother had made a parental responsibility agreement with the co-parent after the couple entered into a civil partnership when the child was four.[40] Until the child was five, the adults sustained positive relationships comprising lengthy contact visits several times a year (the father, who lived in the USA, stayed with the couple in the family home during these visits) and joint holidays. Relations were disrupted when disagreements arose over the discipline and parenting of the child. The father, wishing to have more staying contact and 'be recognized as an equal parent',[41] applied for shared residence and parental responsibility. The mother and her partner objected and submitted a cross-application for joint residence in an effort to cement their status as the child's joint parents and primary carers. Supporting agreed contact of no more than fifty days a year, the judge rejected the parental responsibility application. He stated that, although the father had obviously enjoyed a meaningful relationship with the child, he could not be said to have co-parented him and his position was different to that of a father in a separated heterosexual family. The judge also dismissed the shared residence application, but the lesbian couple's joint residence application was seen as a way of confirming to the child that his primary home was with the couple and was granted.

T V T (SHARED RESIDENCE)[42]

This was the first case to reach the Court of Appeal. Two children were conceived using the same donor, who made parental responsibility agreements with the mother shortly after each child's birth. Before proceedings were initiated, the children had regular contact with the father, including a fortnightly overnight stay. The father wanted more, however, and the case involved the lesbian couple's appeal against a County Court decision to make a shared residence order in favour of him and the mother and increase contact to 152 days a year. The judge had also made a parental responsibility order in favour of the lesbian co-parent,[43] but turned down the mother's

---

37. Ibid, at 1023.
38. [2010] EWHC 417 (Fam); [2010] 2 FLR 383.
39. Since December 2003, fathers named on their child's birth certificate have automatically obtained parental responsibility under s 4(a) Children Act 1989 (as amended by the Adoption and Children Act 2002). The child in this case was born before the relevant amendment came into force.
40. Section 4A(1)(a) Children Act 1989 makes provision for parental responsibility to be extended in this way to step-parents in civil partnerships.
41. [2010] 2 FLR 383 at 392.
42. [2010] EWCA Civ 1366; [2011] 1 FCR 267. For detailed discussion of this decision, see L Smith 'T v T (shared residence) [2010] EWCA Civ 1366' (2011) 33 J Social Welfare and Family Law 175.
43. This was possible under s 4A Children Act 1989 because the lesbian couple had by then entered into a civil partnership.

application for restrictions to be placed on the father's ability to exercise his parental responsibility (as in *Re D*).

The lesbian couple argued that the order was not in the children's best interests because it would undermine the co-parent and because the eldest child had expressed reservations about more overnight stays.[44] The Court of Appeal rejected these arguments, upholding the shared residence order and contact arrangements. The appeal was allowed to the limited extent that the shared residence order was substituted for an order in favour of the mother, father and co-parent. Black LJ stated that she had been persuaded to make this alteration in response to an offer from the father to agree to a residence order in favour of all three adults and an argument that, without this adjustment, the father would be free to remove the children from the co-parent's care in the event of their mother's death.

RE P AND L (MINORS)[45]

The father already had parental responsibility following an earlier court order and the mother had made a parental responsibility agreement with the co-parent after they formed a civil partnership. It was unclear how much prior contact had taken place between the father and children but it had included some overnight stays and shared holidays and was considered to be enough to establish a parenting role. By the time of the hearing, which concerned the amount of contact and, by extension, the nature of the relationship, between the father and children,[46] litigation had been ongoing for some three years, having been initiated when the children were aged three and seven. Relationships between the parties were particularly acrimonious and it was noted that the eldest child, who was staunchly opposed to contact with the father, had 'suffered significant emotional harm' as a result.[47]

Whilst warning that giving general guidance for known donor cases is 'fraught with risk',[48] Hedley J took the view that contact arrangements must reflect the original intentions of the parties and that the father's position should therefore be differentiated from that of a divorced father.[49] He introduced a concept of 'principal and secondary parents' to assist in differentiating between the adults' roles.[50] This approach led him to order indirect contact (as a minimum) with the eldest child and staying contact of a weekend per month and one annual holiday with the youngest.[51]

44. The child was seven years old and the CAFCASS officer had advised against forcing the issue.
45. [2011] EWHC 3431 (Fam). This judgment needs to be read in tandem with an earlier one in which interim contact was awarded: *ML and another v RW and another* [2011] EWHC 2455 (Fam).
46. The father's application for a residence order had been dismissed in the earlier hearing (see above).
47. [2011] EWHC 3431 (Fam) at [3]. The judge comments on the possibility that this could in theory lead to public law proceedings several times in the judgment, though he doesn't go so far as to say that they are actually necessary.
48. Ibid, at [5].
49. Ibid, at [8].
50. Ibid, at [5]. The concept is explained in more depth in the earlier judgment, above n 45.
51. It was made clear that it would be preferable for both children to have direct contact with the father but noted that, unless and until the lesbian couple could be persuaded to present her with a more positive view of the benefits of contact, it would not be in her interests to force it against her will.

A V B AND C[52]

The most recent decision is from the Court of Appeal. Again, the father, A, already had parental responsibility.[53] Relations broke down before the child's birth when he developed expectations that there would be weekly overnight contact from the outset. He applied for contact shortly after the birth and the lesbian couple applied for joint residence.[54] Approving and following Hedley's *Re P and L* approach, Jenkins J asserted that the father's relationship with the child should be limited and made an order for fortnightly contact of a few hours. There were to be no overnight stays and it was suggested that there should be no expectation of an increase to such a regime in the near future.[55] It was on this point that A appealed, claiming that there should be an opportunity to build contact to a point where frequent overnight stays and a full parental relationship would be possible.

The appeal was unanimously allowed and the case remitted for further consideration by a Family Division judge. Thorpe LJ rejected as inappropriate Hedley J's concept of 'principal and secondary parents', describing it as 'demeaning' to known donors. The idea that the quantum of contact should reflect the initially planned role for a known donor was also rejected. Emphasising that the only principle to be applied in resolving parenting disputes is that the child's welfare is paramount, Thorpe LJ stated that it is not necessarily disadvantageous for a child to have three parents. Every case should be decided on its own facts and in this instance, although the father was clearly a secondary carer, he might play a greater role in future.

In terms of the outcomes, what stands out from a collective reading of these cases is the inconsistency between them. Different decisions were reached in relation to whether and why awarding parental responsibility to the fathers was thought to be appropriate, how much contact was considered appropriate in the circumstances, and whether and why shared residence should be used. A full reading of the cases does reveal some factual differences between them, but it is submitted that these do not fully explain the divergent outcomes because the judgments exhibit disagreements and uncertainties on points of principle.

(b) The shortcomings of parental responsibility

One factor complicating the High Court decisions is the judges' differing perceptions of when and why parental responsibility is appropriate. In her *Re D* judgment, Black J noted reasons why it might be undesirable to approach a request for parental responsibility by a known donor in the same way that one would approach a request

---

52. [2012] EWCA Civ 285.
53. The biological mother had a very religious family and feared that they would not accept her pregnancy if she was not married. She and the known donor therefore went through a marriage ceremony prior to the child's birth though there was never a relationship between them and they never lived together. This unusual added complication did not appear to influence decision making either in the High Court or the Court of Appeal.
54. Initially they also sought specific issue orders to restrict A's exercise of parental responsibility, but this aspect of their application appears to have been dropped.
55. There was no order under s 91(4) to rule out further applications, but the Court of Appeal later expressed a view that his comments on future contact would undoubtedly prejudice a future application to extend contact.

from a father who has reproduced naturally.[56] The restricted parental responsibility order was intended to serve the dual purpose of recognising B's status as a parent while supporting the primacy of the child's nuclear family with the lesbian couple. The approach could be viewed as an impressively innovative response to the unusual circumstances of the case, but the pragmatism of the order conceals a problematic paradox.

In issuing the order 'stripped of practical effect' it was suggested that B's visibility to the outside world, and the number of situations in which outsiders might interpret his role as more important than the co-parent's, would be reduced. Thus the parental 'status' of the lesbian couple, which was under threat, would be preserved. It was effectively suggested that, from the lesbian couple's perspective, stripping parental responsibility of practical effect ought to eliminate the objectionable or problematic aspects of conferring status on B. The inference is that status concerns are subordinate to practical concerns when granting parental responsibility.

Yet this was clearly not the case for B, for whom the opposite was true; in his eyes the status aspect of parental responsibility outstripped its practical ramifications in importance. Indeed, the judge's justification for making the order derived from her observation that parental responsibility orders are 'primarily designed to confer status' and status was what B wanted. Invoking a sort of 'doublethink' it was hoped that the parties would perceive the parental responsibility order in very different ways. This seems unrealistic; the solution contrived to fit the circumstances of the case was an imperfect one.

Black J defended her approach, commenting that the situation was unusual and that she was forced to judge 'equipped only with concepts and language which were not designed with this in mind'.[57] Yet it is arguable that parental responsibility was designed to fit exactly this kind of case in that it distinguishes the act of parenting, with all that is necessary to facilitate it, from the fact of parentage.[58] The very existence of the concept represents legal cognizance of the fact that the two need not always coincide and implicit in this is a need to consider whether they do, or ought to, in any given case. Contrary to Black J's assertion, parental responsibility was not primarily designed to confer status (a suggestion often repeated by judges but at odds with the statutory definition of the concept);[59] it was very much concerned with the substantive aspects of bringing up children.

Notwithstanding this, the confused message about the intrinsic value of parental responsibility presented by *Re D* is consistent with a broader incoherence in the

---

56. For example, she noted that the child was deliberately created and all concerned were aware of the couple's intention to be primary carers ([2006] 1 FCR 556 at 561). The potential threat to the stability of the lesbian family unit and the impact on society's perception of the family relationships which might be a consequence of giving parental responsibility to D were also noted (ibid, at 581).
57. [2006] 1 FCR 556 at 565.
58. On a conceptual level, it is significant that it is the investment of parental responsibility in legal parents, not their status as legal parents per se, that cloaks them with the powers necessary to execute day-to-day care. This was acknowledged in *Re S (a minor) (parental responsibility)* [1995] 3 FCR 225.
59. Section 3(1) Children Act 1989 describes parental responsibility as 'all the rights, duties, powers, responsibilities and authority which by law a parent of a child has in relation to the child and his property'.

courts' use of the concept that has attracted widespread critique.[60] As such, the flaws in the outcome of *Re D* appear to be less attributable to the unusual facts of the case than to general ambiguity surrounding the purpose of parental responsibility. Parental responsibility has been used as a catch-all provision with which to recognise the roles of a wide range of individuals involved with children, including fathers, lesbian parents,[61] step-parents[62] and grandparents.[63] This pragmatic, flexible approach has given the courts a valuable tool with which to cement legally stray relationships with children, lesbian co-parents being a pertinent example. However, it has also been used to reflect relationships with children that are qualitatively very different and it is now rare for a father's application for parental responsibility to be turned down in the absence of extraordinary extenuating circumstances.[64] An inevitable consequence of the 'proliferation'[65] of parental responsibility in this fashion is that the significance of holding it has been diluted and the reasons for using it have diversified so that its purpose is unclear. In an effort to paint its implications as very significant to satisfy those seeking it and as less significant for primary carers threatened by it, judicial emphasis has swung from its substantive legal and practical import, to its symbolic significance. This trend has led Reece to write persuasively of 'the degradation of parental responsibility'[66] and the judgment in *Re D* arguably accelerates the process by stripping the concept of almost all its substance and reducing it entirely to a status symbol – and an ambiguous one at that.[67]

The way in which parental responsibility has been used has resulted in frequent failure to consider what justifies an award of parental responsibility, given both its symbolic and substantive ramifications. Flexible use has enabled judges to shy away from difficult questions about how parents in different circumstances should be recognised which should have been central to the development of the jurisprudence surrounding it. The questions concern such matters as the integrity of nuclear families, the autonomy of primary carers, the importance of genetic parentage and the

---

60. Critical accounts can be found in S Gilmore 'Parental responsibility and the unmarried father: a new dimension to the debate' (2003) 15 Child and Family Law Q 21; H Reece 'The degradation of parental responsibility' in R Probert, S Gilmore and J Herring (eds) *Responsible Parents and Parental Responsibility* (Oxford: Hart, 2009) pp 85–102; and P Harris and R George 'Parental responsibility and shared residence orders: parliamentary intentions and judicial interpretations' (2010) 22 Child and Family Law Q 151.
61. As in *Re G (Residence: same sex partner)* [2005] EWCA Civ 462.
62. Section 4A Children Act 1989 permits this. Even after step-parents have separated from the child's parent there are cases in which shared residence has been used as an indirect route to granting them parental responsibility: *Re H (Shared residence: Parental Responsibility)* [1995] 2 FLR 1023; *Re A (a child) (joint residence: parental responsibility)* [2008] 2 FLR 1593.
63. *Re B (a child) (residence order)* [2009] UKSC; [2010] 1 All ER 223.
64. See, eg, *M v M (parental responsibility)* (1999) 2 FLR 737, where the father did not have capacity to exercise parental responsibility because he was left mentally impaired following an accident. The scope for the courts to make decisions about which fathers should qualify for parental responsibility has been heavily circumscribed by, first, the decision to extend parental responsibility automatically to all fathers named on birth certificates (s 4 Children Act 1989, as amended by the Adoption and Children Act 2002) and, second, the decision to make joint birth registration a legal requirement (via changes effected by the Welfare Reform Act 2009, Sch 6).
65. Reece, above n 60, pp 90–94.
66. Reece, above n 60.
67. Further critique of the decision can be found in J McCandless 'Status and anomaly: *Re D (contact and parental responsibility: lesbian mothers and known father) [2006]*' (2008) 30 J Social Welfare and Family Law 63.

interrelationship between each of these. They are of central importance in the context of the new relationships represented in the known donor disputes. It is unsurprising that *Re D* has highlighted the underlying inadequacies in an approach that has been so lacking in principle. The decision exposed the need for unquestioned norms surrounding how parents are recognised through the use of parental responsibility to be challenged. Fortunately, a more reflective approach was taken in *Re B* and *R v E and F*.

Hedley J, it will be recalled, viewed the facts of *Re B* as 'wholly inconsistent with an order of parental responsibility'.[68] He acknowledged that the father in the case met the criteria generally used to judge whether parental responsibility is appropriate.[69] Nevertheless, he said, it was important to remember that 'these applications remain subject to the overriding provision of section 1(1) of the Children Act 1989', particularly 'where the case is outside the ordinary run of parental disputes on separation'.[70] This was such a case and the lesbian couple would perceive parental responsibility for the father 'as a direct threat to their autonomy as a family unit'. Because B's interests and the stability and integrity of the family unit were interrelated, an order for parental responsibility would be 'contrary to his best interests'.[71]

Bennett J followed this approach in *R v E and F*, expressly preferring it over Black J's 'creative' *Re D* decision. Parenting, he said, 'involves not just caring emotionally and physically for a child – important though that is – but also taking decisions and exercising rights and responsibilities in relation to that child'.[72] He went on to observe that when the Law Commission first recommended the introduction of parental responsibility, they hoped that it would 'reflect the everyday reality of being a parent, and emphasise the responsibilities of all those who were placed in that position'.[73] This, he argued, made relevant the question of who had borne responsibility for bringing the child up and taking decisions necessary for his welfare.[74] Because the answer in this case was the lesbian couple, awarding parental responsibility to the father would be inconsistent with his role. In effect he suggested that, at least in unconventional cases, a functional approach to awarding parental responsibility should be taken, meaning that the arrangements for a child's upbringing pertaining at the time of a court application should not be disturbed.

Given how unusual it is for a father's application for parental responsibility to be rejected, the decisions of Bennett J and Hedley J were more striking than Black J's. Each judge emphasised the specificity of the case facts to justify departing from what has become the standard approach. This is ironic given that their approach,

---

68. In doing so he was invoking the relevance of s 1(5) Children Act 1989 to the circumstances of the case. Known as the 'no-order' principle the section states that the court should not make any order relating to the upbringing of a child 'unless it considers that doing so would be better for the child than making no order at all'.
69. [2008] 1 FLR 1015 at 1022. The criteria, as set out in *Re H (Parental Responsibility)* [1998] 1 FLR 855, involve scrutinising the commitment, attachment and motivation of the applicant, though the bar has arguably been set very low in respect of each of them.
70. [2008] 1 FLR 1015 at 1015. Section 1(1) reads: 'When a court determines any question with respect to (a) the upbringing of a child; or (b) the administration of a child's property or the application of any income arising from it, the child's welfare shall be the court's paramount consideration.'
71. [2008] 1 FLR 1015 at 1022–1023.
72. [2010] 2 FLR 383 at 389.
73. *Guardianship and Custody*, Law Com No 172 (London: HMSO, 1988) at [2.4].
74. [2010] 2 FLR 383 at 390.

emphasising the importance of the particular circumstances of the case and the substantive content of parental responsibility, only jars with the use of a diluted form of the concept that is exemplified in *Re D*. It is not in conflict with the originally intended meaning of 'parental responsibility' from which critics have lamented the departure. On the contrary, these decisions are a reminder of how parental responsibility was supposed to function. As such, it is disappointing that the particularity of the circumstances was strongly emphasised as the decisions might otherwise have been harbingers of an appropriate shift to more rigorous and coherent scrutiny of parental responsibility applications. On this point, the judgments in these two cases provide a first indicator of how responses to lesbian parenting could in future prompt reflexive transformation of the principles which underpin law's approach to recognising and regulating parenthood.

The principles (or the lack thereof) governing the use of parental responsibility facilitated the difference between the outcomes of *Re D* and the two later cases.[75] However, this does not explain why Hedley J and Bennett J were prompted by the circumstances to engage with the question of how parental responsibility should be used to recognise different types of parent whereas Black J was not. Underpinning the treatment of the parental responsibility applications is a more fundamental uncertainty concerning what the role of a genetic father should be in these circumstances. Uncertainty over the same issue is evident in the Court of Appeal decisions, which were focused on contact time rather than parental responsibility. Closer examination of this point reveals further distinctions between the judgments and a striking difference between the High Court and Court of Appeal approaches.

(c) Known donors and the nuclear family: the cuckoo in the nest problem

In *Re D* the co-parent was described 'as the most vulnerable person in this situation, whom society will view to some extent as "the cuckoo in the nest"'.[76] The terminology memorably captures the danger of co-parents being seen as 'the odd one out' in lesbian families. Yet the analogy could equally apply to the known donor, as the person most likely to destabilise the primary family and usurp the co-parent in the eyes of society. The very presence of a known donor heightens the vulnerability of lesbian co-parents and the perceived legitimacy of their families, making it difficult for three parents to be accommodated harmoniously on equal terms.[77] Thus the known donor cases present a conundrum. Do the facts of conception give rise to a nuclear family, comprising the lesbian parents and child(ren) and a reasonable expectation that that

---

75. Of course, it is arguable that the outcomes were not substantively very different given the significantly diluted version of parental responsibility that was granted to the father in *Re D*. Linking the 'creative' use of parental responsibility in the first case and the decision to make no order in the other two is a shared view that there is a need to distinguish between the different types of parental relationship in these unusual cases and those in more conventional cases; the comprehensive parental responsibility usually given to fathers was considered inappropriate by all three judges. *Re D* can also be distinguished on the basis that the father was prepared to settle for a diluted form of parental responsibility, whereas the fathers in the other cases gave no indication that this was the case for them. The father in *Re D* could therefore be seen as less of a threat to the lesbian couple's parenting.
76. [2006] 1 FCR 556 at 575.
77. This point is made in L Smith 'Is three a crowd? Lesbian mothers' perspectives on parental status in law' (2006) 18 Child and Family Law Quarterly 231.

family will be shored up against interference from the known donor, who is effectively an outsider? Or, do they create a fragmented family, in which the complications attendant upon negotiating the care and upbringing of a child across two households must be accepted, together with the vulnerability of the co-parent?

In the High Court cases, the judges took pains to emphasise that the lesbian couple and child(ren) constituted a nuclear family. Each judge also made it clear that they felt there was benefit to be gained from the child(ren) having some form of relationship with the father. However, when it came to determining how the roles of the father and the nuclear family should be balanced, the judges were not entirely agreed. Discordance on the answer to the central conundrum can be traced through their judgments and is strongly evident when the analysis is expanded to include the Court of Appeal decisions.

Taking *Re D* first, the concern that the father might undermine the stability of the nuclear family if given too much legal power was accepted as legitimate. The final order did not give him legal parity with the lesbian couple and he was expressly distinguished from 'ordinary' parents as 'a parent of a very different sort'.[78] On the other hand, the decision to grant parental responsibility was justified with the following reasoning:

> 'I am considerably influenced by the reality that Mr B is D's father. Whatever new designs human beings have for the structure of their families, that aspect of nature cannot be overcome.'[79]

This demonstrates reluctance to stray too far from norms dictated by the biological foundations of parenthood. It begins to look like the decision was at least partly motivated by biological determinism, which sees an immutable link between the fact of parentage and the circumstances of child rearing. This leads one to question what the outcome might have been if B had not volunteered to accept a restricted form of parental responsibility. Because he did, Black J was not forced to indicate whether he was entitled as a matter of principle to the same recognition as a father in conventional circumstances. Consequently, there is an unresolved ambivalence about the roles of the parental figures involved.

The *Re B* decision was bolder, the judge stating at the outset that 'general consideration . . . of the continuing role (if any) of the biological progenitors' was needed.[80] Ultimately, he foresaw a role for the father which, based on limited contact, would benefit the child by enabling her to learn about her natural parentage, but definitively stated that it was not a parental role:

> 'The court needs to be clear about the purpose of contact. It is not to give [father] parental status in the eyes of B or indeed anyone else. It is not to allow the development of a relationship which would amount to parental. That would threaten [the lesbian couple] and would not be consistent with their autonomy as a nuclear family.'[81]

The nuclear family and the need to protect it took centre stage and the known donor was positioned in the wings as a peripheral character.

78. [2006] 1 FCR 556 at 583.
79. Ibid, at 582.
80. [2008] 1 FLR 1015 at 1018.
81. Ibid, at 1023.

A clear distinction was also drawn between the role of the father, R, and the lesbian couple's leading role as parents in *R v E and F*. R was known to the child as 'daddy' and contact had been reasonably frequent given that he lived in the USA. He had also been consulted on matters such as schooling. However, the lesbian couple had always been the decision makers and they had always been present during contact. For the judge this was critical. That responsibility for the decisions related to the upbringing of the child, as well as day-to-day care had been borne by the lesbian couple was taken to mean that R 'whilst being committed and loving to D, is not undertaking the role of a parent'.[82]

Whether Bennett J would have concluded differently if there had been evidence that R had taken decisions in relation to the child's upbringing, or enjoyed contact without the presence of the lesbian couple is open to speculation but seems unlikely. In the circumstances presented it was concluded that the lesbian-led family unit constituted 'the nuclear family'. It was observed that this would undoubtedly be the case if a donor was not known and questioned whether 'the known-ness' of the donor should alter the position.[83] Indeed, numerous comments in the judgment align R more closely with an anonymous donor than a conventional parent. For example: '[H]e is trying to equate the instant case with a post divorce or separation situation. In my judgment, each of these perceptions is mistaken.'[84] Furthermore, R's application for contact to develop to encompass half of all the school holidays was rejected because it would send out 'an entirely wrong message to everybody' and restrict the time which the co-parent (who worked full-time) was able to spend with the child.[85] The judgment presents a clear message that the father is not a parent in these circumstances and should have no expectation of a right to be treated as such. The situation was not seen as inconsistent with a relationship between R and the child, but it was seen as inconsistent with legal status and authority for him.

Following these three cases, a consensus appeared to be emerging on the subordinate role of known donor fathers within lesbian-led families. In *Re P and L* Hedley J took a broadly similar but more nuanced approach. He felt that the primary purpose of a contact order in a known donor case is to reflect the parenting roles agreed by the parties. In this case he was in no doubt that a parenting role (albeit a secondary one) had been conceived and established for the father. He therefore took the view that the lesbian couple had never established a standard nuclear family and subjected their attempts to diminish the father's role to as much criticism as the father's attempt to expand it. Nevertheless, the need was emphasised for 'a distinct concept of parenting and parental roles'[86] to provide a basis for orders to reflect the secondary nature of the father's parenting in known donor cases.

The conceptual distinction between principal and secondary parents advanced by Hedley J has the advantage of being flexible and responsive to different types of known donor arrangement.[87] The judgment is progressive in that it sets out to avoid

---

82. [2010] 2 FLR 383 at 400. He also stated that: 'Parenting, in my judgment, involves not just caring emotionally and physically for a child – important though that is – but also taking decisions' (at 389).
83. Ibid, at 394.
84. Ibid, at 400.
85. Ibid, at 402.
86. [2011] EWHC 3431 (Fam) at [5].
87. Indeed, it would in theory be possible, though in practice probably rare, for Hedley's approach to lead to the conclusion that the lesbian couple and the father were all principal parents, if a genuinely equal role for each party was planned.

imposing old concepts of parenthood onto new parenting practices; instead of relying on the usual mantras (such as the need to protect the nuclear family or to promote a relationship with a genetic father), it uses intended and functional relationships as a guide to decision making. Like the earlier High Court decisions, this decision presents the context of the known donor cases as highly relevant to the appropriate outcome. However, it achieves more by carving out a space in which involved known donors can properly be recognised without overriding or invalidating the parenting plans of the lesbian couple.

Unfortunately, the Court of Appeal has taken the opposite approach, rejecting the relevance of the specific reproductive and parenting context in which known donor disputes arise. The amount of contact given to the father through the shared residence order in *T v T* (152 days per year) would have been considerable for a non-resident father in a conventional family and far exceeded what was considered appropriate in the earlier cases. It also constituted a significant extension of the one night per fortnight arrangement that was in place prior to the case so could not be said to reflect a relationship that had already been established. The father was treated as a father in a normal post-separation situation with a legitimate claim to a full parental relationship with the children. The decision is troubling in two key respects.

First, the co-parent in this case had good cause to feel threatened and marginalised by the father's involvement. He had tried to exclude her from proceedings and did not consider her to be a parent. He was also described as bullying and dominating.[88] It is therefore difficult to imagine that the decision to increase his time with the children dramatically will not have brought distress and disruption to the lesbian family. The second concern arises from the reasoning behind the decision to make one concession to the lesbian couple by amending the shared residence order to include the co-parent as well as F and the mother. The modification was not made to avoid the marginalisation of the co-parent, or to express the equality of her position. Rather, it was made for the practical purposes of providing stability in the event of the mother's death.[89] Of particular significance, however, was Black LJ's statement that:

> 'I would still not have treated this as sufficient to interfere with the Recorder's order had it not been for F's offer to agree to a residence order that includes [co-parent] as well as M and himself.'[90]

Effectively, F was given the power to determine the degree of recognition afforded to the co-parent. This is a clear indication that Black LJ did not view the co-parent as a parent in the same way that she viewed the mother and F as parents. Whereas the High Court judges were sensitive to the need to counter the vulnerability of the co-parent, the decision in *T v T* compounded it and in so doing revived the potential for co-parents to be devalued in comparison to genetic parents.

Although the lesbian couple's importance as primary carers was accepted in *A v B and C*, the decision was similarly prejudicial to the viability of known donor arrangements. On the surface, the refusal to accept any guidance on the appropriate role for known donors because it might undermine the overarching principle that child welfare

---

88. [2011] 1 FCR 267 at 272.
89. Note that no indication was given that the children's home ought to remain with the co-parent following such an event. Rather, it was considered that the children should be able to stay where they were until the court was able to settle the question of their future residence. Ibid, at 280.
90. Ibid.

is paramount in every case looks correct. On closer inspection, the reasoning is questionable. The welfare principle is not incompatible with guidance suggesting that agreements about parenting roles made at the planning stage of known donor arrangements should normally be reflected in the outcomes of later disputes. In constructing this guiding principle, Hedley J implicitly linked it with welfare when he said that the case was 'about trying to accommodate the needs of two damaged children in terms of *their experience of parenting*'.[91] In his first instance decision in *A v B and C*, Jenkins J explicitly outlined the ways in which undermining an original agreement could harm the child's welfare.[92] Furthermore, the courts have a long history of using principles to guide their interpretation of what welfare requires in particular circumstances.[93]

There are further flaws in a second strand of the reasoning. Thorpe LJ argued that holding the parties to a known donor arrangement to their plans is inappropriate because they are likely to change their minds about what they want in future. However, this position rests on a rather unsatisfactory circular logic. It is precisely because the parties to known donor arrangements are liable to change their minds about the nature of the relationships they want that a principle restricting their ability to do so is needed. In failing to accept this, the decision strangely denies that there is any role for family law in stabilising and regulating relationships. In line with *T v T*, it also places considerable power in the hands of known donors, who might request a greater role in a child's life at any time, and thereby denies lesbian parents the chance to construct their families in the way they choose. Indeed, Thorpe LJ surprisingly suggested that the desire of the lesbian couple to create a nuclear family 'may be essentially selfish and may later insufficiently weigh the welfare and developing rights of the child'.[94] Orthodox assumptions about the immutable significance of genetic fathers appear to have featured in this decision, which ultimately draws no distinction between known donors and other parents. This underlines a yawning gulf on an important point of principle between the Court of Appeal and High Court approaches to known donor disputes.

The tensions between the judgments demonstrate that a consensus has yet to be reached on how law should recognise the roles of the different adults in lesbian parenting arrangements involving known donors. Instead of introducing clarity, the judgments have created a position of legal uncertainty for known donor families, further tangling the complex web of relationships in which they are embroiled.

3. WHERE NEXT FOR THE LAW ON PARENTHOOD?

It remains to question whether and how the law might respond more constructively and coherently to known donors. In exploring some possibilities, the discussion in this

---

91. [2011] EWHC 2455 (Fam) at [20] (emphasis added).
92. [2012] EWCA Civ 285 at [37] and [38]. Namely, by confusing and destabilising the family unit that was the main source of stability, nurture and security for the child and by amounting to a change in circumstances which would put his emotional needs at risk and have a likely harmful effect on him. It is noteworthy that Thorpe LJ suggests that Jenkins J ignored a number of factors relevant to welfare in his attempt to apply a developing rule to the case, though does not specify what any of these are beyond saying that A was involved in M's conception and wished to be a parent.
93. Examples include the principle that, all things being equal, it is in the interests of children to be raised by their parents when residence disputes arise with third parties and that it will normally be in children's interests for DNA tests to be used to resolve parentage disputes.
94. [2012] EWCA Civ 285 at [27]. This language is disconcertingly reminiscent of the judgemental language used in the very first lesbian parenting cases.

section will tease out practical and theoretical obstacles to alternative frameworks for recognising parents and question the potential for any response to create the kind of reflexive transformation envisioned earlier. First, however, it is important to consider whether the 2008 Act has diminished the significance of the known donor cases.

(a) The impact of the 2008 Act

The 2008 Act's parenthood provisions now enable lesbian couples to conceive in circumstances which will result in them both acquiring the status of legal parents[95] and preclude the donor being treated as the legal father of any resulting child.[96] It is reasonable to suppose that most lesbian couples will now opt to conceive within the terms of the Act in order to benefit from these provisions.[97] However, it would be incorrect to assume that this means lesbian parents will no longer conceive using known donors.

Many lesbians express a preference for known donors[98] and it is not always necessary to choose between that preference and the protection that recognition under the terms of the 2008 Act provides. The sperm of a known donor can be used in the course of fertility treatment provided by a licensed clinic and the Act's parenthood provisions would apply in this situation. Of course, all of the cases discussed above involved 'DIY inseminations', arranged informally, without the assistance of a fertility clinic. In these circumstances, the parenthood provisions of the 2008 Act might apply, but only if the lesbian couple are in a civil partnership at the time of conception.[99]

Leckey has argued that the preference for known donors will diminish now that legislation has established an acceptable framework for lesbian parenting that is built on the two parent norm.[100] He observes that legislation designed to accommodate new family practices can have the 'unintended effect' of assimilating them to standard

---

95. The relevant circumstances are that they are in a civil partnership and the co-parent consents to the insemination (s 42), or that they are treated at a licensed clinic and satisfy 'agreed female parenthood conditions' which concern, inter alia, the provision of valid consent by both parties (ss 43 and 44).
96. Section 41.
97. Note that it was possible for lesbian women to receive treatment as single women under the terms of the earlier Human Fertilisation and Embryology Act 1990. However, using a clinic brings costs, a bureaucratic process and, often, delays. Because lesbian partners could not qualify as legal parents at the end of this process under the 1990 Act, there was not much to dissuade lesbian couples from making informal arrangements if they felt inclined to do so.
98. See Smith, above n 77; K Almack 'Seeking sperm: accounts of lesbian couples' reproductive decision making and understandings of the needs of the child' (2006) 20 Int J Law Policy and the Family 1; G Dunne 'Opting into motherhood: lesbians blurring the boundaries and transforming the meaning of parenthood' (2000) 1 J Gender and Society 14; C Donovan 'Who needs a father? Negotiating biological fatherhood in British lesbian families using self-insemination' (2000) 3 Sexualities 149.
99. It is an anomaly, though perhaps a deliberate one, in the legislation that the provisions do not stipulate that civil partners must receive treatment at a licensed clinic, as other partners must, in order for the parenthood provisions to apply. Provided the mother conceives by artificial insemination, her civil partner will be treated as the resulting parent irrespective of how the insemination was arranged, unless it is shown that she did not consent to the insemination.
100. R Leckey 'Law reform, lesbian parenting and the reflective claim' (2011) 20 Social and Legal Studies 331.

norms[101] and suggests that, following the 2008 Act, 'lesbian parents are likely to feel "channeled" towards the model of two parents in a formalized conjugal relationship'.[102] However normative the parenthood provisions of the 2008 Act are, it seems unlikely that they will prompt *all* lesbians to abandon belief in the benefits of a known donor. It is known that many same-sex couples consciously reject conventional relationship norms and it is difficult to imagine that this culture will lapse entirely in the wake of the legitimation that legal relationship recognition brings.[103] Additionally, intense social and legal emphasis on the importance of fathers and of genetic identity currently creates a climate in which it is likely that the appeal of known donors to lesbian parents will continue to have considerable traction.[104] It is even possible that known donors will look *more* appealing now that the law provides the security of parental status for two female parents.[105] Furthermore, given that the high cost of licensed treatment can be prohibitive and that using a known donor through a clinic prolongs the treatment process,[106] cheap and easy DIY insemination arrangements will remain attractive to some lesbians.

Where known donors are used within the terms of the 2008 Act, it is clear that they will not be legal parents but there are no guidelines to assist in the resolution of potential disputes. In the case of informal arrangements made by couples *not* in a civil partnership, the Act's provisions will not apply at all; the known donor will be the legal father and there is potential for further disputes raising exactly the same issues as the cases discussed above. Add in the fact that known donor insemination arrangements made before the 2008 Act came into force could yet give rise to parenting disputes for a number of years and the problem of whether and how to recognise known donors looks set to remain for the foreseeable future. A principled and coherent framework for recognition is therefore highly desirable.

(b) Possible responses to the known donor problem

(I) REMOVING PARENTAL STATUS FROM ALL KNOWN DONORS

The relationship difficulties highlighted in the cases derive at least in part from the fact that the known donors were legal parents and the co-parents were not. Because this did not correspond to the reality that the lesbian couple were the primary parents in each case, it contributed to the parties' anxieties about their respective roles. It also created the room for conflict to grow with the known donors who were able to play the trump card of legal parenthood when they wished to have more involvement. In different circumstances, with legal parenthood invested in the lesbian couple and not invested in the known donor, there might still be strong emotions to contend with but these are

---

101. Though in this instance it is arguable that the effect was intended. See Sheldon and McCandless, above n 1.
102. R Leckey, above n 100, at 340.
103. See Weston, above n 18, and Weeks et al, above n 15.
104. This point is acknowledged by Leckey, above n 100, at 341–342.
105. This possibility is discussed in Smith, above n 77.
106. In accordance with provisions contained in the HFE Act 1990 (as amended by the HFE Act 2008) and the HFEA Code of Practice relating to license conditions and the storage of sperm and selection of donors, it is necessary for donors to undergo extensive testing and screening processes for transmittable and heritable diseases which require the sperm to be stored for at least six months.

less likely to give rise to protracted conflict because the position of the known donor would be clearer from the outset. Therefore, one of the most obvious practical responses to the known donor cases would be to close the gaps in the 2008 Act which leave some known donor arrangements outside the scope of its parenthood provisions.

Other jurisdictions have taken steps to avoid the gap in English law which means that a known donor will be a legal parent if a woman who is not married or in a civil partnership conceives through informal insemination. Under the Quebec Civil Code, for example, two women who embark on a 'parental project' to conceive[107] will qualify as joint parents and there will be no legally recognised relationship between the donor and child.[108] No formalities need be complied with, meaning that parental status is not dependant on how insemination has been arranged.[109] Australian legislation permitting recognition of two women as parents following assisted conception similarly applies irrespective of whether there has been treatment at a clinic or DIY insemination and the donor is not recognised as a parent in either case.[110] An unusual feature of the Australian legislation is that it also applies retrospectively, so that the parental status of parties to known donor arrangements is consistent across all families, regardless of when they conceived.[111]

There is certainly some appeal in the idea of following the example of these jurisdictions by amending the 2008 Act. However, there are drawbacks in theoretical terms. McCandless and Sheldon outline how the 2008 Act reinforced the heterosexual, nuclear family model through its 'continued adherence to a two-parent model ... and the notion that the couple must be (at least potentially) in a sexual relationship'.[112] Even as it appears to jettison the foundational importance of biological reproduction by recognising two parents of the same sex, the Act perpetuates an exclusionary norm based on the dyadic model of heterosexual reproduction and limits the potential for departure from it.[113] Irrespective of their complexities, and allowing for the fact that they are not a universal preference, multiple parenting models which include known donors constitute a real point of difference in lesbian parenting practices. Insofar as

107. Article 538 CCQ.
108. Article 538.2, [1], CCQ. Article 538.2, [2], even encompasses situations in which a woman, as part of an agreed parental project, conceives through sexual intercourse, though there are some qualifications in such circumstances.
109. Though this regime brings some consistency it also brings its own uncertainties, not least interpretive and evidential problems around establishing the existence of a parental project. For discussion see R Leckey 'Where the parents are of the same sex: Quebec's reforms to filiation' (2009) 23 Int J Law, Policy and the Family 62; and A Campbell 'Conceiving parents through law' (2007) 21 Int J Law, Policy and the Family 242.
110. Section 60H Family Law Act 1975 as amended by the Family Law Amendment (De Facto Financial Matters and Other Measures) Act 2008.
111. The Australian system also brings its own evidential and interpretative difficulties, which are discussed in J Millbank 'De facto relationships, same-sex and surrogate parents: exploring the scope and effects of the 2008 federal relationship reforms' (2009) 23 Australian J Family Law 160.
112. McCandless and Sheldon, above n 1, at 188. See S Sheldon 'Reproductive technologies and the legal determination of fatherhood' (2005) 13 Feminist Legal Studies 349; and R Probert 'Families, assisted reproduction and the law' (2004) Child and Family Law Q 273 on how this trend was also evident in the terms of the preceding Human Fertilisation and Embryology Act 1990.
113. This point is discussed further in F Kelly 'Nuclear norms or fluid families? Incorporating lesbian and gay parents and their children into Canadian family law' (2004) 21 Canadian J Family Law 133.

the current legal framework for recognising parents struggles to accommodate known donors, it fails to value that difference. So, normatively speaking, extending a regulatory framework which does not acknowledge known donors would hardly bring about reflexive transformation.

Moreover, it is not clear that this approach would solve the problem in practical terms. Where a known donor has some contact with a child, there is no guarantee that the absence of parental status will guard against the emotionally charged disputes illustrated in the cases discussed above. Known donors who are not legal parents are not automatically eligible to apply for parental responsibility, contact or residence under the Children Act 1989, but they could seek leave to apply for the latter two.[114] There would be the potential for the case-law to come full circle, with the question of how to recognise someone with a claim to a de facto parental relationship but no legal parental relationship that occupied the courts in *Re G* being raised again, but by the known donor.

Although it is uncertain what the outcome of such a case would be,[115] insight can be drawn from responses to litigated known donor disputes in other jurisdictions. Based on a study of cases across several jurisdictions, Millbank has observed that 'a valorized biological status . . . has meant that donors are received by courts as if they are in fact the other parent'.[116] There are numerous examples of courts awarding high levels of contact and some form of parental recognition to known donors who are not legally fathers – in some instances where there is not even a well established pre-existing relationship.[117] Furthermore, a recent New South Wales case in which a known donor's name was removed from a birth certificate to make way, in accordance with legislation, for the name of a second female parent prompted such a backlash of opinion in favour of the donor that a Parliamentary Inquiry into the desirability of naming donors on birth certificates was set up.[118] It does not appear that removing legal parental status from known donors displaces the belief in the immutable value of the genetic father or generates outcomes less intrusive to the lesbian-led nuclear family than those in the cases discussed above.

(II) EQUAL STATUS FOR MULTIPLE PARENTS

Another possible response would be to do the opposite of excluding known donors from legal parenthood and make legislative provision for recognition of three (or more) legal parents. This would be the logical conclusion of the Court of Appeal's

---

114. See s 10 Children Act 1989.
115. The welfare principle contained in s 1 Children Act 1989 requires that every case be examined and decided on its own facts. It is also possible that interaction between a donor and child might give rise to a relationship that falls within the right to respect for family life under Art 8 of the European Convention on Human Rights.
116. J Millbank 'The limits of functional family: lesbian mother litigation in the era of the eternal biological family' (2008) 22 Int J Law, Policy and the Family 149 at 160.
117. Examples include the US case of *Thomas S v Robin Y* 599 NYS2d 377 (1995), the New Zealand case of *P v K* [2006] NZFLR 22, and the Australian cases of *H and J* [2006] FMCA fam 514 and *Wilson and Anor & Roberts and Anor (No. 2)* [2010] FamCA 734.
118. The case was *AA v Registrar of Births, Deaths and Marriages and BB* [2011] NSWDC 100. The known donor had never been a legal parent but the lesbian co-parent only acquired the right to be named on the birth certificate some years after the child's birth. The Law and Safety Commission 'Inclusion of donor details on the register of births (Inquiry)' was launched in October 2011, but has not yet reported. See http://www.parliament.nsw.gov.au/prod/parlment/committee.nsf/0/7E4018E851966190CA25792D0017F32F?open&refnavid=CO4_1.

reasoning that known donors should be treated as fathers on an equivalent basis to other parents. Although this response would resonate with the reasoning behind cases which did not appear to prioritise the validation of lesbian family forms, it does hold promise in terms of reflexive transformation of parenthood. It would constitute a significant shift in the legal framework for recognising parents and, arguably, a direct response to the innovation in lesbian parenting practices. It would also speak to the criticism that the 2008 Act only extended recognition to parenting arrangements which emulate the two-parent norm of heterosexual reproduction. Though appealing on a conceptual level, however, this solution has serious practical drawbacks.

The cases are testament to the difficulties which can thwart realisation of the desire to share parenting between multiple adults. This should come as no surprise. The practical and emotional difficulties presented by shared parenting following separation occupy enormous amounts of court time and the ongoing attentions of researchers and policy makers. The disagreements behind the reported known donor cases resemble separated parent disputes but they were even more difficult to resolve because the involvement of the fathers threatened the autonomy of a planned and intact family. The disquiet that this prospect engendered in the High Court judges should not be dismissed lightly. The known donor cases should be distinguished from post-separation disputes, where one parent has been displaced from their child's home and their expected position in the child's life, because the donors are peripheral to the child's planned home and parenting from the outset. Though the effective accommodation of three parents in the Court of Appeal judgments could be viewed as progressive (or reflexively transformative), it is just as easily interpreted as a regressive effort to insert identifiable fathers into lesbian families. Such capitulation to the prevailing ideology of essential fathers demeans the parenting capacities of lesbian couples and devalues the integrity of their families.[119]

The viability of multiple legal parents is further undermined by the fact that known donor disputes have the potential to become even more complicated. How much more challenging would the cases discussed above be should the lesbian couple separate and further disputes arise over residence, contact and parental responsibility? And what if there are two known donors (egg and sperm), whose partners might also be involved with the child?[120] Multiplying the holders of legal parental status and parental responsibility multiplies the opportunities for conflict over the care of a child and the idea of dividing a child's time between three (or more) households and warring adults is troubling in the extreme.[121] For this reason the very emphasis on child welfare that

---

119. Of course, it could also be argued that the use of known donors represents a capitulation to the idea that fathers are essential and genetic relationships inalienably important on the part of lesbian parents themselves: R Leckey 'Law reform, lesbian parenting and the reflective claim' (2011) 20 Social and Legal Studies 331; and Kelly, above n 113. As Donovan (above n 98) notes, however, this interpretation risks ignoring some of the legitimate objectives of lesbians who opt to use known donors.

120. In fact, the known donor's long-term male partner was involved in the conception arrangements and in subsequent contact in both *R v E and F* and *A v B and C*.

121. There are already examples of cases in which biological mothers attempt to diminish the roles of lesbian co-parents following separation. *Re G* (above n 8) is an example from this jurisdiction. Millbank (above n 116) has chronicled numerous examples from other jurisdictions. The Australian case of *AA v Registrar of Births, Deaths and Marriages and BB* (above n 118) is an example of a case in which there had been litigation with both the known donor and the lesbian co-parent.

is said to underpin the Court of Appeal decisions facilitating the full involvement of known donors could also militate against recognition of multiple parents.

In the one jurisdiction which has opened up the space for three legal parents, the obstacles to multiple parenting have prevented it being widely supported. The Canadian case of *A.A v B.B*[122] uniquely endorsed the legal recognition of three parents – a mother, her female partner and a known sperm donor – at the request of all three adults involved. It has recently been observed, however, that this remains an isolated case as 'courts and legislatures have resisted any further application of this innovation.'[123] One of the reasons appears to be that another case in which true shared parenting is feasible has yet to arise. As Harder and Thomarat note: '[T]he remarkable privilege and unanimity of purpose among the parties in *A.A.* suggests that the threshold relationship for a finding of status for three parents may be very high indeed.'[124]

(III) THE COMPROMISE

A paradox is emerging. Excluding known donors from legal recognition through a system which recognises only two parents validates and protects lesbian families but also reinforces the dyadic parenting norm based on heterosexual reproduction. Conversely, giving legal recognition to multiple parents undermines the dyadic norm but reasserts heteronormativity by elevating the importance of genetic parentage and fathers. In this catch-22 situation, the hold of the sexual family is not just tenacious, as McCandless and Sheldon assert, but irrevocable and neither option examined above looks theoretically satisfactory. Moreover, in practical terms neither option promises to make the dynamics of the relationships which follow known donor insemination more manageable or less fragile. On this analysis, hopes for a response to known donors which might facilitate reflexive transformation look aspirational at best, futile at worst.

Perhaps the stalemate might be broken and an acceptable way forward found in a compromise solution which recognises known donors but stops short of treating them on an equivalent basis to other legal parents. This would amount to a formalisation of the attempts of the High Court judges to find innovative ways of recognising a new type of relationship to avoid shoehorning it into a legal framework that was not designed for it. There are many ways in which a compromise solution establishing clearly defined but limited roles for known donors could be expressed. They include legislating for a modified, pared-down version of parental responsibility along the lines of what Black J ordered in *Re D*, or for a new category of 'secondary parent' in accordance with what Hedley J envisaged in *Re P and L*. As Millbank has suggested, it is even possible to legislate for a flexible role which would enable women and donors to make agreements encompassing greater or lesser degrees of recognition for the latter.[125]

Proposing a subsidiary role for known donors, which leaves largely undisturbed notions of the primacy of the nuclear family, hardly revolutionises the legal or practical framework for parenthood. Nevertheless, this approach does have progressive potential. Both the response options considered above effectively ignore the difficulties posed by known donors – the two-parent model by simply eclipsing them,

---

122. *A. A v B. B* [2007] ONCA 2.
123. L Harder and M Thomarat 'Parentage law in Canada: the numbers game of standing and status' (2012) 26 Int J Law, Policy and the Family 62 at 78.
124. Ibid, at [3].
125. Millbank, above n 116.

and the multiple-parent model by assimilating them with any other parent. By contrast, the compromise approach would engage directly with the distinctive features of known donor relationships, giving them recognition and legitimacy in a way which would allow lesbian narratives of parenthood to inform the framework for recognition. In practical terms, by providing a template for planning and managing relationships between known donors and parents the compromise approach might forestall the escalation of disputes and limit the potential for misunderstandings about roles. It would not prevent all disputes but, like the two-parent model, would restrict litigation by requiring donors to obtain leave to make contact and residence applications. It would, however, improve on the simple two-parent model by creating a means of recognising known donors which situates them in an expected hierarchy of parental relationships. This would provide judges with a reference point for resolving litigated disputes, thereby inserting principle and predictability into the decision-making process.[126]

Moreover, in terms of reflexive transformation the compromise approach holds more promise than recognising multiple parents. Implicit in it would be recognition that not all parenting relationships are qualitatively the same and that factors other than the existence of a genetic link should influence how they are recognised. The approach would thereby provide a model for recognising a nuanced and varied range of parental relationships which would have the potential to feedback into the regulation of parenthood more generally. For example, it might prompt a rethink of the basis on which parental responsibility should be awarded, facilitating a departure from the tendency to award it to any non-resident parent who asks for it that was criticised earlier. In providing a different model for parenting across different households the compromise solution for recognising known donors might also disrupt the orthodoxy of the belief in the necessity of shared parenting following parental separation. The mantra of shared parenting is now widely promoted as a solution to disputes between heterosexual parents, but its appropriateness has been subjected to scrutiny by researchers, particularly as it has found expression in claims that parenting *time* should be shared.[127] Concerns include the strain and restrictions that sharing decision making and facilitating involvement with the other parent can impose on primary carers (usually mothers);[128] the gendered asymmetry of giving parents equal roles on the basis of (often) unequal contributions to child care;[129] and the lack of evidence supporting (as well as the availability of some evidence refuting) the belief that child welfare always increases when the involvement of a non-resident parent increases.[130]

---

126. As noted earlier, provided principles are treated as guidelines rather than hard and fast rules, principled decision making is not incompatible with s 1 Children Act 1989.
127. Though *equal* parenting time has not yet been supported in this jurisdiction, a commitment to increasing the quantity of time spent with absent parents is to be seen in the judiciary's increased use of shared residence orders. The ideal is likely to have influenced the outcomes of *T v T* and *A v B and C*.
128. C Smart and B Neale *Family Fragments?* (Cambridge: Polity Press, 1999).
129. Ibid; S Boyd *Child Custody, Law and Women's Work* (Oxford: Oxford University Press, 2003); J Wallbank 'Getting tough on mothers: regulating contact and residence' (2007) 15 Feminist Legal Studies 189; S Harris-Short 'Building a house upon sand: post-separation parenting, shared residence and equality – lessons from Sweden' (2011) 23 Child and Family Law Quarterly 322.
130. The overall message here is that certain conditions are necessary to make shared parenting workable and beneficial and they are seldom present among litigating parents. See L Trinder

Rooted in recognition of both the difficulties of splitting care across two families or households and the benefits to children of multiple relationships, the compromise solution for recognising known donors might in some cases provide a rationale for resisting the shared parenting doctrine. This is not to say that it should be directly applicable to post-separation disputes between heterosexual parents – such a suggestion would impose the very erasure of differences between family types that this article has criticised. Rather, the point is to suggest that carving out a special role for known donors could initiate broader reflection on the variation in parental relationships which could in turn undermine the use of normative, standardised solutions which are impervious to difference. The result would be a richer, more principled and more responsive framework for resolving parenting disputes.

CONCLUSION

The cases discussed in this article leave no doubt about the complexity of the family relationships which can result from the decision to conceive using a known sperm donor. It has also been shown that developing a legal framework for recognising known donors is itself a challenge bedevilled by complexities and refining the details of the new, subsidiary form of legal parenthood that has been proposed above would not be easy. The instinctive reaction might therefore be that the use of known donors should be discouraged, rather than facilitated and supported. However, the occurrence of six known donor cases in rapid succession is likely to be a portent of their future significance and numerous reasons to grapple with the challenge, instead of shying away from it, have been highlighted.

One reason is that finding ways of accommodating known donors is an important part of validating lesbian parenting practices. Another is that, to date, the complexity of known donor arrangements has been exacerbated by judicial decisions. The Court of Appeal's refusal to draw any distinction in principle between known donors and fathers in conventional families for the purposes of extending legal recognition is particularly problematic. The result is a common law position that buttresses, rather than challenges, the relationship instability which makes litigation likely. The approach also pathologises the relationship difficulties manifested in the cases, failing to acknowledge how the lack of a legal and regulatory framework facilitating the use of known donors sustains and contributes to them. Without exception, the judges in the cases observed that the failure of the parties involved to make clear, formal and consensual parenting plans prior to conception had fuelled the breakdown in relationships. As a consequence of the decision in *A v B and C*, this practical problem cannot be remedied because the most carefully laid plans will be open to challenge at the whim of the known donor. By contrast, if a legal framework for recognising known donors were to be established, it would provide a basis for structuring much-needed advice and guidance to inform known donor arrangements at the planning stage, as well as bringing stability and clarity.[131]

'Shared residence: a review of recent research evidence' (2010) 22 Child and Family Law Q 475, for a full discussion of the relevant research.

131. Currently, there is little detailed advice available to those seeking to use a known donor. The online information available from the NHS is restricted to the following statement: 'Some couples obtain donated sperm from someone they know. However, in most cases, sperm is obtained from an unknown donor' (http://www.nhs.uk/conditions/Artificial-insemination/

Tangling the web of legal parenthood 381

Finally, it has been suggested that a legal response to known donors could *reflexively transform* the legal recognition and regulation of parenthood in ways which could have ramifications beyond the esoteric circumstances of lesbian parenting arrangements. The fact that all the reported known donor cases to date concern lesbian couples does not mean that the use of known donors is specific to them. Opposite-sex couples can, and sometimes do, use known donors and the question mark over how any potential disputes might be resolved has the potential to be relevant to them.[132] More generally, it is important to acknowledge that the tangled web of relationships seen in the known donor cases is simply a visible form of what is currently concealed by the majority of opposite-sex couples who conceive using donated gametes. They are a consequence of lesbian parents' refusal to shy away from the complexity of the facts of their children's conception. In their efforts to incorporate known donors into their parenting plans, lesbians are also challenging conventional wisdom about the necessity of dyadic parenting models, how parenting should be organised across different households, and whether it is always necessary for fathers to have extensive involvement with their children. All of this means that developing new strands to the legal framework for recognising parents in order to accommodate known donors could generate principles and ideas which are transferrable to the different contexts of solving heterosexual parenting disputes and regulating heterosexual reproduction.

Pages/Introduction.aspx). Information published directly by individual clinics tends similarly to comment on the possibility of using a known donor but not to elaborate on it. Even the HFEA itself publishes very little information about the use of known donors and what is available through their website is very difficult to find. There is no almost no guidance to be found on how to make parenting plans with known donors.

132. Although no specific figures on the number of people using known donors are recorded, the HFEA has reported a rise in the number of patients using gametes donated by someone they know and estimates that up to 16% of newly registered sperm donors may be donating to someone they know: HFEA *Donating Sperm and Eggs. Have Your Say: A Review of the HFEA's Sperm and Egg Donation Policies* (London: HFEA, 2011) pp 4 and 19. Available at http://www.hfea.gov.uk/docs/2011-01-13_Donation_review_background.pdf. Of course, heterosexuals are far more likely to use a known egg donor than a known sperm donor. Often the egg is donated by a sibling, but this is not necessarily a safeguard against relationship difficulties – the sperm donor in *Re B* was the brother of the co-parent.

14

Challenging presumptions: legal parenthood and surrogacy arrangements

Kirsty Horsey

As the law stands, provisions determining parenthood following surrogacy and other forms of assisted conception are inconsistent and reflect – intentionally or unintentionally – a perception that surrogacy is a troublesome, disruptive and less legitimate means of family formation than other methods. In arguing that the law regarding the award of legal parenthood following surrogacy arrangements should be reformulated to recognise pre-conception intentions and commitments to care, this article will attempt to provide an example of a way to iron out those inconsistencies, in part to ensure that some methods of family formation are not reinforced as being superior to others. It will argue that the recognition of the intention to parent should be used as a stable and consistent foundation for all parenthood status provisions in legislation governing assisted reproduction, in turn leading to a greater and easier recognition of 'alternative' family forms. It will also acknowledge that, with surrogacy, intention could be used as the basis of protective enforceable agreements between intending parents and surrogates.

INTRODUCTION

The practice of surrogacy is fraught with practical, legal and ethical difficulties. Despite there having been a number of regulatory events impacting on its governance, the current legal position with regard to surrogacy in the UK is 'thoroughly confused, and there is understandably a good deal of dissatisfaction with it'.[1] Not the least of these problems is that it has long been the case that the legal 'solution' to the 'problem' of surrogacy has been to automatically render the surrogate, as the woman who gives birth to the child, its legal mother. This continues to be the situation under the sections defining legal parenthood (known as 'status provisions') in the Human Fertilisation and Embryology (HFE) Act 2008.[2] Further, notwithstanding the dissatisfaction surrounding surrogacy, the implications of this were not questioned during public consultation undertaken prior to the amendment of the earlier version of the legislation.[3] This is perhaps not surprising, given that comparatively little consideration was given to any of the parenthood or 'status' provisions while the new

---

[1] M. Warnock, *Making Babies: Is There a Right to Have Children?* (Oxford University Press, 2002), at p 91.

[2] Section 33(1) replaces s 27(1) of the Human Fertilisation and Embryology Act 1990, though uses the original wording: 'The woman who is carrying or has carried a child as a result of the placing in her of an embryo or of sperm and eggs, and no other woman, is to be treated as the mother of the child'.

[3] Surrogacy was considered in s 7 of the consultation: here it stated that the government had 'agreed to consider the need to review surrogacy arrangements and [was] therefore keen to gauge public and professional opinions on what, if any, changes may be needed to the law and regulation as it relates to surrogacy' (para 7.14). The Act's determinations of legal parenthood were considered in s 8, but the *only* issue raised regarding parenthood following surrogacy was whether unmarried couples should be able to

legislation was being formulated, either by the public, policymakers or the press.[4] But it *is* particularly surprising that these provisions received so little attention (and the proposed changes so little critique) when they actually work in tandem with one of the more controversial sections of the legislation which commands that the welfare of the putative child should be taken into account by anyone providing licensed fertility treatment services, including the reformed provision that account should be taken of the child's need for 'supportive parenting'.[5]

This perceived 'common-sense' solution to surrogacy engenders a number of complications. First, it serves as an absolute barrier to the automatic legal recognition of the intending mother following surrogacy, even though she will raise the child and when no discussion has been entered into about whether to prevent this is either necessary or desirable, or in the best interests of any prospective child.[6] By extension – and similarly problematic – it prevents automatic recognition of the intending father or female partner. As will be seen, this terminology is problematic in itself and preference would be for both women in such a situation to be 'mothers'.[7] There is also a growing perception that limiting the number of legal parents to two is not to be uncritically accepted.[8]

The legislation covers situations where surrogacy is performed 'formally' – that is where a surrogate is inseminated with sperm (in a clinic or otherwise) or has an embryo or mixed gametes transferred to her.[9] It stipulates that if the surrogate is married, her husband will become the legal father of any child born to her.[10] This is a

---

obtain parental orders (the 1990 Act limited this to married couples) (paras 8.17–8.18). There appears to have been no question of changing the status of the birth mother in any circumstance. (Department of Heath, *Review of the Human Fertilisation and Embryology Act: A Public Consultation* (August 2005), available at http://www. dh. gov.uk/ en/ Publicationsandstatistics/ Publications/ PublicationsPolicyAndGuidance/DH_4123774).

[4] See J. McCandless and S. Sheldon, 'The Human Fertilisation and Embryology Act (2008) and the Tenacity of the Sexual Family Form' (2010) 73(2) *Modern Law Review* 175, at pp 175–176.

[5] Section 14(2)(b).

[6] A principle that is supposed to underpin all clinical assisted reproduction practices, as indicated above (HFE Act 2008, s 14(2)(b)). See also the comments of Edward Webb, a key actor of the Department of Health in the passage of the new legislation, reported in J. McCandless and S. Sheldon, 'The Human Fertilisation and Embryology Act (2008) and the Tenacity of the Sexual Family Form' (2010) 73(2) *Modern Law Review* 175, at note 114. Interestingly, the Department of Health's consultation document expressly stated that 'the Government is aware of arguments that differential treatment in law of different family forms could disadvantage children born in those circumstances' (para 8.11).

[7] See, for example, J. Wallbank, 'Too Many Mothers? Surrogacy, Kinship and the Welfare of the Child' (2002) 10(3) *Medical Law Review* 271; E. Jackson, 'What is a Parent?' in A. Diduck and K. O'Donovan, *Feminist Perspectives on Family Law* (Routledge-Cavendish, 2006), at pp 59–74; R. Mackenzie, 'Beyond Genetic and Gestational Dualities: Surrogacy Agreements, Legal Parenthood and Choice in Family Formation' in K. Horsey and H. Biggs (eds), *Human Fertilisation and Embryology: Reproducing Regulation* (Routledge-Cavendish, 2007), at pp 181–204 and more recently J. McCandless and S. Sheldon, 'The Human Fertilisation and Embryology Act (2008) and the Tenacity of the Sexual Family Form' (2010) 73(2) *Modern Law Review* 175. This paper should not be read as seeking to limit the number of (intentional) legal parents to two.

[8] Among others, see J. Wallbank, 'Reconstructing the HFEA 1990: is blood really thicker than water?' [2004] CFLQ 387 and *ibid*; R. Mackenzie, ibid; J. McCandless and S. Sheldon, ibid.

[9] Confusingly, the idea that a gestationally-defined mother could be carrying a child as a result of the 'placing in her' of *just* sperm (eg by self insemination) is not considered in s 33, though is brought under legislative control in respect of surrogacy by virtue of ss 34 and 35.

[10] Section 35(1) – unless it could be shown that he did not give his consent to her acting as a surrogate. This raises numerous other concerns, which lie outside the scope of this article. Even if the surrogacy was non-formal (ie achieved through sexual intercourse with the intending father), common law presumptions would render the *surrogate's husband* the legal father.

wholly unnecessary legal fiction and, while reinforcing the notion that motherhood is determined by gestation, does not mirror the way that fatherhood following other forms of assisted reproduction is regulated. This seems particularly strange when no substantive reason has been given for why legal parenthood following surrogacy should continue to be treated any differently.

When donor insemination (DI) is used to create a family,[11] the law has long since recognised – and continues to do so – the intention of the male husband/partner of a woman inseminated with donor sperm to be recognised as the child's father, and has in the new legislation extended this recognition to same-sex partners of a woman who conceives using donated sperm.[12] This extension evidenced a deliberate effort to recognise the realities of modern-day uses of assisted reproduction procedures,[13] though has not been without its critics in terms of the terminology used to define the second parent in each situation or the numerically-limited and dimorphic legal constraints placed on (intended) parenthood.[14] The formulation of the new law so as to include a 'second female parent' can be said to reflect 'the law's obsession with a child only having one mother and one father'.[15] In contrast, where a child is born using surrogacy (with or without donor gametes) the law regarding parenthood was left almost entirely untouched. Intending parents can apply to have their intention to become parents legitimated *after* the child is born but no such recognition can be given to them *upon birth*. What are the reasons for separating surrogacy from other forms of assisted reproduction in this way? Does surrogacy raise particular problems that mean that its regulation should differ from other forms of assisted reproduction? While there is argument elsewhere that 'doing' parenting should not equate to legal 'status' as parents,[16] it is at least open to question that it is a different matter when someone initiates conception (perhaps with others) *and* intends to perform the social role of parent. The concept of intentional parenthood I use here does not only encompass the intention to conceive but also an intended social parenthood role after birth.

The law regarding surrogacy appears to be based on assumptions that surrogates are vulnerable, easily exploited and somehow deserve special protection. However, from the limited empirical evidence that is available on the practice of surrogacy, it is arguable that far from being vulnerable, surrogates feel empowered by their ability to exercise control over their bodies and the altruism that underpins surrogacy arrangements.[17] It can also be argued that those who use surrogates are equally, if not

---

[11] In any form – by this I mean either by 'natural' fertilisation following vaginal or intrauterine insemination (IUI) or more technologically assisted fertilisation using in vitro fertilisation (IVF) or intra-cytoplasmic sperm injection (ICSI).

[12] Here s 35(1) replaces s 28(2) of the 1990 Act with regard to married fathers, s 36 replaces s 28(3) in relation to non-married fathers, though adds that this is subject to 'agreed fatherhood conditions' (laid out in s 37). Section 42(1) covers female civil partners, with s 43 extending this to female same-sex partners without a formal civil partnership (as long as 'agreed female parenthood conditions' are met; s 44).

[13] This is evidenced by both the consultation document and the White Paper preceding the 2008 Act – see Department of Heath, *Review of the Human Fertilisation and Embryology Act: A Public Consultation* (August 2005), para 1.4 and Department of Heath, *Review of the Human Fertilisation and Embryology Act*, Cm 6989 (2006), para 2.67.

[14] See J. McCandless and S. Sheldon, 'The Human Fertilisation and Embryology Act (2008) and the Tenacity of the Sexual Family Form' (2010) 73(2) *Modern Law Review* 175, at 190–197.

[15] J. Herring, *Family Law* (Pearson, 4th edn, 2009), at p 339.

[16] See, eg A. Bainham, 'Arguments About Parentage' (2008) 67 *Cambridge Law Journal* 322.

[17] See, for example, quotes from interviews of women who have acted as surrogates in E. Blyth, ' "I wanted to be interesting. I wanted to be able to say 'I've done something with my life'": Interviews with Surrogate Mothers in Britain' (1994) 12 *Journal of Reproductive and Infant Psychology* 189–198.

more, vulnerable, given the lengths they go to in order to have children via surrogacy.[18] If the assumptions about surrogacy and surrogates are unfounded, further weight is given to the contention that surrogacy should be treated the same way as other forms of assisted conception. Not to do so is overly paternalistic and fails to take into account women's ability to control their own bodies and enter into agreements with others.

A rough guide to the problems raised by surrogacy

The available methods of creating children by 'non-natural' means have greatly increased over the last four decades, as has popular awareness and acceptance of them. Even before more medicalised methods of assisted conception were developed, beginning with *in vitro* fertilisation (IVF) in 1978, some alternatives to 'natural' sexual reproduction were possible. Notably these include donor insemination (DI) and the non-technical, or non-medicalised form of surrogacy (often known as 'partial' or 'straight' surrogacy), where the surrogate provides the egg and therefore half of the genetic material of any resulting child. This could, of course, always have been achieved via sexual intercourse, or a surrogate could self-inseminate. The alternative – known as 'full', 'host' or 'gestational' surrogacy, where an embryo created using the sperm and eggs of the intending parents (or with either sourced from donors) is transferred to the surrogate to carry to term – has only been possible since the development of IVF.

Surrogacy is defined as 'an understanding or agreement by which a woman . . . agrees to bear a child for another person or couple',[19] or the situation 'where a woman makes a prior arrangement to carry a child with the intention that it will be handed over to someone else at birth'.[20] As with DI and other developments in medicalised reproduction that include a third party in the reproductive process, there is no question that surrogacy fragments the orthodox or 'natural' reproductive process, though as with those forms of assisted reproduction it is designed to replicate it, at least to an extent. Potentially, the historic or more traditional use of assisted reproductive practices (including surrogacy), which were created and then originally utilised in order to imitate the 'normal' (heterosexual sexual) family has helped to shape the normative values that now saturate their use. In this sense, bar the usual cries of 'slippery-slope' that appear whenever new technologies are introduced, assisted conception procedures have only really become contentious since they began to be used to create 'alternative' family forms. Developments in reproductive science mean that the actions of conception, gestation and child-rearing are now quite easily separated. The potential parents are numerous due to the various combinations of gametes and the roles that can be played. Following surrogacy, a child can have up to six potential 'parents': two gamete providers, the gestational/birth mother and her husband or partner (if she has one) and the two intending parents, where these are different people. Notably, this

---

[18] In parallel interviews to those cited above, see the intending parents' responses in E. Blyth, ' "Not a Primrose Path": Commissioning Parents' Experiences of Surrogacy Arrangements in Britain' (1995) 13 *Journal of Reproductive and Infant Psychology* 185–196. Evidence of intending parents' vulnerability is also apparent in some surrogacy cases: see in particular *Re P (Minors) (Wardship: Surrogacy)* [1987] 2 FLR 421.

[19] D. Morgan, 'Surrogacy: An Introductory Essay' in R. Lee and D. Morgan (eds), *Birthrights: Law and Ethics at the Beginnings of Life* (Routledge, 1989), at p 56.

[20] Department of Heath, *Review of the Human Fertilisation and Embryology Act: A Public Consultation* (August 2005), para 7.1.

number is only limited to six because the law is only prepared to recognise two parents – the number could be greater if this were not the case.[21]

How the law responds to this is an indicator of how surrogacy is more generally regarded – or how it has not been properly considered at all.[22] There has been criticism of the failure to embrace the opportunity to do more with the legal parenthood provisions; partially this is a result of the 2008 Act being a piece of amending legislation rather than a wholesale fresh look at the regulation of assisted conception and embryology. As Julie McCandless and Sally Sheldon point out, the way the status provisions are defined in the legislation is really only a reflection of what lawmakers think that 'a family *should* "look like" ',[23] thereby reflecting common cultural and political norms. In respect of surrogacy, such criticism can be levelled at more than just the parenthood provisions.

Assisted conception generally (and surrogacy in particular) presents challenges to traditional assumptions about parenthood. The law has compensated for this in some situations: for example, as we have already seen, the intending father is legally recognised if a married or otherwise 'stable' couple uses DI to conceive.[24] A mechanism for family courts to transfer legal parenthood following surrogacy to the intending couple also exists, in the form of a 'parental order', in essence a form of fast-track adoption.[25] Nevertheless, it cannot be said that no inconsistencies remain in the way that legal parenthood is defined. The most obvious of these is the certainty that intending parents in a DI situation are given (and also where a woman conceives using donor eggs, as she will always be regarded as the legal mother by virtue of giving birth), compared to the uncertainty regarding not only the outcome of the arrangement but also the acquisition of legal parenthood for those using surrogacy.

Parenthood and the 'natural' biological/genetic relationship have not always co-existed, as historical use of DI and 'partial' surrogacy demonstrates, as well as the perceived necessity – in days long before paternity tests became possible – to invent a presumption that a married woman's husband is the father of her child. The intending parent where DI is used has no immediate genetic relationship with his child(ren).[26] It

---

[21] Hill identified sixteen possible 'reproductive combinations' in addition to 'traditional conception and childbirth'. This total was achieved by varying the sources of both male and female gametes, the location of fertilisation (inside or outside of the body) and the site of gestation (J.L. Hill, 'What Does it Mean to be a "Parent"? The Claims of Biology as the Basis for Parental Rights' (1991) 66 *New York University Law Review* 353, at p 355).

[22] See House of Lords/House of Commons Joint Committee on the Human Tissues and Embryos (Draft) Bill (2007) *Volume 1: Report, Session 2006–2007* (2007), at p 44, and J. McCandless and S. Sheldon, 'The Human Fertilisation and Embryology Act (2008) and the Tenacity of the Sexual Family Form' (2010) 73(2) *Modern Law Review* 175, at p 180.

[23] Ibid, at p 176 [emphasis added].

[24] See fn 12, above.

[25] Section 54 of the HFE Act 2008 replaces s 30 of the 1990 Act in this respect. Gamble and Ghaevart LPP, a leading UK law firm specialising in fertility treatments and surrogacy, refer to parental orders as 'designed to *remedy* parenthood issues following surrogacy' [emphasis added], thereby indicating that the current situation is not only in need of rectification but also problematic to lawyers in practice ('Surrogacy: Parental Orders and Other Options', available at http://www.gambleandghevaert.com/page/Surrogacy:-parental-orders-and-other-options/29/).

[26] This is perhaps the reason that cases were brought in both the UK and the US arguing that the practice of DI amounts to adultery (see *MacLennan* v *MacLennan* 1958 S.C. 105). A discussion of the American courts' uncertainty about the issue can be found in K. Daniels and K. Taylor, 'Secrecy and Ownership in Donor Insemination' (1993) 12(2) *Politics and the Life Sciences* 155, at p 156. Additionally, the Archbishop of Canterbury set up a Commission of Inquiry into the practice of DI in 1945 and, following its report (Archbishop of Canterbury's Commission, *Artificial Human Insemination: the Report of a*

is also common for children to be successfully raised by those who are neither genetically nor gestationally related to them. The legal status of parenthood can be and is conferred on non-biologically related persons by statutory adoption, available since the Adoption of Children Act 1926 and, like the practice of surrogacy, it is highly probable that forms of social or non-institutionalised adoption took place before formal regulatory structures were established.

These examples indicate that we already have a strong cultural tradition in which the social and psychological dimensions of parenthood are recognised, even where a biological connection is absent. The question therefore arises as to which contenders should be recognised as *the* parents of a child born from surrogacy or assisted conception and, more importantly, why.[27] Why do some potential parents seem to have stronger claims to legal parenthood than others? What does this say about the relative legitimacy of various methods of family formation? Does it create or maintain a hierarchy of family forms? Assisted reproductive methods necessitate familial situations outside of the 'cornflakes' ideal,[28] where it can usually be safely assumed that a man and woman who have a child are its parents. This assumption is usually based on the perceived genetic link, even if none exists. It can, however, be questioned whether the definition of 'parent', in circumstances where the acts of parenting and (genetic) creation are separated, should be based on an implied perception of the 'ordinary' and (hetero)sexual two-parent model (as is now the case), on biological component parts (the genetic connection), physical input (eg gestation/birth), or on a social/intentional basis. Here, I take intention to mean not only the intention to bring about conception (as there may be multiple issues regarding this, not least that any clinician involved can also be said to have intended this), but also the intention to *be* the parent – that is to provide care and nurturance – after the child is born.

The remainder of this article will explore whether, in surrogacy and assisted conception, whether or not we remain wedded to the two-parent model, those who *intended* to be the parents of the child should be legally recognised as the parents of that child from birth. It will also consider and weigh this against alternative potential determinants of parenthood, such as genetics or gestation/birth. First, we will look more closely at the theoretical case for intention. In so doing, we will compare parenthood claims based on intention to those based on biological links, both genetic and gestational, arguing that to use either biological basis for determining parenthood would be flawed and inadequate. While a general case can be made for intention-based parenthood, this article will then go on to highlight the practicalities of

---

Commission Appointed by His Grace the Archbishop of Canterbury (1948)), sought to make DI a criminal offence. Similarly, a 1960 report by the Feversham Committee thought that allowing DI might 'lead to indifference towards the marriage vows, and thus weaken the institution of marriage' (*Report of the Departmental Committee on Human Artificial Insemination*, Cmnd 1105 (1960)).

[27] In this sense, I mean both 'parents' in the sense of *being* a parent, ie performing the role of a parent, and *becoming* a parent, ie being legally recognised as such and having parental responsibility from birth. While Andrew Bainham has noted that there are subtle differences between the concepts of parentage, parenthood and parental responsibility and argues that *being a parent* 'should turn on a presumed or actual genetic connection with the child' ('Parentage, Parenthood and Parental Responsibility: Subtle, Elusive Yet Important Distinctions' in A. Bainham, S. Day-Sclater, and M. Richards (eds), *What is a Parent? A Socio-Legal Analysis* (Hart Publishing, 1999), at p 27), I do not believe that this can be applied consistently or fairly to children created by assisted reproduction. This is mainly because, at least implicitly, decisions as to *who* will be the child's parents have been taken before s/he is conceived. These are not decisions being made about an already-born child, where I believe the distinctions are, in the main, worthwhile.

[28] K. O'Donovan, *Family Law Matters* (Pluto Press, 1993), at p 30.

such an approach, by comparing potential alternative claims in the actual contexts of DI, IVF and different forms of surrogacy, showing in realistic terms the problems that recognising intention would solve.

THE CASE FOR INTENTION

I want to argue here that 'intention' should operate as the pre-birth determinant in 'awarding' parental status when a child is born following surrogacy or assisted conception. Intention, here, encompasses the motivation to have a child, initiation and involvement in the procreative process and a commitment to nurture and care.[29] Parenthood within this concept should not have to be 'awarded' at all, nor be based on unchallenged presumptions or perceptions. If it is correct that a strong social tradition acknowledging social and psychological aspects of parenthood exists, then it should be possible to provide a rational alternative to legal and cultural presumptions currently attached to parenthood, when the processes involved in family creation are not typical. The legal concept of intention, a theoretical notion already recognised and enshrined in various areas of law, would, as will be demonstrated, provide the most consistent result in all fragmented reproductive practices, as well as introducing the benefits of equal treatment to all forms of assisted reproduction. Recognising intention would mean that creating families by surrogacy or assisted conception would not cause differential treatment (in terms of how parental status is achieved) of the infertile from the fertile and nor would surrogacy be treated as inferior to other assisted reproductive techniques in the hierarchy of family formation. This is not to suggest that intentional parenthood should be universally recognised; the concept is utilised here solely in relation to surrogacy and assisted conception, thus leaving the parenthood of children conceived and born 'normally' to be treated in the way it currently is. In fact, intention *could* not become a universal factor in determining the parenthood of all children born, whether by assisted conception or 'naturally'. Some children born 'naturally' are not intended (or at least their conception was not); thus the concept would leave them parent*less*. Conversely, this serves to illustrate the potential for using intention as the determinant of the parenthood of children born by assisted conception – all such children will be fully intended.[30]

It might be argued that 'inconsistency' merely equals 'flexibility', in that the law rightly recognises different people as parents in different ways depending on the circumstances of their children's conception. I believe, however, that in this sense, 'inconsistency' really does mean that people are differently treated in that more value is placed on some people's intention to parent than others. For infertile couples seeking to have children, recognition of their difference may be exactly the opposite of what should be done. Furthermore, while some people who need to use assisted conception – and who therefore will assume the role of the child's 'parents' both before and after its birth – are readily granted this status by the law, others are not, despite

---

[29] Gillian Douglas has argued that viewing parenthood as being created by intention reflects a masculine perception of parenthood ('The Intention to be a Parent and the Making of Mothers' (1994) 37 *Modern Law Review* 641). I want to emphasise that intention here includes a commitment to care and is being suggested as a concept that can provide internal coherence to the law while reflecting forward-thinking notions of family and kinship (such as multiple or inter-generational parenthood) and breaking down hierarchies of differently-created families.

[30] Marsha Garrison agrees: '[u]ndeniably, it is easier to assess intention when conception occurs technologically than when it occurs sexually' ('Law Making for Baby Making: An Interpretive Approach to the Determination of Legal Parentage' (2000) 113 *Harvard Law Review* 835, at p 861). This also reflects on 'best interests' or welfare arguments – how can it not be in the good interests of a child to be born to, and legally recognised as the child of, parents who fully intend and desire to raise it?

being similarly situated in terms of both their accepted role and in their intention to create a child. This is particularly true of surrogacy.

Surrogacy has over time been perceived as a direct challenge to both the meaning of motherhood and family. It is *because* of this, rather than in spite of it, that practical issues relating to parenthood, status and rights, and questions regarding who are to be legitimately regarded as parent(s) – and why – are significant. As such, the rules on legal parenthood deserve proper reconsideration, particularly as they have seemingly been overlooked in favour of more general moral and ideological concerns about the overarching regulation. This is illustrated well by the difference in the level of media coverage of the removal of the 'need for a father' provision from the 'welfare clause' of the HFE Act 2008 (s 14(2)(b) now replacing what was s 13(5) of the 1990 Act and replacing the need to consider whether a child born using assisted conception would have a father with the need for 'supportive parenting') with other changes made to status provisions in the new legislation. Similarly, parliamentary debates on the former amounted to some eight hours (and this was curtailed), compared with only about one hour for the latter.[31]

Intention versus biology

The genetic and gestational contributors to the child (if they are different people) undoubtedly possess compelling claims to parenthood. However, it must be asked whether these claims are as strong or as accurately reflect the social situation that will be in place as those of the intending parents. Moreover, even if they were in an individual case, by making any presumption operating towards the intending parents rebuttable, such instances could be resolved. Because, it is assumed, those who intend a child to be born by surrogacy or assisted conception cannot have a child by 'natural' means, the processes of creation will become fragmented, and the way parenthood is defined may not fit comfortably, or even be untenable.[32] Same-sex couples (or groups) who wish to have children will inevitably have to circumvent the 'natural' process and, because of the family that is intended, are unlikely to be content with the mother/father paradigm. The same is true of single people wishing to have children without recourse to sexual intercourse. While this has, to some extent, been addressed in the new legislation with the potential to register a second female co-parent from birth, this model still very much reflects the *only* model seemingly considered valid by lawmakers: that of a two-parent family emanating from the birth mother. Given the paucity of debate on the new status provisions, it is hardly surprising that nowhere in the process of reform was there consideration that where there *are* two female parents they could both be called 'mother'. This is merely another example of the persistent hold that the notion that the woman who gives birth to a child is the mother, *and no other woman*, has on the legal imagination.[33]

Different situations generate different combinations of those with seemingly valid parenthood claims. Those who invest their time (and very possibly their finances),

---

[31] Correlatively, in interviewing Edward Webb, one of the Department of Health officials charged with the drafting and passage of the new legislation, McCandless and Sheldon heard that changes to some of the parenthood provisions, particularly those that maintain preference towards marriage or civil unions might have led to criticisms of 'the Government attacking marriage'. He added '[s]o we always have to be mindful of the bigger political picture as well ...' ('The Human Fertilisation and Embryology Act (2008) and the Tenacity of the Sexual Family Form' (2010) 73(2) *Modern Law Review* 175, at p 190).

[32] For example, the current definitions may not fit at all with transgender parenting, which inevitably will occur through assisted conception. See further J. McCandless and S. Sheldon, ibid, at 199–202.

[33] HFE Act 2008, s 33(1) [emphasis added].

initiate the reproductive process and prepare themselves to gain, raise and care for a child, have the strongest claim. The argument is that:

> 'The use of reproductive technology is an unambiguous indicator of intent. Users of such technology intend to produce a child *and intend to accept the responsibility of caring for it* ... Use of the surrogate method, manifesting procreative intent, should invoke the legal presumption that the child belongs to the intenders.'[34]

There are at least four specific arguments for recognising intention-based parenthood in surrogacy and assisted conception. The first is the 'prima facie importance of the intended parents in the procreative relationship':[35] without their initiative and motivation, the child would not have been created. It is undeniable that *but for* them, the conception and birth of that particular child could not have happened.[36] The intending parents can therefore be said to have:

> 'a unique role as the instigator[s] of the pregnancy. Conception is "ordered" or "commissioned" by the intended parents, who are motivated (it is assumed) by usual parental motivations such as the need for adult status and identity, the opportunity for development of affectionate and intimate relationships, and the need for expansion of the "self".'[37]

The second argument arises from the first: the intending parents created the child *and* intend to be the ones actively involved in its care. While it is possible to argue that childrearing, if recognised in this context, is used merely as a way to legitimise social parenting after birth, it should be remembered that utilising a pre-conception tool to determine legal parenthood offers the only way to achieve internal consistency (and avoid highlighting 'difference') among various types of assisted conception users.[38]

---

[34] J. Levitt, 'Biology, Technology and Genealogy: A Proposed Uniform Surrogacy Legislation' (1992) 25 *Columbia Journal of Law and Social Problems* 451, at p 470 [emphasis added].

[35] J.L. Hill, 'What Does it Mean to be a "Parent"? The Claims of Biology as the Basis for Parental Rights' (1991) 66 *New York University Law Review* 353, at p 414.

[36] See *Johnson v Calvert* [1993] 851 P 2d 774. Hill also argues that '[t]hese arguments should trump the relatively weaker claims of either the gestational host or the biological progenitors' (ibid, at 414).

[37] R. Cook, 'Donating Parenthood: Perspectives on Parenthood from Surrogacy and Gamete Donation' in A. Bainham, S. Day Sclater, and M. Richards (eds), *What is a Parent? A Socio-Legal Analysis* (Hart Publishing, 1999), at p 135. While it could be said that the surrogate also passes a 'but for' test and is undeniably true that many women who act as surrogates have their own initiative and motivation to do so *prior* to the involvement of the commissioning couple, a surrogate's bodily engagement with pregnancy is in the capacity of a donor. Criticism could be made regarding the prioritisation of intention over bodily engagement, but the context is important, as is the intention of the surrogate herself. I thank Sally Sheldon for these points.

[38] Bainham contends that 'social parents' can be afforded recognition by being given parental responsibility for the child and that the 'true' parents of a child are its genetic progenitors. But his arguments tend to be directed at 'social' families outside of the assisted reproduction context. Indeed, he also points out that 'legal parenthood, but not parental responsibility, makes the child a member of a *family*, generating that child a wider kin going well beyond the parental relationship' ('Parentage, Parenthood and Parental Responsibility: Subtle, Elusive Yet Important Distinctions' in A. Bainham, S. Day-Sclater, and M. Richards (eds), *What is a Parent? A Socio-Legal Analysis* (Hart Publishing, 1999, emphasis added) and notes that a 'legal parent will remain a parent for life' (at p 34). This is *exactly* what couples that have children by assisted conception intend, so recognition of parental responsibility only, because they (or perhaps only one out of a partnership) are social rather than biological parents, would again lead to inconsistency and differential treatment. For other social parents (eg step-parents), his formulation may be accurate.

The third argument focuses on the unfairness of permitting the surrogate to renege, when *her* stated intention was always to relinquish the child. Essentially this is an argument founded in contract and/or equity – the principles of which are too broad to go into here – but which clearly both recognise formal or notional intention as an element of exchange and/or enforceable promise. Fourth, there are good pragmatic reasons for acknowledging parenthood before conception, centred upon a need for certainty and uniformity: intending parents would understand from the outset that they will be presumed legal parents and are therefore responsible for the child's well-being. These pragmatic reasons are presumably the reason the law regarding parenthood following the use of donated gametes is formulated as it is. There are already criteria stating what interests should be considered by clinicians treating all fertility patients and these have been subject to extensive review. Why there should be additional criteria for those using surrogacy is a mystery – but is probably explained by the 'hierarchy' point and the fact that surrogacy regulation was initially at least a knee-jerk reaction to perceived abuses of such arrangements in the 1980s and the ongoing perception of surrogates as 'vulnerable' and/or exploited. Extending pre-conception determination of parenthood to surrogacy would mean that parenthood of surrogate-born children need not be settled by court order, rendering unnecessary the additional eligibility assessments currently needed to support a valid parental order application, or by adoption.[39] It may actually be more detrimental to the welfare of children not to do so: our current law means that even '[w]here the surrogate mother is happy to hand over the child at birth, the British approach to parenthood nevertheless demands that the child's life starts with litigation, albeit amicable'.[40] Further, recognising intention as the basis of the presumption may operate to prevent disputes following surrogacy: if it was certain from the outset that the surrogate would not be the parent of the resulting child either legally or socially, arguably only those most committed to bearing a child for someone else would consider becoming a surrogate.[41]

Reasons for not recognising people as parents solely by virtue of either genetic or gestational contributions can also be generalised. If the genetic contributor is not also the intended parent, it can be assumed that s/he acts in the capacity of a donor. Therefore, following the spirit of the legislation as regards donors, s/he should not be recognised as the legal parent. This would extend to a woman acting as a 'partial' surrogate. However, this does not currently apply in the situation where two women have a child together, one providing the egg while the other carries the child. Though the 2008 Act still refers to the woman who provides the egg as a 'donor' in this situation,[42] at best this is a misnomer and at worst it seriously undermines the social reality of lesbian parenting by not recognising both women as mothers.

---

[39] Importantly, this would bring homosexual male couples in line with other couples – an equality seemingly overlooked when the new legislation was formulated. While automatic parenthood is now possible for same sex female couples, in the case of a male couple using a surrogate, the further requirements relating to parental orders would always be an additional hurdle to surmount post-birth. It would be interesting to see whether, in this regard, the new legislation would stand up to a human rights challenge, particularly as parity between different same-sex couples has already been achieved in adoption (in the Adoption and Children Act 2002) and in regards to civil partners and joint parental responsibility (Children Act 1989 as amended by the Civil Partnership Act 2004).

[40] E. Jackson, *Regulating Reproduction: Law, Technology and Autonomy* (Hart Publishing, 2001), at p 270.

[41] Though note that only very few surrogacy arrangements end up with a dispute over parenthood – particularly those cases where the surrogate simply 'changes her mind'. See information provided by the non-profit UK surrogacy agency Childlessness Overcome Through Surrogacy (COTS), 'Do Many Surrogates Keep the Baby?' at http://www.surrogacy.org.uk/FAQ4.htm (last accessed 28 June 2010).

[42] Section 47: 'Woman not to be other parent merely because of egg donation'.

The suggestion is that altruism begets the donation act, whether or not the recipients are known by the donor. Moreover, it is questionable whether the status of parent should be given to someone who wholly donates their genetic material in order to create a child for someone else.[43] The extension of this analysis that best illustrates the point is that of the ubiquitous medical student sperm donor – who would typically donate in return for a small payment, but would have no intention to become the 'father' of all the children his donation(s) may potentially create.[44] The importance attached to genetic ties is as socially influenced as much as anything else is,[45] and prioritising the genetic relationship would maintain artificial constructions of parenthood.[46] Although in numerous surrogacy arrangements the genetic parents are also the intending parents, this cannot be assumed. In many cases only one intending parent will have a genetic link to the child, and to distinguish between parents in this way is wholly undesirable. Similarly, where neither intending parent has a genetic link to the child, as the law is currently formulated, no parental order can be granted. Those creating their family in this way would be forced to use adoption to achieve legal parenthood.[47] The law also does not answer questions that may be posed by emergent technologies, which allow the creation of a child using the genetic material of three people.

Some may believe, however, that the genetic parents of a child should be presumed its legal parents, no matter how the child was created. This may be based on the premise that they share a unique biological relationship with the child. Hill postulates that 'an important aspect of parenthood is the experience of creating another in "one's own likeness" ' and that 'part of what makes parenthood meaningful is the parent's ability to see the child grow and develop and see oneself in the process of this

---

[43] The situation where a known donor's gamete is used, and there is an intention among all parties that the 'donor' will be involved in the child's life is a different one and in fact can be seen as multiple intentional parenting. In the parental responsibility context, the recognition of informal arrangements where more than two parents have been involved in a child's life can be seen in Re D (Contact and Parental Responsibility: Lesbian Mothers and Known Father) [2006] EWHC 2 (Fam) and Re B (Role of Biological Father) [2007] EWHC 1952 (Fam), [2008] 1 FLR 1015.

[44] Arguably, it is absurd to register donors as parents for two simple reasons: (1) they did not intend to become such – their intention, if any, was to allow their 'product' to be used by someone else; (2) A sperm donor may make more than one 'deposit' and as such become the 'father' of many children (it is also unlikely that a single egg would be harvested from an egg donor).

[45] See K. O'Donovan, ' "What Shall We Tell the Children?" ' Reflections on Children's Perspectives and the Reproduction Revolution' in R Lee, and D Morgan (eds), Birthrights: Law and Ethics at the Beginnings of Life (Routledge 1989), at pp 96–114; and O. van den Akker, 'The Importance of a Genetic Link in Mothers Commissioning a Surrogate Baby in the UK' (2000) 15(8) Human Reproduction 1849–1855.

[46] This is not to negate the importance that many people attach to having knowledge of their genetic parents. While this article cannot go into whether having identifiable gamete/embryo donors and surrogates is preferable to anonymity or not, for reasons of space, even identifiable donors would not, and should not, be legal parents. Knowing one's genetic heritage for medical or even 'identity' purposes is important to many, but this does not make one's sperm donor one's father. Social parents who intend a child to be born and who will raise the child from birth should be legally recognised as parents. If such a right exists (knowledge) – and since Rose v Secretary of State for Health [2002] EWHC 1593 (Admin), [2002] 2 FLR 962 it seems that it might – this is independent of the determination of legal parenthood. The difference in importance between the genetic and the social relationship was implicitly acknowledged in the HFE Act 1990, albeit in 'a fairly conservative way' (L. Smith, 'Clashing Symbols? Reconciling Support of Fathers and Fatherless Families after the Human Fertilisation and Embryology Act 2008' [2010] CFLQ 46, at p 42) and continued and extended in the 2008 legislation.

[47] HFE Act 2008, s 54(1)(b).

growth'.[48] Infertility consequently becomes a painful experience and creates a desire that may impel some to use surrogacy or assisted conception, rather than choose adoption. While the genetic presumption is not damaging when applied to those who can conceive naturally, and even to some who cannot, for those who *cannot* have a genetically-related child, it offers no solution to an unfulfilled desire to become parents. Neither does it offer anything to partners in relationships who *cannot* provide genetic material when his/her partner can, and who would then be registered as a parent.

The genetic link is synonymous in many people's minds with normality.[49] It is the way in which most children are connected to their parents. Intuitively, therefore, there is a reason to prioritise this connection. Nevertheless, it is at least arguable that because so many genetic ties are broken (both pre and post-birth) the genetic argument is incapable of universally conferring parenthood on those people who will actually care for a child. Even in 'normal' conception situations the registration of genetic parents can be disputed: one estimate suggests that as many as one in 10 of us may not actually be genetically related to our fathers, even though the connection has been assumed or (mis)represented to us.[50] Parenthood based on genetics would also mean that rapists would be the father of a child conceived within their crime, as would men 'duped' into conceiving children.[51] Registering genetic fathers in situations which would otherwise leave the ubiquitous 'single mother' with a child may seem rational, and seems to be reflected in policy and practice,[52] but it is certainly no guarantee that all men will shoulder responsibility any more so than if they were not registered.

In the context of surrogacy, the law is clear that the gestational mother's claim should be prioritised if she changes her mind and elects to keep the child. Not only is she unquestionably given legal motherhood, further legislation provides that surrogacy arrangements are wholly unenforceable.[53] This is more than a presumption – law has made 'a choice between mothers'.[54] This idea – that the birth mother *is* the mother of a child – is not only deeply entrenched in law but is socially and culturally constructed; thus seemingly intuitive and we tend not to confront it. This is 'deep intuition',[55] based on the supposed logic of long-standing legal and social presumptions that a woman giving birth to a child is undisputedly its mother (reflected as *'mater est quam gestatio demonstrat'*), bonding theory, and in arguments that occasionally surface about the practice of surrogacy more generally. These include the belief that it is universally

---

[48] J.L. Hill, 'What Does it Mean to be a "Parent"? The Claims of Biology as the Basis for Parental Rights' (1991) 66 *New York University Law Review* 353, at 389.

[49] See K. O'Donovan, 'A Right to Know One's Parentage?' (1988) 2 *International Journal of Law and the Family* 27–45.

[50] R. Baker, *Sperm Wars* (Fourth Estate, 1996), at pp 55–61.

[51] S. Sheldon, ' "Sperm Bandits", Birth Control Fraud and the Battle of the Sexes' (2001) 21(3) *Legal Studies* 460–480.

[52] Ibid. This is also linked to the prevailing construction of the 'Single Mother' as financially dependent on the state or others. It begs questions (as does the rape point) about the kind of responsibilities society would prefer to be imposed on people creating children. Unintentional parenthood – especially fatherhood – (outside of the donation situation) seems to justify to policymakers that the father must make financial contributions to the upbringing of the child. This may not be required in all cases (or wanted by the mother, particularly if she is in a same-sex relationship).

[53] Surrogacy Arrangements Act 1985, s 1A.

[54] A. Diduck and F. Kaganas, *Family Law, Gender and the State* (Hart Publishing, 1999), at p 110.

[55] It is only a 'modern understanding that parenthood is as much a social, psychological and intentional status as it is a biological one' (J.L. Hill, 'What Does it Mean to be a "Parent"? The Claims of Biology as the Basis for Parental Rights' (1991) 66 *New York University Law Review* 353, at p 419). As noted above, this has not extended to motherhood in the recent review of the HFE Act.

wrong to agree to bear a child for another, particularly when money (assumed to be linked to exploitation and/or commodification of the reproductive process) is involved,[56] to surrogacy being akin to prostitution,[57] or even slavery.[58]

Moving from the genetic to the gestational biological link, three general reasons can be identified in support of the idea that the gestational claim carries more weight than any other, but each has persuasive counter-arguments:

Bonding occurs between the gestational mother and child

The first argument centres on the claim that an immutable bond develops between mother and child during gestation. There are many different theoretical formulations and interpretations of this supposed bond – in fact there is a 'lack of uniformity (of opinion) [which] has important implications for the claim that bonding is an inevitable concomitant of pregnancy and childbirth'.[59] Notably, the Warnock Committee said while discussing surrogacy (to which it was generally resistant) that 'no great claims should be made' in respect of bonding because of a paucity of evidence about the process.[60] Pregnancy is a different experience for every woman, and although there is both scientific and anecdotal evidence to support the bonding hypothesis, it should be recognised too that there is evidence in direct opposition to it.[61] As far as bonding theory reflects upon the determination of legal parenthood, it could be argued that changing the way this is determined in assisted conception and especially surrogacy may actually serve to negate any bonding process. So-called 'bonding' in the sense it is used here is arguably as much a reflection of social construction as it is of biology so, if for example the surrogate did not ever *expect* to be legally recognised as the parent of the child she carries (and she knows that the intending parents *do*), bonding may not take place at all, not to the same extent, or in a different, more disconnected, way:

> 'Numerous studies indicate that external circumstances affect the bonding process between the surrogate and the foetus. If a surrogate knows from the

---

[56] See generally M. Radin, 'Market Inalienability' (1987) 100 *Harvard Law Review* 1849 and also M. Field, *Surrogate Motherhood: The Legal and Human Issues* (Harvard University Press, 1990), at p 28; V.E. Munro, 'Surrogacy and the Construction of the Maternal-Foetal Relationship: The Feminist Dilemma Explained' (2001) 7 *Res Publica* 13, at p 18.

[57] Among others, see A. Dworkin, *Right Wing Women* (The Women's Press, 1983), at p 182; G. Corea, *The Mother Machine: Reproductive Technologies from Artificial Insemination to Artificial Wombs* (The Women's Press, 1987), at p 39; T. Shannon, *Surrogate Motherhood: The Ethics of Using Human Beings* (Crossroad Publishing, 1988), at p 152; K. Pollitt, *Reasonable Creatures: Essays on Women and Feminism* (Vintage Books, 1995), at p 69.

[58] J. Levitt, 'Biology, Technology and Genealogy: A Proposed Uniform Surrogacy Legislation' (1992) 25 *Columbia Journal of Law and Social Problems* 451, at 459. This idea is also apparent in Margaret Attwood's dystopian future vision of surrogacy in *The Handmaid's Tale*, first published in 1985.

[59] 'What Does it Mean to be a "Parent"? The Claims of Biology as the Basis for Parental Rights' (1991) 66 *New York University Law Review* 353, at p 396.

[60] *Committee of Inquiry into Human Fertilisation and Embryology*, Cmnd 9314 (1984), at 36.

[61] J.L. Hill, 'What Does it Mean to be a "Parent"? The Claims of Biology as the Basis for Parental Rights' (1991) 66 *New York University Law Review* 353, at p 397. Also see more generally D. Eyer, *Mother-Infant Bonding: A Scientific Fiction* (Yale University Press, 1992) and N.M. Else-Quest, J.S. Hyde and R. Clark, 'Breast-feeding, Bonding and the Mother-Infant Relationship' (2003) 49 *Merrill-Palmer Quarterly* 4.

outset that the contract is binding and that the baby belongs to the intentional parents, her expectations and thus emotional ties to the child are therefore likely to be different.'[62]

Supporting this view, Rachel Cook discusses a controlled study undertaken by Fischer and Gillman in 1991, in which surrogates 'indeed showed less attachment to the foetus and different experiences of pregnancy when compared to non-surrogate mothers'.[63] In addition, it could be argued that if bonding is at least in part based on involvement, intending parents who both initiate and continue to be involved with a pregnancy and preparation for birth may actually have a similar or even stronger claim.

The argument that relinquishing a child may psychologically *harm* the gestational mother applies (in this context) only to surrogacy, and is potentially one basis for the rigidity of the legal definition of motherhood.[64] In the main, this argument is based on adoption experiences and studies that show that many relinquishing mothers grieve and/or search for the child that they surrender. Surrogacy is, however, conceptually distinct from adoption: central to any knowledge of relinquishment in adoption is that it came *after* the child already existed. It can also be assumed that the reasons for surrendering a child for adoption are very different to those involved in surrogacy relinquishment: it is largely situational, not based on a pre-conception agreement and does not involve other parties from the pre-conception stage. Additionally, it can be suggested that any harm felt by the surrogate is at least comparable to the 'loss' that may be felt by the intended parents if the child is not passed to them – must these 'losses' be weighed against each other? If so, on what basis would we then determine who was to be regarded as the parent of the child? Does two people's loss outweigh the loss felt by one?

It is generally better for a child to stay with its gestational mother

A second argument raised for favouring the gestational link is loosely based on a 'best interests' argument. Hill notes that every US state has recognised a presumption that it is in the best interests of a child to remain with or be placed with its natural parent(s).[65] This clearly seems to favour a genetic link, though depends entirely on how we define 'natural'. The argument appears to be based on an assumption that children having an uncertain biological legacy, or detachment from their 'natural' mother, may be psychologically harmed. This argument does not stand up for many reasons, mostly because it implies that all adoptees – and potentially stepchildren – would suffer psychological harm, merely through lack of a genetic link to the woman raising them. This therefore adds weight to the argument for favouring intention over the gestational link in the case of a dispute over parenthood. The best interests argument in this sense does not support the claim that gestational mothers (like genetic parents) have a claim to parenthood that trumps the intending parents' claim, although this appears to be a popular belief and is recognised in a legal fiction. In fact the opposite may be true: '[t]o ignore the centrality of . . . intention and instead ascribe *prima facie* parenthood to a

---

[62] J. Levitt, 'Biology, Technology and Genealogy: A Proposed Uniform Surrogacy Legislation' (1992) 25 *Columbia Journal of Law and Social Problems* 451, at p 476.

[63] R. Cook, 'Donating Parenthood: Perspectives on Parenthood from Surrogacy and Gamete Donation' in A. Bainham, S. Day Sclater, and M. Richards (eds), *What is a Parent? A Socio-Legal Analysis* (Hart Publishing, 1999), at p 133.

[64] E. Jackson, *Regulating Reproduction: Law, Technology and Autonomy* (Hart Publishing, 2001), at p 266.

[65] J.L. Hill, 'What Does it Mean to be a "Parent"? The Claims of Biology as the Basis for Parental Rights' (1991) 66 *New York University Law Review* 353, at p 400.

couple that never intended to keep the child may not promote the child's welfare'.[66] Any claim based on the gestational link is clearly a rather speculative empirical assertion: there is no evidence to support the claim that children are better cared for by biological, rather than intentional, parents and, as such, the law should err on the side of protecting the autonomy interests of the adults involved.

The gestational mother contributes most to the creation of the child

The gestational mother's parenthood claim may centre on the fact that she makes the largest single physical contribution to the child. Does sheer physical involvement mean that, in the event of a dispute, a surrogate (or any gestational parent) has the greatest claim to parenthood? One argument is that children 'belong' to the gestational mother on the basis of input.[67] Obviously this is linked to the bonding and relinquishment arguments discussed above, and can probably be dismissed for similar reasons. Again, definition is the key: what is 'involvement'? Intending parents are 'involved' in the creation of the pregnancy *prior* to a surrogate's involvement; they also invest more emotion (and often money) in the pregnancy and in preparation for the child – might this in fact mean that their claim to parenthood is stronger? The significance of social parenthood means that the involvement of the intending parents is essential. Surrogacy agencies both in this country and abroad hold this out to have great importance, and consider it to factor highly in the success of the majority of surrogacy arrangements brokered through them.[68] In addition, '[i]t is suggested that this involvement can simultaneously provide much-needed social support for the surrogate mother as well as a *continued reminder of the identity of the "real" parents*'.[69] This, then, serves the dual purpose of accentuating the physical, mental and financial involvement of the intending parents while encouraging and increasing the surrogate's 'detachment'.

The argument that without the surrogate, pregnancy and birth would not occur seems, but is not, analogous to the argument for recognising the intending parents. In fact, it is more analogous to the position of a donor – she donates gestational time/use of her body – and should be treated similarly. The intending parents initiate the conception, gestation and birth of a child. In that equation, if they need to commission a surrogate, it seems intuitively reasonable to argue that 'but for' the surrogate, the child could not be born. While this is literally true, as a theoretical argument about *how* law chooses to assign legal parenthood, this argument falls short because of the element of *choice*; the difference between the claim of the surrogate and that of the intending parents is that they chose her (presumably, too, she chose to be a surrogate), and could choose someone else. Still, they are the initiators of the arrangement: 'but for' *them*, *that* child would not exist. Surrogates are not passive, they make their choice to be a surrogate deliberately and in the context of altruism, particularly in this country where commercial surrogacy is an impossibility. They make an autonomous decision to have a child for someone else. For this reason, women who act as surrogates should be presumptively held to their agreements: the burden should

---

[66] E. Jackson, *Regulating Reproduction: Law, Technology and Autonomy* (Hart Publishing, 2001), at p 270.

[67] B. Katz-Rothman, *Recreating Motherhood: Ideology and Technology in a Patriarchal Society* (Norton, 1989), at p 44.

[68] COTS, *Comprehensive Guide to Surrogacy* (unpublished, 2000).

[69] R. Cook, 'Donating Parenthood: Perspectives on Parenthood from Surrogacy and Gamete Donation' in A. Bainham, S. Day Sclater, and M. Richards (eds), *What is a Parent? A Socio-Legal Analysis* (Hart Publishing, 1999), at p 136 [emphasis added].

be placed on the surrogate (should she wish to challenge) to show that legal parenthood should be altered and awarded to her.

While the enforcement of surrogates' promises might seem distasteful, there are collateral benefits to be obtained by doing so. Surrogacy arrangements by their very nature appear to be a form of relational contract, yet this aspect of them is denied in substantive law. Grounding the regulation of surrogacy arrangements in contract, relying on the principles of autonomous bargaining, freedom of contract and the built-in ability of contract law to police unconscionable bargains, would offer protection to all parties. In particular, facilitating the making of surrogacy agreements in an environment in which the potential of exploitation is minimised is a constructive use of existing law. Additionally, in surrogacy arrangements, preferences are likely to be expressed by the intending parents, such as a requirement that the surrogate does not smoke, attends certain medical examinations, allows amniocentesis or other medical procedures during pregnancy, or even would terminate the pregnancy if certain eventualities occur.[70]

It is clear, however, that subject to her having capacity, no term taking away a surrogate's ability to control her own body would be supported in law, particularly one that purported to take away her right to a legal abortion. On this, Margaret Radin has argued that the choice of having an abortion is not commodifiable.[71] Similarly, Joan Mahoney argues that '[t]he prospect of women being forced to undergo medical procedures against their will is truly horrifying'.[72] This also begs the question of what happens to children born from surrogacy arrangements who do not end up being cared for in a stable family relationship, or where intentions change. For example, if a child is born disabled, the intending couple may feel that it would be too difficult to raise it. The surrogate, too, may choose not to keep it.[73] Although sad, this is arguably little different to what might happen if a disabled child was born in 'normal' circumstances. The difference is that three people, rather than two, make this choice, but in this circumstance, insisting that any of the parties *must* continue to care for the child would be contrary to the situation and choices faced by fertile people. Nevertheless, current law establishes that the surrogate is the legal mother and, therefore if the situation were to become reality, it will be her, despite the prior intentions of the parties involved, who ultimately has to make this decision. By recognising the intending parents as the legal parents, it would be them who had to make the choice, and the surrogate would be absolved of the responsibility of doing so. Her agreement to become a surrogate presupposes that she did not intend to have parental responsibility or to make such decisions while, by intentionally organising and creating the pregnancy, the intending parents may be taken to have assumed it. Matters of bodily integrity aside, if the contract model was followed, failing to conform to any other accepted term of the

---

[70] In fact such requirements are expressly stated in the 'Information for Surrogates' (p 7) and 'Information for Intended Parents' (p 11) sections of the information booklet provided by COTS (COTS Information Booklet (available online at http://www.surrogacy.org.uk/pdf/COTS%20booklet.pdf).

[71] M. Radin, 'Market Inalienability' (1987) 100 *Harvard Law Review* 1849, at p 1934.

[72] J. Mahoney, 'An Essay on Surrogacy and Feminist Thought' in L. Gostin (ed), *Surrogate Motherhood: Politics and Privacy* (Indiana University Press, 1990), at p 187.

[73] This happened in the US Stiver/Malahoff case: see C. Shalev, *Birth Power: The Case for Surrogacy* (Yale University Press, 1989), at p 97.

contract, not least refusing to hand over the child, would constitute breach of contract and would potentially result in a claim for damages for any lost expenditure and probably also for mental distress.[74]

It has been suggested that there can only be one real reason for maintaining the unenforceability of all surrogacy arrangements: to further discourage the practice of surrogacy: 'surrogacy contracts will seem precarious, and people will be unwilling to risk so much upon such a patently insecure arrangement'.[75] However, given that there is no empirical evidence that surrogacy is in itself harmful, and that the public perception of surrogacy has changed dramatically from its early days, it can be argued that there is no need to deter surrogacy arrangements and so the legal response – and the normative messages implicit within it – must too. If deterrence of surrogacy is not manifestly necessary, then the rigid and absolute unenforceability of all surrogacy arrangements needs to be reappraised. Not to do so implies a fundamental and paternalistic mistrust of the decision-making capacity of women in relation to their own bodies and childbirth.

RECOGNISING INTENTION: PRACTICAL EXAMPLES

Families in general, and children specifically, in surrogacy or other assisted conception situations would benefit from legal reform allowing intention to be the presumptive factor determining parenthood. To recap, intention (broadly encompassing the intention to conceive, raise and care for a child, coupled with the surrogate's intention to gestate it but not raise it) would become the general presumption in such circumstances, and challenges to parenthood would have to be directed *at* the intending parents, instead of *by* them. The remainder of this article will look at the practicalities of determining parenthood in surrogacy, DI and IVF in an internally consistent way, using pre-conception intentions as the starting presumption. Intention will be contrasted to other potentially valid parenthood claims – those of the genetic and gestational 'parent(s)'.

Children by donor insemination (DI)

DI provides a good model to compare potential parenthood claims of genetic contributors with those of the intending parent(s). Here, the intending parent(s) could be a heterosexual couple where there is male sub- or infertility, a lesbian couple wishing to become parents together, a single woman, or even more than two people in a collaborative parenting context. Some *fertile* heterosexual couples might also use DI in a clinical context – to avoid the inheritance of sex-linked (male line) genetic diseases, for example. It is likely in these situations that the woman who becomes pregnant will be genetically related to the child she will raise and will also be the intending mother.[76] Thus, without intention, in any of these formulations the only other participant with a potential claim would be the sperm donor, because of the genetic

---

[74] *Farley v Skinner* [2001] UKHL 49. There are obviously difficulties in this in the sense that a surrogate having to pay damages would potentially not be in the child's best interest. An alternative remedy, specific performance, is also problematic because of autonomy issues – there is no history of its use in contracts for personal services.

[75] E. Jackson, *Regulating Reproduction: Law, Technology and Autonomy* (Hart Publishing, 2001), at p 308.

[76] Though it is possible that both intending parents do not provide gametes. If an egg donor is used, the law will still only support the gestational (intending) mother's parenthood claim, even though the two partners had equal intentions.

link. While the nature and definition of donation should arguably preclude his claim in any case,[77] problems nevertheless arise with his recognition, adding strength to the intending parents' claim.

If the genetic link were held to determine parenthood, absurd legal situations would arise. In the most common DI situation, the genetically-related mother would share parental status, rights and responsibilities with a man who, in his donor capacity, would typically be a stranger, would live outside the home, and who never would have intended to become the child's father.[78] Thus, where a heterosexual couple intends to raise the child together, the legal father of the child would not be the man fulfilling the social role of father. This would, in effect, discriminate against the intending father because of his inability to provide genetic material. It would also fly in the face of the nature and spirit of donation. Where a same-sex female couple use a sperm donor to enable one of them to bear a child that they both intend to raise, without the input of a man, recognising the genetic donor as the father of the child would be entirely unrealistic.[79] And a single woman choosing DI will do so for a variety of reasons, which may even include the desire for her child to remain fatherless. Again, recognising the sperm donor as the father would not fit the intended situation or reflect social reality.

If *intention* was the pre-birth determinant of parenthood, then those who intended to play the social parental roles (whether a heterosexual or lesbian couple, a single person or a collaboration) could legitimately (and more easily) be recognised as parents of the child that they collectively or singly, in all senses other than the doubly biological, created. Moreover, the donor in this circumstance would be exonerated from the responsibilities that parenthood entails – as it would be assumed was always *his* (negative) intention.[80] The way the law was changed in 2008 now almost reflects this position, extending the recognition of both positive and negative intentions in all situations outlined, other than to collaborative parenting arrangements, and subject to certain 'agreed conditions' where a couple are unmarried or not in a civil partnership.

In surrogacy and assisted conception there are two other situations in which genetic links can be said either to not give enough to justify automatic legal parenthood or may give *too much*. Although some of these points have been raised briefly elsewhere, it is worth paying them specific attention here:

Gamete donors would become parents

Usually gamete donors have no other involvement in the creation of any child from their donation than the act of offering their genetic material for use by others. The

---

[77] And in fact already does, according to the HFE Act 2008, s 41(1).

[78] It is helpful to distinguish between the positive intention *to* be a parent, and the negative intention *not* to become a parent during processes of assisted conception. It seems that 'negative intention' is already recognised: when a child is born from DI s 41(1) of the HFE Act 2008 (replacing s 28(6)(a) of the 1990 Act) outlines that the sperm donor will not be the child's legal father. Section 27, by recognising the birth mother as the legal mother in all circumstances, also effectively removes motherhood from egg donors, but does *not* recognise the negative intentions of surrogates. Interesting here is the decision in the case *Leeds Teaching Hospitals NHS Trust v Mr and Mrs A and Others* [2003] EWCH 259 (QB), in which, following a mistake at a fertility clinic, legal parenthood was awarded by the court to the genetic father, who had neither intended to be a father to the twins that resulted, nor would raise them (see further K. Horsey, 'Unconsidered Inconsistencies: Parenthood and Assisted Conception' in K. Horsey and H. Biggs, *Human Fertilisation and Embryology: Reproducing Regulation* (Routledge-Cavendish, 2007).

[79] It has already been argued that the situation where the sperm provider's continued involvement is desired by a same-sex female (or heterosexual, should it arise) couple is not in fact a 'donor' situation but a form of collaborative parenthood. As also stated, none of the arguments made here are intended to preclude the possibility of a child having more than two parents.

[80] Though there is the possibility that a known donor may be part of a collaborative parenting exercise.

commonly understood meaning of 'donation' is to voluntarily give something, requiring nothing in return, inferring that donors gift not only gametes,[81] but the possibility of (legal) parenthood. Gamete donors do not intend to raise the child(ren) that may result from their act. If they did, it is arguable that they should be prevented from donating (this must be misrepresentation), and almost certain that prospective parents would not accept their 'donations' if this were known. This passive contribution to the creation of a child should not be the basis of parenthood, particularly as it cannot be universally applied. This is true of both sperm and egg donors, in spite of the greater physical intervention required in donating eggs.

The genetic claim may be based on property arguments

The potential argument that genetic parents should be legally recognised because of 'property rights' they have in their own material has been dismissed by Hill. Notwithstanding the fact that one cannot actually have property rights in a child, the major premise of this argument appears to be that 'persons possess property rights in the products, processes, and organs of their bodies and in any commodities developed from these sources'.[82] The conclusion drawn would be, therefore, that all genetic contributors would have property (or quasi-property) rights in resultant children. Many arguments arise from this formulation. First, genetic contributors would only have a half-interest in a child, that child being the result of a fusion between two people's genetic material. If the argument were to be logically extended, each genetic contributor would have an equal property share in the child. Therefore, this proposition could only be feasible where both genetic contributors intend to raise the child together – that is, in 'normal' heterosexual conception, conception by insemination or IVF (non-donor), or in full surrogacy where both genetic contributors are the intending parents. It would not work for DI or partial surrogacy and should therefore be rejected as a basis for the presumption of parenthood.

A second and more interesting property argument involves paying for donated gametes. As a consequence of payment, the genetic material would become, according to traditional analysis, the property of the particular clinic or hospital, which would then be free to dispose of it as seen fit.[83] Clearly it would not be expected that as the 'owner' of genetic material provided in assisted conception, a clinic would become the 'parent' of a child. Furthermore, even if gametes were not 'bought' but merely donated, the doctrine of accession, at least in US law, 'might bar the claims of the genetic progenitors',[84] because where a raw material (in this case, 'raw' genetic material) has been altered significantly so as to change its function or increase its value, the doctrine requires that the title or ownership of the goods in question passes to the one who provided the greatest labour input. In assisted conception where donated gametes were used, this would mean that those who gave the greatest input to the resulting pregnancy would have the property-based parenthood claim. For DI this could raise dispute; no great effort is required for s/he who performed the insemination, seemingly leaving the parenthood claim resting with the gestational

---

[81] Or in the surrogacy context, the gestational process.

[82] J.L. Hill, 'What Does it Mean to be a "Parent"? The Claims of Biology as the Basis for Parental Rights' (1991) 66 *New York University Law Review* 353, at p 391

[83] Ibid, at p 392. Note, however, that in the UK gamete donors are not paid, though legitimate expenses may be reimbursed. It is also illegal to pay for gametes (s 12(1)(e) and 41(8) of the HFEA 1990 as amended) though not, obviously, unlawful to pay for the services of clinics who pass on donated gametes.

[84] Ibid, at p 393.

mother.[85] Notwithstanding, there is a more fundamental difficulty with utilising property-based genetic arguments to determine parenthood: '[w]hile people may possess property rights in their genetic issue, they certainly do not possess property rights in the result of their genetic contributions. Put more simply, children are not property'.[86]

Children by IVF

In IVF the intending parents are those who, for one reason or another, cannot conceive 'naturally' and will have unsuccessfully tried to have a baby by other means. They may also require one or other gamete to be provided by a donor. In this section, parenthood following IVF using donors will be considered in addition to IVF using the gametes of the intending parents.

Parenthood after IVF with either a sperm or egg donor (or both) would be subject to the same qualifications as above: the donor in each case is presumed to donate his/her genetic material, while not wishing to become the parent of any resulting child. Conversely, the recipients of the donated gametes do intend to be parents and have initiated the process of becoming so. If intention was not used as the determining factor, then the genetic link may be championed instead, again possibly discriminating against whichever partner was unable to provide genetic material. As with DI, this determination of parenthood would create the unrealistic situation that one of the intending parents (who provided genetic material) will be recognised as the legal and social parent of the child along with the donor of the other genetic material, but not their own partner.

As the law stands, even if the IVF recipient female was not a genetic contributor, she would be the legal mother of the child simply because of the fact that she gives birth to it. Thus, while the genetic link is denied, her intention is implicitly recognised via gestation. The IVF recipient male is presumed to be the father (because he *intended* to be?) of the child of his partner,[87] thus recognising intention would do little to change either status, even if the man was not genetically related. The position is now mirrored for female same-sex couples undergoing IVF treatment.[88] Thus, while intention would have been important under the old legislation as it would have brought in unmarried men and female partners, it may be argued that all this has been done, so the concept of intention is redundant in IVF situations. However, intention retains importance for the concept of universality: an intention-based presumption may produce the same result as existing law in some situations, but has the benefit of being able to be extended to cover all forms of assisted conception, including surrogacy. Further, this result is achieved for the right reasons, not accidentally – that is, where a situation (such as IVF within marriage) fits with traditional belief about what a family 'ought' to be – and would

---

[85] Note that in the case of full surrogacy with gamete donors it would be hard to argue the difference in input between the surrogate, the intending parents, or even the clinic itself if technological assistance (such as IVF or even ICSI) was given.

[86] J.L. Hill, 'What Does it Mean to be a "Parent"? The Claims of Biology as the Basis for Parental Rights' (1991) 66 *New York University Law Review* 353, at p 393.

[87] If married, by virtue of s 35 of the HFE Act 2008. If unmarried, ss 36–37 apply, with the same effect as long as both parties consent. Note however that the parenthood of the *married* man can be rebutted if it is shown that he did not consent, or that his consent was in some way undermined, as in *Leeds Teaching Hospitals NHS Trust v Mr and Mrs A and Others* [2003] EWCH 259 (QB).

[88] If civil partners, by virtue of s 42 of the HFE Act 2008. If not, ss 43–44 apply, with the same effect as long as both parties consent.

mean no distinction would need to be drawn between IVF using donated gametes (which would always be necessary for two females, thus setting them apart) and genetic IVF.

Children by surrogacy

IVF and DI become more contentious when used within a surrogacy arrangement. It therefore becomes necessary to consider surrogacy here in its two separate forms; 'partial' and 'full'. In full surrogacy, the intending couple and/or donors may have provided the genetic material.

Partial surrogacy

Intention in partial surrogacy would eliminate the possibility of the surrogate's legal recognition as the mother – thus reversing the traditional presumption that the legal mother must be the birth mother, at the same time as negating her genetic link to the child. Historically, the maternity presumption was incontrovertible, but the advent and development of sophisticated reproductive technologies and the use of surrogacy in tandem with these now enables it to be challenged.

There have been discussions as to exactly what the surrogate is a substitute for or even whether it is she who is the substitute at all.[89] I would argue that it is more correct to say that the surrogate is a substitute for part of the *process* involved in having a child, not actually for the *person* (mother) herself. Further, if one does not accept the current legal definition of mother, the term 'surrogate mother' becomes incorrect, while 'surrogate' alone does not. A surrogate agrees to carry a child for another person(s) (here a gender-neutral and plural-free definition is best as potentially surrogacy could be for a single person of either sex or either a heterosexual or same-sex (male or female) couple, or a collaboration of potential parents) and to present that child to them after birth. Putting to one side arguments that surrogates are/may be exploited within such a relationship, and other arguments against surrogacy in general, it is the notion of this agreement that motivates the intending parents to initiate that particular pregnancy at the outset, whether this comes about (unusually) by natural conception between the surrogate and the intending father, or by the surrogate being inseminated with the intending father's or donor sperm, either privately or in a clinical setting.

The presumption that the surrogate is the mother can be rebutted on a similar basis as with gamete donors – a surrogate also makes a donation. In partial surrogacy she donates genetic material and time, energy and bodily resources throughout the gestation period. At the time she enters the agreement, she does not intend to parent the child, *despite* the genetic link. In itself this points to the need for change in the legal presumption of parenthood following surrogacy. If the surrogate later wishes to claim parenthood then it should be for her to do so.[90] While this leaves room for argument

---

[89] See in particular D. Morgan, 'Surrogacy: An Introductory Essay' in R. Lee and D. Morgan (eds), *Birthrights: Law and Ethics at the Beginnings of Life* (Routledge, 1989) 55–84, at p 56.

[90] A further argument for reversing the registration of surrogate born children centres on the bizarre combinations of parenthood that can arise after a surrogate arrangement and before a parental order is awarded by the courts (if it is). The husband of a woman acting as surrogate (if she is married) will be registered as the father of the child, when it is unlikely that he will ever have had anything more then a supporting role. He will have made no input genetically or physically to the child, and certainly did not intend to become the father.

that partial surrogacy should not be utilised – that a surrogate should *not* provide any of the genetic material for a child she carries for someone else[91] – that discussion must take place elsewhere.

Full surrogacy

In full surrogacy, a surrogate has no genetic connection to the child she carries (unless she is related to either of the commissioning couple). The child may be the result of the fusion of the gametes of the intending couple in IVF or, if one or both of the couple produces poor quality or no gametes, donor material may be used. Again, donors would not be legal parents and this logic would extend to the surrogate. In full surrogacy the surrogate does not 'donate' her genetic material, but she does still give her time, energy and bodily resources to enable the commissioning couple to have a child. In cases of full surrogacy the child is not linked to the surrogate other than by (donated) gestation and, more importantly, the intending parents are the ones who were motivated to initiate its conception and intend to care for it. They should be legally recognised as the parents of that child, whether they are genetically linked or not.

Using intention to determine parenthood following surrogacy also precludes the necessity for the troublesome 'parental order' device, which is used to transfer parental status to the intending parents between six weeks and six months after the birth of the child when all parties remain in agreement. However, overly stringent requirements exist that serve to limit the availability of parental orders to prospective parents. Given the difficulties already faced by those requiring surrogacy, alongside the fact that commercial surrogacy is criminalised,[92] it has to be questioned whether further hurdles are necessary. While it is no longer the case that to qualify for a parental order a couple must be married,[93] they must be no more than a *couple*, while at least one of them must be genetically related to the child. Why this is the case is unclear. Establishing parenthood in surrogacy on the basis of intention would be fairer to all parties concerned, particularly with the certainty it would give at the outset of the arrangement. The intending couple and the surrogate would be recognised for the actual roles they play: the commissioning parents intend to be parents and the surrogate intends to have the child for others.

CONCLUSIONS

Because methods of creating children by 'non-natural' means or by those requiring medical intervention have greatly increased, and perhaps also because of increased popular exposure to assisted reproductive techniques, it has become necessary for us to rethink how parenthood is defined in such situations. This was clearly the thinking behind the alterations made to the 'status provisions' in the HFE Act 2008, where it was recognised that changes elsewhere in law (for example, in adoption law and in

---

[91] This was in fact proposed in s 5(1)(2) of the Minnesota Assisted Reproduction Act, Bill No 792, March 2003, though this never reached the statute books. Interestingly, the same piece of legislation would have recognised the intending parent(s) as the legal parents (s 6(1)). Information provided by the UK non-profit surrogacy agency COTS (Childlessness Overcome Through Surrogacy) states that 'the advantages of host [full] surrogacy are that the couple, if they use their own egg and sperm, get their own baby *and that a host baby has never been kept by the surrogate against the wishes of the intended parents* (COTS Information Booklet (available online at http://www.surrogacy.org.uk/pdf/COTS%20booklet.pdf), at p 2 (emphasis added). It goes on to say that '[s]tatistically speaking, the dozen or so cases where the baby has been kept by the surrogate since 1988 have all been straight [partial] surrogacy cases.'

[92] Surrogacy Arrangements Act 1985.

[93] Section 54 of the HFE Act 2008 extends to civil partners (of either sex) and also those 'living as partners in an enduring family relationship'.

relation to civil partnerships) made the existing provisions somewhat out of date.[94] However, despite the changes made to legal parenthood in the 2008 Act, there is more to be done, particularly in order to achieve consistency and parity of treatment between all those who utilise assisted reproductive techniques. Because it is possible that many different combinations of people may claim parenthood of a child born from assisted conception, a universal principle enabling consistency and presumptively recognising the people who are most likely to care for the child as parents in any given case is desirable. It seems that a presumption based on intention might be one way of providing this, and it may be that this test has become appropriate following the development of technologies that mean that parenthood, especially motherhood, can be broken down into component parts. Furthermore, because we are able, to a large extent, to control our fertility, 'procreation increasingly involves both the biological process of reproduction *and the intention to become a parent*'.[95]

Though the genetic link argument may engender some support, it does not withstand scrutiny. As has been shown, the claim of the genetically-linked contributor is based upon the premise of a unique biological tie between them and the child. The claim necessarily fails in assisted conception situations because it would mean that donors would become the legally recognised parents of any or all children that their participation helped create. To allow this would contradict the spirit of donation. Recognising donors would also lead to the unrealistic situation that two entirely separate individuals become the parents of a child, when they may be complete strangers. The genetic link is also rejected as the determining factor in parenthood because it could be seen to be a property-based claim, again creating an indefensible situation whereby two unrelated parties may have equal proprietary interests in a child. Additionally, if the property analogy were further extended, a clinic may also claim 'ownership'. In itself the claim is inherently imperfect, as it could not produce a universal outcome for *all* assisted conception techniques.

Claims based on gestation are similarly flawed in a number of respects. The claim merely perpetuates the existing normative constructions of motherhood, and should thus not be a basis for the continued recognition of parenthood. It also prioritises the mother whilst doing nothing for fathers. A 'best-interests' argument is not convincing, especially when turned on its head and the position of the gestational 'mother' is challenged on the basis of her agreement to relinquish the child. For the same reasons, a claim based on the potential harm caused by relinquishment or upon the fact that pregnant mothers might bond with the child they carry must also fail. It would be hard to argue that gestational 'mothers' have *no* claim to the child, but it is not difficult to see that her claim is outweighed by the claim of the intending parent(s). Furthermore, it is suggested that perhaps gestational mothers bond with a child because of an inherently 'natural' expectation of raising it.[96] Thus, a surrogate may potentially 'bond' with the child precisely *because* she always retains the capacity to challenge the claim of genetic or intentional parents because of the entrenched culturally and legally constructed presumption that gestation equals motherhood.

---

[94] Department of Heath, *Review of the Human Fertilisation and Embryology Act: A Public Consultation* (August 2005), available at http://www. dh. gov.uk/ en/ Publicationsandstatistics/ Publications/ PublicationsPolicyAndGuidance/DH_4123774, at paras 8.3, 8.12, 8.13 and 8.21.

[95] E. Jackson, *Regulating Reproduction: Law, Technology and Autonomy* (Hart Publishing, 2001), at p 269 [emphasis in original]. See also S. Sheldon, 'Unwilling Fathers and Abortion: Terminating Men's Child Support Obligations?' (2003) 66 (2) *Modern Law Review* 175.

[96] Although van Zyl and van Niekerk argue that the surrogate may actually perceive 'that the child is not her own' and this perception 'tends to shape her entire experience of pregnancy'. The authors quote surrogates interviewed by Helene Ragone as saying, for example, 'I never think of the child as mine. After

There are, therefore, compelling reasons for not leaving this avenue open – if it is known from the outset that it will be the intending parents who will be the legal parents of the child she carries, the surrogate may not form this bond, or any bond formed will be different.

It is therefore clearly arguable that because the intended parents initiate, plan and prepare for the birth of the child, they should be legally recognised as the parents of that child that, *but for* them, would not exist. It is they who choose to use assisted conception, thus choosing whether to use a donor of genetic material or a surrogate. They are the 'first cause' of the child and as such are of prima facie importance in the procreational relationship.[97] Recognising intentional parenthood depends upon a rejection of biologically-based traditional assumptions: an acknowledgement that parenthood following assisted conception does not depend upon anything inherently biological, but rather upon a pre-conception intention to have a child, and to initiate the process with which that child is to be brought into the world. While '[i]t might be argued that this is a peculiar approach to the determination of parental status since it places a mental element, intention, over the tangible, biological tie',[98] such an argument can be challenged with reference to other areas of law where mental factors (including intention) are given legal weight, including the formation of contractual agreements or the commission of criminal acts. It is also clear from comparisons with other methods of family formation, notably adoption, that although:

> 'other elements [than intention] may be valued, [they] are indeed unnecessary. It is clear from a psychological perspective neither the genetic, sexual or gestational elements are necessary for successful parenting.'[99]

An intention-based argument succeeds because the current law regarding the parenthood of children born from assisted conception, though improved, still fails to recognise the people who will care for the child as the legal parent(s) in all situations, and results in a lack of consistency in parental determination between different forms of assisted conception and between different types of parent(s). This means that a hierarchy of forms of family creation continues to exist. It is not the 'mechanics' involved that are important, but the relationships that will continue.[100]

The causal relationship between intended parents and child (coupled with the negative intention of the surrogate) should mean that they are, legally, 'parents': the recognition of intention would more precisely reflect the expected outcome for all parties concerned. In any assisted reproduction situation it would be inequitable for the genetic contributors or the gestational host to renege on their implied promises to make no further claim on the child. In an agreement such as a surrogacy arrangement, or even an agreement between donor and clinic, all parties make corresponding

---

I had the baby, the mother came into the room and held the baby. I couldn't relate that it had any part of me'; 'I don't think of the baby as my child. I donated an egg I wasn't going to be using'; 'The baby isn't mine. I'm only carrying the baby' (L. van Zyl and A. van Niekerk, 'Interpretations, Perspectives and Intentions in Surrogate Motherhood' (2000) 26 *Journal of Medical Ethics* 404, at p 405).

[97] J.L. Hill, 'What Does it Mean to be a "Parent"? The Claims of Biology as the Basis for Parental Rights' (1991) 66 *New York University Law Review* 353, at p 414.

[98] Ibid.

[99] R. Cook, 'Donating Parenthood: Perspectives on Parenthood from Surrogacy and Gamete Donation' in A. Bainham, S. Day Sclater, and M. Richards (eds), *What is a Parent? A Socio-Legal Analysis* (Hart Publishing, 1999), at p 136. Also see generally S. Golombok, *Parenting: What Really Counts?* (Routledge, 2000).

[100] M. Garrison, 'Law Making for Baby Making: An Interpretive Approach to the Determination of Legal Parentage' (2000) 113 *Harvard Law Review* 835, at pp 878–882.

pre-conception commitments: '[i]nitially it is the intention of all adults in a surrogacy arrangement that the intended parents become the social parents'.[101] It is implicit that both surrogates and donors should refrain from claiming automatic legal parenthood. A surrogate agrees to bear and give birth to a child for someone else – her 'intention is clear, even though her motivations may not be'.[102] The intending parents in a surrogacy arrangement base all expectations upon the agreement and the implied promise contained within it. Thus, it could be argued that it is unfair for the surrogate to break her promise and that there are good reasons for holding her to it and for legally recognising intending parents, based upon their (detrimental) reliance upon her promise, and their expectations:

> 'legal rules governing modern procreative arrangements and parental status should recognize the importance and the legitimacy of individual efforts to project intentions and decisions into the future. Where such intentions are deliberate, explicit and bargained for, where they are the catalyst for reliance and expectations . . . they should be honored.'[103]

Reliance in surrogacy often extends to the payment of a great deal of money to a surrogate (in the form of expenses reimbursed) and, in any case, is likely to involve alternative forms of financial and emotional expenditure in preparation for having a child. Arguments against a contractual formulation are mainly based in arguments previously expounded. For example, if it is argued that the gestational mother should not be held contractually liable to the intending parents if she reneges on the agreement, then this must be based upon arguments that seek to prioritise her claim over any other. Consequently, it must also be based in the presumption of motherhood based on gestation and birth that is currently enshrined in law and deeply embedded in our cultural imagination. An alternative challenge to the reliance or expectation theory may rest on distaste for allowing what is primarily a commercial mechanism to become a defining factor in an inherently private process. However, the use of contractual principles, in conjunction with the acknowledgement of intention, would benefit future surrogacy regulation, in that consistency could be achieved in the determination of legal parenthood, as could some degree of protection for the participating parties.

There are valid reasons to assure the identity of the parents of a child born from assisted conception at the time of conception: it is surely better all round for the parents of a planned child to be determined prior to its birth – and where better than at conception (or pre-conception) to avoid uncertainty or dispute? It is not in a child's best interests to have any or all of its potential parents involved in dispute over parenthood after it is born: 'permitting challenges to the parental status of the intended parents virtually ensures that the child will grow up in the functional equivalent of a broken home'.[104] Making surrogacy arrangements enforceable may also help to prevent disputes, even if this risks fewer women being prepared to become surrogates. Certainty and completeness is obviously important if intending parents are recognised, as it would allow them to prepare for the child that 'but for' them, would not come into

---

[101] R. Cook, 'Donating Parenthood: Perspectives on Parenthood from Surrogacy and Gamete Donation' in A. Bainham, S. Day Sclater, and M. Richards (eds), *What is a Parent? A Socio-Legal Analysis* (Hart Publishing, 1999), at p 135.

[102] Ibid.

[103] M.M. Schultz, 'Reproductive Technology and Intent-Based Parenthood: An Opportunity for Gender Neutrality' (1990) *Wisconsin Law Review* 297, at p 302.

[104] J.L. Hill, 'What Does it Mean to be a "Parent"? The Claims of Biology as the Basis for Parental Rights' (1991) 66 *New York University Law Review* 353, at p 417.

existence. The certainty argument would continue to work in the event of the intending parents refusing to take the child. If, for some reason, they decided that they did not want it: if it were born disabled, for example, they too would be held to their agreement, on the basis of their intention. The current formulation of the law simply *cannot* be correct if it means that a surrogate mother would have automatic parental responsibility if there was a refusal on the part of the intending parents, when the child was one that she never intended to have.[105]

It seems, therefore, that neither the gestational claim nor an argument based upon the genetic link present a clear reason why either should be championed when determining parenthood of a child born from surrogacy or assisted conception. Intending parents in surrogacy and assisted conception have a claim to parenthood that is both stronger and less flawed than the claim of either the genetically related contributor(s) or of the gestational mother (where these processes are separated). In order to accept this, cultural assumptions that current provisions in the law uphold and perpetuate must be challenged. Families in themselves have changed as society has transformed, not only because of technological developments, but also due to modern attitudes and beliefs about what is acceptable in reproduction. In recognition of this, and so as not to treat people seeking parenthood through assisted conception or surrogacy differently, the method of determining legal parenthood must also be reformulated.

---

[105] E. Jackson, *Regulating Reproduction: Law, Technology and Autonomy* (Hart Publishing, 2001), at p 269.

Part IV:

The nature and scope of parental rights

15

The Myth of Parental Rights

Parental rights are commonly regarded as constituting a central moral dimension of the parent/child relationship. I will argue here that this view is mistaken. More specifically, I will offer reasons for denying that biological parents have even presumptive or qualified moral rights to affect the courses of their children's lives in significant respects. I realize full well that this position is almost certain to strike many people as counterintuitive—or even completely crazy. I hope, however, that this initial reaction does not prevent my arguments (and the explanation of moral rights that lies at the heart of these arguments) from being carefully considered.

I begin by establishing a context for my discussion by describing certain actual cases that highlight the practical importance of addressing and answering questions about the existence of parental rights. My argument against such rights (which is developed in sections 2 and 3) can be stated briefly as follows: in virtue of two features necessarily possessed by moral rights, the idea of a parental moral rights would have unacceptable implications for the parent/child relationship; hence there are good reasons for denying the existence of parental moral rights. In section 4, I reply to two objections that are likely to be raised against my position on parental rights, and in section 5, I trace the implications of my account for the actual cases described the first section.

1.

That parents do have rights regarding their children (at least under certain conditions) probably strikes most people as completely obvious. For it seems clear that parents who love and care for their children have rights (perhaps within broad limits) to determine how their children should be educated, what sort of health care they should receive, what (if any) religious doctrines they should be encouraged to accept, and so on. At the same time, however, many people are likely to have certain qualms about endorsing the idea of parental rights wholeheartedly and

48   Phillip Montague

without reservation.[1] Some of the most serious of these qualms are likely to be generated by applying the idea of parental rights to certain actual situations. Here is a sample of these situations.

Baby Doe. In Bloomington, Indiana in 1982, a six-day-old baby (who came to be known as "Baby Doe") was allowed to die of starvation and dehydration in the hospital where she was born. Baby Doe suffered from Down's Syndrome, as well as a physiological defect which prevented her from being fed or hydrated by normal means; and, although the defect was correctable by surgery, her parents decided to withhold their consent for surgery. No surgery was performed, and Baby Doe died.

The children of cult members. The Branch Davidians besieged by the F.B.I. in Waco, Texas included some 38 children, at least 17 of whom died in the ensuing fire. The parents of these children chose a certain kind of life for themselves and for their children—a life which included absolute loyalty and devotion to David Koresh, whom the children were taught was God's prophet. In selecting this kind of life, adult cult members chose to subsume their wills to that of Koresh. The children of the cult members had no opportunity to make this choice, however. Rather, their parents simply placed them in an environment which created serious barriers to the development of their capacities for autonomous decision-making.

Similar remarks could, of course, be made about the children of James Jones's followers. The parents of these children chose to lead a certain kind of life—one characterized by blind obedience to Jones's commands. The children themselves did not choose this sort of life, of course. Their parents chose it for them. And, in doing so, they reared their children in the atmosphere of absolute subservience which led ultimately to the terrible events at Jonestown in 1978.

---

[1]Jeffrey Blustein nicely characterizes one aspect of this ambivalence in the following passage: "[I]mportant to citizens in a democratic society is the idea of parental autonomy, that is, the right of parents to raise their children as they think best, in accordance with their own notions of childrearing. Some of us, perhaps, do not feel comfortable with the mode of childrearing practiced in, for example, the Amish and Hasidic communities, because of the extreme isolation from the larger community it encourages, though we are willing to concede that it is quite arbitrary to limit the scope of parental authority to childrearing that is based on secular values alone. Closer to home, many parents today are uneasy about the right to exercise authority over their own children. We believe that, as parents, we are entitled to command our children's obedience, but we worry that our use of authority may actually be inhibiting our children's growth to autonomy." Jeffrey Blustein, *Parents and Children* (New York: Oxford University Press, 1982), pp. 4-5.

Baby Jessica. Baby Jessica was adopted shortly after her birth with the consent of her mother and a man falsely identified as the baby's father. When the real father learned what had occurred, he sued for custody. He subsequently won his suit, and Baby Jessica—who was two years old by then, and who had become closely attached to her home and her adoptive parents—was returned to her biological parents.

Even the most ardent defenders of parental rights are likely to find cases like these disturbing. For if the parents involved in them are exercising parental rights, then it would appear that they have rights to act in ways that are detrimental to their children—a result that is problematic at best. Thus, if Baby Doe's parents had the right to prevent her from receiving treatment for her life-threatening condition, then they had the right to choose death over life for her. But adults (including adults who are incapable of making rational decisions about their own welfare) who suffer from life-threatening but correctable conditions routinely receive appropriate treatments. They receive treatment because correcting their conditions is deemed to be in their best interests. The question therefore arises of how Baby Doe's parents could have had the right to make a decision which (arguably, at least) was contrary to her interests.[2]

Analogous remarks apply to the children of cult members. For even though the parents of these children don't typically make life-or-death decisions for them (at least not in virtue of their cult membership), they do choose lives for their children that are largely lacking in certain enormously valuable features. These parental choices therefore seem to be contrary to the children's interests—which raises significant problems for the idea that they involve the exercise of parental rights.[3] Similar—even if perhaps less serious—problems arise in connection with Baby Jessica's removal from her adoptive parents, and the home in which she had spent almost her entire life. One must at least wonder whether her best interests were served by the change in custody; and whether, if the change were contrary to her interests, it could have resulted from the exercise of rights on the part of her biological parents.[4]

---

[2] In fact, the federal "Child Abuse and Treatment Act" was amended in 1984 so as to prohibit withholding treatment from infants in cases like that of Baby Doe. This was done by classifying such cases as involving child abuse or neglect, and without reference to parental interests (*98 Stat. 1752*).

[3] Analogous worries are appropriate for religious practices that are not commonly regarded as cults. According to some religions, for example, illnesses should be dealt with by prayer rather than by conventional medical treatments.

[4] As of this writing, a couple is suing for the custody of a six-year-old whom the couple claims is their biological child even though the woman who bore the child

To be sure, the difficulties to which these cases appear to give rise might be only apparent. But determining whether this is so definitely requires clarification of the scope of parental rights (assuming there are such rights), which in turn requires some discussion of the nature of moral rights in general.

2.

Let us begin our examination of moral rights by noting that the rights of interest to us here are "claim rights" rather than "liberty rights." The claim rights of individuals imply corresponding obligations on the part of others. Liberty rights, on the other hand, are simply permissions, where being permitted to act is equivalent to not being obligated to refrain, and implies no obligations in others. Thus, for example, you have a claim right to park in your driveway, and others are obligated not to prevent you from doing so by parking there themselves. In contrast, if you have a moral right to park in public spaces, it is a liberty right rather than a claim right, since others are not obligated to let you park in such spots by refraining from parking there themselves.

One way in which to see the difference between liberty rights and claim rights is by considering the general principles by which rights of each type might be expressed. Examples of principles affirming the existence of claim rights are easy to produce: there is a claim right to life; there is a claim right of self-defense; there is a claim right to privacy. But what about principles that affirm the existence of liberty rights? Bearing in mind that liberty rights to act are equivalent to permissions to act and hence to the absence of obligations to refrain, examples of principles affirming the existence of liberty rights can be formulated by identifying types of actions whose nonperformance is not obligatory. Accordingly, we have: there is a liberty right to eat chocolate cake; there is a liberty right to go hiking; there is a liberty right to read newspapers.[5]

---

believed she was the biological mother. According to the plaintiffs, a fertilized egg of theirs was appropriated without their permission at a fertility clinic, and inserted into the other woman. If their suit is successful, they will obtain custody of a child with whom neither of them has had any contact at all, and hence in the absence even of whatever bonding might occur between mother and child in cases like that of Baby Jessica.

[5] The permissions and obligations to which these remarks refer should be interpreted as presumptive (or prima facie) rather than as permissions and obligations all things considered. I will have more to say about this presently.

The Myth of Parental Rights

Having identified some claim rights and some liberty rights, we can now see how the former imply obligations while the latter do not. Thus, for example, one person's right of self-defense implies obligations in others not to interfere with the person's efforts to defend herself against culpable aggression. But now consider the liberty right to go hiking, say. That is, consider the idea that there is no obligation to refrain from going hiking. Clearly, the mere absence of such an obligation implies nothing about obligations on the part of others. To be sure, one person might lack an obligation to refrain from performing a particular action (that is, the person might have a liberty right to perform that action) and others might be obligated not to interfere in certain ways with that action. But this does not mean that the absence of an obligation to refrain *implies* the existence of obligations of noninterference. Neither does it imply that interference is immoral because it violates a liberty right. Indeed, the idea of liberty rights violations is peculiar at best, since it is equivalent to the idea of violating mere permissions.

Thus, consider the liberty right to go hiking. If you have this right in particular circumstances, then you are not obligated to refrain from hiking in those circumstances. Now, although I am obligated to refrain from interfering with you by tying you to a tree or by running you down with my car, these obligations are not implied by your liberty right to go hiking. Rather, they are implied by your claim rights to not be involuntarily confined and to not be physically injured. Similarly, suppose that someone is picnicking in a public parking space, thereby preventing you from parking there. While the picnicker's action might be morally impermissible in certain circumstances, it would not be impermissible because you have a liberty right to park in public parking spaces.[6] If the person were to prevent you from parking in your driveway by picnicking there, however, then her action would be impermissible in virtue of violating a right of yours—your claim right to utilize your property as you see fit.[7]

I realize that, in common parlance, the distinction between liberty rights and claim rights is often blurred. In particular, the expression "x has a right to do y" is sometimes equivalent to "It is all right (i.e., permissible) for x to do y" while at other times it entails "Others are obligated to refrain from interfering with x's doing y." To avoid

---

[6]Perhaps you have a *legal* claim right to park in the public space, and perhaps the picnicker is legally obligated to vacate the space because of your legal right. Such matters of law are irrelevant to the present discussion, however.

[7]H.L.A. Hart appeals to parallel considerations in explaining how legal liberty rights differ from legal claim rights. H.L.A. Hart, *Essays on Bentham* (Oxford: The Clarendon Press, 1982), pp. 166-69, 171-72.

confusion here, however, all subsequent references to rights will be references to claim rights unless otherwise specified.[8]

There are very good reasons (both theoretical and practical) for distinguishing between presumptive rights on the one hand and rights "all things considered" on the other.[9] Rights that are referred to in general principles (such as "People have a right of self-defense") are necessarily presumptive, whereas rights that are attributed to specific individuals can be either presumptive or rights all things considered. Thus, for example, you might have a presumptive right to defend yourself on a particular occasion but no right all things considered to do so (perhaps because you are a culpable aggressor whose intended victim is "fighting back"). Or you might have a right all things considered to defend yourself against an attack as the innocent target of culpable aggression.

One difference between presumptive rights and rights all things considered is that the former imply presumptive obligations while the latter imply obligations all things considered. Hence, the following propositions are logically compatible: you have a presumptive right to perform some action; and others are *not* obligated (all things considered) to refrain from interfering with your performance. In maintaining that there are no such things as parental rights, I am denying that parents have even *presumptive* moral rights to influence the courses of their

---

[8]I will focus here on claim rights rather than liberty rights because the idea of a parental *liberty* right cannot do the work assigned to parental rights by most writers who emphasize these latter rights. In particular, the existence of mere liberty rights on the part of parents to affect their children's lives in certain ways implies nothing about obligations on the state's part to refrain from interfering with parental decisions.

So, for example, consider the discussion of parental rights in Samantha Brennan's and Robert Noggle's paper "The Moral Status of Children: Children's Rights, Parents' Rights, and Family Justice" (*Social Theory and Practice* 23 (1997): 1-26). They state a "Limited Parental Rights Thesis," and they argue that it is compatible with certain plausible theses concerning the status of children. Nothing in their discussion suggests, however, that the parental rights to which they refer are more than mere liberties, and hence even if their arguments succeed, they do not generate any limitations on state interference with parental decisions—at least none that are tied to features of the parents.

[9]The distinction between presumptive rights and rights all things considered roughly parallels W.D. Ross's distinction between "prima facie" and "actual" duties as explained in his *The Right and the Good* (Oxford: The Clarendon Press, 1930), chap. II. See also Shelly Kagan's discussion of "pro tanto" reasons in *The Limits of Morality* (Oxford: The Clarendon Press, 1989). As it applies to rights, the nature of this distinction and the reasons for drawing it are discussed in Phillip Montague, "Davis and Westen on Rights and Compensation," *Philosophy and Public Affairs* 14 (1985): 390-96, and "When Rights are Permissibly Infringed," *Philosophical Studies* 53 (1988): 348-66.

children's lives in significant ways.

Like obligations, rights can be either special or general. Special rights are conferred on individuals by the voluntary acts of others who thereby become specially obligated to the former, as when people who borrow money confer rights to be repaid on their creditors, and obligate themselves to repay what they have borrowed. No such acts of conferral are required for the possession of general rights, however, and rather than being held against some specific individuals but not others, they are held against "the world at large." The rights to life and to privacy are general in this sense.

In addressing questions about the existence of parental rights, I will be concerned with *general* rights. If, for example, some parent had a right to determine how her child will be educated, it would not be held against some specific individual—certainly not against the child—who conferred the right by obligating himself to act or refrain in certain ways. Rather, it would be held against all those in positions to interfere with the right-holder as she implemented her decisions concerning the child's education; and all of these people would be obligated to refrain from interfering.

A problem facing anyone asking about the existence of rights of specific sorts is that explanations of the nature of rights vary widely from discussion to discussion. According to some writers, for example, rights are equivalent to their implied obligations; while other writers think of rights as composed of intricate (and somewhat bewildering) arrangements of obligations, permissions, "powers," and "immunities." In addition to containing these differing views regarding the structure of rights, philosophical discussions of rights typically incorporate claims about the primary function of rights. We cannot engage here in anything resembling an adequate examination of these various conceptions of rights, or argue in support of one over the others. But neither can we ignore the question of how rights should be interpreted as we consider the existence of parental rights.

Fortunately, discussions of rights—while differing from each other in numerous and significant respects—invariably share a common presupposition that is centrally relevant to the topic of parental rights. The presupposition is that rights are (as I will say) "oriented towards their possessors," and the meaning of this presupposition is clearly explained by L.W. Sumner in his superb book *The Moral Foundation of Rights*.[10]

---

[10]L.W. Sumner, *The Moral Foundation of Rights* (Oxford: The Clarendon Press, 1987). Sumner's discussion is extraordinarily lucid and careful; and it covers the territory occupied by theories of rights both thoroughly and in a manner which clearly reveals how

Sumner's explanation is best understood in light of the distinction he draws between "interest" and "choice" conceptions of rights. He characterizes these two conceptions in this passage:

> The interest conception treats rights as devices for promoting individual welfare. Thus the dominating image here is of the right-holder as the passive beneficiary of a network of protective and supportive duties shared by others . . . . On the other hand, the choice conception treats rights as devices for promoting freedom or autonomy. Thus the dominating image here is of the right-holder as the active manager of a network of normative relations connecting her to others . . ..[11]

While recognizing the respects in which the interest and choice conceptions differ from each other, we must bear in mind that the two conceptions have a significant feature in common. As Sumner points out, the two conceptions

> share a commitment to the root idea that the function of rights is to serve as one kind of constraint on the pursuit of social goals. Thus they share the conviction that . . . rights . . . must protect their holders by imposing normative constrains on others . . ..[12]

This remark matches the spirit (and perhaps even the letter) of familiar claims about the fundamental opposition between rights and utility.[13] It is also reflected, however, in accounts that attempt to embed rights within utilitarian moral theories.[14]

More to the present point, Sumner's remark about the protection that rights afford their possessors implies that rights play a distinctive role in moral theory. They play this role in virtue of possessing a certain essential feature; and it is this feature that I have in mind in referring to rights as oriented towards their possessors.[15] Although centrally important for

---

varied these theories are, and how complex they can be. This appraisal of Sumner's book should not be interpreted, however, as endorsing the particular account of rights which he accepts and for which he argues.

[11]Sumner, p. 47.

[12]Ibid.

[13]For example, Ronald Dworkin focuses on what "might be called the anti-utilitarian concept of a right . . . [which] seems to me very close to the sense of right principally used in political and legal writing in recent years." Ronald Dworkin, *Taking Rights Seriously* (Cambridge, Mass.: Harvard University Press, 1977), p. 269.

[14]See David Lyons, "Rights, Claimants, and Beneficiaries," in David Lyons (ed.), *Rights* (Belmont, Cal.: Wadsworth Publishing Co., 1979), pp. 58-77. This volume also contains H.L.A. Hart's related discussion, "Bentham on Legal Rights" (pp. 127-48).

[15]I am claiming here that rights are necessarily oriented towards their possessors, and I will presently emphasize the importance of clearly distinguishing rights from obligations. This might seem to imply that I regard obligations as necessarily oriented towards individuals other than their possessors—that a person's obligations cannot serve to

moral theory, moreover, this feature of rights is no mere theoretical artifact. It is clearly reflected in laws, policies, and commissions concerned with human and civil rights, as well as in documents such as the Universal Declaration of Human Rights and the Bill of Rights.

Bearing in mind that rights are essentially oriented towards their possessors, let us now attempt to apply the interest and choice conceptions to parental rights.

If the interest conception is to accommodate parental rights, then these rights (or perhaps their implied obligations) must serve as protections of parental interests. As Sumner's remarks suggest, the interest conception would depict a parent "as the passive beneficiary of a network of protective and supportive duties shared by others." But even if the right of parents to care for their children (assuming there is such a right) has *something* to do with protecting parental interests (the interests they have in their children's welfare, presumably) the protection of parental interests could not plausibly be regarded as fundamental—at least not if parental rights comprise a central moral component of the parent/child relation. The interest parents have in their children's welfare is worth protecting because the welfare of their children is worth protecting. Indeed, to the extent that the interest conception is seen as capable of accommodating parental rights, to that extent parental rights become closely associated with property rights. Given that children are nothing like property, however, such an association would be seriously objectionable.

According to the choice conception of rights, parents would have rights to make decisions regarding the well-being of their children only if there is an appropriately corresponding area of activity within which parents have moral discretion whether to act. Bearing in mind that rights are oriented towards their possessors, and also that becoming and being a parent very significantly affects one's life, it seems reasonable to group the areas of activity that correspond to parental rights under the heading of those relative to which right-holders shape their lives in significant respects. Now, we all know about parents who treat their children as vehicles for their own development, but we also recognize that these parents seriously distort the parent/child relationship. Hence, to the extent that parental decisions regarding their children are *properly*

---

protect or benefit that person. In fact, however, I take no stand on this issue—and I need not do so for the purposes of this discussion. I therefore take no stand on whether there are "obligations to self"—whether, for example, there are Rossian "duties of self-improvement" (as referred to in *The Right and the Good*, p. 21).

concerned with the promotion and protection of autonomy, these decisions *directly* relate to the autonomy of the children, and only indirectly concern that of the parents.

The points being made here are reflected in remarks by Jeffrey Blustein in his illuminating discussion of parental rights. As Blustein points out, parental rights might be interpreted in a variety of ways.

> On the one hand, parents' right to raise their children as they think best is thought of as a particular instance of the right to privacy that belongs to every free citizen in a free society. Like the right to be free of annoyance in one's house, or the right to enjoy the use of a piece of property without interference from others, the right to autonomy in child-rearing recognizes the individual's legitimate interest in having a well-defined zone within which one need not be on the alert against possible observations and intrusions. The interest protected by parental autonomy is here the *parent's* interest, just as the interest protected by the right of private property is the property owner's interest.[16]

Blustein goes on to claim, however, that

> [p]arents . . . do have the right to a certain degree of autonomy . . . But such autonomy is justified only insofar as it is not inconsistent with the performance of parental responsibilities . . . individuals do not forfeit all of their responsibility by founding families and becoming parents, but then, as parents, they also have a responsibility to serve their children and so must adjust their individual needs and personal goals to the needs and legitimate demands of their children.[17]

This idea—that the interests or autonomy of parents is worth promoting and protecting only indirectly, and in virtue of its connection with the importance of protecting the interests or autonomy of others—has no parallel for other rights and their possessors. Other rights serve to protect their possessors' interests or autonomy because the autonomy of right-holders is worth protecting in and of itself. For example, the right to privacy can reasonably be viewed as protecting its possessors' autonomy in determining the disposition of personal information about themselves because of the value such autonomy has for the right-holders. Again we have a manifestation of the orientation of rights towards their possessors—an orientation that seriously undermines the very idea of a parental right.

But are there not counterexamples to this idea of rights being oriented towards their possessors? Aren't there clear cases of rights whose possessors are *not* the individuals whose interests or choices the rights are supposed to protect? For example, is it not the case that attorneys have a right to preserve confidence between themselves and their clients

---

[16]Blustein, p. 5.
[17]Ibid., p. 12.

—rights whose purpose is to protect the clients? And don't physicians have a right to recommend what they regard as appropriate treatments for their patients—which rights are supposed to protect the patients? If these questions should be answered affirmatively, then there is no very good reason to doubt that parents have rights whose purpose is to protect the interests of their children.[18] In fact, however, the questions I have posed should be answered negatively: attorneys and physicians *don't* have the rights in question. I will explain why this is so presently, but I must first lay some additional groundwork.

3.

The remarks of the preceding section point to a kind of tension that exists between the concept of a parental right on the one hand, and a certain feature of the parent/child relation on the other. Very roughly, the idea is this: If there are parental rights, then their purpose is to protect the interests of choices of parents. At the heart of the parent/child relationship, however, are responsibilities or obligations that parents have to protect the interests of their children, and to nurture their children's decision-making abilities. A closer look at these parental obligations will shed useful light on the topic of parental rights.

The clearest examples of parental obligations are those incurred by people who deliberately procreate. These parental obligations are "child-centered," in that their being fulfilled consists in parents' performing actions that benefit their children regardless of how these actions affect the parents themselves. If there were parental rights, however, these would be parent-centered, because of the orientation all rights have towards their possessors. The difference here is of considerable practical importance: emphasizing parental rights focuses attention on what's good for parents, while emphasizing parental obligations accentuates the welfare of children.

The question that must be addressed, then, is whether parents who are obligated to care for their children have *rights* to provide that care. And the following argument supports a negative answer to this question: parental decisions regarding their children comprise an area replete with *obligations* on the part of parents to affect the lives of their children in ways that protect their well-being; since parental rights to care for their children are incompatible with parental obligations to do so, there are no

---

[18] I am indebted to an anonymous referee for pointing out the need to address these questions.

parental rights. Although this argument applies only to people who deliberately procreate, if these people do indeed lack parental rights, then such rights certainly could not be possessed by people who procreate unintentionally.

But, one might ask, how does the existence of parental obligations to protect their children's well-being cast any doubt on whether parents have rights in this area? After all, people do often claim to have both rights and obligations (or responsibilities) to perform certain sorts of actions. Why couldn't a proponent of parental rights maintain that parents have *both* rights *and* obligations to care for their children—perhaps agreeing with David Archard when he says that

> if ... [parents] do have a right to rear it is plausible to think that it derives from and is consequently dependent upon the prior duty to give a child the best possible upbringing.[19]

For a statement like Archard's to be true, parental rights must of course be oriented towards both the parents and their children; and the possibility that this is so cannot reasonably be rejected out of hand.

The general point at issue here is sometimes investigated under the heading of whether there are rights which Joel Feinberg has labeled "mandatory." According to Feinberg, mandatory rights are

> best understood as ordinary duties with associated half-liberties rather than ordinary claim-rights with associated full liberties, but ... the performance of the duty is presumed to be so beneficial to the person whose duty it is that he can *claim* the necessary means [to exercise the "right"] from the state and noninterference from others as *his due*. Its character as claim is precisely what his half-liberty shares with the more usual (discretionary) rights and what motivates his use of the word "right" in demanding it.[20]

Half-liberties are permissions to act, and do not include permissions to refrain; whereas full liberties are equivalent to permissions to act or to refrain. Hence, half-liberties are compatible with obligations to act, while full liberties are not.

According to Feinberg, then, mandatory rights are like ordinary duties in that they imply half-liberties rather than full liberties.[21] So what

---

[19] David Archard, *Children: Rights and Childhood* (London: Routledge, 1993), p. 130.

[20] Joel Feinberg, "The Nature and Value of Rights," *Journal of Value Inquiry* 4 (1970): 263-67, p. 253.

[21] Feinberg's emphasis on the distinction between these two types of liberties is particularly appropriate if rights are interpreted within the choice conception. For according to this conception, rights correspond to areas of activity within which right-holders have discretion *whether to act or to refrain from acting*. This discretion is clearly

The Myth of Parental Rights

purpose is served by the label "mandatory right"? Feinberg evidently suggests that this label provides a way in which to identify duties that share a certain feature with rights—namely, that of being oriented towards their possessors. In his words, "the duty is presumed to be . . . beneficial to the person whose duty it is." If Feinberg's construal of mandatory rights is correct (as I believe it is), then if all (or any) parental obligations are interpreted as mandatory rights, then the purpose of those obligations is to benefit the parents. Hence, the result of interpreting parental rights as mandatory would not be a class of rights whose orientation is to individuals other than their possessors, something that I believe is impossible. Rather, the result would be a class of obligations—parental obligations—that are oriented towards their possessors: parents. Relying on the idea that parental rights are mandatory therefore helps not at all to avoid the arguments I am advancing against parental rights.

In addition to equating mandatory rights with duties that are oriented towards their possessors, Feinberg distinguishes them from "more usual" rights. He labels the latter "discretionary" rights in virtue of their relation to full liberties rather than the half-liberties to which mandatory rights are related. The more usual discretionary rights to which Feinberg refers presumably include rights to privacy, to freedom of religious practice, and to bodily autonomy. If there are such things as mandatory rights, then, they differ significantly from rights that quintessentially instantiate the concept of a right.

As noted above, I agree with Feinberg's suggestion that mandatory rights are nothing more than obligations whose orientation is towards their possessors. Perhaps there are such obligations, and perhaps the expression "mandatory right" is of some use in referring to them. But talk of mandatory rights is also a source of considerable confusion, and I think it ought to be abandoned. My main point here is substantive rather

---

equivalent to a *full* liberty, and is therefore incompatible with being obligated to act or to refrain. So if parents are obligated to provide for the well-being of their children, then they cannot have rights to do so. But why, one might ask, could not the choice conception regard rights as associated with *half-* rather than full liberties?

As Sumner persuasively argues, rights do not really protect freedom or autonomy if they imply only the absence of obligations to refrain (Sumner, pp. 27-49, passim). If you are permitted to act but are prohibited from refraining, then there is a significant respect in which your freedom or autonomy is limited. Indeed, if there were such things as mandatory rights—rights which their possessors are obligated to exercise—then the question would arise of how such rights would differ from obligations. And the reply to this question suggested by Feinberg's remarks is that the two would be indistinguishable.

than terminological, however. My substantive claim is not that parental rights (or any class of rights, for that matter) can be legislated out of existence simply by labeling them "obligations" rather than "mandatory rights." What I am arguing is that paradigmatic rights are discretionary, and are oriented towards their possessors; and that there are no such things as parental discretionary rights. That is, there are no parental rights that occupy the same distinctive niche in moral theory as do privacy rights, property rights, the right of self-defense, the right to freedom of religious practice, and so on. The theoretical niche occupied by these rights is importantly different from that occupied by obligations to keep promises, to refrain from harming others, and so on—as well as by "mandatory rights."

So when people affirm the existence of parental rights, do they have discretionary or mandatory rights in mind? My guess is that they have discretionary rights in mind—that is, rights of a type exemplified by rights to privacy and to freedom of religious practice. Answering this factual question is far less important here, however, than is spelling out the implications of there being parental rights, and doing so within a theoretical framework that illuminates both the nature of rights and their relation to obligations.[22]

---

[22] In drawing a sharp conceptual distinction between rights and obligations (including any obligations that belong under the heading "mandatory rights"), there are several things that I am not doing.

First of all, I am not denying that some particular action could be the exercise of a right under certain conditions and the fulfillment of an obligation under others. Consider, for example, your driving to Seattle on a particular occasion. If you promised someone to make the trip, then you are obligated to do so. Typically, however, you would be exercising a right. Although your action could fall within the scope of either of two general principles, one about rights and the other about obligations, this does not imply that your action could be (all things considered) both the exercise of a right and the fulfillment of an obligation. Here is an analogy: depending on circumstances, a particular action of yours could fall within the scope of a principle affirming the obligatoriness of some type of action, or a principle affirming the existence of a prohibition; this would not imply that your action could be both obligatory and prohibited (all things considered).

Nor am I denying that a highly generic *type* of action could be both the exercise of a (standard or "discretionary") right in virtue of its relation to a rights-principle, and the fulfillment of an obligation in virtue of its relation to an obligation-principle. For example, protesting unjust laws could be viewed as a right because of its relation to the (discretionary) right of free speech, and an obligation because of its relation to the obligation to fight injustice. But this would not imply that there is some special kind of right—a mandatory right—which people are obligated to exercise, and which is exemplified by the right to protest unjust laws. Here is an analogy: breaking a promise to avoid harming someone can be viewed as obligatory because of its relation to the obligation to refrain from doing harm, and as prohibited because of its relation to the prohibition against breaking promises. This would not imply that there is a special class of

The Myth of Parental Rights

Now, what has been said here about parental rights applies *mutatis mutandis* to the idea (alluded to above) that attorneys and physicians respectively have rights to keep dealings with their clients confidential and to recommend appropriate treatments for their patients. In fact, lawyers and doctors have *obligations* to do these things because they lack discretion in the areas referred to; and since (as I have argued) there are no such things as nondiscretionary or mandatory rights, attorneys and physicians don't have rights to preserve confidentiality and to recommend treatment. Indeed, a central point about the idea of parental rights that I am making here applies as well to the idea of attorneys' and physicians' rights.

That is, characterizing the roles of attorneys and of physicians vis-à-vis their clients and patients in terms of *rights* has unacceptable implications for the attorney/client and physician/patient relations. These relations should rather be thought of in terms of obligations that attorneys and physicians have to their clients and patients respectively. Not only does this shift in emphasis from rights to obligations have enormous advantages when attempting to explain the moral dimensions of the attorney/client and physician/patient relations, but it has absolutely no disadvantages.

To summarize:

Parental obligations are obligations that are rooted in the parent/child relationship—obligations that people have in virtue of being parents. Broadly speaking, these are obligations that parents have to protect and promote the welfare of their young children; and they are not derived from more basic obligations to protect or promote the welfare of others—of parents in particular. That is, parental obligations are oriented

---

obligations—namely, those that are also prohibitions—a member of which is the obligation to break promises in order to avoid doing harm.

Now consider the following type of action: parents' educating their children. This type of action might fall under two general principles, one of which affirms the existence of a discretionary right (call this principle R), and the other of which affirms the existence of an obligation (principle O). This would not by itself imply the existence of a mandatory parental right to care for one's children, however. To see this, note first of all that O is "Parents are obligated to care for their children." What is R? The most plausible candidates for this principle would refer to the discretionary rights of people to make certain choices about their own lives that happen to overlap with their educating their children. So even if parents' educating their children (interpreted as a general type of action) can fall under a rights-principle and an obligation-principle, this would not imply that parents have a mandatory right to care for their children in virtue of being their parents. It just so happens that our educating our children commonly coincides with acting in ways that are good for us.

towards children rather than parents. Moreover, while parents have broad discretion regarding *how* to fulfill their obligations, they do not have discretion regarding *whether* to fulfill them. That is, parental obligations imply half- rather than whole-liberties. Suppose now that there are such things as parental rights—rights that are rooted in the parent/child relationship that people have in virtue of being parents. Suppose that these are rights that parents have to protect and to promote the welfare of their children. Then, given the nature of rights, parents have discretion whether to protect the welfare of their children; and this conclusion is incompatible with the existence of parental obligations. Introducing the idea that parental rights are mandatory rather than discretionary (assuming that there are such things as mandatory rights) would allow parental rights to be compatible with parental obligations. They would be mutually compatible because mandatory rights are obligations of a certain type—namely, those that are oriented towards their possessors. Parental mandatory rights to protect the welfare or their children would therefore be oriented towards parents rather than children, which is contrary to a fundamental moral feature of the parent/child relationship.

4.

A fairly obvious response to my rejection of parental rights runs along these lines: although the existence of parental obligations implies that parents lack discretion regarding *whether* to care for their children, parents certainly have discretion concerning *how* to care for them; and the existence of this discretion implies that parents do indeed have rights regarding their children. As we shall now see, however, the discretion to which this reply refers can be accounted for within the realm of parental obligations, and without assuming that there are parental rights.

Our first step here is to take note of a certain feature of obligations—namely, that being obligated to act is being obligated to perform a *type* of act rather than any specific token of that type. Suppose, for example, that you are obligated to return a borrowed book by Friday, February 4. You might fulfill this obligation by, say, returning the book in person, on Tuesday, February 1, at 9:03 a.m., in the company of . . . ; or perhaps by returning it by mail on Monday, January 31, ... And you are permitted to select any of these particular actions as the means by which you fulfill your obligation. The fact that you are permitted to determine how exactly you fulfill your obligation does not, however, imply that you have *rights* to act according to these choices. No one is obligated (not even presumptively so) to refrain from interfering with your fulfilling your obligation *in a particular way,* as long as this does not, in the circumstances, prevent you from fulfilling your obligation.

Note too that having discretion regarding how to fulfill one's obligations is very different from having discretion to determine *what counts as* fulfilling one's obligation. For example, if I borrow one hundred dollars from you, and promise to repay you within one week, then I have discretion regarding how to fulfill the obligation I incur by my actions. I may, for example, repay you the next day, or two days later, and so on—as long as I do so within a week of borrowing the money. I may also decide whether to repay you in cash or by check, in person or by mail, and so on. But suppose I send you a one hundred dollar gift certificate to a local restaurant, and that I consider myself as having fulfilled my obligation in doing so. It does not follow that my action counts as having repaid you. Or suppose a student of mine asks me to write a letter on her behalf to a law school, and that I promise to do so. I clearly have considerable discretion regarding how I fulfill my obligation to the student—in particular, regarding what I say in the letter. Suppose that, while I know a great deal about the student's academic and intellectual abilities, I devote the entire letter to recounting the student's considerable athletic accomplishments. Even if I regard myself as having fulfilled my obligation to her, it does not follow that my writing the letter counts as having done so.

So we can deny that there are such things as parental rights while accounting for any latitude that parents have in making certain decisions affecting their children's lives in terms of permissions people have to select the specific ways in which they fulfill their obligations. We can also acknowledge that people are obligated not to interfere with parents as they implement certain decisions regarding their children's welfare while denying that they have rights to implement those decisions.[23] Failure to recognize these points can generate faulty inferences in discussions of parental rights. For example, Archard regards the following excerpt from a Supreme Court decision as "an admirably clear statement" of parents' rights to autonomy and to privacy in the rearing of their children:[24]

---

[23] If, for example, you are obligated to return a borrowed book, then others are surely obligated (presumptively, at any rate) to refrain from interfering with your doing so. Hence, even if people are obligated not to interfere with parents as they implement their decisions concerning their children's welfare, this does not imply that parents have *rights* to implement these decisions.

[24] Archard, pp. 122-23.

it is cardinal with us that the custody, care and nurture of the child reside first in the parents, whose primary function and freedom include preparation for obligations the state can neither supply nor hinder.[25]

Contrary to Archard's suggested interpretation, however, the reference in this passage to freedom in preparation for obligations conforms quite closely to what has been said here about the relation between parental discretion and parental obligations. And the reference is open to a plausible interpretation under which it implies nothing at all about the existence of parental rights.

Even if everything said about parental discretion to this point is true, however, one might question whether it justifies the wholesale rejection of parental rights. For even if apparent parental rights to provide children with educations, with medical care, and so on turn out to be explicable in terms of references to parental obligations and the freedom parents have in choosing how to fulfill their obligations, not all of the rights parents seem to have regarding their children are obviously open to this sort of explanation.

Consider, for example, Al's (apparent) right to determine how if at all his daughter Brenda is to be religiously educated. It seems implausible to regard religious education as within the scope of Al's obligations regarding Brenda—to see him as obligated to provide her with religious training, and as having latitude only in the choice of how to fulfill his obligation. If religious education is not within the scope of his obligations regarding Brenda, and if others are obligated not to interfere with Al as he implements his decisions concerning Brenda's religious training (something which certainly seems to be true), then there is very good reason to believe that Al has a certain right regarding Brenda.

Suppose, however, that the basic tenets of some particular religion are true. Then (other things being equal) it would appear to be in Brenda's best interests to learn these tenets. If, on the other hand, the central doctrines of all religions are false, then (again, other things being equal) Brenda would evidently be better off without religious education than with it. To be sure, Al—like other parents—might have considerable difficulty acquiring knowledge of which of these alternatives is the correct one. And, because of this difficulty, he and other parents should be afforded wide latitude in their choices of whether and (if so) how their children should be religiously educated. But the fact would remain that these choices concern the welfare of children, and hence fall within

---

[25]The passage is quoted by Archard on p. 123. It is from *Prince vs. Commonwealth of Massachusetts*, 321 *U.S.* 158.

the scope of parental obligations rather than rights.

A second potential difficulty associated with the rejection of parental rights concerns the apparently clear presumption in favor of allowing biological parents to rear the children they beget or bear. In the absence of such a presumption, there would seem to be no explaining why children should not be removed from the custody of their biological parents without extremely good reasons. And if parents have no rights regarding their children, then the moral presumption in favor of biological parenthood would appear to be groundless.[26]

One possible reply to this objection is to deny the existence of the presumption to which it refers. Alternatively, one might acknowledge that there is such a presumption and attempt to ground it on certain facts about the bad effects on children of discontinuities in their early development, together with facts about the role biological parents typically play in maintaining continuity. I will not rely on either of these replies here, however. Instead, I will appeal to a feature of obligations appealed to in considering the notion of a mandatory right. I refer to the fact that people are in general obligated (presumptively, that is) not to prevent others from fulfilling their obligations. This feature is possessed by parental obligations no less than by obligations of other sorts, and

---

[26]Ferdinand Schoeman addresses these issues in an important and insightful paper concerned with the existence of parental rights (Ferdinand Schoeman, "Rights of Children, Rights of Parents, and the Moral Basis of the Family," *Ethics* 91 (1980): 6-19). Schoeman argues that people have "a right to intimate relationships"; that "biological parents have a presumptive right to keep their children under their care" (p. 8); and "the parent's right to raise her children in a family stems naturally from the right to intimate relationships" (p. 14). According to Schoeman, parental rights include the right "to make important decisions about the kinds of influences they want the[ir] children to experience," and parents are entitled "to wide latitude in remedying what they regard as faults in the children's behavior" (p. 10). Schoeman's position on parental rights therefore appears to disagree with the one developed here in important respects.

But, immediately after issuing this unequivocal endorsement of parental rights, Schoeman retreats to a much more modest position. He introduces "moral claims as distinct from moral rights, claims being justified on the basis of their importance to our present conditions"; and he says that "rather than arguing that we have a moral right to family autonomy . . ., I will be content in encouraging a kind of appreciation for the meaning of the family over and above the recognition of its accomplishments as an institution dedicated to the production of future citizens" (p. 16).

Contrary to initial appearances, then, Schoeman's position on parental rights—that is, the position for which he argues—is not at odds with the one presented here. Denying that there are parental rights is completely compatible with affirming the existence of good moral reasons for creating and maintaining conditions in which families—as incorporating intimate relationships—endure and thrive. However, whether these good moral reasons should be explained in terms of Schoeman's concept of a claim is impossible to determine without a fuller explanation of the concept than he provides.

hence people are obligated not to prevent parents from fulfilling their obligations to care for their children. We therefore have an explanation of the presumption in favor of biological parenthood that does not presuppose that parents have *rights* to care for their children.

5.

Let us now apply some of the things that have been said here about parental rights to the particular cases described in section 1: the cases of Baby Doe, the children of cult members, and Baby Jessica.

In considering the Baby Doe case, we will find it useful to compare it with other cases in which decisions must be made regarding whether to treat life-threatening but correctable conditions in individuals who are incapable of making rational decisions about their own welfare. Typically in these cases, attempts are made to find appropriate surrogate decision-makers, and the normal choices for such surrogates are the spouses or the adult children or other family members of the patients. One very important reason for selecting these people as surrogates is that they are presumed to be particularly well situated to determine whether treatment would be in the best interests of the patients. And this latter consideration would clearly play a major role in setting policies that stipulate which individuals are to function as surrogate decision-makers in the cases in question.

Now, if individuals designated as surrogates have moral *rights* to serve in that capacity, then the policies should aim at protecting not only the interests of the patients, but also the interests (or choices) of those who have the right to serve as surrogates. But the policies in question have no such aim—nor should they have. Their point is to establish mechanisms that are likely to protect *patient* interests, not the interests of spouses or family members. Hence, assuming that these latter individuals are not designated as surrogates by the patients (in a durable power of attorney, say), they should not be regarded as having rights to serve in that capacity.

The effect of denying that there are parental rights is to locate Baby Doe and her parents in the broader context of incompetent individuals who need life-sustaining treatment, and individuals who are best suited to serve as surrogate decision-makers. Perhaps the selection of Baby Doe's parents as surrogates was a correct one; and perhaps parents in relevantly similar positions should be selected as a matter of policy. But the reasons for such selections would have nothing to do with parental rights and interests; rather, they would concern the infants' interests. So

The Myth of Parental Rights

in determining whether particular cases should count as exceptions to general policies designating surrogate decision-makers, no weight at all should be given to parental interests when treatment of infants is at issue—just as no weight should be given to the interests of spouses or other family members in cases involving incompetent adults.[27]

Similarly, if there are no such things as parental rights, then the decision whether to award custody of Baby Jessica to her biological father should focus on Baby Jessica's interests, and give no weight at all to her father's. To be sure, this sort of focus need not result in a decision different from the one actually reached by the Court. Perhaps Baby Jessica's long term interests are best served by being returned to the custody of her biological parents. The fact remains, however, that—in the absence of parental rights—there is no basis for considering the interests of biological parents in decisions regarding custody of their children.

Cases involving children of cult members are in many respects much more complicated than are those of Baby Doe and Baby Jessica. True, if there are no such things as parental rights, then information about parental interests in these cases is irrelevant to how their children should be treated; but determining whether cults create environments that are contrary to the children's interests is no easy matter. For (as noted earlier) these cases are disturbing partly because the children in them are reared in environments that hinder the development of their capacities for independent thinking and rational decision-making. The extent to which these capacities are developed *outside* of cults is enormously varied, however, and less than maximal development certainly provides no general justification for action.

The problems here are especially evident in the development of public policies aimed at protecting the interests of children. As we all know, such policies often (and perhaps inevitably) function as blunt instruments when applied to particular cases; and the individuals responsible for implementation will find it very difficult to convert these instruments to the scalpels they need in order to do what is best for the children whom the policies are supposed to protect. In the midst of all these complexities (and in the absence of parental rights), however, it

---

[27]One might claim, of course, that children's interests conflict with parental interests in cases like that of Baby Doe, and go on to maintain that, in such cases, children's interests should take precedence. The position being taken here, however, is that parental interests should play no role at all in decisions concerning protecting their young children from being harmed.

remains true that parental interests should be given no weight in decisions regarding what—if anything—should be done with the children of cult members.

The preceding remarks should clearly reveal that rejecting parental rights and explaining putative parental rights in terms of parental obligations is no mere terminological matter. To be sure, the clarity of this revelation depends heavily on how rights are explained, and on how rights are related to obligations within moral theory. The theoretical position taken here is, I believe, eminently defensible. It emphasizes the discretionary character of rights, together with their orientation towards right-holders; and these two features create a gulf between rights and obligations that is of considerable theoretical and practical importance. If the theoretical claims made here are correct, then emphasizing parental rights necessarily de-emphasizes parental obligations. As a result, parents can quite properly have their own interests primarily in mind as they make decisions that significantly affect the courses of their children's lives. Assuming (as we surely must) that, morally speaking, the parent/child relation centers on the interests of children rather than parents, there are very good reasons to reject the idea of parental rights in favor of the idea of parental obligations.

Phillip Montague

16

Conceptions of Parental Autonomy

COLIN M. MACLEOD

> They fuck you up, your mum and dad.
> They may not mean to, but they do.
> They fill you with the faults they had
> And add some extra, just for you
> —Philip Larkin
> *This Be The Verse*

Larkin's acerbic lines nicely capture the peculiarly ambiguous status of the family in contemporary political discussion and debate. On the one hand, the family is widely celebrated and venerated as the most important and valuable institution of culture and society. The sort of love, personal intimacy, and shared projects that are realizable within the context of a family are goods that many people prize above all others. It is commonplace for parents to report that raising children, though demanding and difficult, is a profoundly rewarding experience. Similarly, participating in the ongoing life of a family can be a source of great

---

I would like thank Avigail Eisenberg, Alistair Macleod, Robert Noggle, John Russell, Karen Wendling, and the editors of *Politics & Society* for helpful comments and advice. Earlier versions of this article were presented at the Centre for Applied Ethics at the University of British Columbia and at the meetings of the Canadian Philosophical Association in May 1995. I am grateful for the opportunities for discussion of my arguments that these occasions afforded. Much of the research for this article was completed while I was a postdoctoral fellow in the Department of Philosophy and the Centre for Applied Ethics at the University of British Columbia. I gratefully acknowledge the financial support I received during this time from the Social Sciences and Humanities Research Council of Canada and the Killam Foundation. Finally, although he is too young even to understand these words, I must also note the added inspiration for this project that was provided by my son, Stefan Mikael Eisenberg Macleod.

value to all its members. The enormous expansion in and demand for access to new reproductive technology provides further evidence of the enduring importance placed on the family. People are prepared to assume significant risks and expend huge sums of money on such technology just to have a family. On the other hand, the family is viewed with justifiable degree of suspicion and mistrust. The family is often the site of hideous violence, abuse, and oppression. Moreover, the enormous power and influence exercised by families over children partly explains the social reproduction of various types of injustice. A child's earliest lessons in bigotry often begin at home. As feminists have long pointed out, patriarchy and misogyny are frequently nourished and perpetuated in the traditional family.

The morally ambiguous reputation of the family has important consequences for various controversies that currently rage. It suggests, for instance, that the rhetoric of neoconservatives who call for a return to traditional family values, at best, reflects naive nostalgia for the patriarchal nuclear family or, at worst, callous indifference to gendered inequality and familial injustice. Yet, even from a radical point of view, it is difficult to accept with equanimity the current crisis of the modern family. The decline of the patriarchal family will be a hollow victory for justice if it is accompanied by a deep fracturing of the affective ties on which the genuine goods realizable in healthy families so deeply depend. The abolition of all family structures in which parents enjoy a measure of authority over their children is not a politically feasible objective, nor is it a desirable one. There is, instead, a pressing need to reconstruct the family in a way that accommodates the opportunities for human flourishing it offers, while ensuring that it does not become contaminated by injustice. Politically, the reconstruction of the family will prove to be an enormously difficult task. But it is also surprisingly difficult to articulate the ideal that we might strive to attain. An adequate theory of justice in the family is remarkably elusive.

THE PROBLEM OF PARENTAL AUTONOMY

The objective of this article is to explore, in a preliminary fashion, one of the deep problems that faces theories that try to grapple with the nature of justice in the family.[1] I call this the problem of parental autonomy. The problem of parental autonomy is motivated by the following three general observations. First, children (especially very young children) are vulnerable, impressionable, and dependent on adults. It is an almost banal truth of developmental psychology that the physical and social environment in which a child grows up can profoundly affect the sort of person she becomes in full maturity. The development of cognitive and physical capacities may be permanently retarded by neglect of a child's health and nutritional needs. Similarly, a social environment in which various beliefs, convictions, and commitments are inculcated in the young through the conscious or unconscious employment of subtle and not so subtle techniques of indoctrination can profoundly influence the sort of person a child may become and the sort of life she can lead. A child's social environment can shape and limit her future options in life. It also may affect the degree to which she is able to acquire the capacities needed for realization of meaningful individual autonomy. Second, young children cannot be given, at least in any unqualified manner, the rights to direct their own lives that are generally thought to be among the legitimate prerogatives of mature adults. The moral, emotional, and cognitive capacities that are necessary for prudent and meaningful exercise of such rights—capacities we generally assume adults to have acquired at least to the minimal degree required— are insufficiently developed in children to warrant full extension of such rights to them. In order to safeguard and promote the present and future interests of children, it is necessary that someone other than the child assume responsibility for many elements of the child's life. Third, those who accept the responsibility of raising children frequently do so because the project of creating and raising a family is an important, indeed often fundamental, element of their own life plans. Viewed from this perspective, parents cannot be seen as mere guardians of their children's interests. They are also people for whom creating a family is a project from which they may derive substantial value. They have an interest in the family as a vehicle through which some of their own distinctive commitments and convictions can be realized and perpetuated. Directing parts of the family's life is tied to the parents' control over their own lives. The basic problem of parental autonomy that these observations generate is: What is the nature and extent of parental prerogatives and responsibilities in raising children in light of the child's interests in leading a good life (both as a child and as a future adult) given independent and potentially conflicting interests parents have in shaping and directly their children's lives.[2]

This is not a merely theoretical problem. Many familiar controversies turn on how the principle of parental autonomy is characterized. Parents have sought to justify controversial traditional practices of foot binding, clitoridectomy, the denial of life-saving blood transfusions, and the administration of corporal punishment by appeal to the special authority and prerogatives that purportedly accompany parenthood. Less dramatically, but perhaps not less significantly, parental autonomy is often said to ground the legitimacy of parental attempts to transmit particular religious values to their children. Thus some parents claim a right to send children to special religious schools or even to exempt children from all but very minimal educational requirements mandated by the state. More generally, parents are often assumed to have the right to insulate children from exposure to values that are rejected by parents. Commentators disagree about how these various controversies should be resolved partly because they disagree about the appropriate contours of the principle of parental autonomy.

Virtually everyone agrees that there are some limits to the scope of parental autonomy. Parents are not allowed to abuse their children physically or emotionally, nor can they deny them access to some form of basic education. In theory this means that the protection of certain basic interests of children enjoys absolute priority over the exercise of parental autonomy. Stated somewhat differently, children have certain rights qua children that cannot legitimately be overridden by the decisions of their parents. Although this view may once have been the subject of controversy,[3] we now recognize that any plausible account of the nature of parental autonomy must be compatible with what I shall call the Minimum Provision Thesis (MPT). It holds that children are entitled, at the very least, to basic nourishment, clothing, shelter, health care, and sufficient education to permit the acquisition of literacy.[4] A satisfactory account of parental autonomy must be compatible with the MPT in the sense that parents are not entitled to exercise their prerogatives in ways that are inconsistent with the requirements of the MPT. Since there is broad acceptance of something like the MPT, I shall restrict my attention to arguments that accept it. The particular aspect of the problem of parental autonomy I will consider surrounds the degree to which parents may exercise their authority in the attempt to transmit to their children distinctive conceptions of *the good*. By conceptions of the good, I mean the various religious, cultural, philosophical, or moral commitments that adults have and that are viewed as important to leading a good life. I am interested in considering different responses to the question: To what degree can parents legitimately undertake efforts to ensure that their children become committed to conceptions of the good favored by their parents?

The rest of the article is devoted to exploring different answers to this question. I will start by briefly identifying some of the general background considerations that are relevant to constructing a more comprehensive account of the nature of parental autonomy. Second, I will describe three competing conceptions or models of the appropriate scope of the principle of parental autonomy that have recently been advanced by different theorists. I will argue that although each conception identifies some important ingredients of a satisfactory account of parental autonomy, they are all unsatisfactory. Indeed, I suggest they are all self-defeating. Finally, I will articulate, in a preliminary fashion, the outlines of an alternative and more adequate conception of the principle of parental autonomy.

BACKGROUND JUSTIFICATORY FRAMEWORK AND ASSUMPTIONS

Disagreement about the appropriate contours of the principle of parental autonomy is driven by competing interpretations of the nature and significance of the different interests that are at stake. In pursuing the problem of parental autonomy I shall assume that such interpretive differences occur within a certain shared fundamental commitment to the essential moral equality of all persons, including children.[5] As Ronald Dworkin describes it, the abstract animating idea is that "the interests of the members of the community matter and matter equally."[6]

If we accept this abstract egalitarian thesis, then the task we face is twofold. First, we need to furnish an account of people's interests "most comprehensively construed," and second, we must try to determine what follows from "supposing that these interests matter equally."[7] The competing conceptions of the principle of parental autonomy that I will examine can all be represented as interpretations of the demands of impartial consideration of everyone's fundamental interests.

If we accept this framework, then a useful place to begin is with the identification of the basic categories of interests that need to be considered in determining the appropriate shape of the principle of parental autonomy. Three basic types of interests are worth distinguishing: children's interests, parental interests, and societal interests.

First, the character of children's interests is quite complex. Like all other members of the community, they have an interest in leading a good life. But, unlike adult members of the community, children do not have, at least initially, any conception of the good. Moreover, their capacity to form a conception of the good is initially constrained by the immaturity of their cognitive and moral faculties and their lack of experience and knowledge of the ends that might be adopted and pursued by them. So children have a certain interest in acquiring the capacities needed to allow them to form, evaluate, and pursue their own ends in an autonomous fashion. Rawls characterizes individuals as having two basic moral powers: (1) a capacity to form and revise a conception of the good and (2) a sense of justice through which persons can recognize and accept the valid claims of others.[8] Children have an important stake in acquiring these moral powers so they may act as independent, responsible members of the community. Yet, before they actually fully acquire these powers, children also have a compelling interest in leading a decent life, that is, in participating in valuable projects as children. Similarly, children must also respect the valid claims of others even when they are not fully able to do so without adult guidance and direction. One's childhood cannot be mere preparation for leading a good and responsible life. Indeed, one's childhood ideally should be a constitutive element of a good life. The leading of a good life cannot simply be postponed until one is an adult.

Second, parents also have distinctive interests. Parents have an interest in leading a good life, yet, unlike children, parents typically have some conception of the good. In other words, they have convictions in virtue of which they are committed to various practices or traditions that they believe are valuable. Adults generally have an interest in pursuing their own conceptions of the good in an unmolested fashion. They have a stake in being able to pursue the ends they voluntarily and freely adopt without significant interference from the state. One of the projects that many adults greatly prize is creating a family. As a corollary of their interest in pursuing their own conception of the good, parents have an interest in including their children in some or all of the elements that constitute their conception of the good. Thus parents often wish to pass onto their children various religious, moral, and cultural commitments. The realization of a parent's conception of the good may consist partly in the degree they succeed in transmitting their way of life or at least significant components of their valued commitments to their children.

Third, members of the community outside the family also have interests that need to be recognized. As children mature, they increasingly become potential actors in the public life of a community. As adults, they will be expected to participate in democratic politics and cooperate productively with other citizens. Members of the community have a substantial interest in ensuring that children grow up to be the sort of adults capable of exercising responsible citizenship. Irresponsible or incompetent citizens can place burdens on society that hamper the opportunity of other citizens to lead good lives. There are, of course, many different dimensions of responsible citizenship, but three relevant general features are (1) a capacity to recognize one's fellow citizens as equals and accord them the respect to which they are entitled; (2) a basic understanding of relevant democratic procedures and how to participate in them; (3) a capacity to take responsibility for the direction of one's own life. For instance, women have a legitimate interest that children do not adopt or display sexist beliefs or attitudes. We have an interest in ensuring that children become citizens who will play their role in upholding the democratic government of the community (e.g., by participating in the electoral system) and in ensuring that they will contribute productively to society and not impose unnecessary burdens on us (e.g., by evading taxes).

The competing conceptions of the principle of parental autonomy to which I now turn all present different interpretations of what it is to give fair consideration to these interests. I will label these conceptions as (1) the conservative conception of parental autonomy; (2) the democratic conception of parental autonomy; and (3) the liberal conception of parental autonomy.

THE CONSERVATIVE CONCEPTION

The conservative conception of parental autonomy assigns to parents absolute discretion in directing the upbringing of children. Essentially this means that the only constraints on the exercise of parental autonomy are those captured by the MPT. On this conception, parents are granted, in the words of Charles Fried, "the discretion to direct the formation of the child's earliest and perhaps most basic value structures and to determine his education so long as minimum standards are met."[9] Fried claims that parents have the "right to form one's child's values [and] one's child's life plans."[10] The state or the community has no authority to monitor or interfere with parental decisions about the upbringing of children. Echoing this sentiment, Loren Lomasky claims that "what parents can demand from all others is a generous quantity of non-interference. It is an infringement of the legitimate claims of parents when either private individuals or agencies of the state intrude on parental liberties to transfer resources to children, educate them in a manner deemed suitable, inculcate religious or moral principles, choose a place of residence for the family, or to engage in other, similar practices with respect to the child's upbringing."[11] Advocates of this position believe that the principle of parental autonomy provides good grounds for opposing state establishment or control and regulation of schools. Instead "each family should, as a matter of basic rights, be at liberty to secure through market transactions the sort of educational package it prefers and that educational entrepreneurs can be induced to provide."[12] So on this conception parental autonomy can be constrained only if exercise of parental prerogatives represents a "clear and present danger" to a child. Thus Schoeman holds that state intervention "should be authorized only if (1) serious physical or emotional harm to the child is imminent and (2) intervention is likely to be less detrimental that the status quo."[13] The characteristic feature of conservative accounts of the principle of parental autonomy is that subject to the modest limitations imposed by the MPT, parents have a right to *fix authoritatively* the conception of the good held by their children. In other words, parents are entitled to uniquely determine the content and character of a child's conception of the good.

The rationale for this conception of parental autonomy has four principal components. First, in asserting the right of parents to attempt to fix authoritatively the ends of their children, conservatives generally posit a deep harmony of the interests of parents and children. Indeed, the right to determine one's child's life plan is billed as a basic extension of the right of an adult to choose and pursue her own convictions. The parental right of self-determination is thought to imply a right of child-determination. Here, the conservative conception rests partly on collapsing the distinction between parent and child. The parent's child is viewed as "an extension of the self," and there is consequently an "identity between chooser and chosen for."[14]

Second, the legitimacy of strong parental discretion is predicated on the special epistemic access by parents to the needs and interests of their children. Conservatives recognize that there is not always a complete identity between the interests of parents and children. However, they argue that the close personal relationship between parents and children permits parents special insight into the distinctive needs of their children. In particular, parents are better placed than any state body or outside agency to judge the idiosyncratic needs of their children. Hence children's interests are best served by assigning unconditional authority to parents.

Third, the epistemic access argument is bolstered by an argument that cites the special and spontaneous motivation of parents to promote their children's welfare. The close bonds of intimate affection that link families together mean that parents will be deeply motivated to act in their children's best interest. Thus because parents love their children, they will seek to promote their best interests. Any discretion about the direction of children's upbringing that is left in the hands of even benevolent state authorities cannot be similarly motivated.

The fourth component of the justification of the conservative conception holds that strong parental discretion must be protected because it is a precondition of the realization of certain intrinsically valuable family goods. According to this argument, intimacy, family integrity, and integration along with valuable shared family projects may be realized only if the family is insulated from outside social intrusion. Schoeman claims, for instance, that "the strength or the very possibility of intimate relationships varies inversely with the degree of social intrusion into such relationships generally tolerated."[15] Children and parents have a substantial stake in enjoying these goods and the benefits they bring, but they can acquire these goods only with minimal constraints on parental autonomy.

The arguments around which the conservative conception of parental autonomy is constructed are important and cannot be entirely rejected. Yet, two objections to the conservative conception seem sufficient to defeat it. To begin with, the attempt to ground parental autonomy in a presumed adult right to self-determination is self-defeating. Fried claims that we all have a right to choose our own values and fundamental commitments. We have no right to force our commitments on other adults because "we recognize the liberty of each to develop his own life plan."[16] Fried's own rhetoric suggests that we have a substantial interest in becoming self-directing agents, capable of rationally reflecting on our commitments and revising them if necessary. But by granting parents the prerogative to fix authoritatively the ends of their children, Fried and other advocates of this conception are not giving sufficient recognition to the child's interest in becoming a self-directing agent. After all, a child whose parents succeed in authoritatively fixing her conception of the good, through effective indoctrination, cannot be the author of her own destiny. The fact that children do not begin life with capacities for self-direction does not imply that children do not have an interest in developing such capacities. Fried's presumption that there is a basic identity of interests between children and parents with respect to the interest of each in pursuing of a conception of the good is unwarranted. Whereas parents may have an interest in making a binding commitment to a given conception of the good that they have chosen, children have an interest in developing the capacities that will permit them to judge the worthiness of ends for themselves. Here, the interests of parents and children may significantly diverge. While what I have called authoritatively fixed ends need not be entirely beyond possible revision, they are likely to be extraordinarily difficult to subject to critical examination. So if children have an interest in becoming self-directing agents (as Fried's argument implies), and if we are to treat children with equal concern, then parents should exercise parental authority in ways compatible with eventual acquisition of this capacity. By viewing children initially as mere ingredients in their parents' life plans, the conservative conception does not give proper recognition to the independent moral status of children.

A second difficulty with the conservative conception of parental autonomy is that it provides insufficient recognition of the interests that "a democratic community has in choosing how a child will be nurtured and educated."[17] The point here is that irrespective of whether it is ever appropriate for parents to seek to fix authoritatively some of the ends of their children, a democratic state may legitimately seek to ensure that the ends adopted by its members are consistent with the requirements of democratic citizenship. The conservative conception allows parents to exercise their discretion in ways that may be inimical to what Gutmann calls the "conscious social reproduction" of democratic institutions.[18] The health of a pluralistic democratic state depends, in part, on the mutual recognition by its members of the diversity of their commitments and convictions. Citizens must be able to tolerate this diversity, and in the public realm they must treat all citizens with respect, regardless of their race, gender, or personal convictions. The worry here about the conservative conception is twofold. First, absolute parental discretion over the content of education and other influences permits parents to insulate, to an unwarranted degree, their children from the pluralism of democratic society. Second, such discretion may be used inappropriately to foster intolerance toward other members of the community. For example, children taught to embrace racist attitudes by their parents will find it difficult to accept and support the equal moral standing of all citizens upon which a just and democratic society depends.

THE DEMOCRATIC CONCEPTION

Sponsors of the democratic conception of parental autonomy are generally sympathetic to the wide discretion assigned to parents under the conservative conception. They appeal to many of the same general arguments in support of their position. However, they attempt to address the perceived democratic deficiency of the conservative conception by amending the conservative conception in the following way. The democratic conception assigns to parents full control over their children with the special and explicit proviso that parental authority must be tempered by the requirement that every child receive a suitable civic education. It is difficult to say precisely what institutional measures might be required to ensure that children acquire the relevant democratic civic virtues of tolerance of diversity and respect for the rights and privileges of other citizens. However, it is clear that the state may regulate both public and private schools in ways that foster in children, as Galston puts is, "the beliefs and habits that support the polity and enable individuals to function competently in public affairs."[19] It is important to note, however, that the democratic conception still gives parents the right to attempt to fix authoritatively their children's ends. The transmission of ideals or commitments to children is now subject to the limitation that the ends that are transmitted must be compatible with acceptance of minimal democratic ideals.

Justification of the democratic conception parallels, in many ways, the justification offered for the conservative conception. Broad parental discretion is still predicated on the epistemic access argument, the motivational argument, and the intimacy and shared goods argument. In Galston's version, the democratic proviso on the transmission of ends is intended to be relatively weak. It is only supposed to ensure that parents "do not act in ways that will lead their child to impose significant and avoidable burdens on the community."[20] So the state has the right to teach children "respect for the law" and may "inculcate the expectation that all normal children will become adults capable of caring for themselves and their families."[21] As I have noted, the democratic conception still permits parents to fix authoritatively the ends of their children. So although the democratic conception aims at discouraging the expression of intolerant or discriminatory attitudes in the public realm, it does not give tremendous independent weight to children's interest in autonomy. Like the conservative conception, the democratic conception sees this largely as an extension of the parents' rights to pursue their conceptions of the good. Indeed, defenders of this conception see such strong parental discretion as flowing from fundamental democratic values.

Advocates of this position also emphasize the importance of strong parental autonomy to the preservation of democratic pluralism. One of the valuable features of a democratic society is the diversity it permits. For some theorists, this pluralism is worth preserving and cultivating on the broadly Millian grounds that diversity is instrumentally valuable in meeting the divergent interests of different individuals. The maintenance of pluralism is viewed as essential to human flourishing. We recognize (or should recognize) that our present convictions about what sort of life is worth leading are fallible. One way we may learn about the value of other conceptions of the good is by being exposed to other ways of life. Pluralism thus assists our deliberations about the good and allows us the opportunity to explore other conceptions that we might decide have more value than our present ends. The value of democratic pluralism thus seems to presuppose that citizens have an interest in engaging rational deliberation about their ends. Pluralism is valuable to members of a democracy partly because it helps them to examine, explore, and evaluate the worth of their own convictions.[22] This idea is plausible and important, but some sponsors of the democratic conception seem to defend strong parental autonomy as necessary to maintaining pluralism in a way that puts the cart before the horse. Jean Elshtain, for instance, defends a strong principle of parental autonomy compatible with the authoritative fixing of children's ends because she views it as "vital to the sustaining of a pluralistic culture."[23] However, Elshtain seems to think that pluralism is worth creating and preserving for its own sake. Consequently, she defends the authoritative fixing of ends as an indispensable tool for the social reproduction of pluralism in a democratic state. But her position depends on a confused understanding of the value of pluralism. We want a spontaneous type of pluralism—one that arises out of and responds to the choices and interests of autonomous individuals. An artificially manufactured pluralism that circumvents considerations of autonomy and that simply reproduces existing diversity is neither particularly valuable nor democratic. After all, democratic citizens must be free and able to examine their views and the views of others. Galston, however, rejects this view about the preconditions of a healthy democracy. He claims that there is no "need for public authority to take an interest in how children think about different ways of life. Civic tolerance of deep differences is perfectly compatible with unswerving belief in the correctness of one's own way of life."[24] Indeed, in his view, children do not need to be able to examine their own commitments reflectively. Thus parents may exercise their prerogatives in ways that grant their children "the right to live unexamined"[25] lives. Galston tries to lend credence to this idea by arguing that it is better for children to have deep and uncritical convictions than to have no deeply held convictions at all. But this is a false dichotomy. Critical inspection of one's ends is not incompatible with profound conviction. Indeed, the opposite is more likely true. Blind faith may be powerful, but it is also shallow and potentially antidemocratic. As Gutmann points out, genuine democratic deliberation requires that citizens have the capacities to reflect rationally and critically on different ends.[26] This means that preparing children for genuine democratic citizenship is inconsistent with authoritatively fixing children's ends. A democratic education that leaves children with conceptions of the good that are immune from critical inspection is unstable and self-defeating. Effective democratic participation depends on citizens who are capable of deliberating about a wide range of values. Consequently, the conditions of a flourishing democracy include conditions conducive to the development of individual autonomy. The Galston-Elshtain vision of democracy that prizes tolerance of diversity but abandons a suitably democratic commitment to individual autonomy is too impoverished to provide an adequate justification of their "democratic" conception of parental autonomy.

THE LIBERAL CONCEPTION

The related difficulties of the democratic and conservative conceptions suggest that greater weight should be given to the child's interest in developing capacities for free and rational deliberation about the good. The liberal conception[27] of parental autonomy attempts to speak directly to the child's interest in becoming an autonomous agent. Indeed, protection of this interest is of preeminent importance from the liberal point of view. Liberals suppose that individuals should, as far as possible, be at liberty to deliberate freely among different ends and choose those ends that they believe have the most value. As we have noted, children lack the capacities needed to exercise this sort of deliberative autonomy and yet they are very impressionable. The liberal conception seeks to permit the development of rational autonomy by severely constraining parental autonomy. Parents may not seek to fix authoritatively their children's ends; indeed, insofar as possible, parents and other educational authorities must not act in ways that "bias the choices of children toward some disputed or controversial ways of life and away from others."[28] Parental autonomy is thus constrained by an ideal of neutrality and the requirement that a child's future freedom to choose between different ends be maximized. As Gutmann describes it, the liberal ideal holds that "a just educational authority must not bias children's choices among good lives, but it must provide every child with an opportunity to choose freely and rationally among the widest range of lives."[29] Liberals recognize that this ideal is not fully realizable because utter neutrality between all ends is impossible in the context of the family. Nonetheless, the liberal conception adopts a mainly instrumental understanding of parental autonomy: it is to be exercised principally to secure the future autonomy of children. The liberal conception is not predicated on skepticism about the good. Rather, it emphasizes the fallibility of our convictions about the good. Since we might be wrong about the good life, we need to be able to critically examine our own views. Similarly, since we might be wrong about the convictions we think our children should adopt, we must ensure that they can also critically examine their own commitments. Also liberals generally believe that we must be able to endorse our life plans if they are to generate value for us. The authoritative fixing of ends by parents seems inconsistent with meeting this requirement of endorsement.[30] It should also be noted that the liberal conception does not require the adoption of a neutral attitude toward all values. Children must be taught to respect and support the public conception of justice that governs relations between citizens. For example, moral education by parents and schools should not be neutral with respect to the values of nonrepression or nondiscrimination.[31] Still, children should not simply be indoctrinated into accepting these core democratic values. Ideally, children should be raised in a way that permits them to endorse critically the principles upon which a democratic society should be predicated.

The liberal conception, at least in this extreme form, is inherently unstable. The principal difficulty is that adopting neutrality as a constraint to the exercise of parental autonomy is inconsistent with the realization of familial intimacy and integrity. A family in which parents must endeavor to refrain from displaying any bias toward different conceptions of the good will be denied the fruits of shared family projects. The family will be fractured and its members will be alienated from one another. The conservative insight into the value—for both parents and children—of an integrated family in which members engage in shared projects cannot be dismissed. Caring parents will be unable to exercise the sort of impartiality toward the potential commitments of their children that the liberal conception requires. As Galston says, "if you believe that you are a fit parent, you must believe that some of the choices you have made are worthy of emulation by your children, and the freedom to pass on the fruits of those choices must be highly valued."[32] Moreover, the alienation of parents from children that the liberal conception generates works to undermine both the special epistemic access to children's distinctive interests that parents otherwise enjoy and the special motivation parents have to promote the welfare of their own children. If the bonds of intimacy between parent and child are weakened, children become more like strangers than vulnerable dependents. Their special needs will be more difficult to discern, and parents will be less motivated to give special attention to their children's needs. Ultimately, of course, alienation of this sort is likely to undermine achievement of the very autonomy that the liberal conception seeks to promote. Children who are deprived of close and enduring affective ties and who have either no commitments to a conception of the good or only vague and uncertain ones are unlikely to become effective rational deliberators. Indeed, the understanding of what it is to embrace serious commitments is difficult to achieve in the absence of some experience in what it is like to adopt and pursue a determinate conception of the good. Thus insofar as the liberal conception of parental autonomy embraces an ideal of parental neutrality, it will, like the other conceptions, be infeasible and self-defeating. In sum, the liberal conception in this form is too crude because it ignores the social conditions that are necessary for the acquisition of autonomy.

A REFINED LIBERAL CONCEPTION OF PARENTAL AUTONOMY

The deep difficulty that is faced by conceptions such as the conservative and democratic conceptions that hold that parents may authoritatively fix their children's ends is that justification of this prerogative depends, in large measure, on an appeal to the right of adults to guide their lives by their chosen values. Yet, we cannot prize parental autonomy as a value and simultaneously permit such autonomy to be exercised in a fashion that is inimical to the development of genuine autonomy in children. If autonomy matters for adults, then, since children are future adults, children must be permitted to become autonomous. In this respect, the liberal focus on the development of autonomy in children is surely correct. But clearly, parental neutrality is a defective ideal for advancement of this objective. Neutrality does not serve the autonomy-related interests of children, and it is unduly hostile to the interests parents and children have in adopting distinctive ideals and participating in shared family projects.

The problem, as I see it, is whether the liberal view can be suitably developed and refined so as to permit both acquisition of autonomy by children and the pursuit of shared family projects and ideals that are, to a significant degree, directed by parents. My proposal is that we should replace the ideal of neutrality with a more permissive conception of parental autonomy that extends to parents the prerogative of *provisionally privileging* the conception of the good that they favor. The idea that parents may provisionally privilege certain ends stands in sharp contrast to the idea that parents may authoritatively fix their children's ends. A refined liberal conception does impose constraints on the strategies that parents may legitimately employ to transmit a conception of the good to children. Yet the constraints operate in a manner commensurate with the parental interest in having children share a familial commitment to a common conception of the good. The general idea is that parents should be permitted to advance a distinctive conception of the good for their children. However, parents must not seek to exempt the ends they wish their children to adopt from rational scrutiny. Nor may parents undertake to foreclose the possibility of deliberation about such matters by tightly insulating children from exposure and access to the social conditions of deliberation. Moreover, as children mature, parents must respect the fact that children may choose to reject or revise the commitments that have been promoted by their parents. This refined liberal conception has two dimensions that correspond to different spheres of social interaction and the parental influence that may be wielded by parents in each sphere. First, within the boundaries formed by family and some limited community sphere, parents may legitimately give expression to their cherished ideals and may legitimately include children in practices associated with the ideal. For example, children may be instructed in particular religious doctrines and cultural traditions, they may be required to participate in ceremonies, to observe distinctive dietary or dress requirements, and to celebrate special holidays. Similarly, children may be required to learn a language that has historical or cultural significance for parents. Within this setting parents may legitimately privilege a particular conception of the good in the sense that they may freely profess their beliefs and encourage their children to pursue the way of life that is associated with these beliefs.[33] Second, outside the boundaries of the family and associated community sphere, in what I shall call the pluralistic public culture, there is a sphere of social interaction in which children can acquire an understanding and appreciation of a wide diversity of commitments and beliefs present in the broader community. On the refined liberal conception, the exercise of parental autonomy is constrained by the requirement that children be afforded free and full access to the deliberative resources available in the pluralistic public culture. In other words, parents may not seek to insulate their children from exposure to conceptions of the good present in the broader human community. In this public realm, children should be permitted to acquire some distance from the familial conception of the good and should develop an awareness that there are potentially viable conceptions of the good besides the one endorsed by the family. In order to ensure meaningful participation in this sphere, children must have access to relatively impartial sources of knowledge about other ways of life and potentially valuable projects (e.g., through access to libraries, museums, art galleries)—and they need to learn how to use these resources in an independent manner. Similarly, in this realm children must be encouraged to accept the idea that their present (i.e., provisionally given) way of life, or indeed any conception of the good, is not especially immune from critical inspection. Participation in a pluralistic public culture affords children a buffer against the potentially cloistering influence of the family, and it helps facilitate the acquisition of the skills and resources that are necessary for both autonomous deliberation and active democratic citizenship. By constraining parental control of children in this way, parents' efforts to fix authoritatively their children's ends are circumscribed. The ends espoused by parents do, of course, have a privileged status within the family, but through exposure to and participation in the pluralistic public culture, children's ends are provisional in the sense that they are subject to reflection, revision, and even rejection.

The constraints on parental autonomy that the refined liberal conception requires are not antithetical to a flourishing and intimate family life in which parents and children share distinctive commitments. In this way, the refined liberal conception accommodates the concerns about the importance of preserving the kind of familial integrity that is built around a shared conception of the good. This is not to say, however, that every aspect of a parental conception of the good is compatible with the refined liberal conception of parental autonomy. There are, after all, some conceptions of the good that seem predicated on denying children access to the social conditions that facilitate the development of autonomy and deliberation. In such cases, the refined liberal conception, unlike the democratic or conservative conceptions, denies the legitimacy of parental efforts to subvert children's autonomy in the name of parental pursuit of a given way of life.

THE SOCIAL CONDITIONS OF AUTONOMY

The position that I have just sketched can be further illuminated through consideration of some recent developments in political philosophy. Liberalism, as we have seen, typically assigns special weight to the recognition and protection of individual autonomy. But we cannot simply assume that all individuals are inevitably autonomous. Indeed, as Charles Taylor has argued, the autonomy so prized by liberals depends crucially on the existence of a social context of a particular kind. The "social thesis" advanced by Taylor holds that the development of autonomy depends on the existence of a diverse public culture that presents an array of alternative choices about matters of fundamental importance.[34] Autonomy is a capacity that a person can acquire and exercise only against a social background that is characterized by the presence of diverse options along with serious discussion and debate about these options. Autonomy depends on being able to conceive and consider alternatives to our current commitments, and only a social environment of a certain character facilitates that possibility. In a similar vein, Joseph Raz has identified a number of different conditions that are necessary to the development of autonomy. Raz conceives of one aspect of autonomy as consisting in the capacity of being the author of one's own life.[35] However, meaningful exercise of this capacity depends on the following conditions obtaining. First, an autonomous person cannot be systematically subject to the will of another person. "One is part author of one's world only if one is not merely serving the will of another."[36] Second, Raz insists that a "person is autonomous only if he has a variety of acceptable options available to choose from."[37] Autonomy is nurtured through the presence of an accessible menu containing a rich repertoire of possible options. Third, autonomy depends on an informed choice between options.[38] Autonomy cannot be secured simply by presenting a range of possible options. An autonomous choice is an informed choice that reflects genuine understanding of the relevant options.

Once such plausible claims about the social preconditions of autonomy are acknowledged, the argument for the refined liberal conception of parental autonomy is deepened. The social thesis clearly implies that the development of autonomy in children cannot occur in an environment that is entirely dominated by a single, parental vision of the good life. Indeed, Taylor's passing observation that "it is very dubious whether the developed capacity for this kind of autonomy can arise simply within the family"[39] is very significant. The requirement of the refined liberal conception that parents refrain from denying their children access to the pluralistic public culture speaks directly to children's interest in becoming autonomous. For it is only through exposure to the public culture that children can gain an understanding of different, potentially valuable, options. By contrast, it is characteristic of a view that extends to parents the right to authoritatively fix the ends of their children that parents are permitted to control rigidly the access of their children to the deliberative resources present in the public culture. Indeed, it is no surprise that parents eager to transmit their conception of the good to their children jealously monitor and regulate exposure to views that diverge from the parental conception of the good. In extreme cases, parents seek to isolate their children completely from the outside world. Yet, if the social thesis is accepted, then such isolation undermines the development of autonomy.

We must be careful not to exaggerate the place of the social thesis within the refined liberal conception of parental autonomy. As I noted earlier, young children do not have the sort of developed cognitive and emotional capacities upon which autonomy also depends. Consequently, mere provision of the social preconditions of autonomy outside the family will not transform pre-autonomous or partly autonomous children into persons who are capable of directing their own lives. It is inevitable, for instance, that a child's early life must be shaped by the will of another. Similarly, children without any initial beliefs about value cannot be expected to adopt a life plan of their choosing from an initial menu of options presented to them in the public culture. Autonomous choice from such a vacuum is not possible. Moreover, children have an ongoing interest in pursuing a conception of the good even before they are fully able to choose one for themselves. It is against the framework supplied by experience of a determinate conception of the good that children will subsequently be able to consider the value of the conception that they have lived as children and other options that present themselves. The refined liberal conception accommodates this point directly. The conception of the good that parents may legitimately privilege within the family provides children with an initial value structure that helps facilitate future deliberation. The commitments that children receive from parents furnish part of what Will Kymlicka has called a "context of choice"—a value structure from which activities and practices have meaning.[40] The context of choice provided in the family consists of a set of shared beliefs about value, namely, those favored by the parents, which provides both a way of life to be pursued but also a perspective from which other values can be compared, explored, and assessed. Before children can engage in deliberation about the value of commitments, they must acquire an initial vocabulary of value through which subsequent possibilities can be presented. So by respecting the prerogative of parents to supply such an initial value structure by privileging a particular conception of the good within the family, the refined liberal conception is conducive to promotion of familial intimacy and integrity while facilitating the development of children's autonomy. I think this view represents the fairest accommodation of the divergent interests that I identified earlier.

AN ILLUSTRATION: THE TRANSMISSION OF RELIGIOUS CONVICTIONS

By way of conclusion, it is instructive to consider briefly the difference between this refined liberal conception of parental autonomy and other conceptions of parental autonomy for controversies concerning the transmission of religious commitments from parents to children. For many people, religious commitments are largely constitutive of their view of the good. Indeed, a person's religious affiliation often plays a central role in defining identity and shaping the kinds of life projects and social practices that a person pursues. The traditional importance of religious commitment is reflected in the constitutional protection freedom of religion receives in many modern liberal democracies. Freedom of religion is a fundamental freedom, and the state may limit the free exercise of an individual's convictions only for exceptional reasons. Given this background, it is unsurprising that parents frequently assume that one of the prerogatives that is implied by their right of freedom of religion is the right to *teach* their particular religious values to their children. It seems difficult to object to the idea that parents may teach their children about the religious doctrine to which the parents subscribe. Yet, it is not always clear exactly what the right to "teach" or "instruct" children about a religious tradition actually entails. On the one hand, it is evident that many parents believe that such a right implies that parents may employ whatever means are necessary to ensure that their children adopt a certain set of religious convictions and an accompanying lifestyle. On the other hand, the right to "teach'" or "instruct" may be interpreted merely as extending to parents the permission to inform children about religious doctrines and commitments and to acquaint them with the lifestyle requirements that may be entailed by the adoption of such commitments. On this construal, "teaching" is not designed to foreclose the consideration or possible adoption of other views of religion. This form of teaching is compatible, therefore, with the possibility of apostasy.

By arguing that parents are not entitled to fix authoritatively their children's conception of the good, I have argued, in effect, that parents do not have the right to "teach" or "instruct" their children so as to foreclose the consideration and possible adoption of competing conceptions of the good. This is not to say that parents must try to refrain from showing any bias between different religious beliefs as the unmodified liberal conception requires. Parents may openly profess and practice their faith subject to the constraint that their children, as they reach maturity, are able to deliberate freely about whether they wish to continue to share the religious convictions of their parents. There is, in effect, a proviso on the transmission of religious convictions from parents to children that requires that the religious practices of parents not undermine the social conditions necessary for free deliberation about religious matters. Children's interest in securing the conditions for the development of autonomy include having access to the resources that permit independent formation of the child's own convictions about a religious affiliation. In my view, this constraint on transmission of religious convictions is stronger than any parental claim to undertake efforts designed to ensure that their children adopt a particular religious faith.

The case of the Old Order of the Amish nicely illustrates the central contrast between the right to authoritatively fix ends and the right to provisionally privilege ends.[41] The Old Order is an isolationist religious group whose members seek to insulate themselves and their children from what they view as the corrosive and corrupting influence of the modern world.[42] The social order of the Amish community is based on the *Ordnung*—a set of rules largely based on interpretation of the Bible. Amish settlements are usually small, self-sufficient, agrarian communities in which the use of modern technology is generally avoided. The Amish church pervades all aspects of Amish life, and there is deep devotion to the Christian faith marked by extremely strict adherence to the *Ordnung*.

One particularly important aspect of the Amish faith is the requirement of separation from significant contact with the beliefs and practices of the non-Amish world. This requirement derives from an interpretation of certain passages of scripture and is deemed essential to the survival of traditional Amish communities. Needless to say, the social reproduction of the Amish community depends on the successful transmission of religious convictions from parents to children. The Amish family and community tightly control the social environment to which children have access in order to ensure that children, upon reaching adulthood, will enter the Amish church and remain in the community.[43] Aside from the geographical and social isolation from the outside world that Amish children experience, Amish parents in the United States have successfully sought to exempt their children from all but the most basic requirements of formal education.[44] In *Wisconsin v Yoder* (406 US 205), the U.S. Supreme Court held that Amish parents could exempt their children from the general state requirement that all children attend school until the age of sixteen.[45]

The ruling of the Court is interesting, in part because the justification for the decision closely corresponds to the democratic conception of parental autonomy. The Court held that parents have a very strong interest in controlling the rearing of children that can be constrained only by the modest but important state objectives of enabling citizens to participate in the political system and to prepare individuals to be "self-reliant and self-sufficient participants in society."[46] Since the Amish community is self-sufficient and since its members are self-reliant in the sense that they do not impose burdens on the state (e.g., the Amish do not collect welfare), the Court was satisfied that legitimate state objectives would be met if formal schooling ended at age fourteen. Indeed, the Court adopted an extremely passive conception of effective and intelligent participation in the political system. The fact that the Amish are law-abiding citizens who live peaceably with their neighbors seemed sufficient to persuade the Court that Amish children are effectively prepared for participation in democratic politics. This reflects a conception of democracy stripped of any requirement that citizens be meaningfully equipped to engage in informed debate and deliberation about political matters.

The Court assumed that parents had the right to form their children's religious values in order to prepare them for continued life in the community. Virtually no weight was assigned to development of independent capacities for deliberation and self-direction. Preparation for *possible* exit from the community was subordinate to the goal of advancing the parents' interests in continued survival of the traditional community. In effect, the court accepted the proposition that parents do have the right to authoritatively fix their children's religious convictions.

The degree to which the Amish have succeeded in insulating and isolating their children from non-Amish beliefs and practices is extraordinary. As one expert notes, in a traditional Amish community, the "Amish child was immersed in a tight plausibility structure where the power of a conforming community and the lack of other options were adequate and convincing forces of socialization."[47] The result of this form of extreme isolation from the outside world is that "the ways of the Ordnung are absorbed by the children as the taken-for-granted assumptions of what it means to be Amish."[48] The establishment of Amish schools has also ensured that even the minimal educational requirements that the Amish accept are pursued in isolation from the non-Amish world. Despite some conflicts with the outside world and the increased encroachment of modernity, Amish communities in North America have flourished. There has been a steady increase in the population of all Amish communities, and the retention rate of members amongst the Old Order is extremely high. The percentage of adult children affiliated with the Old Order Amish is 86 percent.[49]

From the perspective of the refined liberal conception of parental autonomy, the strategies employed by Amish parents to ensure adherence to the Amish faith by their children are wrong. The sort of isolation that Amish parents seek for their children is clearly at odds with provision of the social conditions of autonomy. So although entrance into the Amish church by an adolescent is officially a matter of voluntary choice, it is difficult to see such a choice as the expression of genuine autonomy. After all, the ordinary Amish adolescent can hardly be said to have an informed opinion about other possible life choices and for most of her life has, in effect, been subjected to the will of her parents and community. Consequently, the refined liberal conception, unlike the democratic conception or the conservative conception, views the decision in *Wisconsin v Yoder* as deeply flawed. The development of autonomy depends on permitting the very exposure to the public pluralistic culture that Amish parents seek to eliminate. Not only should formal education for Amish children extend past age fourteen, but such education should ideally be provided outside the confines of the Amish community. Moreover, Amish children, especially in adolescence, should have ready access to other elements of the broader culture (e.g., libraries, museums, art galleries) that can help facilitate deliberation about matters such as whether to join the Amish church.

It may be objected that the traditional Amish way of life would not survive the effects of eliminating extreme insulation from other ways of life imposed on children. It is possible that children with knowledge of other ways of life might choose to exit the community or urge changes to traditional practices and beliefs. Hence the democratic and conservative conceptions of parental autonomy may seem more attractive than a refined liberal conception because they are more hospitable to the preservation of traditional religious communities. However, I do not think that we should view the mere prospect of change or even transformation of a community that is propelled by the free choices of its members as a tragedy. Every Amish young adult has the right to abandon the traditional community—even if this would result in the demise of the Old Order church. An existing religious community has no claim to survival if its survival depends on denying its members genuine autonomy. We should not suppose that a refined liberal conception of parental autonomy is simply hostile to the Amish faith. After all, the refined liberal view does not require that parents cease from expressing religious convictions to their children or including children in the practices of the faith. Traditional Amish practices, except for the requirement of insulating children from external influences, may be pursued and promoted by Amish parents within the family and a limited community sphere. Amish parents are not completely barred, therefore, from pursuing their religious convictions. The refined liberal conception is built around the idea that within the confines of the family, parents may privilege a conception of the good. However, the reach and extent of parental control outside the family is circumscribed by the need to ensure that children have reasonable access to the nonfamilial social conditions of autonomy. So in this respect, the traditional claims about the extent of parental autonomy advanced by the Amish and accepted by proponents of the democratic and conservative conceptions of parental autonomy are mistaken.

The suggestion that parents should relinquish some of the tight control that they wield over all aspects of the character and content of their children's social environment may strike some as a radical intrusion into the legitimate prerogatives of parenthood. And as we have seen in the case of the Amish, acceptance of a refined liberal conception of parental autonomy can have controversial consequences. However, the views that extend to parents the right to fix authoritatively children's ends are deeply problematic. So although it may have some controversial implications, the suggestion that the contours of an appropriate conception of parental autonomy be built around the idea that parents may provisionally privilege ends is an alternative that is worth exploring.

NOTES

1. As feminist scholarship has established (e.g., Susan Moller Okin, *Justice, Gender and the Family* [New York: Basic Books, 1987]), most contemporary theories of justice (e.g., those of John Rawls, Robert Nozick, Ronald Dworkin, and David Gauthier) offer no systematic analysis of justice in the family. Family structures are diverse and any adequate theory must acknowledge this fact. I do not assume, for instance, that the term "parents" refers only or primarily to the biological mother and father of a child. Nor do I assume that parents are married or heterosexual. For the purposes of this article, I shall suppose that a family is a social institution composed of one or more adults and one or more children in which the adults and children are linked together through close and distinctive affective ties and in which the adults have special responsibilities and a measure of authority in supervising the rearing of the children.

2. In framing the problem in this way, I am setting aside theories that call for the abolition of any family structure and its replacement with some kind of state-directed institutional system.

3. Jeffrey Blustein calls this general condition governing the parameters of parental authority the "priority thesis." He notes that whereas Hobbes rejected the priority thesis, Locke endorsed it. See Jeffrey Blustein, *Parents and Children: The Ethics of the Family* (Oxford, UK: Oxford University Press 1982), 112-13.

4. Children with profound cognitive disabilities may be unable to become fully or even partially literate. Thus the application of the MPT in such cases raises important problems and puzzles. However, I shall not broach them here.

5. I shall set aside those strains of contemporary contractarianism in which children, in light of the fact that they wield no bargaining power, fall, in David Gauthier's memorable phrase "beyond the pale of morality." David Gauthier, *Morals by Agreement* (Oxford, UK: Oxford University Press, 1986), 268.

6. Ronald Dworkin, "In Defense of Equality," *Social Philosophy and Policy* 1, no. 1 (1983): 24.

7. Ibid., 25.

8. John Rawls, *Political Liberalism* (New York: Columbia University Press, 1993), 19.

9. Charles Fried, *Right and Wrong* (Cambridge, MA: Harvard University Press, 1978), 152.

10. Ibid.

11. Loren Lomasky, *Persons, Rights and the Moral Community* (Oxford, UK: Oxford University Press, 1987), 172.

12. Ibid., 175.

13. Ferdinan Schoeman, "Rights of Children, Rights of Parents and the Moral Basis of the Family," *Ethics* 91, no. 1 (1980): 10.

14. Fried, *Right and Wrong*, 152. It is interesting to note that Fried seems also to be supposing that there is an identity of interests between parents. Since parents often disagree about the ends their children should adopt, the child cannot, as Fried suggests, be an "extension of *the* self."

15. Schoeman, "Rights of Children," 14.

16. Fried, *Right and Wrong*, 152.

17. Amy Gutmann, "Children, Paternalism and Education: A Liberal Argument," *Philosophy and Public Affairs* 9, no. 4 (1980): 346.

18. Amy Gutmann, *Democratic Education* (Princeton, NJ: Princeton University Press, 1987), 39.

19. William Galston, *Liberal Purposes* (Cambridge, UK: Cambridge University Press, 1991), 252.

20. Ibid.

21. Ibid.

22. Avigail Eisenberg, *Reconstructing Political Pluralism* (Albany: State University of New York Press, 1995).

23. Jean B. Elshtain, "Family, Politics and Authority," in G. Scarre, ed., *Children, Parents and Politics* (Cambridge, UK: Cambridge University Press, 1989), 69.

24. Galston, *Liberal Purposes*, 253.

25. Ibid., 254.

26. Gutmann, *Democratic Education*.

27. In describing the liberal conception of parental autonomy I am closely following the depiction of the liberal ideal of education provided by Amy Gutmann in *Democratic Education*. In the earlier "Children, Paternalism and Education," Gutmann defended the liberal ideal. However, she now defends a version of the democratic conception of parental autonomy. Thus she maintains that "the discretionary domain for education—particularly but not only for moral education—within the family has always been and must continue to be vast within democratic society" (*Democratic Education*, 69).

28. Gutmann, *Democratic Education*, 34.

29. Ibid.

30. Conservatives and democrats might reply that children whose ends are authoritatively fixed *do* endorse those ends. Here, liberals will want to distinguish between the mere fact of endorsement and critical endorsement; see Ronald Dworkin, "Liberal Community," *California Law Review* 77, no. 3 (1988): 479-504, esp. 484-87.

31. Gutmann, *Democratic Education*, 45-46.

32. Galston, *Liberal Purposes*, 252.

33. Subject to the important constraint that the conception of the good so favored is compatible with the public conception of justice. For example, parents are not morally entitled to privilege racist conceptions of the good within the family.

34. Charles Taylor, *Philosophy and the Human Sciences: Philosophical Papers 2* (Cambridge, UK: Cambridge University Press, 1985), 204-5. Taylor develops the social thesis in the context of a critique of liberalism. He contends that some central liberal doctrines such as the commitment to the primacy of individual rights and the requirement of state neutrality on questions of the good are inconsistent with the social thesis.

35. Joseph Raz, *The Morality of Freedom* (Oxford, UK: Oxford University Press, 1986), 204.

36. Ibid., 155.

37. Ibid., 204.

38. Ibid., 155.

39. Taylor, *Philosophy and the Human Sciences*, 204. It is odd that even the mainstream political philosophers who have advanced these claims about the social prerequisites of autonomy generally ignore consideration of the implications such views have for the organization of the family. Neither Taylor nor Raz give any serious attention to the case of children.

40. Will Kymlicka, *Multicultural Citizenship* (Oxford, UK: Oxford University Press, 1995), 82-83.

41. There are a number of different Amish affiliations that, despite some important similarities, exhibit significant doctrinal differences. The largest, most established, and oldest Amish group is the Old Order. In some senses, the Old Order can be considered the moderate branch of the Amish faith since the smaller, splinter groups are offshoots of the Old Order. The conservative branch of the Amish faith is represented by the small Swartzentruber and Andy Weaver groups. These groups adopt an extremely rigid view of the requirements of the Amish faith. They are, for instance, much more vehemently committed to the rejection of modern technology than Old Order groups, which permit the use of some modern appliances (e.g., the Old Order permits the use of *rental* freezers). The Swartzentruber and Andy Weaver groups also impose much tougher sanctions on excommunicated members of the Church than either the Old Order or the New groups. The New Order Amish represent the "progressive" branch of Amish society. They are more permissive than any other Amish group about the use of technology both on the farm and in the home. Even within a given affiliation there may be some variation on the precise interpretation of the *Ordnung* in different districts and settlements. See Donald B. Kraybill and Marc A. Olshan, eds., *The Amish Struggle with Modernity* (Hanover, NH: University of New England Press, 1994).

42. There are nonisolationist religious groups who also seek to insulate themselves and their children from putatively corrupting aspects of the broader public culture. Some conservative Christian parents have sought to exempt their children from portions of the public school curriculum that the parents find offensive. See *Mozert v Hawkins County Public Schools*, 827 F2d 1058 (6th Cir 1987). In principle, this kind of selective and partial insulation from exposure to information about beliefs and practices is no different in aim than the more wide ranging form of insulation sought by the Amish.

43. The Amish believe in adult baptism, and one does not become a member of the Church until as an adult one voluntarily agrees to subscribe to the tenets of the faith.

44. The degree of education deemed necessary by the Amish consists largely in acquiring the basic reading, writing, and arithmetic skills that are necessary for reading the Bible and working in the traditional occupations in the community.

45. A comprehensive analysis of the decision in *Wisconsin v Yoder* is clearly beyond the scope of this article. I hope only to illustrate some important points of contrast between the position on parental autonomy I defend and the alternative views I have canvassed.

46. *Wisconsin v Yoder*, in Onora O'Nell and William Ruddick, eds., *Having Children: Philosophical and Legal Reflections on Parenthood* (New York: Oxford University Press, 1979), 288.

47. Donald Kraybill, "Plotting Social Change across Four Affiliations," in Donald B. Kraybill and Marc A. Olshan, eds., *The Amish Struggle with Modernity* (Hanover, NH: University of New England Press, 1994), 59.

48. Donald Kraybill, "The Struggle to Be Separate," in Donald B. Kraybill and Marc A. Olshan, eds., *The Amish Struggle with Modernity* (Hanover, NH: University of New England Press, 1994), 5.

49. Kraybill, "Plotting Social Change," 73.

17

Is Anything Now Left of Parental Rights?

ANDREW BAINHAM

INTRODUCTION

ALMOST 20 YEARS AGO, Alexander McCall Smith posed the question: 'Is anything left of parental rights?'[1] It was a good question then and it is a good question now. In the period after McCall Smith was writing, it had become distinctly fashionable, at least in the context of English law, to deny that a parent's position could properly be characterised in terms of rights. The Children Act 1989 set the tone for at least the next decade by abolishing the former notion of 'parental rights and duties'[2] and proclaiming instead 'parental responsibility'[3] as the central organising concept in the law of parent and child. Indeed, the title of this book reflects this very conceptual shift.

If viewed as a change of emphasis from the former proprietorial notions of ownership or possession of children to ideas of stewardship or trusteeship, the transition which the Children Act brought about is hardly controversial. Few people, including the great majority of parents themselves, would be at all comfortable with the notion that parents use children *primarily* for their own benefit. Even so, it might be wise to concede at the outset that the act of procreation, in so far as it is intentional (and many such acts of course are not), is an unquestionably adult-centred act. It is *those adults* who want the child. To say that a child is being planned and created for its own benefit is a distortion to which not many would subscribe. Neither, it must be said, does the claim that adoption is child-centred and exists solely for the child's benefit ring very true either.[4] There is, however, widespread agreement that the *primary* function of

---

[1] A McCall Smith, 'Is anything left of parental rights?' in E Sutherland and A McCall Smith (eds), *Family Rights: Family Law and Medical Advance* (Edinburgh, Edinburgh University Press, 1990).

[2] The Children Act 1975 s 85(1) defined 'parental rights and duties' as 'all the rights and duties which by law the mother and father have in relation to a legitimate child and his property'.

[3] Despite the clear intention to play down the existence of parental rights, the new concept of parental responsibility in the Children Act 1989 s 3(1) was so defined to include within it any such rights as parents might have.

[4] For a recent and, it is suggested, strikingly 'mother-centred' decision by the Court of Appeal on adoption, see *Re C (A Child) v XYZ CC* [2007] EWCA Civ 1206, which effectively upholds a mother's

parenthood is the responsibility to raise children and promote their best interests. The diminution in the significance attached to parental rights is accordingly in perfect harmony with the much greater importance attached first to the welfare of children and then to children's rights.[5]

But does this change of emphasis necessarily involve the abandonment of rights for parents? There have been plenty of those who have thought so. The House of Lords adopted an interpretation of the welfare principle which equated 'paramount' with 'sole' consideration, effectively meaning that any claims that parents might have could only be referable to their child's interests and not to their own and would be subsumed within the court's general investigation of the child's welfare.[6] The Law Commission felt able to state unequivocally that it was 'not only inaccurate as a matter of juristic analysis but also a misleading use of ordinary language' to talk of parental rights.[7] Furthermore, one leading commentator could speak about the 'emergence of children's rights' alongside the 'eclipse of parental rights'.[8] Such views rest on the apparent assumption that there is something inherently inconsistent in being in favour of children's welfare or rights and defending the existence of rights for parents.

In more recent years, substantial doubt has been cast on this position. There is now a growing feeling that parental rights, if not exactly thriving, may at least have been given a premature burial. The single event which has been most instrumental in this change of heart has been the implementation of the Human Rights Act 1998 and the rather quick realisation that the European Convention on Human Rights is, unsurprisingly, about rights. In so far as parents, or for that matter children, are asserting claims under the Convention, they are asserting rights. There is no question that parents, under Article 8, have rights to respect for their family life, which include rights in relation to their children. Admittedly, such rights are qualified by the 'rights and freedoms of others' and, in the balancing act which must be conducted under Article 8(2), there is a respectable view that the welfare of children must necessarily still predominate.[9] Accordingly,

---

decision to opt for a secret or confidential adoption without informing either the father or the wider birth family on either side. Judith Masson has also recently remarked that 'adoption is presented as a service for children who cannot be cared for by their birth families. However, much of adoption practice in the UK and elsewhere has focused on helping people to become parents': J Masson, 'International families: making new relationships at home and away' in R Probert (ed), *Family Life and the Law: Under One Roof* (Aldershot, Ashgate, 2007) 190.

[5] Children's rights as a concept was given a huge boost by the adoption in 1989 and subsequent almost universal ratification of the United Nations Convention on the Rights of the Child (UNCRC).

[6] *J v C* [1970] AC 668; and see generally NV Lowe, 'The House of Lords and the welfare principle' in C Bridge (ed), *Family Law Towards the Millennium: Essays for PM Bromley* (London, Butterworths, 1997).

[7] Law Commission, 'Custody' (Law Com WP No 96, 1986) [7.16]; and 'Illegitimacy' (Law Com No 118, HC 98, 1982) [4.18].

[8] J Eekelaar, 'The emergence of children's rights' (1986) 6 *OJLS* 161; and 'The eclipse of parental rights' (1986) 102 *LQR* 4.

[9] Importance has been attached to the decision of the European Court of Human Rights in *Yousef v The Netherlands* [2003] 1 FLR 210, holding that, where under the European Convention on Human

some conclude that there is not a great deal of difference between this exercise and the process of applying the welfare principle without recourse to the Convention. This seems to be a widely held view among the family judges.[10] It is not one which has found as much favour with academic commentators, who are inclined to feel that the welfare principle itself is in need of a revamp.[11] It is not my intention here to add to this debate.

We should also note that the idea that parents lack rights, so difficult now to defend in the European context, would be even more difficult to defend in the United States. There, the Supreme Court has resolutely and repeatedly asserted the existence of parental rights,[12] latterly alongside children's rights.[13] There is no doubt whatsoever that in the United States parents' rights have strong constitutional dimensions. Indeed, it has been said that parental rights 'have come to be regarded in American constitutional law as among the most protected and cherished of all constitutional rights'.[14] Therefore, there is a real risk that if we in England were to persist in our denial of parents' rights, we would find ourselves rather isolated in the developed world in doing so and not at all in tune with either Europe or the United States.

However, could it be that this is all just a semantic argument? Twenty years ago, I offered the view that:

> the label which the law attaches to parental authority is not nearly as important as the substantive question of its extent and duration.[15]

I still believe this to be the case. The truth is that there can be endless jurisprudential and philosophical arguments about the nature of rights, duties and discretions. Rather than add to this literature, I want to try here to focus on

---

Rights (hereafter 'ECHR') the rights of parents and children conflict, the child's rights will be the paramount consideration. It may be doubted, however, whether the Court had a complete understanding of the English interpretation of 'paramount' as meaning 'sole' consideration. It seems very unlikely given that the jurisprudence under Art 8 is habitually concerned with balancing rights and not ignoring them.

[10] Many examples could be given of the English judiciary's unwavering commitment to the welfare principle in the face of arguments about human rights. However, for a comparatively recent one, see the Court of Appeal decision in *Re S (Adoption Order or Special Guardianship Order)* [2007] EWCA Civ 54, in which the Court said that it was unlikely that in most cases Art 8 would add anything to the court's central task of applying the welfare principle.

[11] See, eg S Choudhry and H Fenwick, 'Taking the rights of parents and children seriously: confronting the welfare principle under the Human Rights Act' (2005) 25 *OJLS* 453; J Herring, 'The Human Rights Act and the welfare principle in family law—conflicting or complementary?' [1999] 11 *CFLQ* 223; and, for the author's view on this question, A Bainham, *Children: The Modern Law* (3rd edn, Bristol, Jordans, 2005) 38–40.

[12] The leading cases being *Meyer v Nebraska* 262 US 390 (1923); *Pierce v Society of Sisters* 268 US 510 (1925); and *Wisconsin v Yoder* 406 US 205 (1972).

[13] For detailed analysis of the leading decisions on children's rights in the United States, see RH Mnookin and D Kelly Weisberg, *Child, Family and State* (5th edn, New York,, Aspen, 2005) ch 1, especially 75 *ff*.

[14] M Guggenheim, *What's Wrong with Children's Rights* (Cambridge, Mass., Harvard University Press, 2005) 23.

[15] A Bainham, *Children, Parents and the State* (London, Sweet & Maxwell, 1988) 60.

26 *Andrew Bainham*

the *essence* of the independent interests which parents may have in relation to their children, reflected in the special legal status conferred upon them, and the extent to which the legal system should recognise them. I will argue that parents *do* have independent interests which are not referable exclusively to promoting their children's welfare and that the legal system should explicitly and unapologetically endorse them. Whether or not these independent interests should be recognised is at the heart of the parental rights debate. I will accordingly refer to parental rights and interests quite interchangeably throughout this chapter. I will go on to argue that the most important interest parents have lies in the defence of their superior status—superior, that is, to all other adults. This arises automatically on the birth of the child and it sets parents apart from all of those others who may have an interest in the child. It will be my case that the term 'social parent' is something of a misnomer, an invention by academics for the benefit of academic analysis, and that the greatest threat to parents' interests lies in the prevalent tendency to confuse *parentage* with *parenting*, as it has recently been put by Thérèse Callus.[16]

DO PARENTS HAVE INDEPENDENT INTERESTS?

One widely held position is that parents have no independent rights or interests because everything they do is derived from the responsibility they have for their children. Commentators agree that parents must discharge certain minimum duties to their children, including feeding, clothing, arranging necessary medical attention and providing an education.[17] Macleod has called this the 'Minimum Provision Thesis'.[18] Beyond this, it is generally acknowledged that parents enjoy a wide discretion in the manner in which they raise their children. It is clear, for example, that although parents must educate their children,[19] the *kind* of education provided is up to them. It is therefore their choice whether or not the child is privately educated or educated within the state school system. Similarly, once we move beyond essential medical care, more routine medical decisions are a matter for individual parents.[20]

A key question is how this parental discretion should be characterised and whether, in exercising it, a parent is entitled to have regard not simply to what is best for the child, but also to his or her own benefit. One view, described by

[16] T Callus, 'First "Designer Babies", Now À La Carte Parents' (2008) 38 *Family Law* 143.
[17] Criminal liability may arise from wilful neglect to attend to these basic needs of the child, principally under the Children and Young Persons Act 1933 s 1.
[18] CM Macleod, 'Conceptions of parental autonomy' (1997) 25 *Politics and Society* 117, 120.
[19] Education Act 1996 s 7: see further Monk, this volume.
[20] Even in the case of serious medical decisions, it has been accepted by the Nuffield Council on Bioethics that 'parents have interests and that it is reasonable for these interests to be given some weight in any relevant deliberations about critical decisions for a child who is, or who will become, severely ill'. See *Report on Critical Care Decisions in Fetal and Neonatal Medicine* (2006) [2.29], and see further Hagger, this volume.

Archard as the 'priority thesis', is that 'any rights that parents do have are constrained by, and derive from, a prior duty to care for their children'.[21] This derivative notion has been applied by Montague to parental discretion. According to Montague, while it cannot be denied that parents enjoy a large amount of discretion, we can account for:

> any latitude that parents have in making decisions affecting their children's lives in terms of permissions people have to select the specific ways in which they fulfill their obligations.[22]

According to this view, the parent who, say, forces his or her children to attend church twice on a Sunday, despite the fact that the children detest church and protest loudly on every occasion, is not acting in his or her own interests at all, but is merely selecting the way in which he or she fulfils his or her parental obligations. Bernard Dickens, in a seminal article, also highlighted the discretion enjoyed by parents and again saw the modern function of parental rights as enabling parents to discharge their duties, albeit that those duties in his view were best characterised as avoiding harm to the child rather than promoting the child's best interests.[23]

Others have doubted that all parental actions can be seen as taken entirely for the child's benefit and see in some of them an element of parental interest. Alexander McCall Smith himself tried to identify a category of 'parent-centred rights'.[24] For him, the key factor was to try to identify the *beneficiary* of the right in question. A 'child-centred parental right' was justified by its furtherance of the child's best interests or welfare. In contrast, a 'parent-centred parental right' touches upon 'the parental response to the basic moral issue of *what sort of child they wish to raise*'.[25] The significance of this latter type of right, into which category McCall Smith placed the above issue of religious direction, appeared to him to be that:

> [T]he parent has a wide range of discretion to pursue goals which society as whole might find undesirable, but which it will tolerate.[26]

Part of the reason for the existence of such rights is that 'they reflect something to which the parent is entitled by virtue of being a parent'.[27] Furthermore, to continue with the example of religion, the infringement of the right to instil religious values in the child 'involves distress to the parent, not necessarily to the child'. In cases like this, it was McCall Smith's view that it was not the exclusive

---

[21] D Archard, *Children, Family and the State* (Aldershot, Ashgate, 2003) 94.
[22] P Montague, 'The myth of parental rights' (2000) 26 *Social Theory and Practice* 47, 63.
[23] B Dickens, 'The modern function and limits of parental rights' (1981) 97 *LQR* 462.
[24] Above n 1, 9–10.
[25] *Ibid*, 9.
[26] *Ibid*.
[27] *Ibid*, 10.

28 *Andrew Bainham*

purpose of parental rights to serve the interests of children. It was also to take into account 'self-serving parental wishes'.[28]

Archard is also fundamentally unhappy with the tendency to speak only in terms of parental duties or to view the parent as 'merely an agent of the child's welfare'. For Archard, the parent also has interests which are bound up with the activity of parenting:

> Being a parent is extremely important to a person. Even if a child is not to be thought of as the property or even as an extension of the parent, the shared life of a parent and child involves an adult's purposes and aims at the deepest level … parents have an interest *in parenting*—that is, in sharing a life with, and directing the development of, their child. It is not enough to discount the interests of a parent in a moral theory of parenthood. What must also merit full and proper consideration is the interest of someone in being a parent.[29]

In a similar vein, Macleod also recognises the independent interests of parents:

> [T]hose who accept the responsibility of raising children frequently do so because the project of creating and raising a family is an important, indeed often fundamental, element of their own life plans. Viewed from this perspective, parents cannot be seen as mere guardians of their children's interests. They are also people for whom creating a family is a project from which they derive substantial value. They have an interest in the family as a vehicle through which some of their own distinctive commitments and convictions can be realized and perpetuated.[30]

I will call this view, shared by McCall Smith, Archard and Macleod amongst others, 'the independence thesis'. It may be contrasted with the 'priority thesis' because it recognises in one form or another that parents have independent interests in relation to their children which cannot be explained away on the basis that they derive only from parental duty. I want to take two topical examples to demonstrate why I prefer the independence thesis to the priority thesis.

My first example is the much-debated, but nonetheless unresolved, question of contact between children and parents.[31] There is an apparently never-ending argument about whether contact is properly described as a right at all and, if so, whether it is the right of the parent or the child. Historically, it was viewed as the former, but since the 1970s the preponderant view has been that it is better described as a right of the child.[32] Certain feminist commentators are particularly hostile to the notion that so-called 'absent fathers' should be able to assert a right

---

[28] *Ibid.* On the issue of parental responsibility in the context of religion, see further Taylor, this volume.

[29] Above n 21, 97.

[30] Above n 18, 119.

[31] On the issues and controversies surrounding the question of contact between parents and children, see A Bainham, B Lindley, M Richards and L Trinder (eds), *Children and their Families: Contact, Rights and Welfare* (Oxford, Hart, 2003).

[32] Wrangham J led the way in 1973 in *M v M (Child: Access)* [1973] 2 All ER 81.

Is Anything Now Left of Parental Rights? 29

of contact[33] and, unsurprisingly, fathers' rights groups are equally insistent that rights are involved in this question.[34] There has also been much discussion about whether there are any meaningful *duties* in relation to contact, which might be seen as the correlative of rights, and sharp disagreement about the extent to which, if at all, it is appropriate for the courts to attempt to enforce contact.[35]

What, then, is the truth of this matter? In order to get to the bottom of the nature of the contact question I want to focus on the position of the divorced, non-resident parent who, I will assume, is the father. It seems likely that many of these men would be the first to recognise that the *most important* interest at stake in maintaining contact following divorce is *the child's* wellbeing. However, it also seems likely that such men will recognise the significance of maintaining contact, not just for the child, but *also for themselves* and for their own future self-esteem and wellbeing. It is unrealistic to assume that the *only* benefit to be derived from contact with a parent is the child's. Surely a much more realistic way of looking at things is that *both* the child and the father will derive independent, or perhaps mutual, benefits from ongoing contact unless there are reasons why this would be harmful. The priority thesis cannot account for post-divorce contact because it is simply not the case that the parent's own interest lies exclusively in discharging a pre-existing obligation to the child. The independence thesis, in contrast, is much more realistic because it acknowledges that *both* child and parent derive benefits from contact. McCall Smith himself used the case of contact as an example of a parent-centred parental right:

> The right to the society of the child is a parental right, and it is appropriately considered as a parent-centred right, and yet it has nothing to do with any consideration of the welfare of the child. This right is accorded to thoroughly disagreeable (though not violent)[36] parents in exactly the same way as it is accorded to those who are more congenial company from the child's point of view.[37]

McCall Smith did not fall into the trap of believing, as many apparently do, that we must jump one way or the other in classifying contact *either* as a right of the

---

[33] See particularly C Smart, 'The ethic of justice strikes back: changing narratives of fatherhood' in A Diduck and K O'Donovan (eds), *Feminist Perspectives on Family Law* (Abingdon, Routledge Cavendish, 2006).

[34] On fathers' rights groups generally, see R Collier and S Sheldon (eds), *Father's Rights Activism and Law Reform in Comparative Perspective* (Oxford, Hart, 2006).

[35] For the view that contact has been over-zealously enforced by the courts, see C Smart and B Neale, 'Arguments against virtue—must contact be enforced?' (1997) *Family Law* 332. The author has expressed the view in 'Contact as a right and obligation' in A Bainham *et al*, above n 31, ch 5, that it is important that attempts should be made to enforce contact and that, indeed, this is required by the European Convention on Human Rights. For the author's view that contact is properly conceptualised as a right and indeed an obligation, see A Bainham, 'Contact as a right and obligation' (1995) 54 *CLJ* 512.

[36] In fact, McCall Smith has turned out to be incorrect about this, at least in England where it is clear that a record of violence by itself does not preclude the courts from (controversially) allowing contact between parent and child. The leading authority is *Re L (Contact: Domestic Violence)* [2000] 2 FLR 334.

[37] Above n 1, 10.

parent *or* as a right of the child. On the contrary, he was at pains to demonstrate that two quite independent rights existed:

> [I]t is true that a child benefits from the society of its parents, but that fact surely is grounds for asserting the *child's* right to parental society, which is another right altogether. In the case of a parental right to a child's society, any infringement of the right deprives the parent of a benefit.[38]

My second example is from the public law and focuses on the recent furore in the media about the young mother whose newborn baby was removed from her (albeit for a very short time as it turned out) in the middle of the night and about two hours after his birth. In *R (G) v Nottingham CC*,[39] Munby J made a peremptory order which required the local authority to reunite mother and child forthwith on the basis that the authority had acted unlawfully in taking the child from the mother without any prior court order. Later that day, the authority did what it should have done in the first place and obtained an interim care order from a judge. How are we to view this unfortunate episode? If we believe in the priority thesis, we are forced into the position that the only legitimate interest at stake here was the baby's interest in not being unlawfully removed from his mother. Any interest or right of the young mother was *exclusively* referable to discharging her duty to her infant son. However, this is not the real world. It is profoundly unattractive to deny that *the mother herself* had independent interests or rights as against the state when threatened with the taking of her child from her. In fact, if the authority had concentrated a little more on assisting the mother with her problems and a little less on taking her child away from her, it might have been better for all concerned, including the baby. The fact that this unlawful practice came to light at all owes much to the fact that the authority was facing an application for judicial review in relation to its statutory 'pathway plan'[40] for the mother on leaving care, which, it was alleged, was so deficient and inadequate as to be unlawful. Could there possibly be a better illustration of the dangers to the fundamental rights of children where the state chooses to ignore the distinctive rights of their parents?

WHY SHOULD THE LAW RECOGNISE PARENTAL INTERESTS?

In the preceding section, I offered the view that there are good reasons for believing that parents have interests in relation to their children which are independent of their children's welfare and which are attributable to their own benefit. One obvious response to this position may be that although it is easy enough to identify parental behaviour which advances a parent's own interests,

---

[38] *Ibid.*
[39] [2008] EWHC 152 (Admin).
[40] As required by Children Act 1989 s 23E, inserted by the Children (Leaving Care) Act 2000.

this does not lead to the conclusion that the law should recognise or support such behaviour unless it is also consistent with the general aim of promoting the child's welfare.[41] I want to suggest that there are perhaps two principal reasons why the law should openly recognise the independent interests of parents.

The first reason relates to honesty and transparency. Of course it would be possible to portray every action which a parent takes, and which the law regards as legitimate, as no more than furtherance of the child's best interests. It could even be said that parents are under a general duty to act at all times with the aim of promoting the welfare of their children, although this immediately runs into the problem that the 'welfare principle' as we know it is of decidedly limited application.[42] However, more importantly, would this be an honest way of looking at things and would it fairly represent the legal position?

Take the central issue of what used to be called the child's 'custody'.[43] It is generally accepted that a most important aspect, perhaps *the* most important aspect, of the powers which parents exercise relates to the physical care and control of the child's movements. The younger the child is, the more obvious this role is. It can be explicitly regulated now by means of a residence order, but more often than not it is subsumed within the wider status of possessing parental responsibility. Are we to believe that in taking decisions relating to such matters as where the child is to live, go on holiday, spend weekends or which friends and relatives the child should visit and when, the parent is legally bound to determine all of these matters with *only* the child's best interests in mind? To characterise these decisions in this way would in my view be at best a distortion of the truth of family life and at worst plainly dishonest. The fact is that decisions like this are *family* decisions and they reflect more often than not the way in which the *parents* wish to spend their time. If the parents decide that Saturday afternoons will be spent shopping and that Sunday lunchtimes will be spent visiting the grandparents, the law supports them in these decisions, however much their objecting children are forced along with them. Only someone with a vivid imagination, surely, could see these decisions as being *just* about the welfare of

---

[41] Dickens rejects any such claim, limiting the general parental duty to the avoidance of harm: above n 23, especially 464.

[42] The welfare or paramountcy principle in the Children Act 1989 s 1 applies only to questions of upbringing or the administration of children's property which are in dispute before the courts. The corresponding provision in Art 3 of the UNCRC is somewhat wider in its application, although the child's welfare is there expressed to be 'a primary consideration' and not the paramount consideration. It is perhaps worthy of note that, whereas the duty to have regard to the child's best interests as a primary consideration applies to 'public or private social welfare institutions, courts of law, administrative authorities or legislative bodies' in their actions concerning children, the imposition of any such duty on parents is conspicuously absent from the list.

[43] 'Custody' was abolished as a concept by the Children Act 1989 to be replaced, at least in the case of court orders, by the new concept of 'residence'. It survives, however, in relation to international child abduction where possessing 'rights of custody' is an essential prerequisite to invoking the Hague Convention. On the old concept of custody and the forms of custody orders which could be made by the courts, see Law Commission, 'Custody' (Law Com WP No 96, 1986) and 'Review of Child Law: Guardianship and Custody' (Law Com No 172, HC 594, 1988).

32 *Andrew Bainham*

the children. Therefore, one good reason for the law recognising explicitly that parents are entitled to act in relation to their children in a way which is not constrained entirely by any notion of promoting their best interests, is that this represents reality and is the honest thing to do.

The second reason for legal recognition of the independent interests of parents is ironically grounded in the responsibilities which they undoubtedly have. Essentially, the argument, which has been described as the 'exchange view' of parenthood,[44] is that parents have rights because they have responsibilities and they have responsibilities because they have rights. Birth parents are automatically charged, both by social convention and (more importantly) the law, with the task of caring and providing for their children.[45] Parents are not licensed[46] and neither does the state take the responsibility for the collective upbringing of children from birth. Any idea that children should be automatically raised from birth by anyone other than what Guggenheim has called the 'causal parents' would be completely alien to our thinking in a Western liberal democracy. Guggenheim describes the established process for 'allocation' of responsibility for children as follows:

> First, every child must be associated at birth with some adult who has caretaking responsibility and will make the major life decisions for him or her so that society will know the allocation of their custody when they are born ... As is well known, biological parents are responsible for their children at birth. They have the right, above all others, to raise them in their home or to authorize another to raise them instead ... Under our rules, parents self-identify by putting their names on a child's birth certificate ... [A] myriad of legally significant consequences follow from the formal recognition of parenthood.[47]

So parental status flows from the fact of birth and the establishment of parentage. It gives rise to a 'status responsibility' and many legal consequences which, as McCall Smith has also pointed out, are 'non-negotiable'. As he put it:

> It is not open for a parent to say: I accept that I must feed my child, but I don't accept that I have any duty to educate him or her.[48]

---

[44] KT Bartlett, 'Re-expressing Parenthood' (1988) 98 *Yale Law Journal* 293.

[45] Until comparatively recently, it could have been argued that this automatic imposition of parental responsibility (leaving aside the issue of child support) did not apply to fathers who were unmarried to the mother of the child. However, in relation to births since December 2003, the naming of the father on the birth certificate will now lead to these men acquiring parental responsibility: Children Act 1989 s 4(1)(a). There remains a small minority of fathers (about 7% of all fathers and 15% of unmarried fathers) who, although liable for child support, will not acquire wider parental responsibility because they are not identified on the birth certificate.

[46] Although licensing parents has been mooted from time to time. See particularly H Lafollete, 'Licensing parents' (1980) 9 *Philosophy and Public Affairs* 182. For a more recent suggestion that there should be some attempt to screen out unsuitable parents at birth, which also puts forward a model statute on how this might be done, see J Dwyer, *The Relationship Rights of Children* (Cambridge, Cambridge University Press, 2006) 254 *ff*.

[47] Guggenheim, above n 14, 20.

[48] Above n 1, 7.

Is Anything Now Left of Parental Rights? 33

The argument is therefore that the accommodation of parents' own interests in the legal regime is appropriate because of the extensive burdens, financial, emotional and practical, which are automatically thrust upon them by law and society. These remain in place at least until the child attains adulthood and sometimes, to a limited extent, for some years after that.[49] Neither should we under-value in this equation the burdens and sacrifices associated with pregnancy, the birth itself and the beginnings of life for the child. Quite rightly, these burdens are seen as falling disproportionately on the mother and might be thought to give the mother an especially strong claim to consideration of her interests.[50] However, in many cases (although clearly not all), the father's contribution throughout pregnancy, at the birth and in the immediate nurturing of the child thereafter is far from negligible. The absence of anything approaching satisfactory paternity leave does not assist this contribution, but there are signs that this may be changing, albeit slowly.[51]

How well, then, are we doing in English law in giving appropriate weight to parents' interests or rights? It would be possible to revisit again the debate about the nature and extent of parental autonomy and its relationship with children's welfare and rights. However, it is not my intention to reopen this debate.[52] Instead, I want to concentrate on how effectively we defend the very status of parent. It will be my contention that it is this issue which is most critical to parents and that it is in this area that we are performing spectacularly badly.

THE DEFENCE OF PARENTAL STATUS

The most fundamentally important issue for parents, more important to them than particular questions surrounding upbringing, is the security which is represented by the superior status which they as parents hold over others who claim to have an interest in the child. Furthermore, it is this status which is now being subjected to an unrelenting attack. This is how two academic commentators have recently described the modern approach to the definition of parenthood:

---

[49] Parents may, eg be held financially responsible in divorce or matrimonial proceedings for adult children who are 'receiving instruction at an educational establishment or undergoing training for a trade, profession or vocation' or 'where there are special circumstances which justify the making of an order': Matrimonial Causes Act 1973 s 29.

[50] I argue below, however, that proper consideration of the mother's interests ought not to extend to giving her the sole decision on whether her baby should be adopted or whether the father and wider family should be informed of the birth. The Court of Appeal has, however, effectively upheld the mother's right to decide this in *Re C (A Child) v XYZ CC* [2007] EWCA Civ 1206.

[51] The Work and Families Act 2006 does seek to improve paternity leave by permitting the father to take some of the mother's unused maternity leave, where she elects to forgo it, but it does not embody any principle of *concurrent* maternity and paternity leave beyond the current statutory two weeks' paternity leave.

[52] But for an illuminating discussion of the different political positions on parental autonomy, see Macleod, above n 18.

34 *Andrew Bainham*

Who are a child's parents? If one posed this question to a group of passengers on the Clapham omnibus, you [sic] would probably elicit a wide variety of responses. One passenger might respond that it is the man and woman who are linked by blood to the child: the genetic parents. Another passenger might respond that it is the woman who gives birth to the child and her husband and partner: the gestational parents. Yet another passenger might respond that it is the people who love, nurture and care for the child: the social parents. The concept of parenthood and who should be regarded as a child's parents is thus a strongly contested question.[53]

As an academic statement of the law's modern attitude to parenthood, it is difficult to find fault with this, although whether it truly represents how ordinary people would react is perhaps open to question. Is it not just as likely that society in general is capable of keeping in separate compartments the child's biological mother and father and the many other people who, while not being the child's parents, may be acting as parent-substitutes? It is a moot point whether many ordinary people, as opposed to academics, would identify these others as 'parents'. The debate about parenthood is in reality not unlike the debate about cohabitation. Those who are married are readily identified as such by the formality of a marriage certificate. Cohabitants on the other hand are an extremely diverse group who may be cohabiting for a host of differing reasons, for longer or shorter periods of time and with widely different attitudes to commitment and legal regulation of relationships.[54] This is perhaps the principal reason why it has proved so difficult to reach a consensus on what is the appropriate form of legal regulation of cohabitation.[55] Likewise, assuming biological parentage is established, all parents can be defined by reference to their part in procreation. However, this is clearly not the case in relation to so-called 'social parents', which, as a single group, defy any easy definition or identification. It is much more difficult to arrive at an appropriate legal status for such a diverse group; to make them all legal parents is clearly not a desirable or practical option.

Nonetheless, we are increasingly being asked to accept that it is the social role of being a parent which makes someone a parent and which should lead to legal parentage being conferred on that person. Thus, Judith Masson has referred to 'parenting by being' and 'parenting by doing' as alternative bases for the recognition of parental status.[56] The question which is frequently posed is whether the genetic link should carry more weight in the allocation of parenthood than should the assumption of the responsibility for raising a child. This is often

---

[53] S Harris-Short and J Miles, *Family Law: Text, Cases and Materials* (Oxford, Oxford University Press, 2007) 665.

[54] See, eg A Barlow and G James, 'Regulating marriage and cohabitation in 21st century Britain' (2004) 67 *MLR* 143.

[55] This has not, however, prevented the Law Commission from trying to devise a scheme to deal at least with the financial and property issues arising on the breakdown of cohabitation: 'Cohabitation: The Financial Consequences of Relationship Breakdown' (Law Com No 307, Cm 7182, 2007).

[56] J Masson, 'Parenting by being; parenting by doing—in search of principles for founding families' in JR Spencer and A Du Bois-Pedain, *Freedom and Responsibility in Reproductive Choice* (Oxford, Hart, 2006).

presented as a set of scales in which biology, the 'mere genetic link' as it is often described, is weighed against the burdensome practicalities of raising a child. Yet, this involves a sleight of hand. The point is that the overwhelming majority of biological parents have *much more* than a 'mere genetic link' with their children. They also perform, in most cases at least for a period of time, a psychological or social parenting role. It is true that a small minority of fathers and the very occasional mother can be said to have little or nothing more than the genetic link arising from a single act of intercourse or the donation of sperm (in the case of fathers)[57] or the act of gestating and giving birth (in the case of mothers).[58] However, even in those cases it is worth exploring further *why* they may have no more than that connection before denying them the status normally accorded to biological parents.[59] In any event, we ought not to allow the tail to wag the dog. The definition of parent should be constructed to reflect the more usual circumstances of parenthood and ought not to be driven by an unrepresentative minority. When we are engaging then in this suggested balancing exercise, we ought in most cases to allow for the fact that the biological parent's claim is likely to rest on a good deal more than biology, whereas the claim of other people can *only* be based on a social or psychological contribution and acting as a substitute parent.

Baroness Hale of Richmond brought this out in an illuminating speech in *Re G (Children)*,[60] in which she analysed the separate components of parenthood. She listed the *genetic, gestational* and *social and psychological* contributions. The biological mother would normally make all three contributions. The biological father certainly makes the first and in the majority of cases also the third. Baroness Hale did not credit him with a gestational contribution, although it can be argued that many biological fathers *do* contribute at the gestational stage, albeit of course not in the much more physically and emotionally substantial way that mothers do. In contrast, the lesbian partner in this case had made an undeniably important social and psychological contribution to the welfare of the two children concerned, but she could not claim to have contributed in the other ways which we may associate with being a parent. While the House of Lords denied that this created a legal presumption in favour of primary residence with the biological mother, it did hold that in applying the welfare principle the

---

[57] Licensed sperm donors are accordingly excluded from legal parentage: Human Fertilisation and Embryology Act 2008 s 41(1). Neither do they have 'family life' with the child for the purposes of the ECHR. See *G v The Netherlands* [1990] 16 EHRR 38.

[58] A rare reported case is *Re B (A Minor)* [2001] UKHL 70, where the mother (who had given up a previous child for adoption) did not look at the baby when born and said that she had no maternal instincts.

[59] In a number of reported cases, it has been quite clear that the reason why the father has had no involvement with the child has been either because the mother did not inform him of the pregnancy or birth or because she refused to allow him to have anything to do with the child. See, eg *Keegan v Ireland* (1994) 18 EHRR 342; and *Re H; Re G (Adoption: Consultation of Unmarried Fathers)* [2001] 1 FLR 646.

[60] [2006] UKHL 43.

'special contribution' of the biological parent should be an 'important and significant factor' in the court's determination.

Re G reveals just how far we have come in raising expectations about parental status in those who are not parents. It should be conceded at the outset that the mother's behaviour following her split with her partner was far from impeccable.[61] Even so, the lesbian partner, the so-called 'co-parent', sought (with some success in the High Court and Court of Appeal) not merely parity with the mother through parental responsibility for the children and a shared residence order,[62] but *more than equality* with her in the form of a time-sharing order which broke 70:30 in her favour. The House of Lords, quite rightly in my view, reversed these percentages leaving the mother as the primary, and her former partner as the secondary, carer. The claim of the partner here is just one example of the doubtful argument that doing some of the things which parents do entitles one to be regarded as a parent.

Where will all of this end? We do not appear to be so far away from the position that anyone living with a parent will demand the right to be regarded as a parent. Indeed, the position of the lesbian partner is a very good example of exactly this trend, which began with the equally fictitious attribution of parenthood to non-biological fathers. The Human Fertilisation and Embryology Act 2008, confers legal parentage on lesbian partners in cases of assisted reproduction, automatically in the absence of objection where they are civil partners[63] and where the 'female parenthood conditions' are satisfied if they have not formalised their relationship in this way.[64] These latter conditions essentially require that both partners consent to the acquisition of parental status by the mother's partner and that the consent has not been withdrawn. Parentage here ostensibly turns on consent, but the essence of the claim to parentage is surely the existence of the relationship itself and the joint enterprise to have a child. How long is it going to be before the lesbian partner of a mother who bears a child outside the licensed system, perhaps as in several reported cases after having intercourse with a readily identifiable man,[65] claims that it is discriminatory for her not also to be recognised as the legal parent? After all, her claim is just as strong if we see it as being based on her position as the supportive partner of the mother in their mutual desire to have a child. I have argued at length elsewhere that it is a fundamental error of policy to go further down this road of deliberately creating more instances in which biological and legal parentage do not coincide, notably because of the distortion of kinship which this involves.[66] I will return to this

---

[61] She had removed the children from Leicester to Cornwall in breach of a court order.
[62] Under the Children Act 1989 s 12(2), the effect of a residence order in favour of someone who is not a parent is to confer parental responsibility on that person which is held while the order lasts.
[63] See s 42(1).
[64] See ss 43 and 44.
[65] See particularly *Re D (contact and parental responsibility: lesbian mothers and known father)* [2006] EWHC 2 (Fam).
[66] A Bainham, 'Arguments about parentage' (2008) 67 *CLJ* 322.

issue briefly below since of course it begs the question of exactly what legal status ought to be given to long-term carers of children who are not parents.

Re G also provokes a reassessment of the division between the public and private law relating to parents and children. The central principle governing the public law is that the state may not compulsorily remove a child from the care of a parent unless it can establish that the child is either suffering, or at risk of suffering, significant harm attributable to a standard of care which is not that of the reasonable parent.[67] The Children Act 1989 explicitly rejected the notion that compulsory action leading to the removal of a child from parental care should be based (as it would be if governed by the welfare principle) only on a professional view that someone else can do better than the parent at raising the child.[68] In private disputes, by contrast, the welfare principle *does* apply and it enables individuals who are not parents, like the mother's partner in *Re G*, to argue that the coercive power of the state (exercised through the courts) should be used to deprive a parent of care, or at least primary care, despite the fact that it is not alleged that the parent represents a threat of harm to the child.

This orthodox distinction between the public and private law was recently illustrated in *Re P (Surrogacy: Residence)*.[69] In this case, Coleridge J had to adjudicate between the claims of a surrogate mother and those of the biological father whom she had deceived into believing that she had miscarried. In ordering that the child should live with the father and his wife, he quite properly distinguished between the different criteria under the public and private law. He held that it was essential to keep at the forefront of the court's mind that the question was not whether the child had suffered or was likely to suffer significant harm at the hands of either parent. In the private law, when choosing between two competing residential parental regimes, the question was rather 'in which home is he most likely to mature into a happy and balanced adult and to achieve his fullest potential as a human?'[70] This was, however, a case in which the competition was between the two biological parents and, as Coleridge J put it:

> The fact that both sides constitute one of the child's natural parents means that both sides start from the same position, neither side being able to claim that the blood tie should favour their claim.[71]

This is also true, self-evidently, of the much more common instance in which it must be determined which of two parents should be the primary carer following

---

[67] The so-called 'threshold conditions' in the Children Act 1989 s 31(2). These conditions must also be satisfied under the Adoption and Children Act 2002 s 21(2) where a local authority seeks an adoption placement order in relation to a looked-after child.

[68] See DHSS, *Review of Child Care Law: Report to Ministers of an Interdepartmental Working Party* (London, HMSO, 1985) [15.10].

[69] [2008] 1 FLR 177, upheld by the Court of Appeal in *Re P (Residence: Appeal)* [2007] EWCA Civ 1053.

[70] *Ibid*, at 181.

[71] *Ibid*.

38 *Andrew Bainham*

divorce. It is inevitable, in the event of a dispute, that the court must resolve it, and to deprive a parent of care in these circumstances clearly does not entail any judgment that that parent represents a threat of harm to the child. However, we may reasonably question whether the harm principle ought not to play a larger role where the dispute is not between parent and parent, but between parents and others. If we could tear ourselves away from legal theory and concentrate instead on the perception of the parent affected, it may not matter to that parent one jot whether the child is removed from him or her in public law or private law proceedings. In each case, the child will be in the primary care of others under the coercive power of the courts. The difference is that in the former proceedings it is normally necessary to demonstrate that the parent is at risk of harming the child,[72] but in the latter it is not.

Does this in any event truly represent what judges do in private law decisions? A case can be made for saying that practice under the welfare principle is in fact largely consistent with the harm thesis, at least in contexts other than those in which it is necessary to choose a home for the child as between two parents, each of whom could provide this satisfactorily. The case of medical decision-making, so often the site of arguments about parents' versus children's rights, demonstrates that in many cases, although not formulated in this way, the courts are committed to the principle that they ought not to interfere with parental discretion unless the position taken by a parent is considered harmful to the child.[73]

It can be argued more generally that where the dispute is between parent and non-parent, it should be resolved in favour of the parent unless it can be shown that the parent is exposing the child to the risk of harm. Otherwise, the danger is that the state acting through the courts is intervening compulsorily in parenting on the basis of a looser and less exacting standard than Parliament has decreed. In the context of adoption too there are concerns that the child's relationship with the biological family (including the father and the paternal family) may be ignored with impunity where the adoption involves a placement by consent and is therefore characterised by the courts as 'private'. In the case of a public law adoption involving a looked-after child, there is in contrast a statutory duty to explore fully the resources of the birth family.[74] However, if it is important to the child that the potential of the wider family be investigated, it is difficult to see why this is less important simply because proceedings are categorised as 'private'.[75] Further, examined from the perspective of the father or extended family,

---

[72] This is subject to the qualification that where a child has been harmed, but it is not clear who has perpetrated the harm, a care order may be made even though it has not been possible to attribute the harm to a parent. See *Lancashire CC v B* [2000] 2 AC 147.

[73] Many examples could be given, but the case of the conjoined twins is perhaps the best: *Re A (Children) (Conjoined Twins: Surgical Separation)* [2001] Fam 147.

[74] Children Act 1989 ss 22(4) and 23.

[75] In *Re C (A Child) v XYZ CC* [2007] EWCA Civ 1206 [82], Thorpe LJ said: 'There are good social policy reasons for accepting the option of a private birth' and was concerned that if the mother's

in each case the state, whether in the guise of an adoption agency, the local authority or the court, is taking a decision either to include or exclude them from involvement as possible carers. It does not matter to them one iota whether this is characterised as a private or public issue.

More generally, the parent's position in relation to adoption may be seen as another example of the recent erosion of parents' rights or interests. First, the circumstances under which an adoption may now be granted *without* parental consent essentially depend on an undiluted application of the welfare principle. Despite academic arguments that the 2002 legislation does contain safeguards for the birth families' interests, both in the statutory checklist of factors[76] and in the statutory requirement that 'the welfare of the child *requires* the [parent's] consent to be dispensed with',[77] there remains a strong suspicion that the former test of parental unreasonableness, despite its close association in practice with the professional view of the child's best interests,[78] did provide a stronger safeguard of the parent's position. Indeed, there were reported cases right up to the enactment of the 2002 legislation in which parents were held not to have withheld their consent unreasonably.[79]

If the proposition is accepted that parents should have a priority over, and superior status to, other carers this still leaves open the question of exactly what status it is appropriate to give to these others. I have argued elsewhere[80] that we need to resolve this question by keeping in mind the important distinction between being a parent (parentage) and discharging the functions of a parent (parenting). The former is closely linked to legal kinship, while the latter is closely associated with the legal concept of parental responsibility. The difficulty as I perceive it is twofold. First, there is a strong cultural cachet attached to being accepted as a parent. The fact is that those who are performing a long-term parenting role want to be regarded as parents and are generally not satisfied with a lesser status or with being called something else. This surely in part explains the continued popularity of adoption, the efforts to which some will go to obtain a child through assisted reproduction and the correspondingly low status of foster care. Secondly, we lack an appropriate intermediate status which might be

---

appeal were dismissed 'we would be effectively precluding private birth as a prelude to fast-track adoption in almost every case'.

[76] Especially factor (c), which refers to 'the likely effect on the child (throughout his life) of having ceased to be a member of the original family and become an adopted person', and factor (f), which refers to the 'relationship which the child has with relatives' and, inter alia, the likelihood of such relationships continuing if adoption were to be granted: Adoption and Children Act 2002 s 1(4).

[77] Adoption and Children Act 2002 s 52(1)(b).

[78] Lord Hailsham started this trend in *Re W (An Infant)* [1971] AC 682, where he expressed the view that a reasonable parent has regard to his or her child's welfare.

[79] An important example being *Re B (Adoption Order)* [2001] EWCA Civ 347, in which Hale LJ (as she then was) emphasised, in the wake of the Human Rights Act 1998, that the Convention requirement of proportionality might mean that adoption was not the proportionate response to the child's long-term needs in some cases and that therefore a parent who appreciated this might not be acting unreasonably in withholding consent.

[80] Bainham, above n 66.

40 *Andrew Bainham*

capable of satisfying long-term carers, but which does not involve misrepresenting them as parents. It is possible of course to acquire parental responsibility and it has been legislative policy in recent years to make this easier, most notably by allowing step-parents and civil partners to obtain it by formal agreement with the legal parents.[81] The problem is that although possessing parental responsibility is certainly a status of sorts,[82] it is not an identifiable one in the way that being a parent is. Moreover, the rules on standing for obtaining parental responsibility by court order (should this prove necessary) are perhaps unnecessarily complex.[83]

What we need is a recognisable status, more easily obtained, with a sound pedigree and long-standing social acceptance. The obvious candidate is guardianship.[84] Guardians in legal terms approximate quite closely to parents, but there is no pretence that they are parents[85] and in particular kinship is unaffected by the appointment of a guardian. Guardian is in fact a perfect description of someone who is acting in place of a parent—which, after all, is what all social carers are in fact doing.[86] The new status of 'special guardian' is designed to reflect these concerns and to provide an alternative to adoption, but the omens are not especially good that this will become a mainstream status for long-term carers.[87] In any event, the special guardianship regime may be thought rather too unwieldy to provide a general solution to the status problem. It is a pity in some ways that the term 'guardian' has been so excessively and confusingly over-used. We have had, for example, 'poor law guardians', 'guardians of the estate', 'guardians of the person', 'natural guardians', 'guardians *ad litem*', 'children's guardians', 'guardians' and 'special guardians'. What this does perhaps confirm is the utility of the essential notion of guardianship in different contexts where a legal status is required for those who protect children and defend their interests, but who are *not* parents. It seems unlikely that, for all its merits, guardianship could displace

---

[81] Children Act 1989 s 4A.

[82] Notably it confers the right to take or participate in major decisions affecting the child and the right to look after the child unless this is restricted by a residence order.

[83] The rules are largely contained in the Children Act 1989 s 10 and distinguish between parents, guardians and persons with parental responsibility; step-parents and former step-parents, civil partners and former civil partners, persons who have had the child with them for three years or have the consent of those with parental responsibility; and everyone else. Special rules also apply to local authority foster parents and, under the Children and Young Persons Act 2008, to relatives.

[84] For detailed discussion of the history of guardianship, which preceded parenthood as a legal status in English law, see Law Commission, 'Review of Child Law: Guardianship' (Law Com WP No 91, 1985). The best account of the current law on guardianship is to be found in N Lowe and G Douglas, *Bromley's Family Law* (10th edn, Oxford, Oxford University Press, 2006) ch 9.

[85] The Law Commission was concerned that a clear distinction should be drawn between parents and guardians and, accordingly, recommended the abolition of the notion of 'natural guardianship' which had vested in the father of a legitimate child: *ibid* [3.2]–[3.4]. The Children Act 1989 s 2(4) gave effect to this recommendation.

[86] The Law Commission did moot the possibility of an extension of the existing concept of guardianship to allow the appointment of *inter vivos* guardians (see above n 84, Pt IV), but the idea did not, at the time, capture the imagination of consultees. Perhaps it ought to be resurrected.

[87] The previous attempt to introduce a status for long-term carers falling short of adoption, custodianship, was very ineffectual and short-lived.

Is Anything Now Left of Parental Rights? 41

the attractions of parenthood in the popular consciousness. It would nonetheless be better if we were to continue to search for an appropriate status for the many different social carers of children rather than to create ever more instances in which biological and legal parentage do not coincide, with the consequent threat to the special position of biological parents which this poses. In the meantime, the new status of special guardian ought to be welcomed and utilised where possible,[88] and there might also be a case for reforming the current definition of 'child of the family'[89] to recognise *informal*, as well as formal, instances of cohabitation with a parent.

CONCLUSIONS

I have argued here that the debate about parental rights is in simple language an argument about whether parents have independent interests in their children which cannot be accounted for entirely on the basis of their duties or responsibilities towards them. I have further argued that they have and that the law should openly recognise these independent interests, or rights if we prefer to call them that, for two reasons. The first is because in reality the law *does* allow parents to take a host of family decisions which are every bit as much about parents living the kind of lives they wish to live as they are about advancing their children's welfare. Secondly, the automatic status of parenthood, which the law confers or imposes on the birth of a child, justifies respect for parental interests. It is simply not reasonable to take the position that those who bear the legal and moral burdens which society expects of a parent should be denied all recognition of their independent claims or interests.

I have identified protection of the special legal status of parent as the most important issue. When we are considering an appropriate legal status for those who, while not parents, are involved in parenting, we need to remember that the law does *not* automatically impose upon them the responsibilities automatically faced by legal parents on the birth of a child. Liability for child support is perhaps the best example.[90] Therefore, while it is perfectly reasonable for someone who is involved in a major way with upbringing to seek out parental responsibility, to go further and make that person the legal parent muddles kinship and threatens the status of birth parents. This is happening too often in the contexts of assisted reproduction and adoption. While there may well be circumstances under which

---

[88] Although the early evidence on its use suggests otherwise: see A Hall, 'Special Guardianship: A missed opportunity—findings from research' (2008) *Family Law* 148.

[89] At present, the definition in Children Act 1989 s 105 covers only those children treated as children of the family by spouses and civil partners, but it must be doubted whether the position of a spouse or civil partner in relation to his or her partner's children is greatly, if at all, different from that of the informal partner.

[90] This still turns on being the legal parent of the child, which in the overwhelming majority of cases will be the biological parent. For a thorough treatment of the moral and legal basis for child support, see N Wikeley, *Child Support: Law and Policy* (Oxford, Hart, 2006) ch 1.

42   *Andrew Bainham*

it is appropriate to reallocate legal parentage, we ought to be strictly confining and not increasing the occasions on which this is done. The search, I have suggested, should rather be for an appropriate intermediate status, like guardianship, which properly recognises *parenting*, but which does not distort *parentage*. The fact is that there is not, and there never can be, true equality or parity as between biological parents and other carers because they are in a materially different position which justifies differential treatment. Parents have a unique role in the creation of the child which can never be true of those who lack this biological contribution.

However, it might be objected that to assert the independent rights or interests of parents, and to place importance on defending the status of biological parents, is to undervalue the commitment to children's welfare or rights. I do not believe this to be the case for two reasons. First, regarding parental autonomy this should be, and clearly is, limited by the harm principle. Where parents cause or threaten harm to their child, this may found a care order or lead to judicial rulings which protect the child in 'single issue' cases, most obviously where a parent is denying the child necessary medical intervention. Secondly, it is surely not in children's interests to pretend that the law is not cognisant of adult claims when in reality clearly it is. Disputes which may be theoretically formulated as being just about children are in reality not just about children. It must be obvious to everyone that the great majority of legal actions concerning children are brought by adults. Truth and transparency are important to children as has been widely recognised, not least by the family judiciary.[91] Therefore, the case for honesty about the legal balance being struck between the interests of children and their parents is a strong one as is the case, increasingly urged by commentators, for reformulation of the welfare principle.[92] We are right to give priority to the rights and interests of children, but we are wrong to imply that no one else, and especially parents, has them too.

---

[91]   For noteworthy judicial statements, see Ward LJ in *Re H (Paternity: Blood Test)* [1996] 2 FLR 65; Sumner J in *Re J (Paternity: Welfare of Child)* [2007] EWHC 2837 at [13]–[14]; and Thorpe LJ in *Re C (Contact: Moratorium: Change of Gender)* [2006] EWCA Civ 1765 at [11].

[92]   Above n 11.

18

The Welfare Principle and the Rights of Parents

JONATHAN HERRING

Parenthood demands enormous sacrifices. But there is not a parent in the country who always places their child's interests before their own—inevitably and quite rightly family relationships involve "give and take". In many families the children's interests are pre-eminent, but on some occasions fairness and practicality demand that the interests of a child must be subordinated to those of the parents or other family members.[1] By contrast, the basis of the law in England and Wales[2] relating to children is section 1 of the Children Act 1989 which states that whenever the courts are required to make decisions concerning the upbringing of a child "the child's welfare shall be the court's paramount consideration". This is commonly known as the welfare principle.[3] It has been interpreted by the courts to mean that the interests of children shall prevail over those of their parents. So the court could make an order for the purpose of promoting a child's welfare, however great the sacrifice demanded of the parents or other members of the family, and even if the benefit to the child would be minimal. Indeed court orders requiring that a parent does not move from a particular geographical area,[4] or that the parent's new partner does not stay overnight in the family home are in theory available, and have been obtained in other jurisdictions.[5]

And that is the topic of this chapter: to consider the extent to which the courts are and should be entitled to make orders that infringe the rights of parents and others in order to pursue the welfare of a child. How can we reconcile the

---

[1] Indeed our society as a whole does not make children's interests a priority in, for example, economic policy.

[2] The welfare principle is a central part of the law relating to children in many countries. See Article 3 of the United Nations Convention on the Rights of the Child, although the interests of the child are to be a "primary" consideration rather than "paramount". There is, of course, great difficulty in many cases in ascertaining what would promote a child's welfare.

[3] There are *dicta* in the House of Lords stating that parents are to exercise their powers in respect of children in order to promote the child's welfare (Lord Fraser in *Gillick v West Norfolk and Wisbech Area Health Authority* [1986] AC 112 at 170D–E).

[4] Courts have on occasions refused to give leave to a parent wishing to take children out of the jurisdiction e.g. *Re K (A Minor) (Removal from Jurisdiction)* [1992] 2 FLR 98; *Re T (Removal from Jurisdiction)* [1996] 2 FLR 352.

[5] e.g. *Parrillo v Parrillo* 554 A 2d 1043 (1989), a case heard in the Rhode Island Supreme Court, USA.

90 *Jonathan Herring*

welfare principle's centrality to the law with the realisation that doing so may require sacrifices of parents that could be unjust or impractical? I will first consider some of the decided cases where the courts have had to balance the interests of the child and parents. Despite the existence of the welfare principle the courts have given weight to the interests of parents and I will attempt to demonstrate the various means by which they have done so. I will then consider whether it would be better to abandon or explicitly limit the application of the welfare principle but conclude that what is required is an understanding of welfare that recognises the importance to a child of relationships based on justice and equality, rather than the current individualised conception of welfare. Before approaching these issues it is necessary to outline briefly the law relating to parents and children.

1. PARENTS' DUTIES AND RIGHTS IN LAW[6]

The law emphasises the responsibilities of parents rather than their rights. Mothers and some fathers[7] are given "parental responsibility" by the law.[8] This is defined as "all the rights, duties, powers, responsibilities and authority which by law a parent of a child has in relation to the child and his property".[9] The "rights" mentioned in this definition of parental responsibility have been held by Lord Fraser in the House of Lords to exist solely for the purpose of promoting the welfare of the child.[10] It is far from clear when these legal parental rights are of practical importance,[11] but it is generally thought that they are most significant when third parties interact with children. For example, only a person with parental responsibility can give effective consent to a doctor to carry out an operation on a child lawfully. It should also be stressed that the nature of parents' legal rights change as the child grows up.[12] A person who does not have parental responsibility but has care of a child (for example a babysitter) may still "do what is reasonable in all the circumstances of the case for the purpose of safeguarding or promoting the child's welfare".[13]

Alexander McCall Smith (1990) has usefully divided parental rights into parent-centred and child-centred rights. The child-centred rights are given to a

---

[6] For a detailed discussion of the law see Bainham (1998). For empirical research on relationships between children and parents after their separation see, for example, Maclean and Eekelaar (1997).

[7] Those fathers who are married to the mother and those who have been awarded parental responsibility under Children Act 1989, s.4.

[8] It is possible for non-parents to apply to the court for a residence order which if granted would award parental responsibility to the applicant Children Act 1989, s.12(2).

[9] Children Act 1989, s.3(1).

[10] *Gillick v West Norfolk and Wisbech Area Health Authority* [1986] AC 112 at 170D–E.

[11] Contrast Children (Scotland) Act 1995, s. 1 which is a little more explicit. It should also be noted that parents cannot sue in tort for interference of their parental rights: *F v Wirral Metropolitan Borough Council* [1991] Fam 69.

[12] *Gillick v West Norfolk and Wisbech Area Health Authority* [1986] AC 112.

[13] Children Act 1989, s.3(5).

parent to ensure that the child receives at least the minimum care expected in our society. Hence the right (and indeed duty) to clothe, feed and provide for the child. The parent-centred rights are given to a parent in respect of those issues over which there is no particular state-approved view, for example what kind of religious education a child should receive from his or her parents. There are benefits to the state from these parent-centred rights. They help the state avoid having to take a controversially interventionist stance over a topic for which there is no agreed societal response. They also encourage a culturally diverse society. In addition to these parental rights parents also have rights as individuals. It is the clash between this third category of parents' rights and the interests of children with which this chapter is particularly concerned.

Mention must briefly be made of the rights of children, a topic of increasing interest amongst commentators, but only acknowledged to a limited extent by the law. For present purposes it is convenient to accept the classification of children's rights as set out by John Eekelaar (1986). He recognises a child as having three categories of interests: "basic interests" (the essential requirements for the nurturing of the child); "developmental interests" (those interests necessary to enable the child to examine and develop his or her potential as a person); and "autonomy interests" (enabling the child to choose a course of action for him or herself). Eekelaar suggests that the autonomy interests must yield to basic or developmental interests if they are in conflict. This version of children's rights could be seen as consistent with the welfare principle.[14] Basic and developmental interests are clearly in line with the welfare principle. Autonomy interests can be brought in line with the welfare approach if it is accepted that the child's welfare can be furthered by allowing children to learn by their mistakes. I will be returning briefly to children's rights later, but the main focus of this chapter is the conflict between parental interests and the welfare principle.

The present core meaning of the welfare principle[15] is usually said to be contained in the speech of Lord McDermott in *J v. C*,[16] who stated:

> "it seems to me that [the welfare principle] must mean more than that the child's welfare is to be treated as the top item in a list of items relevant to the matter in question. I think [it] connote[s] a process whereby when all the relevant facts, relationships, claims and wishes of parents, risks, choices and other cases are taken into account and weighed, the course to be followed will be that which is most in the interest of the child's welfare as that term has now to be understood. That is the first consideration because it is of first importance and the paramount consideration because it rules on or determines the course to be followed".

This seems clearly to place the interests of children always above the interests of parents. Hence it is regularly stated in the case law that the interests of parents

---

[14] Although many argue that the welfare principle creates an image of children as weak and in need of protection which militates against recognition of children's autonomy "rights".
[15] With the checklist of factors listed in Children Act 1989, s.1(3).
[16] [1970] AC 668 at 711. Approved by House of Lords in *Re KD (A Minor) (Ward: Termination of Access)* [1988] AC 806.

are only relevant in a case involving the upbringing of children in so far as they affect the welfare of the child.[17] Welfare is understood in a wide sense and includes emotional, physical and moral welfare. It also includes considering the child's welfare into the future, including adulthood.[18] However, as I hope to demonstrate below, the courts have adopted a rather narrow approach to welfare, considering the welfare of the child as an isolated individual rather than as a person living within a community. This has created difficulties for the courts in accommodating the interests of parents, but they have found various ways of doing so. I will now consider these.

2. HOW THE COURTS HAVE DEALT WITH TENSIONS BETWEEN THE WELFARE PRINCIPLE AND PARENTS' RIGHTS

I will concentrate on four ways in which the law has been able to place weight on parents' interests despite the dominance of the welfare principle.

(a) Non-enforcement of the welfare principle

It is very noticeable that the legal supervision of parents' care for and nurturing of their children is limited. There is no overt attempt by the state to "police" parenting and to ensure that families are promoting the child's welfare.[19] It is interesting to contrast the law's attitude to day-care and child-minding with that of parenting. Day-care centres and child-minders need to be registered with a local authority and are subject to careful regulation and inspection to ensure the protection of the child's welfare.[20] There is no such formal surveillance with parental care.[21]

Generally, a court may become involved with the upbringing of children in three situations. The first is where the child is suffering harm to such an extent and in such circumstances that it is appropriate for the state to intervene to protect the child, for example by taking the child into care or instituting criminal proceedings against a parent.[22] Here the dispute is essentially a state–parent dispute and the aim of the proceedings is to ascertain whether the child needs state protection. The second is where there is a dispute between two adults, normally

---

[17] See, for example, *Re B (Contact: Stepfather's Opposition)* [1997] 2 FLR 579 at 585B.
[18] *Re B (A Minor) (Wardship: Sterilisation)* [1988] AC 199.
[19] Although see for example Donzelot (1980).
[20] Children Act 1989, Part X and Sch. 9. See Department of Health (1991).
[21] Although some professionals that are involved with children (e.g. teachers, health visitors) have guidelines about notification of evidence of unacceptable parental behaviour. See also Home Office (1998).
[22] Even then the courts have limited control over how a child in care is treated. See, for example, *Re T (A Minor) (Care Order)* [1994] 2 FLR 423.

the parents, over the upbringing of a child.[23] Here the role of the courts is to resolve what is usually a parent–parent dispute. The third is where a child brings proceedings against his or her parents. This is rare. Apart from these three situations the law generally does not interfere directly with the standard of parenting children.[24]

In a state–parent dispute the state is generally only entitled to intervene if the child has suffered or is likely to suffer significant harm.[25] In the absence of such harm state intervention is not permitted, even if it would promote the child's welfare. In those cases where there is no significant harm the welfare principle is promoted by the court in parent–parent cases.[26] However the fact that there is a parent–parent dispute does not necessarily indicate that the child is in particular need of court intervention but rather it simply indicates a need to resolve a dispute between adults (Bainham, 1990). Indeed those cases where parents or relatives are in dispute are often instances where there is in fact no order that can be made positively in the interests of the child and the court has to make an order which is least harmful to the child. Further the Court of Appeal has stated that the courts should not be used to resolve disputes concerning "day-to-day" issues.[27] So court enforcement of the welfare principle in private households is very limited (Freeman, 1997).

(b) Protection of parents' rights while using the welfare principle

There are various ways in which the courts have managed to place significant weight on the interests of parents in the process of applying the welfare principle. I am not necessarily criticising the results in these cases but seeking to demonstrate that the use of the welfare principle by the courts at present tends to disguise what is often the real issue—a clash between the interests of parents and the interests of children. The disguises can take various forms. I will consider three.[28]

(a) The first is by merging the interests of parents and children. It is natural that a judge will see a close link between the interests of parents and children. A child cared for by a miserable parent is likely to suffer more than one being cared for by a content parent. But there is always a danger that a court, when considering the welfare of the child, might confuse the welfare of the child with that of the parents.[29]

---

[23] Although it could be, for example, the grandmother who brings the matter before the court *Re W (Contact: Application by Grandparent)* [1997] 1 FLR 793.
[24] Although there are some restrictions relating to education. See, for example, Education Act 1996, s.7.
[25] Children Act 1989, s.31.
[26] Children Act 1989, s.8(1) describes the orders that are available.
[27] *Re P (A Minor) (Parental Responsibility Order)* [1994] 1 FLR 578.
[28] The case law referred to will only be a selection from that available.
[29] As the Court of Appeal has acknowledged in, for example, *Re O (Contact: Imposition of Conditions)* [1995] 2 FLR 124.

94 *Jonathan Herring*

In a recent case, *Re T*,[30] the Court of Appeal considered what should happen to a seriously ill young child who required a liver transplant. The child had already suffered some unsuccessful surgery and the parents decided not to authorise further surgery. The issue was brought before the court by the doctors. The unanimous medical opinion was that the prognosis for the child if the operation were to go ahead was good but that without the treatment the child would die. However the court decided the operation should not go ahead as it would not promote the child's interests. The Court of Appeal closely identified the interests of the child with those of the mother. It was argued that were the operation to be successful the child would require long-term care by the parents. If the parents were not willing to provide the care the child would suffer greatly and it was decided that this was not in the child's best interests:

"She [the mother] will have to comply with the court order, return to this country and present the child to one of the hospitals. She will have to arrange to remain in this country for the foreseeable future. If [the father] does not come she will have to manage unaided. How will the mother cope? Can her professionalism overcome her view that her son should not be subjected to this distressing procedure? Will she break down?"[31]

Butler Sloss LJ went on to say:

"The mother and this child are one for the purpose of this unusual case and the decision of the court to consent to the operation jointly affects the mother and son and so also affects the father. The welfare of the child depends upon his mother".[32]

By so closely identifying the child's interests with those of the mother the court was able to give weight to the mother's interests while appearing to adhere to the welfare principle.[33]

Another example of this is *Re Y*.[34] The case involved a mentally handicapped adult, but would seem to be applicable to children as the principle used in such cases is whether the treatment is in the patient's welfare. In *Re Y* permission was sought and granted to remove bone marrow from Y to give to her sister. It was stated by Connell J that the operation would be in Y's interests because the bone marrow might save the sister's life and this would prolong the life of the mother who was very close to Y. There were fears that were the sister to die the mother's life expectancy would diminish and this would be contrary to Y's best interests.[35]

[30] *Re T (A Minor) (Wardship. Medical Treatment)* [1997] 1 FLR 502.
[31] At 511H.
[32] At 510G.
[33] Contrast *Re C (Medical Treatment)* [1998] 1 FLR 384 where the court approved the doctors' decision not to provide treatment for a severely ill child, despite the parents' request for treatment.
[34] Re *(Mental Incapacity: Bone Marrow Transplant)* [1997] 2 WLR 556.
[35] Other examples could be cases involving disputes between parents over whether a child should be removed from the jurisdiction where a parent with a residence order will be granted permission to leave if the proposals are reasonable—*Re H (Application to Remove from Jurisdiction)* [1998] 1 FLR 848.

The Welfare Principle and Parents' Rights 95

There are two significant concerns with the merging of the interests of parents and children. First it can mean that interests of children are not given sufficient weight. *Re T* is particularly concerning. No doubt the demands placed on the parents if the surgery were ordered would be immense and it might be improper to compel the parents to suffer this sacrifice. However the court seems to have placed insufficient weight on the possibility of the parents requesting that the child be cared for by the local authority or foster parents.

A second danger is that the courts' approach hides the real issues.[36] For example, in *Re Y* merely focusing on the indirect benefit of improving the mother's well-being and so improving Y's welfare seems an unduly narrow way of looking at the issues involved. It was of crucial importance that the bone marrow transplant might save the sister's life. Surely the case would have been quite different if, say, the sister required some bone for cosmetic surgery, even if such a donation might improve Y's relationship with her mother.[37]

(b) The second form of covert recognition of parents' interests using the welfare principle is by means of using various "presumptions" or "well known facts of nature". For example Lord Templeman's dicta are often quoted:

> "the best person to bring up a child is the natural parent. It matters not whether the parent is wise or foolish, rich or poor, educated or illiterate, provided the child's moral and physical health are not endangered".[38]

Similarly there is the assumption that mothers are better than fathers at the task of caring for young children,[39] and an assumption that it is in a child's interests that she maintains contact with both parents.[40] All these assumptions can be viewed as protecting parental rights in that they emphasise interests highly valued by parents. For example, is it really true that wealth is not relevant when deciding the best place of residence for a child or is this really a presumption used to ensure there is fairness between adults?

(c) The third way that the welfare principle can be manipulated is by the court expressing the child's interests in terms as perceived by an adult or a lawyer rather than a child. For example, in *Re F*[41] a father sought a specific issue order that his twin children aged eleven be interviewed by his solicitor to consider whether or not they should be called to give evidence at the father's trial on charges of assault occasioning actual bodily harm and indecent assault against

---

[36] Cf. Montgomery (1989).

[37] Another example of where children and parents interests are conflated could be where there is genetic screening of young children in order to determine whether any further children of the parents will carry a genetic disorder.

[38] *Re KD (A Minor) (Ward: Termination of Access)* [1988] AC 806 at 812 per Lord Templeman. Approved and applied in *Re M (Child's upbringing)* [1996] 2 FLR 441.

[39] This is not however a legal presumption: *Re A (Children: 1959 United Nations Declaration)* [1998] 1 FLR 356, *Brixley v Lynas* [1996] 2 FLR 499 (a House of Lords decision on appeal from Scotland).

[40] *A v L (Contact)* [1998] 1 FLR 361, although this is not an irrebuttable presumption: *Re B (Contact: Domestic Violence)* [1998] 2 FLR 171. See also Family Law Act 1996, s.1(c)(iii), s.11(4)(c).

[41] *Re F (Specific Issue: Children Interview)* [1995] 1 FLR 819.

96 *Jonathan Herring*

the mother. The Court of Appeal granted the order arguing that it would be in the children's interests that their father should have the opportunity of a fair trial.[42] Although this was a criminal trial, in effect it was a dispute between the children's mother and their father. Pitching the children into the centre of this dispute and requiring them to give evidence seems undesirable. How crucial the fairness of the trial was *to the children* is debatable.

Another example is the law concerning changes to a child's surname. This is described by the courts as "a profound issue".[43] Whether to change a child's name is one of the few questions which a lone parent with parental responsibility cannot decide on their own and it requires the consent of both parents, or else a decision of the court.[44] It might be questioned whether changing a name is a more profound issue than, say, determining when and how a child can be educated; the latter is a decision that a lone parent with parental responsibility can make. It appears that the law here is using a perception of the child's welfare to promote interests important to adults.

(c) Limiting the application of the welfare principle by acknowledging parents' rights

In the previous section I have looked at the way in which the courts have applied the welfare principle but in so doing have disguised the real issues and have protected parents' interests. In this section I will consider cases where the courts have held that they ought not to make the requested order, even though it would promote the child's welfare, explicitly because to do so would infringe parents' rights. This is either on the basis that such orders were not contemplated by the Children Act 1989 or that such orders could be obtained from another statute and the safeguards in those statutes should not be circumvented. I will consider one example but there are several.[45]

In *Re E*[46] the Court of Appeal considered an application for an order that the children reside with the mother on condition that she remained in London, unless the non-resident father consented in writing. Although the Court accepted that it had the power to make such an order:

> "a general imposition of conditions on residence orders was clearly not contemplated by Parliament and where the parent is entirely suitable and the court intends to make a residence order in favour of that parent, a condition of residence is in my view an

---

[42] Quite why the trial would be unfair if the child did not give evidence is unclear.
[43] *Dawson v Wearmouth* [1997] 2 FLR 629.
[44] *Re C (Change of Surname)* [1998] 2 FLR 656.
[45] Other examples include *Re D (Residence: Imposition of Conditions)* [1996] 2 FLR 281; *Re D (Prohibited Steps Order)* [1996] 2 FLR 273; *Re M (Minors) (Disclosure of Evidence)* [1994] 1 FLR 760; *D v N (Contact Order: Conditions)* [1997] 2 FLR 797, *B v B (Residence Order: Restricting Applications)* [1997] 1 FLR 139.
[46] *Re E Residence: Imposition of Conditions* [1997] FLR 638.

The Welfare Principle and Parents' Rights 97

unwarranted imposition upon the legal right of the person to choose where he/she will live within the UK or with whom".[47]

So it seems here that despite the fact that the condition might promote the children's interests, it was not imposed out of concern to protect the parent's right to choose where she lived. Quite how placing such weight on this right is consistent with the welfare principle was not explained.[48]

(d) Cases where the welfare principle has been said not to apply

An alternative way that the law has been able to protect parents' interests is to hold that the welfare principle does not apply, although the interests of the child may still be an important consideration. Such circumstances have included divorce; domestic violence; financial redistribution of property on divorce; secure accommodation orders;[49] disclosure of evidence;[50] adoption;[51] medical experiments (Mclean, 1991); anonymity for sperm donors (Bainham, 1989); and blood tests.[52] The welfare principle does not apply in these cases either because it is decreed by statute or because the issue has been said by the courts to be not directly related to the upbringing of children, and so section 1 of the Children Act 1989 does not apply. Two points should be made about this list (which is not exhaustive by any means). First, the list does not necessarily reflect those issues where there is a low level of children's interests: for example, the result of a domestic violence application is of fundamental importance to a child. Indeed it is tempting to see these cases as cases where the *parents'* interests are of particular importance. Secondly, by taking a strict reading of "children's upbringing" the courts have used what can be highly artificial distinctions. For example, there have been a series of cases involving a parent seeking an order concerning publicity about their child. The leading case is *Re Z*,[53] which stated that the law distinguishes two situations. The first is where the publicity directly concerns the child (for example, a case where a disabled child was to be filmed while receiving specialised treatment). In this case the matter "is with regard to the child's upbringing" and so the welfare principle does apply. The second is where the publicity only indirectly concerns a child (e.g. where a television programme is to be made about her parents), in which case the welfare principle does not apply. In such cases the Court of Appeal in *Re H*[54] suggests "the important

---

[47] At 642.
[48] Cf. Hansard (HL), 16 March 1989, col. 346.
[49] *Re M (Secure Accommodation Order)* [1995] 1 FLR 418.
[50] *Re L (Minors) (Police Investigation. Privilege)* [1997] AC 16.
[51] Adoption Act 1976, s.6.
[52] *S v S; W v Official Solicitor* [1972] AC 24.
[53] *Re Z (A Minor) (Freedom of Publication)* [1996] 1 FLR 191. The other important recent cases include. *Re H (Minors) (Injunction. Public Interest)* [1994] 1 FLR 519; *Mrs R v Central Independent Television PLC* [1994] 2 FLR 151.
[54] *Re H (Minors) (Injunction: Public Interest)* [1994] FLR 519.

98 *Jonathan Herring*

question in this appeal is whether the respondent's and the media's freedom to publish matters of public interest outweigh the risk of harm to the children".

This distinction between publicity relating directly and indirectly to the child seems dubious as it reflects neither the level of harm to the child nor the amount of the public interest, although it is comprehensible as an attempt to balance the rights of parents and children.

The law also produces arbitrary results when a case involves two children. In such cases the child whose welfare is paramount is the child who is named in the application before the court as the subject of the proceedings. This is so even though it may be a matter of chance precisely what form the proceedings take.[55]

3. WHEN ENFORCING THE WELFARE PRINCIPLE DOES INFRINGE A PARENT'S INTERESTS

There are, of course, many cases where the welfare principle is used to require parents to act contrary to their wishes in a way that promotes the child's welfare. But it is rare for the courts to make orders that infringe the rights a parent has as an individual. By far the most common circumstance where this does occur is in relation to contact between children and the non-resident parent after the breakdown of a relationship.[56] A court order may, for example, require the resident parent to facilitate contact between the other parent and the child.[57] The clash is between the interests of a child in keeping contact with a parent with whom she is no longer living and the interests of the parent with a residence order for whom a contact order may infringe their freedom to choose whom to meet. The case law in dealing with this tension places great weight on the "right of the child to contact". It requires the court to decide whether the resident parent's objections are justifiable. If the objections are not justified, it is simply "implacable hostility", and contact will be ordered despite the objections of the resident parent.[58] The one exception to this is where the contact would cause such "major emotional harm",[59] to the resident parent, that the child would be harmed. Although such cases can be seen as cases where the interests of the resident parent are sub-ordinated to the interests of the child, it is also possible to see these cases as examples of where the welfare principle is used to prefer the interests of one parent (the non-resident parent) over the interests of another (the resident parent).

---

[55] *Birmingham City Council v H (No.3)* [1994] 1 FLR 224; *Re T and E (Proceedings: Conflicting Interests)* [1995] 1 FLR 581; *Re S (Contact: Application by Sibling)* [1998] 2 FLR 897.

[56] Prohibited step and specific issues orders usually only conflict with the interests of a parent in exercising their rights qua parent rather than their rights as an individual.

[57] Such as reading letters to a child (e.g. *Re O (Contact: Imposition of Conditions)* [1995] 2 FLR 124) or taking a child to visit a father in prison (cf. *Re P (Contact: Discretion)* [1998] 2 FLR 969).

[58] *Re D (Contact: Reasons for Refusal)* [1997] 2 FLR 98; but see *Re H (Contact: Domestic Violence)* [1998] 2 FLR 47.

[59] *Re D (A Minor) (Contact: Mother's Hostility)* [1993] 2 FLR 1 at 7G per Waite LJ.

4. ALTERNATIVE APPROACHES

I have attempted to demonstrate above that although the welfare principle is central to the law relating to children, the courts have still found ways of protecting parental interests. There is no monitoring of parents to ensure the welfare of children is promoted day to day. Where the courts are involved and the welfare principle does apply the judiciary have found ways of placing weight on the interests of parents. The present law is unsatisfactory. It is not that the results in the cases are necessarily wrong but rather that the use of the welfare principle hides the real issues involved. Also, the courts have had to use strained reasoning to avoid applying the welfare principle as they have understood it, because to do so might produce unfairness to parents.

So how should the law deal with these cases which involve clashes between the interests of children, mothers and fathers?[60] I will examine three possible approaches. The first is to abandon the welfare principle and instead openly balance the interests of different parties. The second is to use the welfare principle but understand that there is a limit to the principle and that those orders which infringe "fundamental rights" of a parent are not permitted. The third is to re-examine the welfare principle and consider whether a better understanding of the welfare principle can be utilised. It is this third approach which I will suggest is the most appropriate.

(a) Abandoning the welfare principle

The increasing uneasiness with the welfare principle is revealed by Lord Nicholls's *dictum* in the House of Lords that "the paramountcy principle must not be permitted to become a loose cannon destroying all else around it".[61] The criticisms of the welfare principle are well known. Some commentators deny its practicality: the court lacks the time, objectivity, evidence and foresight with which to make the necessary prediction of a child's future. Even if the court could make the necessary predictions there is doubt whether it could determine which alternative would promote the child's welfare. One response is that the judge should refer to the relevant standards of the community, if these can be ascertained. Even if the judge is able to find an "accepted standard" he or she may simply be perpetuating the inequality in society by enforcing that standard. For example, Helen Reece (1996) in discussing cases involving homosexual parents has recently argued that:

> "the child's need to be protected from teasing has led, not just to the subordination of, but to the total negation of, a far more important and socially significant value, the equal right of lesbian and gay men to be parents".

---

[60] This can be seen as a clash between an approach based on rights or based on utility. See Parker (1992).
[61] *Re L (minors) (Police Investigation: Privilege)* [1997] AC 16 at 33B.

100 *Jonathan Herring*

While not everyone will agree with this balance it highlights the potential dangers of relying on community standards (see also Golombok, Chapter 9 below). A slightly different argument is that the welfare principle is unduly narrow in not being able to incorporate such concepts as children's rights of autonomy or privacy.

Other objections are concerned with the way that the welfare principle operates in practice. As Frances Olsen (1992) has argued, "legal protection of children can be and has been used as a basis for controlling women". Others have argued that the welfare principle's lack of predictability generates and encourages disputes (Schneider, 1989). Some commentators have suggested that the welfare principle is essentially a rhetorical or political device and perhaps not to be taken too literally. Hence it has been suggested that "overstating the importance of [a] child's welfare prevents parents, judges and legislators from systematically undervaluing it" (Altman, 1997).

In the face of such criticism the welfare test has shown surprising durability. The real reason behind the durability of the test is the absence of an alternative. Space prevents a full discussion of the criticisms of the welfare principle but I will focus on the particular criticism which is most relevant to this chapter: can the welfare principle be justified given its lack of emphasis on the interests of adults?

Helen Reece (1996) has argued:

"the paramountcy principle must be abandoned and replaced within a framework which recognises that the child is merely one participant in a process in which the interest of all the participants count".

The difficulty with this approach is the lack of protection for children. The strength of the welfare principle is that it focuses the court's attention on the person whose voice may be the quietest both literally and metaphorically and who has the least control over whether the issue arrives before the court or in which way it does. The child may also be the person with whom the court is least able to empathise. As we have seen from the case law we do not at present have a problem with the interests of children being given excessive weight at the expense of the interests of adults. Indeed it is interesting that despite Helen Reece's attack on the welfare principle in English law there is a notable shortage of cases in her article where she feels the interests of parents were not adequately protected. She focuses on the rare cases of homosexual parents. As we have seen, the courts have in fact put weight on the interests of parents despite the welfare principle. The courts have also shown willingness to value wider principles, for example, free speech. The lack of protection of parents' interests does not require the abandonment of the welfare principle, but there is a need for the welfare principle to be better understood in order to prevent the court's reasoning becoming so strained.

(b) Protecting parent's fundamental rights

A second approach would be to state that orders infringing certain rights of parents are not available. For example orders limiting a parent's right to live where or with whom they choose; restricting a parent's religious practices; or infringing on a right of free speech, could be impermissible. There could be a specific reference to the rights referred to in the Human Rights Act 1998. An example of such an approach has been promoted by Andrew Bainham (1994) who has suggested that it is necessary to distinguish between the "primary" and "secondary" rights of parents and children. He suggests:

> "in some cases the primary interest would be the child's while in others it would be the parents' interests. The more fundamental the interest in question, and the more serious the consequences of failing to uphold it, the more likely it would be that *that* interest would be regarded as the primary interest".[62]

It may then be necessary to require parents (or children) to sacrifice a secondary interest to promote a primary interest.[63] There are two particular difficulties with this approach. First, the test requires the court to perceive the situation as a battle between parents' and children's interests. As will be seen below this is an unnecessarily individualistic approach. Secondly, the welfare principle has carried enormous political significance, not least as a central plank of the United Nations Convention on the Rights of Children. To limit its application explicitly would seem unacceptable; it is better to reconceptualise it.

(c) Reconceptualising the welfare principle

The conception of the welfare principle adopted by the courts is often too narrowly individualist and focuses on a self-centred approach to welfare. A broader version of the welfare principle could allow consideration of the parent's interests. There are two elements to the argument for pursuing a wider understanding of the welfare principle. The first is that it is part of growing up for a child to learn to sacrifice as well as claim benefits. Families, and society in general, are based on mutual co-operation and support. So it is important to encourage a child to adopt, to a limited extent, the virtue of altruism and an awareness of social obligation.[64] It needs to be stressed that it is a very limited altruism that is being sought. Children should only be expected to be altruistic to the extent of not demanding from parents excessive sacrifices in return for minor benefits.

The second element of this approach is that the child's welfare involves ensuring that the child's relationships with the other family members are fair and just

---

[62] At 173.
[63] It is not clear how Bainham would deal with the problem where two primary interests clash.
[64] *Re B (A Minor) (Wardship: Sterilisation)* [1988] AC 199 made it clear that in considering a child's welfare the long-term consequences into adulthood can be considered.

102 *Jonathan Herring*

(Bartlett, 1988). A relationship based on unacceptable demands on a parent is not furthering a child's welfare. As the preamble to the United Nations Convention on the Rights of Children states:

> "the child, for the full and harmonizing development of his or her personality, should grow up in a family environment, in an atmosphere of happiness, love and understanding".

It is in the child's welfare to be brought up in a family whose members respect each other and so, on occasion, sacrifices may be required from the child. An analogy could be drawn by asking whether it would be to our benefit to have a personal slave to perform all our menial tasks for us. From a narrow perception one may say that to have such a slave would promote our welfare, although I imagine that most people would not accept that achieving ease and comfort in this way would be to a person's emotional, moral and general welfare (as well as, of course, being an infringement on the slave's rights). Of course parenthood is not slavery(!), but the point is that conceptions of welfare should take into account the kind of sacrifice demanded of parents to obtain benefits for the children.

The effect of this approach is to move away from conceiving the problem as a clash between children and parents and in terms of weighing two conflicting interests, and towards seeing it rather as deciding what is a proper parent-child relationship. The child's welfare is promoted when he or she lives in a fair and just relationship with each parent. Understood in this way, the welfare principle can protect children while properly taking into account parents' rights.

The argument can also operate where a child's welfare may require a sacrifice for the obtaining of some greater social good. This view has been recognised by Ward LJ:

> "although the welfare of the children is paramount in the sense that it rules upon and determines the course to be followed, that does not mean that when this is the test, the freedom of publication is not to be weighed in the scales at all. Of course it is. It is one of the relevant facts, choices and other circumstances which a reasonable person would take into account. We do not live in a vacuum and our choices have to be made for ourselves as well as for our children in the realisation that we sometimes have to sacrifice self for the greater good of social order".[65]

This understanding of welfare has five particular advantages. First, it is more in accord with practice in many families. As noted at the very start of this chapter most family dynamics involve "give and take" and do not consider exclusively the child's interests. Secondly, it is in accord with what most of us would have wished when we were being brought up. I suspect that most adults would not have wanted their parents to have been obliged to make extraordinary sacrifices to pursue a minor increase in their welfare, but would have expected a fair level of sacrifice by the parents.[66] Thirdly, this approach enables a court to

---

[65] *Re Z (A Minor) (Freedom of Publication)* [1996] 1 FLR 191 at 212G.
[66] Cf. Rawls (1972).

consider explicitly the interests of all family members while still adhering to the welfare principle. This is what is done already, but covertly. Fourthly, this approach enables the interests of adolescents to be better understood. As a child becomes older the relationship with his or her parents changes, but in complex ways. It no longer becomes necessary for the parents to determine the child's own interests—the child can determine this for him or herself. Similarly, the demands that a child can make on a parent can lessen. Andrew Bainham (1993) refers to the "democratic model of decision making", which usefully captures the sense of co-operation within families focused upon by this approach to welfare. Fifthly, by focusing on a child's relationships this may encourage the law to develop ways in which a child's voice may be heard more effectively in proceedings.

It might be helpful to consider briefly how some of the cases we discussed earlier might be perceived with such an understanding of the welfare approach. Take *Re Y* where it will be recalled that the issue was whether it was in the welfare of Y to donate bone marrow to a sibling. The decision of the court was that it was in Y's interest as the bone marrow transplant would potentially save the life of the sibling and this would improve the health and happiness of the mother, and as she was central to Y's well-being this would benefit Y. I mentioned earlier that this argument is rather artificial. Under the suggested understanding of the welfare principle Y's welfare would not be limited to simply a consideration of her own physical well-being but also a decision on whether this was a just exchange for her as a member of this family. This recognises the benefit to individuals of co-operation within communities, of giving and taking. I suspect the answer would be the same as that reached by the court. But in the variation on cosmetic surgery suggested above the court may well feel this was too small a gain for such a sacrifice. This approach it is submitted better raises the real issues for the court than the individualistic understanding of the welfare principle used by the court in *Re Y*.

Consider also *Re E*[67] where it will be recalled that the issue was whether an order should be made requiring a mother to stay in London so that the contact between the child and father could be retained. Here the court simply stated that in most cases the parent's right to choose where to live overrode any interests of the child. It is submitted that the proper question is whether ordering the mother to stay in London would be part of a just and fair relationship between the child and the mother or whether it would create an abusive relationship where the sacrifices to the mother would be too great compared to the benefit to the child. A child brought up in such a one-sided relationship would not be benefited.

Recall also those cases involving publicity and children. As said earlier a rather artificial distinction is drawn between those cases where the publicity relates to the upbringing of the children (in which cases the child's welfare is paramount) and those where it does not (where the child's welfare has to be

---

[67] *Re E (Residence: Imposition of Conditions)* [1997] 2 FLR 638.

taken into account but is not paramount). Again I suggest that this can be dealt with simply under a broader understanding of the welfare concept. As a member of society a child can expect to make some sacrifices for the general good, to benefit society. Learning respect for others and for the values that society holds dear are an important part of the education and development of a child. Experiencing sacrifices, if those sacrifices are appropriate and fair to the child, is in the child's welfare. The question is whether a child's welfare will benefit from being brought up in a society that requires such sacrifices.

5. CONCLUSION

This chapter has considered the legal regulation of parenthood and, in particular, whether the interests of parents should be taken into account when using the welfare principle. The courts have used a rather individualised conception of welfare. This has caused difficulties in cases where the interests of children and parents clash. It has been argued that the courts have in fact found ways of protecting parents' interests despite the prominence of the welfare principle. However in so doing it has been necessary to manipulate or circumvent their narrow view of the welfare principle and thereby disguised the real issues at play.

It has been suggested this need not be so. A full understanding of the welfare principle should include ensuring that the relationship between the parent and child is a fair and just one, with respect of each individual's rights. A child's welfare will be best promoted by being brought up by parents in a family and community based on appropriate mutual co-operation and respect. With this broader understanding of the welfare principle we have no need to seek to undermine or avoid its application and it can take a legitimate and effective pride of place in the law relating to children.

REFERENCES

Altman, S., "Should child custody rules be fair?" (1997) 325 *Journal of Family Law* 354.
Bainham, A., "When is a parent not a parent? Reflections on the unmarried father and his child in English law" (1989) *International Journal of Law and the Family* 208.
Bainham, A., "The privatisation of the public interest in children" (1990) 53 *Modern Law Review* 206.
Bainham, A., "Growing up in Britain: adolescence in the post-Gillick era" in J. Eekelaar and P. Sarcevic (eds.), *Parenthood in Modern Society* (Netherlands, Kluwer, 1993).
Bainham, A., "Non-intervention and judicial paternalism" in P. Birks (ed.), *Frontiers of Liability* (Oxford, Oxford University Press, 1994).
Bainham, A., *Children: The Modern Law*, 2nd edn. (Bristol, Family Law, 1998).
Bartlett, K., "Re-expressing parenthood" (1988) 98 *Yale Law Journal* 293.
Department of Health, *The Children Act Guidance and Regulations, Volume 2* (London, HMSO, 1991).

Donzelot, J., *The Policing of Families* (London, Hutchinson, 1980).
Eekelaar, J., "The emergence of children's rights" (1986) 6 *Oxford Journal of Legal Studies* 161.
Freeman, M., "The best interests of the child? Is the best interests of the child in the best interests of children?" (1997) *International Journal of Law and Family* 36.
Home Office, *Consultation Paper, Supporting Families* (London, HMSO, 1998).
Maclean, M. and Eekelaar, J., *The Parental Obligation* (Oxford, Hart Publishing, 1997).
McCall Smith, A., "Is anything left of parental rights?" in E. Sutherland and A. McCall Smith (eds.), *Family Rights. Family Law and Medical Ethics* (Edinburgh, Edinburgh University Press, 1990).
McLean, J., "Medical experimentation with children" (1991) 9 *International Journal of Family Law* 173.
Montgomerty, J., "Rhetoric and welfare" (1989) 9 *Oxford Journal of Legal Studies* 397.
Olsen, F., "Children's rights: some feminist approaches to the United Nations Convention on the Rights of the Child" (1992) *International Journal of Law and the Family* 192.
Parker, S., "Rights and utility in Anglo-Australian family law" (1992) 55 *Modern Law Review* 311.
Rawls, J. A., *A Theory of Justice* (Cambridge, Massachusetts, Harvard University Press, 1972).
Reece, H., "The paramountcy principle: consensus or construct?" (1996) 49 *Current Legal Problems* 267.
Schneider, C., "Discretion, rules, and law: child custody and the UDMA's best interest standard" (1989) *Michigan Law Review* 2215.

19

Taking the Rights of Parents and Children Seriously: Confronting the Welfare Principle under the Human Rights Act

SHAZIA CHOUDHRY AND HELEN FENWICK

Abstract—This article argues that resistance to the Human Rights Act has built up in the context of disputes relating to children and that such resistance is founded in the attachment of the courts to the welfare or paramountcy principle as currently conceived—the principle that the child's welfare automatically prevails over the rights of other family members. It argues that the failure to take account of Convention arguments could only be a legitimate stance if there was no conflict between the demands of the welfare principle and those of the Convention guarantees, but that in fact the approach of the European Court of Human Rights differs considerably from that of the UK courts since it seeks to balance the rights of different family members. The article goes on to argue that, taking account of the Strasbourg stance and of the already established domestic recognition of the presumptive equality of competing qualified Convention rights, it is time to accept the adoption of a new model of judicial reasoning in the context of disputes over children—the 'parallel analysis' or 'ultimate balancing act'.

1. *Introduction*

Resistance to the Human Rights Act is strongly marked in many areas of law, but that resistance is especially and increasingly apparent in the field of family law, particularly in relation to disputes involving children. This article takes that field of law as a case-study. It seeks to demonstrate that a refusal to engage with the notion of individual rights in a particular field of law—or to tease out the values underlying clashes of rights—tends to single out certain groups for disadvantage.[1] Some fathers currently perceive themselves as forming such a group[2] and fathers' groups have therefore adopted the classic tactics of those that view

---

[1] See M. Minow 'Interpreting Rights: An Essay for Robert Cover', 96 *Yale Law Journal* 1860 at 1890-91 (1987); H. Reece 'The Paramountcy Principle: Consensus or Construct?' (1996) *Current Legal Problems* 267.

[2] Some judges share that perception; in *In the matter of D* [2004] 1 FLR 1226 at para 8 Munby J. said: 'when the system fails—and fail it does—it is disproportionately fathers and not mothers who find themselves, as well as the children, the victims of that failure'.

themselves as marginalized: fathers have marched on the High Court to demand equal parenting rights[3] and there has been a proliferation of fathers' groups claiming that the Family Division takes an anti-father stance.[4]

This article sets out to examine connections between their concerns and the resistance to the Human Rights Act that has built up in this field. Such resistance is founded in the attachment of the courts to the welfare or paramountcy principle as currently conceived—the principle that the child's welfare automatically prevails over the rights of other family members. But the failure to take account of Convention arguments could only be a legitimate stance if there was no conflict between the demands of the welfare principle and those of the Convention guarantees, given the requirements of the duties enjoined on judges by ss 6(1) and 3(1) of the Human Rights Act (HRA). However, in the family law sphere the approach of the European Court of Human Rights differs considerably from that of the UK courts since it seeks to balance opposing rights and does not start from the assumption that the paramountcy principle will determine the issue. As will be argued, the Court affords weight to the Article 8 rights of parents to respect for family life so that in the case of a clash of rights those of the child will not invariably win out and therefore the inception of the Human Rights Act has called the current domestic approach into question. If the current judicial approach to conflicts of interests in the family law domain is viewed in Convention terms it becomes clear that it is flawed, not only because there is an overall failure to recognize the Convention rights dimension of many family law cases, but because it depends on a refusal to afford full weight to an individual right when it comes into conflict with another such right. In many such cases Article 8 remains the dog that fails to bark.

This is not merely a positivist argument. The value of the 'balancing approach' at Strasbourg, it will be argued, is that it allows for an 'express recognition and separation out of specific individual rights [that reveals] the different values in a way that is not so obvious on an application of the welfare principle'.[5] In other words, under that approach the interests of parents, carers and children—viewed as rights—can gain a fair and transparent hearing. This approach provides, it will be contended, a means of addressing those failings of the welfare principle that have been identified, as discussed below, by the leading academics in this field.[6] As will be indicated, that academic concern has *not* led so far to a

[3] See, e.g. the *Guardian* 21, 22 Oct 03 and 5, 6 Nov 03.
[4] They include: Families Need Fathers (FNF, website, www.fnf.org.uk.), the Equal Parenting Council, until recently known as the Equal Parenting Party (EPP, website: www.equalparenting.org,); the UK Men's Movement (UKMM), website: www.ukmm.org.uk., Dads Against Discrimination (DADS); fathers4justice, website: fathers4justice@yahoogroups.co.uk; the National Child Rescue Organisation, www.childrescue.org.uk. For criticism of the actions of some of these groups see the articles by M. Dearle and M. Stowe, *The Times, Law* at pages 6-7, 23.3.04.
[5] A. Bainham, 'Can we protect children and protect their rights?' (2002) *Fam Law* 279 at 288. The comment was made in the context of children's Convention rights but it is equally applicable, it is argued, to conflicts between their rights and those of parents.
[6] For recent criticism see: J. Eekelaar, 'Beyond the welfare principle' (2002) *CFLQ* 237; H. Reece, above n 1; A Bainham ibid.

full acceptance of a rights-based approach under the HRA, although the most recent writing suggests that movement towards such an acceptance is occurring.[7] This article acknowledges that such an approach raises a number of real concerns, but argues—perhaps optimistically—for a whole-hearted acceptance of the HRA, not only as the most effective means of addressing the failings of the welfare principle, but also as providing an opportunity to consider the *diverse* and individual nature of children's interests and to re-evaluate—from a feminist perspective—current understandings of both motherhood and fatherhood in the light of changing patterns of family life and employment.[8] In so doing this article will identify the beginnings of an acceptance of a rights-based approach which is currently occurring, but will also seek to address the criticisms of the approach which have led so far to its failure to take full hold in post-HRA judicial reasoning and in academic writing.

This article thus puts forward a new approach using a rights-based model to be used for the resolution of legal conflicts in this domain, applying this approach particularly, although not exclusively, to conflicts arising in relation to contact[9] and residence disputes. It is also a model that is consistent with the requirements of the UN Convention on the Rights of the Child (CRC), under which those rights are 'primary' (Art. 3(1)), not paramount.[10]

2. *Themes and Theories underlying the Children Act and the European Convention on Human Rights*

In this article family disputes involving children will be translated into Convention terms and viewed as conflicts between the differing Article 8 rights of all those involved. That translation is itself a matter of controversy as will be acknowledged and considered below. But in order to engage in a meaningful examination of such conflicts, it is important to begin by situating the matter in the context of current understandings of the main principles which underlie family law in relation to children. The Children Act 1989 (CA) contains the main statutory provisions which govern applications concerning children, in both private

---

[7] A. Bainham, 'Contact as a Right and Obligation' in A. Bainham, B. Lindley, M. Richards and L. Trinder (eds), *Children and their Families: Contact, Rights and Welfare* (Hart, 2003) ch 5 esp. at 61, 63–67, 74–75 and 83–86. J. Fortin, in *Children's Rights and the Developing Law* (Butterworths, 2nd edn, 2003), esp. ch 19 offers cautious support to a rights-based approach.

[8] See, e.g. C. McGlynn 'Reclaiming a Feminist Vision: the Reconciliation of Paid Work and Family Life in European Union Law and Policy', 7 *Columbia Journal of European Law* 241–72 (2001)..

[9] It may be noted that if the 'early intervention' project to be piloted in 2004 is eventually implemented generally, contact disputes may become less frequent (see the web-site of the Department of Constitutional Affairs—Facilitation and Enforcement Group, Final Report, Recommendation 18).

[10] The CRC is not currently implemented in domestic law, but pressure is being placed on the government to allow its influence to increase. For example, the Joint Committee on Human Rights has recommended that one of the government's key objectives in the Green Paper on inter alia the introduction of a Children's Commissioner in the UK should be to comply with the demands of the CRC. The Green Paper *Every Child Matters*, Cm. 5860, was published in September 2003 (www.dfes.gov.uk/everychildmatters). The recommendation was the seventh of the Joint Committee on Human Rights in its 9th Report of Session 2002–03 on the case for a Children's Commissioner for England.

and public spheres.[11] The CA represented the first real attempt to codify both spheres of the law in one single piece of legislation, but although the overarching principles[12] of the CA will apply to both spheres, their interpretation may differ depending upon the one they are employed in.[13]

Representing the outcome of a number of reviews and consultations,[14] and a major overhaul of the law relating to children,[15] the Act commences with a statement of principle which is central to its ethos: s 1: 'When a court determines any question with respect to- (a) upbringing of a child; or (b) the administration of a child's property or the application of any income arising from it, the child's welfare shall be the court's paramount consideration'. Routinely referred to as 'the paramountcy' or 'welfare' principle, its meaning is well understood amongst family lawyers: in decisions concerning children, the welfare of the child is to be the single deciding factor,[16] that is, paramount over, and in fact displacing, all other considerations.

This principle is not only applied by the courts in disputes relating to children, but has a considerable influence upon all other parties concerned with any application relating to children.[17] In effect, it creates an exclusive cultural framework within which professional decisions concerning children are made. The 'welfare principle' has thus successfully embedded itself in the very core of the legal and multidisciplinary aspects of the upbringing of children. It also forms one of the key principles underlying the Green Paper on the new Children's Commissioner.[18]

But the understanding of the principle, the extent of its entrenchment and the judiciary's apparent unwillingness to question came under challenge due to the inception of the Human Rights Act 1998 (HRA) and specifically Article 8 which provides a qualified right to respect for private and family life, the home and

---

[11] The private sphere is concerned with actions brought by 'private individuals'—parents, carers and children themselves, against each other, in relation to legal questions concerning children, most frequently in respect of contact and residence. The public sphere is concerned with actions brought on behalf of children, such as care proceedings, by the 'state' through local authorities against parent or carers or vice versa.

[12] Often referred to as the 'tripartite principle', s 1 of the Children Act 1989 sets out the principles of no delay, no order and paramountcy.

[13] For example, the concept of 'purposeful delay', e.g. where detailed assessment is required before the court can reach its decision, is rooted largely in public law proceedings under the Children Act 1989 which, arguably, contradicts the principle of 'no delay' referred to in the Children Act 1989, s 1(2) which includes the statement that 'any delay . . . is likely to prejudice the welfare of the child'.

[14] After an initial inquiry into the law relating to children in care by the House of Commons Social Services Select Committee in 1984 the Department of Health and Social Security set up an interdepartmental working party which produced the *Review of Child Law* (1984) which, in turn, informed the Government's White Paper: *The Law on Child Care and Family Services* Cm. 62. Both the Review and the White Paper formed the basis of the public law elements of the Children Act 1989. The Law Commission undertook its own review which resulted in the publication of the *Report on Guardianship and Custody* No. 172 (1988). This report formed the underlying basis of the private law elements of the Children Act 1989 and its central principles, including the 'welfare principle'.

[15] By providing a brand new statutory framework governing at the same time both the public and private law affecting children and removing most of the complex and piecemeal law that had been its predecessor.

[16] *J v C* [1970] AC 668.

[17] These parties include legal representatives, social services, court reporters, the children's guardians and other experts called upon to comment upon aspects of the child's upbringing.

[18] See above, n 10.

correspondence.[19] Article 8, in encapsulating the rights of both parents and children to private and family life, appears on its face to come into clear conflict with the CA, which renders the child's interests paramount. So far the legitimacy of the paramountcy principle has not been *directly* challenged in this context, either by the European Court of Human Rights or by the UK courts under the HRA, although some academics have expressed reservations as to its compatibility with Article 8 under the HRA.[20] This is surprising given the tension between the approaches employed under the CA and those of Article 8 of the ECHR. That tension can be viewed as deriving from the values underpinning the ECHR on the one hand and the CA on the other. A reasonable consensus among family law theorists can be discerned to the effect that s 1(1) of the CA, as it is currently interpreted, reflects a predominantly utilitarian or consequentialist approach.[21] Stephen Parker in his seminal piece on family law and legal theory[22] has analysed the movement of family law from a 'rights–based' to a 'utility-based' approach. Such contrasts between utility and rights-based approaches have often been employed to illustrate the differences between the two instruments in terms of their underlying principles.[23] In the pre-HRA era the 'rights-based' model of family law had, it will be argued, been rejected as a corollary of the increasing dominance of the child-centred approach—an approach that currently reaches its climax in s 1(1) of the CA.

Although this article will argue that this analysis of the differences in reasoning between the CA and the ECHR is broadly correct, it is now apposite in a post-HRA legal context to question the assumptions behind it with a view to introducing modifications to the utilitarian model. The CA, since it identifies the welfare of the child as the sole and decisive consideration, does not correspond to classic utilitarianism: it does not seek to arrive at an outcome which, overall, achieves the best result for the family members or others, but only for the child. It therefore arguably amounts to a form of 'rule utilitarianism'[24] in that an individual's actions are regulated by reference to a general rule: that the child's welfare

---

[19] In full, Article 8 provides: 1. Everyone has the right to respect for his private and family life, his home and his correspondence. 2. There shall be no interference by a public authority with the exercise of this right except such as is in accordance with the law and is necessary in a democratic society in the interests of national security, public safety or the economic well being of the country, for the prevention of disorder or crime, for the protection of health or morals, or for the protection of the rights and freedoms of others.

[20] See: H. Fenwick 'Clashing Rights, the welfare of the child and the Human Rights Act' (2004) 67(6) *MLR* 889–927, which attacks the effect of the principle in the case of clashes between media freedom and the privacy of the child; S. Choudhry, 'The Adoption and Children Act 2002, the Welfare Principle and the HRA 1998—a Missed Opportunity' (2003) 15(2) *CFLQ* 119–38; H. Fenwick, D. Bonner and S. Harris-Short, 'Judicial Approaches to the HRA' (2003) 52 *ICLQ* 549–86 at 572–84 esp. at 582–84.

[21] For a brief overview of the debates within family law and legal theory see J. Dewar 'Family Law and Theory', 16 *OJLS* 725–36.

[22] S. Parker, 'Rights and Utility in Anglo Australian Family Law' (1992) 55 *MLR* 311. See also J. Eekelaar, 'Families and Children: From Welfarism to Rights' in C. McCrudden and G. Chambers (eds), *Individual Rights and the Law in Britain* (Oxford: Clarendon, 1994), ch 10.

[23] J. Herring 'The Human Rights Act and the Welfare Principle in family law—conflicting or complementary?' (1999) 11(3) *CFLQ* 223–35.

[24] For an introduction to utilitarianism see N.E. Simmonds, *Central Issues in Jurisprudence* (Sweet and Maxwell, 2nd edn, 2002) ch 1 and J. G. Riddall, *Jurisprudence* (Butterworths, 2nd edn, 1999) ch 13.

should be paramount, rather than by direct reference to the principle of utility whereby actions that maximize the greatest welfare of the greatest number are preferentially singled out. Thus any decision made on an individual's application under the CA will not be justified by reference to the principle of utility: the 'welfare principle' has been elevated to the status of a 'rule' that determines the outcome of such applications.

At the same time it may be pointed out that the ECHR's approach cannot be said to be fully deontological or 'rights-based'. Although the ECHR is clearly a classically deontological document since it assumes that certain rights and interests are intrinsically valuable and should prima facie be protected, its adherence to a strictly deontological approach may be viewed as undermined in respect of the materially qualified articles—Articles 8–11. Mullender has argued that these Articles exhibit 'qualified deontology',[25] since the qualifications of their second paragraphs allow the rights to be compromised or overridden by sufficiently weighty consequential considerations. Thus, although the ECHR's theoretical underpinnings differ significantly from those of the CA, the differences in their approaches and values may be less irreconcilable than some theorists have acknowledged.

Nevertheless, the recognition of the parents' Article 8 rights which this article is advocating as a first step towards a reconciliation of conflicts between such rights and those of the child, necessitates abandonment of the current rule utilitarian approach under the CA as encapsulated in the welfare principle. Not only, it is argued, is that approach no longer defensible under the HRA, but its consequentialist focus has obscured the protection for rights that it has in fact engendered. The child-centred approach in the UK has assumed in effect an almost complete coincidence of interests between the mother and the child: the rise of the welfare principle, displacing the notion of individual rights, has paradoxically gradually elevated the mother's rights above those of the father, albeit without acknowledgement that this is occurring. Under the guise of promoting welfarism, motherhood is, it is argued, being accorded—in effect—a status far higher than that of fatherhood. Thus while the CA has generally been seen as embracing a utilitarian approach, in contrast to the Convention which, axiomatically, is rights-based, the mother's rights to family and private life have in fact found, indirectly, a strong and effective protection.

That protection can, however, be viewed from a feminist perspective as a double-edged sword. Despite the fact that the welfare of children was a growing societal and thus political concern in the early 19th century, it is generally accepted that this shift from 'rights' to 'welfare' occurred largely as a result of the campaign mounted by women for equal status in relation to their children.[26] Until that time the common law gave fathers sole rights of custody and control

---

[25] See R. Mullender, 'Theorising the Third Way: Qualified Consequentialism, the Proportionality Principle and the New Social Democracy' (2000) 27(4) *J. Law and Society* 493–516.

[26] See S. Maidment *Child Custody and Divorce: The Law in Social Context* (London: Croom Helm 1984) ch 7; S. Cretney, 'What will the women want next? The struggle for power within the family 1925–75' (1996) 112 *LQR* 110.

over their legitimate children and invested mothers with none.[27] It was not until the enactment of the Guardianship Act 1925 that, when applying the welfare principle to the child, the superiority of the father's claim/right to that of the mother was removed. *At the same time,* however, the Act also established that the court should have regard to the welfare of the child as the first and paramount consideration. The coincidence of the equalization of the rights of men and women over their children and the elevation of the concept of the child's welfare over the rights of both father and mother was, as Maidment argues,[28] a tool used to: 'dilute women's demands for equal parental rights to their children. Indeed, the 1925 Act was a political device used to deny women equality of parental rights'. This is not to say, however, that the entrenchment of the welfare principle failed to enhance the role of women as mothers. As a result of the growing influence of psychiatry and psychology on the determination of what was best in terms of 'child welfare' the role of the mother came to be regarded as crucial, which in itself gave a new 'power' to women.[29] Smart has argued, however, that these new power claims present, in fact, new dangers in terms of the issue of equality because they are not rights-based, but are formulated around the uniqueness of motherhood and the 'natural' bond between mother and child. As a result mothers are not heard unless they speak in the 'language of welfare'.[30]

Collier suggests that the law has constructed fatherhood in terms of an economic provider rather than as carer, and that the law at present lends legitimacy to the notion of the participation of fathers in decision-making (facilitated by the concept of parental responsibility) without participation in the day-to-day responsibility of child-care—which is often left to mothers.[31] Thus, the apparently gender-neutral welfare principle supports a particular conception of fatherhood and of motherhood that is ideologically anti-feminist. The greater, indirect protection of motherhood in terms of residence and contact therefore comes at a price. In what follows it is argued that a return to a rights-based model—under

---

[27] See *Cartlidge v Cartlidge* [1862] 2 Sw & Tr 567.
[28] See above n 26 at 107–108.
[29] See C. Smart, 'Power and the Politics of Child Custody' in C. Smart and S. Sevenhuijsen (eds), *Child Custody and the Politics of Gender* (London and New York: Routledge, 1989).
[30] 'The central and determining metaphors in family law have become the welfare of the child and the importance of the father as an instrument of welfare and as an individual who earns legal standing. The mother seems to lose her standing . . . it is not clear to me that there is any longer a language available for mothers to voice their subject position in law. There is an erasure taking place which is based on a form of silencing which arises out of giving the legitimate modes of expression to those who speak of welfare . . . and those who speak of the significance of fatherhood . . . where there is a conflict there is a tendency for the welfare principle to make the moral claims by these mothers, based on the 'caring for', appear to be statements of self interest. Equally, the fathers' rights principle makes such claims appear to resemble the unacceptable and 'old fashioned' appeal to biological motherhood which is now renounced in favour of a policy of equality, C. Smart 'The Legal and Moral Ordering of Child Custody' (1991) 18 *J. of Law and Society* 485–500 at 486 and 494. See also S. D. Sclater and F. Kaganas, 'Contact: Mothers, Welfare and Rights' in A. Bainham, B. Lindley, M. Richards and L. Trinder, *Children and Their Families* (Hart, 2003) for a feminist critique of the 'welfare discourse' which, they argue, perpetuates the tendency for mothers to see their position in terms of needs rather than rights, whereas fathers not only see their position in terms of rights, but are conceptualized by the legal system as the possessors of rights. See also Kaganas and Sclater 'Contact disputes: narrative constructions of "good" parents' *Fem. LS* (2004) 12(1), 1–27.
[31] R. Collier, *Masculinity, Law and the Family* (London: Routledge, 1995) at 20. He finds: 'Fathers are expected only to demonstrate "paternal heterosexual presence"'.

the HRA—with a concomitant re-working of the welfare principle, far from heralding a return to a traditional family hierarchy, would promote the caring role of fathers,[32] since rights entail the acceptance of responsibility. Thus, in arguing for Article 8 rights to respect for family and private life in contact and residence disputes, fathers would have to demonstrate, as argued below, that they had also discharged their caring (day-to day caring for) responsibilities towards the child: their capabilities in terms of economic provision would not alone appear to provide them with a sufficiently powerful argument.

3. *Domestic Legal Reasoning in the pre-Human Rights Act era*

Establishing the distinct theoretical underpinnings of the CA and the ECHR is crucial to an understanding of the difference in the processes of reasoning that occur at Strasbourg and in the domestic courts. A brief chronological overview of judicial pronouncements reveals a gradual shift not only from 'rights' to 'welfare' within the last century,[33] but also a steadily increasing resistance to 'rights-talk' in the family law context.

In *S* v *S*[34] Willmer LJ described contact as 'no more than the basic right of any parent'. However, this characterization of contact was rejected subsequently by Ormrod LJ in *A* v *C*.[35] He found 'So far as access to a child is concerned, there are no rights in the sense in which lawyers understand the word. It is a matter to be decided always entirely on the footing of the best interests of the child'.

This shift from 'rights' to 'principle' was further affirmed by Lord Oliver in *Re K D (Minor) (Ward: Termination of Access)*,[36] a pre-HRA wardship case.[37] He specifically considered the mother's appeal that the right to access was a parental right protected by Article 8, ECHR and that to terminate access with her child would result in a breach of her Article 8 rights.

> Parenthood [confers] . . . on parents the exclusive privilege of ordering . . . the upbringing of children of tender age . . . That is a privilege which . . . is circumscribed by many limitations . . . When the jurisdiction of the court is invoked for the protection of the child the parental privileges do not terminate. They do, however, become immediately subservient to the paramount consideration— . . . the welfare of the child.[38]

Thus, the approach of domestic courts under the CA when making a decision on an issue which would now be viewed under the HRA as concerning Article 8 rights,

---

[32] See A. Bainham, above n 7 ch 5 at 86.
[33] For a comprehensive historical overview of this shift and a chronology of relevant legislation see S. Cretney, above n 26. See also Kricken 'The "Best Interests of the Child" and Parental Separation: on the "Civilizing of Parents"' (2005) 68(1) *MLR* 25–48 who provides a historical overview of the concept of welfare within the context of the emotional constitution of family life.
[34] [1962] 1 WLR 445 at 448.
[35] [1985] FLR 445.
[36] [1988] 1 All ER 577 at 588.
[37] He considered the approach of the CA as formulated in *J* v *C* [1970] AC 668 in determining whether in wardship proceedings a natural parent's access to the child should be terminated and the child placed for adoption.
[38] See above n 36 at 825.

was clear in the pre-HRA era: it was based on the forerunner of the paramountcy principle. Long before the CA came into force, an approach based on a recognition of parental rights had been rejected in that they were viewed as unable to prevail, in an absolutist sense, over the welfare of the child. Under the CA the paramountcy principle took this process even further: the outcome which was evidentially proven[39] to promote that welfare would prevail, notwithstanding the strength of the interests of any other party. Indeed, those interests became—as independent entities—irrelevancies in post-CA reasoning. This point was graphically illustrated by Sir Thomas Bingham MR in considering the inter-relationship between the welfare principle and the court's power to order contact under s 8, CA in *Re O (Contact: Imposition of Conditions)*[40]:

> It [is] . . . worth stating . . . some very familiar but none the less fundamental principles . . . overriding all else . . . the welfare of the child is the paramount consideration . . . it cannot be emphasised too strongly that the court is concerned with the interests of the mother and the father only in so far as they bear on the welfare of the child.

In contact cases the courts would start from the presumption that the welfare of the child would be promoted by contact with both parents; however the presumption could be rebutted if it was demonstrated that allowing the contact applied for would in fact not be in the best interests of the child and thus would not increase the child's welfare. If this conclusion was reached, the application for contact would be denied on that basis alone. In most instances that outcome was readily defensible.[41] However, a significant danger remained that, under the guise of acting in the child's best interests, those of a resident parent might be elevated or promoted by presenting the child's welfare as inextricably bound up with their own.[42] By so doing she or he might achieve an outcome which would not in the long run promote the child's welfare. An example of such a case would arise where due to extreme personal dislike the resident parent was implacably opposed to contact taking place with the other parent.[43]

---

[39] See J. Herring's analysis of the evidential differences between the approach of the HRA and the CA above n 23.

[40] [1995] 2 FLR 124 at 128.

[41] In some cases the reasons for the hostility would be well-founded, as in instances where there had previously been domestic violence. See: *Re D (Contact: Reasons for Refusal)* [1997] 2 FLR 48; *Re M (Minors) (Contact: Violent Parent)* [1999] 2 FCR 56 and *Re C (a child: contact)* [2004] All ER (D) 367 (Jul).

[42] See: *Re W (A Minor) (Contact)* [1994] 2 FLR 441; *Re O (Contact: Imposition of Conditions)* [1995] 2 FLR 124; *Re M (Contact: Supervision)* [1998] 1 FLR 727. For a general critique of Parental Alienation Syndrome and its use within the family courts see C. D. Bruch, 'Parental Alienation Syndrome and Alienated Children—getting it wrong in child custody cases' (2003) 14(4) *CFLQ* 381.

[43] In *Re J (A Minor) (Contact)* [1994] 1 FLR 729, for example, a 10 year old's experience of contact had been characterized by conflict and distress to such an extent that he had refused to see his father. At first instance, the trial judge concluded that the mother's clear, implacable hostility to ordering contact was causing so much distress to the son as to render contact with his father against his best interests. The Court of Appeal implicitly approved the judge's balancing of the harm caused to the child by refusal of contact against the harm caused by allowing contact. The courts have, however, made it plain that the implacable hostility of one parent does not inevitably prevent them from making contact orders, and there are a number of cases where contact has indeed been ordered; see: *Re D (Contact: Reasons for Refusal)* [1997] 2 FLR 48; *Re M (Minors) (Contact: Violent Parent)* [1999] 2 FCR 56; *Re S (Children) (Uncooperative Mothers)* [2004] EWCA Civ 597 [2004] 2 FLR 710 and *V v V (Children) (Contact: Implacable Hostility)* [2004] EWHC 1215 [2004] 2 FLR 851.

In the pre-HRA era, then, it is clear that while the parents' interests were not ignored, and might be viewed as privileges, they were not characterized as rights and the paramountcy principle was the determining factor. It might have been expected that this approach would undergo some modification in the post-HRA era once the courts had to confront the implications of the inception of Article 8 head-on.

4. Post-Human Rights Act Judicial Reasoning: Evading Conflicts between the Children Act and The European Convention on Human Rights

However, the post-HRA judicial reasoning in this field reveals a resistance to the Convention values which is especially marked, even in comparison with those areas of law in which resistance to the Convention and HRA has sometimes been apparent.[44] The House of Lords has directly faced the question whether the paramountcy principle and the rights protected by the Convention are consistent; in *Re KD (A Minor) (Ward: Termination of Access)*[45] Lord Templeman said[46]: 'In my opinion there is no inconsistency of principle or application between the English rule and the Convention rule'. Similarly, Lord Oliver observed:

> Such conflict as exists is, I think, semantic only and lies only in differing ways of giving expression to the single common concept that the natural bond and relationship between parent and child gives rise to universally recognised norms which ought not to be gratuitously interfered with and which, if interfered with at all, ought to be so only if the welfare of the child dictates it.[47]

This approach to the Convention found some favour with family law academics since it provided 'the courts with a simple method of retaining the welfare principle as a means of interpreting Article 8(2)',[48] although the courts' general failure to conduct *any* balancing exercise at all was criticized.[49]

---

[44] See, e.g. G. Phillipson 'Transforming Breach of Confidence: Towards a Common Law Right of Privacy under the Human Rights Act' (2003) 66 *MLR* 726–58 (on resistance to consideration of Article 8); H. Fenwick and G. Phillipson, *Media Freedom under the Human Rights Act* (OUP 2006), forthcoming; H. Fenwick, D. Bonner and S. Harris-Short see above n 20 and S. Choudhry, above n 20. It is suggested that a reluctance to engage fully with the Convention under the HRA in these different areas of law has sometimes been evident but which is much more clearly marked at times in the field under discussion, as the examples from cases used below indicate. At times such reluctance appears to amount to a whole-hearted determination to avoid such engagement.

[45] [1998] AC 806.

[46] Ibid at para 812.

[47] Ibid at para 825.

[48] See J. Fortin, 'The HRA's impact on litigation involving children and their families' (1999) 11(3), *CFLQ* 252. Her recommendation accepted that evidential differences might exist between claims based on rights, as opposed to claims based on welfare (as argued by Herring: see above n 23). Her argument was, however, subject to the view that the courts would at least acknowledge when dealing with contact disputes that the non-resident parent had a prima facie right to family life which would be infringed by an order made refusing him/her contact. Her key concern was that the implementation of the HRA could enable the courts, in deliberating on parental contact disputes, to favour parents' claims regarding infringements of their own rights under article 8(1), at the expense of their children's best interests. Fortin has since acknowledged that some of these concerns were exaggerated, particularly in reference to the removal of children into state care. See J. Fortin, above n 7 at 56–57.

[49] See J. Fortin, above n 7 at 59. She finds: 'the English courts' obvious relief at discovering that the Strasbourg jurisprudence incorporates the welfare principle, has led them to largely ignore the more technical demands of article 8(2).

The decision in *Payne* v *Payne*[50] provides a further example of the prevailing judicial approach. In brief, this case concerned a non-resident father's appeal to the Court of Appeal against a decision to grant leave to the mother of his child to relocate to New Zealand (her country of origin) under s 13(1)(b), CA. The mother's argument centred on her acute unhappiness in England; she made the assertion that to prevent her returning to New Zealand would increase her unhappiness and anxiety and thus adversely affect the welfare of her child. The father's argument was that to grant leave to the mother to relocate, with the inevitable reduction in the level of contact between himself and his child that this would lead to, was not only against the best interests of the child, but also a breach of his Article 8 rights. Basing the decision on the paramountcy principle and its perceived apparent compatibility with both the CRC and the ECHR, the Court refused the father's appeal.

But these assumptions of compatibility were, it is argued, based on misunderstandings of both Conventions. Thorpe LJ not only misquoted the CRC[51] but, as Harris-Short has pointed out, also demonstrated a lack of understanding of the qualifications imposed by the European Court of Human Rights in relation to Article 8,[52] when quoting it as authority for his views on the compatibility of the paramountcy principle with the ECHR:

> Accordingly the jurisprudence of the European Court of Human Rights inevitably recognises the paramountcy principle, albeit not expressed in the language of our domestic statue. In *Johansen v Norway*, the court held that 'particular weight should be attached to the best interests of the child . . . which may override those of the parent.[53]

As Harris-Short observes, these findings may be compared illustratively with the full quote from that case[54]: 'the court will attach particular importance to the best interests of the child, which, *depending on their nature and seriousness*, may override those of the parent'. It is this very wording which Thorpe LJ excludes. It clearly indicates that, contrary to the approach of the paramountcy principle as domestically interpreted, interference in parental rights has to be justified by reference to the particular interests of the child in issue and their weight in the particular circumstances. It would appear, therefore, that the decision to allow the relocation of the child in this case was made without an explicit assessment of the child's interests on an equal footing with that of her father's. In other

---

In particular, they apparently see no need to consider whether the infringement of the parent's rights is proportionate to the child's immediate needs'.

[50] [2001] Fam 473.
[51] Ibid at 487. 'The acknowledgement of child welfare as paramount . . . is of course enshrined in article 3(1) of the United Nations Convention on the Rights of a Child'. The Convention in fact uses the word 'primary'.
[52] See S. Harris-Short, H. Fenwick, D. Bonner, above n 20 at 582–83.
[53] See above n 50 at 487.
[54] [1997] 23 EHRR 134 at para 78.

words, the father's Article 8 rights were not taken seriously.[55] The focus on the welfare principle found in such decisions provides, in turn, an opportunity for the resident parent to enhance her claims: the courts are, in effect, legitimising a 'pecking order' within which the interests of the non-resident parent are unlikely to prevail.

Further confirmation of this approach was recently given by the House of Lords in *Re B (A Minor)*.[56] This case concerned a natural father who alone, with the mother's consent, sought an adoption order in relation to their child in order to increase his own sense of parental security.[57] Hale LJ, who gave the leading judgement in the Court of Appeal, found reinforcement for a restrictive interpretation of s 15(3)(b) of the Adoption Act 1976[58] by rendering it compatible with the rights set out in Article 8 of the ECHR, in accordance with the interpretative obligation under s 3(1) of the HRA.[59] She considered that it would be a disproportionate response to the child's current needs to terminate her legal relationship with her mother (which would have been the effect of the adoption order) in order to provide the security that the father required.

Her approach—to apply Article 8 and the paragraph 2 qualifications to the particular facts of the case as an exercise to be conducted on an individual case-by-case basis—was one that is, as a starting point, consistent with the approach of the European Court of Human Rights, considered below, although she failed to go on to consider the matter from the perspective of the mother's Article 8(1) rights as an independent exercise. This approach was, however, rejected as unnecessary by the House of Lords. The Lords considered, that in the light of the mother's consent to the adoption, the only individual whose Article 8 rights had to be respected was the child. Lord Nicholls summed up the approach adopted:

> Inherent in both these Convention concepts is a balancing exercise, weighing the advantages and disadvantages. But this balancing exercise, required by Article 8, does not differ in substance from the like balancing exercise undertaken by a court when

---

[55] In summarizing the relevant considerations in such cases, Dame Butler-Sloss in *Payne* made it clear that the welfare of the child was always paramount; there was no presumption created by s 13(1)(b) in favour of the applicant parent; there had to be genuine motivation for the move; the effect upon the applicant parent and the new family of the child of a refusal of leave was very important; and that the reasonable proposals of parents with a residence order wishing to live abroad 'carry great weight'. Acknowledgment was also made that not only was the effect *upon the child* of the denial of contact with the other parent 'very important', but in terms of the non-resident parent: 'the opportunity for continuing contact between the child and the parent left behind may be very significant': *Payne v Payne* [2001] Fam 473, at 499–500. *Payne* has subsequently been applied to grant leave to permanently remove children from the jurisdiction without any explicit consideration of the non resident parents Article 8 rights: see *Re S (children: application for removal from jurisdiction)* [2004] All ER (D) 172 (Nov) and *G v G* [2005] EWCA Civ 170.

[56] [2002] 1 FLR 196. For a detailed exposition of *Re B* see S. Harris-Short, '*Re B (Adoption: Natural Parent)* Putting the child at the heart of adoption?' (2002) 14(3) *CFLQ* 325. See also S. Choudhry above n 20.

[57] The application was initially granted but set aside by the Court of Appeal. A residence order was substituted in favour of the father and an order was made prohibiting the mother from making any application under the CA relating to the child without leave of a High Court judge.

[58] Which dealt with adoption applications by natural parents.

[59] s 3(1) provides: 'So far as it is possible to do so, primary legislation must be read and given effect in a way which is compatible with the Convention rights'. If it is impossible to render the legislation compatible with the right(s) it remains valid (s 3(2)(b)) and therefore must be applied.

deciding whether, in the conventional phraseology of English law, adoption would be in the best interests of the child . . . Although the phraseology is different, the criteria to be applied in deciding whether an adoption order is justified under Article 8(2) lead to the same result as the conventional tests applied by English law.[60]

The Lords thus assumed that a straightforward application of the paramountcy principle was enough to satisfy Article 8, without any need to make a further assessment as to whether the individual facts of the case justified the interference with parental rights. As a result the appeal was allowed and the adoption order restored.

This judgment of the House of Lords, and those discussed previously above, provide a startling illustration of two points: first, with the partial exception of the judgment of Hale LJ just considered, the English courts have simply reconfigured the paramountcy principle so that it becomes an *automatic* justification within Article 8(2). When faced with any question relating to a child, even if parental Convention rights are in play, the court will invariably make the order that caters to the best interests of that child. While the cases typically give Article 8 a cursory glance at the end of the judgment, the view has, in effect, been taken that since the best interests of the child will inevitably outweigh the Convention rights of the parents, there is no need to give detailed consideration to the justificatory process required for interference with the right, since the result is a foregone conclusion. The careful and sensitive balancing act between competing rights and interests that the Convention requires thus becomes, in the hands of the English courts, a brief and mechanical recital to the effect that the interference with parental rights is a necessary and proportionate response in order to pursue the legitimate aim of protecting the child's welfare.[61]

Second, it is clear that this approach provides a marked illustration of the differences between the theoretical underpinnings of the CA and the ECHR discussed above. By refusing to acknowledge the 'rights and interests' of parties other than the child by assessing their value on an equal footing *before* making their decision, the English courts are in effect jumping the theoretical gun: they are taking account of consequentialist arguments which could properly be considered under the qualifications of Article 8(2) without first making an assessment of the deontological foundations—the Article 8(1) rights themselves. Thus they are disregarding the rights-based analysis that Article 8 demands. Failing to adopt that analysis where the outcome might differ depending on the reasoning process would, quite clearly, fly in the face of the court's duty under s 6(1), HRA.[62]

---

[60] See above n 56 at para 31.

[61] See S. Choudhry, above n 20. See also: A. Bainham, 'Taking Children Abroad: Human Rights, Welfare and the Courts' (2001) *CLJ* 489 at 492; A. Bainham, above n 5.

[62] Under s 6(1) 'It is unlawful for a public authority to act in a way that is incompatible with a Convention right'. Courts are public authorities under s 6(3)(a). Courts can only escape this obligation if under s 6(2)(a) 'as a result of one or more provisions of primary legislation, the authority could not have acted differently; or (b) in the case of one or more provisions of . . . primary legislation which cannot be read or given effect in a way which is compatible with the Convention rights, the authority was acting so as to give effect to or enforce those provisions'. s 6(2)(a) or (b) are inapplicable, as argued below, since s 1(1), CA can be interpreted compatibly with the Convention rights, in particular Art. 8.

Some of the ideas underlying the reluctance of the judiciary to engage in talk of 'rights'[63] in family law were revealed by Butler Sloss LJ in *Re L (A Child) (Contact: Domestic Violence)*:

> Furthermore there seem to me to be considerable difficulties with any return to the language of rights . . . the creation of a right of the child does not lead to corresponding duties on parents. The errant or selfish parent cannot be ordered to spend time with his child against his will however much the child may yearn for his company and the mother desire respite . . . it must be recognised that contact is no more than a mechanism for the maintenance and development of relationships and the court's powers are restricted to regulating the mechanism and do not extend to the underlying relationships.[64]

Although the reciprocity argument has some validity it is, for obvious reasons, not relevant in most contact or residence disputes. But the view expressed by Butler-Sloss LJ is not only fully in harmony with the post-implementation jurisprudence, it also appears to have been influential. The decisions in *Payne* and *Re B* have clearly encouraged the Family Division to assume that no change in reasoning is required under the HRA. So despite the possibilities of revising the welfare principle under s 3(1), HRA, or declaring it incompatible with Article 8 under s4, post-HRA judicial resistance to the Convention became strongly apparent in this field.[65] The Family Bench has, it seems, been discouraged from raising creative and imaginative Convention points. Thus, development of a rich *domestic* human rights jurisprudence in this field has been stifled from the outset, precluding the fusion of the Convention and the established domestic jurisprudence, along with all the concomitant possibilities of developing new and more nuanced perspectives that could have arisen.

Indeed, a number of recent judgments suggest that the significance of the Convention seems to be *continuing* to decline in the post-HRA years. Weak and impoverished as most judicial human rights reasoning in this field was, the first two years after implementation nevertheless saw greater acknowledgment of the Convention than is often currently the case. Absence of consideration of the mechanics of the HRA is becoming even more marked. In a selection of recent cases Article 8 was either not mentioned or was barely touched upon—and then in an imprecise and superficial manner—although it would clearly have been relevant. A number of these cases could have provided the opportunity of putting forward Convention-based arguments in much more pressing circumstances

---

[63] Although there is some evidence of a return to the language of rights, it appears to be limited to the rights of the child and does not extend to parents. See, for example, *A v L (Contact)* [1998] 1 FLR 361 at 365 in which Holman J described contact as "a fundamental right of a child".

[64] [2001] Fam 260 CA, at para 294.

[65] As Harris-Short puts it: 'it could certainly be argued . . . that the welfare principle . . . would have to be reinterpreted under s3HRA to give greater recognition to the parents' interests . . . in the period immediately preceding implementation judicial opposition to any such 'watering down' of the welfare principle began to emerge. The opposition now marks the post-implementation jurisprudence'. See S. Harris-Short, H. Fenwick, D. Bonner, above n 20 at 576.

than those which arose in *Re B*. In all of them one parent could have been viewed as asserting and seeking the vindication of their Article 8 rights.[66]

In *C (A Child) (Immunisation: Parental Rights)*[67] Article 8 was referred to briefly in one paragraph,[68] but no analysis of the application of the Article 8(2) tests was undertaken. The court contented itself with the mere assertion that it could interfere with the rights of both parents and children where to do so was to protect the health of the child. Similarly, in *Re S(A Child)*,[69] a contact case, the application of the HRA was briefly adverted to, noting that under it, 'the court has specifically to take into account the rights of each parent and of the child enshrined in article 8'. But without addressing the contradiction involved, the Court of Appeal went on to find: 'The principle of the paramountcy of the welfare of the child is, nonetheless, recognized in the jurisprudence of the European Court of Human Rights'.[70] As discussed below, this was a very selective approach to that jurisprudence which failed to advert to the impossibility of 'taking account' of the parents' rights in any real sense while applying the welfare principle. The Court proceeded to the reassuring finding: 'Article 8 reflects the pre-existing principles of domestic family law. The right to respect for family life is subject to all the factors set out in article 8(2) in respect of which the element of proportionality is highly significant'. However, the doctrine of proportionality demands a balancing of interests rather than an elevation of one interest above all the others so that it becomes the sole determining factor. This judgment is indicative of the stance of the courts post-implementation: a confused, impoverished and imprecise understanding of the doctrine is used in order to avoid addressing the difficulties that its application in full—as considered below— would create. In *Re P (a child)*[71] the reference to the HRA and Convention was

---

[66] For example, in *Re A (Children): Contact* [2003] WL 214 91866 no mention was made of the father's Article 8 right to respect for his family life in relation to the level of contact allowed with his children. Similarly, in *Re B (Children) (Removal from Jurisdiction)* [2003] 2 FLR 1043 the father's Article 8 right to respect for family life was not mentioned in relation to the mother's intention to leave the country with her new partner so that he could return to his country of origin where they could both settle, with the child. Again, in *In the matter of W (a child)* [2003] EWCA Civ 117 the Court of Appeal made no reference to the Article 8 right to respect for family life of the mother who was seeking an order for contact with her child. No contact had been allowed on the basis of the father's unremitting hostility towards her. No contact order was made but the proceedings were adjourned with a view to seeking the aid of social services in addressing the father's attitude to the mother. In *Wilson v Auld* [2004] All ER (D) 80 (Nov) a mother successfully appealed a decision refusing her leave to temporarily remove her child from the jurisdiction for two years due to the undervaluing of the effect the refusal would have on her career development and prospects and the application of too high a test: *Payne* v *Payne* (it being applicable to applications concerning permanent removals). Here no mention was made of the fathers Article 8 rights. See also *G* v *G* [2005] EWCA Civ 170 where a mothers appeal from refusal for leave to return to Argentina with the children was allowed, again, without any express consideration of the fathers Article 8 rights.

[67] [2003] 2 FLR 1054. See on this case—O'Donnell 'Re C (Welfare of Child: Immunisation)—room to refuse? Immunisation, welfare and the role of parental decision making' (2004) *CFLQ* 16(2) 213–29 and Huxtable 'Medical treatment—children—welfare principle—immunisation—expert evidence—parental rights' (2004) *J Soc Wel & Fam L* 26(1) 69–77.

[68] Ibid at para 337.

[69] [2004] WL 62115 at paras 15 and 27.

[70] The court relied on *Yousef* v *Netherlands* [2003] 36 EHRR 20, para 73 to the effect that if any balancing of interests is necessary, the interests of the child must prevail.

[71] [2003] EWCA Civ 17979 A father was seeking to establish a right of indirect contact—which had been denied in the lower court—with his four-year old child. He also sought to have the period within which he could make no

even more brief, oblique and imprecise, finding merely that a 5-year ban [on applying for direct contact] was 'clearly disproportionate to the circumstances of this case'.[72]

But some indications of a change in this prevailing stance are becoming apparent. In *In the Matter of D*,[73] an intractable contact dispute, Munby J not only demonstrated a receptivity to Convention-based arguments, but also accepted that in the context of such disputes, the courts may not be meeting the standards demanded by Article 8.[74] However, while noting that Article 8 protects both 'the father's right to contact with his daughter . . . [and] also her right to contact with her father',[75] he did not go on to consider the difficulty of affording full protection to the father's Article 8 right in the domestic context—a context in which the right can only be acknowledged through the prism of the child's best interests. Clearly, contact with a father can be and is viewed as an aspect of those interests, but the more sensitive and transparent method of taking account of the father's right argued for in this article could provide the higher level of protection Munby J favoured. While decrying the failures of the domestic system in graphic terms,[76] he did not, in other words, proceed to draw one of the conclusions implicit in his own argument.

As these decisions illustrate, once a court starts from the premise that the parents' interests need be considered only in so far as they coincide with those of the child, examination of the parents' rights is rendered a largely redundant exercise within a family law process which will *always* elevate one party's interests—the child's—in *all* circumstances over the other's. The fundamental basis for a rejection of a real engagement with a rights discourse appears, it is submitted, to be the concern rooted in the history of family proceedings, that a return to a rights-based approach would represent a movement away from the levels of protection of the child's welfare currently attained. Below it is suggested that this

---

application for direct contact reduced from five years to two years. The Court of Appeal found in favour of the father's application.

[72] Ibid at paras 9 and 12.

[73] 2004] 1 FLR 1226. Subsequent intractable contact disputes dealing with implacable hostility appear to have been influenced by Munby J's comments, but they do not mention the Article 8 rights of the family members or rely on ECHR jurisprudence. See: *Re S (Children) (Uncooperative Mothers)* [2004] 2 FLR 710; *V v V (Children) (Contact: Implacable Hostility)* [2004] 2 FLR 851.

[74] He said, at para 35: 'Not least in the light of the Strasbourg jurisprudence there is no room for complacency about the way in which we handle these cases'. The Court of Appeal has sounded the wake-up call. As Thorpe LJ said in *Re T (Contact: Alienation: Permission to Appeal)* [2002] EWCA Civ 1736, [2003] 1 FLR 531 at para 25: 'I reject [counsel's] dismissive submission that the Strasbourg cases add nothing to the domestic jurisprudence. Those cases as they stand suggest that the methods and levels of investigation that our courts have conventionally adopted when trying out issues of alienation may not meet the standards that Arts 6 and 8 . . . require. There are policy issues here that the Government and the judiciary may need to consider collaboratively'.

[75] At para 26.

[76] He said (para 3) 'I now hand down this judgment in public as a contribution to what Wall J in *A v A* [2004] EWHC 142 (Fam) at para. 22 referred to as "the ongoing debate about the role of the courts in contact and residence disputes". On 11 November 2003 a wholly deserving father left my court in tears having been driven to abandon his battle for contact with his seven year old daughter D. (para. 1) . . . [He is entitled to . . . express the view that] the last two years of the litigation have been an exercise in absolute futility . . . (para. 2) . . . Those who are critical of our family justice system may well see this case as exemplifying everything that is wrong with the system. I can understand such a view (para. 4)'.

is a mistaken view and that adoption of such an approach may be capable of providing higher levels of such protection—broadly conceived. But it is also suggested that recognition of the Article 8 rights of parents, considered independently from those of the child, need not lead to a diminution of such protection and that, moreover, the quality of reasoning in family cases would tend to rise once the issues at stake were more precisely and transparently delineated under the approach advocated.

5. *The Post-HRA Academic debate*

The academic debate resembles the judicial one in one respect—there is unease with the notion of placing family disputes involving children in a rights-based framework under the HRA.[77] But the two debates differ in that a number of the leading academics have raised serious concerns about the welfare principle.[78] Those concerns were raised well before the inception of the HRA,[79] but they gathered strength in the HRA era,[80] albeit without—in most instances—situating themselves in the Convention jurisprudence or taking account of the HRA mechanisms. Thus, while many of the judges can still be termed 'welfarists', the leading academics appear to be looking for alternatives to the welfare principle. They therefore either place the notion of welfare under strain in seeking to encourage it to accommodate other interests,[81] or they reject the principle altogether without, however, fully embracing the Convention rights-based alternative.[82] In her very recent writing Fortin has perhaps come closest to embracing that alternative, from a child-centred perspective.[83]

Bainham rejects the predominance of children's interests within the welfarist paradigm.[84] Central to his thesis is that children as well as parents should accept

---

[77] See: S. D. Sclater and F. Kaganas in A. Bainham, B. Lindley, M. Richards and L. Trinder, above n 30; A. Bainham, B. Lindley, M. Richards and L. Trinder, above n 7, ch 5; J. Masson 'Thinking about contact: A social or a legal problem?' 12 *CFLQ* 15; J. Herring, above n 23 esp. at 233. Although Fortin in her very recent work (see above n 7) expresses sympathy with a rights-based approach, she has also earlier expressed unease: see J. Fortin, above n 48 at 255; J. Fortin, 'Rights Brought Home for Children' (1999) 62(3) *MLR* 350 esp. at 369–70. See: S. Harris-Short esp. at 584; H. Fenwick and S. Choudhry, above n 20.

[78] The comment does not imply that all judges unreservedly embrace the welfare principle: see, e.g. Lord Nicholl's adverse dictum in *Re L(minors) (Police Investigation: Privilege)* [1997] AC 16 at 33B. For academic criticism see J. Herring 'Parents and Children' in *Family Law, Issues, Debates and Policy* (Willan, 2001) 164–66 for an outline of the main problems with the principle. In summary it is argued that: the principle produces a narrow perception of welfare; it is too uncertain, thereby leading to unpredictable outcomes and frequently obscuring the real basis of the decision; further, its unpredictability has led to an increase in the costs of litigation. See also J. Herring, *Family Law* (Longman, 2001) at 349–50; A. Bainham, above n 5; J. Eekelaar, above n 6. H. Reece, above n 1, argues that the principle allows the courts to disregard the interests of homosexual parents or carers on the basis of a particular view of the welfare of the child.

[79] See, e.g. A. Bainham, 'Non-intervention and judicial paternalism' in P. Birks (ed), *Frontiers of Liability* (Oxford, OUP, 1994); H. Reece, above n 1.

[80] See, e.g. J. Eekelaar, above n 6.

[81] See J. Herring, above n 78 at 164–66.

[82] See J. Eekelaar, above n 6; his position is discussed below.

[83] See J. Fortin above n 7 esp. at 248–52.

[84] See A. Bainham, above n 79. See also A. Bainham, 'Honour Thy Father and Thy Mother: Children's Rights and Children's Duties' in G. Douglas and L. Sebba (eds), *Children's Rights and Traditional Values* (Aldershot: Dartmouth, 1998).

duties to take account of the interests of others. Therefore in order to balance the interests at stake, he categorizes parents' and children's interests as either primary or secondary. A child's secondary interest would have to give way to a parent's primary interest, and vice versa. He also offers a third category of 'collective family interest' and argues that all these interests should be taken into account in the balancing exercise. Bainham was writing in the pre-HRA era, but his thesis is clearly consistent with the Strasbourg 'balancing' stance discussed below.[85]

In contrast, Herring offers as a theoretical construct a reconceptualization of the welfare principle which nevertheless takes the welfare of the child as a starting point. His position differs from the judicial one in that he views 'welfare' as a more developed and nuanced concept.[86] In providing his analysis of the evidential differences between the CA 1989 and the ECHR, he rejects an approach that sees the question as one of weighing up two competing rights or interests, on Bainham's model, on the basis that it is in essence one based on conflict, whereas the values to be promoted, in Herring's view, are those of union and mutual supportiveness. He finds that the law should seek to focus on the nature of the relationship between the children and parents. His construct is based on two premises. First, that it is part of growing up for a child to learn to suffer sacrifices as well as claiming benefits: children should be expected to be altruistic to the limited extent of abjuring the demand of excessive sacrifices from parents in return for minor benefits. Second he argues that the child's welfare involves ensuring that her relationships with other family members are fair and just. He moves on to advocate an approach founded on 'relationship-based welfare' which sees the balancing of the interests of children and parents, not in terms of a conflict, but as an aspect of promoting an effective and satisfactory parent-child relationship.

Rather than offer another reconceptualization of the welfare principle, Eekelaar rejects it entirely in a seminal piece.[87] He argues that the way in which the principle is currently being interpreted does not give proper attention either to children's interests or to the interests of others. Building on Bainham's analysis of the interests of the relevant parties, he offers an alternative model which focuses on their well-being. Under his model, 'if the choice was between a solution that advanced a child's well-being a great deal, but also damaged the interests of one parent a great deal', as opposed to a solution under which 'the child's well-being was diminished, but which damaged the parent's interests to a far lesser degree', the second option would be chosen 'even though it was not the least detrimental alternative *for the child*'.[88] He offers, however, two qualifications to this proposal: that the interests of children should be privileged,

---

[85] See in particular the approach in *Johansen* v *Norway* [1997] 23 EHRR 134, discussed below.
[86] See J. Herring, above n 78.
[87] See J. Eekelaar, above n 6.
[88] Ibid at 244.

although not paramount, in the calculus; and that the degree of detriment to which the child is to be subjected should be 'appropriate'—in other words, that all the circumstances pertaining to a particular case should be taken into account, rather than applying the test in a rigid fashion. His analysis could readily be termed one based on the doctrine of proportionality and therefore at first glance it appears strange that he does not simply advocate a Convention-based approach which would also have the attraction of being legally enforceable via ss 6 and 3 of the HRA. However, he takes a particular view of the values encapsulated in that approach—one that is, it is argued below, coming under question at the present time. Basing his argument on this view,[89] Eekelaar acknowledges the attraction of the 'Convention approach', but argues that it has two limitations. First, in his view it accords too little weight to the interests of children—the 'lack of fairness' objection—since under Article 8 it is necessary first to have regard to the rights of adults (para 1) and apply them unless it can be shown that their infringement is justifiable as necessary in a democratic society in order to further the interests of the child. Second, he finds that the welfare principle, operating, under the Convention approach, as a qualification to the parents' rights under Article 8(2), might allow other interests to predominate in an unacknowledged fashion (as, he argues, currently occurs under the orthodox application of the welfare principle), or it might merely displace them. Thus the Convention approach is equally open to objection on grounds of 'lack of transparency' since it is 'likely to oscillate between a dubious preference for adults' rights and their virtual submergence under the welfare principle'.[90]

These concerns would indeed be relevant to a Convention-based approach which resulted in the application of the welfare principle as a qualification under Article 8(2) to the primary rights guaranteed in Article 8(1). However, this is precisely *not* the approach that is being advocated in this article, and indeed it now appears to be established that although this approach is correct in relation to clashes between Convention rights and societal interests, it should not be applied in relation to clashes of Convention rights, although so far this finding has been made only in the context of conflicts between Articles 8 and 10.[91] The correct Convention approach is, it is submitted, one that places all parties involved in a dispute on a presumptively equal footing under the 'parallel analysis', which is discussed below. One of the most significant aspects of this new reasoning process is that it *is* transparent—unlike reasoning under the welfare principle—(whether viewed in orthodox fashion or as qualifying the Article 8(1) rights) since *all* the rights and interests involved have to be examined in a step-by-step and fact-sensitive fashion. As to the more significant objection that children's

---

[89] This approach discussed by Eekelaar was that as set out by J. Fortin, above n 48 at 250.
[90] Above n 6 at 242.
[91] See: *Re S(a Child)* [2003] 2 FCR 577; *Campbell v MGN* [2004] May 6 HL. The idea of a dual exercise in proportionality was first put forward by H. Fenwick and G. Phillipson, 'The Doctrine of Confidence as a Privacy Remedy in the Human Rights Act Era' (2000) 63 (5) *MLR* 660–93; for recent discussion see: G. Phillipson, above n 44; H. Fenwick, above n 20, and see further text to n 144–47 below.

interests would not receive sufficient protection—under the parallel analysis children's interests would not merely be considered under Article 8(2), but under Article 8(1): in other words, children themselves would be viewed as rights-holders. Therefore *one* of the exercises to be conducted under the parallel analysis would take as its starting point the inherent 'good' of the child's interests—viewed as a right to respect for her family life, subject to exceptions (the parents' rights) to be narrowly applied.

It is concluded that the underlying aims of the approaches advocated by Bainham and Eekelaar can be realized within the Convention-based 'parallel analysis' approach advocated in this article which relies on the model of judicial reasoning utilized by the European Court of Human Rights, one that affords a careful consideration to all parties' rights and interests, but also provides for special consideration to be given to those of the child. That approach would also acknowledge the duties enjoined on the judiciary under ss 6 and 3 of the HRA. The approaches of Eekelaar and Bainham harmonize with the 'parallel analysis' in terms of both the reasoning process and the likely outcomes. Fortin's work, which places differing aspects of childhood in a rights-based framework, is of especial significance in relation to the ongoing debate this article is seeking to promote as to the balance between the rights of children and of adults.[92] Thus, although the academic debate has not yet fully embraced the Convention approach discussed below, a number of the leading figures have paved the way towards it.

6. *Resolving Conflicts between Differing Article 8 Rights to Respect for Family Life under the Human Rights Act: the New Approach*

Under the Human Rights Act, the courts are bound by the Convention rights under s 6(1) of the HRA, and must take the Convention jurisprudence into account under s 2. Where that jurisprudence is clear and consistent it should be treated as binding.[93] The discussion below demonstrates that the current approach of the domestic courts in disputes concerning children is out of kilter with that taken at Strasbourg, although it is fair to say that the application of the margin of appreciation doctrine has some obscuring effect on the conclusions to be drawn from that jurisprudence. Thus it is argued that there is a missing dimension in domestic reasoning in such disputes. First, it is argued that the paramountcy principle requires re-evaluation in the light of the Strasbourg jurisprudence and in order to accept fully the implications of receiving Article 8 into domestic law. Second, as a correlative step, the structure of domestic reasoning, as well as its underpinning values, requires significant modification in order to follow the

---

[92] Above, n 7 esp. chs 1 and 19.
[93] Lord Slynn in *R (on the application of Alconbury Developments Ltd) v Secretary of State for the Environment* [2001] 2 WLR 1389 found: 'In the absence of some special circumstances it seems to me that the court should follow any clear and constant jurisprudence of the European Court of Human Rights' (at para 26).

contours of Article 8(2) in engaging in the 'parallel analysis' or 'ultimate balancing act' discussed below.

A. *The Developing Strasbourg Jurisprudence*

The Strasbourg approach is not founded upon a particular conception of fatherhood as distinct from motherhood since fathers are presumptively in the same position as mothers under the Convention (and the CRC)[94] in the sense that they do not normally have to *establish* a claim to the Article 8(1) right to respect for family life.[95] In contrast to the domestic reasoning discussed above, the European Court of Human Rights approaches any question concerning Article 8 by starting from the stance that wherever family life is found to be in existence, each of the family members will be entitled independently to respect for their family life. It does not regard the child's interests in this respect as paramount, that is, as displacing considerations of other members' rights. Each family member's right to respect for family life is accorded equal weight[96] before a decision is made as to what extent, if at all, such rights are in conflict. The Court will then consider whether any interference with the rights of family members is justified as 'necessary' under Article 8(2); it is only at this point that the welfare of the child becomes relevant and will not inevitably result in the child's interests prevailing. As discussed below, this process of reasoning, which is open to criticism,[97] is inevitable at Strasbourg but need not and should not be followed domestically.

The margin of appreciation doctrine is also inapplicable in domestic courts, allowing for an enhanced scrutiny of the issues at stake. In the family law field, in determining whether the measures taken are indeed 'necessary in a democratic society', Strasbourg will consider whether, in the light of the case as a whole, the reasons adduced to justify them were relevant and sufficient for the purpose of paragraph 2 of Article 8.[98] In making this assessment, the Court will afford the

---

[94] In Articles 7, 8, 9 CRC there is no differentiation between the mother and the father in terms of caring responsibilities.

[95] There are significant exceptions to this position: for example, a father who is not married to the mother and who has had no involvement with the child is unlikely to be viewed as having family life that requires respect: *G v the Netherlands* [1990] 16 EHRR 38 (the link between a sperm donor and a child was not found to establish family life). The inferior legal position in the UK of an unmarried father compared to that of the mother does not violate Article 8: *B v UK* [2000] 1 FLR 1.

[96] Private life is not usually considered separately, although in some circumstances this might be a significant possibility. A private life claim would also be balanced against a family life one on a basis of presumptive equality. This approach is also taken to clashes with the other qualified Convention rights: see *Twenty-Twenty-Television v UK* [1998] 25 EHRR CD 159, discussed below—text to and within n 112. The approach would differ in relation to the unqualified or non-materially qualified rights: for example, if a father and mother were opposed as to a form of education or as to religious practices it would be a violation of Art 2, Protocol 1 (education of children in accordance with parental convictions) or Art 9 (freedom of religion) read with Art 14 to enable—through the courts—the father's wishes to prevail over the mother's. An Article 8 claim of a family life right to chastise a child would fail: see *A v UK* [1999] 27 EHRR 611 (a violation of Art 3 was found in respect of the beating of a boy by his step-father, with an implement where the law had failed to protect the boy; reference was made to Art 19 CRC).

[97] See Eekelaar, above n 6.

[98] See *Olsson v Sweden (No. 2)* (A/250) [1992] 17 EHRR 134 at para 68.

national authorities a margin of appreciation, in recognition of the fact that they are better placed to make the primary judgement as to the needs of the parties involved and the appropriate balance to be struck between them.[99] The extent of the margin of appreciation to be accorded to States in such circumstances will, however, vary in the light of the nature and seriousness of the interests at stake.[100] In *Elsholz* v *Germany*[101] the Court clearly found that the margin of appreciation to be conceded to the state authorities would be narrower where family life had already been circumscribed by the decision to take a child into care and further circumscription in respect of access had occurred.[102] The margin also varies according to the *context* of the individual facts of a case. In this field, and specifically in relation to those cases involving children, the European Court has indicated that cases in the public law sphere may attract a wider margin of appreciation than those in the private sphere.[103]

Nevertheless, the Court still accords significant weight to the Article 8 rights of the parents, even in instances in which the child appears to be at risk. In *K* v *Finland*[104] the Grand Chamber of the Court had to consider inter alia a care order removing a new born child from the mentally ill mother immediately after the birth on the ground that the child was at risk. Even conceding a margin of appreciation to the state, the Grand Chamber found that 'the reasons relied on by the national authorities were relevant but, in the Court's view, not sufficient to justify the serious intervention in the family life of the applicants'.[105] It is clear that the margin conceded where clashes between the Article 8 rights of the child and the parent occur, is not as wide as in certain 'clash of rights' instances in other contexts.[106]

---

[99] For a general discussion of the concept of the margin of appreciation see C. Ovey and R.C.A. White, *Jacobs & White, The European Convention on Human Rights* (Oxford, 3rd edn, 2002) at 210–15, and for an example of its application concerning Art 8 of the ECHR see *Soderback* v *Sweden* [1998] EHRR 342; the Court held that, due to the infrequent and limited nature of the contact between the applicant father and his child, there had been no violation of the father's Art 8 rights: the decision to place the child for adoption was not only clearly justified on the facts of the case but also that it fell well within the State's margin of appreciation to do so.

[100] *K and T* v *Finland* [2001] 31 EHRR 18, para 166 and *Kitzner* v *Germany* [2002] 35 EHRR 25, para 67.

[101] [2000] 2 FLR 486.

[102] '[T]he authorities enjoy a wide margin of appreciation, in particular when assessing the necessity of taking a child into care. However, a stricter scrutiny is called for in respect of any further limitations, such as restrictions placed by those authorities on parental rights of access . . . Such further limitations entail the danger that the family relations between the parents and a young child would be effectively curtailed'. Ibid at para 49. See also *Haase* v *Germany* [2004] 2 FLR 39 [2005] 40 EHRR 19 at para 89.

[103] For example, in *Johansen* v *Norway* 23 EHRR 33, at para 64 the Court stated: 'perceptions as to the appropriateness of intervention by public authorities in the care of children vary from one Contracting State to another, depending on such factors as traditions relating to the role of the family and to State intervention in family affairs and the availability of resources for public measures in this particular area . . . the Court recognises that the authorities enjoy a wide margin of appreciation in assessing the necessity of taking a child into care'.

[104] [2003] 36 EHRR 18.

[105] The Court said: 'Even having regard to the national authorities' margin of appreciation, the Court considers that the making of the emergency care order in respect of J and the methods used in implementing that decision were disproportionate in their effects on the applicants' potential for enjoying a family life with their new-born child as from her birth. This being so, whilst there may have been a "necessity" to take some precautionary measures to protect the child J, the interference in the applicants' family life entailed in the emergency care order made in respect of J cannot be regarded as having been "necessary" in a democratic society'(at para 168). See also *Johansen* v *Norway* [1997] 23 EHRR 134

[106] See *Otto–Preminger Institut* v *Austria* [1994] 19 EHRR 34; *Tammer* v *Estonia* [2003] 37 EHRR 43.

Thus the use of the margin of appreciation doctrine fails to obscure the balancing act that is occurring in the family cases. In *Elsholz v Germany*,[107] the applicant father claimed that his Article 8 rights had been breached by the refusal of the national court to allow him access to his child when it relied on statements made by the child when he was aged five, took into account the strained relations between the parents, considered that it did not matter who was responsible for the tensions, and found that any further contact would negatively affect the child. This breach was further exacerbated, he claimed, since the court had decided that it was unnecessary to obtain an expert opinion, on the ground that the facts had been clearly and completely established for the purposes of domestic law. The European Court of Human Rights, in finding that a violation of the father's Article 8 rights had occurred, reiterated the principle from *Johansen v Norway*[108] that a fair balance must be struck between the interests of the child and those of the parent, and that in so doing particular importance must be attached to the best interests of the child which, depending on their nature and seriousness, can override those of the parent. Thus the father's Article 8 rights were afforded weight in the sense that a justification for infringing them had to be convincingly established. On the facts this had not occurred. The Court, to an extent, considered the curtailment of the father's family life, not merely from the point of view of his Article 8(1) rights, but also from the point of view of the child. It is noteworthy that the applicant father argued that the denial of contact was not only a violation of his interests but also of those of the child, since contact with the non-resident parent was in the child's best medium and long-term interests. In other words, although the case could be viewed as concerning a clash of rights—even though it was not argued in those terms—the Court discerned an underlying harmony between the two claims of rights:

> The Court further recalls that the mutual enjoyment by parent and child of each other's company constitutes a fundamental element of family life, even if the relationship between the parents has broken down, and domestic measures hindering such enjoyment amount to an interference with the right protected by Article 8 of the Convention.[109]

Spurious or trivial reasons had been adduced for the abrogation of the father's rights; the true interests of the child might have been better served by allowing the father access. In determining under Article 8(2) that the interference in the

---

[107] [2000] 2 FLR 486.
[108] [1997] 23 EHRR 134.
[109] Ibid at para 43. This reasoning was also adopted in *Kosmopolou v Greece* [2004] 1 FLR 427 in finding a violation of the applicants Art 8 rights had occurred due to failures in the procedural approach, adopted by the domestic courts, in adequately determining the question of access to her daughter. The applicant, despite possessing visiting rights, had, consequently, been unable to see her daughter or establish regular contact with her. At para 27 the Court stated: 'The Court reiterates in this respect that it is of paramount importance for parents always to be placed in a position enabling them to put forward all arguments in favour of obtaining contact with the child and to have access to all relevant information which was at the disposal of the domestic courts'.

father's rights was unnecessary in a democratic society, the Court concluded that the combination of the refusal to order an independent psychological report and the absence of a hearing before the Regional Court revealed that the applicant had been insufficiently involved in the decision-making process, and thus the national authorities had overstepped their margin of appreciation, thereby violating the applicant's rights under Article 8 of the Convention.

In a significant decision which has so far gone largely unnoticed by academics, the European Commission on Human Rights gave consideration to a challenge to the UK paramountcy principle itself where it came into conflict with the mother's Article 8 right to respect for her family life. In *A and Byrne and Twenty-Twenty Television v United Kingdom*[110] the first applicant, who was the mother of the child (C), argued that she had suffered a breach of her Article 8 right to respect for family life as a result of the refusal of the domestic courts, based on an application of the paramountcy principle, to accept her decision that C should take part in a television programme about her development and education in an institution catering for her special needs.[111] The decision to refuse to allow C to participate had been taken on the basis that—contrary to the mother's view—it was not in C's best interests to do so.

In relation to the question whether the interference could be considered 'necessary' under paragraph 2 of Article 8, the Commission afforded a certain margin of appreciation in assessing whether the need existed. It took into account the purpose of the documentary programme and the acceptance of the applicants' bona fides in this respect. The first applicant submitted that since her decision to allow C to participate in the television programme was taken in good faith, for C's benefit and with the proper advice, the courts should have followed her decision unless they found it irrational or in bad faith.[112] The Commission found that it was for the national authorities to strike a fair *balance* between the relevant competing interests (emphasis added): what would be decisive would be whether the national authorities had made such efforts 'as can be reasonably demanded under the special circumstances of the case' to accommodate the parents' rights.[113] The Commission concluded that, in the circumstances of the present case and in view of the margin of appreciation accorded to states in this area, the imposition by the courts of their view as to the best interests of C was supported by 'relevant' as well as 'sufficient' reasons.[114] The domestic courts had made such efforts as could be reasonably demanded to accommodate the

---

[110] [1998] 25 EHRR CD 159.

[111] The mother and the media applicants both also complained of a breach of Art 10 (the guarantee of freedom of expression) but the argument was conducted under Art 8.

[112] She further submitted that the courts were not well placed to make the assessment that they had; the judges were elderly males of an elite class unlikely to have had experience of raising children with handicaps like C and they could not possibly know how the transmission of the programme would affect C.

[113] *Olsson* v *Sweden* (No. 2) [1994] 17 EHRR 134, para 90 and *Hokkanen* v *Finland* [1995] 19 EHRR 139, para 57.

[114] The Commission took into account the fact that the High Court had taken the view that any short-term benefit for C deriving from the publicity was outweighed by the 'serious consequences' which transmission of the programme would entail for her in terms of extended publicity.

first applicant's rights and the interference was accordingly proportionate to the legitimate aim pursued. The restriction was not therefore found to create a breach of the Article 8 right to family life of the mother. Thus the clash of rights which arose was resolved in favour of the Article 8 rights of the child (although the case was not argued in those terms), but it was also—most significantly— made clear that even where, in domestic terms, the paramountcy principle had applied, the child's welfare does not take *automatic* priority over a parent's independent Article 8 right.

In other words, the balancing approach is in harmony with the tendency of the Court of Human Rights to accord special importance to the best interests of the child. This tendency of the Court has become more marked; the Court has recently demonstrated a greater willingness to give special consideration to children's rights,[115] which in turn has been attributed to the growing influence in the Strasbourg jurisprudence[116] of the United Nations Convention on the Rights of the Child (the CRC).[117] Article 3 of the CRC states: 'in all actions concerning children, whether undertaken by public or private courts of law, administrative authorities or legislative bodies, the best interests of the child shall be a *primary* consideration'. Both the Commission and the Court have referred to the provisions of the CRC in children's cases since it came into force in 1990, and this development in approach is evidenced by the findings discussed in *Johansen* v *Norway*[118] and *Elsholz* v *Germany*.[119]

The Court recently referred to the principle of paramountcy itself in *Yousef* v *The Netherlands*[120] (a private law dispute):

> the court *reiterates* that in judicial decisions where the rights under Art 8 of parents and those of a child are at stake, the child's rights must be the paramount consideration. If any balancing of interests is necessary, the interests of the child must prevail (see

---

[115] The ECHR itself contains few explicit references to children and their rights, which is generally believed to be due to the era of its inception. There are only two explicit references—Art 5 (which guarantees the right to liberty) makes additional provision for the detention of a minor in para 1(d) and Art 6 (which guarantees the right to a fair trial) which provides an exception to the right to a public hearing in the case of juveniles if necessary.

[116] See U. Kilkelly, 'The best of both worlds for Children's rights? Interpreting the European Convention on Human Rights in the light of the UN Convention on the Rights of the Child' (2001) 23 *Human Rights Quarterly* 308–326 and M. Woolf 'Coming of Age?—The Principle of the Best Interests of the Child' (2003) 2 *EHRLR* 205– 21 for an overview of how the principle has been interpreted by the European Court of Human Rights and the UK courts within the context of the UN Convention on the Rights of the Child 1989.

[117] The UK has ratified the CRC and is therefore bound under international law to comply with its requirements. It is still, however, not part of UK law. For a feminist critique of the CRC see F. Olsen, 'Children's Rights: Some Feminist Approaches to the UN Convention on the Rights of the Child' in P. Alston, S. Parker and J. Seymour (eds), *Children, Rights and the Law* (Clarendon Press, 1992). See also J. Eekelaar, 'The Importance of Thinking That Children Have Rights' in the same volume, for a theoretical explanation of the significance of the rights declared by the CRC on behalf of children.

[118] It was found: 'a fair balance has to be struck between the interests of the child in remaining in public care and those of the parent in being reunited with the child. In carrying out this balancing exercise, the court will attach particular importance to the best interests of the child, which, depending on their nature and seriousness, may override those of the parent' [1996] 23 EHRR 33, at para 78. See also *Gorgolou* v *Germany* [2004] 1 FLR 894 para 37; *Kosmopolou* v *Greece* [2004] 1 FLR 427 para 23 and *Haase* v *Germany* [2004] 2 FLR 39.

[119] [2000] 2 FLR 486 at para 50. In *L* v *Finland*, Application No 25651/94, at para 118 (another public law case) the Court stated: 'the consideration of what is in the best interests of the child is of crucial importance'.

[120] [2003] 36 EHRR 20.

Elsholz v. Germany . . . and *TP and KM v. United Kingdom* . . . This applies also in cases such as the present.[121] [emphasis added]

At first sight this statement appears to contradict the previous authority of the Court in relation to the issue of paramountcy. However, the use of the term 'reiterates' is clearly questionable since in the two cases referred to the Court did not explicitly refer to the principle.[122] More significantly, in succeeding judgments the Court has reaffirmed the established position whereby the varying Convention rights of the parties concerned are considered by starting from a basis of presumptive equality. Thus, in *Hansen v Turkey*,[123] a case in which the mother argued that failure to enforce contact had breached her Article 8 right to respect for family life, the Court found, citing *Hokkanen*[124] and *Ignaccolo-Zenide*:[125] 'the rights and freedoms of all concerned must be taken into account, and more particularly the best interests of the child and his or her rights under Article 8 of the Convention. Where contacts with the parent might appear to threaten those interests or interfere with those rights, it is for the national authorities to strike a *fair balance* between them' (emphasis added). In other words, within the margin of appreciation of the member state, a fair balance must be struck between the Article 8 rights of the child and those of the parent, thereby ruling out the use of a presumption that precludes that balancing exercise, although the welfare of the child will be of especial significance. That approach was also taken in *Gorgulu v Germany*,[126] *Hoppe v Germany*,[127] *Haase v Germany*[128] and *Kosmopolou v Greece*.[129] In all of these judgments *Yousef* went unmentioned, and the *Johansen* stance was adopted as the accepted position. It is argued therefore that *Yousef* is out of line with the Court's established and continuing line of reasoning on the interests of the child.

Thus, the approach of the ECHR must be distinguished from the application of the paramountcy principle *simpliciter* for this reason: in a choice between two outcomes for a child, the application of the principle would require that if one option would be even slightly preferable from the child's perspective compared to that of the parent, that outcome should be chosen even though it would cause a substantial infringement of parental rights, where the other one would not.[130] Hence, if it is accepted that the European Court of Human Right's approach is influenced by the CRC, as discussed above, then it also has to be accepted that

---

[121] Ibid at para 73.
[122] See S. Choudhry, above n 20 at 130.
[123] [2004] 1 FLR 142 para 98.
[124] [1996] 1 FLR 289.
[125] [2001] 31 EHRR 7.
[126] [2004] 1 FLR 894 at para 43.
[127] [2004] 38 EHRR 15 at para 44.
[128] [2004] 2 FLR 39.
[129] [2004] 1 FLR 427.
[130] Although courts may *consider* the impact of their decisions on parents when reaching such decisions there is, however, no requirement to do so within s 1 of the Children Act 1989 or indeed the statutory checklist contained in s 1(3).

the Court is responding to a Convention that clearly refers to the child's interests as 'primary', not 'paramount'. Thus, by approaching the issue of 'fair balance' as an opportunity to weigh *all* interests in the scales, the European Convention is still intrinsically opposed to the UK paramountcy approach, which rejects any notion of balance, since interests *other* than those of the child appear not to weigh in the scales at all. In contact disputes the Strasbourg approach may indirectly benefit fathers since their interests are—to a greater extent than those of the mother—prone to be viewed by domestic courts as opposed to those of the child since the father tends to be the non-residential parent.

B. *Abandoning the Paramountcy Principle as Currently Conceived*

The exposition of the jurisprudence above makes it clear that the European Court of Human Rights will seek to strike a fair balance between each family member's Article 8 rights, in the light of the individual facts of the case and the view of the national authorities on the case, although the welfare of the child will be a primary consideration. In contrast to the approach taken under the Children Act 1989, this approach ensures that no one 'rule' (that of the best interests of the child) prevails automatically and that if the best interests of the child *do* prevail it is only after a detailed consideration of all the parties' rights and interests on a *presumptively equal footing* has taken place. Although, as indicated above, the margin of appreciation doctrine plays a significant part in family law decisions at Strasbourg, it is narrowed in certain instances, thereby giving greater guidance to the domestic courts under the HRA. Moreover, the general principle, that Article 8 rights—other than those of the child—must be accorded some weight, is not in doubt and therefore it should be applied in the domestic courts.[131] The decision of the Commission in *Twenty-Twenty Television* gives important guidance under s 2 of the HRA to domestic courts in situations in which a clash of Article 8 rights arises *and* the paramountcy principle applies. The Commission made it clear that the restriction intended to protect the child's welfare had to be justified within the tests under Article 8(2), thereby implicitly rejecting the paramountcy principle as interpreted domestically.

It is argued then that the paramountcy principle as it is currently conceived and applied is incompatible with the demands of Article 8 and therefore requires reinterpretation under s 3(1) of the HRA in accordance with the interpretative obligation under that section and also with the courts' duty under s 6(1), taking account of the relevant Strasbourg jurisprudence under s 2. The term 'paramount' in s 1(1) of the CA would undergo re-definition, but such re-definition would not need to be radical since the word 'paramount' arguably, as one of the authors has already argued, more naturally conveys the notion of 'pre-eminency', rather than the meaning the courts have so far given it under the CA,

---

[131] See above n 93.

whereby it has in reality meant 'sole'.[132] However, given the scope for ambiguity that the courts might discover in the term 'pre-eminent', the term 'primacy' might capture the Strasbourg stance more readily. Adoption of that term could be viewed as a possible interpretation of the term 'paramount' and would obviate the need for a declaration of incompatibility under s 4 of the HRA. A new primacy principle would accord with the jurisprudence of the European Court of Human Rights discussed above without, it is argued, detracting from the new value to be accorded to the rights of other family members. Its abandonment in the face of the demands of the HRA thus necessitates an acceptance of a shift from welfare to rights or, in other words, from a form of rule utilitarianism to the qualified deontological approach of the Convention, in which there is an acceptance of the prima facie entitlement of individuals to family (and private) life. But within this rights-based approach the child's interests would still be fully protected, as indicated below.

Clearly, it has been open to the judges to take this step since the HRA came into force and they have declined so far to do so. One of the purposes of this article is to challenge that prevailing judicial stance. However, in instances in which the welfare principle applies, but which are atypical family cases, there is already some tentative judicial support for a change of stance. Dicta of Hirst LJ in *R v Secretary of State for Home Department, ex parte Gangadeen and Khan*[133] indicate that there is some judicial understanding of the incompatibility between the paramountcy principle as currently conceived and the relevant Convention jurisprudence. These two cases raised the question whether where a decision to deport the appellants affected the interests of their child, the Secretary of State was obliged to give preference to those interests as the paramount consideration in the process, having regard to the principles of Article 8 of the Convention. A large number of Convention cases were cited in argument and reviewed in the court's judgement. Hirst LJ stated that, in his view, the Convention case law cited to him[134]

> demonstrates quite clearly that, in their interpretation of Article 8 in the present context, the human rights court and the Commission approach the problem as a straightforward balancing exercise, *in which the scales start even*, and where the weight to be given to the considerations on each side of the balance is to be assessed according to the individual circumstances of the case; thus they do not support the notion that paramountcy should be given to the interests of the child (emphasis added).

Thus the court specifically found that the Convention did *not* guarantee the paramountcy of the child's interests. There is a clear inconsistency in the approach taken here in a *pre*-HRA decision and that taken by the Court of

---

[132] See S. Choudhry, above n 20.
[133] [1998] 1 FLR 762, CA.
[134] Ibid at 773–74.

Appeal post-HRA in *Payne*. The fact that, had the paramountcy principle been applied in *Gangadeen*, the Secretary of State's broad discretion to deport—traditionally respected by the courts under the *Wednesbury* grounds of review—would have been radically curtailed, may explain this inconsistency. Nevertheless, whatever the motivating factors behind the reasoning, it is clear that a more accurate understanding of Article 8 was reached in *Gangadeen*. Further, in the context of clashes between Articles 10 and 8 in the domain of child welfare there has been some tentative judicial acceptance of the need for the abandonment of the principle as currently conceived[135] or of the need to manipulate the notion of 'up-bringing'—either using s 3(1) of the HRA[136] or ordinary principles of statutory interpretation[137]—with a view to narrowing it down so as to avoid a clash between the principle and Article 10. In that context, as one of the authors has already argued, the tension between the principle and Article 10 is such that its reconfiguration under s 3(1) is eventually likely to become inevitable[138] when a case arises in which it is impossible to avoid invoking the principle, but media freedom under Article 10 is also at stake. It is difficult to see how a principle requiring the automatic abrogation of Article 10 could be sustained in such an instance unchanged, especially given the significance accorded to media freedom by the courts. Merely viewing the application of the principle as an automatic justification under Article 10(2) for the breach—as appears to be occurring under Article 8(2) post-HRA—might be less likely in the context of media freedom to strike the courts as a satisfactory solution. Once that had been accepted, the modification of the principle would also be likely to be accepted in the context of the family cases in order to ensure consistency of approach to s 1(1) of the CA and the Convention.

C. *Weighing up Competing Article 8 rights—the 'Parallel Analysis': Dual or Tripartite Exercises of Proportionality*

It is clear from the Strasbourg cases considered that an individual right cannot figure merely as an exception to another individual right. Still less can it be almost entirely abrogated without a full application of the paragraph 2 tests. However, in the cases considered above where Article 8 rights clashed, Strasbourg had to follow the approach of treating one right as primary due to the particular procedure of bringing applications to the Court. The position of the domestic judiciary is fundamentally different since they have a full opportunity

---

[135] Hedley J in the Family Division of the High Court in *Re S*, unrep, February 19, 2003. He found that the principle did not apply but considered that even if the child's welfare *had* been the paramount consideration, he would have decided that the press reporting could not be curbed even though he had the power to curb it. The Court of Appeal disagreed ([2003] 2 FCR 577; [2003] 147 SJLB 873), Lady Justice Hale finding that when the child's welfare *is* the paramount consideration, 'it rules on or determines the issue before the court. *It* is the trump card' (emphasis in the original) at para 62.
[136] *Medway Council* v *BBC* [2002] 1 FLR 104.
[137] The Court of Appeal in *Re S*, above n 135.
[138] See H. Fenwick, above n 20.

to address the clashing rights issue. The established domestic recognition of the presumptive equality of competing qualified Convention rights discussed below demands adoption of the parallel analysis as the model for the process of reasoning to be followed.

(i) *Presumptive equality between Articles 8 and 10*

The 'parallel analysis'—the dual exercise of proportionality—has already found judicial and academic favour in the context of conflicts between Articles 8 and 10. Outside the domain of child welfare the presumptive equality approach[139] is now dominant.[140] The decision in *Re S*[141] is of especial significance since it concerned the right of a child to private life. In *Re S* the Court of Appeal sought to weigh up Articles 8 and 10 against each other in an instance in which, while the child's welfare was engaged, the paramountcy principle was found not to apply. The Court found, in a highly significant break with the previous line of authority, that they must be considered as independent elements, on the basis, following *Douglas* v *Hello!*[142] and *A* v *B plc*,[143] that one does not have pre-eminence over the other (despite s 12(4), HRA). In the lower court it had been assumed that press freedom would be afforded primacy and that the Article 8 rights of the child would figure merely as exceptions under Article 10(2). It was accepted that this was clearly the wrong approach. Lady Justice Hale then went on to consider the proportionality of the proposed interference with freedom of expression[144] before proceeding to consider the matter from the perspective of the child's Article 8 rights, media freedom figuring this time as an exception to them under Article 8(2). In considering the proportionality of the proposed interference with the right of the child to respect for his private and family life, the judge had to take account of the magnitude of the interference proposed. Lady Justice Hale came to the conclusion that since the first instance judge had not considered each Article independently, and so had not conducted the difficult balancing exercise required by the Convention, the appeal should be allowed, in order that

---

[139] The concept is argued for by H. Rogers and H. Tomlinson, 'Privacy and Expression: Convention Rights and Interim Injunctions' (2003) *EHRLR* (Privacy—Special Issue) 38 at 41.

[140] In *Cream Holdings* v *Bannerjee* [2003] 2 All ER 318 at para 41 SimonBrown LJ, speaking for the majority, said: 'It is one thing to say . . . that the media's right to freedom of expression, particularly in the field of political discussion, 'is of a higher order' than 'the right of an individual to his good reputation'; it is, however, another thing to rank it higher than competing basic rights [Convention rights]'.

[141] *Re S (a Child)* [2003] 2 FCR 577.

[142] [2001] QB 967 1005 at para 24.

[143] [2003] 3 WLR 542 at para 6. Lady Justice Hale (as she then was), who gave the leading judgement, relied on Lord Woolf's dicta in *A* v *B* to the effect that '[the court must] attach proper weight to the important rights which both articles are designed to protect. Each article is qualified expressly in a way which allows the interests under the other Article to be taken into account'.

[144] She had to consider under Art 10(2) what restriction, if any, was needed to meet the legitimate aim of protecting the rights of the child. If prohibiting publication of the family name and photographs was needed, the court had to consider how great an impact that would in fact have upon the freedom protected by Art 10, taking into account the greater public interest in knowing the names of persons convicted of serious crime than of those who are merely suspected or charged.

the exercise could be properly carried out by the first instance Family Division court.[145]

The majority judges endorsed Lady Hale's analysis, which was then applied in the lower courts;[146] it was subsequently endorsed by the House of Lords in *Campbell* v *MGN*.[147] In that instance Lord Hope and Baroness Hale in the majority conducted a balancing exercise,[148] amounting to an application of the parallel analysis, between the Article 8 and 10 rights in question on a basis of their presumptive equality. *In Re S (a child)*[149] itself the House of Lords also endorsed the use of the parallel analysis in all instances in which the issue of open justice in criminal cases does not arise. (The question of paramountcy was not addressed since it had been accepted by both sides that the principle was inapplicable.) Referring to the parallel analysis, Lord Steyn found that in clashes between the Convention rights, 'the proportionality test must be applied to each. For convenience I will call this the *ultimate balancing test*' (emphasis added).[150] Since this analysis has been endorsed in two decisions of the House of Lords it is now clear that it must be viewed as the correct approach to all clashes of the qualified Convention rights, including, it is argued, clashes between two or more rights-holders claiming the same right.

(ii) *Presumptive equality between varying Article 8 rights*

Since, in the context of a child's private and family life, *Re S* (in both the House of Lords and Court of Appeal) took as its starting point the presumptive equality of Articles 8 and 10, relying on paragraph 2 of each Article in order to resolve the conflict between them, it is an extremely significant decision since it creates a new model for judicial reasoning. But the *Re S* approach, while demonstrating up to a point a sensitive understanding of the Convention values, is revealed to be logically flawed since it advocates presumptive equality for two of the qualified Convention rights (Arts 8 and 10), but appeared to be prepared to abandon its own underlying premises had the paramountcy principle come into play. It is therefore in that respect out of accord with the Strasbourg jurisprudence discussed above. The departure from *Re S* argued for here, therefore, is that its reasoning model should also be adopted in an instance in which the paramountcy principle *does* apply, necessitating, as indicated above, the reconfiguration of that principle as one of primacy. Further, it is argued that if the presumptive equality

---

[145] The two judges in the majority disagreed with this finding, considering that although the balancing exercise outlined by Lady Justice Hale was the correct approach, and should have been carried out, the result reached at first instance—that the restraining order should be discharged—would have been reached even if it had been properly carried out. They considered that the first instance judge had not carried out the exercise correctly, but had had factors relevant to the question of proportionality under Art 8 sufficiently in mind.

[146] In *Angela Roddy (A Minor)* [2004] EMLR 8; [2004] 1 FCR 481 the parallel analysis from the CA decision in *In Re S* was applied by Munby J.

[147] [2004] judgment of May 6, 2004.

[148] Ibid see paras 12 and 113 of the judgment.

[149] Judgment of October 29, 2004 [2004] UKHL 47. Lord Steyn gave the leading judgment which was unanimously endorsed by the other four Law Lords

[150] At para 17.

approach is the right one in relation to conflicts between Articles 8 and 10, it surely follows that this approach should be adopted to clashes between differing Article 8 rights to respect for family life, bearing in mind the Strasbourg 'balancing' approach outlined above. This approach to such rights also strongly accords with the theoretical constructs put forward by leading academic lawyers as alternatives to the paramountcy principle.[151]

Following this reasoning model, a child's Article 8 right cannot figure merely as an exception to the parent's right, and vice versa. Still less can the parent's right be almost entirely abrogated—as the paramountcy principle currently demands—without a full application of the paragraph 2 tests. Following this argument, in a significant development of the *Re S* model, the rights of all parties should be considered in turn, the rights of others figuring in each instance as exceptions to the Article 8(1) right in question, applying all the tests within Article 8(2) in each instance. Each analysis would therefore *parallel* the other ones. This is clearly in essentials a parallel exercise in proportionality. It may well be a tripartite analysis where, for example, the parents or carers are in conflict and the child's rights require independent consideration, as they normally would do.

In conducting this reasoning process—the ultimate balancing act—it would be important to examine the underlying values at stake in any particular instance. The question of underlying harmony between the asserted claims can most appropriately be considered in relation to the exercise of proportionality. Below, the example of a standard application for increased contact by a non-resident parent in relation to his/her child is considered in terms of the steps that should be taken. The court would have to undertake a detailed consideration of each relevant party's Article 8 rights which would, in line with the ECHR approach, mean taking each one in turn and applying all the tests under Article 8. The likelihood that underlying harmony will be found between the rights asserted indicates that a rights-based model need not be viewed merely as one based on conflict.[152]

(a) *The child's Article 8(1) right*

In respect of the child (with the aid of the Court Reporter) the question posed would be: would the granting of the application interfere with the child's right to respect for his or her family or private life under Article 8(1)? In other words, would increased contact create a detriment in terms of the child's welfare which could be viewed as amounting to such an interference? It might be, depending on the findings in respect of the non-resident's parent's Article 8 rights below, that this question would be answered in some instances in the negative on the basis that increased contact had been found to be either neutral or beneficial in terms of its impact on the child. Where this seemed to be a possibility it would be sensible to conduct that exercise first. If so, there would be no need to proceed to

---

[151] See in particular J. Eekelaar, above n 6; see also text to n 77 and n 84 above.
[152] See D. Archard, *Children, Rights and Childhood* (1993, Routledge) esp. at 89.

the Article 8(2) tests since no interference with the child's private or family life would be threatened. However, where there would be clear or arguable detriment to the child, at least in the short term, it would be necessary to consider the tests.

The court would go on to consider whether the interference was justified under para 2. Clearly, it would be viewed as 'in accordance with the law' via s 8 of the CA. Any decision which would result in an interference would have the legitimate aim of protecting the 'rights of others'—the right of the non-resident parent to respect for his or her family and/or private life. In considering the test of 'necessary in a democratic society' the court would have to accept as axiomatic the pressing need in principle to afford protection to the parent's Article 8 right to family life since the Convention as a deontological document has already taken that stance. The key question would concern the matter of proportionality. Would the proposed increase in contact be highly beneficial to the parent in Article 8 terms while creating only a minor and probably short term detriment to the child? If so, the interference with the child's Article 8 right represented by increasing the level of contact would be justifiable since to do otherwise would be disproportionate to the aim pursued. In seeking to answer the question a number of factors could be taken into account. What would be the benefits, if any, of the contact requested for the child and what would be the impact, if any, on the child's family life in granting the application? What were the reasons for the current level of contact and are they still pertinent? Consideration of this question would invite an examination of the opposing arguments; it would enable the Court to consider at this stage if there was any issue of harm to the child's welfare and to elevate this to the 'crucial importance' test discussed in *Johansen v Norway*. What is the age of the child and her ascertainable wishes and feelings towards contact?[153] Finally, taking the findings gleaned into account, the court would consider whether there were sufficient compelling reasons to justify an interference in the child's Article 8 rights by granting the non-resident parent's application. The key point is that the child's interests as recognized under Article 8(1) are not viewed in monolithic terms. The true value of the proposed solution or action in relation to the individual child is considered and weighed up against the extent to which it necessitates invasion of the parent's rights. While avoiding a return to the paramountcy principle as currently conceived, the strength of the child's interests is clearly relevant: it should be asked whether an especially 'core' aspect of a child's private or family life is under consideration. His or her interests would be privileged within the processes of reasoning described,[154] in accordance with the Strasbourg stance discussed above, within which

---

[153] See F. Raitt 'Judicial discretion and methods of ascertaining the views of a child' (2004) *CFLQ* 16(2) 151–64 on how this aspect is currently dealt with in Scotland and V. May and C. Smart, 'Silence in court?—hearing children in residence and contact disputes' (2004) *CFLQ* 16(3), 305–15 for evidence of concern about the lack of opportunity for children, particularly younger children, to have an influence on proceedings.

[154] See J. Eckelaar, above n 6 and text to n 87 above.

those interests have primacy. In a manner reminiscent of the model put forward by Herring, and discussed above,[155] the long term benefit to the child of non-invasion or more limited invasion of the parent's rights should also be taken into account.

(b) *The non-resident parent's Article 8(1) right*

The Court should then move on to conduct the *same* exercise in relation to the other parties involved and would consider the claim of the non-resident parent that refusal of the claim for increased contact would amount to a failure to respect his or her private and family life under Article 8. This exercise, beginning with an acceptance of the *prima facie* entitlement of the non-resident parent to family (and private) life, is highly significant since it shifts the emphasis of the court's reasoning from a preoccupation with welfare to an understanding of the value and *content* of this right. The Court would have to consider first whether there had been an interference with the applicant's right to respect for his or her family life under Article 8(1) of the Convention. Usually it would be found that refusal of an application for increased contact would create such an interference (*Keegan v Ireland*,[156] *Johansen v Norway*[157] and *Bronda v Italy*).[158] However, it might be possible in exceptional instances at the extremes to resolve the matter within, or largely within, paragraph 1 of Article 8. For example, a claim for contact by a physically or sexually abusive parent can readily be excluded from the ambit of the guarantees under Article 8(1) since such a parent cannot expect that his or her family life should be respected.[159] This argument is strengthened if other Convention Articles are taken into account. If direct contact was ordered in such a circumstance, placing the resident parent or child at risk, it is arguable that the court as a public authority could itself breach Articles 2 or 3 ECHR.[160] Since Articles 2 and 3 are not materially qualified, or unqualified, they outweigh Article 8 and, following the model argued for here, they cannot figure merely as exceptions under Article 8(2). Therefore the Article 8(1) right of the non-resident parent would be displaced. A claim for contact by an emotionally abusive parent might be viewed as engaging the parent's right to respect for family life and therefore as

---

[155] See n 87 and associated text.
[156] [1994] 18 EHRR 342 para 44.
[157] [1997] 23 EHRR 134 para 52.
[158] [2001] 33 EHRR 4 para 51.
[159] For an example of such a case where the outcome would remain the same if the parallel analysis was utilized, see *Re C (a child: contact)* [2004] All ER (D) 367 (Jul). In this instance the father was disallowed contact for 3 years due to his violence to the mother and child and the mother needed time for psychotherapy in order to be able to deal with contact.
[160] Art 2 guarantees the right to life, Art 3 guarantees freedom from torture, inhuman or degrading treatment. A physical attack on a child or woman could readily be viewed as degrading treatment (*Costello-Roberts v UK* A 247-C [1993]). Arguably, the court is itself bound (s 6(1), HRA) to avoid placing a child or woman at risk where such a risk is readily foreseeable (see *Osman v UK* [1998] 5 BHRC 293; *A v UK* [1999] 27 EHRR 611). This is clearly a controversial argument that cannot be fully developed here: see further H. Fenwick, *Civil Liberties and Human Rights* (Cavendish, 3rd edn, 2002) at 39–40. These arguments, of course, apply equally to a man who is at risk from his partner. The court is also under a duty to consider the child's physical and emotional needs (s 1(3)(b), CA). The term 'consider' could be strengthened by reference to the requirements of these Articles under s 3(1), HRA so that the risk to the child was diminished.

requiring justification under paragraph 2 for its denial, but it could be viewed as a form of family life that only marginally deserves to fall within that term and therefore interferences with it would be very readily justifiable. In certain instances the family relationship claimed might be viewed as so remote or tenuous that the applicant's Article 8 right to family life could not be viewed as engaged.[161] Conversely, in certain circumstances it might be argued that the matter at stake represented a particularly significant aspect of the applicant's family life. There might also be circumstances in which it was worth arguing also that an interference with the applicant's right to respect for his *private* life under Article 8 had occurred in the sense that the intimacy of the relationship with the child formed an aspect of that life. The court would go on to consider whether the interference was justified under paragraph 2. The first two tests—'in accordance with the law' and the identification of 'a legitimate aim' could be disposed of readily, as above. Any decision which would result in an interference with the parent's Article 8 rights would clearly be aimed at protecting the 'rights and freedoms' of the child. Such an aim has been held to be a legitimate aim within the meaning of paragraph 2 of Article 8 (*Ezholz* v *Germany*).[162] In some instances the general societal aim of protecting 'health or morals' might also be relevant.

In deciding on the necessity of the interference 'in a democratic society' the court would be readily satisfied that the rights of the child should be protected since they are Convention rights. In an 'implacable hostility' case, however, it might argued that the child's right was not at stake but that the maintenance of the current level of contact would protect the resident parent's Article 8 right to respect for private and family life, considered *separately* from the child's interests. In either instance the test of proportionality would be most significant. For example, a compromise could be reached in an implacable hostility case whereby the level of contact was increased but measures were taken, such as collecting and returning the child from the home of a third party, to ensure that the resident parent had no contact at all with the non-resident parent. In general the court would consider whether, in the light of the case as a whole, the reasons adduced to justify a non-increase in contact in order to protect the rights of the child are relevant and sufficient. In doing so, it should, as the European Court of Human Rights has done,[163] ensure that a fair balance is struck between the interests of the child and those of the parent and that in striking it particular importance is attached to the best interests of the child which, depending on their nature and seriousness, may override those of the parent. In particular, the parent cannot be entitled under Article 8 of the Convention to have such measures taken as would harm the child's health and development.[164] For example, the effect on the child of awareness

---

[161] However, a family relationship might be found to exist in a range of circumstances: in *Boyle* v *UK* [1994] 19 EHRR 179 it was found to exist in respect of an uncle who had known the child from birth.
[162] [2000] 2 FLR 486 para 47.
[163] *Olsson* v *Sweden (No. 2)* (A/250); [1992] 17 EHRR 134 para 90.
[164] See *Johansen* v *Norway* [1997] 23 EHRR 134 para 78.

of emotional or even physical abuse of the resident parent —where the child was not present at the time and was not directly affected—would have to be taken into account in relation to the question of proportionality.[165] This element of the exercise would, it is submitted, ensure that a decision that would be ultimately of positive harm to the child would not be made. This exercise would mean that the case for increased contact would be looked at in a positive light: the non-resident parent would have a full opportunity to put forward the short and long term benefits of increased contact in terms of his or her family life, bearing in mind the significance of preserving family life in a democratic society.[166]

In determining the proportionality of the interference with the aim pursued, the court could consider the findings in respect of the questions considered at the proportionality stage above, but from the opposing perspective. The Court could in particular consider the degree of contact the non-resident parent is asking for and the impact on his family life of not granting his application or of allowing only a slight increase in contact. Again the reasons for the current level of contact and their continuing pertinence in terms of the crucial importance of the child's welfare would be examined. The *benefits* and detriments, long and short term to the child, of increased contact, should be considered. It would be at this point that the harmony between the claims in question could be evaluated. Once these factors had been considered it might become apparent that a modest increase in contact, far from creating detriment in terms of the child's welfare, might be likely to be beneficial in the long term. At the same time, it might be clear that no increase in contact would be severely detrimental in terms of the non-resident parent's family life in the sense that he or she would be likely to begin to feel estranged from the child as it grew older.[167] In such an instance the failure to increase contact would represent a disproportionate interference with the non-resident parent's family and (arguably) private life. Therefore in such an instance sufficient and compelling reasons to justify an interference in the non-resident parent's Article 8 rights by refusing to grant his application would not have been established.

(c) *The resident parent's Article 8(1) right*

In some instances it may also be necessary to consider the Article 8 rights of the resident parent. This exercise provides an opportunity to take account of this parent's interests *separately* from those of the child, that is, the mother (who is usually, although not invariably, the resident parent)[168] does *not* have to speak

---

[165] See the discussion of this issue in H. Rhoades and M. Harrison *The Family Law Reform Act 1995: the first three years*, Final Report (2000), University of Sydney and Family Court of Australia. It may be noted that in *Re L (A Child) (Contact: Domestic Violence)* [2001] Fam 260, the Court of Appeal found that a small degree of domestic violence would *not* result in an automatic denial of contact.

[166] See *Hansen* v *Turkey* [2004] 39 EHRR 18 para 97.

[167] See B. Simpson, J. Jessop and P. McCarthy, 'Fathers After Divorce' in A. Bainham, B. Lindley, M. Richards and L. Trinder (eds), *Children and Their Families* (Hart, 2003) ch 11.

[168] See C. Smart, V. May, A. Wade and C. Furniss, *Residence and Contact Disputes in Court*, Research Unit Dept of Constitutional Affairs No 6/03 (2003) at 16.

only in the language of welfare. She could for example claim—on her own behalf—that further contact of the child with the father would be disruptive of her private and family life *even if* the child would benefit from it in the long term.[169] This circumstance might arise if for example there had been some emotional or physical abuse involving her, but not the child. The question posed would be: would granting the application amount to an unjustified interference with her right to respect for her family life? It might be possible to satisfy the requirements of proportionality by reaching a compromise which took account of the benefits of increased contact for both the child and the father, but which minimized the effect on her private and family life, perhaps by allowing only increased indirect contact for a certain period. The key point would be that the court would start by acknowledging that her Article 8 rights should be afforded weight, *independently* of those of the child. There is evidence that mothers at present have to hide their emotional response to the situation and are forced to present themselves as 'good mothers' who always put their children first since they have to argue against contact or increased contact only through the prism of the child's interests.[170] Taking account of the impact on the mother of increased contact as well as on the child might obviate the danger of characterizing all mothers opposed to increased contact as selfish and manipulative—as prepared to use the child as a weapon against the father regardless of the benefit to the child of increased contact.[171]

D. *Judicial Reasoning and Outcomes under the Parallel Analysis in Practice*

Clearly, the 'parallel analysis' or ultimate balancing act argued for here is likely to strike some domestic judges—even independently of concerns relating to the proposed reconfiguration of the paramountcy principle—as a rigid, complex and over-technical method of approaching family law—a 'wintry process'.[172] Concern on those lines was recently expressed in a different context by Laws LJ[173] as part of an argument for the development of a domestic human rights jurisprudence. In this context it is readily arguable that a semi-autonomous domestic human rights jurisprudence could eventually develop—one that might fashion the

---

[169] See M. Hetherington, M. Cox and R. Cox 'Long Terms Effects of Divorce and Remarriage on the adjustment of children', 24 *Journal of the American Academy of Child and Adolescent Psychology* 518-30 (1985).

[170] See S.D. Sclater and F. Kaganas, above n 30 esp. at 161-69. See also J. Wallbank, 'Castigating Mothers: the Judicial Response to Wilful Women in Cases Concerning Contact' (1998) 20(4) *J Soc Wel & Fam L* 357-77.

[171] H. Rhoades '"No contact mothers": Reconstructions of motherhood in the era of the "New Father"' (2002) 16(1) *IJLPF* 71-94.

[172] See *Ministry of Home Affairs* v *Fisher* [1980] AC 319 at 328.

[173] In the Court of Appeal in *R (on the Application of the Prolife Alliance)* v *British Broadcasting Corporation* [2002] 2 All ER 756, paras 33 and 34. He said: 'Our duty is to develop, by the common law's incremental method, a coherent and principled domestic law of human rights. In doing it, we are directed by the HRA (s6) to insist on compliance by public authorities with the standards of the Convention, and to comply with them ourselves. We are given new powers and duties (HRA, ss.3 and 4) to see that that is done. In all this we are to take account of the Strasbourg cases (s2) . . . The need to make good an autonomous human rights jurisprudence is prompted by a further consideration. Treating the ECHR text as a template for our own law runs the risk of an over-rigid approach. Travelling through the words of provisions like Article 10(2), with stops along the way to pronounce that this or that condition is met or not met, smacks to my mind of what Lord Wilberforce once condemned as the "austerity of tabulated legalism"'.

Convention into a workable tool for the protection of both adults' and children's rights, addressing its deficiencies by looking in particular to the provisions of the CRC.[174] But, it is argued, the 'wintry process' has to be undergone first, in order to bring about in full the shift from a welfarist to a rights-based stance.

If this approach eventually takes hold, the question of adhering to a notion of a 'discretionary area of judgment' to which the courts will defer may arise. As courts in other areas of law begin to engage more closely with the Convention under the HRA, this doctrine has attained greater prominence[175] although, clearly, the underpinnings of the doctrine of deference in the domestic courts differ markedly from those underlying the international margin of appreciation doctrine,[176] and therefore the level of scrutiny would continue to differ from that available in the Court of Human Rights. In this instance the courts already defer to the opinions of social workers and other professionals as the experts in the area.[177] Thus at present a discretionary area of judgment already impliedly arises, due, precisely, to the operation of the welfare principle as it stands. The Court Reporter and Children's Guardian have a significant influence on decision-making in this context since their expertise in 'welfare science' allows them to determine the application of the welfare principle to the facts, currently the overriding factor for the courts.[178] In the face of a closer engagement with the HRA, the opinions of experts would clearly remain relevant in respect of the 'parallel analysis', although due to the shift in values argued for here, they would be somewhat less crucial to the outcome in any particular instance.

Finally, it must be asked whether outcomes would change or whether this whole discussion has merely sought to replace one reasoning process with another. The example of *Re D (Children) (Removal from Jurisdiction)*[179] is taken—an instance of relocation, not to the country of origin of the mother, but to that of her new partner, South Africa. It would be probable that the father would lose virtually all direct contact with his child: his Article 8 right would be almost entirely abrogated. In order to justify such a sweeping abrogation, very weighty reasons would have to be advanced. In terms of the parallel analysis the detriment to the mother if she was unable to move abroad (prima facie an infringement of her Article 8(1) right) would have to be weighed up against that to the father if his family life was completely destroyed. The detriment to the child if either solution was taken would have to be considered in

---

[174] See U. Kilkelly, above n 116 at 313; she finds that a number of features of the ECHR make the use of the CRC 'as an interpretive guide both possible and valuable'.

[175] For a recent, comprehensive discussion, see R.A. Edwards, 'Judicial Deference under the Human Rights Act' (2002) 65(6) *MLR* 859–82.

[176] See *R v DPP, ex parte Kebilene and others* [1999] 3 WLR 972 at 1043, *per* Lord Hope.

[177] For the notion of deference in respect of special expertise, see in a different context *R (on the application of Pro-life Alliance)v BBC* [2003] 2 WLR 1403, HL..

[178] The application of the welfare principle and the 'welfare science' represents in effect an area of discretion—on the basis of deference to welfare expertise. There is now an established automatic reference to the Court Reporter as the 'judge' of what is in the child' best interests and there is authority to the effect that judges have to explain why they have not followed the recommendations of the Reporter and the Childrens' Guardian.

[179] [2003] EWCA Civ 1149; [2003] 2 FLR.

terms of his independent Article 8(1) right. *D* was decided—apparently—on the basis of an application of the welfare principle although, in Eekelaar's words (in relation to *Payne*), the decision 'demonstrates the classic signs of the lack of transparency objection: that is that the interests of others are protected under the guise of the child's welfare'.[180] In other words, the mother's interests were furthered while the father's were minimized and this was dressed up as a welfare-based solution. Under the rights-based analysis all the claims would be considered on a presumptively equal and transparent basis. It was clear that the mother's family life would be adversely affected by staying, while the father's relationship with the child would be virtually destroyed if she relocated to South Africa. The child's well-being would be affected by either solution: relocating would mean that he would lose his father—with whom he had had substantial contact—but have the opportunity of a new, settled family life in his new father's country of origin. Staying would mean that the relationship with the father would be maintained but that that opportunity would be lost. The decision would be finely balanced, but it is argued that it would come down against relocation since the detriment the father would suffer otherwise would be disproportionate to the benefit to the mother. In other words, although the virtually complete abrogation of his Article 8 right would be justifiable in certain circumstances (where, for example, he had not been a strongly involved father and had had minimal direct contact after the break down of the relationship), it would not, by a small margin, be justifiable in the circumstances in question. Given the strong relationship between father and child, it is arguable that on balance the child would have benefited more from remaining in England than from relocating.[181]

7. Conclusions

Although the discussion above has proceeded on gender-neutral lines it is probable that the application of Article 8 in the manner argued for would not have a gender-neutral impact in practice, especially in one of the areas most susceptible to Article 8-based analysis—contact disputes. At present mothers rather than fathers tend to be the resident parent.[182] Therefore it is the father's relationship with the child rather than the mother's which tends to be most vulnerable and most in jeopardy after the breakdown of the relationship.[183] There is therefore greater leeway to afford it further protection. The argument for placing disputes over children in a rights-based framework can be situated in the context of

---

[180] See J.Eekelaar, above n 6 at 242.

[181] See *Re H (Application to Remove from Jurisdiction)* [1998] 1 FLR 848 and *Re B (Children) (Removal from Jurisdiction)* [2003] 2 FLR 1043 as further examples of the situation discussed which might have been decided differently under a rights-based analysis. See also *Re C* [2000] 2 FLR 457 where leave to relocate was refused.

[182] See B. Simpson, J. Jessop, P. McCarthy, above n 167, ch 11 at 203.

[183] Munby J made this point in *In the matter of D* [2004] 1 FLR 1226 at para 8.

broader, ongoing changes in cultural expectations of parenting.[184] The proposed unpacking and reconfiguring of the paramountcy principle in relation to the Article 8 rights of parents would mean that while fathers are likely to find that the importance of their relationship with their child gains greater legal recognition, societal perceptions of fathers may also change.[185] Closer examination of the competing claims of the parties under the parallel analysis may tend to aid in changing cultural constructions of the father and of parenting.[186] While feminist thought has been highly critical of liberal conceptions of rights, it is, it is argued, time to recognize the utility and power of rights; rather than eschewing rights-talk, feminism should seize the opportunities provided by the Human Rights Act and mould them with feminist ideas and strategies in mind.

This article is seeking to promote a more transparent reasoning process within which, while the child's best interests remain prominent, discourse from perspectives other than those of the child would be acknowledged. But it is also suggesting that that process would provide a more effective means of furthering the child's *individual* interests, broadly conceived[187] and that the notions of caring, intimacy, unity associated with the apparently benign welfare principle can in fact be more effectively realized within a rights-based framework.[188] The change argued for here is based on notions of individuality, in contrast to the hidden premises underlying the paramountcy principle—a change akin to that in the position of married women whose individuality was until quite recently viewed as subsumed within that of their husbands.[189]

---

[184] See, e.g. S. Bridge, ch 1 esp. pp 41–43 in J. Herring (ed.) 'Parents and Children' in *Family Law, Issues, Debates and Policy* (Willan, 2001). See also Krieken, above n 33 who provides a historical overview of the concept of welfare within the context of the emotional constitution of family life, charting the turn to a co-parenting model from the 1970s onwards and the rise of the concept of the 'civilized di,vorce'.

[185] See R. Collier 'A Hard Time to be a Father?: Law, Policy and Family Practices' (2001) 28(4) *Journal of Law and Society* at 520–45; R. Collier, 'In Search of the 'Good' Father: Law, Family Practices and the Normative Reconstruction of Parenthood' in J. Dewar and S. Parker (eds), *Family Law: Processes, Practices and Pressures* (Kluwer, 2003).

[186] See further R. Deech, 'The Rights of Fathers: Social and Biological Concepts of Parenthood' in J. Eekelaar and P. Sarcevic (eds), *Parenthood in Modern Society* (London: Martinus Nijhof, 1993); J. Wallbank 'The Campaign for Change of the Child Support Act 1991: Reconstituting the "Absent" Father' (1997) 6(2) *Social and Legal Studies* 191–216 and J. Wallbank 'Clause 106 of the Adoption and Children Bill: Legislation for the "good" Father' (2002) 22(2) *LS* 276–296 at 277. See also F. Olsen, above n 117 at 204 in which she notes Carol Gilligan's point that 'growth for men may well lie in their adoption of an ethic of care while growth for women may lie in a greater adoption of an ethic of rights'.

[187] As B. Neale puts it: 'the continuing dominance of the welfare orientation in private law proceedings seriously limits children's participation': 'Dialogue with children: children, divorce and citizenship', 9(4) *Childhood* 455–475.

[188] See J. Fortin, above n 7 esp. chs 1, 2 and 19.

[189] See further on the rise of the 'new individuality' in family law: J. Lewis, 'Family Policy in the Post-War period' and S. Katz, 'Individual Rights and Family Relationships' in S. Katz, J. Eekelaar and M. Maclean (eds), *Cross Currents* (2000, OUP) who describe the rise of individualism as the most important event in family law in the last 50 years.

Part: V

Shared parental responsibility

20

THE MEANING AND ALLOCATION OF PARENTAL RESPONSIBILITY – A COMMON LAWYER'S PERSPECTIVE

N. V. LOWE

ABSTRACT

The concept of 'parental responsibility' has gained world wide recognition as the term to be used to describe the modern view of the parents' position in relation to their children. However, the concept is neither easy to define nor is it beyond argument as to who should be vested with responsibility. This article first explores whether a domestic statute or international instrument can or should attempt to define what parental responsibility means and, if so, what that definition should be. It concludes that a meaningful definition can and should be given and that a good model can be found in the Children (Scotland) Act 1995 (though the more succinct definition as recommended by the Council of Ministers in 1984 might be more appropriate for an international instrument).

The second issue explored by the paper is the allocation of parental responsibility and in particular the case for and against vesting automatic parental responsibility in unmarried fathers. It concludes that there does seem to be a strong case (though not yet an obligation under the European Convention on Human Rights) for allocating automatic parental responsibility to *all* parents regardless of marital status.

1. INTRODUCTION

One of the more notable trends in modern child law has been the shift away from parental power as encapsulated by such expressions as 'parental rights and duties' or 'parental power and duties' to that of parental care as encapsulated by the concept of 'parental responsibility'. Such a change was effected for instance in West Germany when 'parental power' (*elter Gewalt*) was replaced by 'parental care' (*elterliche Sorge*) back in 1970.[1] International impetus for a change of stance was first given by the First European Conference on family law in 1977 organized by the Council of Europe and by the Parliamentary Assembly in 1979 which recognised the need to improve the law relating to parental responsibilities.[2] It was further boosted by the Committee of Ministers' adoption in 1984 of a Recommendation specifically dealing with the topic,[3] it being agreed 'that the term "parental responsibilities" described better the modern concept according to which parents are, on the basis of equality between the parents and in consultation with their children, given the task of educating, legally representing, maintaining etc their children. In order to do so they exercise powers to carry out duties in the interests of the child and not because of an authority which is conferred on them in their own interests.'[4]

It was in part influenced by this Recommendation[5] that the term 'parental responsibility' was introduced into English Law by the ground breaking Children Act 1989. The term has subsequently been adopted in the domestic legislation of other UK jurisdictions such as the Isle of Man,[6] Northern Ireland[7] and Scotland[8]. It has also recently been adopted in Australia.[9] World wide recognition of the concept of parental responsibility has been given by its use in the UN Convention on the Rights of the Child.[10] The term is used in the 1993 Hague Convention on Protection of Children and Co-operation in Respect of Intercountry Adoption,[11] while under the redrafted 1996 Hague Convention on the Protection of Children[12] the meaning and allocation of parental responsibility will be determined by the State in which the child is or becomes habitually resident.[13]

This last mentioned Convention raises the two issues that will be the focus of this paper, namely, what does parental responsibility mean and in whom is or should that responsibility be vested? In pursuing these questions this paper seeks to present a common lawyer's perspective based on the experience England and Wales, Scotland and, to a lesser extent, Australia. However, in view of the increasing reference to 'parental responsibility' in international instruments the issues raised in this paper are of equal importance outside the common law world.

2. THE MEANING OF PARENTAL RESPONSIBILITY

Although the term 'parental responsibility' is gaining international acceptance it is an elusive concept to define. In part this is because the concept is concerned not just with the parent-child relationship but also the parent's relationship with the State and with other individuals. In his leading analysis of the concept, Eekelaar[14] concentrates on the first two relationships arguing that parental responsibility embraces two ideas, namely, that parents must behave dutifully towards their children, and that responsibility for the child's care belongs to parents and not to the State. Of course these two aspects are very important and indeed the latter is of particular concern to international instruments protecting human rights.[15] However, it is important not to overlook the relationship between parents and other individuals for the former equally need to be able to act without interference by others as by the State. For example, it could not be right allow third parties to remove children from their parents at will. Equally it is important for the parents to be able to authorize others to look after or help the child, for example, schools to teach them or doctors to treat them medically.

Another complicating factor is the very novelty of the concept. How does or should the concept of 'responsibility' differ from parental 'rights and duties'?

The first issue that will be briefly pursued in this paper is whether the State, or in the case of an international instrument, the international body, can or should attempt to define what is meant by the term parental responsibility, and if so, what that definition should be.

A. *Should Parental Responsibility Be Defined?*

It is obviously necessary that parental responsibility be definable by one means or another for how else will parents know what they can or cannot do in relation to their child? Can they, for instance, choose their child's religion? Can they discipline the child? Can they object to their child being removed into local authority care? Can they object to their child's adoption, veto the issue of a passport or prevent their child's marriage without their consent? Just as importantly how can others know what the parents' position is? Are schools, for example, obliged to send to the parents reports on their child's progress? Do they need to obtain parental permission to take a child on an educational trip? Do doctors need parental consent before medically treating the child and is that consent binding on the child?

Quite apart from the individual's position the Court's powers can sometimes be dependent on the scope of parental responsibility. In English law, for example, a court can only make a 'prohibited steps order' to prevent any 'step which could be taken by a parent in meeting his parental responsibility for a child'[16] and a 'specific issue order' to determine 'a specific question which has arisen, or which may arise in connection with any aspect of parental responsibility for a child'.[17]

Notwithstanding the demonstrable need to be able to define what parental responsibility comprises the question remains as to whether this should be done by means of a general statutory provision or simply left to case-law and statutory provisions dealing with specific points. The Scottish Law Commission considered that there are advantages in having a general statutory statement of parental responsibilities which they saw as being:[18]

(a) that it would make explicit what is already implicit in the law
(b) that it would counteract any impression that a parent has rights but no responsibilities and

(c) that it would enable the law to make it clear that parental rights are not absolute or unqualified, but are conferred in order to enable parents to meet their responsibilities.

These arguments seem convincing. It is surely right that as a matter of principle some attempt be made to give some general statutory guidance on the meaning of what after all is a new and pivotal concept of child law. There also seems need for such guidance to be given in international instruments using the term if only to ensure that, notwithstanding their different backgrounds and traditions, states are in broad agreement over what each is undertaking. This seems particularly pertinent to the 1996 Hague Convention on the Protection of Children which, as we have said, will vest exclusive jurisdiction to determine the meaning of parental responsibility in the state of the child's habitual residence.[19]

B. *Can there be a Meaningful General Definition?*

In contrast to the Scottish Law Commission the earlier inquiry of the English Law Commission concentrated on whether there could be a comprehensive definition. In this respect it concluded that although there was a superficial attraction of providing a comprehensive list of the incidents of responsibility it was impracticable to do so.[20] It pointed out that such a list would have to change from time to time to meet differing needs and circumstances and would have to vary with the age and maturity of the child and circumstances of the case. While there is some validity in this view, particularly if it is sought to provide a comprehensive definition, it is by no means convincing that *some* useful guidance cannot be made but this more limited approach was not apparently considered by the Commission. In the event the Children Act 1989 follows the strategy recommended by the Law Commission and through s3(1) simply provides:

'Parental responsibility' means all the rights, duties, powers, responsibilities and authority which by law a parent of a child has in relation to the child and his property.

The English 'solution' seems a poor one for not only might it rightly be said to be a 'non-definition'[21] it immediately throws one back to the rights and duties concept which 'responsibility' was supposed to replace.

The Australian 'solution' is little better. There, s61B of the Family Law Act 1975 (Cth), as amended, provides:

'parental responsibility' in relation to a child, means all the duties, powers, responsibilities and authorities which, by law, parents have in relation to children

Some commentators have said,[22] that with the significant omission of the term 'rights', the Australian definition is better than the English, but even if that is so, which is debatable, it clearly does not advance the debate very much.

In stark contrast the Children (Scotland) Act 1995, implementing the recommendation of the Scottish Law Commission,[23] provides first by s1(1):

A parent has in relation to his child the responsibility —

(a) to safeguard and promote the child's health, development and welfare;
(b) to provide, in a manner appropriate to the stage of development of the child —
   (i) direction;
   (ii) guidance,
   to the child;
(c) if the child is not living with the parent, to maintain personal relations and direct contact with the child on a regular basis; and
(d) to act as the child's legal representative,

but only in so far as compliance with this section is practicable and in the interests of the child.

To enable a parent to fulfil those parental responsibilities, s2(1) provides that a parent:

has the right —

(a) to have the child living with him or otherwise to regulate the child's residence;
(b) to control, direct or guide, in a manner appropriate to the stage of development of the child, the child's upbringing;
(c) if the child is not living with him, to maintain personal relations and contact with the child on a regular basis; and
(d) to act as the child's legal representative.

In this writer's submission the Scottish legislation does show that it is possible to provide meaningful and helpful general guidance as to the meaning of parental responsibility. It neatly handles the problem of dealing with children of different ages and maturity by the simple expedient of stating that the responsibility to give direction and guidance should be 'in a manner appropriate to the stage of development of the child' and by making separate provisions for responsibilities and rights it grapples with the problem of having to deal with the parent-child relationship not simply as between parent and child (in which context the expression "responsibility" seems absolutely right) but also as between the parents themselves and between parents and third parties (in which context the expression 'rights' seems appropriate). It also avoids the problem of being too specific, which perhaps is best left to the courts to work out and develop and for hapless authors to attempt to define.[24]

In short, the Scottish legislation is vastly superior to the English and Australian and should act as a model for other legislatures desirous of introducing the concept of 'parental responsibility'. Whether the Scottish approach is also appropriate to international instruments is perhaps more debatable, if only because it is too long for such a context. In this respect it is suggested that the Recommendation adopted by the Committee of Ministers of the Council of Europe in 1984[25] provides at least a working basis for a definition with their definition of parental responsibilities as:

a collection of duties and powers which aim at ensuring the moral and material welfare of the child, in particular taking care of the child, by maintaining personal relationship with him and by providing for his education, his maintenance, his legal representation and the administration of his property.

3. THE ALLOCATION OF PARENTAL RESPONSIBILITY

Given that children, particularly young children, cannot look after themselves it is obvious that someone else should do so. Any rational legal system must therefore decide who should have responsibility for bringing up the child and the authority to act on the child's behalf. Although the most obvious candidates, at any rate in a democratic society,[26] in whom to vest parental responsibility are the child's parents the allocation issue is by no means simple. For example, should responsibility *automatically* vest in all parents whether they are married or not? Should persons (or bodies) other than parents be able to acquire parental responsibility and if so, who, how, and in what circumstances? If such third parties do acquire parental responsibility what is or should the legal position of parents then be? These questions have engendered not inconsiderable debate in England and Wales, Scotland and Australia and the solutions adopted differ in some important respects.

A. *The Parents' Position*

In the three jurisdictions with which I am specifically concerned there was no dispute that parental responsibility should automatically be vested in all mothers regardless of whether they are married to the father and in married fathers (ie those who were married to the mother at the time of or subsequent to the child's birth).[27] The debate centred on whether the unmarried father should automatically be vested with parental responsibility. In the event whilst both the English and Scottish jurisdictions seriously considered treating all parents equally but ultimately stopped short of doing so, Australia[28] provides that both parents have joint parental responsibility by operation of law irrespective of marital status.[29] What then were the arguments for and against discriminating between the married and unmarried father and can they still be justified?

(i) *The pros and cons of treating all fathers equally*

(a) The English debate: So far as England and Wales are concerned the major debate about the father's legal position over his child took place not in the context of allocating parental responsibility but in relation to the reform of the legitimacy laws. In its 1979 Working Paper[30] the English Law Commission favoured what was then considered to be the radical proposal of abolishing the status of illegitimacy altogether with the consequence that all fathers should be treated equally. However, whilst there was general agreement that children should not be discriminated against on the basis of their parents' relationship with one another, there was a hostile reaction to giving all fathers automatic parental rights.[31] The Law Commission summarized these objections as follows:[32]

(i) It was thought that a growing number of mothers would be concerned to conceal the identity of the child's father to ensure that in practice he could not exercise any parental rights. As the Commission pointed out, if that were to happen 'it would detract from the desirable objectives of establishing, recognising and fostering genuine familial links.'

(ii) It was argued that vesting unmarried fathers with automatic rights could cause particular distress and disturbance where the mother had subsequently married a third party who had put himself in *loco parentis* to the child, with the possible result that the mother and new partner would seek court orders to forestall any possible intervention by the father thus prematurely denying the child the possibility of establishing a genuine link.

(iii) The automatic investiture of rights in an unmarried father could, it was argued, put him in a position to harass or even blackmail the mother at a time when she might well be exceptionally vulnerable to pressure. The Commission recognized as a strong argument that what was important was not so much what the law was but how it might be perceived by a fearful and perhaps ill-informed mother. In that regard the Commission took special note of the evidence of the National Council for One Parent Families of the hundreds of enquiries that the Council received from unmarried mothers and single pregnant women seeking to be reassured about their rights over the children and of their assurance upon being informed of the general lack of rights in the father.[33]

(iv) Vesting rights in unmarried fathers would create practical problems in connection with local authority care, in that fathers could end any voluntary arrangements, and with regard to adoption because of the need formally to dispense with his consent; and

(v) It observed that even in those countries which have sought to abolish discrimination against children born of unmarried parents most did not automatically vest all fathers with the full range of parental rights.

In view of this hostile reaction the Law Commission felt that they could no longer recommend treating all fathers equally. As they put it:

> we have come to the conclusion that the advantages of abolishing the status of illegitimacy are not sufficient to compensate for the possible dangers involved in an automatic extension of parental rights to fathers of non-marital children.[34]

Although the Law Commission later made recommendations to make it easier for unmarried fathers to acquire parental responsibility, first by being able to apply for what is now known as a parental responsibility order[35] and secondly by making a parental responsibility agreement with the mother,[36] it regarded the question of automatically allocating parental responsibility to unmarried fathers as having been thoroughly canvassed and rejected.[37]

(b) The Scottish debate: When considering the reform of illegitimacy the Scottish Law Commission concluded, as the English Law Commission eventually did, that it was not desirable to confer automatic parental rights on unmarried fathers.[38] This recommendation was based on four arguments which the Commission later summarized as follows:[39]

1. It would be inappropriate to give parental rights to fathers where the child had resulted from a casual liaison or even rape.
2. Automatic parental rights for unmarried fathers would cause offence to mothers who had struggled alone to bring up their children with no support from the fathers.
3. Mothers of children born outside marriage might feel at risk from interference and harassment by unmeritorious fathers in matters connected with the upbringing of the children.
4. The unmarried father would have to be involved more often in care or adoption proceedings even in cases where it would be inappropriate to give any weight to his views.

However, unlike its English counterpart the Scottish Law Commission was prepared to examine the question afresh when considering further reform of child law. Addressing these four arguments the Commission observed:[40]

1. It was not self evident that where a child is born as a result of a casual liaison the unmarried father should not have parental responsibility. As they put it: 'some fathers . . . will be uninterested but that is no reason for the law to encourage and reinforce an irresponsible attitude'.

2. The argument that conferring automatic parental responsibility on the unmarried father would cause offence to mothers struggling to bring up their children without the support from the fathers was not thought to be a weighty argument for denying responsibility to all unmarried fathers for as they observed: 'the important point in all these cases is that it is not the feelings of one parent in a certain type of situation that should determine the content of the law but the general interests of children and responsible parents.'

3. The Commission dismissed the argument that there might be a risk of interference and harassment by the father if he had automatic responsibility,[41] essentially because it was a parent-centred rather than a child-centred approach. In the Commission's view it: 'seems unjustifiable to have what is in effect a presumption that any involvement by an unmarried father is going to be contrary to the child's best interests'. In any event the Commission did not believe that the risk of harassment would be increased by the proposed change of law.

4. The argument that it is undesirable to involve all unmarried fathers in care and adoption proceedings was countered by pointing out that it could equally be said to be a grave defect that a man who has been the social father to the child should have no legal position in such matters merely because he and the child's mother have not married each other.

The Commission additionally observed that provided each holder of parental responsibility can exercise that responsibility independently of the other[42] then the completely absent parent (whether married or not) is not a problem since the care-giving parent can make any decision about the child's upbringing without consulting the other.

Having set out the arguments, the question of giving unmarried fathers automatic responsibility was put out for public consultation.[43] In contrast to the earlier English experience, more agreed than disagreed with the idea. Furthermore support came from a wide variety of sources including, significantly, from several women's groups. Encouraged by this response and clearly influenced by the UN Convention on the Rights of the Child (see further below) the Commission recommended that:

In the absence of any court order regulating the position, both parents of the child should have parental responsibilities and rights whether or not they are or have been married to each other.[44]

As the Commission powerfully observed:

The question is whether the starting position should be that the father has, or has not, the normal parental responsibilities and rights. Given that about 25 percent of all children born in Scotland in recent years have been born out of wedlock,[46] and that the number of couples cohabiting outside marriage is now substantial, it seems to us that the balance has now swung in favour of the view that parents are parents, whether married to each other or not. If in any particular case it is in the best interest of a child that a parent should be deprived of some or all of his or her parental responsibilities and rights, that can be achieved by means of a court order.[45]

Despite what would appear to be a carefully argued case the Government rejected the Commission's recommendation so that under the Children (Scotland) Act 1995, as under the English Children Act 1989, the unmarried father does not automatically have parental responsibility though he can acquire it *inter alia* by making an agreement with the mother or by obtaining a parental responsibility order.[47]

(c) The Australian 'debate': In contrast to England and Scotland the issue of vesting automatic parental responsibility in all fathers attracted little recent debate. Indeed, as one commentator has pointed out:

Arguments based on equality and non discrimination on the basis of marital status has been given more weight in family law in the antipodes in the past decade than they have in the UK.[43]

In point of fact under amendments made in 1987 to the Family Law Act 1975 (Cth)[49] all parents had equal rights under the guardianship provisions. These have now been replaced by provisions expressly dealing with parental responsibility.[50]

(d) The international dimension: One of the arguments relied upon by the Scottish Law Commission in favour of treating all fathers equally was that there is an obligation to do so under the UN Convention on the Rights of the Child. Specifically, the Commission pointed[51] to Art 9(3), under which States Parties are obliged to respect the child's right to contact with both parents, and Art 18(1) which obliges States Parties to:

Use their best efforts to ensure recognition of the principle that both parents have common responsibilities for the upbringing and development of the child.

Although on the face of it Art 18 seems to oblige states parties to treat all parents equally it has nevertheless been queried whether 'common responsibilities' means common and equal or common but different.[52] Another complication is the UK's reservation and declaration that it:

interprets the reference in the Convention to 'parents' to mean only those who, as a matter of national law, are treated as parents.

While this reservation might well be taken as justifying not treating an unmarried father as a 'parent' for the purpose of adoption[53] it would surely be straining the extent of the reservation as justifying not giving unmarried fathers automatic parental responsibility notwithstanding that they are regarded as 'parents' for the purpose of the Children Act.[54] Accordingly, it is submitted that there is a strong case for arguing that UN Convention does oblige the UK, along with all Contracting States, to treat all fathers equally. However, since there is no mechanism for enforcing the Convention the argument that the UK is in breach is not likely to be treated as a serious inducement to change the law.[55]

In contrast to the UN Convention, the European Convention on Human Rights, whilst not directly applicable within the UK, does carry a State obligation to change the law if the State is found to be in breach.[56] Accordingly, a potential breach of this Convention is likely to be treated much more seriously. The question remains, however, whether there is an obligation under the Convention to give all unmarried fathers automatic parental responsibility. There are certainly commentators who believe it is. Perhaps the most outspoken is Norrie who unequivocally asserts that by failing to treat all fathers equally the UK is in breach of its international obligations.[57] Norrie bases his argument on the application of Art 14 which provides that the rights and freedoms under the Convention 'shall be secured without discrimination on any ground such as sex . . ., birth or other status.'

Having acknowledged that in *McMichael* v *UK*[58] the Court has held that the applicant's exclusion from a children's hearing considering the case of his child was not in breach of Art 14 either in conjunction with Art 6 or 8,[59] he nevertheless contends that had the case been argued upon the basis that the law discriminates between fathers and mothers rather than between married and unmarried men, the decision might well have been different. For this proposition he relies on an earlier decision, *Schmidt* v *Germany*,[60] in which it was held:

For the purpose of Art 14 a difference of treatment is discriminatory if it has no objective and reasonable justification, that is if it does not pursue a legitimate aim or if there is not a reasonable relationship of proportionality between the means and the aim sought to be realised. Although Contracting States enjoy a certain margin of appreciation in assessing whether and to what extent different treatment is justified, *very weighty reasons would have to be put forward before the Court could regard a difference of treatment based exclusively on the ground of sex as compatible with the Convention.* [Emphasis Added]

In Norrie's view no such weighty reasons can be forwarded for, as he puts it, why should men have to prove their parenting merit when women do not and why is marriage in itself a determinant of parental merit?

With respect to Norrie, while it is a possible attack on the law that it discriminates on the basis of sex, it is by no means beyond argument that it does so. At any rate it is a perfectly tenable argument that the discrimination is based on marriage rather then gender (or, possibly on a mixture of both). Furthermore, *Schmidt* itself was concerned with a

Bavarian requirement that all male adults had to serve as firemen or to pay a service levy instead, so at the very least caution is needed for using it to support the argument that not vesting parental responsibility in the unmarried father is equally a breach.

Even if *Schmidt* is thought to be relevant Norrie's arguments do not gainsay the actual decision in *McMichael*, namely, that the aim of the relevant legislation[62] was to provide a mechanism for identifying 'meritorious fathers' thereby protecting the interests of the child and the mother, which was held to be a legitimate aim for the purpose of the Convention.

Meulders-Klein[62] used a different approach to suggest that there is a Convention obligation to treat all parents equally. Basing her views on *Marckx v Belgium*,[63] in which it was held that Belgian law violated Art 8 (which provides that 'Everyone has the right to respect for his private and family life') since it failed to acknowledge an unmarried mother's maternity from the moment of birth,[64] she contended that there is a positive obligation for domestic laws to provide legal safeguards which render possible the child's integration in his family from the moment of its birth. Furthermore she contends that in the light of *Marckx* it is difficult to see 'why the father whose paternity is ascertained should be discriminated against with regard to the mother.'[65]

Bainham,[66] having noted Meulders-Klein's arguments, referred to *Berrehab v The Netherlands*,[67] in which the Court held that the deportation of a Moroccan father following the refusal to give him a residence permit after his divorce from his Dutch wife, violated Art 8 because it inhibited further contact between the father and daughter. In reaching that decision the Court held cohabitation was not a *sine qua non* of family life between parents and minor children, but existed from the moment of birth unless subsequent events broke that tie. *Berrehab* was specifically concerned with married, albeit divorced parents, but Bainham suggested that it could equally apply to unmarried parents[68] thus scotching the argument that it is permissible under the Convention to distinguish between the unmarried father who is cohabiting with the mother and the father who is not. Even so Bainham was cautious in asserting that it is a Convention obligation to treat all fathers equally, though he does point out that decisions such as *K v United Kingdom*[69] and more significantly *Johnstone v Republic of Ireland*[70] do establish that parents and children have mutual rights to respect for their family life so that discrimination against the former is also discrimination against the latter.

O'Donnell[71] also seems to accept that it is unclear whether the failure to give the unmarried father automatic parental responsibility violates the Convention. She refers *inter alia* to *B. R. & J. v Federal Republic of Germany*[72] in which the *Commission* held that state provision for the recognition of paternity was sufficient to satisfy any positive obligation upon the State to promote family life while insofar as the absence of any provision allowing the unmarried father to share care and custody with the mother constituted an 'interference' with family life it could be justified as promoting the child's interests by ensuring that any disputes between unmarried parents would come before the Court.

Since the above mentioned commentaries there have been two further significant Court decisions. In the first, *Keegan* v *Ireland*,[73] Irish law was held to have violated Art 8 by not providing a mechanism by which an unmarried father could challenge the making of an adoption order. In that case a couple who began living together and intending to marry, deliberately planned the pregnancy. The relationship, however, broke down before the child's birth. At birth the child was placed for adoption without the father's knowledge or consent.

Irish adoption law did not require the unmarried father's consent and his attempt to be appointed a guardian failed in the face of evidence that the child would be harmed if the placement was disrupted. In reaching its decision the Court accepted that a child born out of a *de facto* relationship which in this case had lasted over two years, was part of the family unit from the moment of birth, apparently regardless of the fact that the parents' relationship had ceased. Whilst accepting that the placement without consent was pursuing the legitimate aims of protecting the rights and freedoms of the child the consequential interference with family life was not necessary in a democratic society.

In the second case, *Kroon* v *The Netherlands*,[74] a child was born of a stable relationship between a man and a woman while the woman was married to another man. Under Dutch law it was impossible to obtain recognition of the biological father's paternity unless the mother's husband denied paternity. This was held to violate Art 8. The notion of family life was not confined to marriage based relationships but encompassed other *de facto* family ties. Normally, to establish such *de facto* ties required evidence of living together but other factors, such as the couple, as here, having had other children, can *exceptionally* be sufficient to demonstrate sufficient constancy to create family ties. In such cases a child born of such a relationship is *ipso facto* part of that family unit from the moment of its birth. Since the relationship between the father and child qualified as 'family life' the competent authorities were under a positive obligation to allow complete family ties to be formed as quickly as possible. A system which in effect demanded that the father had to be married to create a legal tie with the child was not compatible, in the Court's view, with the notion of 'respect' for family life.

Both *Keegan* and *Kroon* lend support to the argument that the absence of automatic parental responsibility in the unmarried father who has or has had an established relationship with the mother (the so-called 'meritorious' father) violates Art 8. However, they do not unequivocally establish such a proposition and they certainly do not establish that responsibility ought automatically be vested in all fathers regardless of their relationship with the mother.

What can be said is that a child born of a *de facto* relationship between the parents as evidenced by some constancy of cohabitation is part of the family unit from the moment of birth and that the relationship between that child and the father qualifies as 'family life' for the purposes of Art 8. Furthermore it seems likely that the absence of *any* mechanism by which the father can acquire parental responsibility would violate Art 8. However, what has yet to be established in whether a system such as that operating in England and Scotland by which unmarried fathers can acquire parental responsibility either by agreement with the mother or by a court order would be regarded as anything but a justifiable mechanism for identifying meritorious fathers and thus protecting the child's interests. In short English and Scottish law cannot yet be said to be in breach of the European Convention on Human Rights. On the other hand the European Court does seem to be moving towards the position that at least so-called meritorious unmarried fathers (ie those having cohabited for some time with the mother) ought to be treated no differently to married fathers or to unmarried mothers. At any rate it ought to occasion no great surprise if it does eventually so decide.

(ii) *Should the UK Think Again?*

Although it seems unlikely that the Government would readily reconsider the position of unmarried fathers, given their recent rejection of the Scottish Law Commission's recommendation, nevertheless the question needs to be asked whether the UK should think again.

Quite apart from the arguable international obligation to do so there are two lines of argument why at any rate the position in England should be reconsidered. The first is that given the relative ease with which unmarried fathers can acquire parental responsibility under the Children Act 1989 there seems little point in making him go through legal hoops to do so. Secondly, the arguments accepted by the English Law Commission against treating all fathers equally are simply no longer valid.

So far as acquisition of parental responsibility is concerned English law puts the unmarried father in the privileged position[75] of being able to do so either by making an agreement with the mother or under a court order.[76] The ability to make parental responsibility agreements was one of the innovations of the 1989 Act.[77] Before then it was only possible to obtain a court order.[78] However, as the English Law Commission had pointed out[79] the need to resort to judicial proceedings seemed unduly elaborate, expensive and unnecessary unless the child's mother objected. Accordingly, s4(1)(b) now allows for agreements to be made, the procedure[80] being that the parties should complete a prescribed form, having their signatures witnessed in court,[81] and send the form to the Principal Registry for registration. It is to be noted that these formalities are minimal. In particular there is no investigation of whether the agreement is in the child's best interest nor of why the parents are entering into it. Since its introduction there has, at least until 1995, been a growing number of agreements registered.[82]

Perhaps more unexpectedly there has been the growing number of parental responsibility orders. In 1995 around 4,450 such orders were made.[83] Case-law on s4 orders is extensive[84] but the bottom line, so far as the appellate courts are concerned,[85] is that provided the father has shown the requisite attachment and commitment to the child[86] then the court will regard it as being prima facie for the child's welfare that the order be made.[87] Accordingly, acrimony between the parents is not a necessary bar to the making of an order[88] nor should much weight be given to the mother's objection to an order being made because of the consequential power it would give the father.[89] At the extremes an order has been made even though the father was denied contact with his child,[90] while in another case[91] it was said that the father's inability to enforce most of his 'rights' was not necessarily a decisive reason for denying him an order. In short once at any rate the *Re H* test is satisfied a s4 order is normally made, the only reported example of refusals being where the father is violent.[92]

In one of the latest decisions, *Re H (Parental Responsibility: Maintenance)*,[93] a judge adjourned an application for a s4 order by a father who had never paid maintenance to allow him to demonstrate his commitment to the children by paying maintenance. On appeal, however, it was held that the judge had been wrong since the Court ought not to use the weapon of withholding a s4 order for the purpose of exacting from the father his financial dues. The order was accordingly granted.

The decision in *Re H* has led one leading commentator to question whether, given the rarity of refusals, there is any longer much point in refusing to vest automatic responsibility in unmarried fathers.[94] While there is a good deal to be said in favour of this view it might be pointed out that, as yet, there has been no decision on the position of the father who has never seen the child, as where the birth took place after the ending of his relationship with the mother. It may well be that the fact that the father is concerned enough to apply: and this, coupled with the Court's recognition of the child's right to know the father's identity and to have some continuing relationship with him,[95] would lead to an order being granted. However, at this stage, to argue that *all* fathers should have automatic responsibility based on the ease with which s4 orders can be obtained overlooks the fact that unmarried fathers seeking to establish a relationship with a child they have never seen are not yet certain of obtaining such an order.

What then of other arguments? Reflecting now on those that convinced the English Law Commission to shy away from treating all fathers equally, one is struck as to how parent-centred they were. The predominant motive was to protect mothers but not directly to promote the child's interests. Many telling points refuting the English Law Commission's reasoning were made by the Scottish Law Commission, which were discussed earlier. To this writer at least the latter's report makes a convincing case for change. But further arguments have been well marshalled by another commentator, Helen Conway, in a recent article,[96] namely:

1. Like the Scottish Law Commission she argues that given the increasing numbers of couples cohabiting rather than marrying, an increasingly larger proportion of fathers are excluded from having automatic parental responsibility. She comments: 'The effect is to judge as a class all who do not conform to the "Victorian family values" so beloved of the Conservative right wing.' This is discriminatory. Also it runs against the intentions of many cohabitees in long term relationships.'

2. She refutes the argument that vesting unmarried fathers with automatic responsibility will encourage people to cohabit rather than marry, by pointing out that since it is relatively easy to obtain a parental responsibility order, 'a hurdle that is so easily overcome, surely cannot be a strong buffer supporting marriage.'

Furthermore

3. With growing numbers of cohabitants it is important to encourage a secure family unit with two involved parents. Vesting each parent with responsibility could help to do this.

4. It is hypocritical of the State to place the burden of financial support on fathers simply by reason of their paternity without also giving them a more general responsibility. Furthermore the argument that mothers would refuse to name fathers if they were to be vested with parental responsibility loses much of its sting given the sanctions under the Child Support Act 1991 of reducing benefit to those mothers who unreasonably refuse to name the father.

5. Finally, she maintains that it is not for the child's welfare for unmarried fathers not to have automatic responsibility since being so vested would foster a culture of responsibility, namely, that fathers have a duty to provide for their children's emotional and moral development as well as their financial needs.

Conway concludes that the time has come to reconsider granting unmarried fathers parental responsibility automatically. However, she couples this proposal with the idea that all parents should have *revocable* responsibility, though leaving the grounds for revocation to be developed by the Courts.

Revocable parental responsibility would deal with the point made by others[97] that just as it may be wrong to deny automatic parental responsibility to 'meritorious' unmarried fathers so it is questionable to vest it in unmeritorious married fathers, as for example where conception took place as a result of rape within the marriage. Although not provided for under the Children Act 1989 (the only way a parent can lose automatic parental responsibility for a child under eighteen is by the child's adoption),[98] provision is made for divesting even parents of their parental responsibility in the Children (Scotland) Act 1995.[99] It is submitted that whilst it would seem a reasonable safeguard of the child's interests to balance the automatic investiture of responsibility in unmarried fathers with a power of divesting it, it also seems appropriate to treat *all* parents equally and therefore to have a general divesting power.

In conclusion the arguments to review the position of unmarried fathers seem compelling and it is therefore urged that the matter be taken up again by the English Law Commission and in turn tested on the public.

B. *The Position of Those Replacing Parents*

If it is right that parents be vested with automatic parental responsibility what about the position of those replacing parents? For those such as adopters and guardians, who permanently replace parents it seems uncontroversial that they too should automatically have parental responsibility. There is, however, more scope for argument with respect to those who do not legally replace the parents but who nevertheless look after the child more or less permanently.

(i) *Adopters and guardians*

In all three jurisdictions adoption transfers parentage thus vesting parental responsibility in the adopters and extinguishing that previous vested in the former parents.[100] This seems unarguably right. So far as guardianship is concerned since at any rate in both England and Scotland the appointee replaces the deceased parent again it seems absolutely right that such an appointment automatically vests parental responsibility in the appointee.[101] The only curiosity is that whereas court appointments are subject to a merits test based on the child's welfare, private appointments of guardians are subject to no public controls whatsoever.[102]

(ii) *Step-parents*

In none of the three jurisdictions do step-parents automatically acquire parental responsibility. Instead under English law the only way such persons can acquire parental responsibility is by being granted a residence order.[103] In Scotland, parental responsibility will automatically follow the making of a residence order,[104] but in addition the Children (Scotland) Act 1995 will allow a court to make a parental responsibility order in favour of a step-parent even without a residence order.[105] A similar position obtains in Australia.[106]

However, if it is possible for a parent to be able to confer parental responsibility without public scrutiny on anyone they choose to appoint as a guardian, ought it not be possible to do so in favour of new marital (or even non marital) partner? Indeed in this writer's view a plausible case can be made out for the automatic vesting of parental responsibility in the new marital partner of the care-giving parent.[107] Indeed it seems rather odd to treat such step-parents as if they were complete strangers to the child, by according them no special status at all.

Pleas for any automatic parental status for step-parents have been resisted.[108] However, in the proposed Adoption Bill provision is made for the step-parent who is married to the child's parent to acquire responsibility either by agreement or by a court order.[109] In effect under this proposal such step-parents would be put in the same position as the unmarried father. This seems not an unreasonable compromise though the question might well be asked as to why non marital step-parents should not be similarly treated?

(iii) *Other care-givers*

In both England and Scotland the granting of a residence order (an order which determines with whom the child lives) automatically confers, for the duration of the order, parental responsibility on the person in whose favour the order is made.[110] That responsibility is shared with the parents but the latter cannot act incompatibly with any court order. While this seems relatively uncontroversial for clearly those given formal sanction to look after the child need the associated powers and authority to be able to do so, in Australia a different attitude is taken. There, a residence order does not automatically confer parental responsibility though the Court can make a 'parenting order', which will vest parental responsibility, if it so chooses.[111] Whether this is a good idea can be debated though as one commentator has put it: 'One could argue that the Australian provision in this respect attempts to make an even more fundamental break with the old concept of custody; residence means simply what it says'.[112]

(iv) *The need for a general power both to confer and remove parental responsibility*

Unlike both Scottish and Australian law[113] English law does not vest in the courts *general* power to make parental responsibility orders. Experience in that jurisdiction strongly suggests that such a power is needed. A good example is *Re WB (Residence Orders)*[114] where a man, who thought he was the father and only discovered he was not as a result of paternity test, found that because the child was to live with the mother there was no way in which he could be given parental responsibility.[115] The power could also be useful in the case of orphans.

Again, unlike Scottish Law,[116] there is no general power under English law to divest a parent[117] of parental responsibility. Whether there should be a general divesting power can be debated. Certainly there are cases where a parent has behaved so appallingly either towards the child or other members of the family, that one could certainly argue that that person should no longer have responsibility.[118] On the other hand a general divesting power cuts across the principle that responsibility should be enduring.[119] On balance, however, provided any divesting power is subject to the overarching principle of the paramountcy of the child's welfare, there does seem a case for amending English Law.

4. CONCLUSIONS

As we have seen, the concept of 'parental responsibility' has gained world wide recognition as the term to be used to describe the modern view of the parents' position in relation to their children. However, this concept is not without its problems. It is not easy to define nor is it beyond argument as to who should be vested with responsibility.

With regard to its definition it does seem incumbent upon legislatures to provide some meaningful guidance not least because of the need to steer public opinion away from the idea that power and authority over children exist for the parents' benefit and to emphasize instead that, in the words of the British Department of Health:

the duty to care for the child and to raise him to moral, physical and emotional health is the fundamental task of parenthood and the only justification for the authority that it confers.[120]

In this respect the Children (Scotland) Act 1995 provides a model for other jurisdictions, though a more succinct definition along the lines recommended by the Council of Ministers of the Council of Europe in 1984 might provide a more appropriate model for international instruments.

The allocation issue admits of no simple solution but there does seem a strong case for allocating automatic parental responsibility to *all* parents regardless of marital status it also seems right that those who look after children pursuant to a court order should also have parental responsibility for the duration of that order. Whether step-parents should have automatic parental responsibility can be debated as can the question of how far parents themselves should by means of formal agreements be able to vest responsibility in others. In this writer's view, however, it seems right that, as is proposed for England, such agreements should be possible in respect of new marital partners of the care-giving parent.

NOTES

[1] See Frank: 'Family Law and the Federal Republic of Germany's Basic Law' (1990) 4 *IJLF* 214, as noted by Eekelaar: 'Parental responsibility: State of Nature or Nature of the State?' [1991] *JSWFL* 37, 38. In Norway, the term 'parental responsibility' was introduced in their Children Act 1981, replacing terms such as 'parental authority' or 'parental power'. See Smith and Lodrup *Children and Parents: The relationship between children and parents according to Norwegian Law* (ad Notam, Oslo, 1991) ch 5. Although formal statutory changes were not effected until implementation of the Children Act 1989 similar shifts from parental authority to responsibility can be discerned in English case-law during the 1980's in particular. See further below.

[2] Ie by Recommendation 874 (1979) as explained by Killerby: 'The Council of Europe's Contribution to Family Law (Past, Present and Future)' in Lowe and Douglas, Martinus Nijhoff (eds) *Families Across Frontiers* (1996) 13, 19.

[3] Recommendation No R(84)4, for details of which, see below.

[4] See para 6 of the Explanatory Memorandum.

[5] See eg Thorpe: 'The Influence of Strasbourg on English Family Law' in *Family Across Frontiers* at 849, 850.

[6] Under the Manx Family Law Act 1991.

[7] The Children (Northern Ireland) Order 1995, which came into force on 4 November 1996.

[8] The Children (Scotland) Act 1995, which came into force with regard to the parental responsibility provisions on 1 November 1996.

[9] See the Family Law Reform Act 1995 (Cth), which came into force in June 1996.

[10] See in particular Art 18(1) which states:
'States Parties shall use their best efforts to ensure recognition of the principle that both parents have common responsibilities for the upbringing and development of the child. Parents or, as the case may be, legal guardians, have the primary responsibility for the upbringing and development of the child. The best interests of the child will be their basic concern'. See also Arts 5 and 9.

[11] See Art 21(1)(b).

[12] Now fully entitled: Convention on Jurisdiction, Applicable Law, Recognition, Enforcement and Cooperation in respect of Parental Responsibility and Measures for the Protection of Children.

[13] See in particular Art 16(1).

[14] 'Parental responsibility: State of Nature or Nature of the State?' [1991] *JSWFL* 37.

[15] See eg Art 8(2) of the European Convention on Human Rights which basically provides that there be no indiscriminate interference with the right to respect for private and family life by a public authority.

[16] Children Act 1989, s 8(1). It is to be noted that under this provision an order can be made against anyone provided *the order* relates to an aspect of parental responsibility.

[17] Children Act 1989, s 8(1). The equivalent powers to make interdicts and specific issue orders in Scotland are similarly restricted to aspects of parental responsibility, see the Children (Scotland) Act 1995, s 11(1)(e) and (f), as is the power to make a specific issue order in Australia under the Family Law Act 1975 (Cth), ss 64(b)(7) and 65P.

[18] See Scot Law Com: Discussion Paper No 88, *Parental Responsibilities and Rights, Guardianship and the Administration of Children's Property* (1990) para 2.3

[19] At the moment there is no definition but the Lagarde report (Preliminary Document No 7 of 1996) at 43 draws attention to the concerns of the Canadian and UK delegation that the term is not precise enough. The UK proposal (Working Docs No 52 and 114) suggested a definition along the lines contained in the Children (Scotland) Act 1995, for details of which, see below.

[20] See Law Com No 172, *Review of Children Law and Guardianship and Custody* (1988) paras 2.6ff.

[21] So described by Lord Meston in the debate on the legislation: *HL Debs* Vol 502, col 1172.

[22] Viz Bailey-Harris, 'Family Law Reform Act 1995 (Cth): A New Approach to the Parent/Child Relationship' (1996) 18 *Adelaide Law Review* 83 and Dewar: 'The Family Law Reform Act 1995 (Cth) and the Children Act 1989 (UK) Compared – Twins or Distant Cousins' (1996) 10 *Australian Journal of Family Law* 18.

[23] Scot Law Com No 125, *Report on Family Law* (1992) paras 2.1ff. The Scottish approach may also be compared with the much earlier Norwegian attempt to define parental responsibility under s 30 of their Children Act 1981 which provides:

[212] 'The child is entitled to care and consideration from those who have parental responsibility. They have the right and the duty to make decisions for the child in personal matters ... Parental responsibility shall be exercised giving due consideration to the interests and needs of the child. Those who have parental responsibility have a duty to give the child a proper upbringing and maintenance. They shall ensure that the child receives an education according to aptitude and ability.

The child must not be exposed to violence or in any be treated so that its physical or mental health suffers injury or is hazarded.'

See Smith and Lodrup at 66ff and 172.

[24] In Bromley and Lowe's *Family Law* (8th ed, 1992) 301 the following components of parental responsibility were identified:

'a Providing a home for the child.
b Having contact with the child.
c Determining and providing for the child's education.
d Determining the child's religion.
e Disciplining the child.
f Consenting to the child's medical treatment.
g Consenting to the child's marriage.
h Agreeing to the child's adoption.
i Vetoing the issue of a child's passport.
j Taking the child outside the [country] and consenting to the child's emigration.
k Administering the child's property.
l Protecting and maintaining the child.
m Agreeing to change the child's surname.
n Representing the child in legal proceedings.
o Burying or cremating a deceased child.
p Appointing a guardian for the child.'

This list has been more succinctly stated by Barton and Douglas: *Law and Parenthood* at 114 to be:

'(1) physical possession, home, protection and contact;
(2) name;
(3) education and religion;
(4) discipline and punishment;
(5) medical treatment;
(6) travel and emigration;
(7) property and contracting;
(8) legal proceedings;
(9) services;
(10) marriage;
(11) disposing of the child's corpse.

See also Eekelaar's scholarly analysis, 'What Are Parental Rights?' (1973) 89 LQR 210.

[25] Recommendation No R (84) 4.

[26] Ie it is unlikely that in a free and democratic society it would be thought appropriate that responsibility should primarily vest in the State. In any event the right to respect for private and family life is guaranteed by Art 8(1) of the European Convention on Human Rights, while Art 18(1) of the UN Convention on the Rights of the Child clearly states that: 'Parents, or as the case may be, legal guardians, have the *primary* responsibility for the upbringing and development for the child'. [Emphasis Added]

[27] But note the English Law Commission's summary dismissal of the suggestion that in certain instances (eg lengthy absence) the rights of *all* parents whether married or unmarried should be restricted. As the Commission put it: 'Our law (in common with that of other common law countries) is firmly based on the principle that the family is a unit in which there exists a broad parental authority. Whilst we are aware that there will be occasion on which even married parents abuse that authority, we believe that the law follows the right course in relation to them by providing machinery for intervention when necessary, rather than by imposing rigid and artificial limitations when not strictly necessary'. Law Com No 118, *Illegitimacy* paras 4.41–4.42 (1982).

[28] With the exception of Western Australia.

[29] Family Law Act 1975 (Cth), s 61C(1), as amended by the Family Law Reform Act 1995 (Cth). For the position in certain European countries as of 1990 see Meulders-Klein: 'The Position of the Father in European Legislation' (1990) 4 *International Journal of Family Law and the Family* 131, 148–50.

[30] Law Com Working Paper No 74, *Illegitimacy* (1979).

[31] It should be noted that at the time of this debate the law was still very much framed in terms of parental rights and duties rather than of responsibilities.

[32] See their Final Report, Law Com No 118, *Illegitimacy* (1982) at para 4.26. See also Hayes (1980) 43 *MLR* 299.

[33] This was indeed a telling point since there is little point for a body concerned to achieve a consensus to put forward proposals that are going to be opposed by a leading interest group. For this and many other dilemmas faced by the Law Commission, see Cretney: 'The Law Commission: True Dawns and False Dawns' (1996) 59 *MLR* 631.

[34] See para 4.49. It might be noted that the Law Commission felt unable to recommend defining a class of 'meritorious' fathers who would automatically be entitled to 'parental rights' see paras 4.13–40.

[35] This was first recommended in their second report in *Illegitimacy*, Law Com No 157 (1986), and enacted first by s 4 of the Family Law Reform Act 1987 (as a parental rights and duties order, and then under s 4(1)(a) of the Children Act 1989 (a parental responsibility order). See further below.

[36] This was recommended by the Law Commission in their Report on Custody and Guardianship see Law Com No 172 (1988) para 2.18 and implemented by s 4(1)(b) of the Children Act 1989 – see further below.

[37] See Law Com No 172, ibid, at para 2.17.

[38] See Scot Law Com No 82, *Illegitimacy* (1984).

[39] See Scot Law Com, Discussion Paper No 88, *Parental Responsibilities and Rights, Guardianship and the Administration of Children's Property* (1990) para 2.23.

[40] See Discussion Paper No 88 paras 2.24ff and Scot Law Com No 135, *Report on Family Law* (1992) paras 2.38ff, and discussed inter alia by Bainham: 'Reforming Scottish Children Law – sense from North of the border' (1993) 5 *J of Child Law*, 3, 5–7.

[41] This was an argument which weighed by heavily with the English Law Commission, see above.

[42] As they can under English law, see s 2(7) of the Children Act 1989, though note *Re G (A Minor) (Parental Responsibility: Education)* [1994] 2 FLR 964, commented upon by White, Carr and Lowe: *The Children Act in Practice* (2nd edn 1995) paras 3.66–3.67. The position in Scotland is similar, see the Children (Scotland) Act 1995, s 2(2). For the position in Australia see s 61C of the Family Law Reform Act 1975 (Cth), as amended, which merely provides that each parent has parental responsibility notwithstanding any changes to their relationship which as Bailey-Harris, 'Family Law Reform Act 1995 (Cth): A New Approach to the Parent/Child Relationship' (1996) 18 *Adelaide Law Review* 83, 90, observes, does not expressly state whether that responsibility can be exercised by one parent *severally* as well as by both *jointly*. See also Dewar: 'The Family Law Reform Act 1995 (Cth) and the Children Act 1989 (UK) Compared – Twins or Distant Cousins?' (1996) 10 *Australian Journal of Family Law* 18 at 26–8.

[43] Viz by the Scottish Law Commission's Discussion Paper No 88 see para 2.31.

[44] Scot Law Com No 135, *Report Family Law* (1992) para 2.50.

[45] Ibid at para 2.48.

[46] The percentage of such children is even higher, namely, almost 34 percent in England and Wales, in 1995, according to the latest figures from the Office of National Statistics.

[47] See respectively ss 4 and 11.

[48] See Bailey-Harris: 'Family Law Reform – Changes Down Under? [1996] *Fam Law* 214.

[49] See what was formerly s 63F(1), which in turn reflected what had been the position in South Australia for some time under that State's Guardianship of Infants Act 1940–75.

[50] Namely under what is now s 61C(1), which came into force on 11 June 1996 in all States save Western Australia.

[51] Scot Law Com No 135 para 2.49.

[52] See Van Bueren *The Best Interests of the Child – International Co-operation on Child Abduction* (1993) 45, 49–53.

[53] As established in England and Wales by *Re M (An Infant)* [1955] 2 QB 479.

[54] See *Re C (Minors) (Adoption: Residence Order)* [1994] Fam 1.

[55] As we have seen it seemed to cut no ice with the UK government when legislating for Scotland, since it rejected the Scottish Law Commission's recommendation.

[56] Namely under Art 53. See generally Harris, O'Boyle and Warbrick: *Law of the European Convention on Human Rights*, 23–6, 703ff.

[57] See his commentary on the Children (Scotland) Act 1995 in Current Law Statutes 1995 Vol 3, at 36–13.

[58] (1995) 20 EHRR 205.
[59] For the reasons for this conclusion, see below.
[60] (1994) 18 EHRR 513, para 24.
[61] Namely the Law Reform (Parent and Child) (Scotland) Act 1986.
[62] 'Cohabitation and Children in Europe' (1981) 29 *American Journal of Comparative Law* 359.
[63] (1979) 2 EHRR 330.
[64] At that time Belgian law required the mother to undertake a formal legal process of recognition or to bring legal proceedings for that purpose. That law has now changed – see Meulders-Klein: 'The Position of the Father in European Legislation' in (1990) 4 *International Journal of Law and the Family* 131 at 138.
[65] Nor why he should be in a comparatively weaker position than the mother *vis-à-vis* the State: see Bainham: 'When is a Parent not a Parent? Reflections on the Unmarried Father and his Child in English Law' (1989) 3 *IJLF* 208 at 212.
[66] 213ff.
[67] (1988) 11 EHRR 322.
[68] A view subsequently vindicated by *Keegan* v *Ireland* (1994) 18 EHRR 342 and *Kroon* v *The Netherlands* (1994) 19 EHRR 263, discussed below.
[69] Application No 11468/85.
[70] (1986) 9 EHRR 203.
[71] 'Parent-Child Relationships within the European Convention' in Lowe and Douglas (eds) *Families Across Frontiers*, 135ff.
[72] Application 9639/82 D & R 36.
[73] (1994) 18 EHRR 342.
[74] (1994) 19 EHRR 263.
[75] Ie no one else can acquire responsibility by agreement or by a specific court order, though for possible reforms see further below.
[76] Unmarried fathers can also acquire responsibility by being appointed a guardian under s 5 and, if the court makes a residence order in their favour it is obliged to make a *separate* parental responsibility order under s 12(1).
[77] Similar provision is made under the Children (Scotland) Act 1995, s 4(1).
[78] For what was then a parental rights and duties order under s 4 of the Family Law Reform Act 1987.
[79] See Law Com No 172, para 2.18.
[80] As laid down by the Parental Responsibility Agreement Regulations 1991 (SI 1991/1478) as amended.
[81] This requirement was introduced as from 3 January 1995 as a safeguard against forged signatures, see White, Carr and Lowe, above at para 3.41.
[82] Namely there were 2,941 agreements in 1992, 4,411 in 1993, 'around' 5,280 in 1994 and an 'estimated' 3,455 in 1995 – see the Children Act Advisory Committee Reports 1993/94 and 1994/95. The reason for the drop in 1995 was the change of procedure introduced that year.
[83] See CAAC Report 1994–5, Appendix 1 and Table 4. Even so this still only represents a tiny proportion of the overall numbers of unmarried fathers, who presumably do not bother to take steps to acquire responsibility, see Butler, Douglas, Lowe, Noakes and Pithouse: 'The Children Act 1989 and the unmarried father' (1993) 5 *Journal of Child Law* 157 at 158.
[84] See the discussion in White, Carr and Lowe, above, paras 3.42ff.
[85] There is some evidence that magistrates and county courts are not quite so ready to grant orders as case law would suggest they ought.
[86] Ie they can satisfy the so-called '*Re H* test', namely, to satisfy the court as to (1) commitment (2) degree of attachment to the child and (3) bona fide reasons for applying for the order: *Re H (Minors) (Adoption: Putative Father's Rights) (No 3)* [1991] Fam 151, to which considerations the Courts should make express reference: *S* v *R (Parental Responsibility)* [1993] 1 FCR 331.
[87] See *Re G (A Minor) (Parental Responsibility Order)* [1994] 1 FLR 504.
[88] *Re P (A Minor) (Parental Responsibility)* [1996] 1 FLR 562.
[89] See *Re S (Parental Responsibility)* [1995] 2 FLR 648.
[90] *Re H (A Minor) (Contact and Parental Responsibility)* [1993] 1 FLR 484.
[91] *Re C (Minors) (Parental Rights)* [1992] 1 FLR 1.
[92] As in *Re T (A Minor) (Parental Responsibility: Contact)* [1993] 2 FLR 450. See also *Re P (Terminating Parental Responsibility)* [1995] 1 FLR 1048.
[93] [1996] 1 FLR 867.
[94] G. Douglas [1996] *Fam Law* 402.

[95] See eg *Re H (Paternity: Parental Rights)* [1996] 2 FLR 65 and *Re R (A Minor) (Contact)* [1993] 2 FLR 762 which respectively prayed in aid Arts 7(1) and 9(1) of the UN Convention on the Rights of the Child.

[96] Helen Conway: 'Parental responsibility and the unmarried father' (1996) 146 *NLJ* 782.

[97] Eg The Scottish Law Commission, see Scot Law Com No 88, para 2.47, and Barton and Douglas: *Law and Parenthood* 93–4.

[98] Or a result of a parental order made under s 30 of the Human Fertilisation and Embryology Act 1990.

[99] See S 11(2)(a). Under the Australian Family Law Act 1975 (Cth) as amended, the exercise of parental responsibility can be subject to any court order (see s 61C(3) which is similar to the English position).

[100] In England, see the Adoption Act 1976, ss 12 and 39. In Scotland, see the Adoption (Scotland) Act 1978, s 12 and in Australia see the Family Law Act 1975 (Cth) s 61E.

[101] See respectively the Children Act 1989, s 5 and the Children (Scotland) Act 1995, s 7.

[102] In this respect see the discussion by Douglas and Lowe: 'Becoming a Parent in English Law' (1992) 108 *LQR* 414 at 427–8.

[103] See s 12(2) of the Children Act 1989.

[104] See s 11(12) of the Children (Scotland) Act 1995.

[105] Under s 11(2) which gives the court a general power to make such an order in favour of any on it thinks fit. This builds on a similar power to make a 'parental rights' order under the Law Reform (Parent and Child) (Scotland) Act 1986, s 3(1). See further below.

[106] See the Family Law Act 1975 (Cth), ss 61D and 65C–F.

[107] See eg the arguments of Masson: 'Old families into new: a status for step-parents' in Freeman (ed) *State Law and the Family* 237ff.

[108] Cf Law Com Working Paper No 91, *Guardianship*, paras 4.15 to 4.19 which canvassed views about the possibility of step-parents acquiring responsibility by administrative rather than judicial means but did not pursue the point because it attracted little support at the time: Law Com No 172, *Guardianship and Custody*, para 2.22. Such reform has, however, since been proposed in the Adoption Bill – see below.

[109] See Cl 85 of the Draft Adoption Bill attached to 'Adoption – Service for Children' (1996).

[110] See respectively s 12(2) of the Children Act 1989 and s 11(12) of the Children (Scotland) Act 1995. Similarly under English law a care order vests parental responsibility (which it shares with the parents) in the local authority. See s 33(3) of the Children Act 1989. Cf Scotland in which parental responsibility is transferred to the local authority under s 86 of the Children (Scotland) Act 1995.

[111] Under s 61D of the Family Law Act 1975 (Cth) as amended.

[112] Bailey-Harris: 'Family Law Reform – Changes Down Under' [1996] *Fam Law* 214.

[113] The powers to make respectively a parental responsibility or a parenting order are conferred by s 11(2) of the Children (Scotland) Act 1995 and s 61D of the Australian Family Law Act 1975 (Cth).

[114] [1995] 2 FLR 1023. For a different type of example see *Re W (Arrangements to Place for Adoption)* [1995] 1 FLR 163.

[115] Ie the court refused to grant him a shared residence for the 'artificial' purpose of allocation responsibility, cf *Re H (Shared Residence: Parental Responsibility)* [1995] 2 FLR 883, where such an order *was* made to alleviate confusion in the child's mind.

[116] See 11(2)(a) of the Children (Scotland) Act 1995.

[117] Ie mothers and married fathers. Parental responsibility orders and agreements can be ended by the court under s 4(3). Those that acquire responsibility via a residence order only have it for the duration of the order.

[118] Cf *Re P (Terminating Parental Responsibility)* [1995] 1 FLR 1048 in which the (unmarried) father inflicted permanent brain damage on his child. This is the only reported case where the Court exercised its powers under s 4(3) to end a parental responsibility agreement. See also *Re M (A Minor) (Care Orders: Threshold Conditions)* [1994] 2 AC 424 in which the father murdered the mother in front of the children.

[119] The enduring nature of responsibility is emphasized in the case of an unmarried father acquiring responsibility by virtue of a residence order made in his favour by the requirement under s 12(1) to make a *separate* parental responsibility order so that the subsequent ending of the residence order will not *ipso facto* end the responsibility.

[120] *Introduction to the Children Act 1989* (HMSO, 1989) para 1.4.

21

The Degradation of Parental Responsibility

HELEN REECE

INTRODUCTION

IN THIS CHAPTER I argue that the concept of parental responsibility in the Children Act 1989 has moved further and further away from its predecessor, parental rights. First, I look at this in general, focusing on the background to the introduction of the term 'parental responsibility'. Then I turn to an examination of the allocation of parental responsibility. In this context, I suggest that parental responsibility has moved away from meaning *parental authority* towards meaning *legitimation*. I illustrate this with a recent case, *Re D (contact and parental responsibility: lesbian mothers and known father)*,[1] which I argue is indicative of three trends away from parental authority, namely the proliferation of parental responsibility, the degradation of parental responsibility and the shift in the reasons given for granting parental responsibility. In my conclusion, I query whether this is merely a staging post on the way to parental responsibility meaning nothing whatsoever.

THE CHANGING MEANING OF PARENTAL RESPONSIBILITY

Although parental rights still form an aspect of the definition of parental responsibility,[2] there is no doubt that with the advent of the Children Act 1989, parental responsibility ousted parental rights as the dominant legal conception of the parent–child relationship.[3] Writing about the United States, Martha Fineman

---

[1] [2006] EWHC 2.
[2] Children Act 1989 s 3(1).
[3] H Reece, 'From Parental Responsibility to Parenting Responsibly' in M Freeman (ed), *Law and Sociology: Current Legal Issues 2005* (Oxford, Oxford University Press, 2006).

has given an explanation for this development[4] that is far more elegant than, but substantively similar to, one that I have previously given.[5] Fineman notes that the 'charge often leveled is that the law treats children as though they are the property of their parents'.[6] Her rejection of equality in the context of the family enables her to take a robust attitude to this charge. While Fineman recognises that the parent–child relationship is inherently unequal,[7] she suggests that nothing follows from this inherent inequality as to the extent to which we value children.[8] Nor does it follow that the parent–child relationship is exploitative: it is wrong to equate the lack of a legal voice with the lack of an actual voice.[9] Not only is exploitation not a necessary consequence of inequality, but Fineman also posits that, in practice, relationships between caretakers and dependants are interactive, with caretakers typically considering dependants' needs.[10]

Accordingly, she believes that the charge that the law treats children as though they are the property of their parents is 'an inflammatory characterization that does more to obscure than to illuminate the issues'.[11] Nonetheless, she explains that this charge has resulted in suggestions for recasting the relationship between parent and child, for example by substituting concepts such as stewardship or trusteeship for the more traditional notion of parental authority, in order to level out the relationship.[12]

Fineman's description of US developments maps very well onto the United Kingdom. In the United Kingdom, the charge that the law treated children as though they were the property of their parents was levelled at parents' rights: the concept of parents' rights was accused of treating children as though they were the property of their parents. For example, Jonathan Herring interprets the shift from parental rights to parental responsibility as demonstrating that 'children are not possessions to be controlled by parents, but instead children are persons to be cared for'.[13] Writing in 1991, Michael Freeman expressed the accusation vividly:

> The shift from parental rights and duties (a property concept, almost) to parental responsibility, with parents as trustees for their children, the beneficiaries, has to be welcomed. We clearly have to get away from the notion of children as consumer durables, completing a family after the C.D. player and video recorder.[14]

---

[4] MA Fineman, *The Autonomy Myth: A Theory of Dependency* (New York, The New Press, 2004).
[5] Reece, above n 3.
[6] Fineman, above n 4, 301.
[7] *Ibid*, 304–5.
[8] *Ibid*, 304.
[9] *Ibid*, 305.
[10] *Ibid*, 305.
[11] *Ibid*, 301.
[12] *Ibid*, 301.
[13] J Herring, *Family Law* (3rd edn, Harlow, Pearson Education, 2007) 376. See also NV Lowe, 'The Meaning and Allocation of Parental Responsibility—A Common Lawyer's Perspective' (1997) 11 *IJLPF* 192, 192 for the association between parental responsibility and parental care.
[14] M Freeman, 'In the Child's Best Interests? Reading the Children Act Critically' (1992) 45 *Current Legal Problems* 173, 185.

The Degradation of Parental Responsibility   87

Despite characterising the consensus, this charge is a caricature of the role of parents' rights. In living memory, the idea that children are their parents' possessions has never been legally endorsed; nor has the idea that children are persons to be cared for ever been legally doubted. When I read Michael Freeman's depiction, I cannot help bringing to mind the old joke:

> Question: What is the difference between an elephant and a post-box?
>
> Answer: I don't know. What is the difference between an elephant and a post-box?
>
> Riposte: Well, if you don't know I won't ask you to post my letters.

There is no danger of confusing children with CD players, no comparison between the way in which children and video recorders complete a family. Indeed, parents commonly lament children's lack of an off switch, volume control or even a pause button.

More seriously though, the charge was wrong because it was crystal clear that, far from parental rights' treating children as property, the law treated parental rights as existing for the benefit of the child, not the parent. This approach was entrenched in the law by the House of Lords in the celebrated case of *Gillick v West Norfolk and Wisbech AHA* in the mid 1980s.[15] Thus, according to Lord Fraser:

> [P]arental rights to control a child do not exist for the benefit of the parent. They exist for the benefit of the child and they are justified only in so far as they enable the parent to perform his duties towards the child, and towards other children in the family.[16]

The House of Lords made quite clear that they were making explicit a long-standing principle, which they traced back to *Blackstone's Commentaries* of 1830.[17] Accepted on all sides, this was not one of the points of contention in *Gillick*.[18]

Despite the fact that the principle that parental rights existed for the benefit of children was settled beyond peradventure, it was concern to emphasise this principle further that provided both the initial and main impetus for switching from parental rights to parental responsibility.[19] However, originally, the shift was conceived of as 'largely a change of nomenclature',[20] the Law Commission assuring that it 'would make little difference in substance'.[21] The strong connection with parental rights is evident in the definition given in the Children Act

---

[15] [1986] AC 112. See SM Cretney, JM Masson and R Bailey-Harris, *Principles of Family Law* (7th edn, London, Sweet & Maxwell, 2003) 522; and Herring, above n 13, 377.
[16] [1986] AC 112 at 170. See also *ibid*, at 184 (Lord Scarman).
[17] *Ibid*, at 170 and 184–5.
[18] *Ibid*, at 170.
[19] See further Reece, above n 3, 462–3.
[20] Lord Mackay, 'Perceptions of the Children Bill and beyond' (1989) 139 *NLJ* 505, 505.
[21] Law Commission, 'Family Law: Review of Child Law, Guardianship and Custody' (Law Com No 172, 1988) 6. See also Cretney, Masson and Bailey-Harris, above n 15, 522.

88 *Helen Reece*

1989 itself,[22] which 'immediately throws one back to the rights and duties concept which "responsibility" was supposed to replace',[23] the first word used to describe parental responsibility being 'rights'.[24] So in other words, parental responsibility originally had a lot of parental rights left in it. Accordingly, in 1991 John Eekelaar could quite plausibly describe 'parental responsibility' as synonymous with 'parental authority', embodying ideas of freedom of parents from government.[25]

Fineman warns, though, that the ideals embodied in the substitution of egalitarian concepts for parental authority:

> amorphously appealing on a rhetorical level, seem harmless enough as aspirations. The problems arise when they are implemented into laws that can be used at the relatively unfettered discretion of various state actors to undermine, even usurp, parental decision-making authority.[26]

This is what we have witnessed in the United Kingdom. The shift from parental rights to parental responsibility set the stage for the current approach, which has switched from the idea that parental authority exists purely for the benefit of children to the idea that parental authority *itself* is antithetical to children's welfare. I have previously looked at this shift in relation to parental responsibility for children's crimes and misdemeanours and I have argued that in this context parental responsibility now means parental accountability to external agencies.[27] In the remainder of this chapter, I look at this shift in relation to the allocation of parental responsibility.

ALLOCATION OF PARENTAL RESPONSIBILITY

Since most of the legal disputes concerning parental responsibility are over its acquisition as opposed to its exercise, examining the allocation of parental responsibility takes us right into the heart of the legal meaning of the concept.

The dominant view among commentators who have investigated the meaning of parental responsibility in the context of allocation is that it is 'a confused, contradictory concept'.[28] There is much force in this view. The allocation of parental responsibility performs a diverse array of different roles, and the case law

---

[22] Children Act 1989 s 3(1).
[23] Lowe, above n 13, 195.
[24] Herring, above n 13, 376.
[25] J Eekelaar, 'Parental Responsibility: State of Nature or Nature of the State?' (1991) 13 *JSWFL* 37. See further Reece, above n 3, 460–61.
[26] Fineman, above n 5, 301.
[27] Reece, above n 3.
[28] J Bridgeman, 'Parental Responsibility, Responsible Parenting and Legal Regulation' in J Bridgeman, C Lind and H Keating (eds), *Responsibility, Law and the Family* (London, Ashgate, 2008) 237. See also Herring, above n 13, 385; and S Gilmore, 'Parental Responsibility and The Unmarried Father—A New Dimension to the Debate' [2003] 15 *CFLQ* 21, 38.

reflects these many meanings. One enduring strand of the meaning of parental responsibility in this context is undoubtedly parental authority: the law still needs to delineate who has the power to decide which school a child will go to or which medical treatment the child will have.

However, I would not wholly endorse the chaotic account. I believe that, even among the many strands of meaning, it is possible to discern a dominant trend, *away from* parental responsibility as parental authority *towards* parental responsibility as legitimation. In relation to the allocation of parental responsibility, an increasingly significant element of the meaning of parental responsibility is 'a pat on the back, official confirmation'.[29]

I want to illustrate this with the case of *Re D*.[30] This case concerned a lesbian couple, Ms A and Ms C, who advertised for a man interested in fathering a child: Mr B responded. From an early stage it transpired that the three adults had different expectations of Mr B's involvement with the child:

> Mr B was expecting something of the role of the absent parent after divorce who might share the child's leisure time equally with the child's mother and participate in decisions about the child whereas Ms A and Ms C intended that he should complement their primary care of the child by being a real father but by doing so through no more than relatively infrequent visits and benign and loving interest.[31]

These differing expectations led Mr B to apply for parental responsibility.

The court granted him parental responsibility hedged with conditions, the specific ones being that unless he had the prior written consent of the primary carers, he was not allowed to visit or contact the child's school or any of her health professionals for any purpose. Black J made plain to Mr B that these were by no means the only situations from which he was excluded:

> The court has power to regulate others, should they arise, through Children Act orders. Given that Mr B will know, following this judgment, the sort of context that the court anticipates there will be for his involvement in D's life, he will be able to forecast the likely consequences of attempts to become involved in areas of her life not covered by the proposed conditions and it is my judgment that that ought to be a brake upon his conduct.[32]

Black J decided that 'the fundamental nature of these restrictions on Mr B's parental responsibility'[33] would be reflected by setting out in the parental responsibility order that the order was made in reliance upon them.[34] Arguably *de trop*, Black J added that Mr B had no role in D's day-to-day care, 'whether in relation to decision making or otherwise'.[35]

---

[29] Herring, above n 13, 384.
[30] [2006] EWHC 2, [2006] 1 FCR 556.
[31] [2006] 1 FCR 556 at 557 (Black J).
[32] *Ibid*, at 582.
[33] *Ibid*, at 582.
[34] *Ibid*, at 582.
[35] *Ibid*, at 583.

I would regard the approach taken in *Re D* as fundamentally inconsistent with the granting of parental responsibility.[36] It is a 'now you see it, now you don't' approach to parental responsibility. Rather than Mr B having any authority or decision-making power over D, he has actually been ordered to keep away. In a sense, he has even fewer powers over the child than 'the man on the Clapham omnibus', who has not been barred from the sites of decision making about her. Mr B has degraded parental responsibility, with the courts telling him exactly how much he has and precisely what he can do with it.

Clearly, *Re D* is highly atypical. Black J commented:

> None of the authorities has so far dealt ... with the sort of situation that exists in this case where a same sex couple has deliberately decided to create a family and, with the knowledge of all concerned that it is their intention that they should be the primary carers, involves a man to father a baby.[37]

However, this only strengthens the point that I am making: the fact that even Mr B could be granted parental responsibility shows that parental responsibility has become debased. Moreover, although the case itself is unusual, I want to suggest that *Re D* is indicative of three aspects of the trend away from parental responsibility as parental authority, namely the proliferation of parental responsibility, the degradation of parental responsibility and a shift in the reasons given for granting parental responsibility.

Proliferation of Parental Responsibility

The categories of people who have parental powers automatically and who may acquire parental powers have been expanded at regular historical intervals. The Children Act 1989 represented a significant extension; nevertheless, the categories have been further stretched since, particularly in relation to unmarried fathers and step-parents.[38]

The Family Law Reform Act 1987 allowed unmarried fathers to acquire parental powers for the first time ever.[39] The Children Act 1989 maintained this position, but diversified the ways in which this could happen.[40] The Adoption and Children Act 2002 extended parental responsibility to all unmarried fathers who sign the birth register.[41] The recent government White Paper, 'Joint birth registration: recording responsibility', proposes to make joint birth registration

---

[36] See J McCandless, 'Status and Anomaly: *Re D (contact and parental responsibility: lesbian mothers and known father)* [2006] EWHC 2 (Fam), [2006] 1 FCR 556' (2008) 30 *JSWFL* 63, 67.

[37] [2006] 1 FCR 556 at 561. But see *Re B* [2007] EWHC 1952 (Fam), [2008] 1 FLR 1015.

[38] In what follows, the term 'step-parent' refers to a partner of a parent who has taken on a parenting role in relation to the parent's child, irrespective of whether he or she has married or entered into a civil partnership with the parent.

[39] Family Law Reform Act 1987 s 4(1).

[40] Children Act 1989 s 4.

[41] Adoption and Children Act 2002 s 111.

for unmarried parents compulsory unless it is impossible, impracticable or unreasonable, so that almost all unmarried fathers would have parental responsibility.[42] The Adoption and Children Act 2002 also introduced acquisition of parental responsibility by step-parents, defined as those persons who are either married to or in a civil partnership with one of the parents.[43]

By judicial fiat, *Re G (shared residence order: parental responsibility)*[44] stretched parental responsibility still further so as to include step-parents who are no longer or never have been married to or in a civil partnership with one of the parents. This case concerned the breakdown of a lesbian relationship, and specifically an application by the non-biological parent, W, for a shared residence order in order to gain parental responsibility for the couple's two children. Thorpe LJ explained that it was common ground in the hearing that:

> A significant feature of the fact that the parties to this appeal had been in a same-sex relationship was that the appellant could only achieve parental responsibility in relation to these two children if she succeeded in her application for a residence order.[45]

With respect, this explanation is misleading. It is true that the only way in which W could gain parental responsibility was through a residence order, but it is not true that this was because she was in a same-sex relationship. Rather, the reason was that she was not in a civil partnership with the children's biological mother. W thus had this feature in common with heterosexual step-parents who are not married to one of the parents.

From the fallacious premise that it was because W was in a same-sex relationship that she could only achieve parental responsibility through a residence order, the Court of Appeal drew the conclusion that it would be unfair not to grant W parental responsibility, their reasoning being that she would have been granted parental responsibility had she been an unmarried father:

> Although [counsel for W] has not asserted discrimination against his client he has made the general observation that, had the case concerned the two children of a heterosexual couple who had cohabited between 1995 and 2003 and the father, being the absent parent, had sought the parental responsibility order on the strength of the same degree of past and proposed future commitment as has been demonstrated by Miss W, the outcome would have been evident.[46]

Accordingly, the Court of Appeal treated her application for a shared residence order as an application for parental responsibility, so much so that they applied the threefold test developed in *Re H (minors) (local authority: parental rights) (No 3)*[47]

---

[42] Department for Work and Pensions, 'Joint birth registration: recording responsibility' (Cm 7293, 2008); see now cl 44 of the Welfare Reform Bill 2009.
[43] Adoption and Children Act 2002 s 112; and Civil Partnership Act 2004 s 75(2).
[44] [2005] EWCA Civ 462, [2005] 2 FLR 957.
[45] [2005] 2 FLR 957 at 959.
[46] *Ibid*, at 964–5.
[47] [1991] Fam 151.

for determining whether or not to grant a parental responsibility order to an unmarried father, namely the degree of commitment shown to the child, the degree of attachment with the child and the reasons for applying for the order.[48]

However, the correct comparator in *Re G* was not the unmarried father, but the unmarried heterosexual step-parent. While the precedents established that an intact couple consisting of a cohabiting parent and step-parent might be granted shared residence primarily or even solely as a means for the step-parent to gain parental responsibility,[49] at that time the precedents suggested that slightly more stringent criteria applied when the couple had separated, as was the case in *Re G*.

Re WB (minors) (residence orders)[50] concerned the relationship breakdown of a heterosexual couple who had lived together for about 10 years, during which time the mother had given birth to two children. N had brought up the children believing them to be his biological children, but after the couple separated blood tests revealed that this was not the case. Like W 10 years later, N applied for a shared residence order as his only route to parental responsibility. Thorpe J, as he then was, described N's appeal against the justices' refusal to grant his application as 'devoid of any merit'.[51] Once the justices had reached the unchallengeable conclusion that shared care was inappropriate, it would have been:

> quite wrong had they expressed their conclusion in the shape of a shared residence order for no other reason than to arrive at a finding of parental responsibility in the appellant.[52]

Re WB was distinguished in *Re H (shared residence: parental responsibility)*.[53] Here the husband met the mother when she was pregnant with her eldest child, whom he accepted as his own. They later had a child together. When the couple separated, the trial judge made a shared residence order in relation to both children, which the mother appealed. Ward LJ distinguished *Re WB* on the basis that there the making of a shared residence order would have been 'quite artificial and unreflective of the reality'.[54] In contrast:

> This is a case where a shared residence order is not artificial but of important practical therapeutic importance. This is a case where its making does reflect the reality of the father's involvement ... Here it was important that the boys retain the perception that they lived with their father when they did not live with their mother. ... Here it was necessary for the boys to know they lived with the respondent and that they did not just visit him.[55]

---

[48] *Ibid*, at 158.
[49] See, eg *Re AB* [1996] 1 FLR 27.
[50] [1995] 2 FLR 1023.
[51] *Ibid*, at 1026.
[52] *Ibid*, at 1027.
[53] [1995] 2 FLR 883.
[54] *Ibid*, at 889.
[55] *Ibid*, at 889. See also in the context of a lesbian relationship *G v F* [1998] 2 FLR 799.

In the light of these precedents, it seemed that, after a couple had separated, a shared residence order might be made primarily in order to confer parental responsibility on the step-parent, so long as shared care was otherwise considered appropriate. Accordingly, it may well be that shared residence was justifiable on the facts of *Re G*. However, the case was not decided by examining whether shared care was otherwise suitable, but on the legally incorrect basis that a lesbian co-parent should be treated equivalently to an unmarried father when awarding parental responsibility.

Although neither the specific precedents nor the general comparator of heterosexual step-parents was mentioned in *Re G*, the case has already been held to apply in this wider context. In *Re A (a child) (joint residence: parental responsibility)*,[56] as in *Re WB*, A had brought up the child on the assumption that he was the biological father, but during contact proceedings it emerged that this assumption was false. At first instance, despite the fact that shared care was not considered appropriate, the recorder made a shared residence order with regard to the child, in order to give A parental responsibility. Dismissing the mother's appeal against the shared residence order in a unanimous Court of Appeal judgment, Sir Mark Potter P. drew from *Re G* the following, unqualified, legal principle:

> it is ... clear the making of a residence order is a legitimate means by which to confer parental responsibility on an individual who would otherwise not be able to apply for a free-standing parental responsibility order.[57]

By judicial fiat, parental responsibility has thus been extended to step-parents who are not married to or in a civil partnership with one of the parents.

The proliferation of parental responsibility has become more significant as a result of another recent body of case law. Despite the fact that the Children Act 1989 s 2(7) provides that a person with parental responsibility is allowed to act alone and without the other or others in meeting his or her responsibility, the courts have developed a group of what they regard as important decisions that may only be taken with the agreement of everyone with parental responsibility. In *Re J (specific issue orders: child's religious upbringing and circumcision)*,[58] in which the issue was whether the child should be circumcised given the parents' disagreement on this matter, Butler-Sloss LJ considered that the group included sterilisation, change of surname[59] and circumcision itself.[60] In *Re C (welfare of child: immunisation)*,[61] the Court of Appeal added immunisation to the list.[62] Although one view is that this case law has augmented the authority aspect of

---

[56] [2008] EWCA Civ 867, [2008] 2 FLR 1593.
[57] [2008] 2 FLR 1593 at 1613.
[58] [2000] 1 FLR 571.
[59] See *Re PC* [1997] 2 FLR 730.
[60] [2000] 1 FLR 571 at 577.
[61] [2003] EWCA Civ 1148, [2003] 2 FLR 1095.
[62] [2003] 2 FLR 1095 at 1099.

parental responsibility, the better view is that these precedents have further diluted parental authority, since they are likely to lead to more decisions being taken by courts, as opposed to parents.

The watering down of parental responsibility perhaps provides an explanation for the recent liberalisation of the circumstances in which shared residence orders may be made.[63] Part of the hope behind the Children Act 1989 was that after separation or divorce the endurance of parental responsibility would lead orders about children to be made less frequently than had been the case.[64] As parental responsibility has been diluted, shared residence orders have arguably come to represent the new way of giving separated parents equal authority.[65]

Current ease with the proliferation of parental responsibility presents a marked contrast with historical unease: the Guardianship of Infants Act 1925 rejected equal parental authority for mothers primarily on the basis that any splitting of parental authority at all would be divisive.[66] This contemporary ease indicates that parental responsibility has shifted away from its origins in parental authority. When the meaning of parental responsibility is closely tied to parental authority, it is important for external agencies to limit the holders of parental responsibility so that everyone knows who is in charge. Conversely, the proliferation of parental responsibility demonstrates that parental responsibility is no longer predominantly about parental authority or decision-making. The fact that the law is quite relaxed about giving parental responsibility to an ever-widening circle, even the father in *Re D*, strongly suggests that parental responsibility no longer represents a buffer against the law; no longer to the same extent does parental responsibility signify parental freedom from legal intervention.[67]

Degradation of Parental Responsibility

As I have already recognised, *Re D* is an extreme case. However, in this section I suggest that *Re D* is the nadir of a line of cases in which parental responsibility has been given only a minimal connection with parental authority. This line of cases, about the circumstances in which parental responsibility should be awarded, have all been concerned with unmarried fathers because until recently they were the only group entitled to apply for parental responsibility.[68]

Much of the case law dealing with unmarried fathers' applications for parental responsibility makes plain that their parental responsibility has little to do with authority. This is apparent in *Re D*, but it is also apparent in the cases that form

---

[63] See *Re D* [2001] 1 FLR 495; and S Gilmore, 'Court decision-making in shared residence order cases: a critical examination' [2006] 18 *CFLQ* 478.
[64] See Law Commission, above n 21, 7–8 and 14.
[65] I am grateful to Jonathan Herring for this point.
[66] S Cretney, *Law, Law Reform and the Family* (Oxford, Clarendon Press, 1998) ch 7.
[67] See Herring, above n 13, 343.
[68] See above, text at nn 39 *ff*.

the foundations of *Re D*. Unlike *Re D*, it would be fair to describe *Re P (a minor: parental responsibility order)*[69] as a run-of-the-mill unmarried father case. In *Re P*, the magistrates refused to grant the father a parental responsibility order because they felt that he would be able to use such an order to question aspects of the child's upbringing, to the child's detriment. However, Wilson J allowed the father's appeal, stating:

> It is important to be quite clear that an order for parental responsibility to the father does not give him a right to interfere in matters within the day-to-day management of the child's life.[70]

It is true that Wilson J continued:

> There is, of course, an order for residence in favour of the mother under the Act and that invests the mother with the right to determine all matters which arise in the course of the day-to-day management of this child's life.[71]

This meant that the father's use of his parental responsibility was in any case restricted, given the provision in the Children Act 1989 s 2(8) that parental responsibility does not entitle the holder to act incompatibly with a Children Act order. However, in *Re S (parental responsibility)*,[72] a Court of Appeal decision the following year that confirmed and extended Wilson J's reasoning, the mother did not have a residence order. The Court of Appeal placed no significance on this distinction.

In *Re S*, the mother objected to the unmarried father's application for parental responsibility because he had been convicted of possessing child pornography. The Court of Appeal overrode this objection and granted parental responsibility, not because of any newly found permissiveness about child pornography, Ward LJ describing it inter alia as an 'appalling activity',[73] but rather on the basis that granting the father parental responsibility really did not entitle him to do very much. Ward LJ emphasised:

> It is wrong to place undue and therefore false emphasis on the rights and duties and the powers comprised in 'parental responsibility' and not to concentrate on the fact that what is at issue is conferring upon a committed father the status of parenthood.[74]

Despite the Law Commission's earlier assurance that the shift from parental rights to parental responsibility would make little substantive difference, *Re S* marks a significant break with parental rights. According to Ward LJ, the decision in the Children Act 1989[75] to define parental responsibility with reference to parental rights gave 'outmoded pre-eminence'[76] to rights, exhibiting:

---

[69] [1994] 1 FLR 578.
[70] *Ibid*, at 584.
[71] *Ibid*, at 585.
[72] [1995] 2 FLR 648.
[73] *Ibid*, at 649.
[74] *Ibid*, at 657. See also *Re C and V* [1998] 1 FLR 392 at 397.
[75] Children Act 1989 s 3(1).
[76] [1995] 2 FLR 648 at 657.

a most unfortunate failure to appreciate the significant change that the Act has brought about where the emphasis is to move away from rights and to concentrate on responsibilities.[77]

Butler-Sloss LJ agreed with Ward LJ's judgment, adding a short judgment of the same tenor if less forcefully expressed, in which she referred to a parental responsibility order as one of 'duties and responsibilities as well as rights and powers'.[78]

In both *Re S* and *Re P*, it was emphasised that to the extent that parental responsibility did give fathers rights, any misuse could be controlled by the granting of specific issue or prohibited steps orders.[79] In neither of these cases were such orders deemed necessary. However, in the later case of *Re H (a child: parental responsibility)*,[80] Thorpe LJ granted the father parental responsibility, hedged by both a specific issue order giving the mother sole responsibility for decisions about the child's medical treatment and a prohibited steps order preventing the father from trying to find out the child's address. Following *Re S*, he confirmed that giving this father parental responsibility was 'essentially an acknowledgment and declaration of his parental status'.[81]

These cases were relied upon in *Re D*,[82] but *Re D* also takes them further. McCandless explains that while attaching section 8 orders to parental responsibility orders seems similar to the decision in *Re D* to make the parental responsibility order in reliance on certain restrictions, there are 'subtle but important differences'[83] between the methods. If circumstances changed so that limitations on parental responsibility were no longer called for, in *Re H* the section 8 orders could be removed to leave the parental responsibility order intact, but in *Re D* parental responsibility itself would have to be reviewed. Relatedly, regulating parental responsibility with section 8 orders implies that the father is prima facie entitled to parental rights, but current circumstances dictate particular restrictions; there is no equivalent implication of entitlement in *Re D*.[84]

It is right to recognise that there is other case law that ascribes more potency to unmarried fathers' parental responsibility. In the recent case of *Re B (role of biological father)*,[85] in which a man who had fathered a child for a lesbian couple applied for parental responsibility, the court declined to grant the order in what were apparently similar circumstances to *Re D*. Hedley J's brief reasoning on this point seems to have been that the father should not be granted parental

---

[77] *Ibid*, at 657.
[78] *Ibid*, at 659.
[79] *Ibid*, at 657; and *Re P* [1994] 1 FLR 578 at 585. See also *Re C and V* [1998] 1 FLR 392 at 397.
[80] [2002] EWCA Civ 542.
[81] *Ibid*.
[82] [2006] 1 FCR 556 at 582.
[83] Above n 36, 69.
[84] *Ibid*.
[85] [2007] EWHC 1952 (Fam), [2008] 1 FLR 1015.

responsibility precisely because it was inappropriate for him to exercise parental responsibility in this situation; if the father were granted parental responsibility, he would inevitably seek to use it.[86] Another instructive example is *M v M (parental responsibility)*.[87] In this case, the father had very severe learning difficulties. Wilson J refused him a parental responsibility order, mainly on the basis that he was incapable of exercising parental responsibility:

> for example to weigh up the merits of rival schools or to balance the potential benefits and risks of a surgical operation.[88]

Wilson J stressed that parental responsibility was not trivial, following Butler-Sloss LJ[89] in emphasising its weight.[90] Even so, this was a highly unusual case, in which the father's disability unsettled the presuppositions on which parental responsibility is based.[91]

Moreover, the current government proposal to make parental responsibility compulsory for almost all fathers is inextricably linked to the diminishing parental authority element of parental responsibility.[92] Compelling almost all fathers to have parental responsibility would inevitably mean that those fathers who are unwilling, unavailable or seen as unsuitable to make decisions about the child's upbringing or otherwise exercise parental authority would be endowed with parental responsibility. The fact that the government regards this as a desirable outcome indicates the dwindling authority aspect of parental responsibility.

Indeed, if almost all unmarried fathers are compelled to hold parental responsibility, their parental responsibility will no longer even imply official approval of them,[93] at least as individual fathers.[94] Nevertheless, parental responsibility as legitimation will remain an important strand in the meaning of the term. Since the case law so far exclusively concerns unmarried fathers, it would be possible to regard this conceptualisation of parental responsibility as specific to unmarried fathers. However, I believe it is more general. Even if the government proposal is implemented, I expect a similar account of parental responsibility to emerge in step-parents' future applications for parental responsibility.

---

[86] [2008] 1 FLR 1015 at 1022–3.
[87] [1999] 2 FLR 737.
[88] *Ibid*, at 743.
[89] *Re S* [1995] 2 FLR 648 at 659.
[90] [1999] 2 FLR 737 at 743.
[91] *Ibid*, at 743.
[92] Department for Work and Pensions, above n 42.
[93] I am grateful to Kathryn Hollingsworth for this point.
[94] On the status of fatherhood generally, see R Collier, 'A Hard Time to Be a Father? Reassessing the Relationship Between Law, Policy and Family (Practices)' (2001) 28 *Journal of Law and Society* 520.

98   *Helen Reece*

The Shift in Reasons for Granting Parental Responsibility

Since the Children Act 1989, there has been a shift in the reasons given by the courts for granting unmarried fathers parental responsibility. In the earlier cases, the main reason for giving an unmarried father parental responsibility was to give him decision-making power. In the more recent cases, the reasons are less to do with decision-making and more to do with feelings and emotions.

In 1991, in the leading case of *Re H*,[95] which set out the criteria for granting parental responsibility orders, the question to be determined was the extent to which the father's parental rights needed to be enforceable for them to be granted. The Court of Appeal found no difficulty in disagreeing with the trial judge's view that parental rights should only be given if all the rights were immediately capable of being exercised.[96] However, the stronger argument against granting parental rights was that since the judge had already decided on the merits that the children would be freed for adoption irrespective of the father's opposition, there was little point in making a parental rights order just to give the father *locus standi* to oppose the freeing order: all that this would mean was that his parental rights and duties would be given and then immediately taken away. The Court of Appeal accepted the force of this argument. Their reason for rejecting it was to point to certain limited rights that a parent still had even after a child had been freed for adoption, for example to receive progress reports and to apply to revoke the freeing order in certain circumstances.[97] It was these residual rights that could later become of benefit to the father that justified making a parental rights order.[98] Feelings and emotions played no part in the Court of Appeal reasoning, not even warranting a mention in the judgment.

The following year, in *Re C (minors)*,[99] the Court of Appeal confirmed that unmarried fathers should be granted parental rights even if those rights were unenforceable, partly on the basis that married fathers with automatic parental rights might also be unable to exercise their rights for a variety of reasons. Although the court did make passing reference to the father's 'peace of mind'[100] as a hypothetical factor, their main reason for giving parental status to a father who could not exercise it was that this parental status would have 'real and tangible value ... as a status carrying with it rights in waiting':[101]

> Though existing circumstances may demand that his children see or hear nothing of him, and that he should have no influence upon the course of their lives for the time being, their welfare may require that if circumstances change he should be reintroduced

---

[95] [1991] Fam 151.
[96] *Ibid*, at 159–60.
[97] *Ibid*, at 160.
[98] *Ibid*, at 161.
[99] [1992] 2 All ER 86.
[100] *Ibid*, at 89.
[101] *Ibid*, at 89.

as a presence, or at least an influence, in their lives. In such a case a PRO, notwithstanding that only a few or even none of the rights under it may currently be exercisable, may be of value to him and also of potential value to the children.[102]

In the 1994 case of *Re G (a minor) (parental responsibility order)*,[103] the emphasis was still very firmly on decision-making. Balcombe LJ regarded the father's reason for seeking parental responsibility, that the father wanted to have 'the ability to have a say in the life of his child',[104] as a perfectly proper reason and wholly appropriate factor to take into account. He viewed it as clearly in the interests of the child that 'her natural father should be given a proper part to play in her life by being given a *locus standi*'.[105] Beldam LJ similarly based his judgment on decision-making:

> It must ... be in a child's interest that a devoted father should have the degree of involvement in her future given by a parental responsibility order, which would enable him to contribute to the promotion of her welfare and to play the natural part of her father in the future.[106]

The turning point came in 1995 with *Re S*,[107] which we have already seen marked a significant rupture between parental responsibility and parental rights.[108] In this case, Ward LJ introduced an entirely new reason for granting parental responsibility, which had never been given in any previous case. This was to confer upon the father a *stamp of approval*:

> I have heard, up and down the land, psychiatrists tell me how important it is that children grow up with good self-esteem and how much they need to have a favourable positive image of the absent parent. It seems to me important, therefore, wherever possible, to ensure that the law confers upon a committed father that stamp of approval, lest the child grow up with some belief that he is in some way disqualified from fulfilling his role and that the reason for the disqualification is something inherent which will be inherited by the child, making her struggle to find her own identity all the more fraught.[109]

Ward LJ also suggested that emphasis should be:

> placed upon children growing up in the knowledge that their father is committed enough to wish to have parental responsibility conferred upon him.[110]

---

[102] *Ibid*, at 89.
[103] [1994] 1 FLR 504.
[104] *Ibid*, at 508.
[105] *Ibid*, at 508–9.
[106] *Ibid*, at 510.
[107] [1995] 2 FLR 648.
[108] See above, text at nn 71 ff.
[109] *Re S* [1995] 2 FLR 648 at 657. See also *Re H* [1995] 2 FLR 883 at 889; and *Re C and V* [1998] 1 FLR 392 at 397.
[110] *Re S* [1995] 2 FLR 648 at 659.

100   *Helen Reece*

Later that year in *Re H*,[111] Ward LJ adopted similar reasoning, describing it as important, given the child's shock on discovering the truth about his paternity,[112] that:

> the benefits of the parental responsibility order ... be impressed upon the boy to give him the confidence that he has not suffered some life-shattering blow to his self-esteem.[113]

Likewise, in *Re M (contact: family assistance: McKenzie friend)*,[114] Ward LJ emphasized that:

> the important thing to recognize is that it is essential for the well-being of the children ... to begin to know that their father was concerned enough to make an application to be recognised as their father, and that his status as their father has the stamp of the court's approval.[115]

In the subsequent case of *Re H*,[116] Thorpe LJ took the same approach, granting the father parental responsibility, hedged with conditions, in the hope that this would benefit the child 'in years to come so that she knows she has two parents'.[117]

The stamp of approval reason in *Re S* marks the start of a process of psychologising the reasons for granting parental responsibility, of granting parental responsibility for therapeutic purposes. At this juncture, the therapeutic reasoning focuses on the child's needs. However, the extent to which a child's feelings and emotions would be affected by a legal order with no tangible effect on him or her is highly questionable.[118] Certainly, in the cases just mentioned, there was no hard evidence that granting or refusing parental responsibility to the father would affect the child's feelings in the manner depicted.[119] As Herring rightly points out, 'the order is more likely to affect the father's image of himself than his child's'.[120]

Therefore, there seems to be a certain logic in the main reason for granting parental responsibility in *Re D*[121] being that the *father* needed recognition:

> For Mr B, to be D's father is simply not enough; he wishes to be recognised as a father and a parent and he perceives that a parental responsibility order would bring this recognition.[122]

---

[111] [1995] 2 FLR 883.
[112] See above, text at n 53.
[113] [1995] 2 FLR 883 at 889.
[114] [1999] 1 FLR 75.
[115] *Ibid*, at 80.
[116] [2002] EWCA Civ 542.
[117] *Ibid*.
[118] See Herring, above n 13, 339.
[119] *Re S* [1995] 2 FLR 648; *Re H* [1995] 2 FLR 883 (CA); and *Re H* [2002] EWCA Civ 542.
[120] Herring, above n 13, 339.
[121] [2006] EWHC 2, [2006] 1 FCR 556.
[122] [2006] 1 FCR 556 at 561.

Mr B's motives for applying for a parental responsibility order are complex and I do not insult him by attempting to reduce their sophistication to a list for this judgment. I am quite satisfied that they do not include any trace of malice but have at their root his feelings for and about D and his wish to be recognised as belonging to her and to do all that he can towards securing her welfare.[123]

Once we have realised that the courts are on occasion deciding parental responsibility on the basis of adults' need for recognition, a hypothesis emerges as to why the apparently similar case of *Re B*[124] was decided differently. Arguably, in both *Re D* and *Re B*, the courts balanced the father's and the lesbian couple's need for recognition. In *Re D*, the balance came down in favour of granting Mr B parental responsibility partly because Black J was confident of the couple's robustness.[125] In contrast, in *Re B*, Hedley J found that granting the father parental responsibility would lead the couple to 'feel assailed and undermined in their status as parents'.[126]

It is highly regrettable that 'recognition' switches to considering adults' feelings and emotions in deciding whether to grant parental responsibility.[127] I have previously argued that adults' interests should be taken into account in deciding disputes about children,[128] and no doubt on occasions their needs should also be considered. However, in this instance the argument for granting parental responsibility is not that an adult needs the *effects* of a legal order, but that an adult needs the *legal order itself*, irrespective of any tangible effect. Truly, this is parental responsibility as legitimation.

In a different context, Andrew Bainham has aptly described this need to be recognised as 'status anxiety', a term he attributes to de Botton.[129] Bainham notes that while one prevalent view is that status is of decreasing importance, with a new emphasis on contract and the private ordering of family affairs,[130] the opposite is in fact the case, reflecting a contemporary desire to secure for family relationships the 'imprimatur of the law'.[131] In *Re D*, the father's need to be recognised was an illegitimate basis for giving him parental responsibility. Parental responsibility should not be granted in order to prevent adults feeling that the law has emotionally neglected them: parental responsibility should be awarded to adults if and only if they deserve parental responsibility.

---

[123] *Ibid*, at 581.
[124] [2007] EWHC 1952 (Fam), [2008] 1 FLR 1015.
[125] [2006] 1 FCR 556 at 575.
[126] [2008] 1 FLR 1015 at 1023.
[127] See McCandless, above n 36, 69.
[128] H Reece, 'Paramountcy Principle: Consensus or Construct?' (1996) 49 *Current Legal Problems* 267.
[129] A Bainham, 'Status Anxiety? The Rush for Family Recognition' in F Ebtehaj, B Lindley and M Richards (eds), *Kinship Matters* (Oxford, Hart Publishing, 2006) 47.
[130] *Ibid*, 47.
[131] *Ibid*, 48.

CONCLUSION

In this chapter I have argued that, so far as the allocation of parental responsibility is concerned, there is a trend away from parental responsibility as parental authority towards parental responsibility as nothing more than official approval, at least in some cases. While I have argued against the view that parental responsibility is at present an incoherent concept, it may be that the process of degrading parental responsibility will continue until parental responsibility is not so much incoherent as completely devoid of any meaning.[132] Certainly, some commentators have seen the decision in *Re D*[133] as being the first case to award 'pure status',[134] blurring the distinction between parenthood and parental responsibility by awarding parental responsibility simply on the basis of biological fatherhood.[135] Perhaps, if the government proposals to make parental responsibility compulsory for almost all unmarried fathers are implemented,[136] we will see parental responsibility come full circle to Eekelaar's original description of it as meaning nothing more than 'acting responsibly'.[137] However, if this happens, this phrase will not return to the meaning ascribed to it by Eekelaar, that parents are expected to behave responsibly.[138] Rather, 'acting responsibly' will have acquired the New Labour meaning that parents are regarded as needing support to behave responsibly.[139]

---

[132] See Bridgeman, above n 28, 242.
[133] [2006] EWHC 2.
[134] McCandless, above n 36, 67.
[135] C Lind, 'Responsible Fathers: Paternity, the Blood Tie and Family Responsibility' in Bridgeman, Lind and Keating, above n 28, 192. See also Herring, above n 13, 339.
[136] See above n 42.
[137] Above n 25.
[138] *Ibid*.
[139] See Bridgeman, above n 28, 242. See further V Gillies, 'Meeting parents' needs: discourses of "support" and "inclusion" in family policy' (2005) 25 *Critical Social Policy* 70; and V Gillies, 'Perspectives on Parenting Responsibility: Contextualizing Values and Practices' (2008) 35 *JLS* 95.

22

LEGISLATING FOR SHARED TIME PARENTING AFTER SEPARATION: A RESEARCH REVIEW

BELINDA FEHLBERG, BRUCE SMYTH, MAVIS MACLEAN AND CERIDWEN ROBERTS

ABSTRACT

This article reviews research on post-separation shared time parenting and on outcomes of legislating to encourage shared time parenting, drawing mainly on Australian experience. The research shows that children benefit from continuing and regular contact with both parents when they cooperate, communicate, and have low levels of conflict. However, there is no empirical evidence showing a clear linear relationship between the amount of parenting time and better outcomes for children. Rather, positive outcomes have more to do with the characteristics of families who choose shared time and who can parent cooperatively and in a child-responsive way. In contrast, research post-2006 legislative change in Australia encouraging shared parenting suggests use of shared time by a less homogenous group, including a marked increase in shared time orders in judge-decided cases. This is of concern as emerging Australian research also suggests that shared care is more risky for children than other arrangements where there are safety concerns, high ongoing parental conflict, and for children younger than 4 years. Australian research also reveals widespread misunderstanding of the law, leading many fathers to believe that they have a right to shared time and many mothers to believe that they cannot raise issues relevant to children's best interests, especially family violence. Overall, the research points to the complexity in legislating to encourage shared time parenting and shows that subtle changes can have important effects.

INTRODUCTION

Shared parenting time after separation (defined in this paper as the child spending at least 30 per cent of nights with each parent)[1]

The authors thank the colleagues who provided valuable feedback on earlier drafts. This paper draws on a Briefing Paper prepared for the Department of Social Policy and Intervention, University of Oxford, and funded by the Nuffield Foundation.

continues to attract much policy and community interest, both in the UK and more broadly, due mainly to pressure from fathers' groups. For example, currently in the UK, there are two private members bills before the Parliament aimed at introducing presumptions to increase fathers' time with their children after separation.[2] The Ministerial Taskforce on Childhood and the Family is looking at ways of encouraging agreements about shared parenting, while the Family Justice Review's (2011) Interim Report has argued against legislation that 'creates or risks creating the perception that there is an assumed parental right to substantial shared time or equal time for parents' (p. 159). Meanwhile in Australia, legislative changes introduced in 2006 to encourage shared time continue to be the subject of intense research focus and scrutiny.

The wider backdrop to these developments is that in many Western countries, including those without legislative intervention, shared time arrangements have been steadily increasing over the past decade, particularly among cooperative parents, as part of broader social and cultural change, including women's greater workforce participation and increasing involvement of fathers in their children's daily lives. However, the pace of change within families is less rapid than we might like to think (Australian Institute of Family Studies, 2010) and consistent with this, shared time arrangements remain unusual, both in countries without legislative intervention like the UK[3] and in jurisdictions that have legislated to encourage it such as Australia[4] and the US state of Wisconsin.[5] While there is still a lot we do not know about shared time arrangements and interpreting the research is not straightforward (Gilmore, 2006; McIntosh, 2009; Smyth and Wolcott, 2003; Trinder, 2010), the evidence so far does not suggest that changing the law to encourage shared time leads more families to enter shared time arrangements, let alone 'workable' arrangements (ie manageable for parents and appropriate for children's needs at different points in their childhood). For example, there was no spike in shared time arrangements in the *general* population of separated parents after the Australian changes in 2006, and the most significant increase in incidence has been in *litigated* cases, which although a small slice of the separating population are of significant concern because they are likely to be characterised by high ongoing parental conflict—a contra-indicator of workable shared time parenting (discussed later in this article).

A further aspect of the wider backdrop is that while governments in Western countries are increasingly being called on to legislate for shared time, few jurisdictions have so far done so. Overall, the legislative trend has been more clearly and consistently towards encouraging both parents to be actively involved in their children's lives post-separation, including maximising contact, rather than specifically towards legislating for shared time. UK developments have followed this trend: during the passage of the 2006 Children and Adoption Act through parliament, proposals to introduce a legislative presumption of minimum contact were debated and subsequently rejected, while reforms aimed at maximising contact when in the best interests of the child were enacted. A non-prescriptive approach sits alongside increasing community and legal recognition of diverse family forms, including cultural diversity.

Ongoing interest in legislating for shared time parenting is, however, understandable. After all, '50/50' (or thereabouts) seems 'fair' to children and parents—especially non-resident parents (mostly fathers). On the other hand, what seems fair to fathers may be viewed as disruptive and even damaging to children, especially by some resident parents (mostly mothers). In reality, children's and parents' lives and preferences are varied, complex, and evolving. Each child and each family is different and a 'one size fits all' approach ignores diversity (Lye, 1999; Ricci, 1997). All this makes any proposal to legislate for shared parenting time a highly charged and contested issue. It is also a very important issue as any legislative shift, however subtle, may have far-reaching consequences for children and their parents (Allen and Brinig, 2011).

Yet there are also some points on which most people (including researchers) agree. These include that it is good for children to maintain continuing and regular contact with both parents when they cooperate and communicate and have low levels of conflict (Ahrons, 2004; Hunt and Roberts, 2004; Johnston et al, 1989; Lamb, 2005; Pryor and Rodgers, 2001; Ricci, 1997; Shaffer, 2007).

However, valuing and facilitating the ongoing role of both parents in their children's lives in most cases is different from *legislating for* shared time. The former is accepted as a 'given' throughout this article. Our focus is on what the key research tells us about the benefits and risks of *legislating for shared time*. We look at Australia more closely because its 2006 shared parenting changes go further than many other countries and have been the subject of detailed research and evaluation. Overall, the research points to the complexity in legislating to encourage shared time parenting and shows us that subtle changes can have important effects.

WHEN DO CHILDREN DO BEST?

Research consistently shows that the best interests of children after parental separation are most strongly connected to the quality of parenting they receive, the quality of the relationship between their parents, and practical resources such as adequate housing and income—not any particular pattern of care or amount of time (Irving and Benjamin, 1995; Lye, 1999; Moyer, 2004; Pryor and Rodgers, 2001; Shaffer, 2007; Smyth and Wolcott, 2003).

For example, Amato and Gilbreth's (1999) statistical review of 63 studies on parent–child contact and children's well-being found that the *quality* of contact is more important than the *frequency* of contact. Good outcomes for children were more likely when non-resident fathers had positive relationships with their children and had an 'active parenting' approach, including both warmth and setting boundaries. Drawing on interviews with 173 adult children of divorced parents in the USA, Ahrons (2004) found that:

[Children] were far less concerned about the specific number of days per week or month they spent living with one parent or the other than they were about how their parents' relationship infused the emotional climate surrounding their transitions between parental households . . . . Most of all, what children want is to have relationships with both of their parents. They want to feel safe and secure. . . . (pp 66–67)

Of course, some time is needed to sustain close relationships. It has also been suggested that children benefit from a range of activities with non-resident fathers who are actively involved in their children's daily lives (Dunn et al, 2004; Whiteside and Becker, 2000; see also Lamb and Kelly 2001). But the research is not clear on just how much time is needed or optimal for children. There is no empirical evidence showing a clear linear relationship between shared time and improving children's outcomes (Shaffer, 2007; Smyth, 2009). While it has been recently argued that '[a]n emerging consensus is that . . . a minimum of one third time is necessary to achieve [the benefits of two involved parents] and that benefits continue to accrue as parenting time reaches equal (50–50) time' (Fabricius et al, 2010: 227–28) the evidence offered is drawn from studies focusing on shared parental *responsibility* rather than shared *time* parenting, so does not support this claim.

Bauserman's (2002) US review comparing joint and sole custody is frequently used as evidence that children in shared time arrangements are significantly better off than those in sole custody. However, his review does not distinguish between 'consensual' and court-imposed shared time parenting, and most of the studies relied on were unpublished student theses. Bauserman's analysis was also unable to deal with 'self-selection' effects—meaning that, as a group, families who voluntarily opt for shared time parenting tend to have characteristics that make positive outcomes for their children more likely, independent of their parenting arrangements (Bruch, 2006; Emery et al, 2005).

WORKABLE SHARED TIME: WHAT HELPS?

Shared time parenting is likely to work well when arrangements are child-focused, flexible, and cooperative. These same characteristics also mean that parents are likely to move away from shared time to accommodate their children's evolving needs and wishes.

The research suggests that families with such arrangements tend to involve parents with features not typical of the broader separating population. These features include being tertiary educated, being socio-economically well-resourced, having some flexibility in working hours, living near each other, fathers who have been involved in children's daily care prior to separation and children of primary school age (although the features present vary from case to case) (Irving and Benjamin, 1995; Masardo, 2009; McIntosh et al, 2010; Shaffer, 2007; Singer, 2008; Smyth, 2004). Studies also repeatedly find that parents in this group have agreed to shared time arrangements without recourse to lawyers or the courts (Irving and Benjamin, 1995; Rhoades et al, 2000; Shaffer, 2007; Smyth, 2004).

Children's views of shared time arrangements vary but are broadly consistent with research findings on workable shared time. They are more likely to feel positive when shared time arrangements are flexible and child-focused when their parents get along and when they have input into decisions about their living arrangements (Cashmore et al, 2010; Haugen, 2010; Lodge and Alexander, 2010; McIntosh et al, 2010; Neale et al, 2003; Pruett and Barker, 2009; Smart et al, 2001).

Children's experiences of moving between households are influenced by a similar range of factors. According to a recent Australian study, frequent moves between households 'bring added practical difficulties . . . in terms of having to pack up and move from house to house, physically and emotionally' (Cashmore et al, 2010: 108), but the level of difficulty depended on a range of factors including the distance between homes, frequency of moves, level of conflict between parents, and the child's personality and preferences (Cashmore et al, 2010; Haugen, 2010; Tucker, 2006).

However, shared time families do not comprise a single homogenous group, even in countries that have not legislated for shared time. The research suggests that without legislation, it is mainly—but not exclusively—cooperative flexible parents that opt for shared time but also that some parents with high ongoing conflict use it too (e.g., Smart and Neale, 1999; Smyth, 2004). The existence of a highly conflicted group has certainly been alluded to in the UK context:

Co-parenting, then, is not necessarily the product of shared commitment to its ethos but may represent an uneasy compromise or deadlock in a context where neither parent has managed to assert authority over the other. (Smart and Neale, 1999: 60)

WHEN IS SHARED TIME UNWORKABLE FOR CHILDREN?

The 'warning flags' for when shared time parenting is not workable (meaning that the stress and burden for children outweighs the benefits for them) are essentially the flipside of those that facilitate it: in particular, high ongoing parental conflict, family violence and abuse, and rigidity. Early indications of these factors began to emerge from US research in the mid-1980s (eg Steinman, 1983; see also Elkin, 1991).

Of course, highly conflicted and highly cooperative parents represent two extremes on the continuum of separated parents. Unfortunately, we lack clear information about the workability of shared time for families in between these extremes (Chisholm, 2001; Haugen, 2010) and the extent to which they are influenced by the 'radiating messages' of legislative change (Dewar, 2004; Parkinson, 2011; Walker, 2003). At present, we simply do not have the evidence 'to establish where the balance of advantage lies' (Hunt and Roberts, 2004: 6) for a large proportion of the separating population.

A more pressing question is whether there are factors that, when present, make shared time *more* damaging for children than other parenting arrangements. There is increasing evidence that shared time arrangements present particular risks for children when mothers express ongoing 'safety concerns', where there is high ongoing parental conflict and when children are very young—or some combination of these.

1. SAFETY CONCERNS

Recent Australian research has found that where mothers report safety concerns, child well-being is lower regardless of the care arrangement, but that the position is worse for children in shared time arrangements than in more traditional contact arrangements (Kaspiew et al, 2009). In the same study's sample of 10,000 recently separated parents registered with the Child Support Agency, a significant minority of mothers and fathers with shared time arrangements (16–20per cent) expressed safety concerns for themselves and their children (Kaspiew et al, 2009). Although self-defined by participants in the study, most who reported 'safety concerns' also described physical or emotional abuse by the children's other parent. While these trends were not as clear when the same respondents were followed up 1 year later (Qu and Weston, 2010), a similar link between lower child well-being and mothers' safety concerns was found in another recent Australian study (Cashmore et al, 2010).

2. HIGH ONGOING CONFLICT

There is strong evidence that high ongoing post-separation parental conflict is damaging for children (Cummings and Davies, 1994; Emery,

1982; Fabricius and Luecken, 2007; Grych and Fincham, 1990; McIntosh, 2003; Reynolds, 2001; Shaffer, 2007). There is also growing evidence that shared time arrangements involving ongoing high levels of parental conflict are more damaging than other parenting arrangements with entrenched high conflict.

For example, two recent Australian studies identified a link between shared time arrangements involving high conflict and poor outcomes for children (cf Kaspiew et al, 2009). The first study, by McIntosh et al (2010), focused on a high conflict sample and found that:

Children's experience of living in shared care over 3–4 years was associated with greater difficulties in attention, concentration and task completion by the fourth year of the study. Boys in *rigidly* sustained shared care were the most likely to have Hyperactivity/Inattention scores in the clinical/borderline range. (p 14)

The study also found that children in shared time arrangements reported higher levels of parental conflict than other children and were more likely to report feeling caught in the middle of the conflict. Across this high conflict sample, children in shared time arrangements were the ones least happy with their parenting arrangements and most likely to want to change them. For example, 43 per cent of children in continuous shared time arrangements said that they wanted more time with their mother compared with 7–21 per cent of children in other arrangements (McIntosh et al, 2010: 49).

We also know that children often feel responsible for their parents' happiness, believe they should share themselves and want to avoid parental conflict. As a result, children who are unhappy with their shared time arrangements may be very reluctant to raise the possibility of changing these arrangements (Cashmore et al, 2010; Haugen, 2010; Neale et al, 2003, Singer, 2008; Tucker, 2006) and may be left to 'absorb the pressures' (Neale et al, 2003).

It has been suggested that to avoid harm to children in shared time arrangements, parental conflict needs to at least be 'contained' (see, eg Emery et al, 2005). At a minimum this requires 'passive cooperation', involving not 'demonising' the other parent in front of children or using children as 'messengers' or 'spies' (Smyth et al, 2004). But this is likely to be difficult to achieve because ongoing high conflict is often a sign of deeper problems between parents. For instance, when parental acrimony is high (ie parents despise each other and lack respect for each other as people and as parents), conflict also tends to be high and ongoing (McIntosh and Long, 2006). Under these conditions, children are likely to be 'caught and used' in any conflict (Johnston et al, 1989: 579) and shared time arrangements are particularly likely to be harmful to them. 'Parallel parenting' (where separated parents have minimal interaction with each other, including the avoidance of direct handovers) is sometimes suggested as a means of containing high parental conflict, but clinicians generally agree that parallel parenting places additional strain on children (Ricci, 1997: 116; Seddon, 2003; Tucker, 2006; see also Birnbaum and Fidler, 2005).

3. YOUNG CHILDREN

There has been debate, particularly in the USA, about whether shared time parenting is developmentally risky for infants and young children (eg Solomon and George, 1999; cf Kelly and Lamb, 2000, Warshak, 2000; see also McIntosh et al, 2010). Recent Australian research, drawing on national random samples—albeit with a predictably small number of infants and young children in shared time arrangements—found in the affirmative:

[R]egardless of socio-economic background, parenting or inter-parental cooperation, shared overnight care of children under four years of age had an independent and deleterious impact . . . (McIntosh et al, 2010: 9)

This finding challenges the view that cooperation and goodwill are enough to make shared time 'work' regardless of children's developmental stage. Rather, these new data suggest that shared time arrangements have special risks for children younger than 4 years.

SHARED FINANCES AND SHARED PARENTING?

Any discussion of shared time parenting raises important questions about money. Does legislating for shared time encourage more strategic bargaining over parenting time, child support and property division? Does shared time encourage fathers to financially support their children? (Fabricius et al, 2010) Or is it a means of minimising child support liability and gaining access to a larger property settlement? (Fehlberg et al, 2009; Haugen, 2010; Singer, 2008; Singer and Reynolds 1987–88) To what extent do parents trade-off time, money, and property (eg do some mothers not pursue child support or a property settlement in order to avoid fathers seeking shared time)? Where reductions in child support payments occur at different thresholds of parenting time, will parents focus on the financial implications of reaching those thresholds rather than on their children's welfare?

Researchers have just begun to explore these questions, which are not easy to answer empirically, mainly because motivations are often complex and hard to assess. However, recent Australian research suggests that negotiation and trade-offs between children, money, and property occur across the board, including in cooperative circumstances, and that they may undermine or facilitate positive ongoing relationships

(Fehlberg et al, 2010; Smyth et al, 2010). In the UK, Bell et al's (2006) study of links between parenting time and money suggested that parents often sought to avoid conflict by making child support concessions.

Another question is whether the tendency of shared time arrangements not to last and for children to 'drift' back to primary mother care over time (Juby et al, 2005; Kaspiew et al, 2009; Maccoby and Mnookin, 1992; McIntosh et al, 2010; Smyth et al, 2008) means that property settlements reached when shared time is in place will result in longer-term economic disadvantage for separated mothers and children and increased social security costs.

Currently, there is little research on the financial implications of shared time parenting. The research that has been done suggests that consistent with research findings in the child support context (Melli, 1999), shared time does not necessarily lead to fathers providing greater financial support for their children (Fehlberg et al, 2010; Singer, 2008). Qualitative evidence suggests that mothers in shared time arrangements often carry more of the responsibility than their former partners for management of children's daily lives, including paying school-related expenses, medical, and dental costs (Cashmore et al, 2010; Fehlberg et al, 2009; Lacroix, 2006). Other recent data collected in 2009 from a large national random sample of 623 adolescents in separated families found that everyday expenses were usually paid by the parent they lived with for most of the time (Lodge and Alexander, 2010). In the case of equal time parenting, the 'vast majority' of adolescents said that both parents made a contribution to their everyday expenses.

LEGISLATING TO ENCOURAGE SHARED TIME PARENTING: THE AUSTRALIAN EXPERIENCE

The headline finding of the major evaluation of Australia's 2006 shared parenting changes was that 'overall the recent reforms are working well for the majority of children and their parents' (Australian Institute of Family Studies, 2009). However, a careful reading of this along with other Australian research suggests the risks rather than the benefits of legislating for shared time.

1. BACKGROUND TO THE 2006 SHARED PARENTING CHANGES

In 2006, significant reforms were introduced in Australia to encourage and support shared time parenting (Family Law (Shared Parental Responsibility Act 2006 (Cth)). The changes were part of a major overhaul of the entire family law system, including wide-ranging procedural changes (most notably, the introduction of compulsory pre-filing mediation in most cases as well as new services and 'less adversarial' court processes) and a new child support scheme (Commonwealth of Australia, 2003; Fehlberg and Maclean, 2009; Ministerial Taskforce on Child Support 2005; Parkinson, 2007).

The stated reason for parenting law reform was concern about 'father absence'—around one quarter of the one million children younger than 18 years with a parent living elsewhere in Australia sees that parent less than once a year or never (although this has gradually improved over time, from 30 per cent in 1997 to 24 per cent in 2010: Australian Bureau of Statistics, 1998, 2004, 2008, 2011). While the changes were the result of formal and detailed inquiry and consultation, politically, fathers' groups played a key role in prompting these review processes and in shaping the amendments (Parkinson, 2010; Rhoades, 2006).

The 2006 shared parenting changes operate as two interrelated—and complex—steps (Fehlberg and Behrens, 2008; O'Brien, 2010). First, a presumption that equal shared parental *responsibility* is in the best interests of children was introduced. The presumption does not apply in cases involving family violence or child abuse and can be rebutted by evidence that equal shared parental responsibility would not be in the child's best interests. Second, when a court decides to make an order for equal shared parental responsibility, it must also consider whether it would be in the best interests of the child and 'reasonably practicable' to order *equal time* or *substantial and significant time* with both parents.

2. EVALUATING THE CHANGES: THE AUSTRALIAN EXPERIENCE

A large research program was funded by the Australian Government to monitor the impact of the 2006 changes. As a result, a shared parenting evidence base has developed in Australia after rather than before the 2006 changes. By far the largest study is the AIFS Evaluation (Kaspiew et al, 2009), which was funded by the Australian Government as part of the 2006 family law reform package.

A. Key Findings

Three key findings emerged from the post-2006 Australian research on shared time parenting.

1. There has been a marked increase in judicially imposed shared time.
2. Complex legislation has led to professional and community misunderstanding that the law says, 'The starting point is shared time'. While professional views vary, family lawyers are most likely to

emphasise that this has encouraged: (i) increased focus on parents' (especially fathers') rights over children's best interests and (ii) increased reluctance of mothers to disclose violence and abuse.
3. Family members' experiences of shared time arrangements vary depending on who is being interviewed.

Key finding 1: increase in judicially imposed shared time. Before the Australian 2006 changes, it appeared that shared time was mainly used by a small minority of parents who parented cooperatively with the resources to make it workable, with a gradual increase in incidence over the past decade (see, eg Smyth, 2004).

Both before and after the reforms, the majority of separating parents in Australia do not go to court, and of those who do only a small minority have judge-determined arrangements (around 10 per cent of those who file for final orders in the Family Court of Australia (2010)). Most shared time (and other) parenting arrangements are reached mainly through discussion between parents (Kaspiew et al, 2009). In the broader separated parent population, shared time arrangements have continued to gradually increase post-2006 but remain unusual (around 12 per cent, as noted earlier). However, following the changes, a marked increase in shared time arrangements has occurred in judicially determined cases (Family Court of Australia, 2009; Kaspiew et al, 2009), rising from 4 per cent to 34 per cent of cases where contact hours were specified (Kaspiew et al, 2009, 133).

Although numerically they represent a small minority of separating families, the marked increase in judicially imposed shared time arrangements is of concern because of the high level of conflict typically associated with fully litigated cases along with research consensus that workable shared time is more likely when parents operate cooperatively and flexibly. It is now well-documented that family violence and safety concerns, mental health problems, and issues related to drug, alcohol, and other addictions feature frequently in families using Australia's family law system (Kaspiew et al, 2009). Allegations of family violence and/or child abuse are raised in a majority of judicially determined cases (Kaspiew, 2005; Kaspiew et al, 2009; Moloney et al, 2007). Thus, as McIntosh and colleagues point out:

[t]he attributes that increase the likelihood of shared arrangements working smoothly ... are not typically characteristic of parents who litigate or otherwise require significant support to determine and administer their post-separation parenting plans (McIntosh et al, 2010: 30–31).

Concerns also surround the viability of court-imposed arrangements. The same researchers suggest that shared time arrangements reached by parents outside of formal dispute resolution processes may be more durable than other shared parenting arrangements, and note that when shared time arrangements were in place prior to mediation, they were twice as likely to last as shared time arrangements put in place for the first time in mediation (McIntosh et al, 2010). Consistent findings on a smaller scale were evident in Trinder's UK in-court conciliation study (Trinder et al, 2006). This said, durability is not an inherently 'good' or 'bad' thing—change may be indicative of a child-focused approach or of continuing conflict and upheaval. Rather, the suggestion here is that shared time negotiated without involvement of the family law system appears to be more workable and more long-lasting.

Early work in the UK (eg Eekelaar et al, 1977) and the USA (eg Gardner, 1991; Maccoby and Mnookin, 1992; Singer and Reynolds 1987–88;) suggested that shared time orders might be made by judges 'as a compromise solution' between warring parents (Eekelaar et al, 1977: 68). Maccoby and Mnookin considered their 'most disturbing finding' to be the tendency for shared time court orders to be 'used by high conflict families to resolve disputes' (p 159). There are some indications in qualitative research that shared-time-as-a-compromise in high conflict cases is occurring in Australia (eg Fehlberg et al, 2009) and also in Sweden (eg Singer, 2008) following legislative change encouraging shared time.

More broadly, Australian researchers have observed that post-2006, '[i]t is increasingly evident that shared care families are not a homogenous group' (McIntosh et al, 2010: 98; see also Smyth, 2009), meaning that that shared time arrangements now appear less uniformly consensual and cooperative. The AIFS evaluation found that:

there is a significant minority of children in shared care-time arrangements who have a family history entailing violence and a parent concerned about the child's safety, and who are exposed to dysfunctional behaviours (Kaspiew et al, 2009, Summary report: 11).

Approximately one quarter of the shared time arrangements described by parents separating post-2006 were in this category.

Key finding 2: legislative confusion and resulting risks. The research consistently identifies three risks flowing out of the Australian experience of legislating to encourage shared time parenting.

Mixed messages. The 2006 Australian changes grafted a shared parenting goal onto an existing 'best interests of the child' framework. The legislative goal(s) were not clearly stated and the drafting added significant new layers of complexity (O'Brien, 2010). This has produced considerable confusion for decision-makers, family law professionals, and families themselves (Chisholm, 2009; Fehlberg et al, 2009; Kaspiew et al, 2009).

The Australian experience suggests significant dangers in even subtle legislative encouragement towards shared time arrangements, such as references to 'equal' and 'time', which give litigating parents something new and concrete to fight about. A further problem is that although the legal starting point is equal shared parental *responsibility* or decision making, not *time*, drafting complexity has encouraged the distillation of a simple message: that the law now says there is a starting point of equal time (Chisholm, 2009; Fehlberg et al, 2009; Kaspiew et al, 2009). Given that the greatest increase in shared time arrangements has occurred in fully litigated cases, there is some basis for this belief.

Parental rights vs children's welfare. The AIFS evaluation found that the 2006 legislative changes have encouraged more fathers to seek shared time and more mothers to feel pressured into agreeing to it (Chisholm, 2009; Fehlberg et al, 2009; Kaspiew et al, 2009). These findings were based mainly on the perceptions of legal professionals and to a lesser extent, family mediators. Legal professionals were particularly likely to mention the difficulty involved in shifting client (especially father) expectations and achieving child-focused outcomes following legislative change. According to AIFS, a 'common view' among legal professions 'was that negotiation and litigation had become more focused on parents' 'rights' rather than children's best interests and needs' (Kaspiew et al, 2009: 216). There is some qualitative support, based on interviews with fathers and mothers, for these views (Fehlberg et al, 2009).

Disclosure of violence and abuse. Despite an increased emphasis on the significance of family violence and child abuse in the 2006 reforms, research has consistently indicated that mothers have felt discouraged from disclosing family violence and child abuse concerns partly because of their belief that there is a legal starting point of shared time, so there is no point disclosing violence—particularly given problems of proof and the risk of being viewed as an 'unfriendly parent' (Bagshaw et al, 2010; Chisholm, 2009; Fehlberg et al, 2009; Kaspiew et al, 2009).

Relevant here is the dual emphasis in the 2006 changes on the benefit to the child of having a 'meaningful involvement' with both parents and recognising family violence. While the new emphasis on 'meaningful involvement' suggested that 'attention should be paid to the quality of time parents spend with their children and not just to its quantity' (Fehlberg and Behrens, 2008: 242), these two key legislative objectives often compete for priority in litigated cases. The Australian Government's recognition that the right balance has not yet been achieved is evidenced by its introduction of a bill to amend the Family Law Act 1975 to prioritise the safety of children over meaningful relationships, encourage people to disclose evidence of family violence and child abuse and help members of the public and family law professionals to understand, disclose, and act on family violence and child abuse (Family Law Legislation Amendment (Family Violence and Other Measures) Bill 2011).

Key finding 3: divergent views and experiences: Fathers, mothers and children. Consistent with previous US research (eg Irving and Benjamin, 1995), the Australian research converges on the finding that most parents express satisfaction with shared time arrangements (Cashmore et al, 2010; Dickenson et al, 1999; Kaspiew et al, 2009). However, this overall finding conceals significant differences within the group. Thus, parents are more likely to be satisfied than children (Cashmore et al, 2010; McIntosh et al, 2010) and fathers are more likely to be satisfied than mothers (Cashmore et al, 2010; Fehlberg et al, 2009; Kaspiew et al, 2009; McIntosh et al, 2010). Mothers' satisfaction also varies according to the circumstances (eg declining where there is high conflict, safety concerns, or shared time has been court-imposed) (Cashmore et al, 2010; Fehlberg et al, 2009; Kaspiew et al, 2009), while fathers express satisfaction with shared time even in the face of ongoing high conflict (McIntosh et al, 2010). Children's dissatisfaction with inflexible shared time arrangements that involve high ongoing parental conflict appears consistent with mothers' views (McIntosh et al, 2010).

Most research, however, hinges on adults' reports of children's well-being. A careful reading of recent Australian research findings on children's well-being suggests that positive conclusions about shared time arrangements are being drawn out of data that more clearly suggest mixed outcomes (Cashmore et al, 2010; Kaspiew et al, 2009). For example, the AIFS evaluation found that children in shared time arrangements were doing 'no worse' or 'marginally better' than children in other arrangements (p. 273). However, the suggestion that children were doing marginally better was based solely on fathers' reports. Mothers' reports indicated no difference between shared time and primary mother residence. To complicate the story, teachers' reports suggested that children seemed to be doing best in primary mother residence. As noted earlier, it also seems that apparent advantages for children's well-being when in shared time have more to do with other factors associated with consensual shared time, such as socio-economic resources and parental characteristics (Cashmore et al, 2010).

CONCLUSIONS

The key points to emerge from our analysis of the research are as follows:

1. OTHER THINGS MATTER MORE THAN COUNTING TIME

Research consistently finds that the best interests of children are closely connected to parental capacities and skills and to practical resources, such as adequate housing and income. The quality of relationships between parents and between parents and their children, as well as the level of resources, are more important determinants of children's well-being than 'mathematised' parenting time (ie a myopic focus on time as a percentage, including 'equal' time).

2. POSITIVE OUTCOMES FOR CHILDREN IN SHARED TIME ARE MORE TO DO WITH THE SORTS OF FAMILIES WHO CHOOSE THIS ARRANGEMENT

There is no evidence establishing a clear link between shared time and better outcomes for children. Indeed, there is no clear evidence that any particular post separation parenting arrangement is most beneficial to children. Rather, there is consistent evidence that positive outcomes for children in shared time arrangements have more to do with the fact that families who opt for shared time parenting tend to be well-resourced and parent cooperatively, flexibly and without reference to lawyers or courts.

3. SHARED TIME IS WORKABLE FOR SOME FAMILIES BUT RISKY FOR OTHERS

Any parenting arrangement can be good or bad for children, depending on the circumstances. There is mounting evidence, however, that shared time is more risky for children than other parenting arrangements where there are safety concerns, where there is deeply entrenched inter-parental conflict and/or when children are very young. These circumstances are likely to be evident in cases where legislation needs to be used to make a decision. Ironically, legislation promoting shared time is likely to be most directly applied in contexts where shared time is least likely to be beneficial for children.

Society and families are ever-changing and that evolution is increasingly encouraging us toward more child-focused ways of fostering children's best interests post-separation. While shared time parenting is one of many possibilities, empirical support for legislating to prioritise shared time over other parenting arrangements is lacking. The more crucial project is to identify ways to assist separated parents to think laterally about arrangements that will best serve their children's changing needs (Chambers, 1984: 480).

NOTES

[1] Definitions of shared parenting vary widely. In the USA (where much of the relevant research has been conducted), the terms 'joint physical custody', 'dual residence', 'alternating residence',

and 'shared physical placement' are all used to describe shared time arrangements. These rarely mean 50/50 timeshare arrangements—rather, the research generally defines shared parenting time as an arrangement when children are with each parent between 30 per cent and 50 per cent of the time (Ellman et al, 2010). Australian legislative and research definitions of shared care reflect a similar range of time-sharing arrangements. Most of the recent Australian research defines shared care as children spending 35–65 per cent of nights with each parent (eg Cashmore et al, 2010; Kaspiew et al, 2009), consistent with child support reform. In contrast, the Family Law Act 1975 (Cth), which contains the provisions relevant to determining private law children disputes, refers to 'equal' time but offers a qualitative definition of 'substantial and significant time'. The way in which 'shared care' is defined is an important preliminary point because prevalence is affected by the definition adopted. For example, prevalence will be higher if shared care is defined as each parent having care of the child for at least 35 per cent of the time than if the threshold is set at 50 per cent of the time. Prevalence will also be higher if the definition is cast in terms of time rather than nights.

[2] In July 2010, Brian Binley MP introduced a Private Member's Bill, the Shared Parenting Orders Bill, which would introduce a presumption that shared parenting orders should be the default arrangement unless certain exceptions apply. In March 2011, Charlie Elphick MP introduced a second Private Member's Bill, the Children's Access to Parents Bill, which would introduce a presumption in favour of parent–child contact. Both were due to be read a second time in June 2011, but the House of Commons ran out of time and they were re-listed for their second reading on 9 September and 25 November 2011, respectively.

[3] Ermisch et al (2001) found 3.1 per cent of non-resident parents described equal time parenting, while Peacey and Hunt (2008) found that 12 per cent of respondents reported equal time parenting.

[4] In a recent major study, 7 per cent of respondents reported an equal time arrangement and 9 per cent reported a substantial shared time arrangement (Kaspiew et al, 2009: 25).

[5] Melli and Brown (2008), using court files, found that 32 per cent of divorce applications had substantial shared time; 22 per cent had equal time.

REFERENCES

Ahrons, C. (2004) *We're Still Family: What Grown Children Have to Say About Their Parents' Divorce*, New York: Harper Collins.

Allen, D. W. and Brinig, M. (2011) 'Do joint parenting laws make any difference?', *Journal of Empirical Studies* 8, 304–24.

Amato, P. R. and Gilbreth, J. G. (1999) 'Non-resident fathers and children's wellbeing: a meta-analysis', *Journal of Marriage and the Family* 61, 557–73.

Australian Bureau of Statistics (ABS) (1998) *Family Characteristics Survey 1997*, Catalogue No. 4442.0, Canberra: Australian Bureau of Statistics.

Australian Bureau of Statistics (ABS) (2004) *Family Characteristics Survey 2003, Australia*, Catalogue No. 4442.0, Canberra: Australian Bureau of Statistics.

Australian Bureau of Statistics (ABS) (2008) *Family Characteristics and Transitions, Australia, 2006-07*, Catalogue No. 4442.0, Canberra: Australian Bureau of Statistics.

Australian Bureau of Statistics (ABS) (2011) *Family Characteristics Survey 2009-10, Australia*, Catalogue No. 4442.0, Canberra: Australian Bureau of Statistics.

Australian Institute of Family Studies (2009) *Media Release: Evaluation of the 2006 Family Law Reforms Finds Mixed Results, 28 January*. Available at http://www.aifs.gov.au/institute/media/media100128.html

Australian Institute of Family Studies (2010) *The Best Start: Supporting Happy, Healthy Childhoods, Facts Sheet to Support 2010 National Families Week*. Available at http://www.aifs.gov.au/institute/pubs/snapshots/ssbrochure10/ssbrochure10.html

Bagshaw, D., Brown, T., Wendt, S., Campbell, C., McInnes, E., Tinning, B., Batagol, B., Sifris, A., Tyson, D., Baker, J. and Arias, P. F. (2010) *Family Violence and Family Law in Australia: The Experiences and Views of Children and Adults From Families Who Separated Post-1995- and Post-2006*, Canberra: Attorney-General's Department.

Bauserman, R. (2002) 'Child adjustment in joint-custody versus sole-custody arrangements: a meta-analytic review', *Journal of Family Psychology* 16, 91–102.

Bell, A., Kazimirski, A. and La Valle, I. (2006) *An investigation of CSA Maintenance Direct Payments: Qualitative study (Research Report No. 327)*, Leeds: The National Centre for Social Research on behalf of the Department for Work and Pensions.

Birnbaum, R. and Fidler, B. J. (2005) 'Commentary on Epstein and Madsen's "Joint Custody with a vengeance: the emergence of parallel parenting orders', *Canadian Family Law Quarterly* 24(3), 337–49.

Bruch, C. (2006) 'Sound research or wishful thinking in child custody cases? Lessons from relocation law', *Family Law Quarterly* 40, 281–314.

Cashmore, J., Parkinson, P., Weston, R., Patulny, R., Redmond, G., Qu, L., Baxter, J., Rajkovic, M., Sitek, T. and Katz, I. (2010) *Shared Care Parenting Arrangements since the 2006 Family Law Reforms: Report to the Australian Government Attorney-General's Department*. Sydney: Social Policy Research Centre, University of New South Wales.

Chambers, D. L. (1984) 'Rethinking the substantive rules for custody disputes in divorce', *Michigan Law Review* 83, 477–569.

Chisholm, R. (2001) *'Softening the Blow—Changing Custody to Residence'*. Paper given at The Third World Congress on Family Law and Children's Rights, Bath, England, 2001.

Chisholm, R. (2009) *Family Courts Violence Review*, Canberra: Attorney-General's Department.

Commonwealth of Australia (2003) *Every Picture Tells a Story: Report on the Inquiry into Child Custody Arrangements in the Event of Family Separation*, Canberra: Standing Committee on Family and Community Affairs.

Cummings, E. M. and Davies, P. T. (1994) *Children and Marital Conflict: The Impact of Family Dispute and Resolution*, New York: The Guilford Press.

Dewar, J. (2004) Regulating families' in Piper C., Scott C., Lacey N. and Braithwaite J. (eds), *Regulating Law*, Oxford: Oxford University Press, 83–84.

Dickenson, J., Heyworth, C., Plunkett, D. and Wilson, K. (1999) 'Sharing the care of children post-separation: family dynamics and labour force capacity'. Paper presented at the Family Strengths Conference, University of Newcastle.

Dunn, J., Cheng, H., O'Connor, T. G. and Bridges, L. (2004) Children's perspectives on their relationship with their non-resident fathers: influences, outcomes and implications', *Journal of Child Psychology and Psychiatry* 45, 553–66.

Eekelaar, J., Clive, E., Clarke, K. and Raikes, S. (1977) *Custody After Divorce: The Disposition of Custody in Divorce Cases in Great Britain*, Oxford: Oxford University.

Elkin, M. (1991) Joint custody: In the best interests of the family' Folberg J. (ed), *Joint Custody and Shared Parenting*, 2nd edn, New York: Guilford Press, 11–15.

Ellman, I. M., Kurtz, P. M., Weithorn, L. A., Bix, B. H., Czapanskiy, K. and Eichner, M. (2010) *Family Law: Cases, Text, Problems*, 5th edn, LexisNexis.

Emery, R. E. (1982) Interparental conflict and the children of discord and divorce, *Psychological Bulletin*, 92, 310–330.

Emery, R. E., Otto, R. K. and O'Donohue, W. (2005) A critical assessment of child custody evaluations: Limited science and a flawed system', *Psychological Science in the Public Interest* 6(1), 1–29.

Ermisch, J., Iacovou, M. and Skew, A. J. (2001) Family relationships' in McFall S. L. and Garrington C. (eds), *Understanding Society: Early Findings From the First Wave of the UK's Household Longitudinal Study*, Colchester, UK: Institute for Social and Economic Research, University of Essex, 7–14.

Fabricius, W. V., Braver, S. L., Diaz, P. and Velez, C. E. (2010) Custody and parenting time: Links to family relationships and wellbeing after divorce' in Lamb M. (ed) *The Father's Role in Child Development*, 5th edn, New Jersey: Wiley and Sons, 201–60.

Fabricius, W. V. and Luecken, L. J. (2007). Post-divorce living arrangements, parent conflict, and long-term physical health correlates for children of divorce', *Journal of Family Psychology* 21, 195–205.

Family Court of Australia (2009) Shared parental responsibility statistics—2008/2009, available at: http://www.familycourt.gov.au/wps/wcm/connect/FCOA/home/about/Court/Admin/Business/Statistics/SPR/FCOA_SPR_2008

Family Court of Australia (2010) *Annual Report 2009-2010*, Melbourne: Family Court of Australia.

Family Justice Review (2011) *Family Justice Review: Interim Report*, London: Ministry of Justice.

Fehlberg, B. and Behrens, J. (2008) *Australian Family Law: The Contemporary Context*, Melbourne: Oxford University Press.

Fehlberg, B. and Maclean, M. (2009) Child support policy in Australia and the United Kingdom: changing priorities but a similar tough deal for children?' *International Journal of Law, Policy and the Family* 23, 1–24.

Fehlberg, B., Millward, C. and Campo, M. (2009) Post-separation parenting in 2009: an empirical snapshot', *Australian Journal of Family Law* **23**(3), 247–75.

Fehlberg, B., Millward, C. and Campo, M. (2010) Post-separation parenting arrangements, child support and property settlement: exploring the connections', *Australian Journal of Family Law* **24**(2), 214–41.

Gardner, R. A. (1991) Joint custody is not for everyone' in Folberg J. (ed), *Joint Custody and Shared Parenting*, 2nd edn, New York: Guilford Press, 88–96.

Gilmore, S. (2006) Contact/shared residence and child well-being: research evidence and its implications for legal decision-making', *International Journal of Law, Policy and the Family* **20**(3), 344–65.

Grych, J. H. and Fincham, F. D. (1990) Children's appraisals of marital conflict: initial investigations of the cognitive-contextual framework', *Child Development* **64**, 215–30.

Haugen, G. M. (2010) Children's perspectives on everyday experiences of shared residence: time, emotions and agency dilemmas', *Children and Society* **24**, 112–22.

Hunt, J. and Roberts, C. (2004) *Child Contact With Non-Resident Parents Family Policy Briefing, 3*, Oxford: Department of Social Policy and Social Work, University of Oxford.

Irving, H. H. and Benjamin, M. (1995) 'Shared parenting: critical review of the research literature' in Irving H. H. and Benjamin M. (eds) *Family Mediation: Contemporary Issues*, 1st edn. Thousand Oaks, CA: Sage Publications, 229–76.

Johnston, J. R., Kline, M. and Tschann, J. M. (1989) Ongoing postdivorce conflict: effects on children of joint custody and frequent access', *American Journal of Orthopsychiatry* **59**, 576–92.

Juby, H., Le Bourdais, C. and Marcil-Gratton, N. (2005) Sharing roles, sharing custody? Couples' characteristics and children's living at separation', *Journal of Marriage and the Family* **67**(1), 157–72.

Kaspiew, R. (2005) Violence in contested children's cases: an empirical exploration', *Australian Journal of Family Law* **19**, 112–43.

Kaspiew, R., Gray, M., Weston, R., Moloney, L., Hand, K. and Qu, L. the Family Law Evaluation Team. (2009) *Evaluation of the 2006 Family Law Reforms*, Melbourne: Australian Institute of Family Studies.

Kelly, J. and Lamb, M. E. (2000) Using child development research to make appropriate custody and access decisions', *Family and Conciliation Courts Review* **38**(3), 297–311.

Lacroix, C. (2006) Freedom, desire and power: gender processes and presumptions of shared care and responsibility after parental separation', *Women's Studies International Forum* **29**, 184–96.

Lamb, M. E. (2005) 'Divorce and parenting' in Fisher C. B. and Lerner R. M. (eds), *Encyclopedia of Applied Developmental Science*, **Vol. 2**, Thousand Oaks, CA: Sage, 794–796.

Lodge, J. and Alexander, M. (2010) *Views of Adolescents in Separated Families: A Study of Adolescents' Experiences After the 2006 Reforms to the Family Law System*, Melbourne: Australian Institute of Family Studies.

Lye, D. N. (1999) *The Washington State Parenting Plan Study: Report to the Washington State Gender and Justice Commission and Domestic Relations Commission*, Washington State: Washington Courts.

Maccoby, E. E. and Mnookin, R. H. (1992) *Dividing the Child: Social and Legal Dilemmas of Custody*, Cambridge: Harvard University Press.

Masardo, A. (2009) Managing shared residence in Britain and France: questioning a default 'primary carer' model' in Rummery K., Greener I. and Holden C. (eds), *Social Policy Review 21: Analysis and Debate in Social Policy*, Bristol: Policy Press, 197–214.

McIntosh, J. (2003) Enduring conflict in parental separation: pathways of impact on child development', *Journal of Family Studies* **9**(1), 63–80.

McIntosh, J. (2009) Legislating for shared parenting: exploring some underlying assumptions', *Family Court Review* **47**(3), 389–400.

McIntosh, J. and Long, C. (2006) *Children Beyond Dispute: A Prospective Study of Outcomes From Child Focused and Child Inclusive Post Separation Family Dispute Resolution*, Canberra, ACT: Australian Government, Attorney-General's Department.

McIntosh, J., Smyth, B., Kelaher, M., Wells, Y. and Long, C. (2010) *Post-separation Parenting Arrangements and Developmental Outcomes for Infants and Children*, Canberra: Attorney-General's Department.

Melli, M. S. (1999) 'Guideline review: child support and time sharing by parents', *Family Law Quarterly* **33**, 219–34.

Melli, M. and Brown, P. R. (2008) Exploring a new family form—The shared time family', *International Journal of Law, Policy and the Family* **22**, 231–69.

Ministerial Taskforce on Child Support (2005) *In the Best Interests of Children—Reforming the Child Support Scheme*, Canberra: Commonwealth of Australia.

Moloney, L., Smyth, B., Weston, R., Richardson, N., Qu, L. and Gray, M. (2007) *Allegations of Family Violence and Child Abuse in Family Law Children's Proceedings: A Pre-reform Exploratory Study* (Research Report No 15), Melbourne: Australian Institute of Family Studies.

Moyer, S. (2004) *Child Custody Arrangements: Their Characteristics and Outcomes (Background paper: 2004-FCY-3E)*, Ontario: Department of Justice Canada.

Neale, B., Flowerdew, J. and Smart, C. (2003) 'Drifting towards shared residence?', *Family Law* **33**, 904–12.

O'Brien, R. (2010) 'Simplifying the system: family law challenges—can the system ever be simple?', *Journal of Family Studies* **16**, 264–70.

Parkinson, P. (2007) 'The future of child support', *University of Western Australia Law Review* **33**(2), 179–206.

Parkinson, P. (2010) 'Changing policies regarding separated fathers in Australia' in Lamb M. (ed), *The Father's Role in Child Development*, 5th edn, New Jersey: Wiley and Sons, 578–614.

Parkinson, P. (2011) *Family Law and the Indissolubility of Parenthood*. New York: Cambridge University Press.

Peacey, V. and Hunt, J. (2008) *Problematic Contact After Separation and Divorce? A National Survey of Parents*, London: One Parent Families/Gingerbread.

Pruett, M. K. and Barker, C. (2009) 'Joint custody: a judicious choice for families—but how, when and why?' in Galatzer-Levy R. M., Kraus L. and Galatzer-Levy J. (eds), *The Scientific Basis of Child Custody Decisions*, 2nd edn, New Jersey: Wiley, 417–62.

Pryor, J. and Rodgers, B. (2001) *Children in Changing Families: Life After Parental Separation*, Oxford: Blackwell Publishers.

Qu, L. and Weston, R. (2010) *Parenting Dynamics After Separation: A Follow-up Study of Parents Who Separated After the 2006 Family Law Reforms*, Melbourne: Australian Institute of Family Studies.

Reynolds, J. (ed) (2001) *Not in Front of the Children? How Conflict Between Parents Affects Children*, London: One Plus One Marriage and Partnership Research.

Rhoades, H. (2006) Yearning for law: fathers' groups and family law reform in Australia' in R. Collier and S. Sheldon (eds), *Fathers' Rights Activisim and Law Reform: A Comparative Perspective*, Oxford: Hart Publishing, 125–146.

Rhoades, H., Graycar, R. and Harrison, M. (2000) *The Family Law Reform Act 1995: The First Three Years*, Sydney: University of Sydney and Family Court of Australia.

Ricci, I. (1997) *Mom's House, Dad's House: Making Two Homes for Your Child*, New York: Simon and Schuster.

Shaffer, M. (2007) 'Joint custody, parental conflict and children's adjustment to divorce: what the social science literature does and does not tell us', *Canadian Family Law Quarterly* **26**, 286–313.

Seddon, E. (2003) *Creative Parenting After Separation: A Happier Way Forward*, Sydney: Allen and Unwin.

Singer, A. (2008) Active parenting or Solomon's Justice? Alternating residence in Sweden for children with separated parents', *Utrecht Law Review* **4**, 35–47.

Singer, J. B. and Reynolds, W. L. (1987–88) 'A dissent on joint custody', *Maryland Law Review* **47**, 497–523.

Smart, C. and Neale, B. (1999) *Family Fragments?* Malden, MA: Blackwell Publishers.

Smart, C., Neale, B. and Wade, A. (2001) *The Changing Experience of Childhood: Families and Divorce*, Cambridge: Polity Press.

Smyth, B. (ed) (2004) *Parent–child contact and post-separation parenting arrangements (Research Report No 9)*, Melbourne: Australian Institute of Family Studies.

Smyth, B. (2009) 'A five year retrospective of post-separation shared care research in Australia', *Journal of Family Studies* **15**(1), 36–59.

Smyth, B., Caruana, C. and Ferro, A. (2004) Fifty-fifty care' in B. Smyth (ed), *Parent–Child Contact and Post-separation Parenting Arrangements (Research Report No 9)*, Melbourne: Australian Institute of Family Studies, 18–29.

Smyth, B., Rodgers, B., Temple, J., Esler, M. and Shephard, A. (2010) *Bargaining and Negotiations Over Child Support and Parenting Time Among Separated Parents Registered With the Child Support Agency*. Paper presented at the 11th Australian Institute of Family Studies Conference, 7–9 July 2010, Melbourne.

Smyth, B., Weston, R., Moloney, L., Richardson, N. and Temple, J. (2008) 'Changes in patterns of parenting over time: Recent Australian data', *Journal of Family Studies* **14**(1), 23–36.

Smyth, B. and Wolcott, I. (2003) *Submission of the Australian Institute of Family Studies to the House of Representatives Standing Committee on Family and Community Affairs Inquiry into Child Custody Arrangements in the Event of Family Separation*, Melbourne: Australian Institute of Family Studies.

Solomon, J. and George, C. (1999) The place of disorganization in attachment theory in Solomon J. and George C. (eds), *Attachment Disorganization*, New York: Guilford Press, 3–32.

Steinman, S. B. (1983) 'Joint custody: what we know, what we have yet to learn, and the judicial and legislative implications', *University of California at Davis Law Review* 6, 739–62.

Trinder, L. (2010) 'Shared residence: a review of recent research evidence', *Child and Family Law Quarterly* 22(4), 475–98.

Trinder, L., Connolly, J., Kellett, J., Notley, C. and Swift, L. (2006) *Making Contact Happen or Making Contact Work? The Process and Outcomes of In-court Conciliation*, London: Department for Constitutional Affairs.

Tucker, A. (2006) 'Children and their suitcases', *Australian Family Lawyer* 18(4), 16–19.

Walker, J. (2003) 'Radiating messages: an international perspective', *Family Relations* 52, 406–17.

Warshak, R. A. (2000) 'Blanket restrictions: overnight contact between parents and young children', *Family and Conciliation Courts Review* 38(4), 422–45.

Whiteside, M. F. and Becker, B. J. (2000) 'Parental factors and the young child's post-divorce adjustment: a meta-analysis with implications for parenting arrangements', *Journal of Family Psychology* 14, 5–26.

Part: VI

Parental rights and the state

23

Licensing Parents Revisited

HUGH LaFOLLETTE

ABSTRACT *Although systems for licensing professionals are far from perfect, and their problems and costs should not be ignored, they are justified as a necessary means of protecting innocent people's vital interests. Licensing defends patients from inept doctors, pharmacists, and physical therapists; it protects clients from unqualified lawyers. We should protect people who are highly vulnerable to those who are supposed to serve them, those with whom they have a special relationship. Requiring professionals to be licensed is the most plausible way of doing that. Given the overwhelming support for the licensing of these professionals, I find it odd that so many people categorically reject proposals to license parents. Although the relationship between a parent and her children is different in some respects, it is also relevantly similar to that between a professional and those she serves. To defend these claims, I show how and why the rationale for licensing parents parallels the rational for licensing professionals. I then ask whether such a program could be justifiably implemented. Finally, I describe and reject what I see as the flawed view of the relationship between parents and their children.*

I have an idea. Let's stop requiring physicians to be licensed. The practice is unreliable because it does not guarantee that all doctors will be competent. It is unfair because it bars admission to some who would be competent or even excellent. Moreover, by limiting the number of physicians, we harm or seriously inconvenience some needing health care. Finally, the practice is intrusive. Those wanting to be physicians must study for years, work insane hours as residents, and take extensive exams. Even if they succeed, this will take a significant toll on them. If they fail, they are financially strapped and their goals are thwarted. Arguably it is unfair to prohibit people from fulfilling their dreams just because we predict that they would not be competent. To intervene because they merely risk harming others violates their rights.

We should also cease similarly flawed practices of licensing dentists, pharmacists, chiropractors, lawyers, counselors, and physical therapists. These licensing systems mistakenly admit some unqualified professionals and deny licenses to others who would be competent. Let's demolish these ineffective and invasive practices; let's remove the obstacles impeding those wanting to be professionals. Surely we can do that.

We could. However, that would be imprudent and immoral. For although these systems are far from perfect, and their problems and costs should not be ignored, they are justified as a necessary means of protecting innocent people's vital interests. Licensing defends patients from inept doctors, pharmacists, and physical therapists; it protects clients from unqualified lawyers. We should protect people who are highly vulnerable to those who are supposed to serve them, those with whom they have a special relationship. Requiring professionals to be licensed is the most plausible way of doing that. That is why most people desiring to be professionals embrace this rationale and are willing to demonstrate their competence.

Given the overwhelming support for the licensing of these professionals, I find it odd that so many people *categorically* reject proposals to license parents. Although the relationship between a parent and her children is different in some respects, it is also relevantly similar to that between a professional and those she serves.[1] Doubtless most objectors think that, despite obvious similarities, licensing parents relevantly differs from standard professional licensing. In my experience, though, objectors rarely spell out and defend this belief. In the end, I suspect that most objectors simply find the idea so odd that they assume that professional licensing must be legitimate while parental licensing is not — even if they cannot say why. I also think many people embrace, at least in attenuated form, a flawed view of the relationship between parents and children.

To defend these claims, I show how and why the rationale for licensing parents parallels the rational for licensing professionals. I then ask whether such a program could be justifiably implemented. Finally, I describe and reject what I see as the aforementioned flawed view of the relationship between parents and their children.

Theoretical Reasons for Licensing

The theoretical rationale for licensing certain activities has been with us for a long time; as stated in US law: 'When practice of a profession or calling requires special knowledge or skill and intimately affects public health, morals, order or safety, or general welfare, legislature may prescribe reasonable qualifications for persons desiring to pursue such professions or calling and require them to demonstrate possession of such qualifications by examination on subjects with which such profession or calling has to deal as a condition precedent to right to follow that profession or calling'.[2] Similar ideas are found in the laws of other developed countries.

Following this law, we can specify two conditions that theoretically justify licensing an activity:

- People are engaged in an activity that may harm those they serve, either directly or by failing to fulfil their fiduciary duties; the harm can be significant and life-altering.
- People can safely perform these risky activities only if they are competent.

These conditions, by themselves are powerful, but insufficient to justify licensing. They ignore the possibility that there are countervailing theoretical reasons against licensing (i.e. requiring licenses for certain activities). There is always one *general* (and in that sense, 'theoretical') countervailing reason against licensing: it is costly to society and individuals. Licensing, like all regulatory activities, is expensive and government coffers are not bottomless. It also limits people's options, and it does so not because the individual *will* harm others, but because she is *statistically likely* to do so. This general theoretical cost does not rule out all licensing. However, it places the burden of proof on those defending it. Defenders must show that the benefits of licensing would outweigh its costs. Thus, a program is theoretically justified only if it also satisfies a third condition:

- The benefits of the licensing program outweigh any theoretical reasons against it.

Let's examine each condition in more detail.

Actions Risky to Others

Most of our actions are relatively benign. What I choose to eat, read, where I choose to walk, and when I choose to sleep do not ordinarily put others are risk. That is why we do not and should not generally consider regulating these human behaviours. However, some activities regularly put innocent people at risk. The risk of significant harm is high when the parties have a special relationship like that between professionals and their patients or clients. Incompetent physicians can significantly harm their patients; ill-prepared lawyers may condemn their clients to imprisonment or financial ruin.

Professionals can cause so much harm because their clients are especially vulnerable to them. Few of us can accurately diagnose our own complex medical problems, give ourselves astute legal advice, or design our own bridges. So we must seek those with the requisite competence. We must entrust them with our health, life, financial security, infrastructure, freedom, etc. That is why we should license these activities. It is the most feasible way of protecting vulnerable citizens.

People Can Safely Perform Risky Activity Only If They Are Competent

These professionals can perform their tasks efficiently and safely only if they have the relevant knowledge, abilities, judgment, and dispositions.

Knowledge

A professional cannot safely carry out her role unless she has basic facts ready to hand. A physician cannot diagnose or propose treatments for diseases or conditions of which she is ignorant. An attorney cannot make plausible arguments or file compelling motions if she does not know rules of evidence, legal procedure, or the relevant statutory, common, and judicial law. Of course we cannot specify exactly what she must know to perform each task competently. However, we know that a professional needs considerable knowledge before she can perform her tasks competently, and even more knowledge to perform them excellently.

Abilities

Bare knowledge does not guarantee competence. The professional also needs certain skills. A surgeon must have steady and accurate hands. Competent attorneys need verbal and written facility. We do not know exactly which skills — and to what degree — a professional needs to perform her tasks. However, we know that she can perform her professional tasks competently only if she has considerable abilities; she needs even greater skills to perform them excellently.

Judgment

It is not enough for an aspiring professional to have the requisite knowledge and abilities; she also needs judgment to make appropriate decisions. A physician must use her knowledge and abilities to decide whether the rash she sees is a common and innocent cellulitis or a rare and dangerous necrotizing fasciitis.[3] If she does not know, she must know where to find that information; otherwise, her patient may die. An attorney must decide which of two motions to make before Judge Jones. If she makes the wrong motion, the client may lose her livelihood or freedom. A civil engineer must decide which bridge design is strongest given the local geology and climate. If she chooses the wrong design, people may die when the bridge collapses. Of course we cannot exactly know the nature and extent of judgment that a professional needs. Still, we do know that if someone's judgment is severely defective, then she cannot reliably, competently, and safely carry out her professional tasks.

Dispositions

Even if someone has the requisite knowledge, ability, and judgment, she may lack the appropriate dispositions; that makes her unlikely to regularly perform her tasks competently. An incurious physician may not take the time to use her knowledge and abilities to correctly diagnose a potentially lethal condition. An insufficiently self-critical lawyer may fail to see that she is not vigorously defending her client because the client unconsciously reminds her of a mean-spirited elementary (primary) school teacher. Of course we do not know exactly which dispositions — and to what degree — any professional must have. Still, we know that if she has (or lacks) certain dispositions, then she is less likely to perform her tasks competently.

In short, the nature and extent of knowledge, skills, judgment, and dispositions that a professional needs vary from profession to profession and from task to task within the same profession. Nonetheless, we know that a competent professional needs some degree of each. That is why it is so important for us to license her. That will not guarantee that she never harms her clients. It would, however, make it less likely.

Theoretical Costs Do Not Outweigh Its Benefits

All licensing programs cost money. All limit individual choices. They admit some ill-prepared professionals and deny licenses to others who are qualified. Since the former are incompetent, they will harm some they serve. Since the latter are denied access to a job they desire, they are harmed. Because these are general features of all licensing programs, this is best seen as a theoretical cost of licensing, an explanation of why we need good reasons for licensing an activity.

At least one scholar has argued that these costs are so high that we should not tolerate licensing.[4] Few buy this view. For as significant as these 'theoretical' costs are, we continue to license physicians because we think it is a necessary means of protecting innocent individuals from risk. Without licensing '[Q]uacks [will] abound like locusts in Egypt'.[5]

No licensing system could be perfect. If we set the requirements for a license very high in an effort to guarantee that no incompetent people are licensed, then we will reject a larger number of deserving candidates. If we lower standards to decrease the chance that deserving candidates are excluded, we increase the number of incompetent applicants who are licensed. This is unfortunate, but not surprising. It is what we should expect as fallible creatures in a complicated world.

There may also be special costs of some licensing programs. After first explaining the rationale for licensing parents, I will discuss one purported special cost of licensing parents.

Why License Parents?

The reasons for licensing parents are the same as those for licensing people seeking entrance into the paradigm professions.

Parenting Is Risky

As a group, children are the most vulnerable members of a society. That is why it is especially important that someone shield them from harm. Normally parents bear this responsibility. They should protect their children from physical harm and provide for their basic needs. Not all parents do what they should do. Some directly harm their children; others harm their children by failing to fulfil their fiduciary duties to them. Since a parent has almost exclusive control of her children over many years, children are especially vulnerable to their parents.

The Costs to Children Are Substantial

We license physicians because they can seriously, and sometimes permanently, harm their patients. Parents can likewise significantly, pervasively and irrevocably harm their children. There are nearly two million cases of *substantiated* child abuse and neglect in the US each year.[6] Authorities speculate that the real number of incidents is three times higher.[7] One national study found that each year one in seven children is abused or neglected.[8] That number is rising, at least in the United States.[9] Parents were responsible for nearly 80% of child maltreatment, while their unmarried partners account for another 4%.[10] Some portion of the remaining cases could have been prevented by adequate parental supervision.

The results are devastating. In the US, more than four children a day die from abuse and neglect.[11] Others suffer significant long-term physical effects. 'Individuals who have been maltreated during childhood are more likely to develop diabetes, cancer, cardiovascular disease, et cetera'.[12] Recent studies suggest 'that childhood traumatic stressors represent a common pathway to a variety of long-term behavioural, health, and social problems' including premature death.[13] Many others are emotionally scarred for life.[14]

The damage does not stop with the victims. Their maltreatment affects how they will treat others when they grow up. They are far more likely to abuse their own children,[15] and they are more likely to become criminals. Some researchers claim that child abuse creates 'an additional 35,000 violent criminals and more than 250 murderers'.[16] Others found that 'child maltreatment roughly doubles the probability that an individual engages in many types of crime'.[17] This is much higher than the effects of factors normally thought to cause criminality — including unemployment and crack cocaine use (Currie & Tekin, 2007, p. 20).

Someone might wonder why I focus on abuse and neglect.[18] After all, a parent may fail to love, care for, encourage, and guide her children in many ways, ways that can cause them serious harm. We all know adults haunted by memories of an inattentive, self-absorbed, or unsympathetic parent. Why not focus on *these* parental failings? There are two reasons. One, as the statistics in the previous paragraphs reveal, harms from abuse and neglect are typically highly significant. Working to prevent them will yield the greatest benefits with the least intrusion. Two, although we might disagree about the appropriateness of some parental behaviours, we can all agree that abuse and neglect are inappropriate. This is a similar approach we take when evaluating professionals. We hope that our system of training and licensing will yield a professional who not only does not harm her patients or clients, but significantly promotes their interests. Nonetheless, our primary aim is to ensure that a physician does not directly harm her patients, or seriously (i.e. negligently) fails to care for their medical interests. It is sensible to do the same with parenting. That explains why we should legally focus on abuse and neglect. At the same time, we should urge a parent to do more than simply not maltreat her children; we should find ways to empower her to provide the care, direction, support, and love her children need.[19]

The Need for Competence

We license professionals because they need knowledge, abilities, judgment, and dispositions to competently discharge their tasks. A parent needs similar characteristics to competently rear her children.

Knowledge

A parent cannot adequately care for her children if she does not know — or know how to meet — their needs. If she does not understand infants' biological needs, she may fail to provide appropriate nutrition or she may feed them something dangerous (e.g. peanuts). If a parent is ignorant about childhood diseases, she might overreact to a minor problem while ignoring a potentially lethal one (e.g. Reyes Syndrome). If a parent does not know the importance of introducing young children to language, she may hinder their development. Or course no parent knows all that she must know. We should not set impossibly high standards. Still, a parent needs a basic repository of knowledge if she has any hope of adequately caring for her children.

Abilities

Since no parent can know everything, she needs the ability to find information she lacks. She must know where to look or whom to ask, and she must have the intellectual wherewithal to comprehend what she finds. When children are very young, the parent also needs the physical ability to feed them, change their diapers, cuddle them, etc. We cannot specify all abilities that a parent must have. However, we know that someone lacking most of these cannot adequately care for a child by herself.

Judgment

A parent needs more than a repository of knowledge and an array of physical and intellectual abilities. She needs to be able to use these to make wise judgments about the care of her children. She must be able to judge what food to introduce when, how to discipline them, and how to develop their intellectual and social skills. Of course some fine parents have less judgment than others; we should not hold parents to impossibly high standards. Still, we know that the less judgment a parent has, the more likely she will harm or inadequately care for her children.

Disposition

A parent with knowledge, abilities, and judgment may still put her children at risk if she lacks the appropriate intellectual and emotional dispositions. If she is impatient, easily frustrated, or violence prone, she might hit her children. If she is excessively self-absorbed, she may not reliably provide adequate care. If she is inattentive or insufficiently self-critical, she may not notice the ways that she ignores or downplays her children's needs. Of course, we should not expect too much from a parent. Still, the more deficient a parent's dispositions, the more likely that she will harm her children, the less likely she is to love them or adequately fulfil her fiduciary duties to them.

At some point the risk of neglect, abuse, or other malfeasance becomes sufficiently great that we should consider intervening. That is why we must consider licensing parents.

Theoretical Objections to Licensing Parents

All licensing programs cost money, have false positives and false negatives, and limit people's options. However, this does not stop us from licensing physicians, lawyers, or engineers; we think the benefits of these programs outweigh their costs. Neither should these costs stop us from licensing parents. The risks to children (and the adults they will become) of ignorant, bungling, maladapted, or malicious parents are widespread and significant — likely as great as the risks to patients being treated by incompetent physicians. Barring any special considerations, the theoretical reasons for licensing parents are as strong as those for licensing professionals.

Parenting Differs from the Paradigm Professions

Some objectors claim that parenting relevantly differs from the paradigm professions. Although there are some disanalogies between these practices, these differences do not undermine the theoretical case for licensing parents. Let me explain.

Someone might claim that we license those in the paradigm professions because they can harm large numbers of patients or clients; in contrast, although a parent can harm her children profoundly, the number of children she can harm is relatively small. However, I do not see that or how this undercuts the theoretical argument for licensing. One, the general rationale for licensing does not depend on a professional being able to harm large numbers of people, but only that she can profoundly harm those she serves. Two, some professionals serve only one or a small number of clients. Three, children are more vulnerable to their parents than patients are to (most of their) doctors. Since children are with their parents longer and in more varied circumstances, then the opportunities for a parent to harm her children are especially high. Four, whereas patients can (usually) leave their physicians, lawyers, etc. to find another; children cannot normally leave their less-than-competent parents. These differences strengthen — not weaken — the case for licensing parents.

Perhaps, though, the objector has something different in mind. She may think that people have a right to their children, whereas people do not have a right to be professionals.

A Right to Have Children

Many think people have the right to be parents and that this right bars any parental licensing program. To assess this claim we must first disambiguate it. It could mean three different things:

- If people are able to procreate, then no one should forbid them from doing so (right to procreate).
- If people have children under their control (whether by procreation or other means), then no one should forbid them from rearing them (negative right to rear).
- If people are incapable of having children, then the state (or others) should provide them with a child (positive right to rear).

Do people have a right to procreate? Even if they do, the right is not unqualified. A man does not have a right to father 500 children just so he can be recognized in *Guinness Book of World Records*. Of course there are reasons why we should be leery of coercively limiting procreation. Nonetheless, any plausible right to procreate has to be 'contingent [on their] having or making some feasible plan for their children to be adequately reared by themselves or by willing others'.[20] However, if an adult has made plausible plans, then arguably she has a strong — albeit qualified — right to procreate. Many people desperately want children. If licensing were to limit procreation, then thwarting people's desires is a cost of the program that should not be disregarded or discounted. I say more about this cost in the next major section of the paper.

What about a positive right to rear? Some people talk in ways that might suggest there is such a right. However, the only plausible related right is a right of access to reproductive services.[21] That is far short of a robust positive right to children. I don't know any serious thinker who avers that the state must give children to any person who wants them. Even if there is a positive right to rear, it, like the previous one, would have to be qualified in the same ways that a negative right to rear must be.

A Negative Right to Rear

Does a parent have a right to rear the children under her control, without interference from the state? Although it would be disastrous if the state regularly interfered in the day-to-day decisions of parents, it is implausible to think that parents have an unqualified negative right to rear. For sure, some parents disagree. In several cases chronicled by DeCourcy and DeCourcy,[22] parents thought that it was not only permissible, but also mandatory, for them to beat their children. However, even if they were sincere we would not — and should not — let them act on that belief. That is why we have laws against child abuse.

That is why, if there were such a negative right to rear, it must be qualified. Law and morality forbid a parent from abusing her children. It mandates that she have her children vaccinated for common childhood diseases (unless explicitly excused) and that she insure they are educated. We need not pretend that these requirements are precisely specified or perfectly enforced. Nonetheless, they reflect our unflagging belief that any right to rear children under one's care must be qualified.[23]

This qualified right resembles the right to become a professional. Jerri's right to become a physician is conditional on her demonstrating the requisite competence. The right, although qualified, is significant because it forbids any ad hoc bar to her being a physician. The qualification is critical because it protects those she serves, those especially vulnerable to her. Jerri's right to parent is also qualified. The right, although conditional, is significant because it forbids any ad hoc prohibition against her being a parent. The qualification is critical because it protects children, those especially vulnerable to her.

Is the Right Conditional only on Actual Abuse?

Someone might claim that the right is conditional not on our *predicting* that she will abuse and neglect her children, but only on her *actually* abusing or neglecting them. However, since this is not true of professional licensing, barring special considerations, there is no reason to think this should be true of parental licensing either. Moreover, this objection assumes that licensing laws are an arm of the criminal law. In the criminal law, we standardly punish people only if they actually commit a crime, not because we judge that they are likely to do so.

However, this objection misconstrues the nature of and rationale for licensing. Although both the criminal law and licensing aim to protect innocent people, they seek this end in importantly different ways. Even though the aim of the practice of punishment is to protect citizens by curbing crime, we punish individual criminals (actions falling under that practice) because of their actions, not primarily to protect others. In that sense the criminal justice system is retributive, past oriented.[24] In contrast, licensing programs are future-directed in both aim and execution. Not only are the programs designed to protect innocent people from risky actions, the decision to bar a specific person from becoming a physician, lawyer, or engineer is also future-oriented. We deny her a license because we think she is ill-equipped to serve the clients or patients with whom she would have a special relationship.

We see the same contrast if we compare reasons for licensing a parent with those for punishing an abusive one. We punish an abusive parent for what she did; we would license parents to protect children. This difference is manifested in different judgments a court might make against an abusive parent. The court might imprison the parent or it might remove her children. It would do the former to punish her. It would do the latter to protect the children. In the latter cases, the court predicts that she would likely re-abuse her children. Doubtless this prediction is based largely on her past actions. But not entirely. Courts sometimes leave children with their abusive parents. In so doing the courts show that we can employ other factors to predict a potential parent's future behaviour. It is akin to laws forbidding an 11-year-old from rearing a child by herself. We bar her from being a parent at that age, not because she previously abused children, but because we think she lacks the requisite knowledge, abilities, judgment, and disposition. This shows that we already recognize that the negative right to rear children is qualified. So does the practice of adoption.

Adoption

It is neither easy nor cheap to adopt a child. An aspiring parent must apply to an adoption agency. The agency scours her background and financial records, and then conducts home visits. These intrusive procedures are designed to protect children, to increase the chance that they will have supportive, loving, and stable homes. The results are impressive. Because of the trauma children face before they are adopted, many have problems. Yet they are less than half as likely to be maltreated compared to children reared by their biological parents.[25] Of course adoption programs are not perfect. They exclude some people who would have been fine parents, let some abusive parents adopt, and there is intentional abuse of the system.

Yet we continue to use this process because we think its benefits are greater than the costs. That gives us powerful reason to think that the licensing of parents is at least theoretically defensible. Notice, too, that the purported disanalogies between being a professional and being a biological parent are equally disanalogies between being a professional and being an adoptive parent. The disanalogies do not show that adoption programs are impermissible. Nor do they show that a program of licensing parents is theoretically indefensible.

Others may claim, though that the relevant difference is between natural parenting and adoption. They may think biological parents have a natural affection or love for their children and that the strength of this affection makes it unlikely that a parent will maltreat her children. Even if many parents do feel a natural affection for their children, this is insufficient to keep all biological parents from maltreating their children. Nearly 92% of parental abusers are biological parents.[26] Other studies indicate that biological parents are no better parents than their adoptive counterparts.[27] Consequently, if we continue current adoptive practices — and certainly we should — we are rationally compelled to establish a licensing program for all parents unless we have special reasons for thinking there are unique practical problems with licensing parents.

The Argument So Far

I have argued that it is theoretically appropriate to license parents. That does not yet show that we should establish a licensing program. We must still decide if it is practical. Nonetheless, this tentative conclusion is extremely important. It shows that we should regulate parenting (a) if we can specify criteria for a competent parent, (b) if we have moderately accurate methods for determining competence, and (c) if there are no special reasons for thinking that the program's costs exceed its benefits. If any of these conditions is not satisfied, then we should not license parents. However, were that so, we should lament it since, by not regulating parenting, we subject innocent children to significant risks. Therefore we should diligently seek ways to more accurately determine competence while lowering regulatory costs.

The Practicality of Licensing: Worries about Implementation

Many who object to licensing parents claim that we cannot satisfy all (or any) of these conditions. I am not so pessimistic.

Criteria of Competence

A competent parent must be knowledgeable, and have the requisite abilities, judgment, and dispositions. The problem is specifying the precise nature and degree of each quality required. Nonetheless, although there is a continuum of possibilities, there are crystal clear cases at the extremes and many clear cases in between. A competent parent must have enough intelligence to identify and know how to satisfy children's basic needs. She requires the abilities and judgment to meet those needs. And she must have the appropriate dispositions: she cannot be violent or exceedingly self-absorbed. We can, of course, disagree about the degree of each trait necessary to be a competent parent. However, they must have them all in some degree.

There are other traits about which thoughtful people might disagree, in part because they disagree about the central goals of child-rearing. Feinberg — and more recently Brighouse and Swift — argue that a parent should rear her children in ways that promote their autonomy when they become adults.[28] Nonetheless, this claim is sufficiently contentious that we should not immediately make it a legal criterion for obtaining a parenting license. We should permit some experiments in parenting just as we should permit 'experiments in living'.[29] We cannot fully specify criteria for being a good parent. We also cannot exhaustively specify criteria for a good physician or lawyer. However that does not prevent us from licensing these professionals. Neither should this prevent us from licensing parents.

Determining whether Prospective Parents Meet Those Criteria

Determining whether prospective parents meet these criteria is difficult but not impossible. We know competent parents need a modicum of intelligence, and we have ways of identifying those with significant mental limitations. We know they need some knowledge about children and child development. We can test for that. We have tests to determine if someone is violent or exceedingly self-absorbed; these would identify the most dangerous potential parents. We have even more fine-grained tests, but arguably nothing that gives us the predictive power we might want before establishing a robust licensing program. However, we should not put too much weight on this. After all, we have made little effort to identify the requisite knowledge, abilities, judgment, and dispositions that competent parents need. The first attempt to do something in this ballpark — the 'Child Abuse Potential Inventory' — appears to be reasonably accurate.[30] With further study we could likely devise a reliable test.[31]

Costs and Benefits of Licensing

Even if that were true, some think the costs of licensing parents would be too high. They aver that the program would be intentionally abused by unscrupulous or biased bureaucrats and unintentionally abused by inattentive ones. I was concerned about this possibility when I wrote the original essay thirty years ago. I am more worried now. Events of the past decade made me more aware of ways that an administration can take a sensible goal (controlling terrorism) and pervert it. Other administrations could pervert the legitimate aims of a robust parental licensing program.

I wonder, though, whether these worries are sufficient to reject parental licensing. After all, I know that adoption programs favour rich, white Christians, yet I am not tempted to scupper them and let aspiring parents 'adopt' (i.e. purchase) children at the local superstore. Rather, I think adoption programs do considerable good that we could not achieve in any other way. I do not want to forego these gains. I would prefer to alter adoption policies to avoid ignorance, bias, and hanky-panky. We should do the same with a general parental licensing program.

In doing so, however, we should not forget the costs of parental licensing. For many people, the desire to have a child is central to their sense of self. That is not a reason to categorically reject licensing. After all, we think adoption agencies should not let unacceptable applicants adopt, even if they have strong desires to parent. Nonetheless, recognizing the strength and centrality of this desire gives us reason to move cautiously before instituting parental licensing on a grand scale.

An Intermediate Conclusion

Licensing parents is theoretically appropriate. We can categorically reject parental licensing only by rejecting the licensing of all professionals. That would be imprudent and immoral. Still, we have reasons to worry about mistakes within or abuse of the system. Additionally, a sizable segment of the population would vehemently resist a robust licensing program. That resistance could easily undermine the program's aims.

However, we should not stand by and do nothing. The costs to children are too high. So how to proceed? One approach, advocated by David Archard, is to seek a less intrusive means of achieving (roughly) the same results.[32] If there were such means, I would support them. Unfortunately, I fear this strategy would fail to protect children or would (partly) succeed only by instituting unacceptably intrusive measures. First, as I understand this scheme, it would not limit incompetent parents until they had already harmed children. That resembles forbidding someone from practicing medicine only after she had harmed patients. Taking this approach would thus undermine a key aim of licensing parents.[33] Second, 'extensive' monitoring can damage the parent-child relationship in the same ways that that monitoring can alter any intimate relationship.[34] This is a cost we should try to avoid.

In short, we need more than mere monitoring, although we would be wise to employ relatively unintrusive means. So I propose a limited licensing scheme. Try it out and see if it works. Depending on what we find, we can jettison it, sustain it, or expand it.

A Limited Licensing Program

What would a limited licensing program look like? I am no social engineer, so I cannot say with any certainty. Here, though, is one option: set minimal requirements for a license, then reward those with licenses — say with special tax breaks — rather than punish those without. This could entice most prospective parents to seek licenses, while being less intrusive than a more robust scheme. This approach would resemble one insurance companies employ to encourage adolescents to take a driver's education course. Insurance companies give lower rates to adolescents who successfully complete driver's education. Few people complain about these programs. They see them as an attractive way to lower their rates. If we give tax breaks to licensed parents, then prospective parents might see a license as a benefit rather than a burden.

The centrepiece of this program might be free-standing or high school parenting courses. People successfully completing the course would be licensed. If the course were rigorous, it would insure that more parents have vital knowledge about children's needs and development. Perhaps some people think this is not a serious problem: they think most parents have sufficient knowledge to competently rear their children. They are mistaken. A recent study discovered that one-third of US parents lack basic knowledge about child-care and development.[35] Parents lacking such knowledge are far less likely to have quality interactions with their children. This will make parents more frustrated with their children, and subsequently more likely to abuse or neglect them.

What, though, could this course do to insure that parents have the appropriate abilities, judgment, and dispositions? Enhancing people's abilities and judgment could be a significant aim of the course. Although there is no simple test for these traits, we can find ways to insure that prospective parents don't wholly lack them. The fourth is more difficult to assess. Still, we might try this: students might take a self-graded personality inventory. The teachers could then discuss the potential problems parents with certain personality traits might have caring for children.

This system would give most people a reason to seek a license. If the program gained public support, even those who failed the course would feel social pressure to retake the course before becoming parents.

This approach would not be problem-free. It arguably favours the rich since they are better able to forego the tax breaks. However, most wealthy people will want these tax breaks as much as anyone else. Therefore, I think this could be a relatively cheap, relatively effective, and a relatively unintrusive way of lessening abuse and neglect and generally improving children's lot. Still, we might worry that children will suffer. Since unlicensed parents will pay more money in taxes, then they will have less money to care for their children. Nonetheless, if the tax breaks for licensed parents were sufficiently large — larger, say, than the current deduction for dependents — then parents will be motivated to become licensed. Moreover, children in licensed families will be financially better off than they are currently.

Additionally, we might establish a program to assist — and, as a side effect, monitor — parents with young children, say a scheme like the UK Health Visitors program.[36] This program assigns a nurse to every home in the country with a child under five. The nurse is available for home visits to examine and care for the child, and to offer advice on nutrition, parenting, development, etc. This is a service many people find beneficial. When providing this supportive care, the nurse can watch for potential problems. If there is an immediate and pressing problem, she can initiate an intervention. That is especially important since nearly half of all maltreatment involves children less than four years of age.[37]

Finally, we can protect children indirectly by strengthening public education, expanding health care, and bolstering children's services. For even if some parents are likely to abuse or neglect their children come what may, many who maltreat their children do so while economically, socially, or interpersonally stressed. A strong 'safety net' would lessen parental stress.

If after some years, we see that this multi-faceted approach fails, we can jettison or modify it. On the other hand, if it is successful, we could consider trying something more robust. Nonetheless, this would be a serious start that would avoid many costs of a full-bore licensing program and would be more likely to garner significant public support.

Some might contend that this approach loses the appeal of a more developed licensing program, and that it abandons the view advanced in my original paper. I reject both contentions. First, there are compelling reasons to worry about starting a rigorous parental licensing scheme. We need to move incrementally as we did with professional licensing generally; those schemes were not implemented all at once, but emerged and morphed over decades.[38] Second, the central aim of the original paper was to argue that licensing is theoretically justified. I thought that getting people to acknowledge *that* would be significant since doing so would, among other things, undermine the familiar view that children are their parents' property.

Children as Property

Once we brush away extraneous considerations, most who categorically reject parental licensing do so because they think it fails to recognize a parent's 'natural dominion' over her children. English common law — on which most US law is founded — explicitly treated children as their father's property.[39] In some countries, this view of children is still widely accepted. In western countries that view is rarely openly embraced, but it still shapes many people's views of children.[40] In the original paper, I described this 'natural dominion' view thusly:

> [P]arents legitimately exercise extensive and virtually unlimited control over their children. Others can properly interfere with or criticize parental decisions only in unusual and tightly prescribed circumstances — for example, when parents *severely* and *repeatedly* abuse their children. In all other cases, the parents reign supreme.[41]

Although I thought that view was lurking just beneath the surface, I assumed few would openly acknowledge its sway. However, Albert Mohler, president of the most prestigious seminary of the US's largest Protestant denomination, finds that the above description 'of parental rights and parental authority is both concise and accurate. Indeed, belief in parental sovereignty over children has been one of the most important means by which the state has acknowledged the primacy of the family, and thus the limits of its own power'.[42] For every person like Mohler, who openly acknowledges this view of children, I have no doubt that there are many more who silently embrace it.

Jettisoning the belief in natural dominion will eliminate attitudes, dispositions, and laws that make abuse more likely by leading parents to believe their interests are paramount.[43] Attenuating this belief will make parents more willing to seek assistance and encourage them to give children a serious voice in shaping their futures.

This view is closely linked to another dangerous view, namely that biological parents have a special moral claim to their children, a claim that outweighs the interests of children in all but rare cases.[44] This leads child protection agencies to assume it is almost always best to reunite children with their biological parents. It leads parents and the states to ask irrelevant questions and make detrimental decisions. Consider the following fictional case: two babies are inadvertently swapped at birth. When they are twelve years old, the parents discover the error. Should the parents exchange children so that each now has 'theirs'? I would hope not. If they did, that would show that something was profoundly wrong with them as parents. In any meaningful sense the child they have been rearing *is* 'theirs'. Unfortunately, the law would likely support a parent who wanted 'her' child 'returned'. This is a view of children we must abandon.

Conclusion

The theoretical reasons for licensing are compelling. Acknowledging them forces us to rethink parent-child relationships, to reject the idea that parents have natural dominion over their children. This will not insure that parents are always loving, caring, knowledgeable, and supportive. But it will help. I also think there are reasons to try a moderate form of licensing. This is better than leaving children in the hands of ignorant, selfish, inept, short-sighted, and short-fused parents.

Hugh LaFollette, University of South Florida St. Petersburg, 140 7th Ave. S., St. Petersburg, FL 33701, USA. hughlafollette@tampabay.rr.com

Acknowledgements

For their time, insight, support, and feedback, I am indebted to David Archard, William Aiken, David Benatar, Jeffrey Gold, George Graham, Chris Hackler, Eva LaFollette, James Rachels, Adam Swift, members of the University of Tennessee Philosophy Department, and two anonymous reviewers for this journal.

NOTES

1 Although this is the offspring of 'Licensing parents' (*Philosophy and Public Affairs* 9 (1980): 182–97), it is a new essay. Rather than summarize the original essay and then respond to criticisms point by point, I through-composed it. This should make it easier for readers to follow, especially those unfamiliar with the earlier essay. The view taken here differs somewhat from the one I advanced earlier. The argument has also been corrected, expanded and revised throughout, largely in response to criticisms.
2 50 SE 2nd 735 (1949). Earlier statements of the same idea can be found at 199 US 306, 318 (1905) and 123 U8 623, 661 (1887).
3 A. Gawande, *Complications: A Surgeon's Notes on an Imperfect Science* (New York: Henry Holt and Company, 2002), pp. 229–48.
4 D. B. Hogan, 'The effectiveness of licensing: History, evidence, and recommendations', *Law and Human Behaviour* 7,2/3 (1983): 117–138.
5 As quoted in R.H. Shyrock, *Medical Licensing in America, 1659–1965* (Baltimore, MD: The Johns Hopkins Press, 1967), p. 5.
6 US Department of Health and Human Services, *Child Maltreatment 2006* (Washington, DC: US Department of Health and Human Services, 2008), p. xiv.
7 Childhelp, *National Child Abuse Statistics* (Scottsdale, AZ: Childhelp, 2005).

8 D. Finkelhor et al., 'The victimization of children and youth: A comprehensive, national survey', *Child Maltreatment* 10,1 (2005): 5–25, at p. 10.
9 Associated Press, 'Report: Child-abuse deaths rising', *MSNBC.com* (2009), http://www.msnbc.msn.com/id/33405080.
10 US Department of Health and Human Services op. cit., Table 5-2.
11 US Department of Health and Human Services op. cit., p. 65.
12 Centers for Disease Control, 'Transcript: Press conference on maltreatment of infant study', (2008), http://www.cdc.gov/od/oc/media/transcripts/2008/t080403.htm (statement by Dr. Illeana Arias).
13 D.W. Brown et al., 'Adverse childhood experiences and the risk of premature mortality', *American Journal of Preventive Medicine* 37,5 (2009): 389–396, at p. 395.
14 P. DeCourcy & J. DeCourcy, *Silent Tragedy* (Sherman Oaks, CA: Alfred Publishing Company, 1973).
15 R. J. Gelles, 'Child abuse as psychopathology: A sociological critique and reformulation', *American Journal of Orthopsychiatry* 43,4 (1973): 611–621, at p. 619.
16 Fight Crime, 'New hope for preventing child abuse and neglect: Proven solutions to save lives and prevent future crime', (Washington, DC: Fight Crime: Invest in Kids, 2006), p. 4.
17 Janet Currie & Erdal Tekin. 'Does child abuse cause crime?', *NBER Working Paper* (2007), p. 20.
18 In this essay I rely on a common understanding of child abuse and neglect. Those seeking a more detailed account could examine the World Health Organization's attempt to define these terms in their 2006 report (Geneva: WHO Press) found online at: http://whqlibdoc.who.int/publications/2006/9241594365_eng.pdf). I do not see that or how minor squabbles about definition affect the argument herein.
19 L. Cassidy, 'That many of us should not parent', *Hypatia: A Journal of Feminist Philosophy* 21,4 (2006): 40–57.
20 O. O'Neill, 'Begetting, bearing, and rearing' in O. O'Neill & W. Ruddick (eds) *Having Children: Philosophical and Legal Perspectives on Parenthood* (New York: Oxford University Press, 1979), p. 25.
21 D. W. Brock, 'The Moral Bases of a Right to Reproductive Freedom' in P. Tittle (ed.) *Should Parents Be Licensed?* (Buffalo, NY: Prometheus Books, 2004), pp. 224–29.
22 DeCourcy and DeCourcy, op. cit.
23 H. Brighouse & A. Swift, 'Parents' Rights and the value of family', *Ethics* 117 (2006): 80–108, at p. 105.
24 J. Rawls, 'Two concepts of rules', *The Philosophical Review* 64 (1955): 3–32. Rawls distinguishes the justification of a practice from the justification of actions falling under that practice.
25 Compare these sources: R. Barth, 'The value of special needs adoption' in R. J. Avery (ed.) *Adoption Policy and Special Needs Children* (Westport, CT: Auburn House, 1997); and US Department of Health and Human Services op. cit. Table 5-4.
26 US Department of Health and Human Services, op. cit.
27 L. Hamilton, S. Cheng & B. Powell, 'Adoptive parents, adaptive parents: Evaluating the importance of biological ties for parental investment', *American Sociological Review* 72 (2007): 95–116.
28 J. Feinberg, 'The child's right to an open future' in W. Aiken & H. LaFollette (eds) *Whose Child?: Children's Rights, State Power, and Parental Authority* (Totowa, NJ: Rowman & Littlefield, 1980), pp. 124–53; Brighouse & Swift, op. cit. I have made similar arguments in: 'Circumscribed autonomy: Children, care, and custody' in J. Bartkowiak & U. Narayan (eds) *Having and Raising Children* (State College, PA: Penn State University Press, 1999), pp. 212–37; and in 'Freedom of religion and children', *Public Affairs Quarterly* 3 (1989): 75–87.
29 J. S. Mill, *Utilitarianism*, ed. G. Sher (Indianapolis, IN: Hackett, 1979), p. 54.
30 C. P. Mangel, 'Licensing parents: How feasible?' in P. Tittle (ed.) *Should Parents Be Licensed?* (Buffalo, NY: Prometheus Books, 2004), p. 106.
31 Michael T. McFall discusses this is and other tests in *Licensing Parents: Family, State, and Child Maltreatment* (Lanham, MD: Lexington Book, 2009), esp. pp. 119ff.
32 D. Archard, *Children: Rights and Childhood*, 2nd edn. (Milton Park: Routledge, 2004), p. 191.
33 Michael McFall, op cit., argues that the needs of children demands that we do something before abuse and neglect occurs. See especially p. 112.
34 J. Rachels, 'Why privacy is important', *Philosophy and Public Affairs* 4,4 (1975): 323–33; Brighouse & Swift, op. cit.
35 H. Paradis, G. Montes & P.G. Szilagyi, 'A national perspective on parents' knowledge of child development, its relation to parent-child interaction, and associated parenting characteristics', in *Pediatrics Academic Society Publication* (Honolulu, HI: The Society, 2008).
36 Department of Health, *Facing the Future: A Review of the Role of Health Visitors* (Crown Copyright, 2007).
37 US Department of Health and Human Services op. cit., Table 3.3.

38 Shyrock op. cit.
39 M. A. Mason, *From Father's Property to Children's Rights* (New York: Columbia University Press, 1994).
40 S. Grover, 'Children as chattel of the state: Deconstructing the concept of sex trafficking', *The International Journal of Human Rights* 11, no. 3 (2007): 293–306; American Academy of Pediatrics, 'The child in court: A subject review', *AAP Policy Statements* (1999), http://aappolicy.aappublications.org/cgi/reprint/pediatrics;104/5/1145.pdf, p. 2.
41 LaFollette 1980 op. cit., p. 196.
42 A. Mohler, 'Should parents be licensed? An ominous new debate', (2005), http://www.almohler.com/commentary_read.php?cdate=2005-04-28.
43 D. I. Bonina & R.A. Bahe-Jachna, 'The treatment of children as chattel in recent adoption decisions', *Human Rights Magazine* 28, 2 (1999): http://www.abanet.org/irr/hr/sp99bonina.html.
44 Bonina op. cit.

24

Child Abuse: parental rights and the interests of the child

DAVID ARCHARD

ABSTRACT *I criticise the 'liberal' view of the proper relationship between the family and State, namely that, although the interests of the child should be paramount, parents are entitled to rights of both privacy and autonomy which should be abrogated only when the child suffers a specifiable harm. I argue that the right to bear children is not absolute, and that it only grounds a right to rear upon an objectionable proprietarian picture of the child as owned by its producer. If natural parents have any rights to rear they derive from duties to bring their children into rational maturity where they can exercise rights for themselves. The presumption that natural parents are best suited to rear their own children should be discounted, as should the assumption that alternatives to natural parenting are unacceptably bad. I reject the suggestion that parents should be 'licensed' but argue for a much closer monitoring of the family. Familial privacy, which such monitoring breaches, is shown to have a culturally specific and, given the facts of abuse, dubious value. In conclusion, I briefly specify the forms of monitoring I approve.*

A familiar complaint of social workers is that they are, in their everyday work, impaled on the horns of a dilemma. Over-zealous intrusion into the lives of families whose behaviour does not in fact warrant such interference brings the charge that rights to privacy have been violated and innocents caused unnecessarily to suffer. On the other hand adequate failure to monitor the private activities of abusing parents has meant children being left to suffer lives which are, in every sense, 'solitary, poor, nasty, brutish and short'. This dilemma—protect children even at the cost of wrecked families or lose children out of respect for the sanctity of the family—sometimes finds expression as a question of balancing rights, those of the parent against those of the child.

I want to register scepticism about this balance. I want to do so by urging the view that insofar as the best interests of the child are of paramount importance the supposed rights of parents and of families should count for little or nothing. I think that talk of getting a balance right concedes a weight and significance to these latter rights which they should not be accorded.

The present debate in Britain about the abuse of children within the family has quite obviously found a focus in the events surrounding the Cleveland crisis, when, during a few months, many children in the Cleveland area of Northern England were diagnosed as having been sexually abused, and removed from the care of their parents. There are many reasons to regret this and to despair of the terms in which the issues have been discussed. The major problem of the Cleveland controversy has been the difficulty of keeping its various elements separate. One could easily talk at length about the diagnostic value of certain alleged means of detecting sexual abuse; about the role that each agency involved—police, social services, voluntary organisations, doctors—can and should play both individually and in concert with the others; about the proper use of the various statutory orders available to these agencies. Unfortunately, it would often seem as if there is only one motion to be debated with one's views on a range of questions following automatically from one's position on this main motion. It is even more unfortunate that the depressingly familiar British custom of personalising important issues should have meant that the main motion is currently worded in terms of unconditional support for (or repudiation of) Doctor X, Reverend Y, or the MP for Z.

Behind the arguments about particular personalities, events and decisions in Cleveland there is at stake the value of a certain widely accepted norm or ideal of child care policy. I should add that, as in so many matters theoretical, there is a considerable similarity between British and American approaches to the matter. It is this norm of family policy, recognisably liberal in character, which I want to lay bare and criticise. In simple terms, the ideal commends the minimum state and social intervention compatible with an adequate protection of the child's interests. Let me now spell out its elements.

First, there is a clear statement of the paramountcy of the best interests of the child. In the United Nations Declaration of the Rights of the Child, formally adopted in 1959, we find Principle 2 urging the child's protection by laws which will enable him or her to develop in a healthy and normal manner. It continues, "in the enactment of laws for this purpose the best interests of the child shall be the paramount consideration" [1]. This sentiment has found continuous re-expression in legislation, agency reports and general statements of intent. A Bill currently being considered in the UK begins with a formulation of general principles, the very first of which is that when a court determines any question with respect to the upbringing of a child or the administration of its property "the child's welfare shall be the court's paramount consideration" [2].

The second element in the ideal under scrutiny is the rights of parents or guardians with respect to the children under their care. Parents are those individuals who, in the first instance, are accorded responsibility for the welfare of their children. This entitles them, subject as we shall see to standard conditions, to autonomy and privacy. Autonomy in this context means the freedom to bring up children, educate and rear them as is seen fit; privacy in this context means the absence of unconsented intrusion upon the family's domain. An admirably concise, and influential, statement of these rights was given by the United States Supreme Court in the case of *Prince v. Massachusetts*, 1944. The case arose out of the attempt by Massachusetts to use its child labour legislation to prevent a family of Jehovah's Witnesses sending its child out upon the streets to sell religious literature. The judge commented: "it is cardinal with us that the custody, care and nurture of the child reside first in the parents, whose primary function and freedom include preparation for obligations the state can neither supply nor hinder. And it is in recognition of this that [previous] decisions have respected the private realm of family life which the state cannot enter" [3].

The third and final element in the liberal ideal is a specification of the threshold of state intervention, that is a statement of those conditions satisfaction of which would warrant State agencies in breaching the rights to parental privacy and autonomy. These conditions can obviously vary but they nearly always require that the child should have been subjected to, or be in immediate and real danger of being subjected to actual and specific harms. By way of representative example, the present Children Bill states that a court may make care, supervision and emergency protection orders—all of which abrogate in different ways existing parental rights—only if satisfied that "the child concerned has suffered significant harm or is likely to suffer such harm". Significantly, the Bill adds that the harm, or likelihood of harm, should be attributable to "the standard of care given to the child... being below that which it would be reasonable to expect the parent of a similar child to give to him" [4]. Evidence that a child is being harmed must also be evidence that a parent is neglecting or abusing the child.

The three elements of this ideal can be shown as mutually reinforcing one another in the following way: it is in the immediate best interests of any child to be reared by its parents as they deem appropriate and in a family context protected against intrusions upon its life; however, when the child is treated in certain deleterious ways by its parents, these parents must forego their erstwhile rights of autonomy and privacy, and the best interests of the child may now be served by its guardianship passing from parent to state.

Before I proceed to criticise this ideal, a brief word about the use of the adjective 'liberal' is in order. It seems clear to me that what the liberal prescribes as the proper relation between State and individual citizen is also viewed as most appropriate for the relation between State and family. Famously, J. S. Mill thought the individual should be guaranteed freedom from interference with his self-regarding action, that is accorded a private and protected domain of behaviour insofar as this does not adversely affect anyone else. Only when an individual's acts harmfully intrude upon others is the State permitted to intervene. Mill believed that such a guaranteed private space was necessary to the flourishing of individuality, and thereby to the improvement of society as a whole. Similarly, the liberal ideal of family policy guarantees a space for the life of an individual family within which what is done is both unsupervised by State and freely chosen. The flourishing of the family, and its members, is argued to be secured by such a guarantee of non-interference. Only when harms are directly occasioned to the child does the family become accountable to the State for its private behaviour.

The analogy between individual citizen and individual family has one important, and instructive, limitation. Autonomy and privacy are conceded to individual citizens and it is for their acts within the public domain that they are responsible to the State; in the case of the individual family, privacy is given to the family but autonomy to the parents, that is, to individuals *within* the family. And again it is for harms done *within* the private familial space by *some* members of the family to *other* members of the same family that the family as a whole loses its right to privacy. This important difference between the cases of the individual and of the family is obscured by writers who speak as if the rights to privacy and autonomy are both possessed by the family as a single unit. Thus, for example, in their influential text, *Before the Best Interests of the Child*, Goldstein *et al.* speak of the value of "family integrity" which encompasses both parental autonomy and privacy [5]. Their conflation of quite distinct rights can only spring from a tendency to view the separate interests of child and parents as unified into that of a single familial interest. This is a not uncommon tendency in liberal writing on the family.

What is to be said in favour of the liberal ideal of family policy? That it is both justified and obviously preferable to any other feasible alternative will be the likely response. I propose now to challenge this answer. Justifications of the liberal ideal seem to me to be of two broad kinds, which are mutually reinforcing rather than exclusive alternatives. The first kind of justification attempts to ground a right such as parental autonomy in some other prior right; the second kind of justification is teleological in character and appeals to the morally desirable ends which are served (and which can only or can best be served) by this ideal. I begin by examining the first kind of justification.

It may be argued that a human being has a right to have children. Indeed, some such right seems to be recognised and enshrined in various famous charters, such as the U.N. Declaration. Unfortunately, this is not an obvious or straightforward right. It comprises at least two rights: the right to *bear* children and the right to *rear* children. (It should be obvious that the right to have children cannot, as Hugh LaFollette points out, mean that the infertile should be given children [6].) If there is a right to bear children—and, strictly speaking, only women could be possessors of such a right—it is clearly not absolute. There may be moral reasons for denying an individual her right to procreate. This seems to be the case if a new human being would by its existence threaten the lives or seriously worsen the welfare of other human beings already existing. Thus, a society might be justified in imposing birth control policies where unlimited population growth in a context of scarce resources jeopardised the well-being of its present and future citizenry (and where non-coercive policies will not or have already failed to work). More imaginatively, we could think of a woman whose highly dangerous and contagious illness is known to be automatically transmitted to the fetus.

Since one gives birth to another human being who presumably *also* has rights, chiefly of course rights to life and liberty, a right to bear would have to be circumscribed by an obligation to ensure that the life of this new being is both secure and free. Thus, Onora O'Neill, for instance, thinks that the right to beget or bear "is not unrestricted but contingent upon begetters and bearers having or making some feasible plan for their child to be adequately reared by themselves or by willing others" [7].

Even conceding a limited right to bear children, what relation does this right have to one to rear children? On one account of parentage, the relation is direct and foundational. Those children I bear I may also rear, and do so *because* I bore them. This account is a proprietarian one. It reasons that whatever I produce I justifiably own. Such an account may employ a Lockean theory of property entitlements as grounded upon labour and ownership of one's own body (and rejoice in the felicitous association of the word 'labour' with childbirth). Whatever the theoretical foundations, it seems clear that in previous centuries at least the view of children has been as the property of their parents, or, more specifically within patriarchal societies, of the father. Thus, for instance, "under ancient Roman law the father had a power of life and death (*patria potestas*) over his children that extended into adulthood. He could kill, mutilate, sell, or offer his child in sacrifice" [8]. In the *Nicomachean Ethics* Aristotle speaks of children as being a part of their parents—"for the product belongs to the producer (e.g. a tooth or hair or anything else to him whose it is)" [9].

Viewing any human being as the property of another is deeply, and rightly, repugnant to present Western culture. It is important to add that the proprietarian thesis is extremely hard to defend. If begetting did generate ownership, then it is hard to see why ownership should not be lifelong, how we would apportion property rights between mother and father, and how we might acknowledge the productive contributions of medical staff. I foreswear consideration of all the questions raised by donation of semen, *in vitro* fertilisation and surrogate motherhood. Again, it would be curious to argue that someone who is owned has legitimate claims against their owner in respect of their treatment. Yet not only do we accord children such claims against their parents, but also believe that as third parties we are justified in enforcing these claims.

Nevertheless, it is probably, if regrettably true that some shadow of the proprietarian thesis stalks even current thinking about the rights of parents to rear their own children. In the absence of a proprietarian justification, it is difficult to see how the bearing of a child would ground a right to rear it. The only justification I can see as remaining is that the best interests of the child are served by remaining with those who begat him. That is, it may be argued that ties of natural affection ensure that a child's best chance of developing and prospering lies in his staying with his biological parents. Or, at least, that this is the presumption we should act upon. I will return to this claim.

Before I do so, it should be noted that no-one can or will defend a right to rear *simpliciter*. Standardly, philosophers and lawyers writing on this subject speak of a right which is conditional upon the fulfilment by the rearers of duties and responsibilities in relation to the children. In other words parents may bring up a child only insofar as and to the extent that they provide those conditions necessary for the child to enjoy a normal physical and emotional development. Some indeed have argued that the relation between parents and their children should be thought of in fiduciary terms: the parents acting as trustees, the rights they exercise belonging not to them but to their children, this exercise of rights lasting only as long as the trust, namely up to that point where the trust's purpose has been accomplished and the children are able to exercise their own rights for themselves [10].

I am very sympathetic to this view. I certainly believe that it gets the right way round the relationship between rights and duties. It is not that a right to rear pre-exists but is circumscribed by a duty to meet certain minimum conditions of upbringing. For one thing as I have tried to argue it is hard to see what that pre-existing right would be based upon. It is rather that given a general duty to ensure that children are given a normal and protected development into adulthood, those who undertake that duty in relation to a specific child thereby acquire certain rights to make decisions and choices for that child.

It may well seem that I have been too summary in my dismissal of a natural parent's right to rear his own children. So I shall try again. In general, an individual's right to something is based upon, and derives its value from the individual's having a strong interest in that thing. Joseph Raz, for instance, writes, "a law creates a right if it is based on and expresses the view that someone has an interest which is sufficient ground for holding another to be subject to a duty" and "to be a rule conferring a right it has to be motivated by a belief in the fact that someone's (the rightholder's) interest should be protected by the imposition of duties on others" [11]. But, of course, for us to recognise a right it is further required both that the interest should be of value and that its protection does not interfere with the securing by other individuals of things they have a valuable and comparable interest in. We are right, so the argument runs, to have an interest in being as free as possible, and it is consequently evident that we may claim a right to the maximum liberty compatible with a like liberty for others.

How is it with parenthood? There are many possible reasons for a human being to have an interest in rearing children: to bring about a life that avoids the errors of its begetter, to create a companion and an assistant for one's dotage, to add another soldier to the army of the motherland or another true believer to the ranks of the faithful, to prove it can be done, to spite another adult. None of these interests in rearing a child are of self-evident value or obviously consonant with the interests of existent adults. An interest in having a child that we might recognise as of real value would be to bring into existence another human who could be the object of our disinterested love, concern and care. Such an interest would seem to merit the protection of a right to rear. But is this not the same in effect as arguing that such a right is generated by the adequate discharge of a certain responsibility owed the child?

To summarise: I have argued that the right to bear children is not absolute, and that it only grounds a right to rear upon an objectionable proprietarian picture of the child as owned by its producer. If there are any rights to rear they derive from duties to bring children into rational maturity where they can exercise rights for themselves. If then natural parents have a right to rear their own children it is because they are or may be presumed to be best at discharging the duty of upbringing in relation to these children.

This neatly brings us to teleological justifications of parental autonomy. Parents are justified in taking decisions about the upbringing of a child insofar as they thereby promote the best interests of the child. It follows that natural parents are justified in deciding for their offspring only if they are the best persons to care for the child. Our culture presumes that this is normally the case. It is a deep-rooted and understandable presumption. However, those who offer themselves as foster or adoptive parents must satisfy the State through its social service agencies that they can provide an adequate home background, within which the child will be given all reasonable opportunities to flourish. We do not ask natural parents to pass a similar test. If we do not—and discounting any unconscious resort to a proprietarian view—it can only be due to a belief on our part that biology alone equips a person to pass the test of adequate parenthood.

There are two things to be said about such a view. First, it is badly mistaken. Natural parents do abuse and neglect their children. They have done so throughout history and continue to do so today. They do so in such numbers that talk of rare exceptions to a general rule appears naive at best and dangerously misguided at worst. Secondly, the presumption of natural affection is counter-productive. It is often our very reluctance to believe that parents could ill-treat their own children which blinds us to the reality of what is actually happening. Our deep shock before the facts of incestuous sexual abuse remains as much *who* is doing it as *what* is done. But our unwillingness to accept that our neighbour is anything other than a loving father may very well inhibit our investigating further—even in cases where we might have initial suspicions.

My own view then is that we should discount any presumption of natural affection, and assess the capacities of natural parents to rear their children as we would any potential surrogate guardians. Two imporant disclaimers are in order. First, I do not ignore the importance to the child of a stable, permanent and affectionate home background. I say only that this may be provided by natural parents, foster or adoptive parents, or even within forms of community care. What I am concerned to deny is the assumption that, *in advance of any other information*, the best interests of children are served by their remaining with their natural parents.

The defender of the liberal ideal may nevertheless reply that the natural parents, for all their faults, represent "the least detrimental alternative" (the phrase is from Goldstein *et al.*, and has been widely adopted). We should, so it is argued, recognise that even if natural parents are not the best for the child, they may be the 'least worst'. And for two reasons: the available options are unacceptably poorer than natural parentship, and the trauma of separation will involve harms for which a reallocation of guardianship cannot compensate.

The first claim if true is so only contingently. Institutional alternatives to the family can be and have been very poor, but this is for two reasons, a historical and an ideological one. Such alternatives owe their form to their historical roots—as custodial and preventative responses to juvenile delinquency and orphanhood. Ideologically, society remains unwilling seriously to support non-familial structures for the upbringing of children. Were society to be convinced that an alternative to the family is needed in the case of very many children who need not as a result be stigmatised as 'misfits', then the first claim would fail to be persuasive. Moreover, such a conviction might draw strength precisely from a recognition that a child is not necessarily best served by remaining with its natural parents.

It is also worth adding that some studies cast direct doubt on the presumption that, in all cases, natural parenting does better for the child than any alternative. Barbara Tizard, for instance, has shown that within a group of initially institutionalised children those adopted fared better than those who were returned to their natural parents [12].

The second claim—that separating the child from its parents does irreparable harm—is an empirical, psychological one. It is thus no accident that the defenders of the liberal ideal rely heavily on psychoanalytic theories of the parent–child relation, such as those of John Bowlby and Anna Freud. They also, it must be added, make use of studies of institutionalised children where the institutions in question were those operating immediately after the Second World War in conditions of Dickensian austerity [13]. 'Revisionist' child psychologists such as the Clarkes, Michael Rutter and Jerome Kagan are currently far more sanguine about the adaptability of children to changes in their environments. They have also argued against the alleged importance of the parent–child bonding to the long-term health and development of the child [14].

At this point it is worth briefly responding to a possible double-edged criticism of my argument thus far. This is, first, that talk of parental and children's *rights* is not the only and is perhaps an overstrong way to understand the problem; and, secondly, that the relationship between natural parent and child displays an emotional reality which is very unlikely to be true of that between an unrelated guardian and child, this reality being misrepresented by talk either of ownership or of grounding rights to rear.

My use of the language of rights to the apparent exclusion of any other moral discourse should not be taken to imply an acceptance that the former represents the only legitimate means of representing the problem of familial privacy and child abuse. However, it remains a fact that it is in terms of parental and children's rights that the legal and social policy debate about families has been conducted. Moreover, it seems clear that the attribution of putative rights to parents and children is the strongest way in which to express and defend the moral concerns of these individuals. If only standard considerations of overall social welfare prevail then the case for children to stay with their natural parents may be a much weaker one. There is, after all, no right to rear which might trump these considerations.

Nevertheless, there may be reasons for children to remain with their natural parents which have not to do with any ownership of the former by the latter, and which do not ground parental rights. It will be said that parents are emotionally bound up with, involved with, and attached to their children in ways that are simply not true, or are very unlikely to be true of mere guardians. Parents *feel* for their own children. They need not view them as owned, nor does their feeling automatically give them rights over their own. However, to neglect this emotional reality would, it can be argued, be implausibly to conclude that natural parents and guardians do not differ in any interesting respects.

I suspect that this alludes to an important feature of human relationships which deserves a more careful and extended treatment than is possible here. For the purposes of my argument a terse, and probably unsatisfactory rejoinder is in order. Feeling bound up with another is no guarantee that one is the best person to promote that other's good. Parents may be more willing than others to tend their own, and be so on account of their parental feelings. But this fact, if it is a fact, does not acquit them from the responsibility of showing that they are good guardians, and better guardians than others who might be available. The ways in which foster and adoptive parents can care for children shows that the feeling of being bound up with another is not exclusive to blood ties. Indeed, the absence of blood ties may make for more sagacious and judicious parenting.

We should not be blind to the reality of parental love, but equally we should not be blinded by it. Social policy should not ignore feelings, but it should also learn to discriminate between feelings. The danger is that an ideology of blood love is self-confirming. Our unwillingness to explore and encourage feasible alternatives to the natural parent may rest on the mistaken belief that the love only a natural parent can feel for its own must be a necessary condition of a good upbringing. I cannot see that it is necessary, and my argument thus far is to the effect that it is certainly not sufficient.

To reiterate, my view is that the capacities of any natural parent to rear their children should be viewed neutrally, that is by discounting any presumption of their biologically grounded superiority as guardians. My second disclaimer, announced earlier, concerns the practical import of this view. One practical proposal would be that advocated by Hugh LaFollette in an admirably provocative article, namely the licensing of parents [15]. LaFollette defends the view that the rearing of children is an activity which, being potentially harmful to others and requiring demonstrated competence in its execution, demands regulation. Someone, LaFollette argues, should not be able to rear children unless they acquire a licence to do so, and such a licence should only be granted on evidence of the requisite ability safely to bring up a child.

Although LaFollette's point of attack is the right to rear, his argument could be extended to the right to bear children, and would thus appear to warrant a licensing of procreation. This would raise enormous difficulties. How, for instance, should an unlicensed recidivist begetter of children be treated? Compulsory abortion and/or sterilisation suggest themselves as obvious but extremely unpalatable solutions. It will be practically impossible to prevent all human beings who might be deemed unfit to bear children from having them. Or at least it will require a machinery for the detection and punishment of offenders that few would be prepared to countenance.

Any practical questions then concern what to do *after* children have been born. LaFollette would presumably re-allocate children from parents who are unlicensed to those who are. A criticism of LaFollette is that he, unreasonably, requires a person's future skills (as a parent) to be predicted, whereas licensing normally requires only that a person's present performance be assessed [16]. We cannot know how people may be as parents in the future. I would make a related but slightly different criticism. LaFollette concedes that we may neither agree what counts as nor be able successfully to predict who actually will be a 'good parent'. But, he says, his scheme "is designed to exclude only the very bad ones" [17]. Now he also rightly suggests that we are gaining a better idea of the profile of the person who is likely to abuse their children. This means, in effect, that we know of some people that they will most probably be very bad parents, even if we may not know of any one of the others that they will not be a bad parent. Thus, licensing alone will not guarantee that all parents are adequate, and licensing of everyone is not needed to exclude in advance the palpably bad parents. The argument against licensing is completed by recognising its costs and outlining a more feasible alternative which serves the same ends just as well.

LaFollette's scheme requires that licenses be fairly and efficiently granted upon the basis of an agreed and workable criterion of 'fitness to parent' which can cover all eventualities. There are obvious, and perhaps insuperable difficulties with such a proposal. However, my practical suggestion prevents those harms LaFollette wishes to see prevented by his scheme and does not involve the difficulties his does. Those who are brought to the attention of society as obviously bad prospective parents may be prevented from rearing their own or anybody else's children. Such persons fit either the profile for an abusing parent of which LaFollette speaks, or a more general profile such as would disqualify them as adequate parents. I am thinking here of something like a previous history of extremely violent behaviour.

For the rest, a child will remain with its parents, but only subject to an extensive and rigorous monitoring of their development after birth. Such monitoring is required by the logic of LaFollette's own argument. Any licence may be revoked upon evidence of subsequent and seriously harmful incompetence in the activity for which the licence was originally granted. Thus, LaFollette would have to be assured that even licensed parents were still fit to care for their children. My point is that, having already excluded those who can be confidently picked out as very bad prospective parents, monitoring alone does all the work that LaFollette's more cumbersome and impractical licensing scheme is designed to do.

Since such extensive monitoring clearly represents a direct challenge to the alleged familial right to privacy, I must now turn to consideration of the grounds for such a right. A familiar defence of the right to privacy in respect of individuals urged by people like Charles Fried is that it permits the intimacy which is essential to relationships of love and friendship [18]. Similarly, it has been argued that familial privacy is necessary for the healthy development of the normal, loving relationships between parent and parent, parent and child which characterise a healthy family [19]. It may further be argued that such familial bonds are "critical to every child's healthy growth and development" [20].

My reply is two-fold. First, the kind of privacy to which the twentieth century Western family feels entitled and which it has come to expect is historically and culturally very specific. It is worth emphasising the degree to which the private nuclear family, a self-contained household of kin only living within its own well-defined space, is a peculiarly late twentieth century Western phenomenon, a compound of various changes in society—the separation of home and work activities, a decline in the number of children born per family, an end to apprenticeship and the 'putting out' of children, the demise of servants as household members, the emergence in various architectural forms of the family house, and the development of entertainments which are or can be home-based [21].

Families in previous times and in other types of society have enjoyed a quite significantly smaller degree of privacy. Of course it can be shown that in all cultures and societies there is some line drawn to divide space, demarcate activities, specify roles in terms of a distinction between public and private. Thus, for example, a particular tribal culture may involve households comprising several kin groups preparing and eating food together, sleeping in the same unpartitioned building, but with some 'private' spaces and times associated with sexual activity and enforced through rules of non-encroachment [22].

However, it is only in this century in the West that the line between private and public has been so clearly and sharply drawn around the nuclear family in so many of its aspects. Importantly, there is little or no evidence that these significant differences in the scope of familial privacy are correlatable with equally significant differences in the degree to which children develop into normal healthy adults.

Secondly, whilst privacy may serve as the precondition for a healthy and loving intimacy, it can equally function as a cloak for abuse and neglect. The ill-treatment of children takes place in a 'private' space, the family home, and to the very extent that it is a private space, it may continue undetected and unsuspected. In response to Richard Wasserstrom's views on privacy Lorenne Clark has written, "Wasserstrom points out ... that 'we have accepted the idea that many things are shameful unless done in private'. The irony is that such shameful things go on just because they are left in private" [23]. The 'privacy' of the family protects the abuser in a number of ways. The abuse is literally unobserved, and whilst physical abuse may display itself through the consequent bruises and burns upon the child, sexual abuse has no obvious public face. Abused children may have no sense that what is 'privately' happening to them is radically and terribly different from what would be 'publicly' acceptable. So many victims of incest have subsequently reported that they did not think of their abuse as anything other than natural, as what happened within even 'normal' families. Finally, the abused child within the 'private' space of the family will probably be pressurised not to reveal the abuse, or to retract previous accusations of abuse. It is sometimes tragically ironic to read about accusations of social workers bullying confessions of abuse from children, when no mention is made at the same time of the brutal means by which abusing parents so frequently secure the silence of their victims.

All these are reasons why abused children will not—as our society sometimes seems to expect—step forward and publicly identify themselves as victims of abuse. They are also thus reasons why the disclosure of abuse will have to involve intrusions upon the privacy of the family prescribed by the liberal ideal. It is important—before I specify something of the intrusiveness upon the family which I favour—to emphasis the extent of the evil which it would help to prevent. The abuse of children—especially sexual abuse—ruins lives, and not just those of the victim. Abuse is deeply traumatising, and its scarring effects last well into, if not throughout adulthood. There is increasing evidence of a cycle of abuse—abusers being themselves very frequently the victims of previous abuse. There is also evidence linking subsequent criminality, alcoholism, drug addiction and violent behaviour to a history of childhood abuse.

So what intrusions upon family privacy would I favour? I would give those social workers who specialise and are trained in child abuse statutory powers of entry into family homes and access to children. It is of course significant that the biggest percentage of referrals to social services of suspected abuse in the United Kingdom comes from health workers who currently enjoy *de facto* rights of access into homes and to children. I would strive to redraw the line that separates the 'private' family from the public domain by creating 'spaces' in which the health of children can be reviewed and monitored with a view to possible abuse. By this, I mean that family doctors, consultants, emergency medical personnel, police and teachers—all those who for professional or statutory reasons may come into contact with children—must be specifically trained in the diagnosis of abuse, educated in the importance of detecting abuse and persuaded as to the need for their contact with the child to present opportunities for the diagnosis of possible abuse. The reporting of cases of suspected abuse to social services by such professionals must also be made mandatory.

It is clear that presently the vast majority of these professionals honour the liberal ideal for familial privacy, are loath to suspect parents of ill-doing, and favour interference only as a last resort. In their study of how the agencies concerned with child welfare operate within the UK, *The Protection of Children* (1983), Robert Dingwall *et al.* conclude: "We have clearly shown that, at each and every stage, the structures of the organisations involved and the practical reasoning of their members have the effect of creating a preference for the least stigmatising interpretation of available data and the least overtly coercive possible disposition. Officially-labelled cases of mistreatment are, quite literally, only those for which no excuse or justification can be found. Compulsory measures are employed only in those cases where parental recalcitrance or mental incompetence leave no room for voluntary action" [24].

Closely related to my preference for a greater intrusiveness upon the family is a dislike for the liberal ideal's threshold for statutory action: the occasioning or risk of specific harms to the child. The criterion is essentially 'negative'. Parents are given the benefit of the doubt, and the onus is upon the State to establish neglect and abuse of a concrete form. I would rather that the State established affirmative duties of care which guaranteed the best possible conditions for the development of the child. This ideal is enshrined within the ancient prerogative of *parens patriae* whereby the State may assume, in the last analysis and last resort, the protective role of parent to its infant citizens. In turn, this doctrine justifies the jurisdiction of High Courts over minors in cases of wardship. Wardship has been defined as "essentially a parental jurisdiction" wherein the "main consideration to be acted upon in its exercise is the benefit or welfare of the child ... the Court must do what under the circumstances a wise parent acting for the true interest of the child would or ought to do" [25]. My point might be expressed rather baldly as follows: the liberal ideal requires that parents be shown to be palpably bad before the State will intervene. I would rather that the State requires its parents to be good, and act accordingly when they are not.

There is much talk nowadays of the emergence of children's rights, and the correlated fragmentation or disappearance of parental rights [26]. As I have noted, the paramountcy of the child's best interests is, at least formally, insisted upon in the rhetoric of legal and social welfare provision. Interestingly, however the doctrine of paramountcy derives principally from custody cases, in which the family *has already broken down*. Similarly, the liberal ideal of family policy presumes the benevolence of existing parental control and intervenes only when there is proven familial failure. If we are to take seriously the notion of the child's best interests, and the reality of children's rights, then we cannot continue uncritically to speak of competing rights to family privacy and parental autonomy. On the contrary, respect for these latter rights serves only to perpetuate the very conditions under which children, out of sight and too often out of the 'public' mind, suffer the 'private' hell of preventable abuse. Despite all the obfuscations and distortions of the facts, I still hope that the events of Cleveland will help to teach us that invaluable lesson [27].

David Archard, Department of Philosophy & Politics, University of Ulster at Jordanstown, Newtownabbey, Co. Antrim, BT37 0QB, United Kingdom.

NOTES

[1] U.N. Declaration of rights, in: O. O'NEILL & W. RUDDICK (Eds) (1979) *Having Children: philosophical and legal reflections on parenthood* (Oxford, Oxford University Press), pp. 112-114.
[2] *Children Bill* (1989), Part I, 1(1).
[3] Quoted in: M. D. A. FREEMAN (1983) Freedom and the welfare state: child-rearing, parental autonomy and state intervention, *Journal of Social Welfare Law*, p. 71.
[4] *Children Bill* (1989), Part IV, 26(2).
[5] J. GOLDSTEIN, A. FREUD & A. J. SOLNIT (1980) *Before the Best Interests of the Child* (London, Burnett Books), p. 5.
[6] HUGH LAFOLLETTE (1980) Licensing parents, *Philosophy & Public Affairs*, 9:2, pp. 186-187.
[7] ONORA O'NEILL (1979) Begetting, bearing and rearing, in: O. O'NEILL & W. RUDDICK (Eds) (1979).
[8] MASON THOMAS (1972) Child abuse and neglect. Part I: Historical overview, legal matrix, and social perspectives, *North Carolina Law Review*, 50, p. 295.
[9] ARISTOTLE, *Nicomachean Ethics*, Book VIII.12, 20-25.
[10] C. K. BECK, G. GLAVIS, S. A. GLOVER, S. A. JENKINS & R. A. NARDI (1978) The rights of children: a trust model, *Fordham Law Review*, XLVI:4, pp. 669-780.
[11] J. RAZ (1984) Legal rights, *Oxford Journal of Legal Studies*, 4:1, pp. 13-14.
[12] BARBARA TIZARD (1977) *Adoption: a second chance* (London, Open Books).
[13] J. BOWLBY (1965) *Attachment and Loss. Vol. 1: attachment* (London, Hogarth Press & Institute of Psycho-Analysis); J. BOWLBY (1973) *Attachment and Loss. Vol. 2: separation—anxiety and anger* (London, Hogarth Press & Institute of Psycho-Analysis); A. FREUD & D. BURLINGHAM (1944) *Young Children in War Time: a year's work in a residential nursery* (London, Allen & Unwin); A. FREUD & D. BURLINGHAM (1944) *Infants Without Families: the case for and against residential nurseries* (London, Allen & Unwin).
[14] A. M. CLARKE & A. C. B. CLARKE (1976) *Early Experience: myth and evidence* (London, Open Books); M. RUTTER (1972; 2nd edn 1981) *Maternal Deprivation Reassessed* (Harmondsworth, Penguin Books); J. KAGAN, R. B. KEARSLEY & P. R. ZELAZO (1978) *Infancy: its place in human development* (Cambridge, MA, Harvard University Press).
[15] HUGH LAFOLLETTE (1980), pp. 182-197.
[16] LAWRENCE FRISCH (1981) On licentious licensing: A reply to Hugh LaFollette, *Philosophy & Public Affairs*, 11:2, pp. 173-183.
[17] HUGH LAFOLLETTE (1980), p. 190.
[18] CHARLES FRIED (1970) *An Anatomy of Values* (Cambridge, MA, Harvard University Press), Ch. IX.
[19] FRANCIS SCHRAG (1976) Justice and the family, *Inquiry*, 19, pp. 193-208; FERDINAND SCHOEMAN (1980) Rights of children, rights of parents and the moral basis of the family, *Ethics*, 91, pp. 6-19; IRIS MARION YOUNG (1983) Rights to intimacy in a complex society, *Journal of Social Philosophy*, 14, pp. 47-52.
[20] J. GOLDSTEIN, A. FREUD & A. J. SOLNIT (1980), p. 10.
[21] BARBARA LASLETT (1973) The family as a public and private institution: an historical perspective, *Journal of Marriage and the Family*, 35, pp. 480-492.
[22] IRWIN ALTMAN (1977) Privacy regulation: culturally universal or culturally specific?, *Journal of Social Issues*, 33:3, pp. 66-84.
[23] LORENNE CLARK (1978) Privacy, property, freedom and the family, in: RICHARD BRONAUGH (Ed.) *Philosophical Law* (Connecticut, Greenwood Press), p. 182.
[24] ROBERT DINGWALL, JOHN EEKELAAR & TOPSY MURRAY (1982) *The Protection of Children: state intervention and family life* (Oxford, Basil Blackwell), p. 207.
[25] LORD JUSTICE KAY (1893) Reg. v. Gyngall, quoted in: S. M. CRETNEY (1984) *Principles of Family Law*, 4th edn (London, Sweet & Maxwell), p. 326.
[26] JOHN EEKELAAR (1973) What are parental rights?, *Law Quarterly Review*, 89, pp. 210-234; SUSAN MAIDMENT (1981) The fragmentation of children's rights, *Cambridge Law Review*, 4:1, pp. 135-158; JOHN EEKELAAR (1986) The emergence of children's rights, *Oxford Journal of Legal Studies*, 6:2, pp. 161-182.
[27] My grateful thanks to Bernarde Lynn, Jim Brown and the members of Bristol University Philosophy Society for comments on a previous draft of this article.

25

Making and Breaking Family Life: Adoption, the State, and Human Rights

Sonia Harris-Short

This article explores the extent to which the state's duties and responsibilities in the context of adoption are framed and reinforced by a rights-based discourse. It argues that the human rights paradigm plays an invaluable role in the pre-adoption process by identifying and imposing ever more exacting obligations on the state – obligations which are currently not being fully met by the Adoption and Children Act 2002. The application of a rights-based discourse to the post-adoption context proves, however, to be considerably more problematic. Indeed, it is argued that rather than extend and strengthen the state's responsibilities towards the child and the adopted family, liberal rights-based doctrine tends towards a more traditional model of adoption in which a minimalist state and the privacy, autonomy, and self-sufficiency of the new adoptive family are further entrenched. It is thus concluded that a human rights analysis provides no secure basis for challenging the Adoption and Children Act's rather limited provisions on post-adoption support.

INTRODUCTION

The state bears a heavy responsibility when it seeks to place looked-after children for adoption. Having removed a child from his or her family of birth, the state thereby instigates a legal process aimed at irrevocably terminating family life between the child and his or her birth parents. Following termination of family life with the birth parents, the child is then legally 'reborn' into a new adoptive family. Through adoption the state is thus uniquely engaged in the process of creating and destroying family life.

The state's role in transforming the child's core familial relationships gives rise to substantial duties and responsibilities on the part of the state owed not only to the child but to all members of the 'adoption triad'. The purpose of this paper is to explore the extent to which the duties and responsibilities of the state in the context of adoption are framed and reinforced by a rights-based discourse and whether, in light of that discussion, the current law on adoption, as contained within the Adoption and Children Act 2002 (ACA 2002), meets the normative imperatives of that discourse. It will be argued that a rights-based approach plays an invaluable role in helping to delineate, extend, and reinforce the state's duties and responsibilities throughout the adoption process. In this context, the application of a liberal rights-based discourse is relatively straightforward. The imperative of non-intervention into the private family life of both the birth family and the child underscores the essential responsibility of the state to respect the autonomy and integrity of the family. Thus adoption as an extreme measure of state intervention into the birth family will only be capable of justification on overriding welfare grounds, the responsibility for establishing such grounds resting firmly with the state. To the extent that it is argued the state holds more extensive responsibilities during the adoption process, including obligations of a more positive nature, these responsibilities are inextricably linked with the far-reaching responsibility on the state to justify its intervention or fall largely within the familiar and relatively uncontroversial realm of procedural rights, with a right-based discourse reinforcing the responsibility of the state to ensure due process and fairness in all its decision-making bodies. In order to justify an adoption, a rights-based discourse thus demands that all the various rights and interests of the parties are carefully articulated and properly and fairly considered at every stage of the decision-making process. Other core liberal principles now embodied in the human rights paradigm, such as equality and non-discrimination, reinforce these responsibilities on the state when acting in the pre-adoption context. In contrast, because of the socio-economic nature of the rights in question and continuing ambivalence concerning the appropriate role of the state in the provision of family support, the application of the human rights paradigm to the post-adoption context is considerably more problematic. Indeed, it will be argued that rather than imposing more extensive and exacting duties on the state, particularly with respect to the provision of post-adoption support, a rights-based approach helps to underpin a more traditional and conservative model of adoption in which a minimalist state, respect for family autonomy, and the negative obligation of non-intervention into the private family life of the adoptive family are regarded as key.

HUMAN RIGHTS AND THE ADOPTION PROCESS: PROTECTING THE INDIVIDUAL RIGHTS OF THE PARTIES

It is widely recognized that a rights-based analysis may have important things to say about the adoption of a child from care.[1] An adoption order is the most drastic and potentially devastating order that can be made in the field of family law. It has life-changing legal effects on all members of the adoption triad. The child's legal status is permanently and fundamentally changed.[2] The 'very parenthood'[3] of the birth parents is terminated[4] and the prospective adopters are transformed into the child's legal parents as if the child had been born their natural legitimate child.[5] Against this legal background, a rights-based discourse can be relied upon to impose ever more exacting duties and responsibilities on the state. Thus, the state's core responsibility to respect the autonomy and integrity of the existing family unit is driven home by a discourse of rights imposing both substantive and procedural obligations on the state and its agents. As noted above, given the importance of the interests at stake, the state will bear a heavy duty of non-interference, rendering adoption a decision of last-resort and demanding that the rights and interests of all members of the adoption triad are carefully identified and properly considered by the various decision-making bodies throughout the process. One of the most important advantages of employing a rights-based discourse is that it ensures these key obligations are met, thereby providing important safeguards for all three members of the adoption triad – all of whom are potentially vulnerable at various stages of the process. Prospective adopters, for example, may face arbitrary and even discriminatory decisions as to their suitability to adopt. Birth parents, often demonized by policy-makers in this area,[6] can be marginalized in the drive towards achieving permanency for the child. Children can find their own rights and interests subsumed within the interests of the adult parties, particularly the adoptive parents. The state thus bears a heavy responsibility to ensure the individual rights and interests of all these parties are properly articulated and considered before an adoption order can be justified. This responsibility is underpinned and reinforced by the human rights paradigm and, as we shall see, more specifically by the demands of Article 8 of the European Convention on Human Rights.

---

1 See, for example, S. Harris-Short, 'The Adoption and Children Bill – a fast track to failure?' (2001) 13 *Child and Family Law Q.* 405 and S. Choudhry, 'The Adoption and Children Act 2002, The Welfare Principle and the Human Rights Act 1998 – A Missed Opportunity?' (2003) 15 *Child and Family Law Q.* 119.
2 Adoption and Children Act (ACA) 2002, s. 67(3).
3 *M v. C and Calderdale Metropolitan Borough Council* [1994] Fam 1.
4 ACA 2002, ss. 46(2) and 67(3).
5 ACA 2002, s. 67(1).
6 Harris-Short, op. cit., n. 1, p. 424, nn. 155-6.

1. What does a rights-based discourse demand?

The 'right to respect for family life' contained within Article 8 gives rise to both positive and negative, substantive and procedural, obligations on the part of the state.[7] In the process leading up to an adoption many of these obligations will be of particular importance to the birth parents. As soon as the state intervenes to remove a child from his or her parents,[8] the parents' rights and interests are afforded vital protection by Article 8.[9] It is firmly established in the Strasbourg jurisprudence that the taking of a child into care should generally be regarded as a temporary measure with the ultimate aim being to reconcile the child with his or her family.[10] The decision to proceed to adoption should therefore be viewed as a last resort when all reasonable attempts at reconciliation have failed. Moreover, pending the final decision as to the child's adoption, the state must seek to promote and support a meaningful relationship between the birth parents and the child. Any limitations or restrictions placed on contact will therefore be subjected to particularly close scrutiny.[11] The 'radical' step to completely terminate contact with the family of birth will only be justified in exceptional cases, albeit the matter becomes more complicated once the child has been placed for adoption and the need to consolidate that placement becomes of primary importance.[12] Article 8 also demands that the birth parents are fully involved throughout the decision-making process. This procedural dimension to Article 8 provides vital protection for the parents by ensuring that at every stage of the process all relevant rights and interests are taken properly into account.[13] Hence the requirement that unless there are strong countervailing reasons to the contrary, a child's natural father must be notified of the adoption proceedings even against the wishes of the child's mother.[14] Finally, before making the adoption order itself, the court must be satisfied that adoption constitutes a proportionate response to the needs and interests of the child, with less extreme alternatives such as special guardianship or a

---

7 See, for example, *Johansen v. Norway* (1997) 23 E.H.R.R. 33; *Scott v. UK* [2000] 1 F.L.R. 958; *Soderback v. Sweden* [1999] 1 F.L.R. 250; *Pini and Bertani; Manera and Atripaldi v. Romania* [2005] 2 F.L.R. 596; and *Down Lisburn Health and Social Services Trust (AP) v. H (AP)* [2006] U.K.H.L. 36.

8 Usually pursuant to a care order or emergency protection order (Children Act (CA) 1989, s. 31 or s. 44).

9 See, generally, *Haase v. Germany* [2004] 2 F.L.R. 39.

10 id., [93].

11 *Johansen*, op. cit., n. 7. Whilst the child is in care, contact between the child and the birth parents is governed by CA 1989, s. 34 and Sch. 2, para. 15. Once the child has been placed for adoption, contact is governed by ACA 2002, s. 26.

12 *S and G v. Italy* [2000] 2 F.L.R. 771, [169]–[170] and *Down*, op. cit., n. 7, [33] (per Baroness Hale).

13 *Johansen*, op. cit., n. 7, [65]–[66] and *Scott*, op. cit., n. 7, pp. 967–8.

14 *Re H; Re G* [2001] 1 F.L.R. 646.

residence order under the Children Act 1989 given careful consideration.[15] Thus Wall LJ has held[16] that although there is no presumption that a special guardianship order, as a less-interventionist measure, is preferable to adoption in any particular category of case,[17] one 'material feature' of special guardianship to which the courts should have regard is that it constitutes a less drastic interference with the existing legal relationship between the natural parents and the child. In the language of Article 8 of the European Convention, it may therefore represent a more proportionate response to the child's need for an alternative family home.[18] And although Wall LJ takes the view that in most cases Article 8 will add nothing to the balancing exercise carried out under the welfare checklists, he does acknowledge that 'the fact that the welfare objective can be achieved with less disruption of existing family relationships can properly be regarded as helping to tip the balance'.[19]

Understandably, in the process leading up to adoption, concern tends to focus on the rights and interests of the birth parents. That is not to say, however, that prospective adopters do not also enjoy important protection under the Convention. Thus, although it is clear that the Convention does not guarantee a right to adopt as such,[20] if the state provides for a system of adoption, any restrictions as to who may adopt and associated selection procedures must not discriminate against particular individuals and groups contrary to Article 14 of the Convention.[21] Furthermore, where the child has lived with the prospective adopters preceding the adoption, it is possible that the adopters will be able to establish the existence of family life for the purposes of bringing themselves within the protection of Article 8. In accordance with *Lebbink,* the prospective adopters must simply be able to demonstrate the 'real existence in practice of close personal ties' of 'sufficient constancy' to give rise to de facto family life with the child.[22]

---

15 Although it has been held that there is no presumption in favour of the lesser alternative: *Re S (a child)(adoption order or special guardianship order)* [2007] EWCA Civ 54, [47].

16 id.

17 A point reiterated in *Re M-J (a child) (adoption order or special guardianship order)* [2007] EWCA Civ 56 [17]–[19].

18 *Re S (a child) (adoption order or special guardianship order)* [2007] EWCA Civ 56 [2007] 1 F.C.R. 329, [49].

19 id.

20 Either under Article 8 or Article 12. It is, for example, clear that the mere desire to found a family does not fall within the scope of the right to respect for family life under Article 8. See *X* v. *Belgium and Netherlands* (1975) 7 DR 75 and *Frette* v. *France* [2003] 2 F.L.R. 9, [32].

21 See *Frette,* id., where these general principles were endorsed, albeit the Court found on the facts that the decision of the French authorities to reject a single homosexual applicant on the grounds of his sexuality was justified under Article 14 on the basis of the child's welfare.

22 *Lebbink* v. *the Netherlands* [2004] 2 F.L.R. 463, [36].

Once the adoption order is made, the formal de jure relationship of parent and child thereby created will be sufficient in and of itself to give rise to family life under the Convention.[23] Moreover, the European Court has made it clear that adoptive families are to be treated in the same way as all other families, it being held in *Pini* that 'the relations between an adoptive parent and an adopted child are as a rule of the same nature as the family relations protected by Art 8'.[24]

For the third member of the adoption triad, adoption can prove particularly complex and challenging. Adoption for the child means the loss of one family but the chance of a secure and happy home with another. For this reason adoption from the child's perspective can be riddled with tensions and contradictions. Rights-based reasoning cannot simply resolve these inherent tensions but it can help to illuminate the various and often competing rights and interests involved. Thus, mirroring the rights of the various adults, it is clear that the child enjoys family life rights with both the birth and the adoptive families. These rights can, and often do, co-exist, sometimes but not always in conflict. The state has a responsibility to respect, in so far as it can, this complexity in the child's familial relationships. A rights-based analysis thus serves as a constant reminder that the interests of one party to the adoption cannot be promoted and prioritized to the exclusion of all others. This becomes of particular importance when the child is placed for adoption. At this stage of an adoption English law has tended to focus its efforts upon supporting and consolidating the adoptive family. Whilst this is clearly important, the child may also retain a vitally important interest in maintaining relations with his or her family of birth – a right protected under Article 8 of the European Convention.[25] Yet, under English law, the child's right to maintain his or her family relationship with the birth parents has tended to be marginalized. Indeed, the courts' approach to contact with the birth parents during and after an adoption remains a particularly worrying example of how the rights and interests of the child can be subsumed within the rights and interests of the various adults, particularly the adoptive parents. Article 8 of the European Convention can help to redress this balance.

The human rights paradigm as embodied by Article 8 of the European Convention thus gives rise to a diverse range of rights and interests which the state must recognize and respect throughout the adoption process. However, English law does not always live up to these demands. In particular, there are three key issues of particular concern where the ACA 2002 arguably falls short of what a rights-based analysis requires.

---

23 *Pini*, op. cit., n. 7, [136]–[148].
24 id., [140].
25 See, for example, *Odievre* v. *France* [2003] 1 F.C.R. 621.

2. Does the ACA 2002 meet the demands of the human rights paradigm?

(a) Reconciling a looked-after child with the birth parents

As noted above, from the moment a child is taken into care, Article 8 imposes important duties and responsibilities on the state to uphold and respect both the child's and the parents' rights to respect for family life. The European Court has thus held that taking a child into care, unless clearly contrary to the child's best interests, should be viewed as a temporary measure with the state under a duty to seek to reconcile the child with his or her parents.[26] This duty has been reiterated in the domestic case law.[27] The duties and responsibilities imposed on the state in the context of care proceedings have important implications for adoption. In accordance with this approach, permanent placement outside the family should be seen as a very last resort, with the local authority seeking first to secure a reconciliation with the birth parents and only if such a reconciliation is clearly unachievable or the risks of returning the child to the family unacceptably high should adoption be considered. There are, however, several key provisions of the ACA 2002 which run counter to these requirements.

At the heart of the government's reform agenda as now enshrined in the ACA 2002 was a drive for permanency, with adoption the clearly preferred option for children who could not return home.[28] The Prime Minister was personally committed to increasing the number of children adopted out of care each year and to eradicating delays throughout the system.[29] The objectives behind these reforms were clearly laudable. Growing evidence as to the poor outcomes for looked-after children in state care, when compared to the very positive outcomes for adopted children, gave strong justification for the government's pro-adoption stance.[30] Moreover, empirical research pointing to the increased vulnerability of an adoption the older the child and the more disruption they have experienced in the pre-placement period,

---

26 *Haase v. Germany* (App. No. 11057/02) [2004] 2 F.L.R. 39, [93].
27 See, for example, Re C and B [2001] 1 F.L.R. 611, [30]–[34] (per Hale LJ).
28 Performance and Innovation Unit, *Prime Minister's Review of Adoption* (2000) 3, 5. The ACA 2002 was hailed as the 'most radical overhaul' of adoption in 25 years. It came into force in December 2005.
29 id.
30 As to the outcomes for looked-after children see, Department of Health, *Adoption – A New Approach. A White Paper* (2000; Cmnd. 5017) 16. As to the outcomes for adopted children, see J. Castle, 'Infant adoption in England. A longitudinal account of social and cognitive progress' (2000) 24 *Adoption & Fostering* 24; M.H. van IJzendoorn and F. Juffer, 'Adoption Is a Successful Natural Intervention Enhancing Adopted Children's IQ and School Performance' (2005) 14 *Current Directions in Psychological Sci.* 326; B. Maughan, S. Collishaw, and A. Pickles, 'School Achievement and Adult Qualifications among Adoptees: A Longitudinal Study' (1998) 39 *J. of Child Psychology and Psychiatry* 669; and A. Brand and P. Brinich, 'Behavior Problems and Mental Health Contacts in Adopted, Foster, and Nonadopted Children' (1999) 40 *J. of Child Psychology and Psychiatry* 1221.

increased anxiety as to the delays between a child coming into care and successful placement with prospective adopters.[31] The ACA 2002 and accompanying Department of Health guidelines therefore contain a number of provisions aimed at facilitating 'more adoptions, more quickly'.[32] Local authorities are now subjected to much tighter timescales for decision-making, forcing them to address the possibility of adoption much earlier in the care process.[33] This is reinforced by s. 22 of the ACA 2002 which places a clear duty on the local authority to apply for a placement order authorizing them to place a child for adoption as soon as they are satisfied that a looked-after child ought to be placed for adoption. This duty applies regardless of whether or not a care order is in force, has been applied for, or the child is simply in voluntary care under Part III of the CA 1989. The only proviso is that the local authority must be satisfied the threshold conditions for state intervention into family life set down in s. 31 of the CA 1989 are met.[34] This means that it is perfectly possible for a child to be placed for adoption against the wishes of his or her birth parents without a care order ever being made.

No one would take issue with the introduction of measures aimed at tackling the problem of 'drift in care' and eradicating unnecessary delays in placing a child for adoption. There is, however, legitimate cause for concern if these measures are introduced at the expense of affording due consideration to the child's relationship with the birth parents. In particular, there is a danger that by focusing too quickly on achieving permanence through adoption, efforts to reunite the child with the birth family, as demanded by Article 8, will be compromised, with local authorities adopting a more robust approach to the need for parents to address their problems within specified (and perhaps unrealistic) timescales and diverting resources away from the vital provision of services, help, and support to the birth parents. This is a particular concern if the child is in voluntary care and, as a result of the duties enshrined within s. 22 of the ACA 2002, the birth parents are deprived of services and support under the auspices of a care order – a serious problem where local authority resources remain focused on the provision of services to children in care under Part IV of the CA 1989 at the expense of providing effective preventative services to children and their families under Part III.[35]

---

31 J. Triseliotis, 'Long-term foster care or adoption? The evidence examined' (2002) 7 *Child & Family Social Work* 23, at 25; C. Dance and A. Rushton, 'Predictors of outcome for unrelated adoptive placements made during middle childhood' (2005) 10 *Child & Family Social Work* 269; D. Howe et al., 'Age at placement and adult adopted people's experience of being adopted' (2001) 6 *Child & Family Social Work* 337.
32 Harris-Short, op. cit., n. 1, p. 407.
33 DoH, *National Adoption Standards for England* (2001) para. 2.
34 ACA 2002, s. 22(1).
35 S. Harris-Short and J. Miles, *Family Law: Text, Cases and Materials* (2007) 1010–12.

(b) The welfare test and dispensing with consent

A further core feature of the government's reform agenda was its commitment to placing the child at the centre of the adoption. In the parliamentary debates leading up to the enactment of the ACA 2002 there was a clear view that too much attention was currently being paid to the wishes and feelings of the birth parents, with adoptions being delayed by social workers prevaricating over repeated attempts at reunification and birth parents selfishly standing between their child and a happier, more secure future.[36] The ACA 2002 thus seeks to address these concerns by making the child's welfare the paramount consideration throughout the adoption process and minimizing any remaining obstacles to adoption once the local authority has determined that adoption will best serve the child's interests.

The government's decision to entrench the paramountcy principle in the ACA 2002 was not unexpected. The previous legislation had been criticized for being out of line with both s. 1 of the CA 1989 and Article 21 of the United Nations Convention on the Rights of the Child, the latter of which provides that any state recognizing or permitting the system of adoption must ensure that the best interests of the child are paramount. The paramountcy principle as enshrined in s. 1 of the ACA 2002 is of wide application binding any 'court or adoption agency' whenever it is 'coming to a decision' relating to the adoption of a child. Again, on the surface, this decision to render the child's welfare paramount throughout the adoption process seems perfectly laudable. However, by making the child's welfare paramount, there is a legitimate concern that sufficient opportunity is not being provided for the birth parents' rights and interests to be taken into account by the key decision-makers – rights and interests which for parents facing the irrevocable termination of their 'very parenthood' are profoundly important.

The problem derives from the meaning of the term 'paramount' as understood in English law.[37] It is widely accepted that 'paramount' means that the child's interests must be the decision-maker's *sole* consideration.[38] The rights and interests of others are therefore only relevant in so far as they bear upon the welfare of the child. Thus, strictly applied, the birth parents' *independent* rights and interests must be disregarded unless the parents can establish they impact upon the child's welfare. This is very different to the test enshrined in the previous legislation which rendered the child's welfare

---

36 See, for example, speeches of Julian Brazier MP: 360 *H.C. Debs.*, col. 588 (21 December 2000) and cols. 744–6 (26 March 2001); Desmond Swayne MP, 360 *H.C. Debs.*, col. 771 (26 March 2001).

37 See S. Harris-Short, '*Re B (Adoption: Natural Parent)* Putting the child at the heart of adoption?' (2002) 14 *Child and Family Law Q.* 325, at 335–9 and S. Harris-Short, 'Family Law and the Human Rights Act 1998: Judicial Restraint or Revolution?' (2003) 17 *Child and Family Law Q.* 329, at 352–8.

38 *J* v. *C* [1970] A.C. 668.

the *first* but not the *paramount* consideration.[39] The concern as to the impact this has on the parents' Article 8 rights is to some extent assuaged by the welfare checklist contained within the ACA 2002 through which the paramountcy principle is to be interpreted and applied.[40] Included within the checklist are specific provisions pointing to the effect of the adoption on the child's legal status[41] and the child's existing and likely future relationships with members of the birth family. Thus, s. 1(4)(f) provides:

> The court or adoption agency must have regard to the following matters (amongst others) ...
> (f) the relationship which the child has with relatives, and with any other person in relation to whom the court or agency considers the relationship to be relevant, including –
> (i) the likelihood of any such relationship continuing and the value to the child of its doing so,
> (ii) the ability and willingness of any of the child's relatives, or of any such person, to provide the child with a secure environment in which the child can develop, and otherwise to meet the child's needs,
> (iii) the wishes and feelings of any of the child's relatives, or of any such person, regarding the child.

Clearly this should ensure that the wishes and feelings of the birth parents are not wholly ignored in the decision-making process. However, whether it is sufficient to meet the demands of Article 8 is more doubtful. Under the ACA 2002, the wishes and feelings of the birth parents must still be mitigated through the framework of the welfare principle. They are not afforded any *independent* weight in the decision-making process such that, even if the parents' interests run counter to the welfare of the child, they will still be afforded due consideration and respect. In contrast, it is clear from *Johansen* that Article 8(1) of the European Convention requires that the parents' rights and interests are given this kind of independent consideration.[42] Moreover, such are the importance of these rights and interests in the context of adoption that it is also clear from *Johansen* that the child's welfare will not always be sufficient under Article 8(2) to justify any prima facie breach of the birth parents' rights under Article 8(1).[43] Strong 'overriding' welfare considerations, that is, more than a simple tipping of the welfare balance in favour of the adoption, will sometimes be required if this 'particularly far-reaching' interference with the birth parents' rights is to be deemed necessary and proportionate.[44]

These potential problems with the paramountcy principle have been compounded by the reformed provisions on dispensing with parental con-

---

39 Adoption Act 1976, s. 6.
40 ACA 2002, s. 1(4).
41 ACA 2002, s. 1(4)(c).
42 *Johansen*, op. cit., n. 7.
43 id., [78]–[84].
44 id., [78]. See, also, the comments of Baroness Hale in *Down*, op. cit., n. 7, [33]–[34].

sent. The starting position under the ACA 2002 is that no child can be placed for adoption or made subject to an adoption order unless every parent or guardian of the child has consented.[45] Parental consent can, however, be dispensed with by the court if satisfied that: (i) the parent or guardian of the child cannot be found or is incapable of giving consent, or (ii) the welfare of the child *requires* the consent to be dispensed with.[46] Again this constitutes an important change from the previous legislation where the most widely used ground for dispensing with parental consent was that the parent or guardian was withholding his agreement unreasonably.[47] Although the child's welfare was a very important consideration in determining whether agreement was being unreasonably withheld, it was generally clear from the case law that a parent taking into account his or her own rights and interests in deciding whether or not to withhold consent would not be acting unreasonably.[48] In other words, the child's welfare was not the only relevant factor. This contrasts sharply with s. 52 of the ACA 2002 which appears to provide that parental consent can be dispensed with on the basis of a simple welfare test. There has been some academic speculation as to whether the use of the term 'requires' in s. 52 may be interpreted to impose a higher threshold for dispensing with consent than a straightforward welfare test.[49] However, early case law following implementation of the ACA in December 2005 is not encouraging. Although reaching no final view on this point, in *Re S*[50] the Court of Appeal gave a strong indication that a straightforward welfare test will be applied. Consequently, once adoption has been found to be in the best interests of the child, parental consent should pose no further obstacle – dispensing with consent will follow logically from a finding that adoption is in the child's best interests.[51] This decision, in combination with the paramountcy principle, is deeply concerning. It pays absolutely no regard to the legitimate rights and interests of the birth parents.

(c) Post-adoption contact

One of the key advantages of a rights-based approach is that it forces decision-makers to focus on the child not only as a member of a family but as an autonomous individual with separate and perhaps competing rights and interests to which the state must have regard. Nowhere is this more important than with respect to the issue of post-adoption contact. One of the most

45 ACA 2002, ss. 19(1), 21(3), and 47(2). Only the consent of a parent with parental responsibility is required: ACA 2002, s. 52(6).
46 ACA 2002, s. 52(1).
47 Adoption Act 1976, s. 16(2).
48 *Re W (An infant)* [1971] A.C. 682; *Re H; Re W (Adoption: Parental Agreement)* (1983) F.L.R. 614; and *Re C (A Minor) (Adoption: Parental Agreement: Contact)* [1993] 2 F.L.R. 260.
49 Choudhry, op. cit., n. 1, pp. 122–4.
50 *Re S*, op. cit., n. 15.
51 id., [71]–[72] (per Wall LJ).

crucial questions the court must address when making an adoption order is whether the adoption will effectively terminate all ongoing relations with the birth family or whether some provision should be made for retaining the child's familial links through some form of contact. Concerns about adopted children's sense of identity have underpinned clear moves in the social work profession towards the promotion of greater openness in adoption.[52] A positive image of, and links with, the family of birth are thus kept alive through the use of various tools such as story books, letter-box schemes, and direct contact. However, despite these developments, the child's right to maintain his or her links with the birth family have traditionally been marginalized within the law.

The right to post-adoption contact arguably falls within the scope of both the private and family life limbs of Article 8. The concept of private life under Article 8 is extremely broad. It is described in the case of *Bensaid* v. *UK* in the following terms:

> Article 8 protects a right to identity and personal development, and the right to establish and develop relationships with other human beings and the outside world.[53]

It has consistently been held in the Strasbourg case law that Article 8 protects the right to access information about one's genetic parentage, albeit that right must be balanced against and may sometimes have to give way to competing interests.[54] As it was expressed in *Odievre* v. *France*:

> Matters of relevance to personal development include details of a person's identity as a human being and the vital interest protected by the Convention in obtaining information necessary to discover the truth concerning important aspects of one's personal identity, such as the identity of one's parents ... Birth, and in particular the circumstances in which a child is born, forms part of a child's, and subsequently the adult's, private life guaranteed by art 8 of the Convention.[55]

Although the question of post-adoption contact has not been explicitly addressed by the European Court, the right to respect for private life has been found to include 'the right to establish and develop relations with others'.[56] The right to maintain relations with members of the birth family in order to preserve and protect established links with one's family of origin, would seem a relatively straightforward extension of the accepted principle that an individual has the right to access information about his or her genetic parentage.

---

52 C. Smith, 'Autopoietic Law and the "Epistemic Trap": A Case Study of Adoption and Contact' (2004) 31 *J. of Law and Society* 318, at 330–3. As to the pervasiveness of post-adoption contact, see J. Masson, 'Thinking about contact – a social or legal problem?' (2000) 12 *Child and Family Law Q.* 15, at 19–20.
53 *Bensaid* v. *UK* (2001) 11 BHRC 297, [47].
54 *Odievre*, op. cit., n. 25.
55 id., [29].
56 *Bensaid*, op. cit., n. 53.

The question of whether a right to post-adoption contact can be brought within the scope of the right to respect for family life is more difficult. This is of course the basis on which arguments in favour of contact are advanced in the context of disputes over contact between natural parents. The proposition that a child has a right to contact with his or her birth parents, and vice versa, is well-established, at least where the relationship between parent and child is sufficient to give rise to the existence of family life.[57] There is nothing in principle to suggest that this right does not prevail in the placement period, albeit subject to welfare considerations in accordance with Article 8(2). The issue is, however, complicated in the post-adoption period by the uncertainty over the continuing 'family' status of the birth parents. The formal legal position is clear. Once the adoption order has been made, the birth parents become 'former parents': they are no longer regarded in law for any purpose as the child's parents and any de jure claim to family life vis-à-vis the child is presumably thereby extinguished. Certainly in domestic law any claim to post-adoption contact is dealt with on the basis that the parents are now to be regarded as legal strangers to the child.[58] However, the approach of the European Court to the existence or non-existence of family life allows for greater flexibility than this. There is no direct authority as to the status of the relationship between the birth parents and the child following an adoption. In *Odievre*, a case concerned with the practice of anonymous birth, the court refused to consider the issues under the family life arm of Article 8.[59] *Odievre* was, however, solely concerned with the provision of information and was a case in which there had never existed any relationship between the birth parents and the child which could even tenuously be argued to amount to the existence of family life. There is no Strasbourg authority dealing with the situation where a de facto relationship has continued between the child and the birth parents leading up to and following an adoption. It is, however, significant that the European Court has more generally been willing to move beyond the formal constraints of legal relationships to find the existence of family life based on the existence of de facto ties between the parties.[60] The fact that the formal legal relationship between the birth parents and the child has been or is about to be terminated should not therefore prove decisive. As it is expressed in *Lebbink*, what is required to establish the existence of family life is 'sufficient constancy' in the relationship and 'the real existence in practice of close personal ties'.[61] Cohabitation as a family is not required.[62] Although cases dealing with the

---

57 See, for example, *Hokkanen v. Finland* [1996] 1 F.L.R. 289 and *Glaser v. UK* [2001] 1 F.L.R. 153.
58 See *M v C & Calderdale Metropolitan Council* [1993] 3 All E.R. 313.
59 *Odievre*, op. cit., n. 25 [28].
60 See, for example, the seminal case of *Marckx v. Belgium* (1979–80) 2 E.H.R.R. 330 and *Lebbink*, op. cit., n. 22.
61 *Lebbink*, id., [36].
62 id.

existence of de facto family ties are decided in a very different context – with individuals seeking to establish the existence of family life, not determine whether it has been extinguished – the same general principles should apply. Thus it is difficult to see why, if the birth family have remained in contact with the child throughout the adoption process and beyond, the de jure position should prevent recognition of the continuation of de facto family life between the birth parents and child.

A positive finding that the child and the birth parents have reciprocal rights to both pre and post-adoption contact under Article 8 of the European Convention is significant, bringing a very different dimension to the question. Where post-adoption contact is disputed, English law has tended to focus almost exclusively on the needs and wishes of the adoptive parents, with the courts being extremely reluctant to make a contact order in the face of the adoptive parents' opposition.[63] Even where the parties are agreed on contact, the courts have been reluctant to fetter the adoptive parents' future discretion by enshrining the agreement in an order.[64] In light of clear changes in social work philosophy and practice regarding post-adoption contact, supported by a growing body of empirical research regarding the benefits of open adoption,[65] the ACA 2002 arguably sought to shift the balance in favour of making greater use of contact orders in the post-adoption context.[66] Thus, in addition to enshrining the right of birth parents, amongst others, to make an application for a s. 26 contact order at the placement stage,[67] the court may order contact of its own motion and is under a clear mandatory duty to consider the adoption agency's proposals for contact before making the placement order.[68] These provisions should ensure more birth parents are able to maintain regular contact with their children throughout the crucial placement period.[69] This, in turn, should strengthen the birth parents' case for post-adoption contact at the final

---

63 See *Re C (a minor) (adoption: conditions)* [1988] 1 A.C. 1, pp. 17–18.
64 *Re T (Adoption: Contact)* [1995] 2 F.L.R. 251.
65 See, for example, J. Fratter, *Adoption with contact – Implications for Policy and Practice* (1996) and M. Ryburn, 'In whose best interests? Post-adoption contact with the birth family' (1998) 10 *Child and Family Law Q.* 53. For a more cautious assessment of the research evidence, see D. Quinton and J. Selwyn, 'Contact with birth parents in adoption – a response to Ryburn' (1998) 10 *Child and Family Law Q.* 349. For more recent summaries of current research, see C. Smith, 'Trust v Law: Promoting and Safeguarding Post-Adoption Contact' (2005) 27 *J. of Social Welfare and Family Law* 315, at 315–17 and D. Quinton and J. Selwyn, 'Adoption: research, policy and practice' (2006) 18 *Child and Family Law Q.* 459, at 470–3.
66 Not everyone would agree that greater use of court orders is the most appropriate or most effective approach to maintaining positive post-adoption relationships with the birth family. See Masson, op. cit., n. 52 and Smith, id.
67 ACA 2002, s. 26(3).
68 ACA 2002, ss. 26(4) and 27(4).
69 As to the potential benefits of contact in this context, see *Re E (A Minor) (Care order: contact)* [1994] 1 F.L.R. 146, pp. 154–5.

hearing. At this stage, the statutory provisions on post-adoption contact have again been strengthened. The court is under a clear mandatory duty to consider the proposals as to post-adoption contact and must consider the full range of powers available to it, including contact orders under s. 8 of the CA 1989.[70] The court should be further encouraged towards the making of a contact order by s. 1(4)(f) of the welfare checklist which, as discussed above, directs the court's attention to the child's existing relationships with members of the birth family, the value of those relationships continuing, and the wishes and feelings of the child's relatives.

Whether or not these provisions are, however, strong enough to bring about a fundamental change in the court's approach to post-adoption contact is doubtful.[71] The problem does not lie with the courts' ability to make the appropriate orders, but with their firmly entrenched resistance to doing so. Without much stronger guidance from the legislature as to the desirability of post-adoption contact, it is highly unlikely that this resistance will be broken down, particularly if the adoptive parents are opposed. These doubts have been borne out by subsequent case law. In *Re R (Adoption: Contact)*, Wall LJ made it clear that despite the new legislative provisions and changing views on the merits of post-adoption contact, the courts' approach would remain essentially unchanged.[72]

The question therefore remains whether the somewhat cautious provisions on contact in the ACA 2002 are sufficient to ensure consistency with the European Convention, particularly if interpreted and applied as suggested by Wall LJ in *Re R*. Again, as with other issues already explored, the European Convention would seem to demand a more robust approach. If the child and the birth parents have a prima facie right to contact, any interference with that right must be justified by the state in accordance with Article 8(2). The courts' typical rationale for refusing to impose post-adoption contact on unwilling adoptive parents is, in the name of the child's best interests, to protect the new and possibly fragile family unit from any destabilizing interference, tension, and stress caused by the birth parents.[73] This is, of course, a fundamentally important consideration. A failed adoption would be devastating for both the adopters and the child. Underpinning this consideration is the undoubted right, protected by Article 8, of both the adoptive parents and the child to respect for their family life vis-à-vis each other.[74] Clearly, if the adoption placement is at risk of breaking down, the adoptive parents' Article 8 rights, as well as the child's rights and interests, may well demand that there is no further contact with the birth family. The balance of rights will come down in favour of the

---

70 ACA 2002, s. 46.
71 See Harris-Short, op. cit., n. 1, at p. 417.
72 *Re R (Adoption: Contact)* [2005] EWCA Civ 1128, [48]–[49]. Compare the more positive comments of Baroness Hale towards post-adoption contact in *Down*, op. cit., n. 7.
73 *Re C*, op. cit., n. 63.
74 *Pini*, op. cit., n. 7.

adoptive family. Where, however, there is no actual threat to the stability and security of the adoption, or contact is nevertheless found to be in the child's best interests, it is difficult to sustain the argument that the interference with the child and/or the birth parents' rights can be justified as a proportionate response to the adoptive family's interests or the legitimate need to protect the child's welfare. Again a rights-based analysis brings a different and vitally important dimension to the debate.

THE LIMITS OF THE DISCOURSE: HUMAN RIGHTS IN THE POST-ADOPTION CONTEXT

Given the far-reaching effects of an adoption order on the child's core familial relationships, it is clear that a rights-based analysis can make an important contribution to our understanding of the duties and responsibilities of the state throughout the adoption process. It is less clear what, if anything, a human rights analysis can add to our understanding of the duties and responsibilities of the state in the post-adoption context. It may be hoped that a rights-based discourse will provide the normative basis for imposing more extensive duties and responsibilities on the state, in particular, that it will provide the basis for strengthening the state's role in the provision of post-adoption support for adopted children and their families. However, given the nature of the rights in question, the application of the human rights paradigm to the post-adoption context proves considerably more difficult.

1. *Post-adoption support under the ACA 2002*

The need for effective post-adoption support services formed a central plank of the government's reforms. It was recognized that if greater use was to be made of adoption for looked-after children, better support would be needed to prevent these often difficult and challenging placements from breaking down. However, as several commentators have noted, under the previous legislation the provision of post-adoption support was woefully inadequate.[75] Adoptive parents reported difficulties in accessing appropriate services, with many observing that once the adoption order had been made they were simply left alone to get on with the job of raising their children without further assistance or support.[76] It was intended that the ACA 2002 would help to redress these problems.

---

75 N. Lowe et al., *Supporting Adoption. Reframing the Approach* (1999) 430; A. Rushton, 'Support for adoptive families. A review of current evidence on problems, needs and effectiveness' (2003) 27 *Adoption & Fostering* 41, at 46.
76 Rushton, id., and J. Selwyn and D. Quinton, 'Stability, permanence, outcomes and support. Foster care and adoption compared' (2004) 28 *Adoption & Fostering* 6, at 12.

In many ways the ACA 2002 sought to shift the balance away from a traditional model of adoption, what has been termed a privacy/autonomy model, to embrace a model of adoption more attuned to the contemporary needs of today's adopted children, what has been termed in the literature a contract/services model.[77] The privacy/autonomy model sees the role of the state in the post-adoption context as minimal. It is founded on the traditional concept of adoption whereby there is a total and absolute transplanting of the legal relationship of parent and child.[78] This has important consequences in terms of the ongoing duties and responsibilities of the state in the post-adoption period. From the perspective of the state, one of the major advantages of this model of adoption is that once the adoption order has been made, the adoptive family is legally and socially reconstituted as an ordinary autonomous family, protected from any outside interference from the state and, just like any other family, neither expecting nor requiring any additional assistance or support.[79] So strongly is this concept of the new autonomous family embedded within society's understanding of adoption that many adoptive parents actively resist post-adoption services and support, believing such intervention stigmatizes them as somehow less than the ideal.[80] Lowe terms this approach the gift/donation model of adoption.[81] However, Lowe and Murch argue that if adoption is to meet the needs of children in care, this 'mindset' of adoption has to change.[82] They therefore reconceptualize the role of the state in the post-adoption context to what they term the 'contract/services' model.

The contract/services model of adoption developed out of recognition of the changing profile of adopted children.[83] Children adopted out of care today often have a range of physical, emotional, social, and educational needs requiring skilled and sensitive parenting. Adoptive parents face a difficult and demanding task for which ongoing professional help and support can be vitally important. As Luckock and Hart explain, adoption in the contemporary context demands a form of 'reparative parenting' from adoptive parents whereby not only are adopted children provided with a

---

77 B. Luckock and A. Hart, 'Adoptive family life and adoption support: policy ambivalence and the development of effective services' (2005) 10 *Child and Family Social Work* 125, at 127. See, too, B. Luckock, 'Adoption Support and the Negotiation of Ambivalence in Family Policy and Children's Services' in this volume, pp. 3–27.
78 ACA 2002, ss. 46 and 67.
79 Luckock and Hart, op. cit., n. 77. M. Ryburn, 'A New Model of Welfare: Reasserting the Value of Kinship for Children in State Care' (1998) 32 *Social Policy and Administration* 28, at 37.
80 Rushton, op. cit., n. 75, p. 46.
81 N. Lowe, 'The changing face of adoption – the gift/donation model versus the contract/services model' (1997) 9 *Child and Family Law Q.* 371.
82 id., and Lowe et al., op. cit., n. 75, pp. 429–30.
83 Lowe et al., id.

secure and permanent home but are compensated through quality, skilled parenting for their earlier damaging experiences.[84] Having removed these troubled children from their birth parents it can thus be argued that the state should not be allowed to simply walk away: that it has continuing duties and responsibilities to support and assist the child and the adoptive parents as they face the many challenges of adoption. As Lowe and Murch explain:

> There needs to be an acceptance that, at the very least with regard to older children (if not for all children), adoption is not the end of the process but only a stage ... in an ongoing and often complex process of family development. We think that the adoption of older children out of care is best understood as some kind of informal 'contract' between the birth family, the child and the adoptive family – a 'contract' which brings with it a pattern of reciprocal obligations between the 'parties' and the adoption agency, which performs a brokering role as well as providing continuing support, while the court holds the ring in this process and puts an important symbolic and official seal to the arrangements.[85]

Under this 'contract/services' model the state should expect to provide substantial support to all members of the adoption triad before, during, and after the adoption.[86] Thus the state cannot expect that its obligations towards adopted children will be discharged by the making of the adoption order. To the contrary, it is contended that the duties and responsibilities of the state to support adopted children and those who take on the task of looking after them must, prima facie, continue into the post-adoption period. Thus, of fundamental importance to the contract/service model of adoption is the state's responsibility to provide a comprehensive post-adoption support service including, where appropriate, financial support, and facilitating and supporting post-adoption contact. The contract/services model also has particularly important implications for the adoptive parents. As Lowe suggests, the adopters should expect that adoption will not necessarily mean the end of contact with members of the birth family and, perhaps most controversially, the adoptive parents may need to accept that they may not be in complete control of the child's upbringing in the same way as the child's natural parents may usually expect.[87]

The ACA 2002 certainly seeks to improve the provision of post-adoption support services. The legislation now enshrines a clear statutory duty to provide adoption support services to adopted children and their families which includes post-adoption support.[88] This duty is particularized in the Adoption Support Services Regulations 2005 which explicitly provide that in addition to 'counselling, advice and information', adoption support services must, amongst other things, include: (i) the payment of adoption allowances;

---

84 Luckock and Hart, op. cit., n. 77, p. 127.
85 Lowe et al., op. cit., n. 75, pp. 429–30.
86 Lowe, op. cit., n. 81, p. 383.
87 id.
88 ACA 2002, s. 3(1).

(ii) providing assistance in relation to arrangements for contact between an adopted child and his or her birth family; (iii) assisting the adoptive family where the placement is at risk of disrupting; and (iv) meeting the 'therapeutic needs' of an adoptive child.[89] Support services will thus include practical help, professional advice, financial assistance where needed, and information about local and national support groups and services. Every local authority must appoint an adoption support services adviser who is responsible for advising those affected by an adoption as to how to access appropriate support services.[90]

These clear statutory duties should lead to a substantial improvement in services. There are, however, weaknesses in the legislative scheme. Most importantly, under s. 4(1) of the legislation the local authority must, at the request of the adopted child, the adoptive parents, or the birth parents,[91] carry out an assessment of that person's needs for support services. However, the local authority is under no duty to meet those assessed needs. It must simply decide whether or not to provide the person with appropriate support.[92]

More fundamentally, it has been argued that the ACA 2002 has failed to truly embrace a contract/services model of adoption. Although the legislation has gone some way towards recognizing the ongoing responsibilities of the state, it is pointed out that the legislation contains many contradictions.[93] Thus, whilst the legislation does introduce more extensive provisions on post-adoption support, the traditional legal concept of adoption as a 'total legal transplant' remains firmly entrenched. In particular, what Parkinson refers to the as the 're-birthing' of the child into the adoptive family remains enshrined within s. 67.[94] As Luckock and Hart argue, this ambiguity in the legislation reflects continuing ambivalence about the nature of adoptive parenthood and the appropriate role for the state in the post-adoption context:

> Government tries to have it both ways. It has reinforced the traditional expectations of the autonomy of the adoptive family and explicitly distinguished adoption from 'corporate' parenting and its instability. But it has also emphasised the importance to the success of adoption of additional support. This leads to mixed messages being received on the ground and some confusion about which way to move services forward.[95]

---

89 Adoption Support Services Regulations 2005, S.I. 2005/691, reg. 3.
90 id., reg. 6.
91 Amongst others. See ACA 2002, s. 4(1).
92 ACA 2002, s. 4(4)
93 Luckock and Hart, op. cit., n. 77.
94 P. Parkinson, 'Child Protection, Permanency Planning and Children's Right to Family Life' (2003) 17 *International J. of Law, Policy and the Family* 147, at 161.
95 Luckock and Hart, op. cit., n. 77, p. 126.

2. Does a rights-based discourse demand more?

For those who argue that the state must play a much greater role in the post-adoption context, it may be hoped that the human rights paradigm can be successfully employed to reinforce the contract/services model of adoption and strengthen and extend the state's duties and responsibilities to provide effective post-adoption support beyond those currently enshrined within the ACA 2002. However, given the socio-economic nature of the rights in question, this is difficult territory for human rights. Indeed, rather than challenging the ACA's fairly limited model of state responsibility in the post-adoption period, a rights-based approach tends to reinforce the traditional gift/donation model of adoption and the minimalist approach to post-adoption support that follows. Liberal rights-based doctrine sits easily with a model of state-family relations which promotes and prioritizes the protection of family privacy and autonomy. It is trite law that Article 8 of the European Convention imposes both negative and positive obligations on the state.[96] However, it is the state's negative obligation to refrain from intervening into autonomous family life which lies at the heart of a liberal rights-based framework. As it was put by the European Court of Human Rights in *Pini*, it is the negative obligation of non-intervention that forms 'the essential object of Article 8'.[97] This negative obligation is certainly less challenging to traditional rights orthodoxy than the positive obligations which may be enshrined within Article 8, the scope and extent of which are considerably less certain. The 'total legal transplant' model of adoption and a conceptualization of welfare which perceives the state's role as supporting and consolidating the new adoptive family unit by protecting them from any potentially destabilizing outside interference thus fits neatly and easily with the 'core' obligations enshrined under Article 8(1). As discussed earlier, the right of the child's adoptive family to respect for their private and family life has been firmly established by the Strasbourg court.[98] As it was put in *Pini*, 'the relations between an adoptive parent and an adopted child are as a rule of the same nature as the family relations protected by Article 8 of the Convention'.[99] There is thus little within this jurisprudence to suggest the adoptive family will attract differential treatment under the Convention to that received by a natural biological family. A model of non-intervention predominates.

This is clearly not encouraging if one is looking to a rights-based discourse to help underpin and strengthen the provision of post-adoption support. However, given the traditional foundations of the human rights discourse, to invoke rights-based arguments in an effort to impose more

---

96 See, for example, *Marckx*, op. cit., n. 60, [31].
97 *Pini*, op. cit., n. 7, [149].
98 id., [140].
99 id.

extensive socio-economic obligations on the state, whilst not impossible, will always be problematic. The field of social welfare assistance, including family support, is not a natural home for the human rights paradigm. It can, of course, be argued as a matter of legal principle that the state has a positive obligation under Article 8(1) of the Convention to provide help and support to an adoptive family in need, particularly if the outcome of refusing support will be the breakdown of the family unit. However, imposing positive obligations on the state to provide help and support in the form of financial, professional, and therapeutic services raises the intractable problem of the allocation of scarce state resources: socio-economic questions with which liberal rights doctrine is traditionally reluctant to engage. The European Court has yet to deal with the question of whether a state's positive obligations under Article 8 include the provision of social welfare assistance in order to prevent family breakdown - whether the family is adoptive or otherwise.[100] This absence of authority reflects the difficulty of making these arguments within the framework of the Convention. In the domestic context, the House of Lords have accepted the principle that the state may be under a positive obligation to provide social welfare assistance to a class of individuals (in this case in-country asylum seekers) who have been deprived of this assistance by the state and who would otherwise be rendered destitute to a degree of severity that it constitutes inhuman and degrading treatment under Article 3 of the Convention.[101] This is, however, a long way from establishing the principle that there is a right to social welfare assistance under Article 8. Moreover, even if a right to social welfare assistance to prevent family breakdown could be established in principle, as a qualified right it would be subject to the state's right to balance this against competing interests as permitted under Article 8(2). It is therefore not surprising that in *R (on the application of G)* v. *Barnet London Borough Council et al.*, the House of Lords, in determining the nature and scope of the state's duties and responsibilities to 'children in need' under s. 17 of the CA 1989,[102] gave extremely short shrift to the Article 8 arguments.[103] The three conjoined cases were all concerned with the accommodation of 'children in need'. In

---

100 The Strasbourg jurisprudence suggests, however, that a positive outcome to such an argument is extremely unlikely. It has, for example, rejected the argument that Article 8 gives rise to the right to be provided with a home by the state. See *Chapman* v. *UK* (2001) 33 E.H.R.R. 399.
101 *R (Limbuela)* v. *Secretary of State for the Home Department* [2005] U.K.H.L. 66.
102 Section 17(1) provides:
   It shall be the general duty of every local authority (in addition to the other duties imposed on them by this Part) – (a) to safeguard and promote the welfare of children within their area who are in need; and (b) so far as is consistent with that duty, to promote the upbringing of such children by their families, by providing a range and level of services appropriate to those children's needs.
103 *R (on the application of G)* v. *Barnet London Borough Council; R (on the application of W)* v. *Lambeth London Borough Council; R (on the application of A)* v. *Lambeth London Borough Council* [2003] U.K.H.L. 57.

the first case, two disabled children had been assessed as in need of accommodation under s. 17 because of the unsuitability of their present accommodation. The local authority decided it was unable to provide the accommodation. In the second and third cases, the children were assessed as in need of accommodation because their mothers were homeless and did not qualify for assistance under the homelessness legislation. Two keys issues arose for consideration: (i) whether once a child had been assessed as in need of accommodation, the local authority were under a duty to meet that assessed need; and (ii) whether the local authority were acting lawfully in only offering to accommodate the two homeless children without their mothers.[104] On the first issue the House of Lords held that the duty referred to in s. 17(1) is a 'general' or 'target' duty owed to all children in need within the local authority area. They went on to dismiss the argument that this general duty 'crystallizes' into a specific duty once the child has been assessed and a particular need identified. This means in practice that the s. 17(1) duty cannot be enforced at the suit of individual children and the local authority is thus under no enforceable duty to provide a particular service to an individual child following an assessment of the child's need under s. 17. On the second issue, the House of Lords held that the local authority was acting perfectly lawfully in refusing to accommodate both mother and child together, there being no duty under the Children Act to accommodate a homeless parent. In reaching these conclusions, both Lord Nicholls in dissent and Lord Hope giving judgment for the majority made only cursory reference to the Article 8 arguments.[105] This is despite what is prima facie a strong argument that, at least with respect to the second issue, the right to respect for family life under Article 8 of the Convention strengthens and prioritizes the duty on local authorities under s. 17(1) to seek to promote the upbringing of children within their families, something manifestly not achieved by refusing to accommodate both parent and child together.

On the basis of the existing jurisprudence there is therefore very little to suggest that a rights-based analysis could be successfully employed to strengthen the provisions on post-adoption support as contained in the ACA 2002. In particular, on the specific question of whether the ACA 2002 could be interpreted to impose an individualized duty on the local authority to actually meet the assessed needs of an adoptive family, there is no reason to

---

104 Pursuant to their duty under s. 20(1) of the CA 1989 which provides:
   Every local authority shall provide accommodation for any child in need within the area who appears to them to require accommodation as a result of – (a) there being no person who has parental responsibility for him; (b) his being lost or having been abandoned; or (c) the person who has been caring for him being prevented (whether or not permanently, and for whatever reason) from providing him with suitable accommodation or care.
105 *R (on the application of G)* v. *Barnet*; *R (on the application of W)* v. *Lambeth*; *R (on the application of A)* v. *Lambeth*, op. cit., n. 103, [52]–[53] (per Lord Nicholls), [69] (per Lord Hope).

suppose the legislation would be interpreted any differently from the House of Lords interpretation of s. 17 of the CA 1989 in *R (on the application of G)* v. *Barnet*. Indeed, although in general terms one would wish the state's obligations to assist and support adoptive families to be as rigorous as possible, there is no immediately apparent reason why the state's obligations to adoptive families *should* be any more extensive or rigorous than the state's obligations to other families in need. The fact that adopted children, unlike children seeking assessment under s. 17 of the CA 1989, have the right to be assessed for support and assistance has already been the subject of convincing criticism on the grounds that it may lead to the needs of adopted children being unjustifiably prioritized over the needs of other vulnerable families.[106] Without cogent reasons for distinguishing the needs of adoptive families from other vulnerable families, the latter may well have legitimate grounds for complaint. So, do any such cogent reasons exist? There are a few possibilities, but none of them convincing.

It could be argued that the needs of adoptive families as a group are greater than those of other vulnerable families, something which, on the empirical evidence regarding the positive functioning of adoptive families, may be difficult to sustain.[107] Similarly, the fact that adopted children may have a range of complex and challenging needs does not explain why they cannot be dealt with on the same basis as children suffering from similar difficulties but who fall to be dealt with under the CA 1989. Alternatively, it could be argued that the state's unique role in the creation of adoptive family life underpins distinctive obligations to provide more extensive assistance and support: in essence, a 'once engaged, always engaged' argument. However, it is not self-evident why the fact of the state's participation in the creation of adoptive families should, in and of itself, impose ongoing obligations of support on the state and elevate the family's needs above those of other vulnerable families in need. No such calls are made in the context of assisted reproduction where the state is similarly engaged in the creation of families. Indeed, it is likely any such calls would be met with strong hostility and surprise. Finally, on a similar 'once engaged, always engaged' premise, it could be argued that the duties and responsibilities of the state in the post-adoption context are derived from the duties and responsibilities assumed by the state to a looked-after child when the child was in local authority care. In other words, having assumed the role of corporate parent, the state's duties and responsibilities will continue to persist throughout the child's childhood. However, such an approach again raises difficult questions as to the justification for treating previously looked-after children differently based on

---

106 J. Masson, 'The Impact of the Adoption and Children Act 2002 – Part 2 – the Provision of Services for Children and Families' (2003) 33 *Family Law* 644, at 646–7.
107 id. See, also, K. O'Brien and K. Zamostny, 'Understanding Adoptive Families: An Integrative Review of Empirical Research and Future Directions for Counseling Psychology' (2003) 13 *The Counseling Psychologist* 679, at 690.

their particular route out of care. It is difficult to provide a convincing answer as to why a natural parent to whom a child is returned following discharge of a care order should not be entitled to the same elevated level of support services as an adoptive family, particularly as it may be anticipated that, despite the challenges of adoption, a natural parent in such circumstances may well be more vulnerable to recurring family breakdown.

There is thus little scope within the traditional rights paradigm to push the duties and responsibilities of the state beyond those contained within the ACA 2002. Indeed, a rights-based analysis would tend to reinforce rather than challenge a more traditional approach to adoption in which family autonomy is respected, the role of the state is kept to a minimum, and adoptive families are treated as equal to, not different and distinct from, the natural family norm.

CONCLUSION

Rights are a valuable tool. In the context of adoption they play an invaluable role in protecting the vulnerable and marginalized, ensuring their interests and needs are fairly and properly considered. Article 8 of the European Convention can be successfully employed throughout the adoption process to impose ever more exacting standards on the decision-makers, strengthening and extending the state's duties and responsibilities to all three members of the adoption triad and illuminating important deficiencies in the current law. However, human rights do not always provide a 'better' answer. There are important limitations to the discourse. Enthusiasts of the human rights paradigm[108] are sometimes accused of looking to a rights-based discourse to do too much. The problematic application of rights-based reasoning to the post-adoption context and the issue of post-adoption support in particular provide a pertinent example. Rights enthusiasts may well have hoped that a rights-based discourse would not only reinforce the existing obligations of the state, but may be relied upon to provide the normative basis for strengthening and extending the state's duties and responsibilities towards adopted children and their families. However, such enthusiasts will be disappointed. Given continuing ambivalence about the role of the state within the post-adoption context, the socio-economic nature of the rights in question, and the difficult policy questions to which such issues give rise, rights-based arguments provide no secure basis for demanding more from the state than the ACA 2002 already requires. However, whilst in many ways a disappointing conclusion, when viewed within the wider context of the state's policies on family support, the level of support and assistance provided to adoptive families within the ACA 2002 is not only defensible but probably right.

---

108 Of which the author is one.

Index

A and Byrne and Twenty-Twenty Television v United Kingdom 422, 425
A. A. v B. B. 282
abandonment, paternal 117
abortion 60
abuse *see* child abuse
adoption 3, 10–11, 65, 104, 123, 125–6, 134, 208, 212–13, 217, 296, 361, 376–7, 379, 389, 514; and adjustment 78; adoption allowances 149–50, 153–4; agency practice 154–5; of babies 142; changing legal position on 146–52; changing nature of 142; changing organisation of 142–4; changing practice of 145–6; contract/services model of 153–4, 551–4; exclusive view of 155; fast-track 240, 245, 257; full vs. simple 174; and genetic parenthood 166; gift/donation model of 141–2, 152–3; individual human rights issues in 537–50; inroads into severance 146–52; involvement of the state in 535–558; judicial approach to 154; legal 30, 102; and legal parenthood 167, 169–70, 174–6; of older children 141–2, 153, 156, 217; open 145–7, 175–6; out of care 541, 551; overturning 107; post-adoption contact 147, 545–50; post-adoption human rights issues 550–8; post-adoption support 150–2, 550–3; privacy/autonomy model of 551; protocol for 244–5; regulation of 143–4; by same-sex couples 241, 252; by step-parents 247–8; suggestions for reform 152–6; in surrogate parenting arrangements 21–2; tracing parents 148; transplant model of 217, 256; by unmarried couples 241; voluntary 82
Adoption Act: (1949) 146; (1976) 143, 146, 148–50, 154
Adoption Agencies Regulations 151
Adoption Allowance Regulations 149–50
Adoption and Children Act (ACA; 2002) 251–2, 536, 541–3, 545, 556, 558; post-adoption support under 550–3
Adoption Contact Register 148, 241
Adoption of Children (Regulation) Act (1939) 143
Adoption of Children Act: (1926) 142; (1949) 143, 291–2; (2002) 470–1
Adoption Support Services Regulations (2005) 552
Adoption: The Future 151
adoptive parents and families 30, 63–4, 117, 121, 131, 155, 163, 199–200, 530; due process rights of 57n153; parental responsibilities of 457; and post-adoption contact with birth family 147, 545–50; rights of 537; support for 550–3, 557–8
alternate reproduction methods 31; *see also* assisted reproduction
American Civil Liberties Union 98
Amish society 354–7, 359nn41–43
Ampthill Peerage case 214
Anderson, Elizabeth 116
Archard, David 326, 366
Aristotle 526
Article 8 (ECHR) 402–3, 544; and the adoption process 537–8, 542, 545–9, 554–5, 558; and conflict resolution 418–19; conflict with Article 10 417; disregarding of 412, 414; in domestic law 418; interpretation of 408, 410–11; judicial reasoning and outcomes 435–7; parallel analysis 427–35; and the paramountcy principle 425–7; and parental rights 414; respect for family rights 402–3, 406, 409, 413, 461n26; Strasbourg approach 419–25; violation of 453
artificial insemination 29, 51, 80; by donor (AID) 29, 29n1, 30n9, 43, 50, 109, 163, 194, 208; by husband (AIH) 29n1; *see also* donor insemination
assisted conception 2, 14n38, 193, 290–1; and the law 291; *see also* assisted reproduction; in-vitro fertilisation
assisted reproduction 4, 100, 121, 160, 190, 230, 244–5, 253, 377, 379; and genetic parenthood 166; and legal parenthood 174;

and the rights of the child 171; and same-sex parentage 239–53, 374; *see also* assisted conception; in-vitro fertilisation
attachment 77; *see also* bonding
attachment theory 114–16; *see also* bonding hypothesis/theory
Australia: birth registration in 237; parental responsibility in 442, 446; responsibilities of fathers in 450; shared time parenting in 484, 491–6
authority of parents *see* parental authority
autonomy: of the child 8, 244, 254, 347–9, 383; personal 61; social preconditions of 351–2; *see also* parental autonomy
A v. B and C 268, 276, 284–5
A v B plc 428
A v C 406

babies, premature 77
Baby Doe 316–17, 334–5
Baby Jessica 317, 335
Baby M case 32n13, 62, 64, 93, 111
baby-selling 86
Bainham, Andrew 218, 393, 395, 415, 416, 418, 481
Becker, Lawrence 20
being a parent 160–2, 220, 377; legal status of 163–4
Belsito case 216
Bensaid v. UK 546
Berrheab v The Netherlands 452
best-interests-of-the-child argument 39, 76–81, 101; *see also* children, best interests of
Bingham, (Sir) Thomas 407
biological family 376; *see also* birth family/ies
biological fathers 51–5, 220, 232–3, 246, 249, 373, 375, 473, 476–7; *see also* genetic fathers; natural fathers
biological mothers 206, 246, 255, 260–1, 373; *see also* birth mothers; genetic mothers; natural mothers
biological parents/parentage 1, 4–5, 10, 21, 34, 79, 125, 128, 160, 176, 225, 230, 237–9, 241, 244–5, 253, 258, 317, 372–3, 379–80; biological 134, 138–9; *see also* biological family; biological fathers; biological mothers; genetic parents
biological relationships, importance of 254

birth family/ies 10, 376, 536; post-adoption contact with 545–8; reconciling child with 541–5; *see also* biological family; birth mothers; birth parents
birth mothers 75, 208, 218, 220, 294; legal rights of 47–8; and the physical-involvement argument 83–5; *see also* birth parents; natural mothers
birth parents 121, 133–4, 193, 199–200; and the adoption process 537, 539, 547; *see also* biological parents/parentage; birth mothers; natural fathers; natural mothers
birth registration(s) 235–7, 241, 247, 250, 470–1; access to 148
blood tests, for paternity 209
blood tie *see* genetic link(s)
Blunkett, David 229
Blustein, Jeffrey 324
bodily integrity 61
bonding 114–16, 123, 299–300; and the critical-period hypothesis 75; postnatal 74–5; prenatal and postnatal 70–1; *see also* attachment
bonding hypothesis/theory 71, 77, 84, 92, 94–5, 298; *see also* attachment theory
Bowlby, John 529
B. R. & J. v Federal Republic of Germany 452
Branch Davidians 316
Brazier Report 212
British Agencies for Adoption and Fostering 145
Bronda v Italy 432
"but-for" causal relationship 119
Buzzanca, Jaycee 212–13
Buzzanca, John 212–13, 224
Buzzanca, Luanne 212–13
Buzzanca case 212–13, 215–6, 224
B v. B (Custody, Care and Control) 193

CA *see* Children Act (1989)
Caban v. Mohammed 54–6
California courts, and the determination of motherhood 97–102
Callus, Thérèse 364
Calvert, Chrispina 98
Campbell v MGN 429
caregivers: and parental responsibility 458; state's selection of 134
causalism 120–1

causal theory 121
causation 129
child abuse 7, 10, 77, 135–6, 509–10, 512–14, 523, 528
childbirth: forced 127–8; planned 126–7
child maltreatment *see* child abuse
children: adaptability of 529; and the adoption process 540; Article 8(1) rights of 430–2; attachment to parent figures 200; autonomy of 8, 244, 254, 347–9, 383; best interests of 39, 216, 231, 235, 238, 242, 288, 309, 343, 365, 370, 377, 400, 424, 485–6, 524, 545; biological heritage of 80, 170–3, 176, 199; change of name of 473; changing names of 387; conceived after death of father 222; of cult members 316–17, 335; custody of 369–70; development of 338–9; with disabilities 389, 556; disabled 302, 312; duty to care for 127; genetic link with parents 161; informing about adoption 242; informing about donor conception 242–3; interests of 341, 343–4, 381, 383, 387, 403, 416–18, 426, 438; as property 518–19, 526–7; psychological harm to 77; reconciling with birth family 541–5, 558; regulation of upbringing 135–6; relational rights of 133–9; relinquishment of 300; rights of 9, 133–9, 231, 340, 362, 366, 380, 382–3, 529, 533, 537; right to know parents 226, 235n30, 237, 253, 265–6, 297n46, 455, 546; view of shared time arrangements 496; violence against 136–7; welfare of 6, 8, 382, 495; *see also* best-interests-of-the-child argument; child abuse
Children Act (CA): (1975) 143, 149; (1989) 100, 146–7, 169–70, 178, 184, 190, 196, 280, 361, 369n42, 375, 378n73, 381, 388, 406–7, 411, 416, 425, 442, 450, 454, 457, 465, 467–8, 470, 473–5, 478, 539, 542–3, 556; (Scotland 1995) 441, 445, 450, 459; underlying themes and theories 401–3
child support 167, 185, 207, 235, 379
Child Support Acts (1991 and 1995) 163, 181–2, 456
citizenship 207
Civil Partnership Act (2004) 263
civil partnerships 263, 309
claim rights 318–19, 320n8
Clark, Lorenne 532
Clarke, A.C.B. 529

Clarke, A.M. 529
cloning 207
cohabitation 51, 175, 372, 456
collaborative reproduction 94; *see also* assisted conception; assisted reproduction
Colorado Supreme Court 107
common law 48–9, 56, 97, 209
compelled-relinquishment argument 92
Conaway, Helen 456
confidentiality 329
contraception, failed 3, 129–31
contraceptives 60
contract motherhood 105
Cook, Rachel 300
co-parents 266–7, 275, 374; parental role of 261; *see also* lesbian couples; lesbian parenting; same-sex parents/parentage
CRC *see* United Nations Convention on the Rights of the Child
Cretney, Stephen 142
critical-period hypothesis 75
custodial parents 3, 121–3
custody issues 105, 369–70, 369n43
C v C 260

democratic pluralism 346, 350
Department of Health and Rehabilitative Services v. Privette 210
Dickens, Bernard 365
discretionary rights 327
DNA fingerprinting/testing 209, 231
doctrine of accession 69
domestic violence 387–9, 493, 495–6
donated/donor gametes 159, 172, 217, 289, 296; *see also* egg donors/donation; sperm donors
donated sperm 208, 211; *see also* sperm donors
donor insemination (DI) 289–90; and intentionality 303–6; *see also* artificial insemination
Douglas v Hello! 428
Due Process Clause 41, 52
Dworkin, Ronald 340

ECHR *see* European Convention on Human Rights (ECHR)
ectogenesis 105
education 7, 38, 182, 342–3, 345, 358n27; in Amish communities 355–6

Eekelaar, John 229, 383, 416–18, 442, 468, 482
egg donors/donation 4, 31, 47–8, 64–9, 98, 191, 193, 206, 218, 224, 230, 240, 296; rights of 106. *See also* gamete donors; genetic donors
eggs, sources of 67–8
Ellis, Tom 229
Elsholz v. Germany 420, 421, 423, 433
Elshtain, Jean 346–7
embryo donation 206
embryos, frozen 68
England: adoption laws in 256; determination of parenthood in 178; parental responsibility in 442; parenthood laws in 189–90; paternity laws in 234–5, 253
Equal Protection 52, 137
European Convention on Human Rights (ECHR) 8–10, 172, 255, 409–11, 413, 416, 422, 424–5, 441, 451, 537–40; underlying themes and theories 403–6; *see also* Article 8 (ECHR)
European Court of Human Rights 159, 232, 245, 400, 403, 413, 418, 421, 423–5, 436
exploitation and commodification arguments 81–3

families: biological 376; influence of 337–8; integrity of 525; right to privacy 41, 111, 531–3, 536, 546; *see also* adoptive parents and families; birth family/ies
family law 39, 99, 216, 400, 405n30; in Australia 493; domestic legal reasoning post-HRA 408–15; domestic legal reasoning pre-HRA 406–8
Family Law Act (1975) 450, 495
Family Law Reform Act: (1969) 209; (1987) 470
family life 10
family policy 525
family relationships: children's rights to enter or avoid 133–5; and the role of the state 134–8
family values, traditional 338
fathers and fatherhood 4, 52–4, 160; abandonment by 117; absence of 250; on child's birth certificate 208, 220, 222, 236, 241, 266, 280; determination of 57–8, 175; and the family relationship 48; identification of 48–58, 190; intentional 208, 210–11; legal approach to 107; moral obligations of 130–1; vs. motherhood 202; natural 107; nature of 105; parental responsibility of 192, 267, 271, 446–54; psychological role of 246; question of marriage to mothers 52–4, 107, 166, 181, 208–10, 212–13; social role of 225, 246; step- 197, 220; surrogate 239; and transsexuals 159; view of shared time arrangements 496; *see also* biological fathers; fatherhood; genetic fathers and fatherhood; legal fathers and fatherhood; paternal rights; unmarried fathers
Feinberg, Joel 326–7
fertility industry 117
fiduciary duty 138
Fineman, Martha 465–6, 468
foetus: interaction with 73; physical relationship to mother 111–12, 114; psychological relationship to mother 114–15
Fortin, J. 415, 418
foster care 377
foster parents 163, 530; due process rights of 57n153
Fourteenth Amendment (U.S.) 41
France: determination of motherhood in 215; determination of paternity in 176–7; paternity laws in 232–4
Freeman, Michael 466–7
Fretté v France 245
Freud, Anna 529
Fried, Charles 342, 344, 531
frozen embryos 68

Galston, William 345–8
gamete donors and donation 100, 109, 191, 214, 223, 229–30; as parents 304–5; *see also* egg donors/donation; sperm donors
gay male couples 195–6, 262, 296n39; *see also* same-sex couples
Gender Recognition Act (2004) 191
genetic connection *see* genetic link(s)
genetic disease, sex-linked 303
genetic donors 64–70; claims for priority 64–70; genetic-identity argument 65–7; property-rights argument 67–70; *see also* egg donors/donation; sperm donors
genetic fathers and fatherhood 107–8, 117, 120, 195, 208–9, 211–12, 223, 225, 298, 469; *see also* genetic parents and parenthood
genetic-identity argument 65–7

genetic information, access to 80, 170–3, 176, 199
geneticists and geneticism 103, 118, 123; monistic 105
genetic link(s) 1, 160, 174, 213, 298, 304, 309, 312, 373; moral weight of 94; presumed 163
genetic mothers and motherhood 30, 97, 105, 108, 208, 214, 216, 218–19; as surrogate mothers 216; *see also* genetic parents and parenthood
genetic parents and parenthood 2–3, 33, 35, 66, 119–20, 122–3, 160–1, 171, 175–8, 193, 199, 215, 217, 223, 229–30, 263, 294, 297, 309, 372–3; and adoption 166; establishment of 166; legal significance of 166; *see also* biological parents; genetic fathers and fatherhood; genetic mothers and motherhood
genetics 291–2
genetic testing 210
Germany: determination of motherhood in 215; determination of genetic paternity in 176
gestation 291–2; and parenthood 2
gestational host's claims: best-interests-of-the-child argument 76–81; exploitation and commodification arguments 85–9; maternal-bonding argument 70–6; physical-involvement argument 83–5; relinquishment argument 81–3; *see also* gestational mothers
gestationalists and gestationalism 103, 106; 118, 123; necessity 108; sufficiency 116–17; *see also* monistic gestationalism
gestational mothers 2–3, 30–3, 35, 64, 68, 86, 97, 101, 105–7, 108, 110–11, 116–18, 120, 122–3, 214, 219, 223, 289, 298, 309; and the best interest of the child 300–1; bonding with child 299–300; change of mind of 21, 44, 47–8, 92; contributions of 301–2; as legal mothers 97n5; moral and legal priority of 70–89, 122–3; necessity of 119; parental claims of 94; parental status of 89; physical involvement argument 83–5; relinquishment argument 81–3; *see also* gestational host's claims; surrogate mothers and motherhood
gestational parents 3, 120, 122, 294, 372–3
gestational surrogacy 21–2, 30n5, 46–7, 58, 97, 105, 199, 216
Gillick v West Norfolk and Wisbech AHA 467

Görgülü v. Germany 255, 424
grandparents 183, 220
Great Britain *see* England
Griswold v. Connecticut 42
guardians and guardianship 167, 170, 378–9; parental responsibilities of 457
Guardianship Act 405
Guggenheim, M. 370
Gutmann, Amy 345, 347–8

Haase v Germany 424
Hague Convention on Protection of Children and Co-operation in Respect of Intercountry Adoption 442
Hague Convention on the Protection of Children 442, 444
Hale, Brenda 177
Hansen v Turkey 424
Herring, Jonathan 221, 416
heterosexual parenting 210–11, 260
Hokkanen case 424
homosexual parents *see* same-sex parents
Hoppe v Germany 424
Horsburgh Committee 143–4
Houghton Committee 143–4, 148–50
HRA *see* Human Rights Act (1998)
Human Fertilisation and Embryology Act 98, 101, 159, 211, 221–2, 252, 259, 287, 374; section 27 97–8; section 28 211; section 30 (fast-track adoption) 213, 240; sections 27–30 190; section 31 241
Human Fertilisation and Embryology Bill 239, 247, 249
human rights 237, 257; and individual rights in the adoption process 537–50; of parents 8; in the post-adoption context 550–8
Human Rights Act (HRA; 1998) 226, 393, 399, 401–3, 410–13, 417, 425–6, 438; academic debate 415–18
Hurst Committee 143–5, 148

identifiability argument 111–12
identity, biological 2
Ignaccolo-Zenide case 424
incest 236
incorporation argument 111–12
independence thesis 6, 8, 366
infertility 34, 298, 303; male 29; secondary 81
In re Baby M 44, 58–9

In re Marriage of Buzzanca 212; *see also* Buzzanca case
insemination, informal 265, 277; *see also* artificial insemination
intended parents 2, 32, 32n12, 33–4, 68, 92, 94–5, 119, 121–2, 215, 223, 291–2, 310–11; as legal parents 213; *see also* intentional parents
intensionalism 118n34
intention 165; as determinant of parentage 99–102; *see also* intentionality
intentional fathers 208, 210–11; *see also* intended parents; intentional parents
intentionalism and intentionalists 104, 118–20, 123; necessity 120; sufficiency 120
intentionality 62–3, 89–94, 98, 206, 211, 215, 219, 289, 293–302; avoidance-of-uncertainty argument 93–4; and the "but for"-causation argument 90–1; contract argument 91–2; and donor insemination (DI) 303–6; and IVF 306–7; practical examples 303–8; and surrogacy 307–8; *see also* intention
intentional/intended mothers 208, 215, 219; *see also* intended parents; intentional parents
intentional parents 3–4, 35, 123, 293–302, 309; *see also* intended parents; intentional fathers; intentional/intended mothers
In the Marriage of Moschetta 216
In the Matter of D 414
in-vitro fertilization 30, 30n4, 43, 90, 98, 206, 215, 219; and intentionality 306–7; IVF surrogacy 206, 215, 219, 222, 290
Islamic law, on adoption 256

Jennifer L. Shultz-Jacob v. Jodilynn Jacob and Carl Frampton 252
Johansen v Norway 421, 423, 431–2, 544
Johnson, Anna 47, 215–16
Johnson v. Calvert 2, 47–8, 58, 97–100, 102, 215–16
Johnstone v Republic of Ireland 452
Joint Committee on the Human Tissue and Embryos Bill 229, 241, 250
Jones, James 316
J v. C 383

Kagan, Jerome 529
Keegan v Ireland 432, 453
known donors 5, 284, 297n43; and lesbian co-parents 272–6; parental status of 278–80; *see also* sperm donors
Koresh, David 316
Kosmopolou v Greece 424
Kroon v. The Netherlands 453
K v Finland 420
K v United Kingdom 452
Kymkicka, Will 353

labour theory 1, 20–1
L'accouchement sous X 232
LaFollette, Hugh 530–1
Lebbink v. the Netherlands 539, 547
Leeds Teaching Hospitals NHS Trust v. Mr and Mrs A 192, 211
legal fathers and fatherhood 162, 210, 213, 214, 232–3; *see also* legal parents and parenthood
legal issues 3–7, 8, 276–7; adoption laws 30, 102; in California 97–102; common law 48–9, 56; compromises 282–3; equal status for multiple parents 280–2; impact of 2008 Act 277–8; on lesbian parenting 260–4; parentage laws 135; and parental interests 368–71; parental responsibility 9; parental status of known donors 278–80
legal mothers and motherhood 213–14, 216; *see also* legal parents and parenthood
legal parents and parenthood 13n25, 121, 133–4, 146, 206, 208, 213, 239, 253, 288–9, 379–80; and the adoption process 174, 537, 547; and assisted reproduction 174; attribution of 166–7; and family relationships 167; identification of 190, 205; intended parents as 213; lesbian parenting arrangements 244, 259–64; multiple 206; need for 182; and parental responsibility 175; significance of 207; social parents as 177; *see also* legal fathers and fatherhood; legal mothers and motherhood
Lehr v. Robertson 54–6
lesbian couples 193–5, 199, 303, 374, 469, 471; as legal parents 259–60; as nuclear family 273–4; *see also* same-sex couples
lesbian parenting 239, 259–60; assisted reproduction cases 264–8; known donors and the nuclear family 272–6; legal issues 244, 259–64; *see also* same-sex parents/parentage

Locke, John 1, 20–1, 25–6, 125
Lomasky, Loren 342
Lord Mansfield's Rule 49

MacLeod, C.M. 364, 366
Mahoney, Joan 302
Marckx v Belgium 452
Masson, Judith 230
maternal-bonding argument 70–6
maternity, determination of 213–17
maternity leave 371n51
McCall Smith, Alexander 361, 365–7, 370, 382
McIntyre, E. Alison 129
McMichael v UK 451–2
Michael H. v. Gerald D. 56, 64
Mikulić v. Croatia 234
Mill, J. S. 525
Minimum Provision Thesis (MPT) 340, 342–3, 364
Mohler, Albert 518
monistic gestationalism 2, 105, 107–9; and the identifiability argument 110–11; incorporation argument 111–12; inherent approach to 109–10; and sweat equity 113–14; and the tracking approach 112–13
Montague, P. 365
Moral Foundation of Rights, The (Sumner) 321
moral rights 6, 318, 333n26; of children 133–9; presumptive 320
mothers and motherhood 4, 108, 160; as biological parents 160; vs. fatherhood 202; identification of 46–8, 190, 208–9; intentional/intended 208, 215, 219; legal approach to 107; multiple 217; natural 107–8; and parental responsibility 446; rights of 403–4, 437; single 298, 298n52; social 219; view of shared time arrangements 496; *see also* biological mothers; genetic mothers and motherhood; gestational mothers; legal mothers and motherhood; surrogate mothers and motherhood
Mullender, R. 404
M v M (parental responsibility) 477

natural (original) fathers 107; *see also* biological fathers
natural (original) mothers 107–8; *see also* biological mothers; birth mothers
natural (original) parents 13n25, 104–6, 108, 121, 123, 160, 247, 375, 527–9; support for 558
nature-nurture debate 66n200, 74
neoconservatism 338
non-consensual sex 236
Norway, paternity laws in 232
Norwegian Act on Children and Parents 232

obligations vs rights 325–30, 333, 336
Olsen, Frances 391–2
O'Neill, Onora 125, 526
organ donation 86
ovum donors 22; *see also* egg donors

paramountcy principle *see* welfare principle
parentage 160, 164; biological 160; determination of 230; genetic 162–4; legal concept of 135, 161–2, 164–5
parental authority 9, 41, 316n1; for non-parents 183; social assumption of 200; *see also* parental rights
parental autonomy: background framework and justifications 340–2; conceptions of 7; conservative conception 342–5; democratic conception 345–7, 358n27; liberal conception 347–9, 358n27; problem of 338–40; protection of 324; refined liberal conception 349–51; social conditions of 351–3; and the transmission of religious convictions 353–7
parental exclusivity 5, 208; advantages and disadvantages of 217–22
parental obligation, institutional theory of 126
parental privilege 6
parental responsibility/ies 9, 125–32, 160–1, 164–5, 191–2, 207, 220–1, 251, 255, 361, 370, 378; agreement 101; allocation of 446–60, 468–70; causal view of 125–9, 131; changing meaning of 465–8; conferring of 168–70; degradation of 474–7; of fathers 108, 267; and guardianship 167; of known sperm donor 265–6; legal 382–4; legal concept of 164–5, 190; legal orders for 455; and legal parenthood 166–70, 175; in lesbian relationships 249; meaning of 441–6; and medical decisions 386; as necessary and/or sufficient 181–4; and parental status 198; vs. parenthood 221; power to remove or revoke 458–9; proliferation of 470–4;

revocable 456–7; and the rights of parents 183–4; shift in reasons for granting 477–82; shortcomings of 268–72; of step-parents 196–7; of surrogate mothers 312; voluntarist view 126–8, 131–2; *see also* parental rights

parental rights 33, 104–5, 108, 207, 218–19, 225, 315–16, 323–4, 329, 331–2, 336, 361–4, 380–1, 467, 529, 533; academic debate 415–18; acknowledgment of 388–9; Article 8 (1) of the ECHR 433–5; child abuse 532–3; vs. children's welfare 495; doctrine of 39–42; of fathers 108; of gamete donors 69; general 321; and medical decisions 413; moral rights 20; and the parent/child relationship 325–6; protection of 385–8, 393; to raise and nurture a child 44–5; right of procreation 42–5; right to have children 512, 526; of sperm donors 66; termination of 63–4; *see also* parental responsibility

parental status 2; creating immaterial legal consequences for 201; expansion of 198–200, 202–3; legal consequences of 201; of lesbian couples 194; meaning of 193; nature of 197; and parental responsibility 198

parental unfitness 40–1

parent-child relationships 325–6, 466, 497, 529

parenthood 1–2, 117, 160, 163; adoptive 132; biological 131–2, 145, 222; components of 246; before conception 296; custodial 104; definitions 36–8; determinants of 103–4; emotional intimacy in 115–16; as exclusively genetic 173–5; forced 3; fragmentation of 197–8; gendering of 197–8; genetic 117–18, 161, 166; gestational 117–18; identifiability argument 110–11; incorporation argument 111–12; inherent approach to 109–10; laws on 276–84; legal 5, 13n28, 104–5, 145, 164; legal concept of 164–5; lesbian couples 193–5; monistic view of 104; natural (original) 104–6, 108, 123; non-exclusive model of 222–5; non-gestational 108; vs. parental responsibility 221; and parental responsibility 166–7; planned 3; pluralistic view of 104; psychological 145, 291–2; same-sex 199, 262; social 102, 104, 108, 118, 123, 161, 163, 291–2; sociological 232; tracking approach 112–13; two-parent ideal 282–3; *see also* parenting; parents

parenting: heterosexual 210–11, 260; parallel 489; post-separation 9; as profession 511–12; and the role of the state 3, 176, 201–2; *see also* parenthood; parents; same-sex parents/parentage; shared time parenting

parents: assisted reproduction 190–1; attempts to define 36–8; autonomy of 528; binary norm 198–200; children's relationship with 195–6; consultation between 184–5;; determination of fitness of 60; genetic link with child 65–6, 161, 206; genetic relationship 291; human rights of 8; identification of 218, 311; infertile 199; legal claim to children 22–5; legal duties and rights of 382–4; legal rights of 41–2, 74–5, 136–8; legitimation of 9; licensing of 10, 506–11, 530–1; multiple 223, 225–6, 280–2; potential 290; practicality of licensing 515–18; principal vs. secondary 274; responsibilities of 20; and the right of procreation 32; two-parent ideal 198; v 290; *see also* adoptive parents and families; being a parent; biological parents/parenting; co-parents; custodial parents; genetic parents; gestational parents; intended parents; intentional parents; legal parents; natural (original) parents; parental rights; parenthood; parenting; parent's interests; psychological parents; social parents/parenthood; step-parents

parent's interests 341–4, 364–71, 379–80, 383–4, 387, 527–8; infringement on 390; protection of 391–6

parity principle 106–9

Parker, Stephen, 403

parthenogenesis 206

paternal rights 52–3, 201, 366–7, 399–400, 403–5, 421–2, 436–7; and the common law 56; legal issues 51–3; of unmarried men 52–3

paternity 5, 230, 253; acknowledgment of 222; of deceased fathers 222; determination of 209–13; establishment of 48–50, 231–9; genetic 173, 176, 211–12, 225; genetic testing for 210; legal 238; legal view of 109; presumption of 50n104, 174, 176, 209–10

paternity leave 371, 371n51

paternity problem 108

Payne v Payne 409, 412, 427

permissibility 138

personhood 87–8

physical-involvement argument 81–3
Pickford, Ros 181
Pini case 554
pluralism: democratic 346, 350; inclusive 122–3; sufficiency versions of 104
Poor Law 169
possession d'état 233
pregnancy, accidental 117–18, 120, 129–31
press freedom 428
presumption of biology 45–6, 64; genetic donor's claims 65–70; and the genetic-identity argument 65–7; gestational host's claims 70–89
presumption of legitimacy 48–51, 57
Prince v. Massachusetts 524
priority thesis 6, 8, 357n3, 365
procreation: and the intention to create 61–2; and parental responsibility 125–32; *see also* right of procreation
property rights argument 20–1, 67–70, 305–6
proportionality: in Article 8 (ECHR) 427–35; and the Article 8(1) rights of the child 430–2; and the non-resident parent's Article 8(1) rights 432–4; presumptive equality between article 8 rights 429–30; presumptive equality between articles 8 and 10 428–9; and the resident parent's Article 8(1) rights 434–5
prostitution 86, 89
psychological parents 4, 40n39, 176, 225, 246–7, 255, 373

Quilloin v. Walcott 53–6
Quinn, Stephen 229

R (G) v. Nottingham CC 368
R (on the application of G) v. Barnet London Borough Council et al. 555, 557
rape 127, 236
Rawls, John 341
Raz, Joseph 351–2
Re A (A Child: Joint Residence/Parental Responsibility) 196, 199–200, 473
Re B (A Minor) 410, 412–13
Re B (Role of Biological Father) 193–4, 199–200, 265–6, 271, 273, 476, 481
Re C (A Child) (Adoption: Duty of Local Authority) 257
Re C (A Child) (Immunisation: Parental Rights) 413, 473
Re C (Contact: Moratorium: Change of Gender) 239n41
Re C (minors) 478
Re D 469–70, 474, 476, 480–1
Re D (a child) 192
Re D (A Minor) (Adoption Order: Validity) 154
Re D (Children) (Removal from Jurisdiction) 436–7
Re D (Contact and Parental Responsibility: Lesbian Mothers and Known Father) 194, 199–201, 250, 252, 265, 268–73, 282, 465
Re D (Paternity) 235
Re E 388, 395
Reece, Helen 391–2
Re Evelyn 199
Re F 387
Re F (A Minor) (Blood Tests: Parental Rights) 210
Re F (Paternity: Jurisdiction) 235n30
Re G (shared residence order: parental responsibility) 193, 196, 246–7, 255, 261, 373–5, 471–2, 479
Re H 389, 478, 480
Re H (Blood Tests: Parental Rights) 225, 235, 239n41
Re H (minors) (local authority: parental rights) (No 3) 194, 196, 471–2
Re H. (Parental Responsibility: Maintenance) 455
Re H (shared residence parental responsibility) 472
Re J (A Minor) (Adoption Order: Conditions) 147
Re J (Paternity: Welfare of the Child) 235n30, 239n41
Re J (specific issue orders: child's religious upbringing and circumcision) 473
Re K (Specific Issue Order) 235n30
Re KD (A Minor) (Ward: Termination of Access) 218, 406, 408
Re L (A Child) (Contact: Domestic Violence) 412
religious values 339, 342–3, 350, 353–7, 383, 473
relinquishment argument 81–3, 95
Re M (contact: family assistance: McKenzie friend) 480
Re O (Contact: Imposition of Conditions) 407

Re P (A Child) 413
Re P (a minor: parental responsibility order) 475–6
Re P (Surrogacy: Residence) 375
Re P and L (minors) 267–8, 274, 282
Re Patrick (2002) 194, 200
reproductive technology 106, 205, 338
Re R (a child) 211
Re R (Adoption: Contact) 549
Re S 479, 545
Re S (A Child) 413, 428–30
Re S (A Minor) (Blood Transfusion: Adoption Order Condition) 152–3
Re S (Parental Responsibility) 196, 475–6
Re T 386–7
Re T (Adopted Children: Contact) 147, 154
Re T (Paternity: Ordering Blood Tests) 200
Review of Adoption Law 150–1
Re WB (minors) (residence orders) 458–9, 472
Re Y 386–7, 395
Re Z 389
right of privacy 59–64
right of procreation 2, 3, 32, 32n14, 33, 42–5; biological interpretation 58–9; identifying participants 45–6; identifying the father 48–58; identifying the mother 46–8; intentionalist interpretation 62–3; and the right of privacy 59–64
rights: of children 9, 133–9, 231, 340, 362, 366, 380, 382–3, 529, 533, 537; choice conception of 323–4; discretionary 327; liberty 318–19; mandatory 326–8, 328n22; of mothers 403–4, 437; vs. obligations 325–30, 333, 336; presumptive 320; specific vs. general 321; *see also* claim rights; human rights; moral rights; parental rights; paternal rights; property rights argument; right of procreation
Rothman, Barbara Katz 109
Rutter, Michael 529
R v E and F (female parents: known father) 266, 271, 274
R v Secretary of State for Home Department, ex parte Gangadeen and Khan 426–7

same-sex couples 241, 263, 294; parental authority of 183; parental status of 197; *see also* gay male couples; lesbian couples
same-sex parents/parentage 4–5, 14n38, 193–5, 230, 239, 252, 255, 392; gay male couples 262; *see also* lesbian parenting
Scandinavia, determination of genetic paternity in 176
Schmidt v Germany 451–2
Scotland, responsibilities of fathers in 448–50
self-determination 344
self-ownership 1, 22, 25–6, 28n18
separation anxiety 81
shared time parenting 9, 483–5; benefits to children 497; best arrangements for children 485–6; legislation encouraging 491–6; and shared finances 490–1; unworkable arrangements 488–90; workable arrangements 486–7; of young children 490
'single mother' construction 298, 298n52
Skinner v. Oklahoma 42–3
Smith v. Jones 47–8
social expectations 116–18
social fathers 225, 246; *see also* social parents/parenthood
social mothers 219; *see also* social parents/parenthood
social norms 116–18
social parents/parenthood 4, 102, 104, 108, 118, 123, 160, 163, 166, 169, 171, 175–8, 215, 217, 219, 225, 230, 244, 246–7, 255, 258, 291–2, 295n38, 372–3; as legal parents 177; *see also* social fathers; social mothers
social thesis 351–2
sociological parenthood 232
Soos v Superior Court of Maricopa 216
sperm, sources of 67–8
sperm banks 67
sperm donors 22, 31, 43, 48, 51, 58–9, 66, 68–9, 109, 193–4, 199, 208, 210, 212, 223–4, 230, 246, 249–50, 297; anonymity for 389; *see also* donated sperm; gamete donors; known donors
Stanley v. Illinois 52–3, 55–6
state: involvement in adoption 535–58; involvement in the raising of children 512–13; and parental autonomy 342–3, 345; and parental responsibility 442–3; and parental rights 10; role of 3, 176, 201–2, 426
stem cells 206
step-fathers 220; parental responsibility of 197

step-parents 4, 163, 170, 177, 183, 195, 199, 220, 247–8; complexities of 195–6; gender of 197; parental responsibilities of 457–8; and parental responsibility 196–7
sterilisation: consent to 215; involuntary 32n14, 42
Strasbourg jurisprudence 419–25
Sturge, Claire 251
Sumner, L.W. 321–2
surrogacy 5–6, 21–2, 30n9, 51, 97n4, 98, 101, 208, 212–13, 215, 217, 222, 310–11; AID 30n9; arguments against 86–7; 'common sense' solutions to 288; defined 290; difficulties associated with 287; full vs. simple 308, 308n91; genetic 43; gestational 21–2, 30n5, 46–7, 58, 97, 105, 199, 216; and intentionality 307–8; IVF 206, 215, 219, 222, 290; and the law 291; and legal parenthood 289; partial 307–8, 308n91; power relations in 122n43; problems raised by 290–3; and same-sex couples 195, 240; *see also* surrogate fathers; surrogate mothers and motherhood
surrogate fathers 239
surrogate hosts *see* surrogate mothers and motherhood
surrogate mothers and motherhood 2, 21–2, 31–3, 43, 62, 82, 105, 109, 195, 223, 239, 309, 312, 375; change of mind of 199, 214–15, 224, 296, 301–2; as genetic mothers 216; husbands of 212–13, 224, 307n90; *see also* surrogacy
surrogate parenting *see* surrogacy; surrogate mothers and motherhood
sweat equity 113–14

Taylor, Charles 351
Thomas S. v. Robin Y. 194, 199–200
three parent triad 199
Tizard, Barbara 529

transsexuals 159, 191
T v T (Shared Residence) 266–7, 275

Uniform Parentage Act (UPA) 50, 56, 98
United Nations Convention on the Rights of the Child (CRC) 171–2, 226, 234, 393–4, 401, 409, 423, 449–50, 524, 543
United States, parental authority in 466–7
unmarried couples 241; *see also* cohabitation
unmarried fathers 181, 183, 185, 196, 208, 220–1, 241, 454; parental responsibilities of 446–54, 464n119
utilitarianism 403–4

violence: domestic 387–9, 493, 495–6; against women 136–7; *see also* child abuse
voluntary contact register 148, 241

Wales, parenthood laws in 189–90
Warnock, Mary 245
Warnock Report 106
welfare principle 8, 258, 276, 363, 369n42, 373, 375–6, 380–3, 400, 402, 407, 415, 437, 544; abandonment of 391–2, 425–7; in Article 8 (ECHR) 425–7; cases where it does not apply 389–90; infringement on parent's interests 390; limiting application of 388–9; non-enforcement of 384–6; and the protection of parents' rights 385–8; reconceptualisation of 393–6
West Germany, parental care in 441
Whitehead, Mary Beth 44, 58, 62, 82
Williams, Bernard 130
Wisconsin v. Yoder 355–6
women, violence against 136–7; *see also* mothers and motherhood

X, Y, and Z v United Kingdom 218

Yousef v The Netherlands 423–4